The Guide to Cooking Schools

Other ShawGuides:

The Guide to Writers Conferences
The Guide to Photography Workshops & Schools
The Guide to Art & Craft Workshops
The Guide to Academic Travel
The Guide to Golf Schools & Camps

The Guide to Cooking Schools

1996

Eighth Edition

Copyright (c) 1988, 1989, 1990, 1991, 1992, 1993, 1994, 1995 by ShawGuides, Inc.

All rights reserved

ShawGuides and The Guide to Cooking Schools are trademarks of ShawGuides, Inc.

Inquiries concerning this book should be addressed to: Editor, ShawGuides, P.O. Box 1295, New York, New York 10023, Phone (212) 799-6464, Fax (212) 724-9287.

Please note that the information herein has been obtained from the listed cooking schools and organizations and is subject to change. The editor and publisher accept no responsibility for inaccuracies. Schools should be contacted prior to sending money and/or making travel plans.

**Library of Congress Catalog Card Number 88-92516
ISSN 1040-2616
ISBN 0-945834-21-7**

Design: Joseph Santoro
Printed in the United States of America by
R. R. Donnelley & Sons Company

Introduction

The Guide to Cooking Schools *is the only comprehensive, international resource to information about culinary and wine educational programs. This eighth annual edition, the largest to date, contains detailed descriptions of 322 career and professional and 448 nonvocational and vacation programs (77 new to this edition), 100 culinary apprenticeships, 65 wine appreciation programs, and 21 food and wine organizations. All schools have stated that they provide instruction in English and all listings are free.*

In June, 1995, we mailed a 36-question survey to more than 1,500 of the top chefs in the U.S. and Europe. The purpose was to gather information about their professional experiences and activities that will help aspiring chefs determine whether to pursue a culinary career. The survey results follow the Table of Contents.

Many of those who responded to the survey said reading was their most important non-cooking activity. To help you keep up with them, we've included a new section of "Recommended Reading" in the Appendix.

Section I, Career and Professional Programs, contains information about programs in 48 states and 11 countries and 100 U.S. Department of Labor-registered culinary apprenticeships in the U.S., Puerto Rico, and the Bahamas. Most are career programs offered by trade schools, colleges, and universities for the aspiring professional cook or chef; some are continuing education programs for the professional who desires more expertise in a particular specialty. In addition to contact name, address, and phone and fax numbers, the following information was requested from each program sponsor: description of institution, months of operation, year culinary program was established, length of program, accreditation, admission dates, total enrollment and number of enrollees each admission period, student to faculty ratio, age demographics, facilities and specialized equipment, culinary courses, daily and weekly schedule, on-the-job training and part-time employment opportunities, post-graduate courses, number and qualifications of faculty members, tuition and fees, cost of lodging, refund policies, number and average dollar amount of scholarships and loans awarded last year, and the percentages of applicants who are accepted, graduates who find jobs, students who work part-time, and financial aid recipients.

Section II, Nonvocational and Vacation Programs, contains information about programs in 42 states and 19 countries in venues that include cookware shops, restaurants, hotels, resorts, and homes. Many (230) are vacation programs that feature daily cooking classes as well as food-related excursions and dining at fine restaurants. In addition to contact information, sponsors provided the following: year established, months of operation, length and focus of programs, emphasis, maximum class or group size, method of instruction, facilities, special activities, faculty names and credentials, and costs.

Section III, Wine Courses, includes the following information about programs taught by wine connoisseurs who are members of the American Wine Society and/or the Society of Wine Educators: year established, course length and frequency, maximum enrollment, cost and vintage range of wines sampled, number of wines sampled at each session, specialties, background and credentials of instructor, cost, location, and contact.

Section IV, Food and Wine Organizations, describes the goals and objectives, publications, activities, dues, and membership services of 21 organizations.

Section V, Appendix, contains accreditation requirements and contacts for 74 schools accredited by the American Culinary Federation Educational Institute, 37 recommended reading resources, tuition rankings for career programs, page-referenced indexes to scholarships, children's classes, and advertisers, and a list abbreviations and currency conversion rates.

Although we've strived to make each listing as accurate and complete as possible, changes do occur. Call or write to the schools to confirm costs, schedules, and programs before enrolling or making travel plans. Request the names of graduates or previous attendees you can contact whose needs are similar to yours. Ask them if the program fulfilled their expectations; what were the weak and strong points; would they enroll in this program again. Please let us know if you feel that any listing is an inaccurate representation of a school's program or if you are acquainted with schools that should be listed in future editions.

The editor and publisher thank the school and organization officials for their cooperation and assistance. We also thank Stacey Shane-Nusbaum and Sandee Cohen for their help and expertise.

We wish you enjoyment and success in all your culinary endeavors.

***Shaw*Guides**

Contents

Introduction v

Survey of leading chefs ix

1. Career and professional programs 1
National apprenticeship program 135
2. Nonvocational and vacation programs 153
3. Wine courses 281
4. Food and wine organizations 295
5. Appendix
Culinary programs accredited by the American
Culinary Federation Educational Institute 303
Recommended reading 309
Career school tuition rankings 318
Scholarships 319
Children's classes 321
Abbreviations and currency conversion 323
Index of advertisers 324
6. Master Index 325

ShawGuides Survey of Leading Chefs

What do top chefs and restaurateurs look for in hiring a new employee? Where do they find qualified candidates? How much can a beginning cook or chef expect to earn? An experienced chef?

We sought answers to these and other questions by conducting a survey of the leading chefs in Europe and the U.S. A 36-question survey was mailed to the executive chefs of 539 European restaurants that are rated 1-, 2-, or 3-star by the 1995 *Michelin* guides and 973 U.S. restaurants that are rated among the top 40 in each of 30 metropolitan areas by the 1995 *Zagat Survey*. A total of 391(29% of the European and 24% of the U.S.)chefs responded.*

What knowledge, personal qualities, education, and experience are most desirable in a new employee?

Each chef was asked to rate 10 abilities/qualities on a scale of 1 (least important) to 5 (most important). The following were rated 4 or 5 by more than half the responders:

- Professional demeanor 93%
- Product knowledge 89%
- References 71%
- Accredited training 62%
- Knowledge of cuisine specific to the region 60%
- Knife skills 5%

What is the starting salary in your restaurant?
- $15,000 to $19, 999   52%

What is the top salary for a chef in your restaurant?
Nearly 65% of the responders have an ownership interest in their restaurant.

- $30,000 to $49, 999   52%
- $50,000 to $74, 999   25%
- More than $200,000   2%

Are/were any of your immediate family members chefs or restaurateurs?
More than 65% have family ties to the profession.

- Parent 33%
- Grandparent 23%
- Uncle or aunt 15%
- Sibling 13%
- Other (mostly cousins and in-laws) 16%

Michelin Guides are published by: Pneu Michelin, Services de tourisme, 46 Ave. de Breteuil, 75324, Paris Cedex 07, France; (33) 1 45 66 12 34, Fax (33) 1 45 66 11 63. *Zagat Surveys* are published by: ZagatSurvey, 4 Columbus Cir., New York, NY 10019; (212) 977-6000. Neither Pneu Michelin nor ZagatSurvey participated in or endorsed this survey.

How old were you when you decided to become a chef and how long have you been involved in your profession?
The average age at which responders made the decision to pursue a culinary career was 18 for both the American and European chefs, but the European chefs had been at it longer – an average of 25½ years versus 19½ years for the U.S. chefs.

Describe your background and training:
- Changed careers 25%
- Started as an apprentice 63%
- Attended a culinary school 58%
- Received part or all of training outside the U.S. 48% (of U.S. chefs)

What do you like most about being a chef?
"Creativity". "Immediate gratification". "Raves from customers". "Making people happy". "Freedom". "Working with and helping others". "Teaching". "Constant learning opportunities". "The changing seasons, each with different menus and foods". "The pace". "Food as art and cooking as love". "Opening new restaurants". "Marrying ingredients without disturbing the integrity of each". "Playing with food". "Using my hands". "The people I work with".

What do you like least?
"The hours". "We never see a sundown". "Being away from family on holidays and special occasions". "Not having time for personal relationships". "The pace". "Business aspects, paperwork, telephone calls". "Having to babysit employees". "Tomatoes in winter". "Dissatisfied customers". "Self-styled food critics". "Hot kitchens". "A half-empty restaurant". "Cooking school graduates who think they know it all". "The people I work with".

What personality traits do you look for in a new employee?
"Passion". "Enthusiasm". "High energy level". "Eager to learn". "Perfectionist". "Strong work ethic". "People skills". "Humility". "Ability to stay calm under pressure". "Team player (preferably captain)". "Athletic ability". "Asks questions". "Keeps their mouth shut". "Clothes reflect a sense of style". "Gets their foot in the door any way they can".

What other qualities do you look for?
"Experience in a high pressure, high quality restaurant". "Well-rounded training from a good culinary school or apprenticeship". "Someone I can learn from". "Someone I can teach from scratch". "Eager to learn, eager to please". "Looks me in the eye". "Likes chaos". "Management ability".

Which aspects of your culinary education were most valuable?
"Good teachers". "Studying under top chefs". "Learning basic techniques". "Eating in many restaurants". "Culinary school". "Learning to taste". "European training". "Reading". "Apprenticeship". "Learning to make a good sauce". "Learning self-discipline". "Gaining a respect for food products".

What advice would you give someone considering a culinary career?
"Get a job in a restaurant before going to school and see if that's really what you want to do". "Work only at the top restaurants (for nothing if necessary)". "Never stop learning or studying". "Make it your <u>life</u>, not your job. "Taste, taste, taste". "Remember who matters most – the guest".

1

Career and Professional Programs

ALABAMA

LAWSON STATE COMMUNITY COLLEGE
Birmingham/September-May

This college offers a 21-month certificate. Program started 1949. Accredited by SACS. Admission dates: quarterly; 23 students per instructor; 50% of graduates obtain employment.

FACULTY: 2 full-time.

COSTS: Tuition is approximately $200. Admission requirements: high school diploma or equivalent and admission test required.

LOCATION: Total enrollment: 2,000 students. 50-acre campus in suburban community, 100 miles from Detroit.

CONTACT: Roosevelt Daniels, Commercial Food Preparation, Lawson State Community College, 3060 Wilson Rd., SW, Birmingham, AL 35221; (205) 925-2515.

WALLACE STATE COMMUNITY COLLEGE
Hanceville

This college offers a 18-month diploma and 24-month degree. Program started 1979. Accredited by SACS. Admission dates: October, January, April, July. Total enrollment 20; 15 students per instructor; 98% of graduates obtain employment.

FACULTY: 2 full-time.

COSTS: Tuition is $1,100 to $1,300 in-state. Admission requirements: high school diploma or equivalent.

CONTACT: Culinary Director, Commercial Foods & Nutrition, Wallace State Community College, P.O. Box 2000, Hanceville, AL 35077; (205) 352-6403.

ALASKA

UNIVERSITY OF ALASKA-FAIRBANKS
Fairbanks/January-April, August-December

This university offers a 2-year certificate and 2-year AAS degree. Program started 1879. Accredited by NASC, ACCSCT. Admission dates: fall, spring. Total enrollment 30-45; 85% of applicants accepted; 8 to 10 students per instructor; 95% of graduates obtain employment.

COURSES: Externship provided.

FACULTY: 3 full-time, 7 part-time.

COSTS: Annual tuition: in-state $69 per credit hour, out-of-state $207 per credit hour. Admission requirements: high school diploma or equivalent required.

CONTACT: Frank U. Davis, CCE, CEC, Tanana Valley Campus, University of Alaska-Fairbanks, 510 Second Ave., Fairbanks, AK 99701; (907) 474-5196, Fax (907) 474-7335.

ARIZONA

PIMA COMMUNITY COLLEGE
Tucson/September-May

This state-supported college offers a 2-year certificate and 2-year AAS degree. Program started 1972. Accredited by NCA. Calendar: semester. Curriculum: core (culinary + general subjects). Admission dates: January, May, August. Total enrollment 50; 22 enrollees each admission period;

ARIZONA
The Guide to Cooking Schools 1996

100% of applicants accepted; 92% part-time students; 18 students per instructor; 90% of graduates obtain employment. Facilities: 1 kitchen, 3 classrooms.

COURSES: Gourmet cooking, garde manger, baking. 72 hours of culinary courses required for graduation. 4-year degree continuation at Northern Arizona Univ.

FACULTY: 11 full-time, and part-time. Includes: Camille Stallings, John Dailey, Martin Kreger.

COSTS: Annual tuition: in-state $28 per credit hour, out-of-state $141 per credit hour. Other fees $20-$40 per semester. Last year 3 scholarships were awarded averaging $500. 12 loans were granted. Average off-campus housing cost $200 to $600 per month. Part time employment available.

CONTACT: Camille Stallings, Dept. Chair, Hospitality, Pima Community College, 1255 N. Stone Ave., Tucson, AZ 85703; (602) 884-6541, Fax (602) 884-6201.

SCOTTSDALE COMMUNITY COLLEGE
Scottsdale/August-May

This state-supported college offers a 9-month certificate and 2-year AAS degree. Program started 1985. Accredited by NCA. Calendar: semester. Curriculum: core. Admission dates: August. Total enrollment 30; 22 enrollees each admission period; 60% of applicants accepted; 30% under age 25; 50% age 25 to 44; 20% age 45 or over; 7 students per instructor; 90% of graduates obtain employment. Facilities: 1 kitchen, 2 classrooms, 1 student-run dining room.

COURSES: Hospitality management, culinary principles, menu planning, hot foods, bakery/pastry, garde manger. 35 hours of culinary courses required for graduation. Schedule: 35 hours per week.

FACULTY: 2 full-time, 2 part-time.

COSTS: Annual tuition: in-state $1,600 out-of-state $5,400. Course fee is $250 per semester. Application deadlines: April 15. Admission requirements: high school diploma and 1 year food service experience. Last year 4 scholarships were awarded averaging $500.

LOCATION: The 10,000-student, 160-acre campus on the Salt River-Pima Indian Community land.

CONTACT: Sarah Labensky, Professor, Culinary Arts Program, Scottsdale Community College, 9000 East Chaparral Rd., Scottsdale, AZ 85250; (602) 423-6241, Fax (602) 423-6200.

SCOTTSDALE CULINARY INSTITUTE
Scottsdale/Year-round *(See also page 154) (See display ad page 3)*

This private institution offers an accelerated 15-month 78-credit-hour AOS degree in Culinary Arts and Sciences and Restaurant Management. Founded in 1986. Accredited by ACCSCT and ACFEI. New sessions begin every 6 weeks. Total enrollment 300; 70% of applicants accepted; average class size of 15 per instructor in all practical classes; 97% of graduates obtain jobs. Facilities: include 5 modern, full-service kitchens, bakery, meat fabrication shop, and student-run Mobil 3-star L'Ecole restaurant.

COURSES: Emphasis is on classic French techniques and the principles of Escoffier. Curriculum covers food preparation and presentation, regional and ethnic foods, continental cuisine, restaurant management, and front-of-house operations. Classes run 7 to 8 hours daily. The final 12 weeks are spent in a national paid externship program with 80% of positions becoming permanent. A Continuing Education program for professionals is available.

FACULTY: Founder and Director Elizabeth Leite developed and implemented a commercial food trades curriculum at Scottsdale Vocational Technical Institute. Her teaching staff consists of 18 American and European-trained professionals selected for their teaching skills. An advisory board of chefs, restaurateurs, and hospitality managers recommend curriculum.

COSTS: Tuition is $15,385. A one-time $785 fee covers uniforms, knives, and textbooks. A $25 fee accompanies application; full tuition is due 30 days prior to class unless other arrangements are

Professional CHEF Training

- Small Classes
- Hands-on Curriculum
- Accelerated A.O.S. Degree

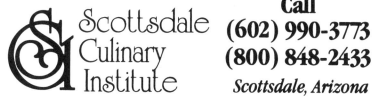

Scottsdale Culinary Institute

Call
(602) 990-3773
(800) 848-2433
Scottsdale, Arizona

made. The financial planning office assists students in obtaining Federal financial aid and scholarships. Part-time placement is available for students. Housing adjoins the campus.

CONTACT: Admissions, Scottsdale Culinary Institute, 8100 E. Camelback Rd., Ste. 1001, Scottsdale, AZ 85251; (602) 990-3773 or (800) 848-2433.

CALIFORNIA

AMERICAN HARVEST WORKSHOP
Napa Valley/Summer)
Established by Cakebread Cellars winery, this annual four-day event is open to ten invited chefs and sommeliers, who plan and produce two 5-course dinners for 50, using local products and Cakebread Cellars wines. Other activities include visits to food growers and a farmer's market.

FACULTY: Workshop director Narsai David, a San Francisco television and radio host, and the Cakebread Cellars staff.

CONTACT: Cakebread Cellars, 8300 St. Helena Hwy., Box 216, Rutherford, Napa Valley, CA 94573-0216; (707) 963-5221, Fax (707) 963-1067.

CALIFORNIA CULINARY ACADEMY
San Francisco/Year-round *(See also page 157) (See display ad page5)*
This proprietary institution offers a full-time 16-month (2,035-hour) AOS degree in Culinary Arts, a 30-week certificate in Baking and Pastry Arts, and over 200 courses a year for professionals and novices. Founded in 1977. Accredited by ACFEI and ACCSCT. Calendar: 16-week terms. Curriculum: culinary. Admission dates: various. Total enrollment 700 students for the degree program; 90 enrollees 6 times a year for degree program, 22 students 6 times a year for certificate program; 85% of applicants accepted; 75% of applicants receive financial aid; 39% of students under age 25; 54% ages 25-44; 7% age 45 and over; 20 to 25 students per instructor; 93% of graduates obtain employment within 6 months. Facilities: 14 commercially-equipped production kitchens, food production demonstration auditorium, 2 full-service restaurants with instructional dining rooms, confiseries, butcher and seafood prep kitchens, garde manger and baking/pastry kitchens.

COURSES: Degree program, modeled after European apprenticeships, covers food preparation and presentation, baking and pastry, nutrition, wine, menu and facilities planning; certificate program covers baking and pastry, chocolate and candies, decorating, and pastillage. Schedule: 7 hours per day, morning and afternoon shifts; rotation through restaurants. Degree students serve a 1-month externship the last semester.

FACULTY: Full-time staff of 30 professionally-trained chefs averaging 15 years experience and 3 professionally-trained maitres d'hotel; 6 part-time faculty; visiting area professionals; no student instructors.

COSTS: Approximately $25,000 ($11,000) for degree (certificate) program, which includes meals, uniforms, textbooks, equipment and student accident insurance. Application fee $35; deposit of $500 due within 15 days of acceptance; balance by first class; deferred payment plans are available. Recommended application deadline 6 months prior; acceptance notification 3 months prior. Admission is competitive and open to those with a high school diploma or equivalent; industry experience recommended. Financial aid and veterans aid assistance are provided to qualified students. Number of scholarships awarded in 1994-95: 40; average amount: $1,500. Part-time employment is available. The housing service provides assistance in finding lodging and transportation. Approximate cost of housing: $5,200.

LOCATION: Near San Francisco's Civic Center, two blocks from City Hall.

CONTACT: California Culinary Academy, Admissions, 625 Polk St., San Francisco, CA 94102; (415) 771-3536 or (800) BAY-CHEF; Fax (415) 771-2194.

Go Professional

Recipe for SUCCESS Choose that program that suits your taste, mix well with your talent and enter one of the world's most exciting careers.

At the California Culinary Academy, we offer:
- 16-month Culinary Arts AOS degree program
  30-week Baking & Pastry Arts certificate program
- Financial Aid available to those who qualify
  Lifetime Placement service for graduates
- ACFEI and ACCSCT accreditation
  San Francisco's diverse food culture
- International Chef/Instructors
  1-800-BAY-CHEF   625 Polk St San Francisco CA 94102

CALIFORNIA
CULINARY ACADEMY

CENTURY BUSINESS COLLEGE
San Diego
This college offers a 6-month diploma and 15-month AOS degree. Program started 1982. Accredited by ACCSCT. Admission dates: every 2 weeks. Total enrollment 300; 90% of applicants accepted; 20 students per instructor; 82% of graduates obtain employment.

FACULTY: 20 full-time.

COSTS: Annual tuition is approximately $7,325.

CONTACT: Wayne Miletta, Culinary Arts Department, Century Business College, 2665 Fifth Ave., San Diego, CA 92103; (619) 233-0184, Fax (619) 233-1302.

CITY COLLEGE OF SAN FRANCISCO
San Francisco/August-May
This college offers a 4-semester AS degree in Hotel and Restaurant Operations. Program started 1935. Accredited by WASC. Calendar: semester. Curriculum: core. Admission dates: August, January. Total enrollment 240; 86 enrollees each admission period; 90% of applicants accepted; 20 students per instructor; 90% of graduates obtain employment. Facilities: 8 kitchens and classrooms, and student-run restaurant.

COURSES: Elementary and advanced foods, bake shop, advanced pastry, meat analysis, garde manger, general education. Schedule: 6 hours per day, 9 months per year. Externship: 240-hour.

FACULTY: 12 full-time.

COSTS: Annual tuition: in state $390, out-of-state $3,720. Full refund possible within deadline dates. Application deadlines: April, November. Last year 30 scholarships awarded averaging $800.

CONTACT: Lynda Hirose, Hotel & Restaurant, City College of San Francisco, 50 Phelan Ave., San Francisco, CA 94112; (415) 239-3152, Fax (415) 239-3913.

COLUMBIA COLLEGE
Sonora/August-May
This college offers a 2-year AS degree in Culinary Arts/Hospitality Management. Program started 1977. Accredited by WASC. Calendar: semester. Curriculum: core. Admission dates: August, January. Total enrollment 75; 30 enrollees each admission period; 99% of applicants accepted; 40% financial aid recipients; 40% under age 25; 50% age 25 to 44; 10% age 45 or over; 20% part-time students; 10 students per instructor; 100% of graduates obtain employment. Facilities: 2 kitchens, 5 classrooms, and a Mobil 3-star restaurant.

COURSES: cooking, baking, wines, bartending, garde manger, sausages and cured meats, service, restaurant management and marketing. 41 hours of culinary courses required for graduation. Other required courses: catering/special events. Schedule: 30 hours per week, 10 months per year.

FACULTY: 2 full-time, 5 part-time. Qualifications: full-time: lifetime teaching credential and industry experience; part-time: full-time employment and 15 years experience.

COSTS: Annual tuition: in-state $286, out-of-state $2,800. Health and student fees $20 per semester. Refund policy: 70% first month of semester. Application deadlines: July, December. Admission requirements: admission test required. Last year 45 scholarships awarded averaging $200; 12 loans were granted averaging $800. On-campus housing: 180 spaces; average cost $400 per month. Average off-campus housing cost $500 per month. Part time employment available.

LOCATION: The 3,000-student campus is 120 miles from San Francisco.

CONTACT: Francis T. Lynch, Program Coordinator, Hospitality Management, Columbia College, 11600 Columbia College Dr., Sonora, CA 95370; (209) 533-5135, Fax (209) 533-5104, E-Mail francis@mlode.com.

CAREER/PROFESSIONAL **CALIFORNIA** 7

CONTRA COSTA COLLEGE
San Pablo

This college offers a 2-year certificate. Program started 1962. Admission dates: August, January. Total enrollment 75 to 100; 90% of applicants accepted; 20 to 25 students per instructor; 90% of graduates obtain employment.

FACULTY: 3 full-time, 1 part-time.

COSTS: Annual tuition: $100. Admission requirements: admission test.

CONTACT: Steve Cohen, Culinary Arts, Contra Costa College, 2600 Mission Bell Dr., San Pablo, CA 94806; (510) 235-7800 ext. 311.

CYPRESS COLLEGE
Cypress/January-May, August-December

This college offers a 1-year certificate, 2-year AS degree in Food Service Management and Hotel Operations. Program started 1975. Accredited by WASC. Calendar: semester. Curriculum: core. Admission dates: August, January. Total enrollment 90; 35 enrollees each admission period; 90% of applicants accepted; 45% financial aid recipients; 25% under age 25; 50% age 25 to 44; 25% age 45 or over; 55% part-time students; 16 students per instructor; 85% of graduates obtain employment. Facilities: 1 kitchen, 4 classrooms, and a student-run dining room.

COURSES: Basic food production, advanced cooking techniques, quantity food production, international gourmet foods, dining room service, food and beverage costing and kitchen management, menu planning and design, and kitchen planning design. Schedule: full, part-time and evenings. Externship: 255-hour, salaried.

FACULTY: 1 full-time, 4 part-time. Includes: D. Schweiger, D. Cotaya, G. Blackwell, F. Albano.

COSTS: Tuition: in-state $13 per unit, out-of-state $114 per unit. Lab fees: $5 per lab. Refund policy: full refund before second week. Application deadlines: Wednesday of the first week of class. Admission requirements: high school diploma or equivalent. Last year 15 scholarships were awarded averaging $500; 10 loans were granted, averaging $1,000. Average off-campus housing cost $250 to $750 per month. Part time employment available.

LOCATION: The 16,200-student urban campus is 35 minutes from downtown Los Angeles.

CONTACT: David Schweiger, Hospitality Management/Culinary Arts, Cypress College, 9200 Valley View St., Cypress, CA 90630; (714) 826-2220, ext. 208, Fax (714) 527-8238.

DIABLO VALLEY COLLEGE
Pleasant Hill/Year-round

This college offers a program in Culinary Arts, Baking & Patisserie, Restaurant Management and Hotel Administration. Program started 1971. Accredited by ACFEI and WASC. Calendar: semester. Curriculum: core. Admission dates: August, January. Total enrollment 600; 40 enrollees each admission period; 25% under age 25; 45% age 25 to 44; 30% age 45 or over; 50% part-time students; 24 students per instructor; 100% of graduates obtain employment. Facilities: include a fully-equipped food production kitchen, demonstration laboratory and 130-seat open-to-the-public restaurant.

COURSES: Advanced food preparation, catering, garde manger, menu planning, costing, nutrition, California Cuisine and baking. Schedule: 8 hours daily, Monday-Friday. Externship:1-semester, at local hotels and restaurants.

FACULTY: 5 full-time, 14 part-time. Includes: Jack Hendrickson, Department Chair Linda Sullivan, Nader Sharkes, Robert Eustes, Paul Bernhardt. Qualifications: BA degrees and 7 years experience in the industry.

COSTS: In-state tuition for first semester is $225. Fees and deposits: $13 per unit for residents,

CALIFORNIA

$127 per unit for non-residents, $135 per unit for international students. Additional fees for books and supplies. Withdrawals within the first 2 weeks of class receive refund. Application deadlines: August, January. Admission requirements: high school diploma or equivalent. Last year 45 scholarships were awarded averaging $750. Average off-campus housing cost $500 per month.

LOCATION: The 23,000-student, 100-acre campus is in a suburban setting off Contra Costa Blvd. and the 680 Freeway.

CONTACT: Jack Hendrickson, Culinary Arts Dept., Diablo Valley College, 321 Golf Club Rd., Pleasant Hill, CA 94523; (510) 685-1230, ext. 555.

EPICUREAN SCHOOL OF CULINARY ARTS
Los Angeles/Year-round *(See page 160)*

This proprietary institution offers a 6-month Professional Chef diploma. Established 1985. Calendar: semester. Admission dates 3 times yearly. 45 enrollees each admission period; 100% of applicants accepted; 35% under age 25; 35% age 25 to 44; 15% age 45 or over; 15 students per instructor. Facilities: teaching kitchen with 5 work stations.

COURSES: Classic French and contemporary cuisines, breads and pastries, food costing and accounting. Schedule: Monday to Sunday; part-time and evening options. A 20-hour externship is provided at a restaurant or catering kitchen. Assistantships available at the school.

FACULTY: The 4 part-time instructors are CIA graduates Carol Cotner, Kim Welch, Teri Appleton, and Patrick Magee.

COSTS: Tuition is $2,300. A 50% deposit is required. Part-time employment is available.

CONTACT: Shelley Janson, Director, Epicurean School of Culinary Arts, 8759 Melrose Ave., Los Angeles, CA 90069; (310) 659-5990, Fax (310) 659-0302.

GLENDALE COMMUNITY COLLEGE
Glendale/January-May, August-December

This college offers a 2-year certificate. Program started 1974. Accredited by State. Calendar: semester. Curriculum: culinary. Admission dates: August, January. Total enrollment 338 per semester; 433 enrollees each admission period; 95% of applicants accepted; 25% under age 25; 60% age 25 to 44; 15% age 45 or over; 50% part-time students; 35 students per instructor; 80-85% of graduates obtain employment.

COURSES: Sanitation & safety, restaurant and cost control management, quantity foods & purchasing. Other Required courses: wine & beverages, catering, baking, dining room service. Schedule: part-time and evening, 18-week semester. Externship provided.

FACULTY: 1 full-time, 5 part-time. Qualifications: BS or MS degree and at least 6 years experience.

COSTS: Annual tuition: in-state $15 per unit, out-of-state $118 per unit. Admission requirements: high school diploma or equivalent. Last year 14 scholarships were awarded.

CONTACT: Yeimei Wang, Prof. of Food & Nutrition and Coordinator, Culinary Arts Dept./Food & Nutrition Studies, Glendale Community College, 1500 N. Verdugo Rd., Glendale, CA 91208; (818) 240-1000 ext. 5597, Fax (818) 549-9436.

GROSSMONT COLLEGE
El Cajon

This college offers a 1-year certificate and 2-year degree. Program started 1969. Accredited by WASC. Admission dates: August, January. Total enrollment 90; 100% of applicants accepted; 20 students per instructor; 100% of graduates obtain employment.

FACULTY: 8 full-time

CAREER/PROFESSIONAL CALIFORNIA

COSTS: Annual tuition: in-state $60 per semester, out-of-state $103 per unit.

CONTACT: Evan Enowitz, Grossmont College, 8800 Grossmont College Dr., El Cajon, CA 92020; (619) 465-1700 ext. 327.

LANEY COLLEGE
Oakland/Year-round

This public institution offers a 2-year AA degree in Culinary Arts and a certificate in Retail baking. Program started 1948. Accredited by WASC. Calendar: semester. Curriculum: core. Admission dates: August, January. Total enrollment 200; 60 enrollees each admission period; 80% of applicants accepted; 70% financial aid recipients; 25% under age 25; 50% age 25 to 44; 25% age 45 or over; 10% part-time students; 18 students per instructor; 100% of graduates obtain employment. Facilities: include 7 kitchens and classrooms, a student-run restaurant, and a retail bakery. Job placement assistance is available.

COURSES: Schedule: 6 hours daily, 4 days per week.

FACULTY: 5 full-time, 4 part-time.

COSTS: Tuition is $110 per unit. Application deadlines: September 1 and January 20. Last year 6 scholarships were awarded averaging $250. Part-time employment is available.

CONTACT: Wayne Stoker, Culinary Arts, Laney College, 900 Fallon St., Oakland, CA 94607; (510) 464-3407.

LE TROU RESTAURANT AND COOKING SCHOOL
(See pages 126, 162, 252) **San Francisco and France/Year-round**

Aux Gastronomes, the cooking school of Le Trou restaurant, offers full-time 8-week apprenticeships in France, 12-week and 6-month apprenticeships in San Francisco, 1- and 2-week courses in San Francisco and France, and master classes. Apprenticeships were first offered in 1983. Those in France are limited to 6 participants. Approximately 25% of applicants are accepted and 100% of graduates obtain employment.

COURSES: Regional, classic, and modern French cuisines, menu planning and marketing, kitchen and business management, dining room service, wines. Schedule: 8 hours daily, Tuesday-Saturday.

FACULTY: Robert Reynolds, the French-trained chef of Le Trou Restaurant, is co-author of *From A Breton Garden*, participated in the Great Chefs Teaching Series, contributed cookbooks, is recipient of an honor from Gault Millau, and is a certified Educational Supervisor in California.

COSTS: The 12-week apprenticeship is $5,500; class and tour programs are $1,250 per week. A 25% deposit is required; refund less $100 fee with 30 days notice. In France, apprentices can live with a Niort family or stay at a hotel or inn.

LOCATION: Deux Sevres, France, north of Cognac and Bordeaux.

CONTACT: Robert Reynolds, Le Trou Restaurant and Cooking School, 1007 Guerrero St., San Francisco, CA 94114; (415) 550-8169.

LEDERWOLFF CULINARY ACADEMY
Sacramento/Year-round

This proprietary vocational school offers a 7-month diploma in Professional Baking, 11-month diploma in Professional Cooking. Program started 1990. Accredited by ACCSCT. Calendar: modular. Curriculum: culinary. Admission dates: year-round. Total enrollment 250; 15 to 25 enrollees each admission period; 80% of applicants accepted; 30% under age 25; 60% age 25 to 44; 10% age 45 or over; 22 students per instructor; 95% of graduates obtain employment. Facilities: include 4 kitchens and 3 classrooms.

… 10 **CALIFORNIA** *The Guide to Cooking Schools 1996*

COURSES: Schedule: Professional Cooking meets 5 days per week 9 am-3:30 pm for 11 months or 6-10:45 pm for 18 months; Professional Baking meets 6-11am weekdays.

FACULTY: 12 full-time.

COSTS: Annual tuition is $15,995 for Professional Cooking and $7,995 for Professional Baking. Application fee is $75; other fees range from $170 to $500; refund policy: pro rata. Admission requirements: high school diploma or equivalent and admission test.

LOCATION: In a 22,000-square-foot historic landmark building.

CONTACT: Ron Lederman, Admissions, Lederwolff Culinary Academy, 3300 Stockton Blvd., Sacramento, CA 95820; (916) 456-7002, Fax (916) 456-7603.

LET'S GET COOKIN'
Westlake Village/Year-round *(See page 162)*

This private school offers a 24-session professional series and a 6-session catering series. Established 1983. Enrollment limited to 12 per session. Job search assistance provided.

COURSES: Include food preparation and presentation, international cuisines, nutrition, business management, and menu planning. Schedule: one session per week.

FACULTY: The more than 25-member guest and regular faculty includes owner Phyllis Vaccarelli and Cecilia De Castro, who coordinated professional chef programs for UCLA.

COSTS: Approximately $2,000 for the professional series, $250 for the catering series. An assistantship program is available.

LOCATION: A 30-minute drive from Los Angeles.

CONTACT: Phyllis Vaccarelli, Let's Get Cookin', 4643 Lakeview Canyon Rd., Westlake Village, CA 91361; (818) 991-3940.

LOS ANGELES CULINARY INSTITUTE
Burbank/Year-round

This proprietary institution offers a 18-month diploma in Culinary Arts. Program started 1991. Calendar: quarter. Total enrollment 75; 24 enrollees each admission period; 90% of applicants accepted; 20% under age 25; 70% age 25 to 44; 10% age 45 or over; 12 students per instructor; 100% of graduates obtain employment. Facilities: include 3 kitchens, 1 demonstration kitchen, and 4 classrooms.

COURSES: Schedule: averages 24 hours per week. Externship: 500-hours.

FACULTY: 6 full-time, 1 part-time. Includes: Chefs Raimund Hofmeister, CMC, David Wentz, Andre Aversleng, Rudy Rossier. Qualifications: industry trained and have a degree or certificate and minimum ACF designation of executive chef.

COSTS: Annual tuition: $12,000. Application fee: $100; books and supplies: $2,000. Admission requirements: high school diploma or equivalent. Last year 6 scholarships were awarded averaging $125. Average off-campus housing cost: $300-$450 per month. Part time employment available.

CONTACT: Mr. Jonathan Goetsch, Los Angeles Culinary Institute, 480 Riverside Dr., Burbank, CA 91506; (818) 840-1315, Fax (818) 840-1321.

LOS ANGELES TRADE-TECHNICAL COLLEGE
Los Angeles/January-May, August-December

This college offers a certificate and a 2-year AA degree in Culinary Arts and Professional Baking. Program started 1941. Accredited by WASC. Calendar: semester. Curriculum: culinary (certificate program) and core. Admission dates: August, January. Total enrollment 200; 60 enrollees each admission period; 75% of applicants accepted; 40% financial aid recipients; 40% under age 25;

CAREER/PROFESSIONAL   **CALIFORNIA**   **11**

40% age 25 to 44; 20% age 45 or over; 25 students per instructor; 80% of graduates obtain employment. Facilities: include 2 kitchens, 6 classrooms and 3 restaurants.

COURSES: Schedule: 21 hours per 4-day week.

FACULTY: 9 full-time. Qualifications: AA degree, ACF certification, industry experience.

COSTS: Annual tuition: in-state $150+, out-of-state $250+. Tuition deposit is $175 per semester. Other fees include $600 for tools, uniforms, and books over 2 years; refund granted before end of second week. Application deadlines: first day of semester. Last year 20 scholarships were awarded averaging $250; 40 loans were granted averaging $50. Part time employment available.

CONTACT: Ernest Green, Director, Culinary Arts, Los Angeles Trade-Technical College, 400 West Washington Blvd., Los Angeles, CA 90015; (213) 744-9480.

NAPA VALLEY COOKING SCHOOL
St. Helena/Year-round

(See page 163) (See display ad below)

The Napa Valley Cooking School . . . Professional Training for Fine Restaurants begins offering a one-year certificate program in 1996. Calendar: three 4-month semesters. Curriculum: culinary. Admission dates: August of each year. Total enrollment: maximum of 18.

COURSES: Basic to intermediate techniques in a variety of cuisines and food and wine education are taught the first two semesters, with special emphasis on skills for entry and advancement in fine restaurant kitchens; the final semester is a paid externship in a Napa Valley restaurant.

FACULTY: Northern California chef-instructors. Guest lecturers include noted area chefs, growers, specialty food producers, viticulturists, and winemakers.

COSTS: Estimated to be $9,000. A high school degree or equivalent is required. At least 6 months industry experience is required; a year or more is preferred.

LOCATION: St. Helena in the Napa Valley, 75 minutes from San Francisco.

CONTACT: Sue Farley, Coordinator, Napa Valley Cooking School, 1088 College Ave., St. Helena, CA 94574; (707) 967-2930, Fax (707) 967-2909.

ORANGE COAST COLLEGE
Costa Mesa

This college offers a 1-year certificate and 2-year AA degree. Program started 1964. Accredited by WASC and ACFEI. Admission dates: August, January. Total enrollment 350; 100% of applicants accepted; 15 students per instructor; 100% of graduates obtain employment.

COURSES: Culinary and cook apprenticeship program. 1,120 hours of culinary courses required for graduation. Other required courses: general education and food service management. Apprenticeship field experience.

FACULTY: 15 full-time.

Costs: Tuition: $120 per year in-state, $102 per unit out-of-state. Admission requirements: high school diploma or equivalent required. Last year 22 scholarships were awarded averaging $400.

Location: A suburban 25,000-student campus in southern California.

Contact: Dan Beard, Professor, Hospitality Department, Orange Coast College, 2701 Fairview Blvd., Box 5005, Costa Mesa, CA 92628-5005; (714) 432-5835, Fax (714) 432-5609.

OXNARD COLLEGE
Oxnard/January-May, August-December

This college offers a certificate and a 2-year degree program. Program started 1985. Accredited by WASC. Calendar: semester. Curriculum: culinary. Admission dates: August, January. Total enrollment 75 to 125; 30 enrollees each admission period; 100% of applicants accepted; 20 students per instructor; 95% of graduates obtain employment.

Faculty: 1 full-time, 5 part-time.

Costs: Annual tuition: in-state $15 per unit, out-of-state $115 per unit. Admission requirements: high school diploma or equivalent. Scholarships: average $2,500. Part time employment available.

Contact: Frank Haywood, Hotel & Restaurant Management, Oxnard College, 4000 S. Rose Ave., Oxnard, CA 93033; (805) 986-5869, Fax (805) 986-5865.

RICHARDSON RESEARCHES, INC.
Hayward/March, June-July, October *(See display ad page 13)*

This product development and research company for the confectionery food industry offers 8 to 10 five-day certificate courses per year in the theoretical and practical aspects of confectionery and chocolate technology. Established 1976. Classes, limited to 18 students with 2 instructors, are held in the company's 4,000-square-foot professional facility, which has 3 kitchen areas, a lecture room, and a specially-equipped laboratory.

Courses: Chocolate Technology, Confectionery Technology, Continental Chocolates, and Lite/Sugar-Free/Reduced Calorie and No Sugar Added. Schedule: 8 hours daily.

Faculty: Terry Richardson, a graduate of London Borough Polytechnic in Confectionery and Chocolate Technology, has worked for major companies and holds patents for new products and processes. He has more than 40 years experience. Margaret Knight has a BS in Food Science.

Costs: Tuition ranges from $1,280-$1,450. A $150 nonrefundable deposit is required with balance due a month prior. Cancellations 10 working days prior forfeit $500.

Location: 30 minutes from the San Francisco Airport, 20 minutes from the Oakland Airport.

Contact: Richardson Researches, Inc., 23449 Foley St., Hayward, CA 94545; (510) 785-1350, Fax (510) 785-6857.

SAN JOAQUIN DELTA COLLEGE
Stockton/August-May

This college offers a 1-semester certificate and a 3-4 semester certificate in Basic and Advanced Culinary Arts, and a 2-semester certificate in Dietetic Services Supervisor. Program started 1979. Accredited by WASC. Calendar: semester. Curriculum: core. Admission dates: rolling. Total enrollment 60; 20 to 30 enrollees each admission period; 100% of applicants accepted; 40% financial aid recipients; 30% under age 25; 60% age 25 to 44; 10% age 45 or over; 40% part-time students; 15 students per instructor; 90% of graduates obtain employment. Facilities: 2 kitchens, 2 classrooms and a student-run restaurant.

Courses: Introduction to culinary arts, baking, restaurant operations, nutrition, menu planning, food purchasing, and catering. Schedule: part-time and evening options are available. Externship: 1-semester, salaried.

World-Renowned, Hands-on Courses in Continental Chocolates, Confectionery Technology and Chocolate Technology

For more information, contact:
RICHARDSON RESEARCHES, INC.
Located in the Bay Area of San Francisco
23449 Foley Street, Hayward, CA 94545
PHONE: (510) 785-1350 • FAX: (510) 785-6857

FACULTY: 2 full-time, 3 part-time. Includes: Char Britto, John Britto. Qualifications: MS or MA.

COSTS: Tuition: $13 per unit in-state, $115 per unit out-of-state. Students must supply their own equipment and supplies. Refunds granted during the 1st 2 weeks of class. Application deadlines: on-going. Admission requirements: high school graduate or age 18. Last year 6 scholarships were awarded averaging $1,000.

CONTACT: Hazel Hill, Ed. D., Division Chairperson, Culinary Arts Department, San Joaquin Delta College, 5151 Pacific Ave., Stockton, CA 95207; (209) 474-5516, Fax (209) 474-5600.

SANTA BARBARA CITY COLLEGE
Santa Barbara/August-May

This public institution offers a certificate and a 2-year AS degree in Culinary Arts and Restaurant-Hotel Management. Program started 1970. Accredited by WASC and ACFEI. Calendar: semester. Curriculum: core. Admission dates: fall, spring. Total enrollment 120; 50 enrollees each admission period; 80% of applicants accepted; 60% financial aid recipients; 70% under age 25; 20% age 25 to 44; 10% age 45 or over; 10 to 15 students per instructor; 100% of graduates obtain employment. Facilities: include 6 kitchens and classrooms, a gourmet dining room, coffee shop, bake shop, lecture/lab room with individual stoves, cafeteria, and snack shop.

COURSES: International cuisine, wines, bar mgt., production service, nutrition, meat analysis, garde manger, baking, restaurant ownership. Schedule: 6:30 am-2:30 pm, Monday -Friday.

FACULTY: 3 full-time, 6 part-time. and 10 lab teaching assistants.

COSTS: Annual tuition: $500 in-state, $3,360 out-of-state. Application deadlines: May, December. Admission requirements: high school diploma or equivalent required. Last year 40 scholarships were awarded averaging $500; 10 loans were granted averaging $600. Average off-campus housing cost $250 per month. Part time employment available.

LOCATION: The 12,000-student campus is in a suburban setting 90 miles from Los Angeles.

CONTACT: John Dunn, Hotel/Restaurant & Culinary Department, Santa Barbara City College, 721 Cliff Dr., Santa Barbara, CA 93109-2394; (805) 965-0581, Fax (805) 963-7222.

SANTA ROSA JUNIOR COLLEGE
Santa Rosa

This junior college offers a 1-year certificate. Accredited by WASC. Admission dates: August, January. Total enrollment 25 to 40; 20 to 24 students per instructor; 100% of graduates obtain employment.

FACULTY: 3 full-time, 10 part-time.

COSTS: 1995 tuition was $60 per semester in-state, $96 per unit out-of-state.

CONTACT: Harriett Lewis, Consumer & Family Studies Dept., Santa Rosa Junior College, 1501 Mendocino Ave., Santa Rosa, CA 95401; (707) 527-4395.

SCHOOL FOR AMERICAN CHEFS
St. Helena/June-September

This nonprofit school, opened in 1989 at Beringer Vineyards' Culinary Arts Center, offers tuition-free 2-week postgraduate courses each summer. 25%-30% of applicants accepted. 4 students per instructor. Facilities: one kitchen for practicing and one for public dinner preparation.

COURSES: Tailored to student requests. Required courses are wine and food pairing, wine tasting, and elementary viticulture. Schedule: 44 hours per week.

FACULTY: School Director Madeleine Kamman was born in Paris and worked at her aunt's Michelin-starred restaurant in the Loire Valley. She has taught French cuisine in the U.S. for 34 years, authored 9 cookbooks, and hosts a PBS television series.

COSTS: Tuition, ingredients, and wines are provided by Beringer Vineyards. Application deadline is 1 year prior to admission. Selection is based on application, a competition based on menu/recipe design, and a statement of goals regarding the future of food professions in the U.S. All must be American citizens at least 21 years of age with a high school diploma or equivalent and at least 2 years of experience as a working chef. Off-campus lodging averages $250 per week.

LOCATION: Beringer Vineyards, in the Napa Valley, 90 minutes from San Francisco.

CONTACT: Administrator, School for American Chefs, 2000 Main Street, St. Helena, CA 94574; (707) 963-7115, ext. 2225, Fax (707) 963-2385.

SHASTA COLLEGE
Redding

This college offers a 1-year certificate and 2-year AA degree. Program started 1975. Admission dates: August. Total enrollment 125; 25 students per instructor; 100% of graduates obtain employment.

COSTS: Annual tuition approximately: in-state $130, out-of-state $100 per unit.$125 per year.

CONTACT: Bill Justice, Culinary Arts, Shasta College, P.O. Box 4960061155 N. Old Oregon Tr., Redding, CA 96049-6006; (916) 225-4600.

SOUTHERN CALIFORNIA SCHOOL OF CULINARY ARTS
South Pasadena/Year-round

This non-profit school offers a 1-year full-time/2-year part-time 1,865-hour Professional Culinary Arts diploma, 3-month Advanced Professional Cooking and Advanced Professional Baking diplomas, and a 608-hour Hospitality Management diploma. Program started 1994. Calendar: quarter. Curriculum: culinary. Admission dates: fall, winter, spring, summer. Total enrollment 100; 36 enrollees each admission period; 75% of applicants accepted; 25% under age 25; 50% age 25-44; 25% age 45 or over; 30% part-time students; 10 students per instructor; 100% of graduates obtain employment. Facilities: free-standing building containing three 1,000-square-foot kitchens with 36 work spaces and newly-equipped baking, hot foods, and garde manger labs.

COURSES: Include culinary arts, garde manger, baking and pastry, food production for restaurants and hotels, nutrition. Externship provided.

FACULTY: Director and Executive Chef Christopher F. Becker, Executive Chefs D. Wentz, A. Averseng, and D. Danhi, and Pastry Chef L. Bilderback.

COSTS: Tuition is $10,716. Registration fee $100, other fees $1,665. High school diploma or equivalent and entrance test required. Last year 2 scholarships were awarded averaging $250 each; 3 loans were granted averaging $5,000 each. Off-campus lodging averages $500 per month.

LOCATION: The 10,000-square-foot school facility is in an historic suburb of Los Angeles.

CONTACT: Christopher Becker, School Director, Southern California School of Culinary Arts, 1420 El Centro St., S. Pasadena, CA 91030; (818) 403-8493, Fax (818) 403-8494.

LEARN TO COOK WITH THE MASTER CHEFS!

*P*repare for a Career at **Tante Marie's Cooking School in San Francisco!** Whether your goal is to become the Chef of a Small Restaurant or a Pastry Chef, Caterer, Cooking Teacher or Food Stylist, **Tante Marie's** is the school for you!

Six-Month Culinary and Pastry Courses start twice a year. Evening and Weekend Courses and Afternoon Demonstrations are ongoing throughout the year. Small class size allows for lots of individual attention.

Call now or write for a free Brochure and Schedule:
271 Francisco Street, San Francisco, CA 94133 (415)788-6699

Tante Marie's Cooking School

TANTE MARIE'S COOKING SCHOOL
(See also page 167) (See display ad above) **San Francisco/Year-round**

This small private cooking school offers 6-month certificate programs in culinary arts and pastry arts as well as nonvocational courses and culinary travel programs. Established in 1979. Admission dates: March and September. Approximately 95% of applicants are accepted and 95% of graduates obtain employment.

COURSES: Culinary courses cover basic French techniques, breads and pastries, desserts, ethnic cuisines, food purchasing and handling, menu planning, and taste refinement. Schedule: culinary course meets from 10 am to 4 pm, Monday through Friday. Mornings are spent in hands-on preparation; afternoons are devoted to guest chef demonstrations. The pastry course is scheduled part-time. Graduates can serve a 4-week apprenticeship in a local quality restaurant.

FACULTY: School founder Mary Risley studied at the Cordon Bleu and La Varenne and taught in the U.S. and Canada; Catherine Pantsios, formerly chef/owner of Zola's, is the instructor for the culinary course; and Cathy Burgett teaches the pastry course. Guest instructors may include Giuliano Bugialli, Jim Dodge, and Alice Medrich.

COSTS: Tuition is $12,000 for the 6-month culinary certificate course, $4,800 for the 6-month part-time pastry course. A $300 nonrefundable deposit is required.

LOCATION: On San Francisco's Telegraph Hill, within walking distance of Fisherman's Wharf and public transportation.

CONTACT: Tante Marie's Cooking School, Inc., 271 Francisco Street, San Francisco, CA 94133; (415) 788-6699.

UCLA EXTENSION, HOSPITALITY/FOODSERVICE MANAGEMENT
Los Angeles/Year-round *(See also page 167)*

UCLA Extension, a self-supported continuing higher education institution, offers 6 certificate programs: Professional Cooking, Professional Catering, Professional Baking, Vintage, Hotel Management, and Restaurant Management. Nonvocational courses are also offered. Hands-on classes are limited to 18 students.

COURSES: All 3 Professional certificate curricula include 6 core business courses and an internship. The Vintage certificate consists of 4 required courses. Schedule: Most courses meet for 3 to 4 hours once weekly for 10 to 12 weeks, weeknights or Saturdays.

FACULTY: Local restaurant chefs, culinary specialists, and graduates of the CIA and CCA, including Laura Weinman, Bart Goldberg, French Sommelier of the Year Award 2-time finalist Paul Ellis and pastry chefs Kathleen Soo Hoo and Julie Nikcevich.

COSTS: Tuition is $7,300 for Professional Cooking, $6,000 for Professional Catering, $4,800 for Professional Baking, and $1,700 for Vintage. A nonrefundable $75 application fee is required. Credit cards accepted.

CONTACT: Hospitality/Foodservice Management, UCLA Extension, Room 515, 10995 Le Conte Ave., Los Angeles, CA 90024-0901; (310) 206-8120.

COLORADO

COLORADO INSTITUTE OF ART — SCHOOL OF CULINARY ART
Denver/Year-round

This proprietary school offers a 18-month AAS degree in Culinary Arts. Program started 1994. Accredited by ACTTS. Calendar: quarter. Curriculum: core. Admission dates: January, April, July, October. Total enrollment 300; 100 enrollees each admission period; 98% of applicants accepted; 20 students per instructor. Facilities: include 5 kitchens, classrooms, and full dining facility.

COURSES: Basic skills, baking and pastry, food production, garde manger, a la carte, dining room, sanitation, nutrition, management, cost control, wines and spirits, facilities design, and general education courses. 1716 hours of culinary courses required for graduation. Schedule: day and evening classes are available.

FACULTY: 11 full-time, 11 part-time. Qualifications: professional certification, AAS degree, and 20 years experience.

COSTS: Quarterly tuition: $2,980. Application fee $50, tuition deposit $100. Other fees: $250 per quarter lab fee, $275 general fee, $510 supply kit. Admission requirements: high school diploma or equivalent.

LOCATION: A 25,000-square-foot free-standing facility in the city of Denver.

CONTACT: Barbara Browning, V.P., Director of Admissions, Colorado Institute of Art, 200 E. 9th Ave., Denver, CO 80203; (800) 275-2420, Fax (303) 860-8520.

COLORADO MOUNTAIN CULINARY INSTITUTE
Dillon/Year-round

This collaboration between Keystone Resort and Colorado Mountain College offers a 3-year AAS and Certificate from ACF in Culinary Arts. Program started 1993. Accredited by NCA. Calendar: trimester. Curriculum: core. Admission dates: June. Total enrollment 45; 15 enrollees each admission period; 25% of applicants accepted; 35% financial aid recipients; 50% under age 25; 40% age 25 to 44; 10% age 45 or over; 6 students per instructor. Facilities: include 10 full-service kitchens and classrooms and 25 food and beverage outlets.

CAREER/PROFESSIONAL COLORADO 17

COURSES: Modern cuisine, garde manger, baking, nutrition, meal planning, sanitation, applied math, and English composition. 6,000 hours of structured work experience combined with 850 hours of classroom lecture required for graduation. Schedule: 40 hours per week classroom work. Rotation every 6 months to a different facililty.

FACULTY: 1 full-time, 12 resort chefs part-time. Includes: Doug Schwartz, Chris Wing, Bob Burden, Julie Licktiege, Alisa Mathews. Qualifications: instructors are all ACF members.

COSTS: Annual tuition: in-district $1,300, out-of-state $4,500. Application deposit is $450, and includes ACF registration and tool kit. Application deadlines: April 1. Admission requirements: applicants must complete an interview. Scholarships average $400. On-campus housing: $250 per month; off-campus housing: $250-$400 per month.

LOCATION: The AAA 5-Diamond Keystone ski resort, 70 miles west of Denver, has 1,300 guest rooms and 18 restaurants.

CONTACT: Admissions, Colorado Mountain College, P.O. Box 10,001, Glenwood Springs, CO 81602; (800) 621-8559.

COOKING SCHOOL OF THE ROCKIES

6 Month Professional Training Program starting January, 1996.
Featuring small classes. Faculty members are Master Chefs & experienced teachers, including Robert Reynolds of Le Trou, San Francisco. Highly personalized, intense hands-on experience. Spend 5 months in Boulder and 1 month in France. Contact Joan Brett, 637 So. Broadway, #H, Boulder, CO 80303, (303) 494-7988.

COOKING SCHOOL OF THE ROCKIES
Boulder/Year-round *(See also page 169) (See display ad above)*

This private school offers a 6-month culinary arts diploma program that consists of 5 months of training in Boulder, the sixth month in St. Remy de Provence in France. Program starts 1996. Admission dates: January and July. Total enrollment 12 students. Facilities: Modern, fully-equipped kitchens.

COURSES: Classical, regional, modern French cuisine. Schedule: 9:30 am to 4 pm, Monday-Friday.

FACULTY: Robert Reynolds, chef/owner of Le Trou Restaurant in San Francisco and director of "aux Gastronomes" Cooking School; Michael Comstedt, chef/owner of the Greenbriar Restaurant in Boulder and former chair of the Rocky Mountain Chefs Apprenticeship Program; Mary Copeland, who was head pastry chef at the Palais du Chocolat and Occidental Grill in Washington, DC, and taught at L'Academie de Cuisine in Bethesda.

COSTS, ACCOMMODATIONS: The $17,500 tuition includes round-trip airfare between France and Denver and room and board in France. A 10% deposit is required with application, $5,000 is due on acceptance, 50% of balance is due 60 days prior, balance is due 30 days prior. A 20% fee is assessed cancellations 30 days prior.

LOCATION: Boulder is 25 miles northwest of Denver in the Rocky Mountain foothills; St. Remy de Provence is 20 miles west of Avignon in the south of France.

CONTACT: Joan Brett, Director, Cooking School of the Rockies, 637 S. Broadway, Ste. H, Boulder, CO 80303; (303) 494-7988, Fax (303) 494-7999.

CULINARY INSTITUTE OF COLORADO SPRINGS
Colorado Springs/Year-round

This division of Pikes Peak Community College (PPCC) offers a certificate, apprenticeship, and a 2-year degree in Culinary Arts/Food Management. Program started 1986. Accredited by NCA. Calendar: semester. Curriculum: core. Admission dates: August, January, June. Total enrollment 35; 10 to 15 enrollees each admission period; 100% of applicants accepted; 90% financial aid recipients; 50% under age 25; 48% age 25 to 44; 2% age 45 or over; 10 students per instructor; 100% of graduates obtain employment. Facilities: include kitchen and student-run restaurant/classroom.

COURSES: Food preparation, restaurant management, wine and spirits, food and beverage management, and sanitation. 54 hours of culinary courses required for graduation. Other required courses: computer, English, math, accounting. Schedule: 8 hours per day, 5 days per week for 11 months. Continuing education: language classes available.

FACULTY: 3 full-time, 1 part-time. Includes: George J. Bissonnette, CCE, CEC, Dept. Chair; Gary Hino, CSC; Robert Hudson, CC. Qualifications: ACFEI certification.

COSTS: Annual tuition: in-state $4,125, out-of-state $5,775. Application deadlines: 1 month prior to each semester. Admission requirements: high school diploma or equivalent and admission test. Last year 4 scholarships were awarded averaging $5,000. 25 loans were granted. Average off-campus housing cost $250 and up.

LOCATION: The 15,000-student campus is in an urban setting 2 miles from Colorado Springs.

CONTACT: George Bissonnette, CCE, CEC, Dept. Chair, TI &S Div., Culinary Institute of Colorado Springs, PPCC, 5675 S. Academy Blvd., Colorado Springs, CO 80906; (719) 540-7371.

JOHNSON & WALES UNIVERSITY
Vail/Year-round *(See page 94)*

This branch offers a one-year accelerated AAS degree in Culinary Arts for those with a bachelor's degree or higher.

CONTACT: Office of Admissions, Johnson & Wales University, 616 W. Lionshead Circle, #101, CO 91657; (303) 476-2993, Fax (303) 476-2994.

SCHOOL OF NATURAL COOKERY
Boulder/Year-round *(See also page 170)*

This private trade school specializing in vegetarian cuisine offers a 5-week Fundamentals course, Teacher's Training and Personal Chef Training certificate programs, and a 2-week Baking and Pastry Course. Program started 1991. Calendar: quarter. Curriculum: culinary. Admission dates January, April, June, September. 8 enrollees each admission period; 95% of applicants accepted; 30% financial aid recipients; 33% under age 25; 50% age 25 to 44; 15% age 45 or over; 5 students per instructor; 98% of graduates obtain employment. Facilities: teaching kitchen.

COURSES: The Fundamentals course covers techniques, grains, energetics of foods, intuitive cooking, and meal composition; Teacher Training includes practice teaching, the Personal Chef Training program covers marketing and business management. Schedule: 3 to 5 hours daily.

FACULTY: Founder and director Joanne Saltzman, author of *Amazing Grains* and *Romancing the Bean*, and Mary Bowman.

COSTS: $2,600 for Fundamentals, $1,340 for Teacher Training, $800 for Personal Chef Training, and $980 for Baking and Pastry. Deposit is $500 and equipment fee is $270. Cancellations 1 month prior receive full refund. Application suggested 3 months prior to admission. Personal or phone interview required. Last year 3 loans were granted at an average of $2,350 each. Off-campus lodging ranges from $300 to $500 per month.

CAREER/PROFESSIONAL   **CONNECTICUT**   **19**

LOCATION: 35 miles from Denver.

CONTACT: Joanne Saltzman, Director, School of Natural Cookery, P.O. Box 19466, Boulder, CO 80308; (303) 444-8068; (303) 494-8068.

WARREN OCCUPATIONAL TECHNICAL CENTER
Golden/August-May

This public institution offers a 1-semester (options for 2nd and 3rd semesters) certificate in Restaurant Arts. Program started 1974. Accredited by State, NCA. Calendar: semester. Curriculum: culinary and service. Admission dates: August, January. Total enrollment 60; 45 enrollees each admission period; 98% of applicants accepted; 2% financial aid recipients; 98% under age 25; 2% age 25 to 44; 1% age 45 or over; 25% part-time students; 20 students per instructor; 95% of graduates obtain employment. Facilities: kitchen, 60-student classroom, 2 dining rooms, restaurant.

COURSES: Production, nutrition, baking, safety, sanitation. 540 semester hours of culinary courses required for graduation. Schedule: Monday-Friday, 7:30 am-2:00 pm. Externship provided.

FACULTY: 3 full-time with master's degree in vocational education.

COSTS: Tuition: in-state $1,600 per semester, out-of-state $2,464 per semester. Parking fee $50, materials $10. Application deadlines: July. Admission requirements: diploma or GED. Last year 5 scholarships were awarded averaging $1,000-$1,500. Off-campus housing cost: $350 per month.

LOCATION: The 1,200-student campus is in a suburban setting.

CONTACT: Sharron K. Pizzuto, C.F.E., Service Instructor, Rest. Arts, Warren Occupational Technical Center, 13300 W. Ellsworth Ave., Golden, CO 80401; (303) 982-8555, Fax (303) 982-8547.

CONNECTICUT

CBI CULINARY ACADEMY
Stratford/Year-round

This proprietary institution offers a 32- to 48-week diploma in Culinary Arts/Food Service. Program started 1988. Accredited by ACICS. Calendar: semester. Curriculum: culinary only. Admission dates: rotating. Total enrollment 20 to 28; 5 to 10 enrollees each admission period; 85% of applicants accepted; 80% financial aid recipients; 50% under age 25; 25% age 25 to 44; 25% age 45 or over; 9 students per instructor; 96% of graduates obtain employment. Facilities: include kitchen, 2 classrooms and a restaurant.

COURSES: Baking, garde manger, cooking principles, stocks, sauces, soups, desserts, fruit and vegetable preparation, menu planning, food service math, and sanitation. Other required courses: externship. Schedule: Tuesday-Friday 8:30 am-2:25 pm (days), Monday-Thursday 5:45-10:15 pm (evenings). Externship: 7-8 weeks

FACULTY: 1 full-time, 2 part-time. Includes: Chefs John Valus, Sr. and Charles Rowland.

COSTS: Annual tuition: $8,000. Application fee is $10. $40 general fee. Refund policy: pro-rata. Admission requirements: high school diploma or equivalent and admission test. Last year 100 loans were granted, averaging $4,000. Part time employment available.

CONTACT: John Valus, Sr., Chef/Director, Culinary Arts/Food Service, CBI Culinary Academy, 7365 Main St., Stratford, CT 06497; (203) 380-4079, Fax (203) 380-4077.

CONNECTICUT CULINARY INSTITUTE
Farmington/Year-round

(See also page 171)

This private school offers 360-hour professional training programs. Founded in 1988. Accredited by the Connecticut Department of Education and the ACCSCT. Curriculum: culinary. Admission dates September, January, March, and June for day students; September and February for evening students. Students per instructor 11; 92% of graduates obtain employment. Farmington facilities include a custom-built 4,500-square-foot area with 2 fully-equipped kitchen-classrooms; another facility is in New Haven county.

COURSES: Emphasis is on the preparation of fine international cuisine and pastry. Topics also include kitchen organization and food identification and purchasing. Schedule: day classes run 12 weeks, 6 hours daily, Monday through Friday; evening classes run 20 weeks, 3 classes per week, 6 hours per class. Home assignments and research are required. Continuing education courses include sanitary food handling and low-cholesterol cooking.

FACULTY: Includes 25 part-time chef/instructors, a director of education, staff instructors, and educational supervisors. Tad Graham-Handley is general manager and Leslie Noury heads the Professional Training Program.

COSTS: Tuition is $5,300. Application fee is $100; materials fee is $345. A $750 deposit is due within 10 days of acceptance, $2,500 is due 30 days prior to class, and balance is due one week prior. Financial aid is available to eligible students. Applicants must have a high school diploma or equivalent and pass an interview.

LOCATION: Suburban Farmington Valley, 10 miles west of Hartford.

CONTACT: Connecticut Culinary Institute, Loehmann's Plaza, 230 Farmington Ave., Farmington, CT 06032; (203) 677-7869 or (800) 76-CHEFS.

GATEWAY COMMUNITY-TECHNICAL COLLEGE
New Haven/Year-round

This college offers a 1-year certificate, 2-year degree in Culinary Arts. Program started 1987. Accredited by State, NEAS. Calendar: semester. Curriculum: culinary only. Admission dates: September, January. Total enrollment 140; 20 enrollees each admission period; 100% of applicants accepted; 40% financial aid recipients; 20% under age 25; 60% age 25 to 44; 20% age 45 or over; 60% part-time students; 15 students per instructor; 100% of graduates obtain employment. Facilities: include 1 lab, many classrooms and a restaurant.

COURSES: Externship provided.

FACULTY: 2 full-time, 4 part-time.

COSTS: Annual tuition: in-state $1,398, out-of-state $4,206. Application fee $10. Admission requirements: high school diploma or equivalent and admission test. Last year 15 loans were granted, averaging $1,200. Average off-campus housing cost $500 per month.

CONTACT: Eugene J. Spaziani, Hospitality Management, Gateway Community-Technical College, 60 Sargent Dr., New Haven, CT 06511; (203) 789-7067, Fax (203) 777-8637.

MANCHESTER COMMUNITY COLLEGE
Manchester/September-May

This college offers a 1-year certificate. Program started 1977. Accredited by ACFEI. Calendar: semester. Curriculum: core. Admission dates: September, January. Total enrollment 54; 20 enrollees each admission period; FCFS acceptance; 25% financial aid recipients; 50% under age 25; 35% age 25 to 44; 15% age 45 or over; 50% part-time students; 18 students per instructor; 95% of graduates obtain employment. Facilities: include classrooms and 2 kitchens.

COURSES: Include 4 culinary, 2 baking, sanitation, nutrition, and coop ed. Schedule: various options available. Externship provided. Continuing education: decorative work, wines and spirits, introduction to hospitality industry, cost controls, and equipment design and layout.

FACULTY: 6 full-time with master's degree or equivalent.

COSTS: Tuition per semester: in-state $820, out-of-state $2,400. Application fee $10. Admission

CAREER/PROFESSIONAL — FLORIDA

requirements: high school diploma or equivalent. Part time employment available.

LOCATION: The 160-acre campus is in a suburban setting 10 miles from Hartford.

CONTACT: G.S. Lemaire, Program Coordinator, Culinary Arts Dept., Manchester Community College, 60 Bidwell St., Manchester, CT 06040; (203) 647-6000.

DISTRICT OF COLUMBIA

THE PASTRY INSTITUTE OF WASHINGTON DC

Discover the Art of Pastry. Ten-month apprenticeship program. Next program begins October, 1996. From basics in pastry to sugar and chocolate work. 10 hours a week. Instructor: Francois Thibaudeau, chef of Le Palais du Chocolat. Year-round workshops for professionals, presented by famous pastry chefs. Call (202) 726-0790.

THE PASTRY INSTITUTE OF WASHINGTON DC
(See also page 174) (See display ad above) — Washington, D.C./Year-round

This private school offers a 10-month pastry apprenticeship, seminars for professionals, and demonstrations that are open to the public. Founded 1993. Total enrollment 15 students; 50% to 70% of applicants accepted; 50% under age 25; 30% ages 25 to 44; 20% age 45 or over; 7 students per instructor; 70% obtain employment. Facilities: professionally-equipped pastry kitchen and 800-square-foot classroom. A one-week trip to Paris in June, 1996, features classes at Bellouet-Conseil (page 174), visits to noted pastry shops and hotel and restaurant kitchens, Fauchon, and the Cacao Barry factory.

COURSES: Include basic to advanced French pastry, chocolate, sugar, and professional decoration. Schedule: the 220-hour program meets for 5 hours on Wednesday evenings.

FACULTY: Dominique Leborgne, owner of Palais du Chocolat, received the first Charles Proust Prize in 1981; Joel Bellouet, principal partner of Bellouet Conseil in Paris and Meilleur Ouvrier de France 1979, taught at Ecole Lenotre in Paris and authored 4 books; Jean Michel Perruchon won the Charles Proust junior prize and is Meilleur Ouvrier de France 1993. Francois Thibaudeau-Sauzeau, pastry chef of Palais du Chocolat and specializes in sugar work and cakes.

COSTS: Tuition is $3,900, payable in monthly installments. A $50 deposit is required. Professional seminars begin at $150. The Paris trip is $3,000, which includes airfare, lodging, and some meals.

LOCATION: About 15 minutes from downtown, a block from the Metro station and 25 minutes from National Airport.

CONTACT: Lawrence Leclerc, Administrator, The Pastry Institute of Washington, DC, 6925 Willow St. NW, Washington, DC 20012; (202) 726-0790, (202) 723-8970.

FLORIDA

ART INSTITUTE OF FT. LAUDERDALE
Ft. Lauderdale/Year-round

This proprietary school offers a 9-month diploma in Baking & Pastry and The Art of Cooking and an 18-month AS degree program in Culinary Arts. Program started 1991. Accredited by ACCSCT. Calendar: quarter. Curriculum: core. Admission dates: January, April, July, October. Total enrollment 180; 15 to 40 enrollees each admission period; 90% of applicants accepted; 20% under age 25; 65% age 25 to 44; 15% age 45 or over; 18 students per instructor; 98% of graduates obtain employment. Facilities: 8 kitchens and classrooms and a student-run restaurant.

COURSES: General education subjects; 1st year courses include basic cooking, product identification, baking and pastry, knife skills, and nutrition; 2nd year includes garde manger, art history, international cuisine, menu planning, kitchen layout, wine appreciation and restaurant service.

FACULTY: 7 full-time ACF-certified instructors.

COSTS: Annual tuition is $8,940. Application fee $50, tuition deposit $100. Application deadlines: open. Admission requirements: high school diploma or equivalent. On-campus housing: $290-$1,150 per quarter. Average off-campus housing: $600 per month. Scholarships available.

CONTACT: The Art Institute of Ft. Lauderdale/School of Culinary Arts, 1799 S.E. 17th St., Ft. Lauderdale, FL 33316; (305) 463-3000, Fax (305) 527-1799.

ATLANTIC VOCATIONAL TECHNICAL CENTER
Coconut Creek/Year-round

This public institution offers a 1,080 hour certificate in Culinary Arts. Program started 1976. Accredited by SACS, ACFEI. Calendar: quarter. Curriculum: core. Admission dates: Open. Total enrollment 130; 90% of applicants accepted; 15 students per instructor; 85% of graduates obtain employment. Facilities: include student-run restaurant.

COURSES: Hot foods, cold foods, bakery, nutrition, sanitation, supervision, dining room, and management. Schedule: 30 hours per week, evening schedule available.

FACULTY: 8 full-time.

COSTS: Annual tuition: $700. Textbook and workbook $35, uniforms $60, and knives. Admission requirements: admission test. Part time employment available.

LOCATION: The campus is in a suburban setting.

CONTACT: Moses Ball, Culinary Arts, Atlantic Vocational Technical Center, 4700 N.W. Coconut Creek Pkwy., Coconut Creek, FL 33066; (305) 977-2066, Fax (305) 977-2019.

DAYTONA BEACH COMMUNITY COLLEGE
Daytona Beach/Year-round

This college offers a 3-year Certificate of Apprenticeship. Program started 1980. Accredited by ACFEI. Curriculum: culinary. Admission dates: open. Total enrollment 130; 80% of applicants accepted; 10% under age 25; 60% age 25 to 44; 30% age 45 or over; 100% part-time students; 25 students per instructor; Facilities: include kitchen and classroom.

COURSES: Culinary and pastry apprenticeship, sanitation, supervision, nutrition. Schedule: culinary course meets for 4 hours on Mondays, pastry course meets for 4 hours on Tuesdays.

FACULTY: 5 part-time. Includes: Brian Clarke, Denise M. O'Brien, Lucille Taylor. Qualifications: vocational teaching certificates from DBCC.

COSTS: State funded vocational program. Fees: $160. Admission requirements: high school diploma or equivalent and admission test.

CONTACT: Denise M. O'Brien, Culinary Arts Department, Daytona Beach Community College, P.O. Box 2811, Daytona Beach, FL 32020-2811; (904) 255-8131, ext. 3735, Fax (904) 254-4492.

FLORIDA CULINARY INSTITUTE
West Palm Beach/Year-round

This proprietary institution, a division of New England Tech, offers an 18-month Specialized Associate degree in Culinary Arts and International Baking and Pastry. Program started 1987.

Accredited by ACFEI and SACS. Calendar: quarter. Curriculum: culinary. Admission dates: January, March, July, October. Total enrollment 450; 175 enrollees each admission period; 80% of applicants accepted; 80% financial aid recipients; 50% under age 25; 40% age 25 to 44; 10% age 45 or over; 18 students per instructor; 95% of graduates obtain employment. Facilities: include 8 kitchens and 8 classrooms.

COURSES: 6 quarters including food preparation, facilities planning, nutrition, purchasing, baking, and classical American and international cuisine. Other required courses: two 4-week internships are served in the practicum facility and Cafe Protege, the Institute's gourmet restaurant. The International Baking and Pastry program includes 3 quarters with courses that are common to the culinary program and 3 quarters that concentrate on advanced baking techniques. Schedule: Six 11-week quarters with 2-week breaks in between. Classes meet 4 hours daily.

FACULTY: 18 full-time.

COSTS: Total cost for the two academic years is $18,000. Admission requirements: high school diploma or equivalent. Advanced credit awarded through a testing program. Last year 5 scholarships were awarded averaging $500. Average off-campus housing cost $400 per month.

LOCATION: 25,000-square-foot facility on Florida's southeast coast.

CONTACT: Scott Spitolnick, Admissions Director, Florida Culinary Institute, 1126 53rd Court, West Palm Beach, FL 33407-9985; (800) 826-9986 or (407) 842-8324, Fax (407) 688-9882.

GULF COAST COMMUNITY COLLEGE
Panama City/Year-round

This college offers a 2-year AS degree in Culinary Management. Program started 1988. Accredited by SACS, ACFEI. Calendar: semester. Curriculum: core. Admission dates: fall, spring. Total enrollment 60; 20 enrollees each admission period; 100% of applicants accepted; 16 students per instructor; Facilities: include a student-run restaurant.

FACULTY: 2 full-time, 1 part-time. Includes: Travis Herr, John Holley.

COSTS: Tuition: in state $30 per credit, out-of-state $110 per credit. Lab fees $8-$9. Refund policy: 100% 4 weeks prior, third day of class 75%. Application deadlines: first day of class. Admission requirements: high school diploma or equivalent. Last year 7 scholarships were awarded averaging $200 part-time, $400 full-time. Part time employment available.

LOCATION: The campus is in a suburban setting in Florida's Panhandle.

CONTACT: Travis Herr, Gulf Coast Community College, 5230 W. U.S. Hwy. 98, Panama City, FL 32401; (904) 872-3850.

INSTITUTE OF THE SOUTH FOR HOSPITALITY & CULINARY ARTS
Jacksonville/Year-round

This 2-year college offers a 1-year diploma and 2-year AS degree. Program started 1990. Accredited by SACS, ACFEI. Calendar: semester. Curriculum: core. Admission dates: August, January, May. Total enrollment 100; 100% of applicants accepted; 30% financial aid recipients; 20% under age 25; 79% age 25 to 44; 1% age 45 or over; 40% part-time students; 20 students per instructor; 95% of graduates obtain employment. Facilities: 3 kitchens, 4 classrooms, 2 restaurants.

COURSES: 64 hours of culinary courses required for graduation. Externship: 2 at 150 hours, throughout the community.

FACULTY: 4 full-time, 6 part-time. Includes: Chefs Rick Grigsby, Joe Harrold, and Al Fricke. Qualifications: ACF certified.

COSTS: Annual tuition: in-state $832, out-of-state $3,328. Admission requirements: high school diploma or equivalent.

CONTACT: Dr. Sharon Cooper, Dean, Florida Community College at Jacksonville, Institute of the South for Hospitality & Culinary Arts, 4501 Capper Rd., Jacksonville, FL 32218; (904) 766-6594, Fax (904) 766-6654.

JOHNSON & WALES UNIVERSITY
North Miami
(See page 94)

This nonprofit university offers a 2 year AAS and 4 year BS program in Culinary Arts and Baking/Pastry Arts. Calendar: quarter. Curriculum: core. Admission dates: rolling. Total enrollment 617; varied number of enrollees each admission period; 77% of applicants accepted; 38% under age 25; 62% age 25 to 44; 5% part-time students; 20 students per instructor; 58% of graduates obtain employment. Facilities: 14 kitchens, 9 classrooms, 2 restaurants; new, modern, labs.

COURSES: culinary fundamentals, advanced culinary technologies, culinary principles. 1,250 hours of culinary courses required for graduation. Other requirements: professional studies, academic courses. Schedule: up to 24 hours per week, 9 months per year; weekend programs available.

FACULTY: 15 full-time

COSTS: Tuition: $13,500. $100 deposit. Application deadlines: rolling. Admission requirements: high school diploma or equivalent. On-campus housing: 250 spaces, average cost: $2,880. Average off-campus housing cost: $350 per month.

LOCATION: The 617-student, 8-acre campus is in South Florida.

CONTACT: Barbara Weiss, Director of Admissions, Office of Admissions, Johnson & Wales University, 1701 N.E. 127th St., North Miami, FL 33181; (800) 232-2433 or (305) 892-7600, Fax (305) 892-7020.

MID-FLORIDA TECHNICAL INSTITUTE
Orlando

This institution offers a 1,800-hour certificate. Program started 1970. Accredited by SACS. Admission dates: open. Total enrollment 80; 100% of applicants accepted; 15 to 20 students per instructor; 100% of graduates obtain employment.

FACULTY: 2 full-time, 6 part-time.

CONTACT: Dale Pennington, Commercial Cooking-Culinary Arts, Mid-Florida Technical Institute, 2900 W. Oakridge Rd., Orlando, FL 32809; (407) 855-5880, Fax (407) 855-5880, ext. 700.

NORTH TECHNICAL EDUCATION CENTER
Riviera Beach/Year-round

This public institution offers a 1,800-hour certificate in Commercial Foods and Culinary Arts. Program started 1970. Accredited by SACS. Calendar: quarter. Curriculum: culinary only. Admission dates: August, October, January, March, June. Total enrollment 40; 20 day and 20 evening enrollees each admission period; 100% of applicants accepted; 50% financial aid recipients; 70% under age 25; 20% age 25 to 44; 10% age 45 or over; 50% part-time students; 15 to 20 students per instructor; 90% of graduates obtain employment. Facilities: kitchen and classroom.

FACULTY: 1 full-time.

COSTS: Annual tuition: in-state $400 to $800. Textbook, uniform and shoes approximately $200. Refund policy: full first week, half second week less $10 fee.

LOCATION: The public vocational school is in an urban setting.

CONTACT: R. Robertson, Commercial Foods & Culinary Arts, North Technical Education Center, 7071 Garden Rd., Riviera Beach, FL 33404; (407) 881-4600.

OKALOOSA-WALTON COMMUNITY COLLEGE
Niceville/Year-round

This college offers a 2-year AAS/AS degree in Restaurant Management. Program started 1973. Accredited by SACS. Calendar: semester. Curriculum: core. Admission dates: August, January, May. Total enrollment 25; 40% financial aid recipients; 40% under age 25; 50% age 25 to 44; 10% age 45 or over; 5% part-time students; 25 students per instructor; 92% of graduates obtain employment. Facilities: include kitchen and classroom.

COURSES: 36 hours of culinary courses required for graduation. Other required courses: 6 hours elective in commercial baking.

FACULTY: 1 full-time, 1 part-time.

COSTS: Tuition: in-state $26 per semester hour, out-of-state $104 per semester hour. Admission requirements: high school diploma or equivalent and admission test. Last year 6 scholarships were awarded averaging $750. Average off-campus housing cost: $225 per month.

CONTACT: Riley Perdue, Commercial Foods-Industrial Education, Okaloosa-Walton Community College, 100 College Blvd., Niceville, FL 32578; (904) 678-5111, Fax (904) 729-5215.

PINELLAS TECHNICAL EDUCATIONAL CENTER
N. Clearwater/Year-round

This college offers a 15-month diploma in Culinary Arts. Program started 1965. Accredited by ADFEI, SACS. Calendar: trimester. Curriculum: culinary only. Admission dates: every 15 weeks. Total enrollment 60; 6 to 10 enrollees each admission period; 100% of applicants accepted; 75% financial aid recipients; 50% under age 25; 25% age 25 to 44; 25% age 45 or over; 15 students per instructor; 100% of graduates obtain employment. Facilities: include 2 kitchens, 2 classrooms and a student-run restaurant.

COURSES: Include employability skills and computer literacy. 1,800 hours of culinary courses required for graduation. Other required courses: transformation class. Schedule: 5 hours per day, 11 months per year.

FACULTY: 4 full-time.

COSTS: Tuition: in-state $213 per trimester. Admission requirements: admission test. Last year 3 scholarships were awarded averaging $213; 150 loans were granted, averaging $213. Average off-campus housing cost $350 per month. Part time employment available.

CONTACT: Vincent Calandra, Department Chair, Culinary Arts Department, Pinellas Technical Educational Center, 6100 154th Ave., N. Clearwater, FL 34620; (813) 538-7167.

PINELLAS TECHNICAL EDUCATIONAL CENTER
St. Petersburg/Year-round

This trade school offers a 1,800-hour diploma in Culinary Arts. Accredited by SACS, ACFEI. Calendar: trimester. Admission dates: open. Total enrollment 52; 10 enrollees each admission period; 100% of applicants accepted; 60% financial aid recipients; 18% under age 25; 70% age 25 to 44; 12% age 45 or over; 17 students per instructor; 95% of graduates obtain employment. Facilities: include kitchen, baking lab and classroom.

COURSES: Schedule: days 7:30 am-2:10 pm, evenings 5:30 pm-9:00 pm.

FACULTY: 3 full-time, 1 part-time. Includes: Dr. Warren Laux, Dr. Tom Maas, Alvin W. Miller, Fred Usher, Fred Lemiesz.

COSTS: Annual tuition: $440. Other costs: books $42. Admission requirements: admission test. Last year 3 scholarships were awarded averaging $450; 25 loans were granted, averaging $980.

LOCATION: The 1,950-student campus is in a suburban setting 21 miles from Tampa.

CONTACT: Alvin Miller, Culinary Arts Dept., Pinellas Technical Educational Center, 901 34th St. South, St. Petersburg, FL 33711; (813) 893-2500, ext.1104.

SARASOTA COUNTY TECHNICAL INSTITUTE
Sarasota

This institution offers a 1,485-hour certificate. Program started 1967. Accredited by SACS. Admission dates: open; 90% of applicants accepted; 100% of graduates obtain employment.

FACULTY: 1 full-time.

CONTACT: Timothy Carroll, Culinary Arts, Sarasota County Technical Institute, 4748 Beneva Rd., Sarasota, FL 34233; (941) 924-1365 ext. 250.

SHERIDAN VOCATIONAL TECH CENTER
Hollywood/Year-round

This school offers a 1-year certificate. Accredited by SACS. Admission dates: each 9-week term. Total enrollment 50; 10-20 enrollees each admission period; 100% of applicants accepted; 50% financial aid recipients; 50% under age 25; 47% age 25 to 44; 1% age 45 or over; 90% of graduates obtain employment. Facilities: cafeteria, snack bar, dining room.

COURSES: Baking & pastries, food production, garde manger, service. 1,080 hours of culinary courses required for graduation. Other required courses: 30 hours each of sanitation, nutrition, supervisory management. Schedule: 7 am-1:45 pm, Monday-Friday.

FACULTY: 2 full-time, 2 part-time. Includes: Program Coordinator/Dept. Head V. Paul Citrullo, Jr., CEC and Odis Herring.

COSTS: Tuition: $135 per term. Admission requirements: basic skills testing.

CONTACT: V. Paul Citrullo, Jr., CEC, Exec. Chef/Culinary Arts Coordinator, Sheridan Vocational Tech Center, 5400 Sheridan St., Hollywood, FL 33021; (305) 985-3262, Fax (305) 985-3229.

THE SOUTHEAST INSTITUTE OF CULINARY ARTS
St. Augustine/Year-round

This public institution, part of St. Augustine Technical Center, offers 1-year 1,080-hour Certificate and 2-year 2,160-hour Diploma programs in Commercial Foods and Culinary Arts. Established in 1976. Accredited by ACFEI and SACS. Calendar: quinmester. Curriculum: core. Admission every 9 weeks. Total enrollment 800; 45 enrollees each admission period; 97% of applicants accepted; 10% financial aid recipients; 1% under age 25; 90% age 25 to 44; 9% age 45 or over; 15 to 20 students per instructor; 100% of graduates obtain employment. Facilities 5 kitchens and 5 classrooms.

COURSES: Students rotate through each station and can then take specific intensives. Curriculum covers cafeteria and continental foods, epicurean service, cold buffet, baking and pastry, and purchasing. A 9-week paid externship concludes the diploma program. Schedule: August to May, Monday through Friday, 8 am to 3 pm; June to August, Monday through Thursday, 7:30 am to 3:30 pm. Specialized Certificates can be earned for portions of the course. Apprenticeship and cooperative education programs are available for those who wish to work part-time.

FACULTY: 21 full- and 2 part-time faculty, all with a minimum of 5 years experience and most with ACF certification.

COSTS: Approximately $155 per quinmester. Nonrefundable registration fee is $15, annual book deposit is $50. Refund within 30 days of completion. Applicants must have a high school diploma or equivalent. Last year more than 10 scholarships were awarded at an average of $200 each; more than 10 loans were granted at an average of $250 each. Part-time employment is available. Off-campus lodging is $400 per month.

LOCATION: St. Augustine, the nation's oldest city and home of the American Culinary Federation.

CAREER/PROFESSIONAL — GEORGIA

CONTACT: Chef Harold Holanchock CEC, CCE, AAC, The Southeast Institute of Culinary Arts, 2980 Collins Ave., St. Augustine, FL 32094-9970; (904) 829-1060/1061, Fax (904) 824-6750.

SOUTHEASTERN ACADEMY
Kissimmee/Year-round

This propriety institution offers a 30-week diploma in Culinary Arts. Program started 1990. Accredited by ACCSCT. Calendar: block system. Curriculum: core. Admission dates: every 5 weeks. Total enrollment 120; 30 enrollees each admission period; 95% of applicants accepted; 90% financial aid recipients; 20% under age 25; 75% age 25 to 44; 5% age 45 or over; 10 students per instructor; 85% of graduates obtain employment. Facilities: include 6 kitchens and classrooms, and a student-run restaurant.

COURSES: Culinary arts, baking/pastry arts, sanitation, nutrition, professional development. Schedule: 5 hours per day, 5 days per week, 1-3 classes per day, year-round. Externship provided.

FACULTY: 10 full-time, 2 part-time. Includes: Mick Young, Ftiz Blumberg, Gerald Krotky, Ann-Marie Marciano, Jeffrey Harriman. Qualifications: ACF certified.

COSTS: Annual tuition: in-state and out-of-state $6,500. Tuition deposit $150. Refund policy: pro-rated except for application fee, uniforms, text and tools. Admission requirements: high school diploma or equivalent. On-campus housing: $2,500; off-campus housing: $4,000 for 30 weeks.

CONTACT: Culinary Director, Southeastern Academy, 233 Academy Dr., Box 421768, Kissimmee, FL 24742-1768; (407) 847-4444.

GEORGIA

ART INSTITUTE OF ATLANTA
Atlanta/Year-round

This proprietary school offers a 18-month AA degree in Culinary Arts. Program started 1991. Accredited by ACFEI, SACS. Calendar: quarter. Curriculum: core. Admission dates: January, April, July, October. Total enrollment 400; 50 to 75 enrollees each admission period; 75% financial aid recipients; 25% under age 25; 70% age 25 to 44; 5% age 45 or over; 10% part-time students; 20 to 25 students per instructor; 100% of graduates obtain employment. Facilities: include 4 kitchens and 3 classrooms.

COURSES: Culinary skills, food production, baking and pastry, garde manger. 72 hours of culinary courses required for graduation. Schedule: 20 hours per week, mornings, afternoons, or evenings.

FACULTY: 17 full and part-time full-time. Includes Director J. Morris, CWC, CCE and Asst. Director K. Duffy, CEC, CCE.

COSTS: Quarterly tuition: $3,088. Application fee $50, tuition deposit $100, quarterly lab fee $250. Application deadlines: rolling. Admission requirements: high school diploma or equivalent and writing sample required. On-campus housing: $440 per month. Part time employment available.

LOCATION: The 1,300-student campus is in the uptown "buckhead" area of Atlanta.

CONTACT: Robin J. Rickenbach, Director of Admissions, Art Institute of Atlanta, 3376 Peachtree Rd., NE, Atlanta, GA 30326; (800) 275-4242 or (404) 266-2662, Fax (404) 266-1383.

ATLANTA AREA TECHNICAL SCHOOL
Atlanta

This institution offers a 18-month diploma. Program started 1967. Accredited by SACS. Admission dates: quarterly. Total enrollment 50; 12 students per instructor; 92% of graduates obtain employment.

FACULTY: 6 full-time.

Costs: Annual tuition: $400 in-state, $700 out-of-state. Admission requirements: high school diploma or equivalent and admission test.

Contact: Barbara Boyd, Culinary Arts-Commercial Baking, Atlanta Area Technical School, 1560 Stewart Ave. S.W., Atlanta, GA 30310; (404) 756-3700, ext. 3727, Fax (404) 756-0932.

AUGUSTA TECHNICAL INSTITUTE
Augusta/Year-round

This state trade school offers a 4-quarter diploma in Basic Culinary Arts and a 6-quarter diploma in Advanced Culinary Arts. Program started 1985. Accredited by SACS. Calendar: quarter. Curriculum: core. Admission dates: September, March. Total enrollment 24; 15 enrollees each admission period; 90% of applicants accepted; 100% financial aid recipients; 10% under age 25; 12 students per instructor; 100% of graduates obtain employment. Facilities: include 1 kitchen, 2 classrooms, and local restaurants.

Courses: Food preparation and baking, garde manger, nutrition, menu management, consumer education. 108 (6 quarters), 69 (4 quarters) hours of culinary courses required for graduation. Other required courses: accounting, computer literacy. Schedule: approximately 30 hours per week, 12 months per year. Internship: 150-hours (concludes Advanced Culinary Arts), salaried, at various food service institutions. Continuing education: catering, cake decoration, sanitation.

Faculty: 2 full-time. Includes Willie Mae Crittenden, CCE and Kathleen Fervam, CCE, CEC.

Costs: Quarterly tuition: $274 in-state, $548 out-of-state. Application fee $15. Cancellations prior to July 5 receive full refund and prior to July 19 receive 75% refund. Application deadlines: summer and winter quarters. Admission requirements: high school diploma or GED. Average off-campus housing cost: $500 per month. Part time employment available.

Location: The 50-acre, 5000-student suburban campus is 7 miles from Augusta.

Contact: Willie Mae Crittenden, Department Head, Culinary Arts, Augusta Technical Institute, 3116 Deans Bridge Rd., Augusta, GA 30906; (706) 771-4000.

SAVANNAH TECHNICAL INSTITUTE
Savannah/Year-round

This public institution offers a 6-quarter and a 4 -quarter diploma in Culinary Arts. Program started 1981. Accredited by SACS, ACF. Calendar: quarter. Curriculum: core. Admission dates: quarterly. Total enrollment 24; 4 enrollees each admission period; 100% of applicants accepted; 54% financial aid recipients; 12 students per instructor; 100% of graduates obtain employment. Facilities: include kitchen, classroom and student-run restaurant.

Courses: Culinary arts, sanitation and equipment, food preparation, baking, garde manger, nutrition, and management. 106 (6 quarters), 69 (4 quarters) hours of culinary courses required for graduation. Other required courses: English, math, psychology. Schedule: 30 hours per week. Externship: 150 hours, restaurant.

Faculty: 1 full-time, 1 part-time. Includes: Marvis T. Hinson, CFBE, M.Ed and John F. Kelley, Executive Sous Chef.

Costs: Tuition: in-state $216 per quarter, out-of-state $348 per quarter. Application fee $15. 2 uniforms $50, shoes $40, knives $60, books $100.

Refund policy: 100% prior to first day of class, 75% first to fourteenth day of class. Application deadlines: 30 days before entry. Admission requirements: high school diploma or equivalent and admission test. Last year full scholarships were awarded to 75% of the student body; full loans were granted to 75% of the student body. Part-time employment is available.

Contact: Marvis Hinson, Department Head, Culinary Arts, Savannah Technical Institute, 5717 White Bluff Rd., Savannah, GA 31499; (914) 351-4553, Fax (912) 352-4362.

HAWAII

HONOLULU COMMUNITY COLLEGE
Honolulu

This college offers a certificate and a 2-year degree. Program started 1920. Accredited by WASC. Admission dates: fall. Total enrollment 50; 25 enrollees each admission period; 100% of graduates obtain employment. Externship provided.

FACULTY: 2 full-time.

CONTACT: Lloyd Yokoyama, Commercial Baking, Honolulu Community College, 874 Dillingham Rd., Honolulu, HI 96817; (808) 845-9138.

KAPIOLANI COMMUNITY COLLEGE
Honolulu/August-May

This college offers a 2-year AS degree in Culinary Arts, Patisserie, School Food Service, and Food Service-Health care, and a 1-year and 1-semester certificate program in Culinary Arts and Patisserie. Program started 1947. Accredited by ACFEI, WASC. Calendar: semester. Curriculum: core. Admission dates: fall, spring. Total enrollment 450; 100 enrollees each admission period; 100% of applicants accepted; 25% financial aid recipients; 25% under age 25; 65% age 25 to 44; 10% age 45 or over; 50% part-time students; 20 students per instructor; 98% of graduates obtain employment. Facilities: 9 kitchens, 8 classrooms, 5 restaurants.

COURSES: Asian/Pacific and international cuisine, garde manger, confisserie. Schedule: day classes 8 am-2 pm, evening lab classes 2:30 pm-9 pm, Monday-Friday. Externship: available at local and neighbor island hotels.

FACULTY: 14 full-time, 6 part-time. Qualifications: Industry experience.

COSTS: Annual tuition: in state $504, out-of-state $3,096. $10 fee per semester; 100% refund up to 5 days prior to class. Application deadlines: July 1 and December 1. Admission requirements: age 18, or age 17 with high school diploma or GED. Last year 75 scholarships were awarded averaging $350. Average off-campus housing cost: $500 per month.

LOCATION: The 7,500-student, 47-acre suburban campus is 2 miles from Waikiki.

CONTACT: Frank Leake, Chairman, Food Service & Hospitality Education Dept., Kapiolani Community College, 4303 Diamond Head Rd., Honolulu, HI 96816; (808) 734-9485, Fax (808) 734-9212.

MAUI COMMUNITY COLLEGE
Kahului/January-May, August-December

This 2-year college offers a 1-year certificate, a 2-year AS degree-Culinary, and a 2-year AS degree-Baking. Program started 1969. Accredited by ACFEI. Calendar: semester. Curriculum: core. Admission dates: August, January. Total enrollment 75- 85; 10 students per instructor; 98% of graduates obtain employment. Facilities: 2 kitchens, 2 classrooms, 1 restaurant, 1 cafe/dining room.

COURSES: Culinary Arts or Baking Specialties. 42-43 hours of culinary courses required for graduation. Schedule: 24-30 hours per week, 2 years. Apprenticeship available.

FACULTY: 4 full-time, 5 part-time.

COSTS: Annual tuition: in-state $522, out-of-state $3,114. Application deadlines: January and August. Last year 10 scholarships were awarded averaging $300.

CONTACT: Karen Tanaka, Coordinator, Culinary Arts Dept., Maui Community College, 310 Kaahamanu Ave., Kahului, HI 96732; (808) 244-9181, Fax (808) 242-1251, E-Mail mccada::tanaka.

IDAHO

BOISE STATE UNIVERSITY
Boise/January-May, August-December

This university offers a 1-year certificate and a 2-year AAS degree. Program started 1969. Accredited by ACFEI. Calendar: quarter. Curriculum: culinary. Admission dates: August, January. Total enrollment 35 to 45; 10 students per instructor; 98% of graduates obtain employment.

FACULTY: 3 full-time, 1 part-time.

COSTS: Tuition is $940 per semester. Admission requirements: high school diploma or equivalent and admission test.

CONTACT: Vern Hickman, CWC, CCE, Culinary Arts Program, Boise State University, 1910 University Dr., Boise, ID 83725; (208) 385-4199.

COLLEGE OF SOUTHERN IDAHO
Twin Falls

CONTACT: Chris Mottern, Program Coordinator, Hotel-Restaurant Management, College of Southern Idaho, P.O. Box 1238, Twin Falls, ID 83303-1238; (208) 733-9554, ext. 408.

ILLINOIS

BLACK HAWK COLLEGE-QUAD CITIES CAMPUS
Moline/Year-round

This college offers a 1-year certificate and a 2-year AAS Degree in Hospitality, Culinary Arts, and Professional Baking. Program started 1988. Accredited by NCA. Calendar: semester. Curriculum: core. Admission dates: September, January. Total enrollment 85; 15 enrollees each admission period; 60% under age 25; 40% age 25 to 44; 70% part-time students; 15 students per instructor; 100% of graduates obtain employment. Facilities: include advanced equipment in several areas of curriculum, and students prepare food for gourmet luncheon and community functions at the college. Part-time employment is available.

COURSES: Sanitation, culinary arts, quantity food, cost/portion control, baking, garde manger, internship, nutrition, general education courses. 34 (certificate), 62 (degree) hours of culinary courses required for graduation. Schedule: days. Externship: 16 weeks, open, individualized. Continuing education: classes for home economic teachers.

FACULTY: 8 full-time. Includes: V. Jones, B. Nevins, K. Davenport.

COSTS: Tuition: in-district $48 per credit hour, out-of-district $109 per credit hour, out-of-state $196 per credit hour. Refund policy: 100% through 6th calendar day of term. Application deadlines: ongoing. Admission requirements: high school diploma or equivalent and admission test. Last year 2 scholarships were awarded averaging $500 to $1,000. Average off-campus housing cost: $250-$300 per month. Part time employment available.

LOCATION: The 161-acre site is in a suburban setting.

CONTACT: Kim Davenport, Culinary Arts, Black Hawk College-Quad Cities Campus, 6600-34th Ave., Moline, IL 61265; (309) 796-1311 ext. 4125, Fax (309) 792-3418.

CLEA'S CASTLE COOKING SCHOOL
Oak Park/Year-round

Founded in 1974, this school offers 12-session cuisine courses, 2-session ice carving courses, 5-session courses in cake decorating, baking, and catering, a 30-hour supervisory development and nutrition course, and a 5-session sanitation and safety course for state certification.

FACULTY: Cleatis V. Wilcox, CCE, CEPC, CWC, AAC, is a member of the Escoffier Society and the Professional Pastry Guild.

COSTS: Tuition ranges from $125-$200.

CONTACT: Clea's Castle Cooking School, 1201 Fair Oaks Ave., Oak Park, IL 60302; (708) 383-8245, (708) 383-1849, Fax (708) 848-8580.

COLLEGE OF DUPAGE
Glen Ellyn/Year-round

This college offers a 1-year certificate and a 2-year AAS degree in Food Service Administration and Culinary Arts. Program started 1966. Accredited by NCA, ADVEI, RBA, NRA Educational Foundation. Calendar: quarter. Curriculum: core. Admission dates: September, January, March, June. Total enrollment 400; 50 to 125 enrollees each admission period; 100% of applicants accepted; 25% financial aid recipients; 40% under age 25; 40% age 25 to 44; 20% age 45 or over; 30% part-time students; 15 students per instructor; 100% of graduates obtain employment. Facilities: include kitchen, many classrooms, restaurant and dining room.

COURSES: Food preparation, classical cuisine, merchandising, cake decorating, garde manger, wines and intl. cuisine. Schedule: students can enroll part-time or evenings. Externship provided.

FACULTY: 4 full-time, 12 part-time. Includes: George C. Macht, CHA, CFE, FMP

Chris Thieman, CWC, Rolf Sick, Jim Zielinski, FMP.

COSTS: In-district $25 per credit hour. Admission fee $10. Texts, uniforms, tools and fees $500. Refund policy: 100% refund before the first day of quarter, 80% refund through the first week of the quarter. Application deadlines: depend on quarter. Admission requirements: high school diploma or equivalent. Last year 10 scholarships were awarded averaging $250. Part-time employment is available. Average off-campus housing cost: $500 per month.

LOCATION: The 33,000-student campus is in a suburban setting 25 miles from Chicago.

CONTACT: Catherine Leveille, Program Assistant, Culinary Arts/Pastry Arts, College of DuPage, 22nd St. & Lambert Rd., Glen Ellyn, IL 60137; (708) 858-2800, Fax (708) 858-9399.

COLLEGE OF LAKE COUNTY
Grayslake/August-May

This college offers a 1-year certificate in Culinary Arts or Food Service Management and an AAS in Food Service Management. Program started 1987. Accredited by NCA. Calendar: semester. Curriculum: core. Admission dates: August, January. Total enrollment 40; 10 enrollees each admission period; 95% of applicants accepted; 10% financial aid recipients; 50% under age 25; 40% age 25 to 44; 10% age 45 or over; 50% part-time students; 10 students per instructor; 98% of graduates obtain employment. Facilities: include 2 kitchens and 3 classrooms.

COURSES: Cooking, baking, nutrition and menu planning. Schedule: 4 days per week, part-time/full-time and evening options available. Externship: 16-week part-time.

FACULTY: 5 full-time. Includes: C. Wener, M. Eskenazy, J. Lempke, J. Bress. Qualifications: minimum 2 year culinary school or formal internship.

COSTS: Tuition: $44 per credit hour. Other fees: lab, equipment, uniforms. Last year 2 scholarships were awarded averaging $500. Part-time employment is available.

CONTACT: Mr. Cliff Wener, Coordinator Food Service Program, Business Division, College of Lake County, 19351 W. Washington St., Grayslake, IL 60030-1198; (708) 223-6601 ext. 2573, Fax (708) 223-7248.

COOKING ACADEMY OF CHICAGO
Chicago/January-December

This institution offers a 6-month and 1-year Culinary Career Certificate, and a 6-month Baking & Pastry Certificate. Program started 1992. Admission dates: January, May, September. Total enrollment 10; 10 enrollees each admission period; 100% of applicants accepted; 10% under age 25; 80% age 25 to 44; 10% age 45 or over; 10 students per instructor; 100% of graduates obtain employment. Facilities: 2 full kitchens, 2 classrooms.

COURSES: Knife skills, soups and stocks, vegetables and starches, meats, fish, and poultry.

FACULTY: 2 full-time. Qualifications: minimum AAS and 5 years experience.

COSTS: Tuition: culinary $3,500, baking & pastry $3,000. Fees: $100. Application deadlines: January 1, May 1, September 1. Admission requirements: high school or GED. Last year 5 scholarships were awarded averaging $1,500.

CONTACT: Nora Christensen, Director, Cooking Academy of Chicago, 2500 W. Bradley Pl., Chicago, IL 60618; (312) 478-9840, Fax (312) 478-3146.

THE COOKING AND HOSPITALITY INSTITUTE OF CHICAGO
Chicago/Year-round *(See also page 182) (See display ad page 33)*

This institution offers a 2-year (70-credit-hour) associate degree in culinary arts, 30-week (28-credit-hour) certificate programs in professional cooking and baking and pastry, a 300-hour certificate program in restaurant management, and a variety of continuing education and nonvocational classes. Established in 1983. Accredited by the ACCSCT. Full-time classes start every 7 weeks; a part-time 16-month program starts 3 times a year. Total enrollment 900 students per year; 80% of applicants are accepted; 25 students per faculty member; 95% of graduates obtain jobs. Facilities: three fully-equipped instructional kitchens and an on-site restaurant.

COURSES: Professional cooking covers qualitative and quantitative cooking, menu planning, recipe development, sanitation, and job search techniques. Baking and pastry covers production techniques, food as an art form, yeast breads, and decoration. Flexible schedules are available.

FACULTY: School founder Linda Calafiore is a past state coordinator of local vocational training programs. Instructors include Mark Facklam, formerly executive chef at Cricket's, and Carl Jerome, author of *Cooking for a New Earth*. Guest chefs occasionally teach.

COSTS: Tuition is $15,500 for the degree program and $6,200 for each certificate program. Registration fee is $100. High school diploma or equivalent required. Pell grants and guaranteed student loans are available.

CONTACT: The Cooking and Hospitality Institute of Chicago, 361 W. Chestnut, Chicago, IL 60610; (312) 944-2725.

THE CULINARY SCHOOL OF KENDALL COLLEGE
Evanston/Year-round

This nonprofit school, a division of Kendall College, offers a 21-month AAS degree in Culinary Arts, 9-month Culinary Professional Certificate, and 2- and 4-year Hospitality Management programs. Founded 1985. Accredited by ACFEI and NCA. Calendar: 11-week terms. Admission dates: September, January, April, June. Total enrollment 350; 40 enrollees each admission period; 80% of applicants accepted; 82% financial aid recipients; 53% under age 25; 39% age 25 to 44; 8% age 45 or over; 22% part-time students; 13 students per instructor; 100% of graduates obtain employment. Facilities include demonstration, production, and display kitchens, dining room, banquet area.

COURSES: Culinary skills, business management, nutrition, menu planning, classic cuisine. Beginning students work in school's cafeteria, bakery, and catering service; advanced students work in the school's open-to-the-public restaurant. A 13-week salaried internship at an approved foodservice establishment is required.

CAREER/PROFESSIONAL — ILLINOIS

THE COOKING AND HOSPITALITY INSTITUTE OF CHICAGO

Chicago's premier culinary school. For information, call 312.944.2725

FACULTY: Includes 15 chef/instructors, hospitality specialists and visiting lecturers and guest chefs.

COSTS: Tuition is $12,801 per year, including equipment and activities fee and 2 meals daily. A $30 nonrefundable application fee is required; $150 nonrefundable deposit is due within 30 days of acceptance. Withdrawals the first week of class forfeit $100. Applicants must have a high school diploma or equivalent and some foodservice experience. Last year 144 scholarships were awarded at an average of $800 each; 300 loans were granted at an average of $2,625 each. Part-time employment is available. Room and board is $1,065 double, $1,829 single per term.

LOCATION: 35 minutes from Chicago's Loop by express train.

CONTACT: The Culinary School of Kendall College, 2408 Orrington Ave., Evanston, IL 60201; (708) 866-1304, Fax (708) 866-6842.

ELGIN COMMUNITY COLLEGE
Elgin/September-July

This college offers a 2-year associate degree in Culinary Arts. Program started 1972. Accredited by Illinois Community College Board, ACFEI. Calendar: semester. Curriculum: core. Admission dates: August, January. Total enrollment 140; 30 to 40 enrollees each admission period; 80% of applicants accepted; 25% under age 25; 65% age 25 to 44; 10% age 45 or over; 30% part-time students; 12 to 30 students per instructor; 100% of graduates obtain employment. Facilities: 4 kitchens, 3 classrooms and a culinary training center.

FACULTY: 3 full-time, 8 part-time. Includes: Michael Zema, CCE, FMP, Director Roland Zwerger, CMC, Stephanie Johnson, CPC. Qualifications: ACF-certification.

COSTS: $35 per credit hour. Books and uniforms $200. Admission requirements: high school diploma or equivalent. Last year 12 scholarships were awarded averaging $300. Part-time employment is available. Average off-campus housing cost: $400-$600 per month.

CONTACT: Michael Zema, Director, Hospitality Department, Elgin Community College, 1700 Spartan Dr., Elgin, IL 60123; (708) 697-1000 ext. 7461, Fax (708) 888-7995.

FOOD ARTS STUDIO
Elmwood Park/Spring, Summer, Fall

Food stylist Donna Lafferty conducts 2- and 4-day certificate courses (limit 10 students) in styling food for the still and motion camera. Facilities: a 250-square-foot professional kitchen with work stations and overhead mirror. Other activities: shopping at specialty stores. Also available: a yearly food-oriented tour to a country where food styling, cooking, and food photography are taught.

COURSES: Weekend (5-day) course offers 16 (40) hours of instruction and a shopping trip.

FACULTY: Donna Lafferty has 16 years experience styling for still and motion advertising. Clients include Edy's Grand Ice Cream, Kraft Foods, and The Oprah Winfrey Show.

COSTS: $400 for 2 days, $800 for 4 days, both with nonrefundable deposit.

LOCATION: U.S. classes: a Chicago suburb.

CONTACT: Donna Lafferty, Food Arts Studio, 2733 N. 75th Ct., Elmwood Park, IL 60635-1433; (708) 456-8415.

JOLIET JUNIOR COLLEGE
Joliet/Year-round

This college offers a 2-year certificate/AAS degree in Culinary Arts. Program started 1970. Accredited by NCA, ACFEI. Calendar: semester. Curriculum: core. Admission dates: August, January, May, June. Total enrollment 200; 100 enrollees each admission period; 98% of applicants accepted; 40% financial aid recipients; 85% under age 25; 15% age 25 to 44; 20 students per instructor; 95% of graduates obtain employment. Facilities: include 3 kitchens, demonstration kitchen, 3 classrooms and a pastry shop.

FACULTY: 9 full-time

COSTS: Annual tuition: in-state $982, out-of-state $4,118. Admission requirements: high school diploma or equivalent and admission test. Part time employment available.

LOCATION: The 11,000-student campus is in a small town setting.

CONTACT: Patrick F. Hegarty, CEC, CCE, Culinary Arts/Hotel-Restaurant Management, Joliet Junior College, 1216 Houbolt Ave., Joliet, IL 60436-9352; (815) 729-9020 ext. 2448, Fax (815) 744-5507.

LEXINGTON COLLEGE
Chicago/September-May

This independent institution offers a 2-year AAS degree in Hotel, Food Service, or Dietary Management. Program started 1977. Accredited by NCA. Calendar: semester. Curriculum: core. Admission dates: September, January. Total enrollment 20; 20 enrollees each admission period; 90% of applicants accepted; 85% financial aid recipients; 75% under age 25; 25% age 25 to 44; 10% part-time students; 4 students per instructor; 95% of graduates obtain employment. Facilities: include a culinary lab, 3 classrooms, library, computer lab, bookstore, off-campus site for quantity foods.

COURSES: Professional baking, pastries, food and beverage sales & service, garde manger, purchasing, quantity foods, basic food production, professional cooking, food service sanitation, and general education, liberal arts and management courses. 8 hours of culinary courses required for graduation. Other requirements: English, management, speech, Western civilization, business

CAREER/PROFESSIONAL　　　　ILLINOIS　　　　35

math, accounting. Schedule: 15-17 credit hours per semester, 17-20 hours of class time per week; part-time options available. Externship provided. Continuing education: evenings and weekends.

FACULTY: 4 part-time.

COSTS: Tuition: $2,700 per semester. Application fee $25, books and equipment $300-350 per semester, lab culinary fees $50-100 per semester. Part time employment available.

No refund after fourth week of class. Application deadlines: rolling. Admission requirements: high school diploma or equivalent, with 2.0 average or above. Average off-campus housing cost $1,600 per semester.

LOCATION: An urban setting, 20 miles from downtown Chicago.

CONTACT: Mary Jane Markel, Director of Admissions, Admissions, Lexington College, 10840 S. Western Ave., Chicago, IL 60643-3294; (312) 779-3800, Fax (312) 779-7450.

TRITON COLLEGE
River Grove/August-May

This college offers a 2-year AAS degree in Culinary Management. Program started 1970. Accredited by NCA, ACFEI. Calendar: semester. Curriculum: core. Admission dates: September. Total enrollment 150; 30 enrollees each admission period; 50% financial aid recipients; 30% under age 25; 60% age 25 to 44; 10% age 45 or over; 30% part-time students; 12 students per instructor; 97% of graduates obtain employment. Facilities: 5 kitchens and classrooms, demonstration kitchen, ice carving facility, and student-run restaurant.

COURSES: Garde manger, international cooking, ice carving, food production, food theory, menu planning, purchasing, cost control, nutrition, service, and baking. Schedule: Monday-Friday 10 months per year; part-time, evening and weekend options available. Externship provided. Continuing education: international cooking, sanitation, and nutrition.

FACULTY: 3 full-time, 10 part-time. Includes: J. Drosos, K. Iverson, Ph.D., J. Nielsen, MA.

COSTS: $36.50 per credit hour. Application fee $25. Other fees: approximately $100 per semester. Refund policy: before classes begin. Application deadlines: Fall: August 25; Spring: January 15. Admission requirements: high school diploma or equivalent. Last year 10 scholarships were awarded averaging $500. Part-time employment is available. Average off-campus housing cost: $300 per month.

CONTACT: Hospitality Industry Administration, Triton College , 2000 Fifth Ave., River Grove, IL 60171; (708) 456-0300.

WASHBURNE TRADE SCHOOL
Chicago

This independent institution offers a 80-week certificate in Chef Training. Program started 1937. Accredited by City Colleges of Chicago. Calendar: 3 phases of 16 weeks per year. Curriculum: culinary only. Admission dates: September, January, May. Total enrollment 150; 25 enrollees each admission period; FCFS applicants accepted; 75% financial aid recipients; 25% under age 25; 25 students per instructor; 98% of graduates obtain employment. Facilities: 6 kitchens, 6 classrooms.

COURSES: Schedule: 8:00 am-1:35 pm Monday-Thursday, 8:00 am-12:20 pm Friday. Continuing education: ice carving.

FACULTY: 7 full-time.

COSTS: Annual tuition: $3,664 and includes books and uniforms. Application fee: $200 if cash-paying student; none if financial aid. Cutlery set: $272. Admission requirements: high school diploma or equivalent and admission test. Part time employment available.

LOCATION: The 4-story campus occupies one-block in Chicago.

CONTACT: Bill Jaeger, Chefs Training Program, Washburne Trade Program, 3233 W. 31st St., Chicago, IL 60623; (312) 579-6108.

WILLIAM RAINEY HARPER COLLEGE
Palatine/Year-round

This college offers a 1-year certificate in Culinary Arts and Baking. Program started 1975. Calendar: semester. Curriculum: core. Admission dates: year-round. Total enrollment 150; 25 enrollees each admission period; 95% of applicants accepted; 50% financial aid recipients; 50% under age 25; 40% age 25 to 44; 10% age 45 or over; 75% part-time students; 15 students per instructor; 100% of graduates obtain employment. Facilities: include 3 kitchens including production bakery, production kitchen, demo lab, and several classrooms.

COURSES: Garde manger, classical cuisine, cake decorating, basic and advanced culinary, basic and advanced baking. 420 hours of culinary courses required for graduation. Other required courses: 200 management contact hours. Schedule: daily August-May; part-time and evening options.

FACULTY: 3 full-time, 4 part-time. Includes: Patrick J. Beach, Gayle Simon. Qualifications: ACF-certified with 4-year or graduate degrees.

COSTS: Annual tuition is $1,000. Other costs: application fee $50, lab fee $200, books $400. Refund policy: 90% 1st week, 80% 2nd week. Scholarship awards: average $500. Part-time employment is available. Average off-campus housing cost: $400-$600 per month.

LOCATION: The 27,000-student, 20-building suburban campus is 35 miles from Chicago's loop.

CONTACT: Bruce Borher, Director of Admissions, William Rainey Harper College, 1200 W. Algonquin Rd., Palatine, IL 60067-7398; (708) 925-6700, Fax (708) 925-6031. E-Mail bborher@harper.cc.il.us

WILTON SCHOOL OF CAKE DECORATING
Woodridge/February-November

This private school offers career-oriented 4- to 10-day cake decoration and candy making diploma courses Founded in 1929. Facilities: the 2,200-square-foot school includes a classroom, teaching kitchen, student lounge, and retail store.

COURSES: The 10-day (70-hour) Master Course, which covers basic cake decorating and design techniques; 5-day courses cover chocolate, the Lambeth method, Australian techniques, and catering; 3- and 4-day courses cover gum paste and pulled sugar. Hours vary and some courses can be taken concurrently. Most are conducted on consecutive days with weekends free.

FACULTY: Sandra Folsom, Susan Matusiak, Nicholas Lodge, Wesley Wilton, and Elaine Gonzalez.

COSTS: Range from $150 for 3 days to $550 for a 10-day course. A registration fee of $25-$75 must accompany application. Refund with 14 days written notice.

LOCATION: A southwestern Chicago suburb, 25 miles from downtown.

CONTACT: School Secretary, Wilton School of Cake Decorating and Confectionery Art, 2240 W. 75th St., Woodridge, IL 60517; (708) 963-7100, ext. 216; Fax (708) 963-7299.

INDIANA

IVY TECH STATE COLLEGE
Fort Wayne/Year-round

This college offers a 2-year AAS degree in Hospitality Administration with Culinary Arts or Pastry Arts Specialty. Program started 1981. Accredited by NCA, ACFEI. Calendar: semester. Curriculum: culinary only. Admission dates: fall, spring, summer. Total enrollment 108; 64 enrollees each admission period; 100% of applicants accepted; 33% financial aid recipients; 15% under age 25;

CAREER/PROFESSIONAL INDIANA 37

75% age 25 to 44; 10% age 45 or over; 42% part-time students; 10 to 12 students per instructor; 100% of graduates obtain employment. Facilities: include 5 kitchens and classrooms, pastry arts lab, and large full service kitchen with top-of-the-line equipment.

COURSES: Basic foods, soups, stocks and sauces, nutrition, meat cutting, special cuisines, classical cuisines, fish and seafood, pantry and breakfast, garde manger, catering, breads and pastries, cake decoration, chocolates and baking. 60 hours of culinary courses required for graduation. Schedule: 8 am-10 pm; part-time evening options are available. Externship: 144-hour, salaried, in an ACF approved site.

FACULTY: 2 full-time, 8 part-time. Includes: Program Chair Bobbi Moghaddam, CC, FMP, CDM and Chef Instructor Elizabeth Watzek-Bougher, a CIA graduate with 21 years industry experience.

COSTS: Annual tuition: $1,835 in-state, $3,335 out-of-state. Other fees: books, uniforms, knife kits, and specialty tools. Refund: full during 1st week of class; partial thereafter. Application deadlines: rolling. Admission requirements: high school diploma or equivalent and admission test. Last year 5 scholarships were awarded averaging $600. Part-time employment is available.

LOCATION: The small campus is in an urban community, 200 miles from Chicago or Indianapolis.

CONTACT: Bobbi Moghaddam, CC, FMP, CDM, Hospitality Administration, Ivy Tech State College, 3800 North Anthony Blvd., Fort Wayne, IN 46805; (219) 482-9171, Fax (219) 480-4177.

IVY TECH STATE COLLEGE
East Chicago, Gary, Valparaiso/Year-round

This college offers a 2-year AAS degree and a 1-year technical certificate in Hospitality Administration. Program started 1981. Accredited by NCA. Calendar: semester. Curriculum: core. Admission dates: January, May, August. Total enrollment 80; 15 enrollees each admission period; 90% of applicants accepted; 30% financial aid recipients; 30% part-time students; 12 students per instructor; 100% of graduates obtain employment. Facilities: include 4 kitchens at 3 campuses, catering facilities, restaurant and bakeshop.

COURSES: Include portfolio program - wine, culinary/hotel specialty, catering, baking. Schedule: 8 am-5 pm, Monday-Friday, or 2 evenings per week; year-round. Externship: 16 week. Continuing education: French studies with the Premier Sommelier and Chef of France, and special interest courses are available.

FACULTY: 2 full-time, 7 part-time. Program director Deborah Ward is the only American to have received France's Cross of Gold award.

COSTS: Annual tuition: $1,810 in-state, $3,621 out-of-state. Admission requirements: high school diploma or equivalent. Last year 8 scholarships were awarded, averaging $4,000. Part time employment available.

CONTACT: Deborah Ward, Hotel & Restaurant Management/Culinary Arts, Ivy Tech State College, 410 East Columbus Dr., East Chicago, IN 46312; (219) 392-3600 ext. 18 or (219) 981-1111 ext. 33, Fax (219)981-4415.

IVY TECH STATE COLLEGE
Indianapolis/Year-round

This college offers a 2-year AAS degree in Culinary Arts, Baking & Pastry Arts, and Hotel Restaurant Management. Program started 1986. Accredited by NCA, ACFEI. Calendar: semester. Curriculum: core. Admission dates: August, January. Total enrollment 200; 40 enrollees each admission period; 100% of applicants accepted; 75% financial aid recipients; 20% under age 25; 70% age 25 to 44; 10% age 45 or over; 40% part-time students; 10 students per instructor; 98% of graduates obtain employment. Facilities: 3 kitchens, classrooms, 1 restaurant.

COURSES: Include basic food theory & skills, sanitation, classical French techniques. 66 hours of culinary courses required for graduation. Externship: 5 months.

FACULTY: 3 full-time, 12 part-time. Qualifications: Associate degree, 5 years experience, certifiable.

COSTS: Annual tuition: $3,000 in-state, $4,650 out-of-state. Admission requirements: high school diploma or equivalent and admission test. Average off-campus housing cost: $300 per month.

CONTACT: Chef Vincent Kinkade, Chair, Hospitality Administration, Ivy Tech State College, One W. 26th St., Indianapolis, IN 46208; (317) 921-4619.

VINCENNES UNIVERSITY
Vincennes/August-May

This public institution offers a 2-year AS degree in Culinary Arts. Accredited by NCA. Calendar: semester. Curriculum: core. Admission dates: open. Total enrollment 60; 30 enrollees each admission period; 100% of applicants accepted; 90% financial aid recipients; 65% under age 25; 35% age 25 to 44; 5% part-time students; 12 students per instructor; 100% of graduates obtain employment. Facilities: include kitchen, 3 classrooms, hands-on lab and restaurant.

COURSES: Quantity foods, pastry and bake shop, haute cuisine, food facility design, hospitality, sanitation, purchasing, supervision, and general education. 44 hours of culinary courses required for graduation. Other required courses: core curriculum 22 to 23 hours. Schedule: 16 to 17 hours per 5-day week. Externship provided. Continuing education: ACF regional chefs conduct hands-on classes.

FACULTY: 2 full-time, 1 part-time. Includes: Chef Robert Bird, CCE, Chef Carol Keusch, CWPC, Phyllis Robison, Dept. Chair, and Lori Marchino. Qualifications: combined 58 years in industry with AS and BA degrees.

COSTS: Annual tuition: $1,800 in-state, $5,000 out-of-state. Application fee $20; housing deposit $150. Student activities fee $18. Refund policy: 100% credit adjustment of tuition and fees during the first week of classes, 75% during second week, 50% during third week, and 25% during fourth week. Admission requirements: high school diploma or equivalent required. Last year 7 scholarships were awarded averaging $250-$500. Part-time employment is available. On-campus housing: 3,000 spaces.

CONTACT: Robert H. Bird C.C.E., Asst. Professor Culinary Arts, Culinary Arts Department, Vincennes University, Hoosier Hospitality Center, Gov. Hall, Vincennes, IN 47591; (812) 888-5742, Fax (812) 888-5868.

IOWA

DES MOINES AREA COMMUNITY COLLEGE
Ankeny/Year-round

This college offers a 2-year AAS degree in Culinary Arts. Program started 1975. Accredited by NCA and ACFEI. Calendar: semester. Curriculum: core. Admission dates: fall, spring. Total enrollment 50; 20 enrollees each admission period; 100% of applicants accepted; 60% financial aid recipients; 50% under age 25; 45% age 25 to 44; 5% age 45 or over; 25% part-time students; 15 students per instructor; 90% of graduates obtain employment. Facilities: include 2 kitchens, demonstration lab, several classrooms and restaurant.

COURSES: Externship provided.

FACULTY: 2 full-time, ACF-certified.

COSTS: Annual tuition: in-state, $1,500, out-of-state, $3,000. Application fee $10. Admission requirements: high school diploma or equivalent and admission test. Last year 2 scholarships were awarded. Average off-campus housing cost $300 per month. Part time employment available.

LOCATION: The 12,000-student suburban campus is 10 miles from Des Moines.

CAREER/PROFESSIONAL IOWA

CONTACT: Robert Anderson, Culinary Arts Department, Des Moines Community College, 2006 South Ankeny Blvd., Ankeny, IA 50021; (515) 964-6532, Fax (515) 964-6486.

INDIAN HILLS COMMUNITY COLLEGE
Ottumwa/Year-round

This college offers a 18-month AAS degree in Culinary Arts. Program started 1969. Accredited by NCA. Calendar: semester. Curriculum: culinary only. Admission dates: fall, spring. Total enrollment 35; 15 to 20 enrollees each admission period; 100% of applicants accepted; 85% financial aid recipients; 20% under age 25; 75% age 25 to 44; 5% age 45 or over; 12 students per instructor; 97% of graduates obtain employment. Facilities: include 3 kitchens, 3 classrooms and student-run dining room.

COURSES: Schedule: 8 hours per day.

FACULTY: 4 full-time.

COSTS: $3,115 annually. Application fee $25. Admission requirements: high school diploma or equivalent and admission test. Last year 10 scholarships were awarded averaging $500. Part-time employment is available. On-campus housing: 472 spaces. Average off-campus housing cost: $350 per month.

CONTACT: Tom Shepard, Program Director, Culinary Arts, Indian Hills Community College, 525 Grandview, Ottumwa, IA 52501; (515) 683-5195, Fax (515) 683-5184.

IOWA LAKES COMMUNITY COLLEGE
Emmetsburg/Year-round

This college offers a 2-year AAS degree in Culinary Arts. Program started 1974. Accredited by NCA. Calendar: semester. Curriculum: core. Admission dates: September, January. Total enrollment 30 to 40; 95% of applicants accepted; 10 to 12 students per instructor; 95% of graduates obtain employment. Facilities: 2 kitchens, 2 classrooms, 1 restaurant.

COURSES: Externship provided.

COSTS: Annual tuition: $2,500 in-state, $3,000 out-of-state. Admission requirements: high school diploma or equivalent and admission test. Dormitory spaces available on campus.

CONTACT: Mr. R. Halverson, Professor/Coordinator, Culinary Arts Department, Iowa Lakes Community College, South Attendance Center, 3200 College Dr., Emmetsburg, IA 50536; (712) 852-3554, ext. 256, Fax (712) 852-2152.

IOWA WESTERN COMMUNITY COLLEGE
Council Bluffs/August-May

This college offers a 2-year AAS degree in Culinary Arts. Program started 1974. Accredited by NCA. Calendar: semester. Curriculum: core. Admission dates: fall, spring. Total enrollment 30 to 40; 10 to 20 enrollees each admission period; 95% of applicants accepted; 80% financial aid recipients; 75% under age 25; 25% age 25 to 44; 1% part-time students; 10 to 12 students per instructor; 95% of graduates obtain employment. Facilities: include kitchen and 2 classrooms.

COURSES: Externship: 8 to 12-weeks.

FACULTY: 2 full-time, 3 part-time. Includes: P. Swope, B. Gauke, B. Leeder, CCE, N. Johnson, L. Harrill.

COSTS: Tuition: in-state $54 per credit hour, out-of-state $81 per credit hour. Application deadlines: August. Admission requirements: high school diploma or equivalent and admission test. On campus housing: $900 per semester. Part time employment available.

LOCATION: The 4000-student school is in a suburban area across the river from Omaha.

CONTACT: Paula Swope, Food Service Management/Culinary Arts/Retail Baking, Iowa Western Community College, 2700 College Rd., Box 4-C, Council Bluffs, IA 51503; (712) 325-3277, Fax (712) 325-3424.

KIRKWOOD COMMUNITY COLLEGE
Cedar Rapids/September-May

This state institution offers a Bakery certificate and a 2-year AAS degree in Culinary Arts and Restaurant Management. Program started 1972. Accredited by NCA, ACFEI. Calendar: semester. Curriculum: core. Admission dates: fall, spring. Total enrollment 55; 40 enrollees each admission period; 100% of applicants accepted; 33% financial aid recipients; 30% under age 25; 50% age 25 to 44; 30% age 45 or over; 1 to 2% part-time students; 23 students per instructor; 97% of graduates obtain employment. Facilities: include 2 kitchens, 2 classrooms, restaurant and bakery.

COURSES: Food production, culinary arts, garde manger, artistic display, bakery, wines, purchasing, menu planning, nutrition, restaurant law, sanitation, and general education courses. 55 hours of culinary courses required for graduation. Other required courses: 14 credit hours. Schedule: part-time or evening options available. Part time employment available.

FACULTY: 3 full-time, 2 part-time. Includes: Carol Wohlleben, CCE, FMP; Mary Rhiner, RD; David Dettman, Chef; Janelle Kamerlin, Pastry Chef; Lisa Pisney, Chef. Qualifications: college degrees and industry experience.

COSTS: Tuition: in-state $53 per credit hour, out-of-state $106 per credit hour. Refund policy: 1st week 80% of tuition; 2nd week 60%. Admission requirements: high school diploma or equivalent and admission test. Last year 2 scholarships were awarded; loans granted averaged $400. Average off-campus housing cost: $375 per month.

LOCATION: The 10,000-student urban campus has 9 off-campus sites and 13 other buildings.

CONTACT: Carol Wohlleben, FMP, CCE, Culinary Arts Department, Kirkwood Community College, 6301 Kirkwood Blvd. S.W., Cedar Rapids, IA 52406; (319) 398-5468, Fax (319) 398-5597 or (319) 398-5667.

SCOTT COMMUNITY COLLEGE
Bettendorf/Year-round

This college offers a 3-year AAS degree and a 6,000-hour apprenticeship in sanitation and cook certification from ACF. Program started 1991. Accredited by ACFEI, U.S. Department of Labor. Calendar: semester. Curriculum: culinary. Admission dates: fall. Total enrollment 30; 10 to 15 enrollees each admission period; 60% of applicants accepted; 75% financial aid recipients; 30% under age 25; 50% age 25 to 44; 20% age 45 or over; 5% part-time students; 10 students per instructor; 100% of graduates obtain employment.

COURSES: Nutrition, sanitation, menu planning, management, beverages, garde manger, hot food, baking, purchasing, and general education courses. Schedule: 8:30 am-9:00 pm, Monday only. Externship: 6,000-hour, salaried, in restaurant or hotel setting.

FACULTY: 1 full-time, 8 part-time. Qualifications: chef instructors certified by ACF, lecture instructors 4-year degrees, all have industry experience and ACF membership.

COSTS: Annual tuition: in-state $1,432.50. Other costs: application fee $25, books, uniform, knives, ACFEI registration $650 (one-time). Refund: tuition only. Application deadlines: May. Admission requirements: admission test. Last year 8 scholarships were awarded averaging $500; 2 loans were granted averaging $1,200. Off-campus housing cost approximately $300-$400 per month. Part time employment available.

CONTACT: Jennifer Cook-DeRosa, Culinary Arts, Scott Community College, 500 Belmont Rd., Bettendorf, IA 52722-6804; (319) 359-7531 ext. 279, Fax (319) 359-8139.

CAREER/PROFESSIONAL **KANSAS** 41

AMERICAN INSTITUTE OF BAKING
Manhattan/September-May

This nonprofit educational and research institution offers a 16-week Baking Science and Technology course and a 10-week Bakery Maintenance Engineering program. Established in 1919. Accredited by NCA. Calendar: semester. Curriculum: culinary. Admission dates August/September, February. 90% of applicants accepted; 25% financial aid recipients; 40% under age 25; 60% age 25 to 44; 15 students per instructor; 95% of graduates obtain employment. Facilities include a bread shop with a 1,500 loaves-per-hour capacity oven, a cake shop with carbon dioxide freezer, and an in-store bakery with mixers, ovens, and display cases.

COURSES: The Baking Science courses include cake and sweet goods production, bread and roll production, and food product safety. The Maintenance Engineering courses include refrigeration, basic electricity, and motor controls. Schedule: Monday through Friday, 8 am to 5 pm. Continuing education and correspondence courses range from the 50-lesson Science of Baking course to the 12-lesson course in Warehouse Sanitation. The Certified Baker Program provides companies with on-the-job training. Scholarships are available.

FACULTY: Seven full-time instructors.

COSTS: The 16-week program is $3,000. Registration fee is $45 and a nonrefundable $100 deposit is required. Application deadlines January 15, August 15. Applicant must have high school diploma or equivalent and at least 2 years of bakery experience (or completion of Bakery Science correspondence course).

LOCATION: The 75,000-square foot facility is on 13 acres overlooking the Kansas State University campus, 120 miles west of Kansas City.

CONTACT: American Institute of Baking, 1213 Bakers Way, Manhattan, KS 66502; (800) 633-5137 or (913) 537-4750; Fax (913) 537-1493.

JOHNSON COUNTY COMMUNITY COLLEGE
Overland Park/Year-round

This college offers a 2- to 3-year AOS degree. Program started 1975. Accredited by NCA, ACFEI. Calendar: semester. Curriculum: core. Admission dates: July, November. Total enrollment 420; 80% of applicants accepted; 20 students per instructor; 100% of graduates obtain employment.

COURSES: Externship provided.

FACULTY: 10 full-time.

COSTS: Annual tuition: $1,400 in-state, $4,200 out-of-state. Admission requirements: high school diploma or equivalent and admission test. Average off-campus housing cost: $500 per month.

CONTACT: Jerry Vincent, Business & Technology Division, Johnson County Community College, 12345 College at Quivira, Overland Park, KS 66210-1299; (913) 469-8500, Fax (913) 469-2560.

KANSAS CITY KANSAS AREA VOCATIONAL TECHNICAL SCHOOL
Kansas City/August-May

This public institution offers a 720-hour certificate in Professional Cooking. Program started 1975. Accredited by State. Calendar: quarter. Curriculum: culinary only. Admission dates: open. Total enrollment 15; 99% of applicants accepted; 60% financial aid recipients; 93% under age 25; 7% age 45 or over; 50% part-time students; 15 students per instructor; 88% of graduates obtain employment. Facilities: include kitchen, classroom, cafeteria and child care center.

COURSES: Food preparation, sanitation, workplace skills, mathematics. Schedule: 4, 5, or 6 hours per day. Externship provided.

FACULTY: 1 full-time; Sharyn Gassmann, BS, MS.

COSTS: Annual tuition: $780. Application fee $25. Other fees: $50. Application deadlines: open. Admission requirements: admission test.

LOCATION: The 4-building campus is 5 miles from Kansas City.

CONTACT: Sharyn Gassmann, Instructor/Program Manager, Professional Cooking, Kansas City Kansas Area Vocational Technical School, 2220 W. 59th St., Kansas City, KS 66104; (913) 596-5500, Fax (913) 596-5509.

NORTHEAST KANSAS AREA VOCATIONAL TECHNICAL SCHOOL
Atchison/August-May

This public school offers a 1-year diploma in Culinary Arts. Program started 1969. Accredited by State. Calendar: semester. Curriculum: core. Admission dates: open. Total enrollment 12; 90% financial aid recipients; 80% under age 25; 20% age 25 to 44; 30% part-time students; 15 students per instructor; 100% of graduates obtain employment. Facilities: kitchen, student-run restaurant.

COURSES: Professional cooking, baking, purchasing, sanitation. Externship provided.

FACULTY: 1 full-time; Craig J. Maxim, CEPC.

COSTS: Tuition: in-state $8 per credit-hour, out-of-state $6,028.

CONTACT: Craig J. Maxim, Northeast Kansas Area Vocational Technical School, 1501 West Riley, Atchison, KS 66002; (913) 367-6204, Fax (913) 367-3107.

WICHITA AREA VOCATIONAL-TECHNICAL SCHOOL
Wichita

This school offers a 9-month certificate. Program started 1975. Accredited by State. Admission dates: August, January. Total enrollment 20; 95% of applicants accepted; 6 students per instructor; 95% of graduates obtain employment.

FACULTY: 6 full-time

COSTS: Annual tuition is approximately $1,500. Admission requirements: high school diploma or equivalent and admission test.

CONTACT: Food Service & Culinary Arts, Wichita Area Vocational-Technical School, 324 N.Emporia, Wichita, KS 67202; (316) 833-4340.

KENTUCKY

JEFFERSON COMMUNITY COLLEGE
Louisville/January-May, August-December

This college offers a 2-year AAS degree. Program started 1974. Accredited by ACFEI, SACS. Calendar: semester. Curriculum: core. Admission dates: August. Total enrollment 22; 90% of applicants accepted; 11 students per instructor; 96% of graduates obtain employment. Facilities: 2 kitchens and 2 classrooms.

COURSES: Food preparation, American and European pastries, garde manger, menu planning, and catering. 42 hours of culinary courses required for graduation. Other required courses: nutrition, sanitation, management, food cost and portion control. Schedule: 14 hours per week. Externship provided.

FACULTY: 2 full-time, 1 part-time.

COSTS: Annual tuition: $880 in-state, $2,520 out-of-state. Admission requirements: high school diploma or equivalent and admission test.

CONTACT: Patricia Heyman, Program Coordinator, Culinary Arts Department, Jefferson Community College, 109 E. Broadway, Louisville, KY 40202; (502) 584-0181.

CAREER/PROFESSIONAL **KENTUCKY** **43**

KENTUCKY TECH ELIZABETHTOWN
Elizabethtown/August-June

This public institution offers a 22-month diploma in Food Service Technology. Program started 1975. Accredited by SACS. Calendar: semester. Curriculum: core. Admission dates: August, January. Total enrollment 18; 18 enrollees each admission period; 100% of applicants accepted; 80% financial aid recipients; 20% under age 25; 70% age 25 to 44; 10% age 45 or over; 18 students per instructor; 95% of graduates obtain employment. Facilities: kitchen, classroom and restaurant.

COURSES: Food service, quantity food production, short order cooking, bakery, and cake decorating. Schedule: 24 hours per week full-time. Externship: 3 months.

FACULTY: 1 full-time.

COSTS: Annual tuition: $600 in-state, $1,200 out-of-state. Admissions fee $20. Refund policy: 1st 10 school days 100% of tuition. Application deadlines: 1 month before start of semester. Admission requirements: high school diploma or equivalent and admission test. Last year 10 scholarships were awarded averaging $206; 7 loans were granted, averaging $2,090.

LOCATION: The 20-acre campus is in a small town 40 miles from Louisville.

CONTACT: Rene J. Emond, Registrar, Food Service Technology, Kentucky Tech Elizabethtown, 505 University Dr., Elizabethtown, KY 42701; (502) 766-5133, Fax (502) 737-0505.

KENTUCKY TECH-DAVIESS COUNTY CAMPUS
Owensboro/August-June

This independent institution offers a 5- to 6-quarter certificate/diploma in Culinary Arts. Program started 1971. Calendar: quarter. Curriculum: core. Admission dates: August. Total enrollment 24; 2 to 6 enrollees each admission period; 100% of applicants accepted; 90% financial aid recipients; 60% under age 25; 35% age 25 to 44; 5% age 45 or over; 50% part-time students; 18 students per instructor; 85% of graduates obtain employment. Facilities: include kitchen and classroom.

COURSES: Include culinary and general education courses. Schedule: 30 hours per week full-time, 15 hours per week part-time. Continuing education: cake decorating.

FACULTY: Includes M. VanVactor. Qualifications: BS in Home Econ., MS in Secondary Ed.

COSTS: $125 per quarter. Application fee $25. Application deadlines: August. Last year 3 scholarships were awarded averaging $500; 100 loans were granted averaging $1,500.

CONTACT: Kaye Evans, Counselor, Student Services, Kentucky Tech-Daviess County Campus, 15th and Frederica St., Owensboro, KY 42301; (502) 686-3255.

SULLIVAN COLLEGE'S NATL. CTR. FOR HOSPITALITY STUDIES
Louisville/Year-round

This division of Sullivan College offers 18-month AS degree programs in Culinary Arts, Baking & Pastry Arts, Hotel/Restaurant Management, Professional Catering, and Travel & Tourism. Established in 1987. Accredited by the SACS and ACFEI. Calendar: quarter. Curriculum: core. Admission dates January, March, June, September. Facilities: a la carte kitchen, 3 bakery labs, international lab, garde manger lab, basic skills lab, computer lab.

COURSES: Include theory and skills, regional and international cuisine and pastry, business management, nutrition and meal planning, and menu design and layout. Schedule: Monday through Thursday. Students also participate in a 400-hour off-premise practicum.

FACULTY: The 45-member resident faculty includes Culinary Chairman Tom Hickey CEC, CCE and Baking and Pastry Chairman Walter Rhea CMPC, CEC, CCE. The school also has a 38-member adjunct faculty.

COSTS: Tuition is $17,550 ($8,775 per 9 months). Comprehensive supplies fee is $800 per lab;

nonrefundable application fee is $100. Applicants must have a high school diploma or equivalent and can apply for financial assistance from state and federal programs. Graduates can re-take any course at no charge. Nearby apartments are $290 per month.

LOCATION: Watterson Expressway and Bardstown Road in suburban Jefferson County.

CONTACT: Sullivan College's National Center for Hospitality Studies, Watterson Expressway at Bardstown Rd., P.O. Box 33-308, Louisville, KY 40232; (800) 844-1354 or (502) 456-6504.

WEST KENTUCKY STATE VOCATIONAL TECHNICAL SCHOOL
Paducah
This institution offers an 18-month diploma/degree. Program started 1979. Accredited by SACS. Admission dates: July, October, January, March, June. Total enrollment 36; 18 students per instructor; 80% of graduates obtain employment.

FACULTY: 2 full-time.

COSTS: Annual tuition: in-state $150, out-of-state $250. Admission requirements: high school diploma or equivalent and admission test.

CONTACT: Mary Sanderson, Culinary Arts, West Kentucky State Vocational Technical School, Blandville Rd., Box 7408, Paducah, KY 42002-7408; (502) 554-4991.

LOUISIANA

BATON ROUGE REGIONAL TECHNICAL INSTITUTE
Baton Rouge/Year-round
This public institution offers a 1-year diploma/certificate in Culinary Arts. Program started 1974. Calendar: quarter. Curriculum: culinary only. Admission dates: year-round; 6 enrollees each admission period; 95% of applicants accepted; 45% financial aid recipients; 30% under age 25; 60% age 25 to 44; 10% age 45 or over; 20% part-time students; 12 students per instructor; 95% of graduates obtain employment. Facilities: include 2 kitchens and classroom.

COURSES: Sanitation, nutrition, food and beverage management. 1,248 hours of culinary courses required for graduation. Schedule: 8:00 am-2:40 pm, Monday-Friday.

FACULTY: 1 full-time; Michael Travasos. Qualifications: bachelor's degree, industry experience.

COSTS: Annual tuition: $420. Application fee $9.50. Books, uniforms, equipment $215. No refunds. Last year 8 loans were granted. Average off-campus housing cost: $275 per month.

CONTACT: Rose Fair, Admissions, Baton Rouge Regional Technical Institute, 3250 N. Acadian Throughway, Baton Rouge, LA 70805; (504) 359-9226, Fax (504) 359-9296.

BOSSIER PARISH COMMUNITY COLLEGE
Bossier City
This institution offers a 9-month certificate. Program started 1986. Accredited by ACFEI. Admission dates: August. Total enrollment 25; 98% of applicants accepted; 13 students per instructor; 100% of graduates obtain employment.

FACULTY: 2 full-time, 4 part-time.

COSTS: Annual tuition: $3,100. Admission requirements: high school diploma or equivalent and admission test.

CONTACT: Tommy Sibley, Culinary Arts Dept., Bossier Parish Community College, 2719 Airline Drive North, Bossier City, LA 71111; (318) 746-9851, Fax (318) 742-8664.

CAMELOT CAREER COLLEGE
Baton Rouge

CONTACT: Clarence Hayes, Culinary Program, Camelot Career College, 2618 Woodale Blvd., #A, Baton Rouge, LA 70805; (504) 928-3005, Fax (504) 927-3794.

THE CULINARY ARTS INSTITUTE OF LOUISIANA

Now degree granting. An Associates Degree may be obtained in just 60 weeks. Monthly enrollments, operate a white linen restaurant 50% of schooltime, ratio 12 students to 1 instructor. Approved for grants and loans, VA, Vo-rehab. Send for free brochure today.

THE CULINARY ARTS INSTITUTE OF LOUISIANA • 427 LAFAYETTE ST., BATON ROUGE, LA 70802
504-343-6233 or 800-927-0839 • FAX: 504-336-4880

CULINARY ARTS INSTITUTE OF LOUISIANA
Baton Rouge/Year-round
(See display ad above)

This proprietary institution offers a 15-month (1,800-clock-hour) certificate in Nutrition, Sanitation, and Restaurant Management. Established in 1988. Accredited by ACCSCT. Calendar: quarter. Curriculum: core. Admission dates: monthly. Total enrollment 60; 10 to 20 enrollees each admission period; 99% of applicants accepted; 75% financial aid recipients; 5% under age 25; 90% ages 25 to 44; 12 students per instructor; 100% of graduates obtain employment. Facilities include 4 kitchens and classrooms. Courses: Include culinary theory and technique, restaurant management, ice carving, nutrition, and general subjects. Schedule: 8 am-2:30 pm and 3-9:30 pm:, Monday through Friday. Continuing education courses: advanced classical French, Cajun/Creole, tableside service.

FACULTY: Founder and president Violet Harrington, who received an MBA from UCLA, teaches restaurant management and operations and sanitation; other instructors include Randall Andre, Ross Headlee, Robert Esseltine, Marc D'Antonio, and Tony Jean-Claude Cantin.

COSTS: Tuition is $17,314, which includes meals, uniforms, cutlery, insurance, and textbooks. A $25 refundable fee must accompany application 30 days in advance. Applicant must be a high school graduate with some cooking experience. Last year 4 scholarships were awarded and 65 loans were granted. Part-time employment is available. On-campus housing for 150 students at the LSU apartment complexes, a 5-minute drive from the Institute, is $250-$350 per month. Off-campus lodging is $200-$400 per month.

LOCATION: A leased hotel building overlooking the Mississippi River.

CONTACT: Vi Harrington, Director, Culinary Arts Institute of Louisiana, 427 Lafayette St., Baton Rouge, LA 70802; (800) 927-0839 or (504) 343-6233, Fax (504) 336-4880.

LAFAYETTE REGIONAL TECHNICAL INSTITUTE
Lafayette
This school offers a program in culinary arts and occupations.

CONTACT: Rafael Galindo, Lafayette Regional Technical Institute, 1101 Bertrand Dr., Lafayette, LA 70502; (318) 362-5122.

NEW ORLEANS REGIONAL VO-TECH
New Orleans

This school offers a program in culinary arts and occupations.

CONTACT: Tom Gourley, New Orleans Regional Vo-Tech, 9800 Nevarre Ave., New Orleans, LA 70124; (504) 483-4626.

SCLAFANI 'S COOKING SCHOOL, INC.
Metairie/Year-round *(See display ad page 47)*

This proprietary school offers a 4-week (120-hour) certificate of completion program in commercial cooking/baking. Program started 1987. Accredited by State of Louisiana. Admission dates: monthly. Total enrollment 95 per year; 8 enrollees each admission period; 85% of applicants accepted; 60% financial aid recipients; 25% under age 25; 50% age 25 to 44; 25% age 45 or over; 8 students per instructor; 98% of graduates obtain employment. Facilities: classroom/dining room, commercial kitchen preparation room, storage area.

COURSES: Culinary arts, baking, food cost math, sanitation & safety, supervisory skills. 120 hours of culinary courses required for graduation. Other required courses: field trips, work assignments, ACF chapter meetings. Schedule: part-time evenings 8:30 am to 3:30 pm, Monday-Friday. Continuing education: 5 points towards ACFEI certification, 120 points towards re-certification.

FACULTY: 2 full-time. Include: Administrative Instructor Frank P. Sclafani, Sr., CEC and chef/instructor Maryanna Kunz.

COSTS: Tuition: $2,145. $150 deposit with application, balance due 14 days before class; full refund for written cancellation within 3 business days. Admission requirements: age 18 or older; must pass 7th grade level reading and math. Average off-campus housing cost: $15 per day and up.

LOCATION: 3 miles from New Orleans.

CONTACT: Frank P. Sclafani, Sr., CEC, President, Sclafani's Cooking School, Inc., 107 Gennaro Pl., Metairie, LA 70001; (504) 833-7861, Fax (504) 834-3524.

SIDNEY N. COLLIER VOCATIONAL TECHNICAL INSTITUTE
New Orleans

This institution offers a 12-month certificate. Program started 1957. Accredited by SACS. Admission dates: open. Total enrollment 20; 100% of applicants accepted; 20 students per instructor; 80% of graduates obtain employment.

FACULTY: 30 full-time, 1 part-time.

CONTACT: Edward James, Culinary Arts, Sidney N. Collier Vocational Technical Institute, 3727 Louisa St., New Orleans, LA 70126; (504) 942-8333, Fax (504) 942-8337.

MAINE

SOUTHERN MAINE TECHNICAL COLLEGE
South Portland/September-May

This state-owned institution offers a 2-year associate degree in Culinary Arts. Program started 1956. Accredited by NEASC. Calendar: semester. Curriculum: core. Admission dates: rolling. Total enrollment 70; 75% of applicants accepted; 50% financial aid recipients; 20% under age 25; 40% age 25 to 44; 40% age 45 or over; 10% part-time students; 16 students per instructor; 90% of graduates obtain employment. Facilities: include 8 kitchens and classrooms, restaurant.

COURSES: Baking, food development, buffet, classical cuisine, dining room management, and general education courses. Schedule: 6 hours per day, 9 months per year, part-time and evening options available. Continuing education: bartending and cake decorating.

FACULTY: 6 full-time with college degrees and/or ACF certification.

COSTS: Annual tuition: in-state $2,088, out-of-state $4,572. Application deadlines: August 1. Admission requirements: high school diploma or equivalent and admission test. On-campus

✔ Consider Money Saving Time and Convenience Factors

Frank P. Sclafani, Sr., C.E.C.

QUICKEN YOUR CAREER !!!

✔ Job ready in four weeks of training.
(Many students are career changers).

✔ Hotels, restaurants, country clubs, casinos, offshore and many other employers accept SCS graduates for immediate employment.

✔ Daily Hands-on kitchen practical experience.

✔ Licensed by the State of Louisiana Department of Education.

✔ Networking throughout your career -
Job assistance and certification development.

✔ **ONLY ONE COST COVERS ALL:** Training, Placement Assistance, Text Book, Chef's Jacket with Logo, Resume and Use of tools, food, linens, paper, lunch, etc.

SCLAFANI
COOKING SCHOOL, INC.
We Train and Place Cooks

(504) 833-7861

housing: 100 spaces; off-campus housing cost: $50 per week. Part time employment available.

CONTACT: Robert Latham, Culinary Arts/Hotel, Motel & Rest. Management, Southern Maine Technical College, 2 Fort Rd., South Portland, ME 04106; (207) 767-9520, Fax (207) 767-9671.

MARYLAND

BALTIMORE INTERNATIONAL CULINARY COLLEGE
Baltimore and Ireland/Year-round *(See also page 257)*

This private nonprofit college specializing in hospitality education offers associate degrees in Professional Cooking, Professional Baking and Pastry, Professional Cooking and Baking, Food and Beverage Management, and certificates in Professional Cooking, Professional Baking and Pastry and Culinary Arts (combines cooking and baking). Founded: 1972. Accreditation: ACCSCT. Calendar: quarter. Curriculum: core. Admission: January, April, July, October. Total enrollment 807; 95% of applicants accepted; 90% financial aid recipients; 61% under age 25; 36% ages 25 to 44; 3% ages 45 and over; 13 students per instructor. Facilities: the 23-building Baltimore campus includes 30 kitchens and classrooms, hotels, restaurants, bakeshops, lecture and demonstration theater, classrooms, library, computer labs, bookstore, 5 open-to-the-public eating establishments, and 3 lodging facilities; the 100-acre Ireland campus comprises The Park Hotel-Deer Park Lodge, an 18th century country estate.

COURSES: Each program builds from a foundation of theories and techniques to advanced techniques and special projects. Core courses include math, science, English, economics, history, and psychology. All degree programs include 3-12 weeks of study at the College's European Educational Centre in Ireland and a 3-month externship or internship. Also available: mini-courses, Summer Institute.

FACULTY: The 45-member faculty includes ACF-Certified Executive Chefs, Working Chefs, Master Pastry Chefs, and Culinary Educators. Academic faculty members hold degrees through the doctorate level. European-trained chedfs at the European Educational Centre hold credentials from the City and Guilds of London.

COSTS: Per semester costs are $3,045 for tuition, $982-$1,260 for fees. Nonrefundable $25 application and $100 deposit fees. High school diploma or equivalent and satisfactory placement test score required. Last year scholarships totaling $898,000 were awarded; loans totaling $2,814,000 were granted. Part-time employment is available. On-campus lodging for 200 students begins at $1,400 per semester.

LOCATION: Baltimore's Inner Harbor area and County Cavan, Ireland, 50 miles from Dublin.

CONTACT: Raymond L. Joll, Vice President of Enrollment Management, Baltimore International Culinary College, 17 Commerce St., Baltimore, MD 21202; (800) 624-9926 or (410) 752-4710.

INTERNATIONAL SCHOOL OF CONFECTIONERY ARTS, INC.
Gaithersburg/Year-round *(See display ad page 49)*

This proprietary school offers 1- to 3-week certificate courses in confectionery arts. Established in 1982 in Zurich, Switzerland. Admission dates: weekly. Total enrollment 400 students per year; 12 to 16 students per course; 100% of applicants accepted; 3% financial aid recipients; 20% under age 25; 70% ages 25 to 44; 10% age 45 or older; 4 students per instructor; 100% of graduates obtain jobs. Facilities: 2,400-square-foot area has 16 individual work stations, overhead mirrors, marble tables, and decorating and candy-making equipment.

COURSES: Sugar pulling, blowing, and casting, chocolate decoration, Swiss candy making, cake decoration, gum paste. Schedule: 8 am- 4:30 pm, Monday-Thursday, 8 am-noon Friday.

FACULTY: Ewald Notter and his wife, Susan, have won gold medals in international competitions and have taught in Japan, Hong Kong, Denmark, Germany, England, Spain, and Finland. They are

CAREER/PROFESSIONAL MARYLAND

authors of *The Text Book of Sugar Pulling and Blowing* and *That's Sugar*.

COSTS: Tuition ranges from $220-$680, which includes breakfast, lunch and materials. A 50% deposit is required. Cancellations 14 days prior receive full refund. Application deadline: 1 month prior. In 1994-95, 10 scholarships were awarded. Assistantships are available. Nearby lodging averages $46 per night.

LOCATION: Two miles from Gaithersburg, 10 miles from Washington, D.C.

CONTACT: Susan Notter, Admissions, International School of Confectionery Arts, 9209 Gaither Rd., Gaithersburg, MD 20877; (301) 963-9077, Fax (301) 869-7669.

EWALD & SUSAN NOTTER

INTERNATIONAL **OF CONFECTIONERY**

Specialized courses in the arts of:
PULLED AND BLOWN SUGAR
CHOCOLATE DECORATION
SWISS CANDY MAKING
WEDDING CAKE DECORATION

All courses taught by internationally acclaimed instructors.

9209 Gaither Road, Gaithersburg, MD 20877
Tel: 301 963 9077   Fax: 301 869 7669
Email: esnotter@aol.com

L'ACADEMIE DE CUISINE
(See also page 188) (See display ad page 50)   **Gaithersburg/Year-round**

This proprietary vocational school offers a 1-year full-time Culinary Career Training diploma program, 9-month part-time certificate courses, courses for continuing education and nonprofessionals, and a vacation program in France. Founded in 1976. Accredited by ACCET and certified by the Maryland Higher Education Commission. Calendar: semester. Curriculum: culinary. Admission dates: January, July, September. Total enrollment: 35 twice a year; 85% of applicants accepted; 50% financial aid recipients; average age 29.7 years; 17 students per instructor; 95% of graduates obtain jobs. Facilities: at the 2 campuses, include a 25-station practice and pastry kitchen and 25-seat demonstration classroom.

COURSES: Curriculum is based on classic French technique. Diploma program covers food preparation and presentation, pastries and desserts, wine selection, catering, and menu planning and kitchen management. First six months consists of daily classes, second six months is a paid restaurant externship. Certificate courses cover theory and techniques of cooking, practical culinary skills, pastry, and practical culinary skills for the professional. Advanced and continuing education courses include marzipan, wedding cakes, sugar, chocolate, catering.

FACULTY: School president Francois Dionot graduated from L'Ecole Hoteliere de la Societe Suisse des Hoteliers in Switzerland, served apprenticeships at Hotel Meister in Lugano and Hotel le Relais in France, was a consultant to Time-Life Books, and is a founder of the IACP. Pascal Dionot is a graduate of the Hotelfachschule D. Speiser in Germany. Bonnie Moore is a graduate of Johnson & Wales and was sous chef at the Inn at Little Washington.

COSTS: Tuition for the diploma program is $13,500. A $75 application fee and $2,500 tuition deposit are required; full deposit refund with 7 days notice. Supplies are $450. Applicants must have a high school diploma or equivalent. Last year, 20 loans were granted at an average of $9,500 each. Certificate course tuition ranges from $2,300 to $4,450; payment plans available. Nearby lodging is approximately $600 per month.

LOCATION: The Gaithersburg branch is 20 minutes north of Washington, DC; the Bethesda branch is 3 miles northwest of D.C.

START YOUR CULINARY CAREER AT THE TOP!

If you're serious about learning both the art and science of cooking, then L'Academie and its European trained chefs are ready and prepared to train you in just that - basic and advanced techniques of food purchasing, preparation, presentation and development of a refined palate.

L'ACADEMIE DE CUISINE

the Academy of Culinary Arts
established in 1976

FULL-TIME PROGRAM • PART-TIME PROGRAMS • AVOCATIONAL PROGRAMS
Write or call for free brochure: 16006 Industrial Drive, Gaithersburg, MD 20877   (800) 66-4-CHEF

CONTACT: Carol McClure, Assistant Director, L'Academie de Cuisine, 16006 Industrial Dr., Gaithersburg, MD 20877; (301) 670-8670 or (800) 664-CHEF, Fax (301) 670-0450.

MASSACHUSETTS

BERKSHIRE COMMUNITY COLLEGE
Pittsfield
This college offers a 1-year certificate and a 2-year AAS degree. Program started 1977. Accredited by NEASC. Admission dates: fall. Total enrollment: 15.

COURSES: Externship provided.

FACULTY: 2 full-time, 3 part-time.

COSTS: Tuition: in-state $2,000, out-of-state $6,300. Admission requirements: high school diploma or equivalent and admission test.

CONTACT: Janet R. Kroboth, Business Division Chair, Culinary Arts Dept., Berkshire Community College, 1350 West St., Pittsfield, MA 01201-5786; (413) 499-4660, Fax (413) 447-7840.

BOSTON UNIVERSITY METROPOLITAN COLLEGE
Boston/September-May *(See also page 189)*
This university offers a 4-month certificate in the Culinary Arts (started 1988) and a Master of Liberal Arts with concentration in Gastronomy (started 1994). Certificate program calendar: semester. Curriculum: core. Admission dates January, September. Total enrollment 24; 12 enrollees each admission period; 60% of applicants accepted; 50% financial aid recipients; 20% under age 25; 60% age 25 to 44; 20% age 45 or over; 6 students per instructor; 100% of graduates obtain employment. Facilities: demonstration room with overhead mirror, classroom, 8 restaurant stations in the laboratory kitchen. Courses: Cover basic classic and modern techniques and theory, ethnic and regional cuisine, food history, dining room theory and practice, purchasing. Schedule: 30 hours per week. Continuing education courses are available. The master program includes four core courses in the history and anthropology of food, nutrition and diet and four electives covering food archaeology, geography of hunger and poverty, culture and cuisine, and food writing.

FACULTY: Two full- and 30 part-time professionals. Guest chefs have included Julia Child, Albert Kumin, Jacques Pepin, Jacqueline Cattani, and Roger Fessaguet.

COSTS: Certificate course tuition is $5,800. Application fee is $35. Full refund less $100 after the first week of class. Applicants must have some foodservice experience. Last year 1 scholarship was awarded; 13 loans were granted. Part-time employment is available.

LOCATION: The 28,000-student campus is in Kenmore Square.

CONTACT: Rebecca Alssid, Director of Special Programs, Boston University Metropolitan College, 808 Commonwealth Ave., Room 109, Boston, MA 02215; (617) 353-9852, Fax (617) 353-4130.

BRISTOL COMMUNITY COLLEGE
Fall River

This institution offers a 1-year certificate. Program started 1985. Accredited by NEASC. Admission dates: September, January. Total enrollment 22 to 24; 80% of applicants accepted; 6 students per instructor; 75% of graduates obtain employment.

FACULTY: 4 full-time.

COSTS: Tuition: in-state $2,000, out-of-state $5,800.

CONTACT: Culinary Director, Culinary Arts Department, Bristol Community College, Fall River, MA 02720; (508) 678-2811 ext. 2111, Fax (508) 678-2811 ext. 2470.

BUNKER HILL COMMUNITY COLLEGE
Charlestown

This institution offers a 1-year certificate and a 2-year AAS degree. Program started 1978. Admission dates: September, January. Total enrollment 125; 8 to 15 students per instructor; 98% of graduates obtain employment.

FACULTY: 6 full-time.

COSTS: Tuition: in-state $750 per semester, out-of-state $2,000 per semester. Admission requirements: high school diploma or equivalent and admission test.

CONTACT: Arthur Buccheri, Dept. Chair, Hotel/Restaurant Management-Culinary Arts, Bunker Hill Community College, New Rutherford Ave., Charlestown, MA 02129; (617) 241-8600 ext. 336.

THE CAMBRIDGE SCHOOL OF CULINARY ARTS
(See also page 189) — Cambridge/Year-round

This proprietary institution offers a 10-month (756-792-clock-hour) Professional Chef's diploma program, a summer program for cooking enthusiasts, and culinary trips to Europe (page 189). Founded in 1973. Licensed by the Commonwealth of Massachusetts Department of Education, accredited by the ACCSCT. Admission dates September and January. Total enrollment 110 to 200; 75 to 100 enrollees each admission period; 80% of applicants are accepted; 5% under age 25; 90% age 25 to 44; 5% age 45 or over; class size is 32 for lectures, 15 for hands-on; 90% of graduates obtain employment. Facilities: 3 large newly renovated kitchens and 3 large demonstration classrooms; gas and electric commercial appliances.

COURSES: Emphasis is on chemistry and principles of fine cooking. Curriculum covers basics, pastry, American and international cuisines, food and business management, butchering, herbs and spices, cheese and wine. Schedule: 21-22 hours per week (attendance 3 times per week) day or evening classes. Continuing education Courses: wedding and specialty cakes, bread sculpture, event planning.

FACULTY: President, founder, and executive chef Roberta Avallone Dowling received diplomas from Julie Dannenbaum, Marcella Hazan, Madeleine Kamman, and Richard Olney, is owner of DeGustibus, Inc., catering company and a member of the ACF, IACP, Academy of Chefs, and Les Amis d'Escoffier Society. Instructors are experienced master chefs, federally accredited and state-certified teachers.

COSTS: Tuition is $9,000, payable in 4 installments; application fee $35. Upon acceptance a $100 deposit is required, refundable within 5 days. Applicants must be at least age 18 and have a high school diploma or equivalent. In 1994-95, a $1,500 scholarship was awarded. Job placement assistance is provided. Nearby lodging ranges from $500-$1,600 per month.

LOCATION: Five miles from downtown Boston, 1 mile from Harvard Square.

CONTACT: Director of Admissions, The Cambridge School of Culinary Arts, 2020 Massachusetts Ave., Cambridge, MA 02140; (617) 354-3836, Fax (617) 576-1963.

ESSEX AGRICULTURAL AND TECHNICAL INSTITUTE
Hathorne/September-May

This public institution offers a 2-year AAS degree in Culinary Arts and Food Service. Program started 1968. Accredited by NEASC. Calendar: semester. Curriculum: core. Admission dates: revolving. Total enrollment 60; 40 enrollees each admission period; 90% of applicants accepted; 33% financial aid recipients; 60% under age 25; 30% age 25 to 44; 10% age 45 or over; 5% part-time students; 15 students per instructor; 90% of graduates obtain employment. Facilities: include 6 kitchens and classrooms, bakery and restaurant.

COURSES: Restaurant operation, baking, garde manger, international cuisine, buffet, specialty food production, cakes and pastries, American regional cuisine, and nutrition. Schedule: 25 hours per week, 15 weeks per semester. Externship provided.

FACULTY: 4 full-time. Includes: Division Chair C. Naffah, P. Kelly, L. Bassett, J. Costello.

COSTS: Annual tuition: $1,650. Application fee $30. Other fees: approximately $1,830. Application deadlines: revolving. Admission requirements: high school diploma or equivalent.

LOCATION: The 180-acre campus is in a suburban setting 20 miles from Boston.

CONTACT: Dr. Donald Glazier, Admissions, Essex Agricultural and Technical Institute, 562 Maple St., Hathorne, MA 01937; (508) 774-0050, Fax (508) 774-6530.

HOLYOKE COMMUNITY COLLEGE
Holyoke/Year-round

This college offers a 1-year certificate in Culinary Arts. Program started 1991. Calendar: semester. Curriculum: culinary only. Admission dates: September, January. Total enrollment 50; 100% of applicants accepted; 20% part-time students; 90% of graduates obtain employment. Facilities: include 2 kitchens, bakeshop and student-run cafeteria.

COURSES: Food production management, advanced food production, and nutrition. Schedule: 7 am-4 pm, Monday-Friday; classes September-May, with field experience in summer; part-time options available. Externship: 14-week, paid. Continuing education: evening courses in advanced baking, food service supervision, nutrition, ice carving, garde manger, and cake decorating.

FACULTY: 4 full-time. Includes: H. Robert, D. Walsh, W. Grinnan, L. Kinney.

COSTS: Annual tuition: in-state $2,605, out-of-state $6,275. Application fee $10. Advance payment fee $30. Refund: 100% prior to 1st day of classes, 90% during add/drop period. Application deadlines: day before classes begin. Admission requirements: high school diploma or equivalent.

CONTACT: Hugh Robert, Hospitality Management, Holyoke Community College, 303 Homestead Ave., Holyoke, MA 01040; (413) 538-7000, Fax (413) 534-8975.

MASSASOIT COMMUNITY COLLEGE
Brockton

This college offers a 2-year degree. Program started 1982. Accredited by State. Admission dates: September. Total enrollment 60; 20 to 35 students per instructor; 93.5% of graduates obtain employment.

COURSES: Externship provided.

FACULTY: 3 full-time, 2 part-time.

COSTS: Annual tuition: in-state $950, out-of-state $1,900. Admission requirements: high school diploma or equivalent.

CONTACT: Culinary Director, Culinary Arts Dept., Massasoit Community College, 1 Massasoit Blvd., Brockton, MA 02402; (508) 588-9100.

CAREER/PROFESSIONAL **MASSACHUSETTS**

MINUTEMAN REGIONAL VOCATIONAL TECHNICAL SCHOOL
Lexington

This independent institution offers a 3-year diploma, 2-year post-graduate course, and 90-day retraining courses in Culinary, Baking, Hotel and Restaurant Management. Program started 1973. Calendar: quarter. Curriculum: core. Total enrollment 150; 25 enrollees each admission period; 95% of applicants accepted; 90% under age 25; 5% age 25 to 44; 5% age 45 or over; 10 students per instructor; 99% of graduates obtain employment. Facilities: 6 kitchens and classrooms.

COURSES: Sanitation, nutrition, management, purchasing, computer skills, applied math, and applied science. Schedule: 6 hours per day, 10 months per year. Externship: 20 weeks, hotel/restaurant.

FACULTY: Includes: P. Denaro, N. Myerow, J. Fitzpatrick, R. Kohlstrom, J. Pitta.

COSTS: Annual tuition: in-state $6,200. Uniform fee: $100. Application deadlines: open. Admission requirements: admission test. Last year 8 scholarships were awarded averaging $500. Part-time employment is available.

CONTACT: John Fitzpatrick, Director, Foodservice/Hospitality Management, Minuteman Tech, 758 Marrett Rd., Lexington, MA 02173; (617) 861-6500, Fax (617) 863-1254.

NEWBURY COLLEGE
Brookline/September-May

This non-profit institution offers a 2-year AAS degree in Culinary Arts and Food Servive Management. Program started 1981. Accredited by NEASC. Calendar: semester. Curriculum: core. Admission dates September, January. Total enrollment 240; 140 enrollees each admission period; 60% of applicants accepted; 80% financial aid recipients; 75% under age 25; 20% age 25 to 44; 5% age 45 or over; 10% part-time students; 17 students per instructor; 99% of graduates obtain employment. Facilities include 7 production kitchens and the college dining room.

COURSES: Include preparation and presentation of international and regional cuisines, equipment, sanitation, and nutrition, menu planning, and general education subjects. A 12- to 18-week salaried externship is provided.

FACULTY: The 10 full- and 6 part-time faculty members are active industry professionals. Culinary arts chairman George Anbinder received a BS degree from Boston University and an AOS from Johnson & Wales University.

COSTS: Annual tuition is $10,500. Tuition deposit is $100 and culinary program fee is $1,150. Refund with written request prior to April 15 or November 15. Rolling application deadline. Applicant must have high school diploma or GED and a 2.0 GPA. Scholarships and part-time employment are available. On-campus room and board are provided for 400 students at $6,200 (double occupancy).

LOCATION: A suburban setting, 4 miles from downtown Boston.

CONTACT: Kimberly Boslego, Admissions Center, Newbury College, 129 Fisher Ave., Brookline, MA 02146; (617) 730-7006; Fax (617) 731-9618.

MICHIGAN

CAREER DEVELOPMENT CENTER
Detroit

CONTACT: Culinary Director, Culinary Arts, Career Development Center, 5961 14th St., Detroit, MI 48208; (313) 894-0610.

GRAND RAPIDS COMMUNITY COLLEGE
Grand Rapids/January-May, August-December

This college offers a 2-year AAAS degree in Culinary Arts, Culinary Management, and Baking and Pastry Arts. Program started 1980. Accredited by ACFEI, NCA. Calendar: semester. Curriculum: culinary, baking and pastry. Admission dates: January, August. Total enrollment 360; 95% of applicants accepted; 60% financial aid recipients; 40% under age 25; 50% age 25 to 44; 10% age 45 or over; 20% part-time students; 15 to 22 students per instructor; 99% of graduates obtain employment. Facilities: include 28 kitchens and classrooms, bar, bakery, bistro, banquet rooms, auditorium, 2 formal storerooms, and 2 student-run restaurants.

COURSES: Schedule: 30 hours per week, 34 weeks per year; part-time options available. Externship: 240-hour, summer semester Continuing education: about 40 non-credit seminars per year on a variety of subjects.

FACULTY: 12 full-time, 7 part-time. Includes: R. Garlough, MS, CEC, CCE; G. Renusson, Master Pastry Chef; A. Campbell, Master Chef; R. Monaldo, CEC, CCE; M. Rango. Qualifications: equivalent of a bachelor's degree and minimum 6 years industry experience in management.

COSTS: Annual tuition: $4,896 in-state, $6,048 out-of-state. Application fee $20. Books, uniforms, cutlery kit: $1,200. Full refund before start of classes. Admission requirements: high school diploma or equivalent and admission test. Last year 24 scholarships were awarded averaging $500. Part-time employment is available. Average off-campus housing cost $250 per month.

LOCATION: The 14,000-student, 11-building campus is in an urban setting.

CONTACT: Robert B. Garlough, Hospitality Education Division, Grand Rapids Community College, 151 Fountain, N.E., Grand Rapids, MI 49503-3295; (616) 771-3690, Fax (616) 771-3698.

HENRY FORD COMMUNITY COLLEGE
Dearborn

CONTACT: Culinary Director, Culinary Arts/Hotel Restaurant Management, Henry Ford Community College, 5101 Evergreen Rd., Dearborn, MI 48128; (313) 845-9651.

MACOMB COMMUNITY COLLEGE
Mt. Clemens

This college offers a 2-year AAS degree in Culinary Arts. Program started 1972. Accredited by State. Admission dates: fall, spring, summer. Total enrollment 112; 16 to 35 students per instructor; 99% of graduates obtain employment.

FACULTY: 3 full-time, 2 part-time.

COSTS: Tuition: in-county $42 per credit hour, out-of-county $165 per credit hour. Admission requirements: high school diploma or equivalent.

CONTACT: David Schneider, Culinary Arts Department, Macomb Community College, 44575 Garfield, Mt. Clemens, MI 48044; (810) 286-2000, Fax (810) 286-2038.

MONROE COUNTY COMMUNITY COLLEGE
Monroe/September-May

This independent institution offers a 2-year AOC degree/certificate in Culinary Skills and Management. Program started 1981. Accredited by NCA, ACFEI. Calendar: semester. Curriculum: core. Admission dates: September. Total enrollment 36; 20 enrollees each admission period; 80% of applicants accepted; 25% financial aid recipients; 35% under age 25; 50% age 25 to 44; 15% age 45 or over; 25% part-time students; 18 students per instructor; 87% of graduates obtain employment. Facilities: include 2 kitchens, classroom and restaurant.

COURSES: Restaurant production, baking, buffet, institutional food, management, sanitation,

CAREER/PROFESSIONAL — MICHIGAN 55

nutrition, garde manger, ice carving, menu planning, purchasing and receiving, a la carte, dining room procedure, general education. Schedule: Monday-Friday, 3 hours daily. Externship provided.

FACULTY: 2 full-time. Includes: K. Thomas, CCE, CEC and H. Stokes, CPC.

COSTS: Annual tuition: in-state $650, out-of-state $962. Application fee $15. Lab fee $20. Refund policy: prorated until 3 weeks after start of semester. Application deadlines: May 21. Admission requirements: high school diploma or equivalent and admission test. Last year 6 scholarships were awarded averaging $250. Part-time employment is available. Average off-campus housing cost: $300 per month.

LOCATION: The 4,000-student campus is in a rural setting.

CONTACT: Herb Stokes III, Culinary Arts Department, Monroe County Community College, 1555 Raisinville Rd., Monroe, MI 48161; (313) 242-7300, Fax (313) 242-9711.

NORTHERN MICHIGAN UNIVERSITY
Marquette/August-April

This public institution offers a 1-year certificate, 1-year AAS degree, and 4-year BS degree, program in Culinary Arts, Restaurant and Institutional Management. Program started 1970. Accredited by NCA. Calendar: semester. Curriculum: core. Admission dates: September, January. Total enrollment 47; 18 enrollees each admission period; 100% of applicants accepted; 80% financial aid recipients; 70% under age 25; 30% age 25 to 44; 25% part-time students; 18 students per instructor; 100% of graduates obtain employment. Facilities: include 5 kitchens and classrooms, computer lab, restaurant and meat-cutting room.

COURSES: Cooking, baking, garde manger, sanitation, purchasing, and general education. Schedule: Monday-Thursday, 8 am-2 pm.

FACULTY: 3 full-time. Qualifications: bachelor's or master's degrees.

COSTS: Tuition: in state $81 per credit hour, out-of-state $152 per credit hour. Application fee $50. Application deadlines: July 1. Admission requirements: high school diploma or equivalent. On-campus housing: 2,000 spaces at $2,300 per year. Off-campus housing cost: $2,000 per year.

LOCATION: The 9,000-student campus is in a small town setting.

CONTACT: Walt Anderson, Department Head, Department of Consumer & Family Studies, Northern Michigan University, College of Technology & Applied Sciences, Marquette, MI 49855; (906) 227-2365, Fax (906) 227-1549.

NORTHWESTERN MICHIGAN COLLEGE
Traverse City/Year-round

This college offers a 2-year AAS degree in Culinary Arts. Program started 1978. Accredited by ACFEI. Calendar: semester. Curriculum: core. Admission dates: open. Total enrollment 75; 100% of applicants accepted; 65% financial aid recipients; 50% under age 25; 50% age 25 to 44; 45% part-time students; 20 students per instructor; 90% of graduates obtain employment. Facilities: includes 3 kitchens, many classrooms, restaurant and bake shop.

COURSES: Externship: 400-hour, salaried.

FACULTY: 2 full-time, 10 part-time. Includes: Fred Laughlin, CCE, Department Chair, Lucy House, CC, Randy Lawton, CCE, William Black.

COSTS: Tuition: in-state $52 per credit hour, out-of-state $83 per credit hour. Application fee $15. Admission requirements: high school diploma or equivalent. Last year 6 scholarships were awarded averaging $800. Part-time employment is available. On-campus housing: 120 spaces; average cost $1,950 with meal plan.

LOCATION: A small town campus, 150 miles from Grand Rapids.

CONTACT: Fred Laughlin, Culinary Arts Department, Northwestern Michigan College, 1701 East Front St., Traverse City, MI 49686; (616) 946-4700, ext. 7025, Fax (616) 946-2772.

OAKLAND COMMUNITY COLLEGE
Farmington Hills/September-June

This college offers a 2-year AAS program in Culinary Arts, Food Service Management, Hotel Management, and Chef Apprentice. Program started 1978. Accredited by ACFEI. Calendar: semester. Curriculum: core. Admission dates: September, January, May. Total enrollment 210; 125 enrollees each admission period; 98% of applicants accepted; 35% financial aid recipients; 20% under age 25; 60% age 25 to 44; 20% age 45 or over; 50% part-time students; 15 students per instructor; 90% of graduates obtain employment. Facilities: includes 10 kitchens and classrooms and restaurant.

COURSES: Cooking, baking, pastries, garde manger, front-of-house service, sanitation, purchasing, menu planning, cost control. Schedule: 6 hours per day 4 days a week. Continuing education: garde manger, culinary competition, meat cutting, baking.

FACULTY: 7 full-time, 6 part-time. Includes: Chairperson Susan Baier, FMP; Kevin Enright, CEC, CCE; Roger Holder, CPC, CCE; Jim Staworn, CCE, CC, MSC; Robert Zemke, RD, MBA; Darlene Levinson, FMP.

COSTS: Annual tuition: in-county $46 per credit-hour. Lab fee $330 for production classes. Last year 25 scholarships were awarded averaging $300. Part-time employment is available.

CONTACT: Susan Baier, Hospital/Culinary Arts, Oakland Community College, 27055 Orchard Lake Rd., Farmington Hills, MI 48334; (810) 471-7786, Fax (810) 471-7739.

SCHOOLCRAFT COLLEGE
Livonia/August-April

This college offers a 2-year certificate/AAS degree in Culinary Arts and Culinary Management. Program started 1966. Accredited by NCA. Calendar: semester. Curriculum: core. Admission dates: January, August. Total enrollment 156; 12 to 78 enrollees each admission period; 100% of applicants accepted; 50% under age 25; 40% age 25 to 44; 10% age 45 or over; 40% part-time students; 14 students per instructor; 100% of graduates obtain employment. Facilities: include 8 kitchens and classrooms, pastry kitchen, butcher shop, bakery, and restaurant.

COURSES: Baking, pastries, a la carte, international cuisine, butchery. Other required courses: sanitation, nutrition. Schedule: 18 hours per week, 8 months per year. Externship: 16-week, salaried, restaurants. Continuing education: sanitation, supervision, olympic cooking trends and concepts, and nutrition.

FACULTY: 5 full-time, 6 part-time. Includes: Joseph E. Decker, CMPC; Jeffrey M. Gabriel, CMC; Kevin P. Gawronski, CMC; Daniel G. Hugelier, CMC; Leopold K. Schaeli, CMC. Qualifications: ACF-certification.

COSTS: Tuition: $70 per credit hour. Application fee $10. Lab fees $35-80. Refund policy: 100% up to 1 week following start. Admission requirements: high school diploma or equivalent, admission test. Last year 10 scholarships were awarded averaging $300. Part-time employment is available.

LOCATION: This 13,900-student suburban campus is 20 miles from Detroit.

CONTACT: Kevin Gawronski, Culinary Manager, Culinary Arts, Schoolcraft College, 18600 Haggerty Rd., Livonia, MI 48152-2696; (313) 462-4423, Fax (313) 462-4519.

WASHTENAW COMMUNITY COLLEGE
Ann Arbor/September-April

This college offers a 1-year certificate in Food Service Production Specialist and a 2-year AAS degree in Culinary Arts and Hotel and Restaurant Management. Program started 1975. Accredited

CAREER/PROFESSIONAL   MINNESOTA

by NCA. Calendar: semester. Curriculum: core. Total enrollment 80 to 120; 50 enrollees each admission period; 90% of applicants accepted; 10% financial aid recipients; 30% under age 25; 40% age 25 to 44; 25% age 45 or over; 60% part-time students; 16 to 25 students per instructor; 95% of graduates obtain employment. Facilities: include kitchen, bake shop, and student-run dining room.

Courses: 50% culinary courses, 25% business courses, 25% general studies. 40 hours of culinary courses required. Other requirements: core. Schedule: 15-20 hours per week full-time; 3-9 hours per week part-time. Externship: 300-hour, salaried. Continuing education: in summer.

Faculty: 4 full-time. Qualifications: bachelor's or master's degree and ACF certification.

Costs: $51 in-district, $73 out-of-district, $92 out-of-state. $23 registration fee per semester and $2 per credit fee. Application deadlines: year-round. Admission requirements: high school diploma or equivalent and admission test required. Last year 6 scholarships were awarded averaging $300. Part-time employment is available.

Off-campus housing cost: $400-$600 per month.

Location: The suburban 11,000-student campus is 40 miles from Detroit.

Contact: David Placey, Director, Admissions, Washtenaw Community College, 4800 E. Huron River Drive, Ann Arbor, MI 48106-0978; (313) 973-3300, Fax (313) 677-5414.

DUNWOODY INSTITUTE
Minneapolis/September-June

This independent institution offers a 2-year AAS degree and 1-year diploma in Baking Production and Management Technology. Program started 1914. Accredited by ACCSCT, NCA. Calendar: quarter. Curriculum: baking only. Admission dates: September 12, December 4, March 9. Total enrollment 45; 6 to 20 enrollees each admission period; 98% of applicants accepted; 50% financial aid recipients; 51% under age 25; 43% age 25 to 44; 6% age 45 or over; 8% part-time students; 15 students per instructor; 100% of graduates obtain employment. Facilities: include 3 labs and 5 classrooms.

Courses: Bread and rolls, ingredient science, cake and pastry, cake decorating, financial and business management, merchandising. Schedule: 6 hours daily. Externship: 12-week, salaried

Faculty: 3 full-, 1 part-time. Qualifications: master bakers with degrees and teaching licenses.

Costs: Annual tuition: $4,650. Application fee $30, tuition deposit $50, tools and uniforms $150-200 per year. Refunds: as per school policy. Admission requirements: high school diploma or equivalent and admission test. Last year 7 scholarships were awarded averaging $1,000. Part-time employment is available. Off-campus housing cost: $300 per month.

Contact: Robert J. Galloway, CMB, Baking Production & Management Technology, Dunwoody Institute, 818 Dunwoody Blvd., Minneapolis, MN 55403; (612) 374-5800, Fax (612) 374-5366.

HENNEPIN TECHNICAL COLLEGE
Brooklyn Park and Eden Prairie/September-June

This college offers a 80-credit diploma/certificate in Culinary Arts. Program started 1972. Accredited by NCA, ACFEI. Calendar: quarter. Curriculum: core. Admission dates: fall, winter, spring. Total enrollment 60; 10 to 20 enrollees each admission period; 100% of applicants accepted; 40% financial aid recipients; 25% under age 25; 60% age 25 to 44; 15% age 45 or over; 8 to 10%% part-time students; 15 students per instructor; 98% of graduates obtain employment. Facilities: include 3 kitchens, 3 classrooms and restaurant.

Courses: Externship: 6- to 8-week and post-graduate assistantships.

Faculty: Brooklyn Park: C. Castagneri, E. Vinkemeier; Eden Prairie: D. Wood, B. Menne, G. Dorn. Qualifications: ACF certified or certifiable.

COSTS: Annual tuition: $2,228 in-state, $4,456 out-of-state. Approximately $550 for supplies. Refund policy: up to 1st 10 days of quarter. Application deadlines: up to start of classes. Last year 1 scholarship was awarded. Part time employment available.

LOCATION: The campus is in a suburban setting, 10 miles from Minneapolis.

CONTACT: Mike Jung, CEC AAC, Culinary Arts Dept., Hennepin Technical College-Brooklyn Park Campus, 9000 Brooklyn Blvd., Brooklyn Park, MN 55445; (612) 425-3800, Fax (612) 550-2119.

MOORHEAD TECHNICAL COLLEGE
Moorhead/September-May

This college offers a 2-year certificate in Chef Training. Program started 1966. Accredited by State, NCA. Calendar: quarter. Curriculum: core. Admission dates: quarterly. Total enrollment 40 to 50; 35 enrollees each admission period; 80% financial aid recipients; 80% under age 25; 15% age 25 to 44; 5% age 45 or over; 10% part-time students; 20 to 25 students per instructor; 89% of graduates obtain employment. Facilities: 2 kitchens, 1 classroom, 2 restaurants.

COURSES: Quantity food preparation, food purchasing and cost controls, menu planning. Schedule: 7 am-3 pm, 9 months per year; part-time options available.

FACULTY: 2 full-time

COSTS: Annual tuition: in-state $616, out-of-state $1,232. Other fees: $20 tuition deposit, $60 per quarter meal fee, $40 per quarter uniform fee. Refund policy: 100% during first 5 days of quarter, 80% 6-10 days, 50% 11-15 days. Admission requirements: high school diploma or equivalent. Last year 30 loans were granted, averaging $2,000. Off-campus housing cost: $125 per month.

LOCATION: The single building campus is in an urban setting.

CONTACT: Kim Brewster, Chef Training, Moorhead Technical College, 1900 28th Ave. S., Moorhead, MN 56560; (800) 426-5603, Fax (218) 236-0342.

NORTHWEST TECHNICAL COLLEGE
Detroit Lakes/August-June

This college offers a 10-month diploma in Commercial Cooking and Baking. Program started 1965. Calendar: quarter. Curriculum: core. Admission dates: August. Total enrollment 20; 9 to 12 enrollees each admission period; 100% of applicants accepted; 89% financial aid recipients; 20% under age 25; 78% age 25 to 44; 2% age 45 or over; 1% part-time students; 20 students per instructor; 96% of graduates obtain employment. Facilities: kitchen, classroom, restaurant.

COURSES: Schedule: 7 hours per day, 10 months per year; part-time options available.

FACULTY: Instructor isSonia Anderson.

COSTS: Tuition: in-state $37 per credit hour, out-of-state $76 per credit hour.

CONTACT: Sonia Anderson, Culinary Director, Chef Training, Northwest Technical College-Detroit Lakes, 900 Highway 34 East, Detroit Lakes, MN 56501; (800) 492-4836, Fax (218) 847-7170.

ST. PAUL TECHNICAL COLLEGE
St. Paul

This college offers a 12-month diploma. Program started 1967. Accredited by NCA. Admission dates: September, December, March. Total enrollment 40 to 50; 14 to 16 students per instructor. Career planning and placement available.

FACULTY: 3 full-time.

COSTS: Tuition: in-state $35 per credit hour, out-of-state $70 per credit hour. Admission requirements: high school diploma or equivalent and admission test.

CAREER/PROFESSIONAL **MISSISSIPPI**

CONTACT: Culinary Director, Restaurant-Hotel Cookery, St. Paul Technical College, 235 Marshall Ave., St. Paul, MN 55102; (612) 221-1300, Fax (612) 221-1416.

SOUTH CENTRAL TECHNICAL COLLEGE
North Mankato/September-July

This college offers a 15-month diploma and 2-year associate degree in Hotel, Restaurant and Institutional Cooking. Program started 1968. Accredited by NCA. Calendar: quarter. Curriculum: culinary only. Admission dates: September, January, March, June. Total enrollment 25; 5-7 enrollees each admission period; 100% of applicants accepted; 70% financial aid recipients; 60% under age 25; 40% age 25 to 44; 5% age 45 or over; 50% part-time students; 17 students per instructor; 95% of graduates obtain employment. Facilities: include 2 kitchens, bakery, classroom.

COURSES: Food preparation, inventory control, cost control, management, menu design, job preparation, and problem solving. Other Required courses: CPR, first aid, microcomputers, problem solving. employment search skills. Schedule: 7 hours per day.

FACULTY: 2 full-time. Includes: J. Hanson, MBA, BSBA.

COSTS: Annual tuition: in-state $40 per credit, out-of-state $80 per credit. Books and uniforms $520. Refund policy: within 5 days of beginning of quarter. Application deadlines: beginning of each quarter. Admission requirements: high school diploma or equivalent. Last year 18 loans were granted, averaging $600. Off-campus housing cost: $400 per month.

LOCATION: The 1,200-student campus is in an urban setting.

CONTACT: Jim Hanson, Instructor, Culinary Arts, South Central Technical College, 1920 Lee Blvd., P.O. Box 1920, North Mankato, MN 56003; (507) 389-7229, Fax (507) 388-9951.

MISSISSIPPI

OFFSHORE COOKING SCHOOL
Ocean Springs/Year-round

This private vocational school offers 1- to 5-week diploma courses in shipboard cuisine. First offered in 1990. Accredited by the State of Mississippi. Admission dates weekly. Total enrollment 4 students per session; 75% of applicants accepted; 50% financial aid recipients (JTPA); 10% under age 25; 50% age 25 to 44; 40% age 45 or over; 95% of graduates obtain jobs. Facilities: large lab/kitchen and 1 classroom in a restored 1911 manor house.

COURSES: Emphasize southern traditional and cajun cuisine. Steward: includes basic scratch cooking and baking, inventory control, cost control analysis, and menu planning. Specialized House husband/wife weekend and evening courses are offered.

FACULTY: President/chef L.J. Couch, a graduate of the CIA, studied in Germany and England, and has worked in hotels and restaurants for more than 30 years; and Jeannie Couch, an experienced traditional southern cook.

COSTS: $400 weekly, specialized courses begin at $100. Payment is due in advance. Lodging ranges from $100-$200 per week.

LOCATION: A coastal town 60 miles from Mobile, Ala., and 98 miles east of New Orleans.

CONTACT: L.J. Couch, Offshore Cooking School, 703 Cox Ave., Ocean Springs, MS 39564; (601) 875-1333, Fax (601) 872-2537.

MISSOURI CULINARY INSTITUTE
Lexington/January-November

This private school offers a 10-week certificate of completion. Program started 1995. Curriculum: culinary. Admission dates: every 10 weeks starting in January. Total enrollment 12; 12 students per instructor. Facilities: 1 demo kitchen/classroom, 1 lab kitchen with 12 work stations.

COURSES: Basic culinary and baking skills, safety, sanitation, nutrition, menu planning. 300 hours of culinary courses required for graduation. Schedule: 9 am-3 pm, Monday-Friday.

FACULTY: 2 full-time, 1 part-time. Includes: Dorothy Kopp, Terry Kopp. Qualifications: Dorothy Kopp has over 50 years of restaurant service. Terry Kopp has operated his own restaurant and studied at Le Cordon Bleu.

COSTS: Tuition: $2,500. Application and registration fees are $150; other fees and supplies are $850. Full refund for cancellations within 3 days of enrollment; withdrawals during first week forfeit 15% of tuition plus $150. Admission requirements: high school graduation, GED, or school examination. Average off-campus housing cost $150-$500.

LOCATION: The school is in a rural setting, 35 miles from Kansas City.

CONTACT: Terry Kopp, Missouri Culinary Institute, Rte.1, Box 224F, Lexington, MO 64067; (816) 259-6464.

ST. LOUIS COMMUNITY COLLEGE-FOREST PARK
St. Louis/August-May

This college offers a 2-year AAS degree and a 3-year apprenticeship in Culinary Arts. Program started 1976. Accredited by NCA. Calendar: semester. Curriculum: core. Admission dates: August, January. Total enrollment 150; 50 enrollees each admission period; 100% of applicants accepted; 20% under age 25; 60% age 25 to 44; 20% age 45 or over; 40% part-time students; 20 students per instructor; 98% of graduates obtain employment. Facilities: include 2 kitchens and classrooms.

COURSES: Meat analysis, garde manger, pastry, baking, nutrition, food specialties, catering, general education, involvement with Junior Chef Organization. 40 hours of culinary courses required for graduation. Other required courses: 20 hours. Schedule: 15 hours per week; part-time and weekend options available. Externship: 150-hour, salaried, each semester.

FACULTY: 3 full-time, 25 part-time. Includes: Kathy Schiffman, Dept. Chair; Scott Vratarich, Instructor; Reed Miller, Chef Instructor. Qualifications: masters degree and industry experience.

COSTS: Annual tuition: $1,200 in-state, $1,700 out-of-state. Parking $16. Refund policy: 100% before classes begin, 50% before 2nd week. Application deadlines: 1 week before classes begin. Admission requirements: high school diploma or equivalent and admission test. Last year 10 scholarships were awarded averaging $500. Part-time and weekend options available. Off-campus housing cost: $450 per month. Part time employment available.

LOCATION: The 7,000-student campus is in an urban setting.

CONTACT: Kathy Schiffman, Culinary Arts Department, St. Louis Community College-Forest Park, 5600 Oakland Ave., St. Louis, MO 63110; (314) 644-9751, Fax (314) 644-9752.

MONTANA

COLLEGE OF TECHNOLOGY — UNIVERSITY OF MONTANA
Missoula/Year-round

This public institution offers a 1-year certificate and 2-year AAS degree in Food Service Management. Program started 1973. Accredited by ACFEI, NASC. Calendar: semester. Curriculum: core. Admission dates: August, January. Total enrollment 50; 25 enrollees each admission period; 90% of applicants accepted; 30% financial aid recipients; 10% under age 25; 70% age 25 to 44; 20% age 45 or over; 5% part-time students; 15 students per instructor; 90% of graduates obtain employment. Facilities: include 4 kitchens and classrooms and 3 restaurants.

COURSES: Cooking, baking, management, and general education. Schedule: 6 hours per day, 12 months per year.

CAREER/PROFESSIONAL — NEBRASKA

FACULTY: Includes: F. Sonnenberg, R. Lodahl, M. Barton, S. Bartos. Qualifications: CEC, CPC, CC.

COSTS: Annual tuition: $1,364 in-state, $2,634 out-of-state. Application fee $20. Other fees: $400. Refund policy: 80% – 2 weeks. Application deadlines: July. Admission requirements: high school diploma or equivalent and admission test. Last year 8 scholarships were awarded averaging $300. Part-time employment is available. Off-campus housing cost: $300 per month.

CONTACT: Frank Sonnenberg, Culinary Arts Dept., College of Technology-University of Montana/Missoula, 909 S. Ave. W., Missoula, MT 59801-7910; (406) 452-6811, Fax (406) 243-7899.

NEBRASKA

CENTRAL COMMUNITY COLLEGE
Hastings/September-June

This college offers a 2-year certificate/AAS degree in Culinary Arts. Program started 1971. Accredited by NCA. Calendar: semester. Curriculum: core. Admission dates: open. Total enrollment 40; 6 enrollees each admission period; 100% of applicants accepted; 80% financial aid recipients; 80% under age 25; 20% age 25 to 44; 20 students per instructor; 95% of graduates obtain employment. Facilities: 1 kitchen, 4 classrooms and restaurant.

COURSES: Bake shop, pantry, entrees, international cuisine, advanced sauces, pastries, and garde manger. Schedule: 8 am-4 pm, Monday-Friday.

FACULTY: 2 full-time.

COSTS: Annual tuition: in-state $996, out-of-state $1,536. Uniform and supplies $40. Admission requirements: high school diploma or equivalent. Last year 4 scholarships were awarded averaging $250. Career planning and placement available. Part time employment available.

LOCATION: The 600-acre campus is 100 miles from Lincoln.

CONTACT: Deborah Brennan, Program Supervisor, Hotel, Motel, Restaurant Mgt., Central Community College, P.O. Box 1024, Hastings, NE 68902; (402) 461-2458, Fax (402) 461-2454.

METROPOLITAN COMMUNITY COLLEGE
Omaha/Year-round

This college offers a 1- to 2-year AAS degree in Food Arts, Foodservice Management, and Chef Apprentice. Program started 1976. Accredited by NCA, ACFEI. Calendar: quarter. Curriculum: core. Admission dates: September, December, March, June. Total enrollment 100; 15 enrollees each admission period; 100% of applicants accepted; 68% financial aid recipients; 40% under age 25; 40% age 25 to 44; 10% age 45 or over; 53% part-time students; 12 students per instructor; 96% of graduates obtain employment. Facilities: include 18 kitchens and classrooms, and restaurant.

COURSES: Schedule: 8 am-10 pm Monday-Friday; part-time options available. Externship: 150-hour, restaurant setting.

FACULTY: 2 full-time, 10 part-time. Includes: Jim Trebbien, CCE and Yvonne Nettelmann, CCE.

COSTS: Tuition: in-state $23 per credit hour, out-of-state $42 per credit hour. Other fees: uniforms, tools. Admission requirements: high school diploma or equivalent. Last year 12 scholarships were awarded averaging $5,000. Part-time employment is available.

CONTACT: Jim Trebbien, Food Arts & Management, Metropolitan Community College, P.O. Box 3777, Omaha, NE 68103-0777; (402) 449-8400, Fax (402) 449-8333.

SOUTHEAST COMMUNITY COLLEGE
Lincoln/Year-round

This college offers a 18-month AS degree in Culinary Arts. Program started 1988. Accredited by NCA. Calendar: quarter. Curriculum: core. Admission dates: September, March. Total enrollment

20; 10 enrollees each admission period; 100% of applicants accepted; 50% under age 25; 50% age 25 to 44; 30% part-time students; 15 students per instructor; 95100% of graduates obtain employment. Facilities: include kitchen and 2 classrooms.

COURSES: Advanced food, buffet, decorating and catering, professional baking. Schedule: 20 hours per week. Externship: 220-hour, salaried.

FACULTY: 1 full-time, 3 part-time. Includes: G. Schreck Kirby, CCE, CWC; J. Taylor, MA, RD; L. Cockerham, BS; E. Coudill, MS RD; K. Cain, CWC. Qualifications: associate degree.

COSTS: Annual tuition: in-state $25.50 per credit hour, out-of-state $30.50 per credit hour. Program reservation fee $25. Student activities fee $12. Refund policy: pro-rated on percentage of total course length. Admission requirements: high school diploma or equivalent. Part-time employment is available.

CONTACT: Jo Taylor, Program Chair, Food Service Program, Southeast Community College, 8800 "O" St., Lincoln, NE 68520; (402) 437-2465, Fax (402) 437-2404.

NEVADA

AREA TECHNICAL TRADE CENTER
North Las Vegas
CONTACT: Ted Doram, Director, Culinary Arts, Area Technical Trade Center, 444 W. Brooks Ave., North Las Vegas, NV 89030; (702) 799-8300.

CLARK COUNTY COMMUNITY COLLEGE
North Las Vegas
This college offers a 1-year certificate and a 2-year degree. Program started 1990. Accredited by NASC. Admission dates: open. Total enrollment 400; 100% of applicants accepted; 18 students per instructor; 95% of graduates obtain employment. Career planning and placement available.

FACULTY: 3 full-time, 6 part-time.

COSTS: Annual tuition: in-state $720, out-of-state $2,220.

CONTACT: Culinary Director, Culinary Arts Dept., Clark County Community College, 3200 East Cheyenne Ave., North Las Vegas, NV 89030; (702) 651-4192.

COMMUNITY COLLEGE OF SOUTHERN NEVADA
North Las Vegas
This school offers a program in Hotel, Restaurant, and Casino Management, and Culinary Arts.

CONTACT: Thomas Rosenberger, Community College of Southern Nevada, 3200 E. Cheyenne Ave., S2D, North Las Vegas, NV 89030-4296; (702) 651-4193.

TRUCKEE MEADOWS COMMUNITY COLLEGE
Reno/August-May
This college offers a 2-year AAS degree in Food Service Technology. Program started 1980. Accredited by State. Calendar: semester. Curriculum: core. Admission dates: January, September. Total enrollment 72; 30 to 40 enrollees each admission period; 100% of applicants accepted; 30% financial aid recipients; 60% under age 25; 25% age 25 to 44; 15% age 45 or over; 70% part-time students; 16 students per instructor; 75% of graduates obtain employment. Facilities: include 8 kitchens and classrooms, and student-run restaurant.

COURSES: Cooking, baking, pastry, garde manger, sauces, business chef, nutrition, sanitation, general education.

CAREER/PROFESSIONAL   **NEW HAMPSHIRE**   **63**

FACULTY: 1 full-time, 5 part-time. Includes: George Skivofilakas, CEC, CCE, AAC.

COSTS: Tuition: in-state $34 per credit hour, out-of-state $1,100 + $31 per credit hour. Application fee $5. Refund policy: no refund after third class. Application deadlines: prior to first class of each semester. Admission requirements: high school diploma or equivalent. Last year 9 scholarships were awarded averaging $500. Part-time employment is available. Off-campus housing cost: $400-500 per month.

CONTACT: George Skivofilakas, Culinary Arts Department, Truckee Meadows Community College, 7000 Dandini Blvd., Reno, NV 89512; (702) 673-7015.

NEW HAMPSHIRE

NEW HAMPSHIRE COLLEGE CULINARY INSTITUTE
Manchester/September-May

This 4-year college offers a 2-year AAS degree in Culinary Arts; this can be transferred into a 4-year Hotel/Restaurant degree. Accredited by ACFEI. Calendar: semester. Admission dates: June. Total enrollment 120; 65 enrollees each admission period; 80% of applicants accepted; 75% financial aid recipients; 80% under age 25; 15% age 25 to 44; 5% age 45 or over; 10% part-time students; 15 students per instructor; 100% of graduates obtain employment. Facilities: include 3 kitchens, bakeshop lab, 2 production labs, and a dining room/classroom.

COURSES: Include culinary skills, bakeshop, food production, garde manger, nutritional cooking, and general education courses. Other required courses: dining room management and classical, regional, and international cuisine. Schedule: 20-30 hours per week; part-time options available. Externship: 600-hour, salaried, with travel opportunities.

FACULTY: 5 full-time, 6 part-time. Includes: Carol Mueller, Vicki Connell, Christine Merritz, Douglas Armstrong, Mary Franz Allen, Richard Petty.

COSTS: Annual tuition: $9,596. Knife set fee $147, books $200, uniforms $100. Admission requirements: high school diploma or equivalent. On-campus housing cost: $4,884 annually.

LOCATION: The 1,200-student campus is situated on 200-wooded acres in a rural setting.

CONTACT: Cindie Farley, Admissions Counselor/Culinary Coordinator, Admissions, New Hampshire College Culinary Institute, 2500 N. River Rd., Manchester, NH 03106; (603) 644-3128, Fax (603) 644-3166.

NEW HAMPSHIRE TECHNICAL COLLEGE
Berlin/Year-round

This college offers a 2-year diploma/certificate/AAS in Culinary Arts. Program started 1966. Accredited by NEASC. Calendar: semester. Curriculum: core. Admission dates: open. Total enrollment 30; 20 enrollees each admission period; 76% of applicants accepted; 89% financial aid recipients; 60% under age 25; 30% age 25-44; 10% age 45 or over; 10% part-time students; 15 students per instructor; 100% of graduates obtain employment. Facilities: 2 kitchens plus classrooms.

COURSES: Soups and sauces, food production, meat fabrication, sanitation, baking, patisserie, classical desserts, garde manger, patisserie internationale, charcuterie, buffet, food sculpture and design, menu analysis and restaurant design, marketing, regional American cuisine, a la carte, international cuisine, general education. Schedule: Monday-Thursday. Externship provided.

FACULTY: 2 full-time. Includes: R. Turgeon, CWC, CCE; K. Hohmeister, working Executive Chef.

COSTS: Annual tuition: $2,296 in-state, $5,408 out-of-state. Other fees: $90. Application deadlines: open. Admission requirements: high school diploma or equivalent. Last year 35 scholarships were awarded averaging $500; 530 loans were granted, averaging $3,000. Off-campus housing cost: $1,440 per semester. Part time employment available.

CONTACT: Roger Turgeon, Department Chair, Culinary Arts Department, New Hampshire Technical College, 2020 Riverside Dr., Berlin, NH 03570; (603) 752-1113, Fax (603) 752-6335.

UNIVERSITY OF NEW HAMPSHIRE
Durham/September-May

This college offers a 24-month AAS degree in Food Service Management. Program started 1966. Calendar: semester. Curriculum: core. Admission dates: fall, spring. Total enrollment 70; 8 to 32 enrollees each admission period; 75% of applicants accepted; 80% financial aid recipients; 50% under age 25; 45% age 25 to 44; 10% age 45 or over; 10% part-time students; 10 students per instructor; 90% of graduates obtain employment. Facilities: include 3 kitchens, multiple classrooms and 2 restaurants.

COURSES: Food preparation, hospitality, facilities and equipment planning, purchasing, nutrition, buffet and banquet service, food service management. Schedule: M-F daily, some evenings.

FACULTY: Includes: R.S. Alonzo, PhD, C.A. Caraminalis, D. O'Brien, M. Murtagh.

COSTS: Annual tuition: in-state $3,550, out-of-state $11,180. Application fee $20 in-state, $40 out-of-state. Enrollment fee $300. Other fees: approximately $850. Application deadlines: rolling admissions after February. Admission requirements: high school diploma or equivalent. On-campus housing: 5,000 spaces; average cost: $2,214. Part time employment available.

CONTACT: Charles Caraminalis, Thompson School of Applied Sciences-Food Service Management, University of New Hampshire, Barton Hall, Room 105, Durham, NH 03824; (603) 862-1073, Fax (603) 862-2915.

NEW JERSEY

ACADEMY OF CULINARY ARTS — ATLANTIC COMM. COLLEGE
Mays Landing/August-May

This college offers a 2-year AAS degree in Culinary Arts. Founded 1981. Accredited by MSA. Calendar: semester. Curriculum: core. Admission dates September, January. Total enrollment 360; 110 enrollees each admission period; 100% of applicants accepted; 54% financial aid recipients; 95% under age 25; 4% age 25 to 44; 1% age 45 and over; 20 students per instructor; 100% of graduates obtain employment. Facilities include 8 kitchens, 4 classrooms, computer lab, a bake shop, retail store, and gourmet restaurant. Courses: Include food purchasing, pastry, garde manger, hot food preparation, and nutrition. Schedule: 5 hours daily, mornings or afternoons and limited evening program. An internship is required. Also offers non-credit culinary arts classes and the ACF Apprenticeship Program in entry level skills.

FACULTY: 15 full-time international faculty with professional designations.

COSTS: Approximately $3,000 per semester. Nonrefundable application deposit of $300. 100% refund before first class, 50% after 2 weeks. Rolling admission. Applicants must have a high school diploma or equivalent. Off-campus part-time employment is available. Housing is available.

LOCATION: Atlantic Community College, a 536-acre campus in New Jersey's Pinelands, is 17 miles west of Atlantic City's boardwalk, 45 miles from Philadelphia and 115 miles from New York City.

CONTACT: Bobby Royal, Admissions Office, Atlantic Community College, 5100 Black Horse Pk., Mays Landing, NJ 08330-2699; (609) 343-5000 or (800) 645-CHEF; Fax (609) 343-4914; E-Mail accadmit@nsvm.atlantic.edu

BURLINGTON COUNTY COLLEGE
Pemberton/Year-round

This college offers a 2-year certificate and a 3-year AAS degree in Hospitality Management/Culinary Arts. Program started 1989. Accredited by MSA. Calendar: semester. Curriculum: core. Admission dates: open. Total enrollment 127; 5 enrollees each admission period; 100% of applicants accepted; 25% under age 25; 65% age 25 to 44; 10% age 45 or over; 50% part-time students; 14 students per instructor; 100% of graduates obtain employment. Facilities: include 14 kitchens and classrooms, pastry kitchen and restaurant.

COURSES: Cooking, baking, nutrition, and sanitation.

FACULTY: 5 full-time. Qualifications: master's degree or state certification.

COSTS: Annual tuition: in-state $605 + fee, out-of-state $51 per credit hour. Tuition deposit $100. Refund policy: 10 days after first day of class. Admission requirements: high school diploma or equivalent and admission test. Last year 1 scholarship was awarded for $1,000.

CONTACT: William White, Program Director, Business Studies, Burlington County College, Route 530, Pemberton, NJ 08068; (609) 894-9311 ext. 441.

HUDSON COUNTY COMMUNITY COLLEGE
Jersey City/January-May, September-December

This college offers a 2-year certificate/AAS degree. Program started 1983. Accredited by MSA. Calendar: semester. Curriculum: core. Admission dates: September, January. Total enrollment 240; 15 students per instructor; 100% of graduates obtain employment. Facilities: 4 kitchens, 3 classrooms, 1 bar.

COURSES: Include bakeshop, garde manger, buffet catering. Externship provided.

FACULTY: 10 full-time.

COSTS: Annual tuition: $1,080 in-state, $2,160 out-of-state. Admission requirements: high school diploma or equivalent and admission test.

CONTACT: Siroun Meguerditchian, Executive Director, Culinary Arts Dept., Hudson County Community College, 161 Newkirk St., Jersey City, NJ 07306; (201) 714-2193, Fax (201) 656-1522.

MIDDLESEX COUNTY COLLEGE
Edison/Year-round

This college offers a 1-year certificate in Culinary Arts. Program started 1987. Accredited by MSA. Calendar: semester. Curriculum: culinary only. Admission dates: January, May, September. Total enrollment 32; 10 enrollees each admission period; 25% financial aid recipients; 50% part-time students; 18 students per instructor; 100% of graduates obtain employment. Facilities: include 2 kitchens and 3 classrooms.

COURSES: Food selection and preparation, baking, food production, garde manger, food and beverage cost controls and purchasing, sanitation, and general education. Schedule: 12 hours per week; part-time and evening options available. Externship: 180 hours.

FACULTY: 6 full-time, 3 part-time.

COSTS: Annual tuition: in-state $2,300, out-of-state $4,600. Application fee $25. Application deadlines: 1 month prior to semester. Admission requirements: high school diploma or equivalent.

LOCATION: The 200-acre suburban campus is 30 miles from New York City.

CONTACT: Marilyn Laskowski-Sachnoff, Department Chair, Hotel Restaurant & Management, Middlesex County College, 155 Mill Rd., P.O. Box 3050, Edison, NJ 08818-3050; (908) 906-2538.

SALEM COUNTY VOCATIONAL TECHNICAL SCHOOLS
Woodstown
This college offers a 1-year certificate. Program started 1976. Accredited by MSA. Admission dates: September, January. Total enrollment 30; 75% of applicants accepted; 15 students per instructor; 80% of graduates obtain employment.

FACULTY: 20 full-time.

COSTS: Annual tuition: $2,150.

CONTACT: Culinary Arts, Salem County Vocational Technical Schools, Box 350, Woodstown, NJ 08098; (609) 769-0101, Fax (609) 769-3602.

NEW MEXICO

ALBUQUERQUE TECHNICAL VOCATIONAL INSTITUTE
Albuquerque
CONTACT: Kayleigh Carabajal, Albuquerque Technical Vocational Institute, 525 Buena Vista SE, Albuquerque, NM 87106; (505) 224-3765.

SANTA FE COMMUNITY COLLEGE
Santa Fe/Year-round
This college offers a 2-year certificate/AAS degree in Culinary Arts. Program started 1985. Accredited by NCA. Calendar: semester. Curriculum: core. Admission dates: August 20, January 10, June 1. Total enrollment 190; 30 enrollees each admission period; 100% of applicants accepted; 20% financial aid recipients; 50% under age 25; 40% age 25 to 44; 10% age 45 or over; 70% part-time students; 14 students per instructor; 100% of graduates obtain employment. Facilities: include 2 kitchens and classrooms, culinary lab and restaurant.

COURSES: Culinary courses, specialty topics, Southwestern cuisine, general studies. 30 hours of culinary courses required for graduation. Other required courses: nutrition, sanitation, food and beverage management, math, English. Schedule: 24 hours per week, 10 months per year, full part-time/evening schedule. Externship provided. Continuing education: 12 courses per semester.

FACULTY: 1 full-time, 8 part-time. Qualifications: working executive chef.

COSTS: Annual tuition: in-county $17 per credit hour, out-of-county $24 per credit hour, out-of-state $45 per credit hour. Other fees: lab fees. Refund policy: pro-rated. Admission requirements: high school diploma or equivalent. Last year 8 scholarships were awarded averaging $250. Part-time employment is available.

LOCATION: The new 9,000-student campus is in a country setting.

CONTACT: Bill Weiland CEC, Culinary Arts Dept., Santa Fe Community College, P.O. Box 4187, Santa Fe, NM 87502-4187; (505) 438-1600, Fax (438) 471-1237.

NEW YORK

ADIRONDACK COMMUNITY COLLEGE
Queensbury/September-May
This proprietary college offers a 1-year certificate and a 2-year AAS degree in Food Service. Program started 1969. Accredited by MSA. Calendar: semester. Curriculum: core. Admission dates: fall, spring. Total enrollment 25; 7080% financial aid recipients; 75% part-time students; 10 students per instructor; 90% of graduates obtain employment. Facilities: include 3 kitchens, classroom and restaurant.

COURSES: 1 year of food preparation, year of spa cuisine, year of American regional cuisine.

Externship: 1,000-1,200 hours. Continuing education: baking, wines and other topics.

FACULTY: 1 full-time and 3 part-time instructors.

COSTS: $1,600 annually. Admission requirements: high school diploma or equivalent required. Last year scholarships were awarded averaging $400-$600. Part-time employment is available.

CONTACT: William Steele, Commercial Cooking/Occupational Education, Adirondack Community College, Bay Rd., Queensbury, NY 12803; (518) 793-4491.

THE CHOCOLATE GALLERY
New York/Year-round

Founded in 1978. This private school specializing in cake decoration and baking offers 2-hour workshops to 2-day hands-on certificate courses. Students may attend one class weekly for 4 weeks or enroll in daily intensives.

Specialties: Beginning to advanced cake decoration, baking, chocolate, confectionery, desserts.

FACULTY: Owner-head instructor Joan Mansour has studied with master cake decorators in the U.S. and abroad for more than 15 years, is a certified Wilton Cake Decorating Instructor, and received the Award for National Enrollment, Northeast Teacher of the Year, and National Teacher of the Year. Guest lecturers include Steven Palumbo and Colette Peters.

COSTS: Range from $35 for 2 hours to $250 for 2 days. Full payment required 7 days prior.

CONTACT: Joan Mansour, The Chocolate Gallery, 56 W. 22nd St., New York, NY 10010; (212) 675-2253.

THE CULINARY INSTITUTE OF AMERICA
Hyde Park/Year-round *(See also page 199) (See display ad page 67)*

This independent, not-for-profit educational institution offers 21-month associate degree programs in culinary arts and baking and pastry arts, bachelor's degree programs in culinary arts management and baking and pastry arts management, and continuing education and nonvocational courses. Founded in 1946. Accredited by the ACCSCT; curricula registered with N.Y. State Education Dept. Associate degree programs begin 16 (8) times per year for culinary (baking and pastry) arts; bachelor's degree programs begin 3 times per year. Total enrollment 2,000; 72 (50) enrollees each admission period for associate (bachelor) degree programs; 97% of applicants accepted; 85% financial aid recipients; student to faculty ratio 18:1. Facilities: 36 professionally-equipped production kitchens and bakeshops, 45,000-volume library, learning resources center, over 1,500 instructional videotapes, nutrition center, student center, bookstore, four student-staffed public restaurants.

COURSES: Associate degree culinary arts curriculum includes American and international cuisines and pastry, nutrition, table service and customer relations, wine and spirits management, and menu and facilities planning; baking and pastry arts curriculum includes culinary courses, breads, desserts, ice carving, and showpieces; bachelor's degree curriculum includes leadership, ethics, management, marketing and communications, finance and economics, advanced cooking and pastry techniques, a senior thesis, and a 4-week food and wine seminar in California. Schedule: 224 days per year. Both associate degree programs include 18-week paid externships. The Continuing Education Department offers 1- to 30-week courses, customized programs, recipe testing and product development, independent learning courses, and travel programs. Fellowships are awarded to a limited number of graduates.

FACULTY: Over 115 chefs and instructors from more than 20 countries, including the highest concentration of ACF-Certified Master Chefs.

COSTS: Estimated cost, including fees and two meals daily, is $24,995 for associate degree programs, $22,400 for bachelor's degree programs, $595–$11,380 for continuing education courses. Nonrefundable application fee of $30; $150 deposit due 90 days prior. Cancellations 90 days prior to registration or within 3 days of signing enrollment agreement receive refund. Applicants require high school diploma or equivalent and at least 3 to 5 months foodservice experience. Financial aid is available from several sources. In 1994–95, 1,271 scholarships were awarded averaging $946 each; 2,793 loans were granted averaging $3,489 each. Four on-campus dormitories house 1,200 students; fees range from $1,225–$1,825 per semester.

LOCATION: The 150-acre campus overlooks the Hudson River on U.S. Route 9 in Hyde Park, about 90 minutes north of New York City.

CONTACT: The Culinary Institute of America, 433 Albany Post Rd., Hyde Park, NY 12538-1499. Admissions Office (800) CULINARY (285-4627). Continuing Education Dept. (800) 888-7850.

ERIE COMMUNITY COLLEGE, CITY CAMPUS
Buffalo/September-May

This college offers a 2-year AOS degree in Hotel Technology/Culinary Arts. Program started 1985. Accredited by MSA. Calendar: semester. Curriculum: core. Admission dates: fall. Total enrollment 80; 80 enrollees each admission period; 60% of applicants accepted; 70% financial aid recipients; 65% under age 25; 20% age 25 to 44; 15% age 45 or over; 10% part-time students; 28 students per instructor; 75% of graduates obtain employment. Facilities: include 5 kitchens and classrooms, computer lab and restaurant.

FACULTY: 5 full-time

COSTS: Annual tuition: in-state $1,980, out-of-state $3,960. Tuition deposit $50. Other fees $100. Refund policy: 100% by 1st week of school. Admission requirements: high school diploma or

The French Culinary Institute

Dean of Special Programs
JACQUES PÉPIN
Former Chef to Charles de Gaulle, Master Chef, TV Personality

Dean of Culinary Studies
ALAIN SAILHAC
Former Executive Chef of Le Cirque

Master Chef/ Sr. Lecturer
ANDRE SOLTNER
Former Owner/Chef of Lutece

"This school is committed as no other to the teaching of the fundamentals of basic French cuisine and its discipline which is indispensable to the start of a successful future in cooking."

DANIEL BOULUD, *Chef/Owner of Restaurant Daniel, NYC*

Learn cooking from the *best!*

If you are serious about becoming a chef or entering the world of food, call our admissions representative at: (212) 219-8890
We have an average of 5 job opportunities for every graduate.

FINANCIAL AID AVAILABLE IF QUALIFIED

FCI AND ITS RESTAURANT L'ECOLE 462 BROADWAY (IN SOHO) NYC
(212) 219-8890 FAX (212) 219-9292
VISIT US ON THE WORLD WIDE WEB AT HTTP://WWW.INTERPORT.NET/FCI/

equivalent and admission test. Last year 40 scholarships were awarded averaging $600. Career planning and placement available.

LOCATION: The 2,000-student campus is in an urban setting.

CONTACT: Paul J. Cannamela, CCE, AAC, Assistant Professor, Hotel Management/Culinary Arts, Erie Community College, City Campus, 121 Ellicott St., Buffalo, NY 14203; (716) 851-1034/35, Fax (716) 851-1129.

THE FRENCH CULINARY INSTITUTE
New York/Year-round *(See display ad page 69)*

This proprietary institution offers a 600-hour 6- or 9-month career program in classic French technique culminating in the Grande Diplome. Founded in 1984 with Le Centre d'Information Technologique des Metiers d'Alimentation Ferrandi in Paris. Accredited by the ACCSCT. Calendar: quarter; new classes begin every 6 weeks. Curriculum: culinary. Total enrollment 320; 18 enrollees each admission period; class size ranges from 8 to 18 per instructor. Placement and career counseling available for graduates.

COURSES: Basic French classical technique with emphasis on fine dining, a la carte preparation, and service. Students may attend full time for 6 months (8:30 am to 2:30 pm Monday through Friday) or part-time for 9 months (5:30 to 10:30 pm, 3 evenings per week).

FACULTY: The 13 full- and 3 part-time instructors include Dean of Special Programs Jacques Pepin, Dean of Culinary Studies Alain Sailhac, Dean of Pastry Arts Jacques Torres, and Master Chef Senior Lecturer Andre Soltner.

COSTS: Tuition for the 600-hour program is $16,850, which includes uniforms, equipment, and registration fee. A $1,000 deposit and $100 application fee are required. Refund policy complies with ACCSCT guidelines. Applicants must have a high school diploma or equivalent. Part-time employment and financial aid are available if qualified.

LOCATION: New York's SoHo district, adjacent to Chinatown and little Italy.

CONTACT: Admissions Department, The French Culinary Institute, 462 Broadway, New York, NY 10013; (212) 219-8890; Fax (212) 219-9292 or (212) 431-3054.

JEFFERSON COMMUNITY COLLEGE
Watertown

This college offers a 2-year certificate/AAS degree. Program started 1975. Accredited by MSA. Admission dates: August, January. Total enrollment 120; 100% of applicants accepted; 25 students per instructor; 95% of graduates obtain employment.

COURSES: Externship provided.

FACULTY: 4 full-time.

COSTS: Annual tuition: in-state $1,470, out-of-state $2,940. Admission requirements: high school diploma or equivalent.

CONTACT: Edward W. Bushaw, Hospitality & Tourism Dept., Jefferson Community College, Outer Coffeen St., Watertown, NY 13601; (315) 786-2200, Fax (315) 788-0716.

JULIE SAHNI'S SCHOOL OF INDIAN COOKING
Brooklyn Heights/Year-round

Julie Sahni offers intensive participation courses (limit 3 students) that meet over a weekend in her specially designed teaching kitchen. Sessions emphasize techniques, spices and seasonings, healthful meal planning, historical background, and religious ideology and include shopping at an Indian grocery. Each course can be taught in any private kitchen in the U.S. as a 1-day introduction for 6 students.

CAREER/PROFESSIONAL — NEW YORK

COURSES: Classic and regional Indian cuisine.

FACULTY: Julie Sahni was executive chef of 2 restaurants in New York City, served on the faculty of New York University and Boston University's culinary arts programs, and is author of *Classic Indian Cooking, Classic Indian Vegetarian and Grain Cooking,* and *Moghul Microwave.*

COSTS: Each session is $900, with materials. A $100 nonrefundable deposit is required 90 days prior. Refund for cancellations 90 days prior or within 3 days of signing enrollment agreement.

LOCATION: Near the Brooklyn entrance to the Brooklyn Bridge.

CONTACT: Julie Sahni, Julie Sahni's Indian Cooking, 101 Clark St., Brooklyn Heights, NY 11201; Tel/Fax (718) 625-3958.

THE KING'S CHOCOLATE HOUSE
Ozone Park/Year-round except summer

The Ultimate Chocolate Candy Class, a 5-day participation course offered 2 times a year, provides instruction to different techniques and brands of chocolate. Emphasis: hand-dipped fruits, truffles, fondant, English toffee, hard candy, tempering, woven baskets, hollow and solid molding.

FACULTY: Proprietor Joan Lipkis studied with Rose Levy Beranbaum, Elaine Gonzales, Ruedi C. Hauser, Albert Kumin, Meta McCall, and Westly Wilton.

COSTS: Fee is $775. A $375 deposit is required; $400 is due 3 weeks before course. Written cancellations 3 weeks prior forfeit 25% of fee; no refund thereafter.

LOCATION: Between JFK International Airport and LaGuardia Airport in Queens.

CONTACT: Joan Lipkis, The King's Chocolate House, 112-09 Rockaway Blvd., Ozone Park, NY 11420; (718) 848-8564.

Mohawk Valley Community College
- Food Service (AOS)
- Food Svc. Admin./Restaurant Mgmt.(AAS)
- Nutrition & Dietetics (AS)
- Chef Training (Certificate)

Excellent facilities, industry contacts. Call/write Dennis Baumeyer, Hospitality Programs, MVCC, Floyd Avenue, Rome, NY 13440. Tel: 315-338-5202.

✪ Good things begin at MVCC.
An equal educational opportunity institution. Affiliated with SUNY.

MOHAWK VALLEY COMMUNITY COLLEGE
(See display ad above) — **Rome/August-May**

This college offers a 1-year Chef Training certificate, a 2-year AOS degree in Food Service, a 2-year AAS degree in Restaurant Management, and a 2-year AS degree in Nutrition and Dietetics. Program started 1978. Accredited by MSA. Calendar: semester. Curriculum: culinary. Admission dates: August, January. Total enrollment 120; 80% financial aid recipients; 25 students per faculty member; 98% of graduates obtain employment. Facilities include 6 kitchens and classrooms, student-run restaurant and cafe. Courses: include sanitation, food preparation, food merchandising, and baking. A 225-hour externship is provided.

FACULTY: 3 full- and 6 part-time instructors. Includes Dennis R. Baumeyer, BS, MS, Linda Irwin, AAS, BS, MS, Marc Lubetkin, AAS,BS.

COSTS: Annual tuition is $2,350 in-state, $4,450 out-of-state. Application fee is $25. Other fees: student activity and insurance fee is $65. High school diploma or equivalent and admission test required. Last year 1 scholarship was awarded for $300; 15 loans were granted averaging $3,000. Part-time employment available.

LOCATION: The 2,500-student college campus is 12 miles from Utica.

CONTACT: Dennis R. Baumeyer, Director, Hospitality Programs, Mohawk Valley Community College, 1101 Floyd Ave., Rome, NY 13440; (315) 339-3470, ext. 210, Fax (315) 339-6934.

MONROE COMMUNITY COLLEGE
Rochester

This college offers a 2-year certificate/AAS degree. Program started 1967. Accredited by MSA. Admission dates: fall, spring. Total enrollment 175; 80% of applicants accepted; 18 students per instructor; 96% of graduates obtain employment.

FACULTY: 8 to 10 part-time.

COSTS: Annual tuition: in-state $2,000. Admission requirements: high school diploma or equivalent.

CONTACT: Eddy Callens, Chairperson, Dept. of Food, Hotel and Tourism Management, Monroe Community College, 1000 E. Henrietta Rd., Rochester, NY 14623; (716) 292-2000, ext. 2586, Fax (716) 427-2749.

THE NATURAL GOURMET COOKERY SCHOOL
New York/Year-round *(See also page 202)*

This private trade school devoted to healthy cooking offers 603-hour Chef's Training and 110-hour Holistic Culinary Arts Assistants certificate programs and courses for professionals and non-professionals. Founded in 1977. Chef's Training 4-month full-time/8-month part-time courses begin 6 times a year. Enrollment 7 to 16 students per session; 95% of applicants are accepted; 10% receive financial aid; 10% are under age 25; 75% are ages 25 to 44; 15% are 45 or older; 10% are part-time; 60% to 70% of graduates obtain jobs. Facilities include 2 kitchens, classroom, and bookstore. Students prepare meals for the Friday Night Dinner Club.

COURSES: Preparation of fresh vegetables, nuts, fruits, whole grains, legumes, and healthful condiments; Eastern and Western nutritional theories. Emphasis is on vegetarian, with some instruction in fish, poultry, butter and eggs. The full-time (part-time) Chef's Training program meets weekdays from 9 am to 4 pm (Tuesday and Wednesday evenings and 3 Saturdays per month). A 95-hour externship is provided. Assistants take at least 1 or 2 classes per week and assist the instructor.

FACULTY: Annemarie Colbin, MA, CCP, CHES, school founder and president, is a syndicated columnist and author of *Food and Healing* and 2 natural food cookbooks. Diane Carlson, vice president, is a graduate of the school and owned a cooking school in Minneapolis. Jenny Matthau, CCP, vice president, is a graduate of the school.

COSTS: Tuition is $8,900 for Chef's Training, $3,400 for Assistants. Applicants must have high school diploma or equivalent; Assistants applicants must have taken a course at the school and have natural food experience. Financing is available. Nearby lodging begins at $500 per month.

LOCATION: Between 5th and 6th Avenues in Manhattan.

CONTACT: Director of Admissions, The Natural Gourmet Cookery School, 48 W. 21st St., 2nd Floor, New York, NY 10010; (212) 645-5170.

NEW SCHOOL CULINARY ARTS
New York/Year-round *(See also page 202)*

The New School for Social Research, founded 1919, offers Master Class Certificate courses in Cooking (25 sessions), Baking (15), Professional Catering (10), Italian Cooking (10), and Restaurant Management (12) and other programs for professionals and nonprofessionals. Calendar: trimester. Maximum enrollment in each Master Class is 12 students; graduates are eligi-

CAREER/PROFESSIONAL **NEW YORK**

ble for apprenticeships. Facilities: a restored landmark townhouse with indoor and outdoor dining areas and a fully-equipped instructional kitchen.

COURSES: The Cooking Master Class stresses high quality cooking and covers basic skills and equipment use, cuisine and pastry preparation, charcuterie and hors d'oeuvres, presentation, and recipe development; Baking covers fine pastries, breads and doughs, cake decoration, and chocolate; Catering combines food preparation with instruction in the business of catering. Schedule: Monday through Friday mornings and evenings. Professional and continuing education courses include restaurant management, commercial cake decorating, and how-to's on opening a coffee bar, creating and selling a new food or beverage, and getting a cookbook published. Restaurant management and finance courses are offered on-line via personal computer in the Distance Instruction for Adult Learners (DIAL) program.

FACULTY: The 50-member professional faculty, headed by food and restaurant consultant Gary A. Goldberg and co-founder Martin Johner, includes Miriam Brickman, Richard M. Glavin, Arlyn M. Hackett, Karen Hanson, Harriet Lembeck, Lisa Montenegro, Robert W. Posch, Marie Simmons, Karen Snyder-Kadish, Jack Ubaldi, and Carole Walter.

COSTS: Master Class tuition is $2,150 (+$425 materials fee) for Cooking, $1,275 (+$190) for Baking, $850 (+$195) for Catering. Most other professional level courses are $45 per session (+$5-$14). A tuition-free kitchen assistant and work/study program are open to selected applicants.

LOCATION: Manhattan's Greenwich Village.

CONTACT: New School Culinary Arts, 100 Greenwich Ave., New York, NY 10011; (212) 255-4141 (Culinary Arts), (800) 544-1978, ext. 20 (New School Bulletin), (212) 229-5690 (registration), (212) 229-5648 (fax registration).

NEW YORK CITY TECHNICAL COLLEGE
Brooklyn/September-May

This college offers a 2-year AAS degree and a 4-year BS degree in Hospitality Management. Program started 1947. Accredited by MSA, State. Calendar: semester. Curriculum: core. Admission dates: September, February. Total enrollment 850; 125 enrollees each admission period; 50% financial aid recipients; 38% under age 25; 59% age 25 to 44; 3% age 45 or over; 50% part-time students; 15 students per instructor; 90% of graduates obtain employment. Facilities: include 5 kitchens, dining room, 3 classrooms and restaurant.

COURSES: Food and beverage cost control, culinary arts, baking and pastry arts, wines and beverage management. Externship: 8-weeks, in Italy, France, Germany if qualify. Continuing education: garde manger, cake decorating, and other subjects.

FACULTY: 13 full-time, 20 to 40 part-time. Includes: Patricia S. Bartholomew, Chair.

COSTS: Annual tuition: in state $2,500, out-of-state $5,000. CUNY fee is $35. Textbooks $1,000, materials fee $10, uniforms $120. Refunds: 100% prior to 1st class. Admission requirements: high school diploma or equivalent and admission test. Last year 25 scholarships were awarded. Average off-campus housing cost $600 per month. Part time employment available.

LOCATION: Downtown Brooklyn.

CONTACT: Patricia S. Bartholomew, Chair, Hospitality Management, New York City Technical College, 300 Jay St., Brooklyn, NY 11201; (718) 260-5630, Fax (718) 260-5997.

NEW YORK FOOD AND HOTEL MANAGEMENT SCHOOL
New York/Year-round

This proprietary institution offers a 9-month certificate in Commercial Cooking and Catering. Program started 1935. Accredited by ACCST. Curriculum: culinary only. Admission dates: every 4 to 6 weeks. Total enrollment 20 to 25; 80% of applicants accepted; 50% financial aid recipients;

50% under age 25; 40% age 25 to 44; 10% age 45 or over; 16 students per instructor. Facilities: include 4 kitchens, 5 classrooms and restaurant.

COURSES: Skills development, quantity food production, food preparation, catering, restaurant operation, food purchasing, sanitation, baking and pastry production, externship. Schedule: 5 hours per day, 5 days per week. Externship: 3-months.

FACULTY: 10 full-time.

COSTS: Annual tuition: $6,715. Registration fee $100. Other costs: books $168, food lab fee $1,080, kits and uniforms $132. Admission requirements: high school diploma or equivalent and admission test. Last year 2 scholarships were awarded averaging $8,195.

CONTACT: Harold Kaplan, Admissions, New York Food and Hotel Management School, 154 W. 14th St., New York, NY 10011; (212) 675-6655.

NEW YORK INSTITUTE OF TECHNOLOGY
Central Islip/Year-round

This independent institution offers a 21-month AOS degree in Culinary Arts. Program started 1987. Accredited by MSA. Calendar: semester. Curriculum: culinary only. Admission dates: fall, spring. Total enrollment 170; 36 to 72 enrollees each admission period; 90% of applicants accepted; 95% financial aid recipients; 90% under age 25; 8% age 25 to 44; 2% age 45 or over; 16 students per instructor; 100% of graduates obtain employment. Facilities: include 3 kitchens, bakery, 10 classrooms, computer software and 2 restaurants.

COURSES: Externship: 3-month, in public restaurants.

FACULTY: 9 full-time, 3 part-time.

COSTS: Annual tuition $25,085. Admission requirements: high school diploma or equivalent. On-campus housing: 150 spaces; average cost: $2,500 per semester.

CONTACT: Prof. Susan Hendee, Dean, Culinary Arts Center, New York Institute of Technology, 300 Carleton Ave., #66-101, P.O. Box 9029, Central Islip, NY 11722-9029; (516) 348-3232, Fax (516) 348-3247.

NEW YORK RESTAURANT SCHOOL
New York/Year-round *(See display ad page 75)*

This private college offers a 16-month AOS degree program in Culinary Arts-Restaurant Management and a 6- to 9-month credit-bearing certificate program in Pastry Arts and Culinary Skills. Program started in 1980. Rolling admission. Total enrollment 400; approximately 40% of applicants are accepted; 30% under age 25; 66% age 25 to 44; 4% age 45 and over; 10% part-time students; 17 students per instructor in labs, 25 in lectures; 93% of graduates obtain employment. The 30,000-square-foot recently renovated facility includes 5 newly-equipped kitchens, 3 classrooms, and resource center. Lifetime job placement assistance and career development course available.

COURSES: Include basic food preparation and knife skills, food handling, meat, vegetable, fish, and seafood preparation, international cuisine, and garde manger. Schedule: 35 hours per week full-time or 17 hours per week part-time. Late night and weekend classes are available. Programs conclude with a 2- to 3-month local externship.

FACULTY: The 28 faculty members all have a minimum of 8 year's experience and many have 4-year degrees and prior teaching background.

COSTS: Tuition is $13,260 for Culinary Arts, $9,426 for Restaurant Management, $7,392 for Pastry Arts, $8,250 for Culinary Skills, and $20,112 for AOS degree program. A $40 application fee and $300 deposit are required. Additional fees for books, equipment, and labs range from $750-$1,050. NYRS follows both New York State refund policy and Federal Pro Rata policy. Admission require-

> ## We're open 24 hrs to help you start the career you've always wanted.
>
> **The New York Restaurant School** is the choice of many of today's top chefs and restaurant managers. The school is fully accredited with state-of-the-art facilities, and offers courses in Culinary Arts, Restaurant Management and Pastry Arts. The New York Restaurant School graduates over 800 students each year!
>
> **Call 212-226-5500 to receive our bulletin and arrange a tour.**
>
> Become part of our winning team!
> **NOW DEGREE GRANTING**
>
> **NYRS**
>
> **The New York Restaurant School**
> 75 Varick Street, NY, NY 10013 212-226-5500
> *A leader in training for the food service industry since 1980*

ments vary. Last year 10 scholarships were awarded at an average of $4,500 each. Part-time employment is contingent on student skills and completion of a month of the program. The Admissions Office provides assistance in obtaining nearby housing.

LOCATION: Just off Broadway, in SoHo.

CONTACT: Stephen Tave, Admission Dept., New York Restaurant School, 75 Varick Street, New York, NY 10013; (212) 226-5500; Fax (212) 226-5644.

NEW YORK UNIV. CENTER FOR FOODS & FOOD MANAGEMENT
New York/February-May, October-December

Established in 1986, the Center offers more than 60 one- to four-session demonstration (limit 12 students) and participation (limit 12) cooking and business courses per year for food professionals and home cooks. Facilities: university kitchen and classrooms.

COURSES: Include food styling, menu writing, nutrition consulting, food public relations, business planning, creating and selling a winning recipe, and wine, coffee, beer, and cheese tastings.

FACULTY: Local chefs, instructors, cookbook authors, foodservice professionals, consultants.

COSTS: Approximately $50-$60 per session.

LOCATION: Washington Square, near Greenwich village.

CONTACT: Marjorie Possick, Special Projects Coordinator, New York University, Center for Foods & Food Management, 35 W. 4th St., 10th Fl., New York, NY 10012-1172; (212) 998-5588/92, Fax (212) 995-4194.

NIAGARA COUNTY COMMUNITY COLLEGE
Sanborn
CONTACT: Samuel J. Sheusi, CEC, CCE, Culinary Arts Dept., Niagara County Community College, 3111 Saunders Settlement Rd., Sanborn, NY 14132; (716) 731-4101.

ONONDAGA COMMUNITY COLLEGE
Syracuse
This college offers a 1-year certificate and a 2-year AAS degree. Program started 1979. Accredited by State. Admission dates: fall, spring. Total enrollment 90 to 100; 16 students per instructor.

COURSES: Externship provided.

COSTS: Annual tuition: in-state $1,350, out-of-state $2,700.

CONTACT: Culinary Director, Culinary Arts Department, Onondaga Community College, Onondaga Hill, Syracuse, NY 13215; (315) 469-7741.

PAUL SMITH'S COLLEGE
Paul Smiths/Year-round
This college grants a 2-year AAS degree in Culinary Arts and a 1-year Bakery Certificate. Programs first offered in 1980 and 1989. Accredited by MSA. Calendar: semester. Curriculum: core. Admission dates September, January. Total enrollment 800; 85% of applicants accepted; 80% financial aid recipients; 14 students per instructor; 99% of graduates obtain jobs or transfer to a 4-year college. Facilities: food laboratories, a la carte kitchen, and 60-seat dining room.

COURSES: After completing first-year course work on campus, students spend one of the remaining semesters in the College's Hotel Saranac, where they learn food preparation and are responsible for the dining room's evening meal. The other semester is spent in an externship. The Bakery Certificate curriculum covers journeyman baker skills, including advertising, merchandising, and management. Students produce goods for an on-campus bakery.

FACULTY: The College has 66 full- and 12 part-time faculty members. The Culinary Arts faculty includes Robert Brown CM, and Paul Sorgule CCE, 1988 Olympic Gold Medalist.

COSTS: Annual tuition is $10,380. The Culinary Arts Program comprehensive fee is $545 per semester. Applications are accepted up to a month before semester and must be accompanied by high school transcript or GED and $20 fee. The Bakery Certificate program is open to those who have industry experience or have completed a culinary arts program. Several scholarships are offered. Housing averages $2,123 per year; board is $2,340 per year.

LOCATION: On Lower St. Regis Lake, in the Adirondack Mountains.

CONTACT: Admissions Office, Paul Smith's College, Paul Smiths, NY 12970; (800) 421-2605 or (518) 327-6227.

PETER KUMP'S NEW YORK COOKING SCHOOL
New York/Year-round *(See page 202) (See display ad page 77)*
This private school offers 20- to 26-week diploma programs in Culinary Arts and Pastry and Baking Arts, 10- to 24-week certificate programs in cooking and baking, continuing education and business courses, and programs for nonprofessionals (page 202). Founded in 1974. Career program curricula licensed by NY State Dept. of Education. Admission dates at least seven times a year. Student to teacher ratio 14 or 16 to 1.

COURSES: In addition to theory and hands-on training in the preparation and presentation of classic cuisines, culinary arts courses cover menu planning, kitchen management, butchering, regional cuisines, and wine; the pastry and baking curriculum includes breads. Schedule: diploma courses meet 5 days per week for 14 weeks or 3 evenings per week for 20 weeks, followed by a

CAREER/PROFESSIONAL — NEW YORK

We Couldn't Have Said It Better Ourselves...

"The graduates of Peter Kump's are intelligent and well-trained. They reflect the dedication and excellence of the school staff."
Michael Romano, Chef-Owner
Union Square Cafe, NYC

"'**Highest caliber**' describes the graduates of Peter Kump's we've had at the restaurant."
Charlie Trotter, Chef-Owner
Charlie Trotter's, Chicago

At **Peter Kump's New York Cooking School** we're getting people ready for top-level careers — and we can do it in as little as 20 weeks

- Accelerated diploma programs in the **Culinary** or **Pastry & Baking Arts**, full or part time
- Includes six-week externship in a top restaurant or pastry shop here or in France
- Small full-participation classes ensure personalized instruction
- Intensive instruction in classic techniques, world cuisine, restaurant management and more
- Many start dates a year — both day and evening
- Study in New York City, the culinary, restaurant and food media center of the country
- Courses taught by expert school faculty, notable visiting chefs and other leading food authorities

No other program offers you so much in such a short time and at such a low price

307 East 92nd Street, New York, NY 10128   (800) 522-4610

6-week apprenticeship at a restaurant or pastry shop in New York City or France; certificate courses meet once weekly for 10 to 24 weeks.

FACULTY: More than 30 chefs and instructors. Founder Peter Kump studied with James Beard and Simone Beck, was president of the IACP and founding president of the James Beard Foundation; Director of Pastry and Baking Nick Malgieri authored 3 cookbooks. Guest faculty includes Guiliano Hazan, Diana Kennedy, Nicole Routhier, Wayne Nish, and Daniel Boulud.

COSTS: Day (evening) diploma course tuition is $8,600 ($6,200). 10% deposit with application; 10% due 30 days prior to course. Proof of 2 years college attendance or 4 years work in the food industry required. Culinary Arts certificate course tuition is $2,500. A work-scholarship program is available.

LOCATION: East 92nd Street and West 23rd Street in New York City.

CONTACT: Bill Grant, Dean of Students, Peter Kump's New York Cooking School, 307 East 92nd St., New York, NY 10128; (800) 522-4610 or (212) 410-4601, Fax (212) 348-6360.

SCHENECTADY COUNTY COMMUNITY COLLEGE
Schenectady/Year-round

This college offers a 2-year degree and a 1-year certificate. Program started 1980. Accredited by MSA, ACFEI. Calendar: semester. Curriculum: culinary. Admission dates: September, January, June. Total enrollment 254; 89% of applicants accepted; 26% part-time students; 22 students per instructor; 84% of graduates obtain employment. Facilities: 7 kitchens, restaurant, 2 dining rooms, banquet room.

COURSES: Other required courses: 600 hours work experience. Externship provided.

NEW YORK

FACULTY: 11 full-time, 22 part-time.

COSTS: Annual tuition: $1,840 in-state, $3,680 out-of-state. Admission requirements: high school diploma or equivalent. Part time employment available.

CONTACT: Toby Strianese, Chair and Professor, Hotel, Culinary Arts & Tourism, Schenectady County Community College, 78 Washington Ave., Schenectady, NY 12305; (518) 346-2611, Fax (518) 346-0379.

SULLIVAN COUNTY COMMUNITY COLLEGE
Loch Sheldrake/September-May

This college offers a 2-year AAS degree in Professional and Hotel Technology. Program started 1965. Accredited by MSA, ACFEI. Calendar: semester. Curriculum: core. Admission dates: September, January. Total enrollment 126; 75 enrollees each admission period; 90% financial aid recipients; 78% under age 25; 20% age 25 to 44; 10% age 45 or over; 22% part-time students; 14 students per instructor; 90% of graduates obtain employment. Facilities: include 7 kitchens and classrooms, restaurant.

FACULTY: 8 full-time. Qualifications: bachelor's or master's degree.

COSTS: Annual tuition: $2,050 in-state, $4,100 out-of-state. Application fee $25. Other fees: $6,500 in-state. Refund policy: according to Federal regs. Application deadlines: rolling. Admission requirements: high school diploma or equivalent and admission test. Last year 142 scholarships were awarded averaging $485; 624 loans were granted, averaging $2,609. On-campus housing: 300 spaces. Average off-campus housing cost: $4,400.

LOCATION: The 405-acre campus is 35 miles from Middletown.

CONTACT: Edmund Nadeau, Hospitality Division, Sullivan County Community College, LeRoy Rd., Box 4002, Loch Sheldrake, NY 12759-4002; (914) 434-5750, Fax (914) 434-5806.

SUNY COLLEGE OF AGRICULTURE & TECHNOLOGY
Cobleskill/August-May

This college offers a 2-year AOS degree in Culinary Arts. Program started 1971. Accredited by MSA, ACFEI. Calendar: semester. Curriculum: culinary only. Admission dates: fall, spring. Total enrollment 100; 60 enrollees each admission period; 85% of applicants accepted; 95% financial aid recipients; 90% under age 25; 8% age 25 to 44; 2% age 45 or over; 15 students per instructor; 98% of graduates obtain employment. Facilities: include 5 kitchens.

COURSES: Externship provided. Fellowship available.

FACULTY: 10 full-time.

COSTS: Annual tuition: $2,650 in-state, $3,900 out-of-state. Admission requirements: high school diploma or equivalent. Part time employment available.

LOCATION: The 750-acre campus is 30 miles from Albany, Schenectady, and Troy.

CONTACT: Dean, Food Service & Hospitality Administration, SUNY College of Agriculture & Technology, Cobleskill, NY 12043; (518) 234-5011, Fax (518) 234-5333.

WESTCHESTER COMMUNITY COLLEGE
Valhalla/September-May

This college offers a 2-year AAS degree in Food Service Administration. Program started 1971. Accredited by MSA. Calendar: semester. Curriculum: culinary and business. Admission dates: all year. Total enrollment 100; 50 enrollees each admission period; 20% financial aid recipients; 50% under age 25; 30% age 25 to 44; 20% age 45 or over; 25% part-time students; 15 students per instructor; 100% of graduates obtain employment. Facilities: include lab/demo kitchen, baking kitchen, production kitchen, bar/beverage management lab, instructional dining room.

COURSES: Food preparation, quantity food production, buffet catering, advanced foods, garde manger, bar/beverage management, and menu planning.

FACULTY: Curriculum Chair D. Nessek, D. Salvestrini, J. Snyder. Qualifications: MS required.

COSTS: Annual tuition: in-state $875 per semester. Lab fees $15. Application deadlines: 2 weeks before each semester. Admission requirements: high school diploma or equivalent. Last year 2 scholarships were awarded averaging $500. Part-time employment is available.

CONTACT: Daryl Nosek, Curriculum Chair, Restaurant Management, Westchester Community College, 75 Grasslands Rd., Valhalla, NY 10595-1698; (914) 785-6551, Fax (914) 785-6765.

NORTH CAROLINA

ASHEVILLE BUNCOMBE TECHNICAL COMMUNITY COLLEGE
Asheville/Year-round

This college offers a 2-year AAS degree in Culinary Technology. Program started 1968. Accredited by SACS. Calendar: quarter. Curriculum: core. Admission dates: begins September of year previous to official enrollment. Total enrollment 70; 35 enrollees each admission period; 100% of applicants accepted; 54% under age 25; 37% age 25 to 44; 8% age 45 or over; 16% part-time students; 11 students per instructor; 100% of graduates obtain employment. Facilities: includes 2 kitchens, 4 classrooms, restaurant 1 day per week.

COURSES: Food preparation, baking, garde manger, classical lab, palate development, butchering, dining room personnel, sanitation, and international cuisine. 61 hours of culinary courses required for graduation. Externship provided.

FACULTY: 2 full-time, 3 part-time. Includes: S. Tillman, BS, MA.Ed.; R. Setayesh; L. Etheridge, Head Baker, Grove Park Inn; M. Grey, chocolatier; S. Howard, Sous Chef, Biltmore Forest Country Club.

COSTS: Annual tuition: $763 in-state, $4,966 out-of-state. Activity fee $7 quarterly. Refund policy: 75% on or before the 20% point. Application deadlines: May 31. Admission requirements: high school diploma or equivalent and admission test. Last year 4 scholarships were awarded averaging $250. Part-time employment is available. Off-campus housing cost: $300 per month.

LOCATION: The 4,000-student, 127-acre campus is in a suburban setting.

CONTACT: Sheila Tillman, Chairperson, Culinary Technology, Asheville Buncombe Technical Community College, 340 Victoria Rd., Asheville, NC 28801; (704) 254-1921, Fax (704) 251-6355.

CENTRAL PIEDMONT COMMUNITY COLLEGE
Charlotte/Year-round

This college offers a 2-year AAS degree in Food Service Management and Culinary Arts. Program started 1974. Accredited by SACS, ACFEI. Calendar: quarter. Curriculum: culinary and core. Admission dates: fall, winter, spring. Total enrollment 500; 100 to 150 enrollees each admission period; 75% of applicants accepted; 10% financial aid recipients; 30% under age 25; 40% age 25 to 44; 30% age 45 or over; 25% part-time students; 15 students per instructor; 98% of graduates obtain employment. Facilities: includes 5 kitchens, TV kitchen, 7 classrooms, baking lab, small quantities lab and restaurant.

FACULTY: 25 full-time.

COSTS: Annual tuition: in-state $800, out-of-state $4,800. Admission requirements: high school diploma or equivalent and admission test. Last year 25 scholarships were awarded averaging $500. Part-time employment is available. Off-campus housing cost: $400-$500 per month.

CONTACT: James E. Cannon, CHA, Culinary Arts Department, Central Piedmont Community College, P.O. Box 35009, Charlotte, NC 28235; (704) 342-6721, Fax (704) 342-6581.

GUILFORD TECHNICAL COMMUNITY COLLEGE
Jamestown/Year-round
This community college offers a 1-year and 2-year program in Culinary Technology. Program started 1989. Total enrollment 48; 25 enrollees each admission period; 90% of applicants accepted; 50% financial aid recipients; 50% under age 25; 45% age 25 to 44; 5% age 45 or over; 50% part-time students; 7 students per instructor; 95% of graduates obtain employment.

COURSES: Garde manger, baking & pastry, dining room management, nutritional cuisine. 106 hours of culinary courses required for graduation. Schedule: day and evening courses.

FACULTY: 2 full-time, 4 part-time. Includes: Ronald Wolf, CWC, CCE and Keith Gardiner, CWC. Qualifications: ACFEI certified and minimum 5 years experience.

COSTS: Tuition: in-state $13 per quarter-hour, out-of-state $108 per quarter-hour. Application deadlines: on-going. Last year 1 scholarship was awarded averaging $500; 12 loans were granted averaging $500. Part time employment available.

CONTACT: Ronald S. Wolf, CWC, CCE, Department Chair, Culinary Technology, Guilford Technical Community College, Box 309, Jamestown, NC 27282; (910) 334-4822, ext. 2302.

WAKE TECHNICAL COMMUNITY COLLEGE
Raleigh/Year-round
This college offers a 2-year associates degree in Culinary Arts. Program started 1985. Accredited by SACS. Calendar: quarter. Curriculum: core. Admission dates: year-round. Total enrollment 45; 30 enrollees each admission period; 75% of applicants accepted; 20% under age 25; 60% age 25 to 44; 20% age 45 or over; 10% part-time students; 10 students per instructor; 98% of graduates obtain employment. Facilities: include kitchen.

COURSES: Foods, nutrition, sanitation, cost control, wine, inventory control, general education. Schedule: 30 hours per week. Externship provided.

FACULTY: 3 full-time, 1 part-time. Includes: Richard Roberts, Fredi Morf, Carolyn House. Qualifications: BS, HRM, certified chefs.

COSTS: Annual tuition: in-state $2,300. Admission requirements: high school diploma or equivalent. Off-campus housing cost: $400+ per month. Part time employment available.

CONTACT: Richard Roberts, Dept. Head, Culinary Technology, Wake Technical Community College, 9101 Fayetteville Rd., Raleigh, NC 27603; (919) 662-3417, Fax (919) 779-3360.

NORTH DAKOTA

NORTH DAKOTA STATE COLLEGE OF SCIENCE
Wahpeton/August-May
This college offers a 18-month diploma/AAS degree in Culinary Arts. Program started 1971. Accredited by NCA. Calendar: semester. Curriculum: core. Admission dates: August, January. Total enrollment 30 to 35; 15 enrollees each admission period; 100% of applicants accepted; 80% financial aid recipients; 80% under age 25; 15% age 25 to 44; 5% age 45 or over; 15 students per instructor; 100% of graduates obtain employment. Facilities: include 2 kitchens and classrooms.

COURSES: Food preparation, baking, catering, gourmet, short order. 49 semester hours of culinary courses required for graduation. Other required courses: 23 semester hours.

FACULTY: 2 full-time. Includes: N. Rittenour, M. Uhren.

COSTS: Annual tuition: $1,701 in-state, $4,293 out-of-state. Application deadlines: rolling. Admission requirements: high school diploma or equivalent. Last year 258 scholarships awarded averaging $527; 2,146 loans were granted. On-campus housing: 1,700 spaces, average cost $840.

CAREER/PROFESSIONAL OHIO

LOCATION: The 2,429-student campus is on 125 acres in a small town, 45 miles from Fargo.

CONTACT: Neil Rittenour, Program Director, Culinary Arts, North Dakota State College of Science, 800 North 6th St., Wahpeton, ND 58076; (800) 342-4325, Fax (701) 671-2145.

OHIO

CINCINNATI STATE TECHNICAL AND COMMUNITY COLLEGE
Cincinnati/Year-round

This college offers a 2-year ASOB degree in Chef Technology. Program started 1980. Accredited by ACFEI, NCA. Calendar: quarter. Curriculum: core. Admission dates: open. Total enrollment 130; 30 enrollees each admission period; 40% financial aid recipients; 40% under age 25; 50% age 25 to 44; 10% age 45 or over; 20% part-time students; 15 students per instructor; 100% of graduates obtain employment. Facilities: include commercial kitchen.

COURSES: 7 culinary courses. Other required courses: 23 other courses. Schedule: day and evening options. Externship provided.

FACULTY: 4 full-time. Includes: J. Kusilla, I. Myatt, J. Sheldon.

COSTS: Annual tuition: $3,025 in-state, $5,000 out-of-state. Application fee $20. Admission requirements: high school diploma or equivalent and admission test. Scholarship awards averaged $400. Part-time employment is available. Off-campus housing cost: $350 per month.

CONTACT: Richard Hendrix, Dept. Chair, Business Div., Cincinnati State Technical & Community College, 3520 Central Pkwy., Cincinnati, OH 45223; (513) 569-1500, Fax (513) 569-1467.

THE CLEVELAND RESTAURANT COOKING SCHOOL
Cleveland/Year-round

This private school offers a 4-month professional program and classes for hobbyists. Founded in 1986. Admission dates January, June, September. Total enrollment 18; 6 enrollees each admission period; nearly all applicants are accepted; 40% under age 25; 40% age 25 to 44; 20% age 45 or over; 6 students per instructor; 100% of graduates obtain employment. Facilities include a teaching kitchen, demonstration area, and a restaurant kitchen. **COURSES:** Cover restaurant planning, food costing and importing, catering management, food journalism, and organic farming. Schedule: 25 hours per week of hands-on cooking. Two months of daily classes are followed by a 2-month externship at Parker's Restaurant.

FACULTY: Chef Parker Bosley, owner of Parker's Restaurant and Catering, and the restaurant staff.

COSTS: $3,200 for the program. Applicant must undergo a personal interview. Parttime employment is available.

CONTACT: The Cleveland Restaurant Cooking School, 2801 Bridge Ave., Cleveland, OH 44113; (216) 771-7130; Fax (216) 771-8130.

COLUMBUS STATE COMMUNITY COLLEGE
Columbus/Year-round

This college offers a 3-year AAS degree in Culinary Apprenticeship. Program started 1978. Accredited by ACFEI, NCA. Calendar: quarter. Curriculum: core. Admission dates: September, January. Total enrollment 60; 35 enrollees each admission period; 100% of applicants accepted; 60% under age 25; 40% age 25 to 44; 95% part-time students; 15 students per instructor; 100% of graduates obtain employment.

COURSES: General education, business, foodservice management, culinary courses. 107 credit (quarter) hours of culinary courses required for graduation. Schedule: one full day of class per week plus 40 hours per week on apprenticeship.

FACULTY: 7 full-time. Includes: Chairperson C. Kizer, M. Sleiskal, D. Cobler, T. Atkinson, A. King.

COSTS: Annual tuition: $1,836 in-state. Application deadlines: May 15. Admission requirements: high school graduate, letters of reference, interview. Last year 15 scholarships were awarded.

CONTACT: Carol Kizer, Hospitality Management Department, Columbus State Community College, 550 East Spring St., Columbus, OH 43216; (614) 227-2579, Fax (614) 227-5146.

CUYAHOGA COMMUNITY COLLEGE
Cleveland/Year-round

This college offers a 2-year AAB degree in Culinary Arts, Restaurant Food Service Management, and Hotel/Motel Management. Program started 1969. Accredited by NCA. Calendar: quarter. Curriculum: core. Admission dates: quarterly. Total enrollment 175; 30 enrollees each admission period; 95% of applicants accepted; 60% financial aid recipients; 20% under age 25; 75% age 25 to 44; 5% age 45 or over; 60% part-time students; 15 students per instructor; 95% of graduates obtain employment. Facilities: include 3 kitchens, 2 classrooms, computer lab and restaurant.

COURSES: Management/food preparation, haute cuisine, garde manger. 35 hours of culinary courses required for graduation. Other required courses: purchasing, accounting, menu planning. Schedule: daily 8 am-5 pm. Continuing education: safety & sanitation, nutrition.

FACULTY: 5 full-time, 9 part-time. Qualifications: degree and industry experience.

COSTS: Annual tuition: in-state $36.50 per credit hour, out-of-state $97 per credit hour. Application fee $10, lab fees $300. Application deadlines: 3 weeks before quarter. Admission requirements: testing in English/math. Last year 10 scholarships were awarded averaging $200-500. Off-campus housing cost: $500 per month. Part time employment available.

CONTACT: Jan DeLucia, Program Mgr., Hospitality Management, Cuyahoga Community College, 2900 Community College Ave., Cleveland, OH 44115; (216) 987-4081, Fax (216) 987-4086.

HOCKING TECHNICAL COLLEGE
Nelsonville

This college offers a 2-year certificate/AAS degree. Program started 1979. Accredited by NCA. Admission dates: September, January, March, June. Total enrollment 150; 15 students per instructor; 95% of graduates obtain employment.

FACULTY: 5 full-time

COSTS: Annual tuition: in-state $1,500, out-of-state $3,000.

CONTACT: Joe Strangis, Executive Chef Instructor, Culinary Arts Department, Hocking Technical College, Nelsonville, OH 45764; (614) 753-3591, Fax (614) 753-9018.

SINCLAIR COMMUNITY COLLEGE
Dayton/Year-round

This college offers a 2-year Associate Degree in Hospitality Management. Program started 1993. Total enrollment 150; 100% of applicants accepted; 30% financial aid recipients; 20% under age 25; 60% age 25 to 44; 20% age 45 or over; 100% of graduates obtain employment. Facilities: 3 kitchens, 150-seat dining room, classrooms.

COURSES: Food preparation, garde manger, butchery & fish management, pastry & confectionery, classical foods. 97 hours of culinary courses required for graduation.

FACULTY: 2 full-time, 5 part-time. Includes: Dept. Chair Steven Cornelius, FMP, CWC and Frank Leopold, CEC, CWPC. Qualifications: certified by ACF and NRA.

COSTS: Tuition: in-county $31, in-state $58. Admission requirements: high school diploma or GED.

CONTACT: Steven Cornelius, Dept. Chair, Hospitality Management, Sinclair Community College,

444 W. Third St., Dayton, OH 45402-1460; (513) 449-5197, Fax (513) 449-4530, E-Mail scorneli@lear.sinclair.edu.

UNIVERSITY OF AKRON
Akron

This university offers a 2-year certificate/AAS degree. Program started 1968. Accredited by State. Admission dates: fall, spring, summer. Total enrollment 245; 18 students per instructor; 95% of graduates obtain employment.

COURSES: Externship provided.

FACULTY: 11 full-time.

COSTS: Annual tuition: in-state $2,430, out-of-state $5,970.

CONTACT: Jan Eley, Coordinator, Hospitality Management, University of Akron, Gallucci Hall #104, Akron, OH 44325; (216) 972-7026, Fax (216) 972-5101.

UNIVERSITY OF TOLEDO
Toledo

This university offers a 2-year AAS degree. Program started 1980. Accredited by NCA. Admission dates: quarterly. Total enrollment 30; 5 students per instructor.

COURSES: Externship provided.

FACULTY: 1 full-time, 1 part-time.

COSTS: Annual tuition approximately: in-state $2,610, out-of-state $3,400.

CONTACT: Benita Wong, Food Svc. Mgt./Culinary Arts, University of Toledo, Scott Park Campus, Toledo, OH 43606; (419) 537-3112, Fax (419) 537-3194.

OKLAHOMA

GREAT PLAINS AREA VOCATIONAL TECHNICAL CENTER
Lawton

This institution offers a 18-month certificate. Accredited by NCA. Admission dates: open. Total enrollment 36; 18 students per instructor;

FACULTY: 2 full-time.

COSTS: Annual tuition: $300. Admission requirements: high school diploma or equivalent.

CONTACT: Sue Maree, Commercial Food Svcs./Fast Foods Mgt., Great Plains Area Vocational Technical Center, 4500 W. Lee Blvd., Lawton, OK 73505; (405) 355-6371.

MERIDIAN TECHNOLOGY CENTER
Stillwater/January-May, August-December

This institution offers a 1,050-hour certificate. Program started 1975. Accredited by State. Calendar: semester. Curriculum: core. Admission dates: August. Total enrollment 36; 18 students per instructor; Facilities: 1 kitchen, 1 classroom, 2 restaurants.

COURSES: 1,050 hours of culinary courses required for graduation. Schedule: 30 hours per week, 10 months.

FACULTY: 3 full-time

COSTS: Annual tuition: in-district $1,250, out-of-district $2,500. Admission requirements: assessment, interview.

OKLAHOMA

CONTACT: Karim Farajollahi, Asst. Supt., Commercial Food Production, Meridian Technology Center, 1312 S. Sangre Rd., Stillwater, OK 74074; (405) 377-3333, Fax (405) 377-9604.

OKLAHOMA STATE UNIVERSITY
Okmulgee

This college offers a 24-month AAS and 20-month diploma in Food Service Management. Program started 1946. Accredited by NCA. Calendar: trimester. Curriculum: core. Admission dates: August, January, April. Total enrollment 120; 35 enrollees each admission period; 90% of applicants accepted; 65% financial aid recipients; 70% under age 25; 20% age 25 to 44; 10% age 45 or over; 10% part-time students; 16 students per instructor; 90% of graduates obtain employment. Facilities: include 4 kitchens and 4 classrooms.

COURSES: Pastry production, food preparation, garde manger, hot food production, meat identification, dining room management, nutrition, and general education courses. 50 hours of culinary courses required for graduation. Schedule: Monday-Friday, 6 hours per day, 12 months per year. Externship provided. Continuing education: includes advanced cooking and sauces, beginning cake decoration, and apprentice meat identification.

FACULTY: 4 full-time. Qualifications: 5 years experience, college level culinary arts, ACF certified.

COSTS: Annual tuition: in-state $44 per credit hour, out-of-state $110. Admission requirements: admission test. On-campus housing: 1,000 spaces, average cost: $200-$250 per month.

LOCATION: The 2,000-student campus is in a small town, 45 miles from Tulsa.

CONTACT: Dean Daniel, Department Head, Hospitality Services Technology, Oklahoma State University, 1801 E. 4th St., Okmulgee, OK 74447; (918) 756-6211, ext. 220, Fax (918) 756-1315.

PIONEER AREA VOCATIONAL TECHNICAL SCHOOL
Ponca City

This institution offers a 1-year certificate. Program started 1972. Accredited by NCA. Total enrollment 36; 6 students per instructor; 100% of graduates obtain employment.

COURSES: Externship provided.

FACULTY: 3 full-time.

COSTS: Annual tuition: $400. Admission requirements: high school diploma or equivalent.

CONTACT: Steve Ellenwood, Commercial Foods, Pioneer Area Vocational Technical School, 2101 N. Ash, Ponca City, OK 74601; (405) 762-8336, Fax (405) 765-5101.

SOUTHERN OKLAHOMA AREA VOC. TECHNICAL SCHOOL
Ardmore

This institution offers a 2-year certificate. Program started 1966. Accredited by State. Total enrollment 40; 20 students per instructor.

FACULTY: 1 full-time, 2 part-time.

COSTS: Annual tuition: in-district $0, out-of-district $1,600.

CONTACT: Georganne Westfall, Culinary Arts, Southern Oklahoma Area Vocational Technical School, 2610 San Noble Pkwy., Ardmore, OK 73401; (405) 223-2070.

OREGON

INTERNATIONAL SCHOOL OF BAKING
Bend/Year-round

Established in 1986, this school offers customized bread making participation courses (limit 2 stu-

CAREER/PROFESSIONAL OREGON

dents) that meet for one or two 6-hour daily sessions in a modern, well-equipped baking facility.

COURSES: Beginning Breads covers ingredient function, bagels, whole grain, pita, fruit and nut bread, and high fiber buns. Intermediate Breads covers brioche, sweet dough, and European breads. Students can select their own curriculum.

FACULTY: Director Marda Stoliar has taught bread making since 1965, is a baking consultant in China for U.S. Wheat Associates, and owned a French bakery.

COSTS: From $300-$400 per day for 1 or 2 students. Half is due 30 days prior; balance is due at class. A list of nearby lodging is provided.

LOCATION: A 3-minute drive from downtown, 15 minutes from the Redmond Oregon Airport.

CONTACT: Marda Stoliar, International School of Baking, 1971 N.S. Juniper Ave., Bend, OR 97701; (503) 389-8553, Fax (503) 389-3736.

LANE COMMUNITY COLLEGE
Eugene/September-June

This independent college offers a 1-year certificate and a 2-year AAS degree in Culinary Arts and Culinary option. Program started 1976. Calendar: quarter. Curriculum: core. Admission dates: open. Total enrollment 85 to 105; 25 to 50 enrollees each admission period; 100% of applicants accepted; 60-70% financial aid recipients; 15% under age 25; 60% age 25 to 44; 25% age 45 or over; 3% part-time students; 18 students per instructor; 95% of graduates obtain employment. Facilities: include 2 kitchens, 1 dining room, deli/bake shop, and 4 to 6 classrooms.

COURSES: Introduction to foods, restaurant lab, buffet, baking, sanitation, safety, menu planning, and general education courses. 107 hours of culinary courses required. Schedule: 25-32 hours per week. Externship: 325-450 hour, in commercial, institutional, or single proprietor settings. Post-graduate study available to students applying to CIA and other postgraduate programs.

FACULTY: 3 full-time, 3 part-time. Includes: Willie Kealoha, Guy Plaa, Don Savoie, Wendy McDaniel, Cort Richer. Qualifications: ACF certifications with BS, AAS degrees, and training from European cooking schools.

COSTS: Annual tuition: $600-$900 per term. Other fees: lab fees, student fees. Admission requirements: limited enrollment. Last year 4 scholarships were awarded averaging $750. Average off-campus housing cost $350-$800 per month. Part time employment available.

CONTACT: Willie Kealoha, Culinary Food Service and Hospitality Program, Lane Community College, 4000 E. 30th Ave., Eugene, OR 97405-0640; (503) 747-4501 ext. 2531, Fax (503) 744-4159.

LINN-BENTON COMMUNITY COLLEGE
Albany/September-June

This college offers a 2-year AAS degree in Culinary Arts/Hospitality Services with Chef Training Option. Program started 1973. Accredited by NASC. Calendar: quarter. Curriculum: core. Admission dates: September, January, March. Total enrollment 30; 15 enrollees each admission period; 100% of applicants accepted; 50% financial aid recipients; 50% under age 25; 50% age 25 to 44; 5% part-time students; 5 students per instructor; 100% of graduates obtain employment. Facilities: include bakery production facility and restaurant.

COURSES: Schedule: 7 hours per day, Monday-Thursday. Fellowships awarded.

FACULTY: 6 full-time. Includes: S. Anselm, M. Whitehead, M. Young.

COSTS: Annual tuition: in-state $1,500, out-of-state $5,355. Application fee $20. Approximately $300 for tools and uniforms. Application deadlines: September. Admission requirements: high school diploma or equivalent. Last year 12 scholarships were awarded; 9 loans were granted. Off-campus housing cost: $250 per month. Part time employment available.

LOCATION: The 16,000-student campus is in a small town setting 24 miles from Salem and 42 miles from Eugene.

CONTACT: Scott Anselm, Culinary Arts/Restaurant Mgt. c/o Aux. Serv., Linn-Benton Community College, 6500 SW Pacific Blvd., Albany, OR 97321; (503) 917-4385, Fax (503) 917-4395.

WESTERN CULINARY INSTITUTE
Portland/Year-round *(See display ad 87)*

This private school offers a 12-month accelerated diploma program in Culinary Arts. Founded in 1983. Accredited by the ACFEI and ACCSCT. Admission dates: every 6 weeks. 85% of applicants accepted; 15 to 30 students per instructor in lab classes; 97% of available students obtain employment within 90 days. Facilities include up-to-date, well-equipped kitchens and an open-to-the-public restaurant. Job placement assistance is provided throughout graduates' careers.

COURSES: Curriculum is 80% participation and based on the principles of Escoffier with emphasis on modern techniques and trends. The 18 courses include culinary fundamentals, purchasing and cost control, intl. cuisines, nutrition, baking and pastry, and wines. The 1491-hour program consists of 44 weeks of instruction and a 6-week internship in an approved foodservice operation.

FACULTY: The 18-member faculty is made up of individuals with international experience and training, many of whom have won culinary awards.

COSTS: Tuition is $12,875, which includes cutlery, uniforms, and lab fees. A $25 nonrefundable application fee and $100 enrollment fee are required. Financial aid and payment arrangements must be made prior to first class. Admissions representatives assist in finding suitable lodging.

LOCATION: Near Portland State University in downtown Portland.

CONTACT: Admissions Dept., Western Culinary Institute, 1316 S.W. 13th Ave., Portland, OR 97201; (800) 666-0312 or (503) 223-2245.

PENNSYLVANIA

BUCKS COUNTY COMMUNITY COLLEGE
Newtown/Year-round

This college offers a 2-year AA degree and a 3-year degree/apprenticeship program. Started 1968. Accredited by MSA. Calendar: semester. Curriculum: core. Total enrollment 180; 40 enrollees each admission period; 80% part-time students; 17 students per instructor; 90% of graduates obtain employment. Facilities: include kitchen, dining room, and lab.

FACULTY: 2 full-time, 4 part-time. Qualifications: ACF-certification and degree preferred.

COSTS: Tuition: $65 per credit-hour in-county, $130 per credit-hour out-of-county. Application deadlines: May. Last year 6 scholarships were awarded averaging $500-$2,000.

CONTACT: Earl R. Arrowood, Jr., Business Dept., Bucks County Community College, Swamp Rd., Newtown, PA 18940; (215) 968-8241, Fax (215) 968-8005.

COMMUNITY COLLEGE OF ALLEGHENY COUNTY
Monroeville

This college offers a 2-year certificate/AAS degree. Program started 1967. Accredited by MSA. Admission dates: open. Total enrollment 175; 15 students per instructor; 100% of graduates obtain employment.

COURSES: Externship provided.

FACULTY: 2 full-time, 5 part-time.

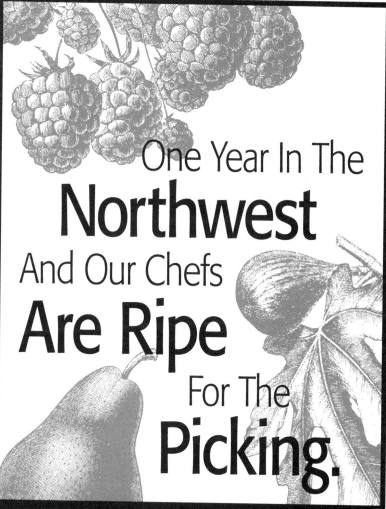

One Year In The Northwest And Our Chefs Are Ripe For The Picking.

Invest twelve months in the kitchen laboratories and classrooms of Western Culinary Institute and you'll be fully prepared to enter the profession of culinary arts. Our curriculum is based on the principles of Escoffier with emphasis on modern technique, a classic foundation from which students can evolve into any number of specialized areas. For more information and a catalog, we welcome your call at 800-666-0312. Financial aid is available for those who qualify.

WESTERN CULINARY INSTITUTE

Accredited by the American Culinary Federation Educational Institute.

1316 SW 13TH AVENUE
PORTLAND, OREGON 97201
(503) 223-2245 (800) 666-0312

COSTS: Annual tuition approximately: in-state $1,272, out-of-state $2,545. Admission requirements: high school diploma or equivalent.

CONTACT: Linda Sullivan, Hospitality Mgmt./Culinary Arts, Community College of Allegheny County, 595 Beatty Rd., Monroeville, PA 15146; (412) 327-1327.

COMMUNITY COLLEGE OF ALLEGHENY COUNTY
Pittsburgh

This college offers a 2-year AAS Degree in Culinary Arts. Program started 1974. Accredited by MSA. Calendar: fall, spring, summer. Curriculum: core. Admission dates: fall. Total enrollment 60; 90% of graduates obtain employment.

COURSES: Includes basic foods, culinary artistry, nutrition, baking, costing. Externship: 240 hours.

CONTACT: Willie Stinson, CEC, AAC, Community College of Allegheny County, 808 Ridge Ave., Jones Hall, Rm. 012, Pittsburgh, PA 15212; (412) 237-2698, Fax (412) 237-4678.

HARRISBURG AREA COMMUNITY COLLEGE
Harrisburg/Year-round

This college offers a 2-year certificate/AA program in Culinary Arts. Program started 1965. Accredited by MSA, ACBSP. Calendar: semester. Curriculum: core. Admission dates: August, January. Total enrollment 250; 48 enrollees each admission period; 100% of applicants accepted; 50% financial aid recipients; 40% under age 25; 50% age 25 to 44; 10% age 45 or over; 50% part-time students; 15 to 20 students per instructor; 100% of graduates obtain employment. Facilities: include production kitchen, demonstration kitchen, culinary classroom and weekly luncheons.

COURSES: Culinary arts, quantity foods, and 20 other courses. Schedule: 12-15 credit hours per semester. Externship: 3-month, salaried.

FACULTY: 3 full-time, 3 part-time. Qualifications: bachelor's degree, master's preferred, certifiable by ACF.

COSTS: Annual tuition: in-state $116.50 per credit hour, out-of-state $175 per credit hour. Tuition deposit $100 after acceptance; $25 to enroll. Equipment and uniforms about $265. Refund policy: full refund before start of classes. Application deadlines: May 1 for fall. Admission requirements: admission test.

LOCATION: The 3 campuses (Harrisburg, Lebanon, and Lancaster) with 11,000 students are 100 miles from Philadelphia.

CONTACT: Marcia W. Shore, M.S., Ed., CCE., Hotel, Restaurant, Institutional Management Dept., Harrisburg Area Community College, One HACC Dr., Harrisburg, PA 17110; (717) 780-2674, Fax (717) 231-7670.

HIRAM G. ANDREWS CENTER
Johnstown/Year-round

This proprietary school offers a 4-month diploma and 18-month AST in Kitchen Helper, Cook's/Baker's Helper, and AST Culinary. Program started 1975. Accredited by ACCSCT. Calendar: trimester. Curriculum: core. Admission dates: every 4 months. Total enrollment 30; 12 to 15 enrollees each admission period; 40% financial aid recipients; 25% under age 25; 50% age 25 to 44; 25% age 45 or over; 15 students per instructor; 100% of graduates obtain employment. Facilities: include 3 kitchens and classrooms and a part-time restaurant.

COURSES: Baking, sanitation, nutrition, food preparation, cooking methods and techniques, menu writing, and table service. Schedule: 6.25 hours per day. Externship: 2 months.

FACULTY: 3 full-time.

COSTS: Annual tuition: $35 per day. Admission requirements: high school diploma or equivalent

CAREER/PROFESSIONAL   PENNSYLVANIA   89

and admission test. On-campus housing: 400 spaces.

LOCATION: The 66-acre campus is in a suburban setting 80 miles from Pittsburgh.

CONTACT: Jack B. Demuth, Voc. Supv., Culinary Arts Program, Hiram G. Andrews Center, 727 Goucher St., Johnstown, PA 15905; (814) 255-8288.

INDIANA UNIV. OF PENN. ACADEMY OF CULINARY ARTS
Indiana/Year-round

This university offers a 16-month certificate in Culinary Arts. Program started 1989. Accredited by MSA and ACFEI. Calendar: semester. Curriculum: culinary. Admission date September; 115 enrollees each admission period; 75% of applicants accepted; 90% financial aid recipients; 90% under age 25; 8% age 25 to 44; 2% age 45 or over; 17 students per instructor; 99% of graduates obtain employment. Facilities include 5 production and 2 demonstration kitchens, computer lab and classroom. Courses: include cuisine and pastry preparation, purchasing, nutrition, wine appreciation, international cuisine, and menu and facility design. Schedule: 35 hours per week. A 450-hour salaried externship is required.

FACULTY: The 6 full- and 2 part-time instructors include Albert Wutsch, director, Timothy Brown, Hilary DeMane, Calvin Fryling, and Martha Jo Geer.

COSTS: Tuition is $4,400 per semester. Application fee is $30 and instructional deposit (upon acceptance) is $75. A $104 activity fee is required each semester. All deposits are nonrefundable. Applicants must have high school diploma or equivalent. Last year 10 scholarships were awarded at an average of $1,000 each. Part-time employment is available. On campus lodging is $2,528 for a double room, $900 single supplement.

LOCATION: 25 miles north of Indiana in rural Punxsutawney.

CONTACT: Kelly Barry, Admissions Coordinator, IUP Academy of Culinary Arts, Reschini Building, IUP, Indiana, PA 15705; (800) 727-0997, Fax (412) 357-6200.

INTERNATIONAL CULINARY ACADEMY
Pittsburgh/Year-round

This division of Computer Tech offers 2-year (1,800-clock-hour) AST degrees in Culinary and Pastry Arts. Accredited by ACICS and ACFEI. Admission dates March, August, October. Total enrollment 250 students; 80% of applicants accepted; 25 students per instructor; 92% of graduates obtain employment. Facilities include professional-size commercial kitchens, classrooms, resource center, executive dining room, student lounge.

COURSES: Culinary arts curriculum covers basic kitchen and storeroom operations and hands-on practice in the preparation and presentation of classic international cuisines. The pastry arts curriculum covers basic baking principles, international and specialty breads, pies and cakes, French pastry, and advanced decoration and design. Schedule: classes meet daily, Monday-Thursday.

FACULTY: Eight ACF-Certified Culinary Educators.

COSTS: tuition for each program is $15,550, which includes uniforms, books, equipment and all food costs. The $50 registration fee is refundable prior to start of class. Applicants must have a high school diploma or equivalent and complete an aptitude test. Student housing is offered.

LOCATION: In Pittsburgh's Golden Triangle, overlooking the Allegheny River.

CONTACT: International Culinary Academy-A Division of Computer Tech, 107 Sixth St., Fulton Bldg., Pittsburgh, PA 15222; (412) 471-9330, Fax (412) 391-4224.

NORTHAMPTON COMMUNITY COLLEGE
Bethlehem/Year-round

This college offers a 30-week specialized diploma in Culinary Arts. Program started 1993.

90 PENNSYLVANIA

Accredited by MSA. Calendar: trimester. Curriculum: culinary only. Admission dates: January, May, September. Total enrollment 60; 20 enrollees each admission period; 100% of applicants accepted; 30% financial aid recipients; 30% under age 25; 60% age 25 to 44; 10% age 45 or over; 20 students per instructor;

Courses: Baking, pastry, nutrition, pantry, skill development, garde manger, and restaurant operations. Schedule: full-time, 30 hours per week.

Faculty: 2 full-time, 1 part-time. Includes: Duncan Howden and Scott Kalamar. Qualifications: culinary degree and 10 years professional experience.

Costs: Annual tuition: in-state $1,770, out-of-state $5,500. Tuition deposit $50. Other fees: uniforms $150, meals $115, books $200, tools $100. Refund policy: 100% prior to start date. Admission requirements: high school diploma or equivalent. Last year 9 scholarships were awarded averaging $1,667; 15 loans were granted, averaging $2,100. On-campus housing: 145 spaces; average cost: $2,400 per year. Average off-campus housing cost $350 per month.

Contact: Duncan Howden, Assoc. Professor, Culinary Arts, Northampton Community College, 3835 Green Pond Rd., Bethlehem, PA 18017; (610) 861-5573, Fax (610) 861-5093.

ORLEANS TECHNICAL INSTITUTE
Philadelphia

This institution offers a 30-week specialized diploma. Program started 1978. Admission dates: open; 85% of graduates obtain employment.

Faculty: 1 to 2 full-time.

Costs: Annual tuition: $3,950. Admission requirements: admission test.

Contact: Chandra Davis, Culinary Arts Dept., Orleans Technical Institute, 1330 Rhawn St., Philadelphia, PA 19111; (215) 728-4488.

PENNSYLVANIA COLLEGE OF TECHNOLOGY
Williamsport/Year-round

This college offers a 2-year AAS degree in Food/Hospitality Management and Baking/Pastry Arts. Accredited by MSA, ACFEI. Calendar: semester. Curriculum: core. Admission dates: fall, spring. Total enrollment 80; 60 enrollees each admission period; 86% financial aid recipients; 15% part-time students; 12 students per instructor; 100% of graduates obtain employment. Facilities: include 15 kitchens and classrooms, retail restaurant, catering and meeting facilities, theatre lounge, and planned bed and breakfast.

Courses: Cooking, baking, service, sanitation, supervision, and nutrition. Other required courses: semester-long internships provided. Schedule: Monday-Saturday; part-time and evening options available.

Faculty: 10 full-time, 4 part-time. Qualifications: college degree and ACF certification.

Costs: Annual tuition: in-state $181 per credit hour, out-of-state $215 per credit hour. Application fee $20, tuition deposit $100. lab fee $13. Refund policy: 100% first week, 30% second and third. Admission requirements: high school diploma or equivalent and admission test. Last year 100 scholarships were awarded averaging $3,667; 97 loans were granted, averaging $2,695. Off-campus housing cost: $250-$450 per month. Part time employment available.

Location: The 53-acre, 4,300-student campus is in a small town 200 miles from Pittsburgh

Contact: Chet Schuman, Director of Admissions, Pennsylvania College of Technology, One College Ave., Williamsport, PA 17701-5799; (717) 326-3761, ext. 4761, Fax (717) 327-4503.

REAL

REAL SKILLS. REAL WORK. BIG FUTURE.

Have you been dreaming about starting a career in food?

Call us. We will show you how your future as a professional Chef or Restaurant Manager can be, in a word, real.

For those seeking a top-level position in a field of unlimited growth and diversity...

- 12 months on campus + paid 4 month externship – you choose the location
- Hands-on-Curriculum
- Advanced Placement Available
- Lifetime Nationwide Job Placement Assistance
- Accelerated AST and ASB Degrees
- Financial Aid for those who qualify
- Located in a dynamic restaurant city – work while in school

JOB 100% PLACEMENT

School of Culinary Arts
School of Restaurant Management

Pennsylvania Culinary

1-800-432-2433 ANSWERS 24 HOURS
THE PENNSYLVANIA INSTITUTE OF CULINARY ARTS
717 Liberty Avenue • Pittsburgh, PA 15222

*Out of the 1,994 graduates available for placement between May 1988 and April 1995, all 1,994 were placed in the field.

THE PENNSYLVANIA INSTITUTE OF CULINARY ARTS
Pittsburgh/Year-round *(See display ad page 91)*

This private institution offers 16-month associate degrees in Specialized Technology in the School of Culinary Arts (73 credits) and in Specialized Business in the School of Restaurant Management (78 credits). Program established 1986. Accredited by the ACCSCT and ACFEI. Calendar: semester. Curriculum: core. Admission dates January, March, May, June, September, October. Total enrollment over 1,100; 135 enrollees each admission period; 85% applicants accepted; 95% financial aid recipients; 70% under age 25; 27% age 25 to 44; 3% age 45 and over; 40 per instructor in lectures, 20 per instructor in labs; 100% of available graduates are placed. Facilities include 7 kitchens, 6 lecture classrooms, computer classroom, library, and full-service restaurant.

COURSES: Include food preparation and skill development, advanced classical and international cuisine, nutrition, wines and spirits, menu planning and dining room management. Schedule: 25 to 30 hours per week on one of 5 schedules, including an evening schedule. Both programs include a 16-week paid externship.

FACULTY: The faculty of 23 certified chefs, maitres d'hotel, and educators is supervised by International Culinary Olympics gold medalist Dieter Kiessling, CMC, AAC.

COSTS: Tuition $3,830 per semester. Application fee $50. High school diploma or equivalent required; foodservice experience desirable. Last year 19 scholarships were awarded averaging $1,000 each; 755 loans were granted at an average of $2,563 each. Part-time employment is available. On-campus housing for 150 students. Off-campus lodging from $200–$400 per month.

LOCATION: Pittsburgh's cultural district.

CONTACT: Charles Day, Director of Admissions, Pennsylvania Institute of Culinary Arts, 717 Liberty Ave., Pittsburgh, PA 15222; (800) 432-2433; Fax (412) 566-2434.

THE RESTAURANT SCHOOL
Philadelphia/Year-round *(See display ad page 93)*

This proprietary institution offers 15-month programs leading to a specialized associate degree in Chef Training, Pastry Chef Training, Restaurant Management, and Hotel Management. Founded in 1974. Accredited by ACCSCT. Calendar: quarter. Curriculum: core. Admission dates February and September. 90% of applicants accepted; 95% financial aid recipients; 25% under age 25; 50% age 25 to 44; 25% age 45 or over; 10% part-time students; 28 students per instructor; 98% of graduates obtain employment. Facilities include 4 new classroom kitchens, two 100-seat demonstration kitchens, pastry shop, and restaurant.

COURSES: The 1,806-clock-hour Chef Training program combines classroom instruction with a 1,080-hour apprenticeship in an approved area restaurant. Courses include culinary arts, business management, dining room service, wines, and nutrition. The 2,200-clock-hour Pastry Chef Training program courses include basic culinary and baking skills, science of baking, business management, and career development. Students produce the inventory for the school's open-to-the-public pastry shop. Both programs include a 7-day culinary tour of France.

FACULTY: The 12-member professional faculty have a minimum of 12 years' experience in the restaurant, foodservice, and hotel industry.

COSTS: The $15,000 cost of each program includes trip. Application and deposit are $200; other fees are $900. Applicant must have high school diploma or equivalent and reference letters. Last year 8 scholarships were awarded at an average of $2,000 each. Part-time employment is available. On-campus dorm is provided for 20 students.

LOCATION: Restored mansion in University City.

CONTACT: Lynne R. Byck, Director of Admissions, The Restaurant School, 4207 Walnut St., Philadelphia, PA 19104; (215) 222-4200, ext. 6; Fax (215) 222-4219.

The Restaurant School

One of the Nation's First
to specialize in fine restaurants, hotels and resorts

Four Nationally Renowned Majors:
Hotel Management ◆ Chef Training
Pastry Chef Training ◆ Restaurant Management

- ❏ Specialized Associate Degree in just 15 months
- ❏ Tuition includes a tour of France or a Cruise and Resort tour
- ❏ Housing available in historic victorian townhouse

Call now for a school catalogue
4207 Walnut Street Philadelphia, PA 19104   215-222-4200 ext. 6

WESTMORELAND COUNTY COMMUNITY COLLEGE
Youngwood/Year-round

This college offers a 2-year and 3-year AAS degree in Culinary Arts Apprenticeship and Culinary Arts Non-apprenticeship. Program started 1981. Accredited by ACFEI. Calendar: semester. Curriculum: core. Admission dates: August, January. Total enrollment 110; 35 enrollees each admission period; 30% financial aid recipients; 64% under age 25; 42.5% age 25 to 44; 9% age 45 or over; 60.5% part-time students; 15 to 20 students per instructor; 100% of graduates obtain employment. Facilities: include 4 specially equipped kitchens and classroom projects simulate student-run restaurant.

Courses: Garde manger, quantity foods, purchasing and storage, baking, food specialties, and hospitality marketing, as well as ACF Laurel Highlands Chapter Membership. Schedule: day and evening, 15-week fall and spring semesters and 6- and 12-week summer sessions. Continuing education: 1 semester externships and 3-year apprenticeships provided.

Faculty: 4 full-time, 18 part-time. Includes: Mary B. Zappone, Marlene Scatena, Cheryl Shipley and Carl Dunkel. Qualifications: ACF certification, experience in field, academic requirements.

Costs: Annual tuition: in-county $1,419, out-of-county $2,838. Application fee is $10, lab fee $20. Refund policy: 100% during first week of term. Admission requirements: high school diploma or equivalent and admission test. Last year 10 scholarships were awarded averaging $2,000; 8 loans were granted, averaging $1,000. Part time employment available.

Contact: Mary Zappone, Culinary Arts Dept., Westmoreland County Community College, Armbrust Rd., Youngwood, PA 15697; (412) 925-4000, Fax (412) 925-1150.

PUERTO RICO

INSTITUTO DE EDUCACION UNIV.
Hato Rey/Year-round

This independent college offers a 12-15 month certificate program in Culinary Arts, Baking, and Food Service Specialist. Program started 1991. Accredited by ACCSCT. Calendar: trimester. Curriculum: culinary only. Admission dates: February, September. Total enrollment 164 (culinary), 60 (baking); 50 to 60 enrollees each admission period; 95% of applicants accepted; 98% financial aid recipients; 95% under age 25; 5% age 25 to 44; 20 students per instructor; 80% of graduates obtain employment. Facilities: include 2 kitchens and classrooms.

COURSES: Include safety & hygiene, cooking methods, basic sauces, menu planning; bread formulas, cost production. 1,440 hours of culinary courses required for graduation. Schedule: 3 blocks of 440 hours. Externship: 120 hours, nearby hotels, restaurants, and bakeries.

FACULTY: 6 full-time culinary, 2 full-time baking.

COSTS: Admission requirements: high school diploma or equivalent. Last year 98 scholarships were awarded; 75 loans were granted.

CONTACT: Willie Lucca, Coordinator of Culinary Arts, Culinary Arts Dept., Instituto de Educacion Univ., Barbosa Ave. #404, Hato Rey, PR 00930; (809) 766-2443, Fax (809) 767-4755.

INSTITUTO DEL ARTE MODERNO, INC.
Hato Rey

This institution offers a 1,000-hour certificate. Program started 1987. Accredited by ACCSCT. Admission dates: January, August. Total enrollment 150; 25 students per instructor;

FACULTY: 5 full-time.

COSTS: Annual tuition: about $2,900. Admission requirements: high school diploma or equivalent.

CONTACT: Miriam Aponte, Culinary Arts Dept., Instituto del Arte Moderno, Inc., Ave. Monserrate FR-5, Villa Fontana, Carolina, PR 00630; (809) 769-7636.

RHODE ISLAND

JOHNSON & WALES UNIVERSITY COLLEGE OF CULINARY ARTS
Providence, RI; Charleston, SC; Norfolk, VA; North Miami, FL; Vail, CO/Year-round

This private, nonprofit institution offers a 1-year certificate program in Culinary Arts (Norfolk), 2-year AAS degree programs in Culinary Arts (Providence, Charleston, Norfolk, North Miami) and Baking & Pastry Arts (Providence, Charleston, North Miami), a 1-year accelerated AAS degree program (Vail) to college graduates, a 2-year AS degree program in Food & Beverage Management (Providence, Charleston, Norfolk), and BS degree programs in Culinary Arts (Providence, North Miami), Food Service Management (Providence, Charleston), Food Marketing (Providence), and Food Service Entrepreneurship (Providence). College of Culinary Arts founded in 1973; International Baking & Pastry Institute in 1982. Calendar: 3-term. Admission dates: March, September, November. Total enrollment over 3,500; about 84% of applicants are admitted to undergraduate programs, 100% to professional programs; most students receive financial assistance; 20 students per instructor for laboratory classes; 98% of graduates obtain employment. Campuses offer modern teaching facilities, including 5 student-run restaurants.

COURSES: Culinary arts courses include basic cooking and baking, classic and international cuisines, quantity food preparation, nutrition, communication skills and menu design; baking & pastry courses concentrate on basic ingredients and production techniques, French pastries and classic desserts, chocolate and sugar artistry, and specialties; food service management combines food preparation and service with specialized management courses. Schedule: 6 hours daily, Monday through Thursday; morning, afternoon, and evening options. Students can apply for a paid externship at a recognized facility and a select group participate in a student exchange program with Ecole Superieure de Cuisine Francaise in Paris and Ireland's Council for Education, Recruitment and Training. Top graduates can study another year or two as Teaching Assistants or Fellows. Continuing education program offerings vary by campus.

FACULTY: The 113 full-time faculty members are oriented toward instruction rather than research. The College of Culinary Arts annually honors outstanding chefs who present lectures and demonstrations.

COSTS: Annual tuition and fees for the culinary/baking & pastry arts AAS programs (Providence campus) are $13,752 for commuters, $18,438 for resident students. Payment options are available. A $100 ($200) nonrefundable commuter (resident) deposit is payable on acceptance. High school diploma or equivalent required; some foodservice experience is desirable. Part-time employment is available for students.

LOCATION: Near Providence's cultural and recreational facilities; Charleston's Port City Center; Norfolk's Westgate Center; North Miami, near Fort Lauderdale; Vail's Gore Creek Valley.

CONTACT: Mark Burke, Director of Enrollment Management, Johnson & Wales University, 8 Abbott Park Place, Providence, RI 02903; (800) 343-2565 or (401) 598-1000, Fax (401) 598-4712.

SOUTH CAROLINA

GREENVILLE TECHNICAL COLLEGE
Greenville/Year-round

This college offers a 1-year certificate and a 2-year degree in Food Service Management. Program started 1977. Accredited by ACFEI, SACS, ABSCP. Calendar: semester. Curriculum: core. Admission dates: quarterly. Total enrollment 85; 5 to 10 enrollees each admission period; 7% financial aid recipients; 5.5% part-time students; 15 students per instructor; Facilities: include kitchen and 3 classrooms.

COURSES: A la carte, bakeshop, buffet, nutrition, food production.

FACULTY: 5 full-time, 2 part-time.

COSTS: Tuition: $500 per semester. Application fee $20. Refund policy: 100% during first week. Admission requirements: high school diploma or equivalent and admission test. Last year 8 scholarships were awarded averaging $500. Part-time employment is available.

LOCATION: The 8,700-student, 57-acre campus is in a suburban setting 150 miles from Atlanta and 170 miles from Charlotte.

CONTACT: Marge Condrasky, Food Science Dept. Head, Food Science Dept., Greenville Technical College, P.O. Box 5616, Station B, Greenville, SC 29606-5616; (803) 250-8404, Fax (803) 250-8506.

HORRY-GEORGETOWN TECHNICAL COLLEGE
Conway/Year-round

This college offers a 2-year degree in Culinary Arts Technology. Program started 1985. Accredited by SACS, ACFEI. Calendar: semester. Curriculum: core. Admission dates: February. Total enrollment 65; 35 enrollees each admission period; 100% of applicants accepted; 60% financial aid recipients; 20% under age 25; 70% age 25 to 44; 10% age 45 or over; 5% part-time students; 12 students per instructor. Facilities: include 3 kitchens, 2 dining rooms and 2 restaurants.

COURSES: Food production, sanitation, nutrition, a la carte, buffet, menu planning. Schedule: 8:00 am-3:00 pm Monday-Friday. Externship provided.

FACULTY: 12 full-time. Includes: Dept. Head C. Catino, K. Hassett, I. Periera

COSTS: Tuition: in-state $500 per semester, out-of-state $1,000 per semester. Application fee $10. Application deadlines: 2 weeks prior to registration. Admission requirements: high school diploma or equivalent and admission test. Average off-campus housing cost: $250-$350 per month.

LOCATION: The 2,800-student campus is in a small town setting.

CONTACT: Carmen Catino, Culinary Arts Dept., Horry-Georgetown Technical College, P.O. Box 1966, Conway, SC 29526; (803) 347-3186, Fax (803) 347-4207.

JOHNSON & WALES UNIVERSITY
Charleston/Year-round

This nonprofit university offers an AAS degree in Culinary Arts. Program started 1984. Accredited by ACICS, NEASC. Calendar: quarter. Curriculum: core. Admission dates: rolling. Total enrollment 642; 75% financial aid recipients; 75% under age 25; 16.3% age 25 to 44; 7.7% age 45 or over; 22 students per instructor; 98% of graduates obtain employment. Facilities: 10 kitchens, 15 classrooms.

COURSES: Culinary Arts. 99 quarter hours of culinary courses required for graduation. Schedule: 25 hours per week, 9 months per year. Other required courses: cooperative education practicum. Externship: 12 weeks, $5 per hour, resorts/hotels/restaurants.

FACULTY: 18 full-time, 2 part-time.

COSTS: Tuition: $8,688. Other costs: $100 tuition and $100 housing deposits, $300 general fee, $2,640 comprehensive fee. Application deadlines: rolling. Admission requirements: high school diploma or equivalent. On-campus housing: 124 apartment units; cost: $2,946. Off-campus housing cost: $375 per month and up. Part-time employment is available.

CONTACT: Ada M. Howell, Director of Admissions, Office of Admissions, Johnson & Wales University, 701 E. Bay St., PPC Box 1409, Charleston, SC 29403; (800) 868-1522 or (803) 727-3000, Fax (803) 763-0318.

TRIDENT TECHNICAL COLLEGE
Charleston/Year-round

This college offers a 4 semester Diploma and Associate degree in Culinary Arts. Program started 1986. Accredited by SACS. Calendar: semester. Curriculum: core. Admission dates: open. Total enrollment 57; 30 to 35 enrollees each admission period; 40% financial aid recipients; 10% under age 25; 75% age 25 to 44; 15% age 45 or over; 5% part-time students; 15 students per instructor; 100% of graduates obtain employment. Facilities: include 10 kitchens and classrooms and student-run restaurant.

COURSES: Schedule: 8 am-5 pm. Continuing education: 6-10 courses per semester.

FACULTY: 3 full-time.

COSTS: Annual tuition: $1,482 in-county, $1,722 out-of-county, $2,544 out-of-state. Application fee $20, tuition deposit $10. Admission requirements: high school diploma or equivalent and admission test. Last year 6 scholarships were awarded averaging $600. Off-campus housing cost: $325 per month. Part-time employment is available.

LOCATION: The 9,700-student campus is in downtown Charleston.

CONTACT: Chrissy Huggins, Division of Hospitality & Tourism, Trident Technical College, P.O. Box 118067, MK-C, Charleston, SC 29423-8067; (803) 722-5541, Fax (803) 572-6109.

SOUTH DAKOTA

MITCHELL TECHNICAL INSTITUTE
Mitchell/September-May

This school offers a 18-month diploma, certificate, or AAS degree in Culinary Arts. Program started 1968. Accredited by NCA. Calendar: semester. Curriculum: culinary only. Admission dates: February. Total enrollment 40; 18 to 24 enrollees each admission period; 90% financial aid recipients; 50% under age 25; 50% age 25 to 44; 18 to 20 students per instructor; 100% of graduates obtain employment. Facilities: include 3 kitchens, 3 classrooms and a 54-seat restaurant.

Courses: Schedule: 7:30 am-3:30 pm, 5 days per week.

Faculty: 2 full-time.

Costs: Annual tuition: $1,260. Application fee $75. Other fees $80. Refund policy 90% within 2 weeks. Admission requirements: high school diploma or equivalent and admission test. Last year 2 scholarships were awarded averaging $500; 21 loans were granted, averaging $3,000. Off-campus housing cost: $4,200. Part-time employment is available.

Contact: John Weber, Cook/Chef, Mitchell Technical Institute, 821 N. Capitol, Mitchell, SD 57301; (605) 995-3030.

TENNESSEE

MEMPHIS CULINARY ACADEMY
Year-round

This private school offers a 40-week diploma program that consists of 10-week basic, 5-week intermediate, and 15-week advanced courses based on classic French and European cuisines. Founded 1984. Class size 12 students.

Courses: Include culinary skills, baking, nutrition, and kitchen rotation. Seminars in pastry, garde manger, kitchen management.

Faculty: Director Joseph Carey, CEC, has worked as an executive chef and culinary arts instructor since 1971. Elaine Wallace-Carey is a professionally trained pastry chef.

Costs: Tuition is approximately $3,000 for the basic course, $300 for the intermediate and advanced courses, $3,600 for all three.

Contact: Joseph or Elaine Carey, Memphis Culinary Academy, 1252 Peabody Ave., Memphis, TN 38104; (901) 722-8892.

ART INSTITUTE OF HOUSTON
Houston/Year-round

This proprietary school offers an 18-month AAS degree in Culinary Arts. Program started 1992. Accredited by ACCSCT. Calendar: quarter. Curriculum: core. Admission dates: January, April, July, September. Total enrollment 199; 40 enrollees each admission period; 65% of applicants accepted; 75% financial aid recipients; 33% under age 25; 50% age 25 to 44; 17% age 45 or over; 10% part-time students; 20 students per instructor; 85% of graduates obtain employment. Facilities: include 4 kitchens, bakery, deli and open-to-the-public restaurant.

Courses: Basic cooking, food production, garde manger, a la carte, baking, nutrition, sanitation, food and beverage, purchasing and cost controls. Other Required courses: 24 credit hours of general education. Schedule: 30 hours per week for 18 months, full-time. Externship provided.

Faculty: 9 full-time.

COSTS: Tuition is $3,160 per quarter. Application fee $50, tuition deposit $100, general fee $250, lab fee $250, kit $515. Application deadlines: rolling. Admission requirements: high school diploma or equivalent and interview. Last year 68 scholarships were awarded averaging $1,200; 189 loans were granted averaging $3,312. On-campus housing: 120 spaces; average cost: $1,130 per quarter. Average off-campus housing cost: $400-$600 per month. Part-time employment available.

LOCATION: The 1,200-student, 70,000-square-foot facility is in Houston.

CONTACT: Cherié R. McNeel, Director of Admissions, Art Institute of Houston, 1900 Yorktown, Houston, TX 77056; (800) 275-4244 or (713) 623-2040, Fax (713) 966-2700.

DEL MAR COLLEGE
Corpus Christi/Year-round

This state supported institution offers a 1-year certificate, 2-year AAS degree, and 4-year BS degree in Restaurant Management and Culinary Arts. Program started 1963. Accredited by SACS. Calendar: semester. Curriculum: core. Admission dates: June, September, January. Total enrollment 175; 15 enrollees each admission period; 100% of applicants accepted; 40% financial aid recipients; 30% under age 25; 60% age 25 to 44; 10% age 45 or over; 30% part-time students; 15 students per instructor; 100% of graduates obtain employment. Facilities: include 3 restaurants, 4 classrooms and laboratory.

COURSES: Saucier, garde manger, elementary baking, advanced pastry, and restaurant management. Schedule: varied, day and night.

FACULTY: 4 full-time, 11 part-time.

COSTS: Annual tuition: in state $1,000, out-of-state $1,800. Admission requirements: high school diploma or equivalent and admissions test. Last year 15 scholarships were awarded averaging $750. Part-time employment is available. Average off-campus housing cost $250-$350.

CONTACT: D.W. Haven, Professor & Chair, Dept. of Hospitality Management, Del Mar College, Baldwin at Ayers, Corpus Christi, TX 78404; (512) 886-1734, Fax (512) 886-1795.

EL CENTRO COLLEGE
Dallas/Year-round

This college offers a 2-year AAS degree in Food and Hospitality Services. Program started 1971. Accredited by SACS. Calendar: semester. Curriculum: core. Admission dates: January, August. Total enrollment 400; 350 to 400 enrollees each admission period; 100% of applicants accepted; 40% financial aid recipients; 30% under age 25; 50% age 25 to 44; 20% age 45 or over; 65% part-time students; 20 to 35 students per instructor; 90% of graduates obtain employment. Facilities: include 3 kitchens and 4 classrooms.

COURSES: Schedule: 20 to 25 hours per week, part-time options available.

FACULTY: 4 full-time, 8 part-time.

COSTS: Annual tuition: in-county $400, out-of-county $800. Admission requirements: high school diploma or equivalent and admissions test required.

CONTACT: C. Gus Katsigris, Food & Hospitality Services Institute, El Centro College, Main at Lamar Sts., Dallas, TX 75202; (214) 746-2202, Fax (214) 746-2335.

GALVESTON COLLEGE
Galveston/Year-round

This college offers a 2-year certificate and a 2-year AAS degree in Food Preparation, Management Development, Culinary Hospitality Management. Program started 1987. Accredited by SACS. Calendar: semester. Curriculum: core. Admission dates: January, September. Total enrollment 15 to 45; 10 to 12 enrollees each admission period; 75% of applicants accepted; 100% financial aid recipients; 25% under age 25; 60% age 25 to 44; 15% age 45 or over; 10% part-time students; 15 students per instructor; 70% of graduates obtain employment. Facilities: include kitchen, bakeshop and classroom.

COURSES: Schedule: 8 am-6 pm, Monday-Friday, 12 months per year; part-time and evening options available. Externship provided.

FACULTY: 2 full-time.

COSTS: Annual tuition: $279 in-state, $459 out-of-state. Admission requirements: high school diploma or equivalent and admissions test.

CONTACT: Phil Harris, Culinary Arts Dept., Galveston College, 4015 Ave. Q, Galveston, TX 77550; (409) 763-6551, Fax (409) 762-9367.

LE CHEF COLLEGE OF HOSPITALITY CAREERS
Austin/Year-round

This independent nonprofit institution offers a full-time 1-year (1,728-hour) Culinary Arts Program, a 6-month Food and Beverage Management Program, and a 72-credit-hour AAS degree in Culinary Arts and Food and Beverage Management. Founded in 1985. Accredited by the ACFEI and SACS. Admission dates: continuous. Curriculum: core and culinary. Total enrollment 100; 60% of applicants accepted; 25 students in each of 3 classes with one or more instructors; 94% of graduates obtain employment. Facilities: a culinary lab, 2 classrooms, audio/visual library, storage room, student lounge.

COURSES: The 1-year program covers cuisine and pastry preparation, pantry production and garde manger, production and control, and planning and presentation. The degree program includes culinary and food and beverage courses as well as general education courses in algebra, English, public speaking, psychology, and computing. Schedule: 5 hours daily, 5 days a week, flexible time frames. The degree program includes a 720-hour paid externship. Short courses and seminars are also offered.

FACULTY: College founder and president Ronald F. Boston, CDM, CFBE, was 1987-1988 Texas Chef of the Year and has chef, management, and instructor experience. Other instructors are James A. Alverson, CEC, Bud Wheeler, CEC, Joseph Schroeder, Andre Touboule, Peter Wabbel, James Fischer, and Charles Collins.

COSTS: Tuition is $12,816 for Culinary Arts, $4,200 for Food and Beverage Management, $15,875 for the degree program. A $50 nonrefundable registration fee is required; 30-day satisfaction guarantee. Thereafter, refunds are pro-rated according to state and federal regulations. Applicants must have a high school diploma or equivalent and a personal interview. Financial aid is available; the school is VA approved.

LOCATION: North central Austin, near transportation, 30 minutes from Texas Hill Country.

CONTACT: Le Chef College of Hospitality Careers, 6020 Dillard Circle, Austin, TX 78752; (512) 323-2511, Fax (512) 323-2126.

ODESSA COLLEGE
Odessa

This college offers a 2-year certificate/AAS degree. Program started 1990. Admission dates: open. Total enrollment 35 to 50; 75% of applicants accepted; 10 to 15 students per instructor; 100% of graduates obtain employment. Externships provided.

FACULTY: 5 full-time.

COSTS: Annual tuition: in-state $550, out-of-state $800-$1,000. Admission requirements: high school diploma or equivalent and admission test.

CONTACT: Jennifer Cochran, Director, Culinary Arts, Odessa College, 201 W. University, Odessa, TX 79764; (915) 335-6583, Fax (915) 335-6860.

ST. PHILIP'S COLLEGE
San Antonio/Year-round

This college offers a 2-year AAS degree and 3-year apprenticeship in Hospitality Management. Program started 1979. Accredited by SACS. Calendar: semester. Curriculum: core. Admission dates: August, January, June. Total enrollment 250; 250 enrollees each admission period; 80% financial aid recipients; 50% part-time students; 50 students per instructor; 85% of graduates obtain employment. Facilities: include 7 kitchens and classrooms and a restaurant.

COURSES: Garde manger, international food preparation, and baking principles. Externship: 8 weeks. Continuing education courses available.

FACULTY: 5 full-time.

COSTS: Annual tuition: in-state $500, out-of-state $900. Admission requirements: high school diploma or equivalent and admission test.

CONTACT: William Thornton, Hospitality Operations, St. Philip's College, 2111 Nevada, San Antonio, TX 78203; (210) 531-3315.

SAN JACINTO COLLEGE NORTH
Houston

This college offers a 2-year and 3-year AAS degree. Program started 1986. Accredited by SACS. Admission dates: September, January. Total enrollment 20 to 30; 90% of applicants accepted; 12 students per instructor; 50% of graduates obtain employment.

FACULTY: 3 full-time.

CONTACT: George J. Messinger, Chef's Apprenticeship Training, San Jacinto College North, 5800 Uvalde, Houston, TX 77049; (713) 459-7150, Fax (713) 459-7100.

UTAH

SALT LAKE COMMUNITY COLLEGE
Salt Lake City/Year-round

This college offers a 2-year full-time and 3-year part-time Apprentice Chef program. Program started 1984. Accredited by NASC. Calendar: quarter (full-time) or semester (part-time). Curriculum: culinary and core. Admission dates: rolling. Total enrollment 110; 40 to 50 per year enrollees each admission period; 90% of applicants accepted; 40 to 50% part-time students; 14 students per instructor; 100% of graduates obtain employment. Facilities: include kitchen, 8 classrooms, video and reference library.

COURSES: Food preparation, sanitation, baking, menu design, and nutrition. Other required courses: AAS degree requires 24 credits in general education. Schedule: full-time Monday-Friday, 5 hours daily; part-time Mondays only 2 pm-8 pm; Aug.-Nov. and Jan.-Apr. Continuing education: specialized classes and workshops available for culinary professionals.

FACULTY: 8 full and part-time full-time. Includes: R. Renzetti, L. Seiferle, R. DeJong, R. Mirabelli, J. Bielefeld.

COSTS: In-state full-time tuition: $482 per quarter, $1,446 per year; part-time program rates: $77 per class, $154 per semester, and $308 per year. A $20 application fee ($5 for part-time program) is required. Admission requirements: high school diploma or equivalent and admission test. Last year 4 scholarships were awarded averaging $500; numerous loans were granted. Part-time employment is available. Average off-campus housing cost $300 per month.

CAREER/PROFESSIONAL UTAH 101

CONTACT: Joe Mulvey, Apprenticeship Director, Salt Lake Community College, P.O. Box 30808, Salt Lake City, UT 84130-0808; (801) 957-4066, Fax (801) 957-4612.

UTAH VALLEY STATE COLLEGE
Orem/August-April

This college offers a 2-year AAS degree in Culinary Arts. Program started 1992. Accredited by NASC. Calendar: semester. Curriculum: core. Admission dates: open. Total enrollment 35; 15 enrollees each admission period; 90% of applicants accepted; 80% financial aid recipients; 50% under age 25; 50% age 25 to 44; 10% age 45 or over; 10% part-time students; 12 students per instructor; 100% of graduates obtain employment. Facilities: include 3 kitchens, 3 classrooms, restaurant and food service operation.

COURSES: Food production, nutrition, sanitation, garde manger, and buffet. Schedule: 8 am-1 pm daily. Externship: 5-week, salaried, in hotels or restaurants.

FACULTY: 3 full-time. Includes: G. Forte, W. Bitters. Qualifications: certified chef, work experience.

COSTS: Annual tuition: in state $579, out-of-state $2,080. Other fees: $130. Refund policy: 100% first week, 75% second week, 50% third week. Admission requirements: high school diploma. Last year 500 scholarships were awarded; 2500 loans were granted, averaging $2,625. Average off-campus housing cost $200 per month. Part-time employment is available.

CONTACT: Greg Forte, Business, Utah Valley State College, 800 West 1200 South, Orem, UT 84058; (801) 222-8000, Fax (801) 226-5207.

VERMONT

NEW ENGLAND CULINARY INSTITUTE
(See also page 217) (See display ad page 102) **Montpelier and Essex/Year-round**

This private institution offers a 2-year AOS degree program in Culinary Arts and an upper level 1-year Bachelors degree in Service & Management. Founded in 1979. Accredited by the State of Vermont and ACCSCT. Curriculum: culinary, service and management. Admission dates August, November, March, May. Total enrollment 448; 84 enrollees each admission period; 90% of applicants accepted; 70% financial aid recipients; 70% under age 25; 28% ages 25 to 44; 2% age 45 or over; student to faculty ratio 7:1; 100% of graduates obtain employment. Facilities: 11 kitchens and 14 classrooms; in Montpelier 2 open-to-the-public restaurants, bakeshop, catering and banquet department, 2 cafeterias; in Essex 2 open-to-the-public restaurants and a catering, banquet, and bakery department. Career counseling and lifetime placement.

COURSES: Students spend 75% of class time preparing food for the public. Remaining class time covers cooking theory, food and wine history, wine and beverage management, tableservice, and service management and purchasing. At least 45 hours are devoted to a structured physical fitness plan. Schedule: 8 to 10 hours per day, 5 to 6 days per week. Each year consists of a 24-week on-campus residency, followed by an 18- to 20-week internship. More than 70% of second-year internships become permanent.

FACULTY: The 40-member faculty are chosen on the basis of experience and teaching ability. They include Jim Dodge, Michel LeBornue, David Miles, and Jozef Herrewyn. The Institute has a 19-member administrative staff and 3 advisory boards.

COSTS: The annual $18,300 fee includes room, board, and uniforms. Other costs include a nonrefundable $25 application fee, a $200 dormitory deposit, $500 for books and equipment. A $100 enrollment deposit is due within 30 days of acceptance, first tuition payment of $5,390 is due 75 days before registration, balance is due at registration. Applicants must have a high school diploma or equivalent and 3 reference letters; advanced placement second year students must pass an exam. In 1994-95, 60 scholarships were awarded averaging $500 each, 70% of students received federal

WHY WE CUT OUR CLASS SIZE TO THE BONE.

Less is more.
The fewer students in a class, the more time the teacher can spend with each student. Our student/teacher ratio is 7 to 1. Our unique, 2 year program also offers:
- Hands-on training
- Paid, personalized internships
- Financial aid for qualified students
- Advanced Placement available
- A.O.S degree in Culinary Arts
- NEW: Bachelor's degree program in Service and Management

Call or write for our four-color catalog.

NEW ENGLAND CULINARY INSTITUTE
250 Main St., Dept. SH
Montpelier, VT 05602-9720
(802) 223-6324

Accredited Member
ACCSCT

loans averaging $3,000 each. Dormitory lodging is available for 160 students; other nearby lodging is $300-$500 per month.

Location: The Montpelier campus, a rural setting, is 3 hours from Boston and 7 hours from New York City; the Essex Junction Campus, at The Inn at Essex country hotel in a Burlington suburb, is 40 minutes north of Montpelier.

Contact: Admissions Department, New England Culinary Institute, 250 Main St., Dept. S, Montpelier, VT, 05602; (802) 223-6324.

VIRGINIA

ATI CAREER INSTITUTE – SCHOOL OF CULINARY ARTS
Falls Church/Year-round

This private school offers a 12-month diploma in Culinary Arts. Program started 1990. Accredited by SACS. Calendar: 6-week terms. Curriculum: core. Admission dates: every 6 weeks. Total enrollment 190; 40 enrollees each admission period; 80% of applicants accepted; 80% financial aid recipients; 25% under age 25; 65% age 25 to 44; 10% age 45 or over; 18 students per instructor; 95% of graduates obtain employment. Facilities: include 3 kitchens and 5 classrooms.

Courses: Culinary theory, nutrition, sanitation, sauces and entrees, baking, garde manger, hospitality management, electronic accounting. Schedule: 5 hours daily. Externship: 12-weeks required.

Faculty: 10 full-time. Guest chefs are frequent lecturers.

Costs: Tuition is $12,530, including books and equipment. Nonrefundable application fee: $65. Admission requirements: high school diploma or equivalent. Last year 3 scholarships were awarded, averaging $1,500. Part-time employment available. Off-campus housing cost $600 per month.

Location: The 20,000 square-foot campus, on the Beltway, is 15 miles from Washington, D.C.

Contact: John W. Martin, Director of Culinary Arts, ATI Career Institute, School of Culinary Arts, 7777 Leesburg Pike, Ste.100 South, Falls Church, VA 22043; (703) 821-8570, Fax (703) 556-9892.

JOHNSON & WALES UNIVERSITY
Norfolk/Year-round

This university offers 12- and 18-month AAS degrees in Culinary Arts. Program started 1987. Accredited by NEASC, ACICS. Calendar: quarter. Curriculum: core. Admission dates: rolling. Total enrollment 352; 62 to 229 enrollees each admission period; 84% of applicants accepted; 72% under age 25; 26% age 25 to 44; 2% age 45 or over; 1% part-time students; 22 students per instructor; 98% of graduates obtain employment. Facilities: 5 kitchens, 6 classrooms, beverage and dining room labs.

Courses: Culinary Arts. 60 hours of culinary courses required for graduation. Other required courses: 8 academic, 2 seminars. Schedule: 24 hours per week, 9 months per year; 19.5 hours weekend/evening. Externship: 1 term, varied salary, food service.

Faculty: 11 full-time, 2 part-time. Qualifications: college degree/ACF certificate.

Costs: Tuition: $8,526 (day), $5,970 (weekend/evening). Fees: $330 general, $2,616 comprehensive, $65 orientation. Application deadlines: rolling. Admission requirements: high school diploma or equivalent. Last year 249 scholarships were awarded averaging $1,232; 474 loans were granted, averaging $2,536. On-campus housing: 123 spaces; average cost $4,380. Off-campus housing cost: approximately $250 per month plus utilities. Part-time employment is available.

Contact: Tammy Jaxtheimer, Director of Admissions, Johnson & Wales University, 2428 Almeda Ave., Ste. 316, Norfolk, VA 22043; (800) 277-2433 or (804) 853-3508, Fax (804) 857-4869.

WASHINGTON

CLARK COLLEGE CULINARY ARTS PROGRAM
Vancouver/Year-round *(See display ad below)*

This community college offers 1-year certificate and 2-year AAS degree programs in cooking, baking, and bakery and restaurant management. Established at its present location in 1958. Calendar: quarter. Curriculum: culinary and core. Cooking program enrolls 30 each admission period, baking program enrolls 20; 80% of applicants are accepted; student to teacher ratio is 5 to 1; 95% of graduates obtain jobs. The modernized culinary arts facility operates like a large hotel kitchen. Students make all food products sold on-campus and prepare meals for evening functions.

COURSES: Cooking curriculum includes basic food preparation, advanced meat cutting, ice carving, wine appreciation, cake decoration and pastillage. Baking students study fundamentals the first year and select from specialized courses the second year. They spend 1 day a week learning theory, merchandising, and bake shop management, and the rest of the week producing goods for the school's retail store. Schedule: 8 am to 1:30 pm, Monday through Thursday.

FACULTY: The 12-member faculty includes cooking instructors Larry Mains, CEC, George Akau, CCE, and Glenn Lakin and baking instructors Per Zeeberg and Jean Williams.

COSTS: Cost for each 2-year program is $2,700 in-state, $10,092 out-of-state. Applicants are admitted on a first-come, first-served basis during any quarter. Financial aid and department scholarships are available.

LOCATION: Minutes from Portland, Oregon.

CONTACT: Larry Mains, Clark College, 1800 E. McLoughlin Blvd., Vancouver, WA 98663-3598; (360) 992-2143.

Clark College Culinary Arts
Vancouver, Washington

Professional Cooking • Professional Baking
Restaurant Management • Bakery Management

Twice chosen as the Best Culinary Arts Program in the Pacific Northwest by the National Restaurant Association

For more information contact: **Larry Mains (360) 992-2143**

EDMONDS COMMUNITY COLLEGE
Lynwood/January-July, October-December

This college offers a 6-quarter ATA or certificate. Program started 1988. Accredited by State. Calendar: quarter. Curriculum: core. Admission dates: fall, winter, spring. Total enrollment 45; 15 enrollees each admission period; 90% of applicants accepted; 25% financial aid recipients; 15% under age 25; 80% age 25 to 44; 5% age 45 or over; 20 students per instructor; 100% of graduates obtain employment. Facilities: 1 kitchen, 1 classroom, 1 restaurant.

COURSES: Contemporary Northwest cuisine, fine dining service, restaurant/food service management. 850 hours of culinary courses required for graduation. Other required courses: service and management. Schedule: 7:30 am-2 pm weekdays, 10 months. Externship provided.

FACULTY: 2 full-time, 2 part-time. Includes: Walter Bronowitz, CWC, CCE; John Casey. Qualifications: CWC, CCE.

CAREER/PROFESSIONAL WASHINGTON 105

Costs: Annual tuition: in-state $435 per quarter, out-of-state $1,313 per quarter. Application deadlines: 1 month prior to start of quarter. Admission requirements: high school diploma or equivalent. Last year 5 scholarships were awarded averaging $450. Part-time employment available.

Location: The 12,000-student suburban campus is 20 minutes from Seattle.

Contact: Walter N. Bronowitz, Chef/instructor, Culinary Arts, Edmonds Community College, 20000 - 68th Ave. West, Lynwood, WA 98036; (206) 640-1329, Fax (206) 771-3366.

NORTH SEATTLE COMMUNITY COLLEGE
Seattle/September-June

This college offers a 1-year certificate and a 2-year AAS degree in Culinary Arts, Hospitality and Restaurant Cooking. Program started 1970. Accredited by NASC. Calendar: quarter. Curriculum: core. Admission dates: quarterly. Total enrollment 80; 25 enrollees each admission period; 90% of applicants accepted; 25% financial aid recipients; 10% under age 25; 80% age 25 to 44; 10% age 45 or over; 15 students per instructor; 90% of graduates obtain employment. Facilities: include 2 kitchens and classrooms, restaurant and bakery.

Courses: Restaurant cooking and commercial cooking. Schedule: 7:30 am-2:00 pm, September through June.

Faculty: 4 full-time.

Costs: Annual tuition: $1,200 in-state, $5,000 out-of-state. Uniform, supplies $750. Admission requirements: high school diploma or equivalent and admission test. Average off-campus housing cost $500 per month. Part-time employment is available.

Contact: Darryl Mihara, Culinary Arts Dept., North Seattle Community College, 9600 College Way North, Seattle, WA 98103-3599; (206) 527-3600.

OLYMPIC COLLEGE
Bremerton

This college offers a 3-quarter certificate and 2-year AAS degree. Program started 1978. Accredited by State. Calendar: trimester. Curriculum: core. Admission dates: continuous enrollment. Total enrollment 32; 20% enrollees each admission period; 85% of applicants accepted; 60% financial aid recipients; 30% under age 25; 70% age 25 to 44; 15% age 45 or over; 15% part-time students; 16 students per instructor; 90% of graduates obtain employment. Facilities: central kitchen, one classroom, two restaurants.

Courses: Classical cooking, restaurant baking, dining room service, restaurant management. 1,170 hours of culinary courses required for graduation. Other required courses: math, English, computers, business. Schedule: 33 hours per week, 9 months per year. Continuing education: English composition, computers, business management.

Faculty: 2 full-time. Includes: N. Giovanni, S. Lammers.

Costs: Annual tuition: in-state $1,296, out-of-state $5,094. $50 lunch fee quarterly. Admission requirements: high school diploma or equivalent. Last year 4 scholarships were awarded averaging $175. Part-time employment is available. Average off-campus housing cost: $275 per month.

Contact: Steve Lammers, Chef Instructor, Commercial Cooking/Food Service, Olympic College, 16th & Chester, Bremerton, WA 98310-1688; (360) 478-4576, Fax (360) 478-4650.

RENTON TECHNICAL COLLEGE
Renton/Year-round

This college offers a 1,620-hour certificate/AAS degree in Culinary Arts/Chef and Culinary Arts/Baker. Program started 1968. Accredited by ACFEI, NASC. Calendar: quarter. Curriculum: culinary only. Admission dates: open. Total enrollment 30; 10 to 30 enrollees each admission period; 100% of applicants accepted; 30% financial aid recipients; 20% under age 25; 75% age 25 to 44; 5% age 45 or over; 12 students per instructor; 100% of graduates obtain employment. Facilities: include kitchen, bakery, demonstration classroom and 3 restaurants.

COURSES: Schedule: 6 hours per day, Monday-Friday. Externship provided.

FACULTY: 2 instructors and 5 assistants full-time.

COSTS: Tuition: $530 per quarter. Registration fee: $25; tuition deposit: $500-$530 per quarter. Other costs: books, uniforms. Refund policy: 80% within first 5 days, 40% sixth to fifteenth day. Admission requirements: high school diploma or equivalent and admission test.

CONTACT: Kristi Frambach, Associate Dean, Culinary Arts Dept., Renton Technical College, 3000 N.E. Fourth St., Renton, WA 98056; (206) 235-2352, Fax (206) 235-7832.

SEATTLE CENTRAL COMMUNITY COLLEGE
Seattle/Year-round

This college offers a 6-quarter Culinary Arts certificate and a 3-quarter Pastry certificate. Program started 1942. Accredited by ACFEI. Calendar: quarter. Curriculum: culinary. Admission dates: quarterly. Total enrollment 100-125; 30 enrollees each admission period; 85% of applicants accepted; 29.8% under age 25; 41.1% age 25 to 44; 29.1% age 45 or over; 2% part-time students; 20 students per instructor; 97% of graduates obtain employment. Facilities: include 3 kitchens, 8 classrooms, cafeteria, cafe and gourmet restaurant.

COURSES: Professional cooking, restaurant cooking, baking, specialty desserts and breads, nutrition, buffet catering, costing, and computerized menu planning. 1,750 hours of culinary courses required for graduation. Schedule: 8 am-2:30 pm, Tuesday-Friday. Continuing education: occasional nutrition courses are offered for culinary professionals.

FACULTY: 7 full-time, 2 part-time. Includes: Keijiro Miyata, CEC, Linda Hierholzer, CCE, Diana Dillard, CIA graduate, David Madayag, CEC, John Balmores, and Melissa Dallas.

COSTS: In-state tuition $426 per quarter, out-of-state $1,692 per quarter. Withdrawals during the first week of class receive full refund. Application deadlines: 2 weeks before beginning of each quarter. Admission requirements: admission test. Last year 11 scholarships were awarded averaging $1,333. Part-time employment is available. Off-campus housing cost: $300-$500 per month.

LOCATION: Campus is located in Capitol Hill district of Seattle, a short walk to downtown.

CONTACT: Joy Gulmon-Huri, Program Manager, Hospitality & Culinary Arts, Seattle Central Community College, 1701 Broadway, Mailstop 2BE2120, Seattle, WA 98122; (206) 587-5424, Fax (205) 344-4390. EMail: jgulmon@sccd.ctc.edu

SKAGIT VALLEY COLLEGE
Mt. Vernon/September-May

This college offers a 1-year certificate and a 2-year ATA degree in Culinary Arts/Hospitality Management. Program started 1979. Accredited by State. Calendar: quarter. Curriculum: core. Admission dates: open. Total enrollment 60; 6 enrollees each admission period; 100% of applicants accepted; 60% financial aid recipients; 20% under age 25; 70% age 25 to 44; 10% age 45 or over; 15 students per instructor; 100% of graduates obtain employment. Facilities: include kitchen, classrooms and restaurant.

COURSES: Schedule: 5 days per week, 9 months per year. Externship provided.

FACULTY: 3 full-time.

COSTS: Annual tuition: in-state $1,125, out-of-state $5,500. Admission requirements: high school diploma or equivalent. Part-time employment is available.

CAREER/PROFESSIONAL WASHINGTON 107

Contact: Culinary Arts-Hospitality Management, Skagit Valley College, 2405 College Way, Mt. Vernon, WA 98273; (206) 428-1612.

SOUTH PUGET SOUND COMMUNITY COLLEGE
Olympia

This college offers a 2-year ATA degree. Accredited by State. Admission dates: September, January, April, June. Total enrollment 40; 20 to 25 students per instructor.

Faculty: 2 full-time.

Costs: Annual tuition: in-state $32 per credit hour, out-of-state $124 per credit hour. Admission requirements: high school diploma or equivalent and admission test required.

Contact: Food Service Technology, South Puget Sound Community College, 2011 Mottman Rd., SW, Olympia, WA 98502; (206) 754-7711, ext. 376.

SOUTH SEATTLE COMMUNITY COLLEGE
Seattle/Year-round

This college offers a 18-month certificate/AAS degree in Food Service Production and Pastry and Specialty Baking. Program started 1975. Accredited by ACFEI, NASC. Calendar: quarter. Admission dates: September, January, March, June. Total enrollment 130 to 160; 100% of applicants accepted; 25% financial aid recipients; 25% under age 25; 65% age 25 to 44; 10% age 45 or over; 15 students per instructor; 98% of graduates obtain employment. Facilities: include 4 kitchens, 6 classrooms and 2 waited service dining rooms.

Courses: Food preparation and theory, restaurant baking, purchasing, meat cutting, and general education. Schedule: 7 am-1:40 pm, Monday through Friday.

Faculty: 7 full-time, 8 part-time. Qualifications: extensive industry experience.

Costs: Annual tuition: in-state $1,304, out-of-state $5,224. Last year 20 scholarships were awarded averaging $500-$1,000. Part-time employment is available. Off-campus housing cost: $400-$500 monthly.

Location: The 35-acre campus is in a suburban setting.

Contact: Daniel Cassidy, Associate Dean, Hospitality & Food Science Division, South Seattle Community College, 6000 16th Ave. S.W., Seattle, WA 98106-1499; (206) 764-5344, Fax (206) 764-5393.

SPOKANE COMMUNITY COLLEGE
Spokane/September-June

This college offers a 2-year AAS degree in Culinary Arts, Pastry, and Baking. Program started 1962. Accredited by NASC, ACFEI. Calendar: quarter. Curriculum: culinary and core. Admission dates: March. Total enrollment 75 to 100; 30 enrollees each admission period; 95% of applicants accepted; 40% financial aid recipients; 70% under age 25; 25% age 25 to 44; 5% age 45 or over; 20 students per instructor; 90% of graduates obtain employment. Facilities: include 2 kitchens, bakeshop, pastry shop, 6 classrooms and restaurant.

Courses: Schedule: 7:30 am-2:30 pm, Monday-Friday, 9 months per year. Externship: 3-6 months, in area hotels and restaurants.

Faculty: 4 full-time.

Costs: Annual tuition: approximately $870 in-state. Admission requirements: high school diploma or equivalent and admission test.

Contact: Doug Fisher, Culinary Arts Dept., Spokane Community College, 1810 N. Greene St., Spokane, WA 99207; (509) 533-7284.

WEST VIRGINIA

GARNET CAREER CENTER
Charleston
CONTACT: Culinary Director, Commercial Foods, Garnet Career Center, 422 Dickinson St., Charleston, WV 25301; (304) 348-6127.

SYMPOSIUM FOR PROF. FOOD WRITERS AT THE GREENBRIER
White Sulfur Springs/March
This 2-day conference for professional food writers (limit 90 participants) consists of lectures, seminars, informal discussions, and receptions. Topics include food writing for newspapers and magazines, recipe development, writing for cookbooks, culinary history, food writing for film.

FACULTY: About 15 noted professionals. Speakers for 1995 included Nancy Barr, Shirley Corriher, Barbara Fairchild, Betty Fussell, and Candy Sagon and guests Julia Child and Anne Willan.

LOCATION: The Mobil 5-star, AAA 5-diamond Greenbrier resort in the Allegheny Mountains of West Virginia, is 15 minutes from the Greenbrier Valley Airport in Lewisburg and 75 miles from Roanoke, Va. Amtrak service is available.

CONTACT: Lynne Bostic, Symposium Coordinator, The Symposium for Professional Food Writers, The Greenbrier, White Sulphur Springs, West Virginia 24986; (800) 624-6070 or (304) 536-7112; Fax (304) 536-7834.

WEST VIRGINIA NORTHERN COMMUNITY COLLEGE
Wheeling
This college offers a 2-year certificate/AAS degree. Program started 1975. Accredited by NCA. Admission dates: open. Total enrollment 26; 100% of applicants accepted; 9 students per instructor; 85% of graduates obtain employment.

FACULTY: 3 full-time.

COSTS: Annual tuition: in-state $42 per credit hour, out-of-state $120 per credit hour. Admission requirements: high school diploma or equivalent and admission test.

CONTACT: James Panacci, Culinary Arts Dept., West Virginia Northern Community College, College Square, Wheeling, WV 26003; (304) 233-5900.

WISCONSIN

CHIPPEWA VALLEY TECHNICAL COLLEGE
Eau Claire
This college offers a 2-year degree. Program started 1978. Accredited by NCA. Admission dates: February. Total enrollment 36; 100% of applicants accepted; 18 students per instructor; 90-95% of graduates obtain employment.

FACULTY: 3 full-time

COSTS: 1995 annual tuition was: in-state $45 per credit hour, out-of-state $295 per credit hour. Admission requirements: high school diploma or equivalent.

CONTACT: Culinary Director, Restaurant & Hotel Cookery; Hospitality Mgmt., Chippewa Valley Technical College, 620 W. Clairemont Ave., Eau Claire, WI 54701-1098; (715) 833-6200.

FOX VALLEY TECHNICAL INSTITUTE
Appleton/September-May

This independent institution offers a 2-year diploma/degree in Culinary Arts and Food Service Production. Program started 1972. Accredited by NCA. Calendar: semester. Curriculum: core. Admission dates: fall, winter. Total enrollment 100; 15 to 25 enrollees each admission period; 90% of applicants accepted; 6080% financial aid recipients; 80% under age 25; 15% age 25 to 44; 5% age 45 or over; 50% part-time students; 6 to 12 students per instructor; 100% of graduates obtain employment. Facilities: include 5 kitchens and classrooms including full quantity production kitchen, full bakery, full restaurant kitchen, and student-run restaurant.

COURSES: Quantity production, catering, restaurant cooking, baking, deli operations, and general education courses. Schedule: 7 hours per day, 4-5 days per week. Externship provided.

FACULTY: 9 full-time. Includes: R. Kimball. H. Dean, A. Exenberger, M. Davis, B. Hinsch.

COSTS: Annual tuition: in-state $1,620, out-of-state $10,000. Application fee $20. Refund policy: 100% before classes, pro-rated after classes begin. Application deadlines: August, November. Admission requirements: high school diploma or equivalent and admission test. Last year 15 scholarships awarded averaging $500; 25 loans were granted averaging $500. On-campus housing: limited spaces; average cost: $250 per month. Off-campus housing (shared apts.): $150 per month.

CONTACT: Donna Elliott, Culinary Arts Dept., Fox Valley Technical Institute, 1825 N. Bluemound Drive, Appleton, WI 54913; (414) 735-5638, Fax (414) 735-2582.

MADISON AREA TECHNICAL COLLEGE
Madison/August-May

This college offers a 2-year AAS degree in Culinary Arts. Program started 1950. Accredited by ACFEI. Calendar: semester. Admission dates: August, January. Total enrollment 60; 36 enrollees each admission period; 75% of applicants accepted; 50% financial aid recipients; 60% under age 25; 35% age 25 to 44; 5% age 45 or over; 20% part-time students; 15 students per instructor; 100% of graduates obtain employment. Facilities: include 3 large labs and classrooms.

COURSES: Baking, sanitation, nutrition, gourmet foods, decorative foods, food costs and purchasing analysis, and general education. 71 hours of culinary courses required for graduation. Schedule: Monday-Friday, 7:30 am-2:30 pm.

FACULTY: Includes: D. McNicol, M. Egan, P. Short. Qualifications: certified by state and ACFEI.

COSTS: Tuition: in-state $48.20 per credit hour. Advanced registration fee is $50. Refund policy: 80% first 14 days, 60% next 15 to 28 days. Admission requirements: high school diploma or equivalent and admission test. Last year 645 scholarships were awarded ranging from $100-$700; 3284 loans were granted, averaging $2,654. Average off-campus housing cost: $400-$870.

CONTACT: Mary G. Hill, Chairperson, Culinary Trades Dept., Madison Area Technical College, 3550 Anderson St., Madison, WI 53704; (608) 246-MENU, Fax (608) 246-6316.

MILWAUKEE AREA TECHNICAL COLLEGE
Milwaukee

This college offers a 2-year AAS degree. Program started 1955. Accredited by NCA, ACFEI. Admission dates: August, January. Total enrollment 150; 80 enrollees each admission period; 20 students per instructor; 98% of graduates obtain employment.

FACULTY: 11 full-time.

COSTS: Annual tuition: in-state $2,260, out-of-state $8,244. Admission requirements: high school diploma or equivalent and admission test.

CONTACT: Culinary Director, Culinary Arts A.A.S., Milwaukee Area Technical College, 700 West State St., Milwaukee, WI 53233; (414) 278-6255.

MORAINE PARK TECHNICAL COLLEGE
Fond du Lac/August-May

This college offers a 2-year AA degree in Culinary Arts, a 1-year vocational diploma in Food Service Production, and Culinary Basics certificate. Program started 1980. Accredited by NCA. Calendar: semester. Curriculum: core. Admission dates: July-August, November-December. Total enrollment 36; 16 enrollees each admission period; 90% of applicants accepted; 40% financial aid recipients; 20% under age 25; 65% age 25 to 44; 15% age 45 or over; 30% part-time students; 6 students per instructor; 95% of graduates obtain employment. Facilities: 3 kitchens, 2 classrooms.

COURSES: Food production, sanitation, meat analysis, restaurant management, catering. 1140 hours of culinary courses required for graduation. Other Required courses: various general education (270 hours). Continuing education: school food service, deli-bakery, IDDA certification.

FACULTY: 3 full-time, 2 part-time.

COSTS: Tuition: for the Culinary Arts degree is $2,511 per year, $1,260 for the certificate program, and $2,470 for the 1-year diploma. Application deadlines: May. Admission requirements: high school diploma, placement test, and interview. Last year 3 scholarships were awarded averaging $500; 6 loans were granted averaging $950. Off-campus housing cost: $300 per month.

CONTACT: Lyle Mercer, Associate Dean, Service Occupations, 235 North National Ave., P.O. Box 1940, Fond du Lac, WI 54936-1940; (414) 924-3269, Fax (414) 929-2478.

NICOLET AREA TECHNICAL COLLEGE
Rhinelander

CONTACT: Lyle Greuning, Coordinator, Hospital Management, Nicolet Area Technical College, P.O. Box 518, Rhinelander, WI 54501; (715) 369-4410.

THE POSTILION SCHOOL OF CULINARY ART
Fond du Lac/Year-round

Madame Liane Kuony offers a diploma course consisting of four 100-hour participation sessions that emphasize classic French technique, economy, and building a chef's larder. Founded in 1951. Accredited by the State of Wisconsin. Class size limited to 8 students. Facilities: the professionally constructed teaching kitchen of a Victorian home.

COURSES: The diploma course consists of 2 weeks (100 hours minimum) each of basic, advanced, menu planning, and cost accounting. A catering course is optional. Other courses: professional pastry, butchering, sausage making, ice cream.

FACULTY: Owner/instructor Mme. Kuony was educated in Belgium, France, and Switzerland.

COSTS: Each 2-week segment is $1,600, which includes meals. Students must begin with the basic class, regardless of experience. A nonrefundable $200 registration fee and a $300 deposit are required with enrollment, with the $1,100 balance due on the date of entry. Class dates are announced at the beginning of the year. Inexpensive lodging is available at nearby motels.

LOCATION: On the south side of Fond du Lac at the southern tip of Lake Winnebago, about an hour from Milwaukee and 120 miles from Chicago.

CONTACT: Mme. Liane Kuony, The Postilion School of Culinary Art, 220 Old Pioneer Rd., Fond du Lac, WI 54935; (414) 922-4170.

WAUKESHA COUNTY TECHNICAL COLLEGE
Pewaukee/September-May

This college offers a 1-year diploma and 2-year associate degree in Culinary Arts, and a 3-year ACF apprenticeship in Culinary Management. Program started 1971. Accredited by NCA, ACFEI. Calendar: quarter, semester. Curriculum: core. Admission dates: August, January. Total enrollment

38; 30 enrollees each admission period; 100% of applicants accepted; 10% financial aid recipients; 60% under age 25; 35% age 25 to 44; 5% age 45 or over; 20% part-time students; 12 students per instructor; 95% of graduates obtain employment. Facilities: include 3 kitchens, 4 classrooms, bar lab, restaurant and computer lab.

Courses: Technical culinary arts training and principles of business management. 68 hours of culinary courses required for graduation. Externship: semester, working under certified ACF chef.

Faculty: 3 full-time, 3 part-time. Includes: James Holden, CEC, CCE, Timothy Graham, CFBE, FMP, Phil Lowry, CHA, Keith Owsiany, Michael Leitzke, CEC. Qualifications: All have college degrees and industry experience.

Costs: Annual tuition: in-state $50 per credit hour, out-of-state $80 per credit hour. Cutlery $150, uniforms $100. Refund policy: 80% within 60 days. Application deadlines: August. Last year 6 scholarships were awarded averaging $500. Part-time employment is available.

Contact: William R. Griesemer, Associate Dean, Center for Hospitality Mgmt. & Culinary Arts Studies, Waukesha County Technical College, 800 Main St., Pewaukee, WI 53072; (414) 691-5254, Fax (414) 691-5190.

AUSTRALIA

CANBERRA INSTITUTE OF TECHNOLOGY
Canberra City

This institution offers a 3-year diploma and a 3-year part-time trade certificate. Program started 1992. Calendar: semester. Curriculum: core. Admission dates: February, July. Total enrollment 450; 25% of applicants accepted; 75% under age 25; 20% age 25 to 44; 5% age 45 or over; 15 students per instructor; 100% of graduates obtain employment. Facilities: 6 kitchens, 4 restaurants, computer lab, butchery, bakery, bars.

Faculty: 30 full-time, 50 part-time. Qualifications: industry and educational.

Contact: Pam Robertson, Head, Hospitality & Travel, School of Tourism and Hospitality, Canberra Institute of Technology, P.O. Box 826, Canberra City 2601, Australia; (61) 6-273125, Fax (61) 6-2073209.

COLLEGE OF TOURISM AND HOSPITALITY
South Brisbane, Queensland

Contact: Christine French, Director, College of Tourism and Hospitality, Corner Merivale and Tribune Sts., South Brisbane, QLD 4101, Australia; (61) 7-8402911.

CROW'S NEST COLLEGE OF TAFE
Sydney, New South Wales/February-November

This college offers 1-year certificate and diploma hospitality courses. Program started 1989. Curriculum: core. Admission dates: January. Total enrollment 135; 8% financial aid recipients; 80% under age 25; 20% age 25 to 44; 40% part-time students; 80% of graduates obtain employment. Facilities: include 3 kitchens, 4 classrooms and commercial bar.

Faculty: 10 full-time, 12 part-time.

Costs: A$150 per year. Refund 3 weeks prior to admission.

Contact: Joan Davis, Tourism & Hospitality, Crow's Nest College of Tafe, West St., Crows Nest, Sydney, New South Wales, Australia; (61) 2-9654434, Fax (61) 2-9654408.

AUSTRALIA

DANDENONG COLLEGE
Dandenong

This institution offers a 3-year diploma. Program started 1986. Accredited by State. Admission dates: February. Total enrollment 200; 20% of applicants accepted; 15 to 20 students per instructor; 100% of graduates obtain employment.

FACULTY: 20 full-time, 10 part-time.

COSTS: 1995 tuition was: in-state A$0, out-of-state A$7,000. Admission requirements: high school diploma or equivalent.

CONTACT: George Hill, Head of Department, Hospitality Studies, Dandenong College, 21 Stud Rd., Dandenong VIC 3175, Australia; (61) 3-7975610, Fax (61) 3-7975458.

WILLIAM ANGLISS COLLEGE
Melbourne/Year-round *(See also page 229)*

This career college specializing in the hospitality, travel and food industries offers certificate programs in Commercial Cookery and Advanced Culinary Skills, and an associate diploma and diploma in Hospitality. Program started 1943. Accredited by National, state, and local. Admission dates: every 1 or 2 months for commercial cookery, 3 times a year for cookery, February and July for advanced certificate course. Total enrollment 3,700; 90% part-time students; 15 students per instructor; Facilities: a $15 million teaching facility with well-equipped bakeries, 6 kitchens, 3 restaurants, bars, computer rooms, butchery and confectionery centers.

COURSES: Cookery, culinary skills, hospitality. Apprenticeship: 3-4-years in breadmaking and baking, pastry, cookery and butchering. Continuing education: short evening courses in cooking and wine.

FACULTY: More than 60 full-time.

COSTS: Courses vary in cost. Cookery open to applicants over 18. Admission requirements: advanced certificate open to those who have completed an apprenticeship.

CONTACT: Chris Coates, Associate Director, William Angliss College, 555 La Trobe St., P.O. Box 4052, Melbourne VIC 3000, Australia; (61) 3-9606211l, Fax (61) 3-96701330.

CANADA

ALGONQUIN COLLEGE
Nepean, Ontario/Year-round

This college offers a 2-year diploma in Culinary Management, a 1-year certificate in Cook Training, and a 40-week certificate in Baking Techniques. Program started 1960. Calendar: semester. Curriculum: core. Admission dates: September, January. Total enrollment 140; 90/50 enrollees each admission period; 50% of applicants accepted; 71% under age 25; 25% age 25 to 44; 4% age 45 or over; 15 to 20 students per instructor; 90% of graduates obtain employment. Facilities: include 2 production kitchens and 3 demonstration labs.

COURSES: Baking, menu planning, food demonstration & applications, storeroom procedures, institutional cooking, business management. 1,500 hours of culinary courses required for graduation. Schedule: 25 hours per week, 8 am-10 pm. Continuing education: cake decorating, bread baking, Italian regional cooking.

FACULTY: 5 full-time, 5 part-time. Includes: Philippe Dubout, Mike Durrer, Serge Desforges, Alain Peyrun-Berron, Roger Souffez, Alan Fleming.

COSTS: Annual tuition: in-state C$560 per semester, out-of-state C$7,365. Books, supplies, uniforms: C$850. Application deadlines: March 1. Admission requirements: secondary school diploma or 19 years of age. Part-time employment is available.

CAREER/PROFESSIONAL **CANADA** **113**

CONTACT: Admissions Office, Algonquin College, 1385 Woodroffe Ave., Nepean, Ontario K2G 1V8, Canada; (800) 565-4723 or (613) 727-0002, Fax (613) 727-7632.

CANADORE COLLEGE OF APPLIED ARTS & TECHNOLOGY
North Bay, Ontario/September-April

This college offers a 2-year diploma in Culinary Management. Program started 1984. Accredited by Canadian Federation of Chefs de Cuisine. Calendar: semester. Curriculum: core. Admission dates: September. Total enrollment 50; 35 enrollees each admission period; 10% of applicants accepted; 75% financial aid recipients; 84% under age 25; 15% age 25 to 44; 1% age 45 or over; 10% part-time students; 20 students per instructor; 90-100% of graduates obtain employment. Facilities: include kitchen with specialized equipment and restaurant.

COURSES: Food preparation, baking, sanitation, food and beverage management, nutrition, wines, contemporary cuisine, cost control, menu planning, quantity cooking, garde manger, international cuisine. Schedule: 28 hours per week, 8 months per year; part-time options available. Externship provided.

FACULTY: 8 full-time.

COSTS: Annual tuition: in state C$1,008, foreign C$8,375. Admission requirements: high school diploma or equivalent.

CONTACT: Neil E. Cornthwaite, Coordinator, School of Hospitality & Tourism, Canadore College of Applied Arts & Technology, 100 College Dr., P.O. Box 5001, North Bay, Ontario P1B 8K9, Canada; (705) 474-7600, Fax (705) 494-7462.

DUBRULLE FRENCH CULINARY SCHOOL
(See also page 232)   **Vancouver, British Columbia/Year-round**

This private school offers two 17-week diploma programs: Professional Culinary Training and Professional Pastry & Desserts. Established in 1982. Certified by the Ministry of Labour under the Private Trade Schools Act. Continuous enrollment: January, May, September. The 6,000-square-foot facility has classrooms and 3 teaching kitchens with fully-equipped working stations and student dining areas.

COURSES: Emphasis is on classic French methods and techniques; 80% practical, 20% theory. Accreditation may be given towards the B.C. Apprenticeship program. Schedule: Monday through Friday, 30 hours per week, day and evening.

FACULTY: Classically-trained chefs.

COSTS: Each course fee is C$6,450. Canadian Student loans are available. Non-residents can obtain a student visa. Accommodation assistance is provided.

LOCATION: A block from Broadway and Granville, 3 hours from Seattle.

CONTACT: Sue Singer, Registrar, Dubrulle French Culinary School, 1522 W. 8th Ave., Vancouver, BC, V6J 4R8, Canada; (604) 738-3155 or (800) 667-7288, Fax (604) 738-3205.

GEORGE BROWN COLLEGE OF APPLIED ARTS & TECHNOLOGY
(See also page 232)   **Toronto/Year-round**

This institution's School of Hospitality offers 20 one- and two-year full-time certificate and diploma programs and 30 part-time programs per year. Full-time culinary courses include the 2-year Culinary Management, the 1-year Pre-Employment Chef Training, the 1-year Baking Techniques, General Food Preparation, Professional Sommelier and Chinese Cooking. Established in 1965. Admission dates September, January. Total enrollment 2,000 for full-time programs, 4,000 part-time. Financial assistance available to Canadian citizens and residents; 95% of graduates obtain employment. Facilities include 12 laboratories, each with 24 individual work stations; demonstration areas with overhead mirrors.

COURSES: Culinary Management covers food preparation and presentation to international standards. Pre-Employment Chef Training includes theory classes, demonstrations by experienced chefs, and preparation of dishes served in the college's open-to-the-public student training restaurant. Baking Techniques covers breads, pastries, cakes, and decorating. Part-time courses include Small Quantity Food, Vegetarian Cooking, and Junior Gourmet. Schedule: Full-time programs meet 5 days per week; most part-time programs meet 1 evening per week for 10 weeks.

FACULTY: The 80 faculty members are professors, most holding Master Chef, Master Patissier, or Chef de Cuisine certification. All have at least 5 years industry experience.

COSTS: Resident (nonresident) tuition for most diploma programs is approximately C$1,150 (C$8,000) for 32 weeks; for certificate programs it's $C26 (C$250) per week; Senior citizen resident tuition is C$50 per part-time course. Cancellation penalty is C$50 (C$416) for full-time programs with 2 weeks notice, C$15 for part-time programs. Minimum requirement for admission to a diploma program is an Ontario Secondary School Diploma or an equivalent from within North America. Furnished room averages C$75-C$125 per week.

LOCATION: The 4-story facility, completed in 1987, is at 300 Adelaide St. E. at the college's St. James campus.

CONTACT: Information Services, George Brown College, P.O. Box 1015, Station B, Toronto, ON, M5T 2T9, Canada; (800) 263-8995 or (416) 867-2225; Fax (416) 867-2501.

GEORGIAN COLLEGE OF APPLIED ARTS AND TECHNOLOGY
Barrie, Ontario/September-April

This college offers a 2-year diploma in Culinary Management. Program started 1988. Calendar: semester. Curriculum: core. Admission dates: August. Total enrollment 45; 24 enrollees each admission period; 50% of applicants accepted; 24 students per instructor; 100% of graduates obtain employment. Facilities: include 1 large-quantity kitchen, 2 small-quantity kitchens, bake lab, classrooms, and student-run restaurant.

COURSES: Bake theory/lab, menu planning, food/beverage control, creative cuisine. Externship provided. Post-graduate study available: Rochester Institute of Technology and Ryerson University.

FACULTY: 7 full-time, 1 to 2 part-time.

COSTS: Annual tuition: in-country C$1,109, out-of-country C$9,215. Application fee C$25. Application deadlines: March until program full. Admission requirements: high school diploma or equivalent. Last year 7 scholarships were awarded. On-campus housing: 252 spaces; average cost: C$400 per month. Average off-campus housing cost: C$400-800. Part-time employment available.

LOCATION: The 7-building, 3,500-student campus is in an urban/rural area.

CONTACT: Bill Gordon, Academic Director, School of Hospitality & Tourism, Georgian College of Applied Arts and Technology, One Georgian Dr., Barrie, ON, L4M 3X9, Canada; (705) 722-1592, Fax (705) 722-5123.

HUMBER COLLEGE OF APPLIED ARTS & TECHNOLGOY
Etobicoke, Ontario

This institution offers a 1-year certificate, 2-year diploma, and a 3-year AS degree. Program started 1975. Admission dates: September, January. Total enrollment 150; 20 students per instructor; 95% of graduates obtain employment.

COURSES: Externship provided.

FACULTY: 14 full-time, 5 part-time.

COSTS: Annual tuition: in-state C$900, foreign C$5,000. Admission requirements: high school diploma or equivalent and admission test.

CAREER/PROFESSIONAL   CANADA

CONTACT: John Walker, Chairman, School of Hospitality, Tourism & Leisure, Humber College of Applied Arts & Technology, 205 Humber College Blvd., Etobicoke, ON, M9W 5L7, Canada; (416) 675-3111, Fax (416) 675-9730.

LE CORDON BLEU PARIS COOKING SCHOOL
(See also page 234)
Ottawa, Ontario/Year-round

This private school offers 12-week certificate courses in French cuisine and pastry, 1-day to 1-month intensives, and specialized evening programs. Operated since 1988 by Le Cordon Bleu-Paris. Calendar: trimester. Curriculum: culinary. Admission dates January, April, July, September. Total enrollment 150 maximum per year; approximately 35 enrollees each admission period; 90% of applicants accepted; 30% under age 25; 40% ages 25 to 44; 15% age 45 and over; 15% part-time (evening) students; 12 to 1 student to faculty ratio; 90% of graduates obtain jobs. Facilities include a demonstration room and a fully-equipped kitchen with individual work spaces and specialized equipment.

COURSES: Basic and Intermediate Cuisine, Basic and Advanced Pastry. Students who wish to receive the Cuisine/Pastry Diplomas or Le Grand Diplome can complete the Superior Cuisine and/or Patisserie courses at Le Cordon Bleu in Paris or London. Schedule: 20 hours per week for full-time classes; customized intensives are available.

FACULTY: All French chefs trained in France. Director is Gerard L. Breissan. Instructors are professional master chefs Philippe Guiet, Jean-Claude Petibon, and pastry chef Michel Denis.

COSTS: Tuition is C$4,500 for Basic Cuisine, C$4,850 for Intermediate Cuisine, C$3,950 for Basic Pastry, and C$4,500 for Advanced Pastry. A C$450 deposit is required; balance due 4 weeks prior. Cancellations 6 weeks prior forfeit C$200. Lodging ranges from C$600-C$1,200.

LOCATION: Chateau Royale Professional Building, about 20 minutes from downtown Ottawa.

CONTACT: Gerard L. Breissan, Le Cordon Bleu Paris Cooking School, 1390 Prince of Wales Dr., #400, Ottawa, ON, K2C 3N6, Canada; (613) 224-8603, Fax (613) 224-9966.

MCCALL'S SCHOOL OF CAKE DECORATION, INC.
(See also page 235)
Etobicoke, Ontario/September-May

This school offers full-time certificate courses in baking, commercial cake decorating (10 days each), and Swiss chocolate techniques (5 days), as well as programs for all levels. Class size is limited to 10 students. Facilities: the 1,000 square feet of teaching space include overhead mirrors and two 20-seat classrooms.

FACULTY: Includes school director Nick McCall, Klara Johnston, and Kay Wong.

COSTS: Professional courses range from C$480-C$700. A 50% deposit is required. Cancellations 1 week prior forfeit 10%.

LOCATION: A western subdivision of Toronto.

CONTACT: McCall's School of Cake Decoration, Inc., 3810 Bloor St. W., Etobicoke, ON, M9B 6C2, Canada; (416) 231-8040, Fax (416) 231-9956.

NIAGARA COLLEGE HOSPITALITY AND TOURISM CENTRE
Niagara Falls/September-June

This college of applied arts and technology offers 3-year cook and baker apprenticeship training and a 2-year diploma in Culinary Skills. Program started 1989. Calendar: semester. Admission dates September, January. Total enrollment 120; 72 and 20 enrollees each admission period, respectively; 50% of applicants accepted; 60% financial aid recipients; 75% under age 25; 20% age 25 to 44; 5% age 45 or over; 24 students per instructor; 100% of graduates obtain employment. Facilities include a production kitchen, baking lab, mixology lab, computer lab, 3 food labs, lecture theatre, learning resource center, and 90-seat student-operated restaurant.

COURSES: The 6,000-hour apprenticeships, administered by the Ministry of Education and Training, include 700 hours of instruction and 5,300 hours as a salaried trainee in a foodservice establishment. The Culinary Skills program covers food theory and preparation, kitchen management, nutrition, sanitation, and general education courses. Schedule: 21 hours per week. Students must complete an approved summer work experience. A variety of continuing education courses are available.

FACULTY: Includes 6 full- and 4 part-time instructors. Chef professors are all Certified Chefs de Cuisine.

COSTS: Annual tuition is C$1,312 for Canadian residents, C$7,750 for non-residents. A C$50 application fee and C$735 equipment fee are required. Withdrawals within 10 class days of start of term receive refund less C$50. Admission deadlines are April 15 and November 15. Applicants must have a secondary school diploma or equivalent. Last year 2 scholarships were awarded averaging C$500 each. Part-time employment is available. Off-campus lodging ranges from C$90-C$100 per week.

LOCATION: Niagara Falls City.

CONTACT: David Davies, Niagara College of Applied Arts and Technology, Hospitality and Tourism Centre, 5881 Dunn St., Niagara Falls, ON, L2G 2N8, Canada; (416) 374-7454, ext. 3600, Fax (416) 374-1116.

ST. CLAIR COLLEGE
Windsor/September-April

This college offers a 4-semester diploma in Culinary Arts. Program started 1993. Accredited by Province of Ontario. Calendar: semester. Curriculum: core culinary. Admission dates: September. Total enrollment 80; 40 enrollees each admission period; 75% of applicants accepted; 50% financial aid recipients; 75% under age 25; 22 to 25 students per instructor; 98% of graduates obtain employment. Facilities: include 4 kitchens and classrooms, 140 seat restaurant.

COURSES: Culinary arts, food preparation, culinary practice, hospitality marketing, nutrition & menu writing, garde manger, management techniques. Schedule: 20 hours per week, 10 months per year. Externship: 16-week, 7 hours per week, in hotels and restaurants. Continuing education: bartending.

FACULTY: 3 full-time. Includes: M. Crouisier, R. Schindler, G. Van Blommestien.

COSTS: Annual tuition: in-state C$1,200, out-of-state C$5,000. Last year 8 scholarships and bursarys were awarded, averaging $350. Part-time employment is available.

LOCATION: An urban setting, 2 hours from London, Ontario.

CONTACT: Diane Fisher, Chairperson, Business Hospitality Department, St. Clair College, 2000 Talbot Road W., Windsor, ON N9A 6S4, Canada; (519) 972-2727, Fax (519) 972-0801.

SOUTHERN ALBERTA INSTITUTE OF TECHNOLOGY
Calgary, Alberta/Year-round

This nonprofit institution offers a 1-year diploma in Professional Cooking and 3-8 week Apprentice Cooking sessions. Program started 1949. Calendar: semester. Curriculum: core. Admission dates: September, January, May (plus November and March for Apprentice). Total enrollment 195 (professional), 216 (apprentice); 65 (professional) and 48 (apprentice) enrollees each admission period; 30% of applicants accepted; 50% financial aid recipients; 15 students per instructor; 99% of graduates obtain employment. Facilities: include 4 large commercial kitchens, 2 commercial bakeries, 2 lab and 7 demonstration classrooms, dining room, 1 computer lab, 2 lecture classrooms, ice plant.

COURSES: Include garde manger, patisserie, kitchen management, fat and ice sculpting. 1,328 hours of culinary courses required for graduation. Other required courses: include breakfast and short order cooking, technical writing, meat portioning. Schedule: 30 hours per week. Continuing education: includes bar mixology, bed & breakfast, fusion cooking.

FACULTY: 31 full-time, 4 part-time. Includes: Helmut Schoderbock, Ian Neilson, Otto Daniels, Gerd Steinmeyer, Fred Malley. Qualifications: Journeymans and Red Seal in Cooking.

COSTS: Tuition: C$1,783; other fees: C$1,073. Application deadlines: accepted year-round. Admission requirements: applicants must submit a transcript, resume and statement of career goals. Last year 32 scholarships were awarded averaging C$500; 90 loans were granted. On-campus housing: 204 spaces; average cost: C$7-C$12 per day. Average off-campus housing cost: C$400-500.

CONTACT: Reg Hendrickson, Dean, Hospitality Careers Dept., Southern Alberta Institute of Technology, 1301 16th Ave. N.W., Calgary, AB T2M 0L4, Canada; (403) 298-8612, Fax (403) 284-7034.

STRATFORD CHEF'S SCHOOL
Stratford, Ontario/November-March

This nonprofit school offers a 2-semester full-time apprenticeship diploma. Program started 1983. Province of Ontario accreditation as Journeyman available upon passing exam. Calendar: semester. Curriculum: culinary. Admission dates: November. Total enrollment 65; 30-35 enrollees each admission period; 25% of applicants accepted; 100% of graduates obtain employment.

COURSES: Gastronomy, nutrition, food styling, wine appreciation, kitchen management, menu preparation, food costing. Other Required courses: 2nd-year students research, prepare and serve theme menus in a restaurant setting. Schedule: 45 hours per week. Externship provided.

FACULTY: 14 full-time. Founders/Directors are restaurateurs Eleanore Kane and James Harris.

COSTS: Annual tuition: C$1,750 for Ontario residents, C$10,00 for others. $300 deposit due 30 days after acceptance. Average off-campus housing cost: $300-400 per month.

LOCATION: A small town, 90 minutes from Toronto.

CONTACT: Elisabeth Lorimer, Programme Administrator, Stratford Chef's School, 150 Huron St., Stratford, ON, N0K 1N0, Canada; (519) 271-1414, Fax (519) 271-5679.

UNIVERSITY COLLEGE OF THE CARIBOO
Kamloops, British Columbia/September-May

This college offers a 12-month certificate in Culinary Arts. Program started 1972. Calendar: 9 months. Curriculum: culinary only. Admission dates: September, November, March. Total enrollment 50; 16 enrollees each admission period; 80% of applicants accepted; 40% financial aid recipients; 50% under age 25; 50% age 25 to 44; 12 students per instructor; 75% of graduates obtain employment. Facilities: include 4 kitchens and classrooms and dining room.

COURSES: Schedule: 30 hours per week.

FACULTY: 6 full-time.

COSTS: Annual tuition: C$1,460. Application fee C$15, student fees C$428. Admission requirements: high school diploma or equivalent. Last year 4 scholarships were awarded averaging C$250; 2 loans were granted. Average on-campus housing cost: C$195 per month. Average off-campus housing cost: C$250 per month. Part-time employment is available.

CONTACT: Kurt Zwingli, Department Chair, Food Training/Tourism, University College of the Cariboo, Box 3010, Kamloops, British Columbia, BC V2C 5N3, Canada; (604) 828-5353, Fax (604) 371-5677.

ENGLAND

BONNE BOUCHE
Devon/Year-round *(See also page 237)*

This private school offers 4-week Bonne Bouche Professional Certificate programs in Catering and Hospitality, an extended Diploma course, and state recognized Vocational Qualifications in Food Preparation & Cooking. Program started 1987. Accredited by National Council for Vocational Qualifications (NVQ). Curriculum: culinary. Admission dates 5 times per year. Total enrollment 30; 6 enrollees each admission period; 85% of applicants accepted; 66% financial aid recipients; 30% under age 25; 50% age 25 to 44; 20% age 45 or over; 6 students per instructor; 100% of graduates obtain employment. Facilities include a working kitchen, demonstration kitchen, lecture room, and wine and food book and video library.

COURSES: Hands-on instruction in the 200-hour certificate program covers all key preparation and cooking techniques, wines, table decoration, business management, and classic, contemporary, vegetarian, and ethnic cuisines. Continuing education courses range from 8 to 40 hours and include food hygiene, such advanced techniques as patisserie and doughs and breads, and specialized cuisines.

FACULTY: The 2 full- and 3 part-time instructors are Anne Nicholls, senior tutor, program coordinator, and NVQ assessor; Gerald Nicholls, business management and internal NVQ verifier; Moira Clarke, food hygiene; Sonia Stevenson, fish and sauces; and Sri Owen, southeast Asian.

COSTS: Range from approximately £1,550-£2,000, including double occupancy lodging and meals (single supplement available). A 25% deposit is required. Last year 30 state awards were granted to appropriate students at an average of £400 each. Local Bed and Breakfasts start at £15 per person per night.

LOCATION: A 16th-century Devon longhouse on 3-acre grounds with gardens, fitness center, croquet lawn; other sports facilities nearby. The rural setting, close to historic sites, is 30 minutes from Exeter and 2 hours from London.

CONTACT: Anne Nicholls, Program Coordinator, Bonne Bouche, Lower Beers House, Brithem Bottom, Cullompton, Devon, EX15 1NB, England; (44) 1884-32257 (phone/fax).

CAKE ICING COURSE
York/Year-round

Audrée Massey offers 4-day courses (limit 4 students) that combine 3 days of demonstrations and practical work in sugarpaste icing with 1 day free for sightseeing. Established in 1985. Facilities include individual work areas and specialized equipment.

FACULTY: Audrée Massey, a qualified home ec. teacher, learned sugarpaste icing in Australia.

COSTS: The £450 cost includes meals and lodging at a Yorkshire farmhouse. A nonrefundable £100 deposit must accompany reservation with balance due on arrival.

LOCATION: Dunnington, 3 miles from York.

CONTACT: Audrée Massey, The Icing Parlour, Chippings, Greenside, Dunnington, York, YO1 5NJ, England; (44) 904 489474.

COOKERY AT THE GRANGE
Frome, Somerset/Year-round

This private school offers 4-week Basics to Béarnaise Certificate course and 1 to 2-week Cooks Refresher (February only). Founded 1981. Curriculum: culinary. Rolling admission. 14 to 16 enrollees each admission period; 65% under age 25; 25% age 25 to 44; 10% age 45 or over; 85% of graduates obtain employment. Facilities: main kitchen, preparation room, herb garden.

COURSES: The 4-week Basics to Béarnaise course takes the student through the methods and principles of cookery. Emphasis is on recipe reading, including omissions and substitutions, shortcuts, pastry and breads, and a variety of cuisines. Schedule: 7 hours daily, Monday through Friday.

FACULTY: Robin Witt and teaching staff.

COSTS: Cost for Basics to Béarnaise, including meals and double occupancy housing, is £1,510 to £1,650; Cooks Refresher is £390 for one week, £720 for two weeks. A nonrefundable £150 deposit is required, balance is due 6 weeks prior. Fees are inclusive of VAT. Students are lodged at The Grange in 2 double bedrooms and at a nearby farmhouse. Single room supplement is £30 per week. Nonresident students (£30 per week less) stay for dinner.

LOCATION: The Grange, situated in a converted coach house in a vineyard in rural England, is 90 minutes from London by train.

CONTACT: Hilary McFarland, Administrator, Cookery at The Grange, Whatley Vineyard, Frome, Somerset, BA11 3LA, England; Tel/Fax (44) 1373 836579.

THE CORDON VERT COOKERY SCHOOL
Altrincham, Cheshire/Year-round

The Vegetarian Society UK, a registered charity and membership organization four 1-week Foundation Courses leading to the Cordon Vert Diploma, a 4-day professional course leading to the Professional Cordon Vert Diploma, and a variety of classes and courses for cooking enthusiasts (page 238).

COURSES: Basic and advanced techniques of vegetarian cookery, international cuisines.

FACULTY: Sarah Brown began the courses in 1982, based on her BBC-TV series, *Vegetarian Kitchen*. Tutors include Ursula Ferrigno, Rachel Tyldsley, Lyn Weller, and Deborah Clarke.

COSTS: Range from £255 nonresident (£315 resident)-£260 (£320) for Foundation Courses; professional courses are £420. Resident tuition includes full board and lodging in twin-bedded rooms in the school's Lodge. A nonrefundable deposit is required. Credit cards accepted.

LOCATION: Ten miles south of Manchester.

CONTACT: Heather Mairs, The Cordon Vert Cookery School, The Vegetarian Society, Parkdale, Dunham Rd., Altrincham, Cheshire, WA14 4QG, England; (44) 161-928-0793; Fax (44) 161-926-9182.

EASTBOURNE COLLEGE OF FOOD AND FASHION
East Sussex/September-July

This private school offers a 1-year diploma course, a 10-week intensive cookery certificate course, a 10-week intensive sugarcraft course, and a 10-week advanced cordon bleu certificate course for girls. Established in 1907 and recognized as efficient by the British Accreditation Council. Admission dates April and September. Class size limited to 12. Facilities include 7 specially-equipped teaching kitchens and a student-run restaurant.

COURSES: Include basic and international cuisines, wines, catering, dress and fashion, typing, home and consumer studies, flower arranging, child care, and first aid. The advanced course covers famous chef methods, advanced pastry, cake decoration, and restaurant presentation. During an optional Paris trip, students work in a fine restaurant and visit markets, food companies, and restaurant kitchens. Schedule: 9 am to 4 pm, Monday through Friday.

FACULTY: Principal Janet E. Jenion, recipient of the La Varenne Advanced Certificate, and a staff of qualified specialist teachers.

COSTS: Costs are £2,750 (£2,000 nonresident) per term for the 1-year course, £2,990 (£2,200) for the intensive, £3,000 (£2,500) for the advanced course. A £50 nonrefundable fee must accompany application. The College provides residential lodging.

LOCATION: In the seaside town of Eastbourne, an 80-minute drive from London.

CONTACT: Eastbourne College of Food and Fashion, 1 Silverdale Rd., Eastbourne BN20 7AA, England; (44) 323-730851; Fax (44) 323-416924.

ELISABETH RUSSELL
London/January-June, September-November

This private school offers a 5-week certificate course, a 10-week diploma course, and 4-week courses for those with basic cookery knowledge. Program started 1963. 6-8 students per class.

COURSES: French cookery suitable for home, entertaining, and chalets. Schedule: 10 am to 4 pm, Monday-Thursday.

FACULTY: Eve Pilon, who has taught for 20 years and consults for food firms, and Ann Russell, daughters of Elisabeth Russell.

COSTS, ACCOMMODATIONS: Tuition is £850 for 5 weeks, £1,620 for 10 weeks. Nonrefundable enrollment fee is £30, tuition is due 3 weeks prior; full refund 5 weeks prior. Lodging is available with nearby families.

CONTACT: Elisabeth Russell, Flat 5, 18 The Grange, Wimbledon, London, SW19 4PS, England; (44) 181-947-2144.

LE CORDON BLEU
London/Year-round *(See also page 241)*

This private school offers 30-week diploma and 5- and 10-week certificate courses in French Cuisine and Pastry, a 10-week summer program for hospital management students, a 5-week catering program, 3- to 5-day hands-on workshops, and evening sessions (page 241). Founded in 1933 and acquired by Le Cordon Bleu-Paris (page 126,251) in 1990. Calendar: quarter. Curriculum: culinary. Facilities: similar to a fine restaurant with kitchens designed to the cuisine requirements; individual work areas with specialized appliances; 2 demonstration theatres with overhead mirrors and video.

Courses: The diploma curricula consist of 3 levels of Cuisine or 3 levels of Pastry certificate courses, taken consecutively or together. Courses cover basic to complex techniques, restaurant-quality dishes, and oenology. Schedule: day sessions begin at 9 am, 1:30 pm or 4:30 pm; Basic Cuisine and Intermediate Pastry can be taken as 5-week intensives, and Initiation to French Cuisine and Pastry in 4 weeks.

FACULTY: School directors are Lesley Gray and Susan Eckstein. The culinary staff consists of French and British Master Chefs from Michelin-starred and other fine establishments. Chef exchanges with Le Cordon Bleu-Paris are possible.

COSTS: Tuition ranges from approximately £3,200- £3,800 for the Cuisine courses, £2,350- £2,750 for the Patisserie courses. A 10% deposit is required and is refundable, less 10% (50%) for written cancellations received 4 (less than 4) weeks prior. Fees include VAT and are payable in sterling unless other arrangements are made. A limited number of working scholarships are available. A list of accommodations is provided.

LOCATION: In London's West End, close to Oxford and Bond streets.

CONTACT: Le Cordon Bleu, 114 Marylebone Lane, London, W1M 6HH, England: (44) 171-935-3503, Fax (44) 171-935-7621. In the U.S.: (800) 457-CHEF.

CAREER/PROFESSIONAL ENGLAND

LEITH'S SCHOOL OF FOOD AND WINE
(See also page 241) **London/October-June**

This private school offers a 1-year diploma consisting of three 10- to 11-week certificate courses, a 10-session restaurant management course, and an advanced wine certificate. Nonprofessional courses also offered (page 241). Founded 1975. Calendar: semester. Admission date: October. 96 enrollees each admission period; 99% of interviewed applicants accepted; 40% under age 25; 55% ages 25-44; 5% age 45 or over; 8 students per instructor; 90% of graduates obtain employment. Facilities include 3 kitchens and demonstration theatre. Career planning and placement available.

COURSES: The Beginner's, Intermediate, and Advanced Certificate in Food and Wine courses run consecutively. Basic cookery methods are taught in the Beginners' course; Intermediate course covers butchery, exotic fish, and commercial catering; Advanced course covers boned poultry dishes, aspics, advanced patisserie, and exotic canapes. Schedule: 10 am-4:30 pm, Monday-Friday.

FACULTY: School founder Prue Leith is a former Veuve Cliquot Business Woman of the Year, Chairman of the Restaurant Association of Great Britain, and has written cookbooks and appeared on TV and radio. The 17 full- and part-time faculty include principals Caroline Waldegrave and Fiona Burrell.

COSTS: Tuition ranges from £2,800-£3,150 per course, the cost for all 3 is £8,250. A £100-£200 deposit is required; equipment fee is £200. All prices include VAT. The school assists in obtaining lodging, which ranges from £80 to £120 per week.

LOCATION: A refurbished Victorian building in Kensington, the center of London.

CONTACT: Judy Van DerSande, Registrar, Leith's School of Food and Wine, 21 St. Alban's Grove, London, W8 5BP, England; (44) 81-2290177; Fax (44) 81-937-0257.

THE MANOR SCHOOL OF FINE CUISINE
(See also page 242) **Widmerpool, Nottinghamshire/Year-round**

This proprietary institution offers a 4-week certificate in Cordon Bleu cookery. Established in 1988. Calendar: 4 weeks. Curriculum: culinary. Rolling admission. Eight enrollees each admission period; 90% of applicants accepted; 5% financial aid recipients; 40% under age 25; 30% age 25 to 44; 30% age 45 or over; 60% part-time students; 8 students per instructor. Facilities include 6 kitchens, lecture room, large dining room, and cooking library.

COURSES: Include cuisine preparation, baking, basic nutrition, and menu planning. Schedule: Monday through Friday.

FACULTY: Principal Claire Gentinetta earned the Cordon Bleu Diploma, served as head chef of noted restaurants, and is a member of the Cookery and Food Association, Craft Guild of Chefs, and Chefs and Cooks Circle.

COSTS: Resident (nonresident) tuition is £1,162.07 (£1,044.57). A nonrefundable deposit of £100 is required, balance is due 6 weeks prior; refund with 6 weeks written notice. Residents are housed in The Manor (except weekends). Recommendations are provided for local lodging.

LOCATION: The Manor, a newly refurbished 17th century coaching inn, is 9 miles from Nottingham City center and 80 minutes from London's Kings Cross train station.

CONTACT: The Manor School of Fine Cuisine, Old Melton Rd, Widmerpool, Nottinghamshire NG12 5QL, England; (44) 1949 81371.

OXFORD SYMPOSIUM ON FOOD & COOKERY
University of Oxford/Fall

This annual 2-day weekend academic program focuses on a specific theme (Cooks and Others in 1995). Attendees are invited to submit papers, which are presented and discussed by participants.

COSTS: Tuition, which covers lunches and distribution of papers, is £45 for one, £72 for two, £25 for students. A $40 ($62 for two) deposit is required.

LOCATION: St. Antony's College, University of Oxford.

CONTACT: Harlan Walker, Oxford Symposium on Food & Cookery, 294 Hagley Rd., Birmingham, B17 8DJ; (44) 121-429-1779 (phone/fax).

SONIA STEVENSON
Cornwall/Year-round

Master chef Sonia Stevenson does consultancy work and conducts 2 - to 4-day participation courses (limit 6-8 students) that focus on sauces and fish cookery.

FACULTY: Founder of The Horn of Plenty Restaurant near Tavistock, Devon, Sonia Stevenson is a Master Chef of Great Britain and Chef Laureate of the British Academy of Gastronomes.

COSTS: Begin at £195.

LOCATION: Includes Glasgow, Inverness, Warwick, London, Cornwallk Guildford, and Somerset.

CONTACT: Sonia Stevenson, The Old Chapel, Bethany, Trerulefoot, Cornwall, PL12 5DA, England; (44) 752 851 813.

SQUIRES KITCHEN SUGARCRAFT SCHOOL
Surrey/Year-round *(See also page 242)*

This private school offers a part-time 1-week school certificate in sugarcraft and cake decorating. Established 1987. Rolling admission. 100% of applicants accepted; 10% under age 25; 40% age 25 to 44; 50% age 45 or over; 100% part-time students; 12 students per instructor. Facilities: a kitchen with specialized equipment and materials.

COURSES: Include royal icing, sugarpaste, flowers, pastillage, chocolate.

FACULTY: 17 full- and part-time faculty, members of the British Sugarcraft Guild, include Peggy Green. Guest tutors include Nick Lodge, Cynthia Venn, and Sarah Gleave. **COSTS:** Range from £20-£40 per day. 25% application deposit required.

LOCATION: A period building in a suburban area, a short walk to train station, 45 minutes from London.

CONTACT: Kirsty Smith, Course Coordinator, Squires Kitchen Sugarcraft School of Cake Decorating, 3 Waverley Lane, Farnham, Surrey, GU9 8BB, England; (44) 252-734309; Fax (44) 252-714714.

TANTE MARIE SCHOOL OF COOKERY
Surrey/Year-round *(See also page 243)*

This private school offers the 36-week or 24-week Intensive Tante Marie Cordon Bleu Diploma. Founded in 1954 by cookery writer Iris Syrett. Accredited by BACIFHE. Calendar: trimester. Admission dates January, April, September. Total enrollment 84; 24 to 72 enrollees each admission period; 100% of applicants accepted; 20% financial aid recipients; 50% under age 25; 45% age 25 to 44; 5% age 45 or over; 12 students per instructor; 100% of graduates obtain employment. Facilities include 5 modern teaching kitchens, a mirrored demonstration theatre, and a lecture room. Career planning and placement available.

COURSES: The 36-week course consists of three 12-week terms for beginners, starting with basic skills and progressing to labor-saving appliances, traditional British cookery, and French cuisine. The Intensive 24-week course for experienced cooks covers practical and theoretical elements. A 4-day wine seminar prepares students for the Wine Certificate examination. Schedule: 9:30 am to 4:30 pm, Monday through Friday.

FACULTY: Beryl A. Childs, FIHEC., Principal. Sue Alexander, Cert. Ed., Head Teacher. The 12 full-

CAREER/PROFESSIONAL **ENGLAND** **123**

and part-time staff members are qualified to work in state schools and many have held catering positions. All undergo teacher training. Well-known TV cookery demonstrators, a noted wine expert, and local tradesmen also present.

COSTS: Tuition is £6,900 (£5,000) for the 36-week (24-week) course, £2,600 for one-term certificate course. Uniform and equipment £100 additional. A nonrefundable £250 deposit is required. The first term's fee is due 4 weeks prior for U.K. residents, 6 weeks prior for others. Application deadline 3 months before term. Part-time employment is available. The school assists students in finding local lodging, which is £75 per week.

LOCATION: A turn-of-the-century country mansion near the center of Woking, a small country town approximately 25 minutes by train from London.

CONTACT: Margaret A. Stubbington, Registrar, Tante Marie School of Cookery, Woodham House, Carlton Rd., Woking, Surrey, GU21 4HF, England; (44) 1483 726957; Fax (44) 1483 724173.

THAMES VALLEY UNIVERSITY
Berkshire/Year-round

This university offers a 3-year NVQ Level 2 International Diploma in Culinary Arts. Program started 1992. Accredited by City and Guilds. Calendar: semester. Curriculum: core. Admission dates: October. Total enrollment 40; 40 enrollees each admission period; 70% of applicants accepted; 10% financial aid recipients; 60% under age 25; 40% age 25 to 44; 15 students per instructor; 100% of graduates obtain employment. Facilities: include 4 kitchens, demonstration kitchen, 2 science labs, 3 restaurants and computer lab.

COURSES: Schedule: 20 hours per week; part-time 7 hours per week.

FACULTY: 60 full-time.

COSTS: Annual tuition: £4,000.

CONTACT: David Foskett, Hospitality Studies, Thames Valley University, Wellington St., Berkshire, England; (44) 7535-34585, Fax (44) 7535-74264.

FRANCE

ECOLE DES ARTS CULINAIRES ET DE L'HOTELLERIE
(See also page 248) (See display ad page124) **Ecully/Year-round**

This school offers programs in cooking and hotel and restaurant management, including the 16-week Cuisine and Culture program, the 2-year Cuisine et Gestion program (taught in French), and short courses for professionals and cooking enthusiasts (page 248). Established in 1990. Calendar: semester. Admission: October for 16-week program, April for 2-year program The school is housed in the restored 19th century Château du Vivier and a modern teaching complex that contains 13 seminar rooms, 2 computer labs, 8 teaching kitchens, pastry and pantry facilities, video-equipped demonstration amphitheatre, sensory analysis lab, open-to-the-public restaurant, and student-faculty dining facility.

COURSES: Include food preparation and processing, pantry, pastry and bakery workshop, basic cooking and catering, and restaurant cuisine. Seminars cover cheese, wine, cost control, French ingredients, and French culinary culture. Excursions and conversational French classes are provided. Students who complete the 16-week program and pass an exam may take the longer programs.

FACULTY: In addition to the Board of Trustees, headed by Paul Bocuse, the permanent teaching staff includes 2 Meilleurs Ouvriers de France, Pastry Chef Alaine Berne, and Restaurant Chef Alain Le Cossec.

COSTS: Tuition for the 16-week program is 56,000 FF, which includes lunch and dinner. Tuition for the 2-year program is 45,000 FF per year. The student residence facility has 114 rooms with private shower; lodging is 2,200 FF per month.

LOCATION: In a 17-acre wooded park in the Lyon-Ecully University-Research Zone, 10 minutes from downtown Lyon.

CONTACT: Ecole des Arts Culinaires et de l'Hôtellerie, Office of International Programs, Château du Vivier, B.P. 25, 69131 Ecully Cedex, France; (33) 78-43-36-10, Fax (33) 78-43-33-51.

ÉCOLE DES ARTS CULINAIRES ET DE L'HÔTELLERIE

Hands-on classes in classical and regional French cuisine, pastry and wine coupled with introduction to and appreciation of France's gastronomic heritage. France's school of culinary arts presided by Paul Bocuse. One-week vacation classes and 16-week, two-year and three-year professional training. French cuisine in France in the Chateau du Vivier. ❦

ECOLE GASTRONOMIQUE BELLOUET-CONSEIL
Paris/Year-round

This school offers 2- and 3-day intensive seminars. The more than thirty individual courses include cakes, individual cakes, petits fours, chocolate, artistic sugar. Schedule: 8:30 am to 6 pm with lunch offered. Class size is 8 to 10 students. Also available: customized classes.

FACULTY: G.J. Bellouet, Meilleur Ouvrier de France; J.M. Perruchon, Meilleur Ouvrier de France.

COSTS: Two-day seminar: 3,200 FF, 3-day seminar 4,800 FF, cooking classes and catering 3,400 FF.

LOCATION: Downtown Paris, accessible by Métro: Duroc or Vanneau.

CONTACT: Ecole Gastronomique Bellouet Conseil, 48, rue de Sevres, 75007 Paris, France; (33) 1-40-56-91-20; Fax (33) 1-45-66-48-61.

ECOLE LENOTRE
Plaisir Cedex/Year-round *(See also page 249)*

Founded in 1970, this French gastronomy school offers more than sixty 1- to 4-day certificate courses. Founded in 1970. Classes are 90% participation and limited to 12 students per instructor.

COURSES: Several courses are available in each of the 9 subject categories: cuisine, catering, oenology and coffee, breads and pastry doughs, patisserie, ice cream and frozen desserts, chocolate and confiserie, sugar and decoration, and gastronomy for amateurs. Schedule: 1 day (8 hours) to 4 days (36 hours). Each course is offered at least twice a year; some are offered once a month. Special a la carte courses for groups of 8 to 12 can also be arranged.

FACULTY: Founded by Gaston Lenotre and managed by Marcel Derrien, Meilleur Ouvrier de France in pastry-confectionery. Four school instructors are recipients of the Meilleur Ouvrier de France in pastry-confectionery, pork butchery, ice cream, and bakery-viennoiserie.

COSTS, ACCOMMODATIONS: Tuition (non-French students), including breakfasts and lunches, ranges from 997 FF (626 FF) to 13,800 FF (12,093 FF). Advance payment is required. The school can reserve rooms in one of Plaisir's hotels, which range from 130 FF-260 FF per night.

LOCATION: About 30 miles from Paris, 6 miles from Versailles.

CONTACT: Marcel Derrien or Odile Fleury, Ecole Lenotre, 40 rue Pierre Curie - BP 6 - 787373 Plaisir Cedex, France; (33) 1-30-8146-34 or 35, Fax (33) 1-30-54-73-70.

CAREER/PROFESSIONAL **FRANCE**

ECOLE SUPERIEURE DE CUISINE FRANCAISE GROUPE FERRANDI
Paris/September-June

This professional hotel/restaurant school offers a bilingual 9-month program, awarding a diploma issued by Paris' Chamber of Commerce and preparing qualified students for the C.A.P. certificate of the French Ministry of Education. Program started 1986. Accredited by the French Ministry of Education. Calendar: trimester. Curriculum: culinary. Admission dates April, August. Total enrollment 200; 10 to 12 enrollees each admission period; 60% to 90% of applicants accepted; 50% financial aid recipients; 10% under age 25; 80% age 25 to 44; 10% age 45 or over; 4 students per instructor; 100% of graduates obtain employment. Facilities include 3 professional kitchens, 4 classrooms, and 2 working restaurants.

Courses: In addition to general theoretical and practical courses, students study cooking, baking, pastry, butchery, delicatessen products, and fish cookery. Other activities include a 3-day wine country excursion. The 9-month program includes visits to museums, markets, bistros, and fine restaurants. Six-week restaurant apprenticeships in Paris and the provinces may be arranged for top students during school holidays. Schedule: 8 am to 4:30 pm daily.

Faculty: The curriculum is supervised by a Board of Advisors including well-known French chefs Joel Robuchon and Antoine Westermann.

Costs: The 9-month program costs 86,000 FF. Deposit of 25% due upon acceptance, 50% due at first class, 25% during second half of program. Written cancellations 1 month prior forfeit 3,000 FF; no refunds thereafter. Admission requirements include proof of full medical and accident coverage, long-term student visa, certified birth certificate, and undergraduate transcript. Last year 1 scholarship was awarded. Off-campus lodging ranges from $500-$800 per month.

Location: Rue Ferrandi in Paris's Latin Quarter, between St. Germain de Pres and Montparnasse. Convenient to 4 major metro stations.

Contact: Stephanie Curtis, Coordinator, Bilingual Program, ESCF Groupe Ferrandi, 10 rue de Richelieu, 75001, Paris, France; (33) 1-40-15-04-57, Fax (33) 1-40-15-04-58.

THE ULTIMATE FOOD & WINE VACATION

Come to Burgundy, France to the Château du Feÿ, as featured on PBS. La Varenne's Visitor Programs, directed by Anne Willan include one-week summer series courses, the *French Cooking Today* series and the fall Gastronomic courses.

La Varenne

US (800) 537-6486
(202) 337-0073
France 86 63 18 34

(See also page 251)

LA VARENNE
Burgundy/Summer

This private school offers two 3-week residential programs (limit 15 students) that focus on French cuisine: the Intensive Orientation Program for beginners and French Cooking Today for professionals. Established in France in 1975, the school is in the 17th-century Château du Feÿ, a registered historic monument owned by founder Anne Willan.

Courses: The orientation program focuses on fundamentals, pastry, and contemporary cuisine and includes vineyard tours and dining at fine restaurants. Students who successfully complete a written and practical exam receive La Varenne's *Diplôme* d'Etudes Culinaires. The professionals' course covers selected topics, such as classical cooking trends, pastry and chocolate, and bistro and regional dishes. Other activities include seminars and escorted excursions to northern Burgundy,

Beaune, and Paris, where students visit wine purveyors, restaurants, and specialty shops. Students who complete the full course graduate with La Varenne's *Diplôme* d'Etudes Gastronomiques

FACULTY: Programs are directed by Anne Willan, whose recent books include the *Look and Cook* how-to series featured on PBS, *Château Cuisine*, and *La Varenne Pratique*. About two-thirds of the curriculum is taught by La Varenne's cuisine and pastry chefs, the rest by noted French restaurant chefs.

COSTS: Fee is $7,545 ($8,895) for beginner (professional) program, including full board, shared twin lodging at the Château, planned excursions, and transportation to and from Paris. A $1,000 nonrefundable deposit is due within 15 days of acceptance; balance is due 60 days prior to course.

LOCATION: The Château du Feÿ is 90 minutes south of Paris. Amenities include a tennis court and an outdoor swimming pool in season.

CONTACT: La Varenne, P.O. Box 25574, Washington, DC 20007; (800) 537-6486 or (202) 337-0073, Fax (703) 823-5438. In France: La Varenne, Château du Feÿ, 89300 Villecien, France; (33) 86-63-18-34, Fax (33) 86-63-01-33.

LE CORDON BLEU
Paris/Year-round *(See also page 251) (See display ad page 127)*

This international private school offers a 30-week culinary diploma including 5- and 10-week certificate courses in French Cuisine and Pastry, 1- and 4-week catering courses, a 10-week Summer Semester Abroad program for hospitality management students, and 1-day and 1-month sessions on a variety of topics. Founded in 1895, Le Cordon Bleu has schools in London and Tokyo. Certificate courses begin in January, March, June, August, and October. Student to faculty ratio is 12 to 1. Facilities include 4 practical classrooms, individual work stations, 2 demonstration theatres with overhead mirrors and video, professional cuisine and pastry ovens.

COURSES: Le Grand Diploma curriculum consists of 3 levels of Cuisine and 3 levels of Pastry certificate courses, taken consecutively or together, followed by a 4-week full-time internship in a fine restaurant. Courses cover basic to complex techniques, restaurant-quality dishes, and oenology. Schedule: 18-20 hours per week for cuisine courses, 10-12 hours per week for pastry courses, some courses can be taken as 5-week intensives. Internships are available for certificate course graduates. The Summer Abroad program includes 4 weeks of classes in Paris and London and a 2-week internship.

FACULTY: Full-time faculty includes Master Chefs who have won national and international competitions and have experience in Michelin-starred restaurants and international restaurants.

COSTS: Tuition ranges from 29,950 FF to 35,950 FF for Cuisine courses, 21,950 FF to 25,950 for Pastry courses. Intensives range from 23,950 FF to 31,950 FF; catering courses are 4,750 FF per week. Multiple course discounts are provided. Nonrefundable deposit of 3,000 FF to 9,500 FF per course is required 2 months prior; balance is due 1 month prior. Equipment & uniform fee ranges from 2,650 FF to 3,250 FF.

LOCATION: A central residential area of Paris in the 15th arrondissement.

CONTACT: Le Cordon Bleu, 8, rue Leon Delhomme, 75015 Paris, France; (800) 457-CHEF (in U.S.), (33) 1-48-56-06-06, Fax (33) 148-56-03-96. In the U.S.: (800) 457-CHEF.

LE TROU RESTAURANT AND COOKING SCHOOL
San Francisco and France/Year-round *(See also pages 9, 162, 252)*

Aux Gastronomes, the cooking school of Le Trou restaurant in San Francisco, has offered full-time 8-week apprenticeships in France since 1983. Approximately 25% of applicants accepted; 100% of graduates obtain employment. Apprentices live with Niort townspeople or at a hotel or inn.

LOCATION: Deux Sevres, France, an area of rolling farmland, bordered by Poitiers to the east, Cognac and Bordeaux to the south, and the Venise Vert canal area to the west.

CULINARY EXCELLENCE AT LE CORDON BLEU

- **Cuisine & Pastry Classic Cycle Diploma**
  Program offered 5 times a year.

- **Master Chef Catering Program :**
  don't miss out on our 1 & 4 weeks program.

- **ICHP Summer Semester Program :**
  June 12 - August 18, 1996
  for Hospitality Management Students.

- **Weekly "Hands-on" Workshops.**
- **Regional Cuisine & Bread Baking.**

PARIS • LONDON • TOKYO
8 rue Léon Delhomme 75015 Paris
114 Marylebone Lane London WIM6HH

Call today for a free school brochure or gift catalogue of our gourmet products : **1-800-457 CHEF**

L'ECOLE DE PATISSERIE FRANCAISE
Uzes/Year-round
(See display ad page 128)

Established 1994. This French pastry shop offers 40 intensive 5-day participation master workshops (limit 2 students/teacher ratio) per year. Schedule and program are according to student's choice of curriculum, minimum 8 hours per day. Nonparticipant can visit olive oil mill, truffle farms, local markets, feudal castles, and participate in sports activities. Facilities: commercial patisserie kitchen with separate ice cream preparation kitchen.

COURSES: Traditional and modern patisserie, including ice creams, sorbets, petits fours, chocolates, celebration cakes, plated desserts, croissants, brioches, croqu'embouches, individual pastries, catering. Individual needs are accommodated.

FACULTY: Didier Richeux, co-founder, has 17 years experience in pastry cooking and is the recipient of 17 international awards, including the Gold Medal, Cordon Bleu de France. He was Executive Pastry Chef at Le Cordon Bleu and The Savoy in London, has worked at Maxim's in Paris, and speaks fluent English.

COSTS: 5,000 FF (Tuesday to Saturday), 9,000 FF (2 weeks). A 25% deposit is required; balance is due 4 weeks before course. Written cancellations at least 4 weeks prior forfeit 1,000 FF.

LOCATION: 30 minutes north of Nimes Airport, 40 minutes southwest of Avignon, and an hour from Montpellier Airport.

CONTACT: Didier Richeux, Director, L'Ecole de Patisserie Francaise, 12 rue de la Republique, Uzes 30700, France; (33) 66-22-12-09, Fax (33) 66-22-26-36.

ITS'S NOT JUST TWO STUDENTS PER TEACHER THAT MAKES LEARNING... 'A PIECE OF CAKE'

it's also our hands-on Masterclass workshops held in our own pastry shop kitchen, using programs especially designed for each student.

L'ECOLE DE PÂTISSERIE FRANÇAISE

FRANCE: TEL (33) 66 22 12 09   FAX (33) 66 22 26 36

PASTRY INSTITUTE OF WASHINGTON DC *(See page 174)*

RITZ-ESCOFFIER ECOLE DE GASTRONOMIE FRANCAISE
Paris/Year-round *(See also page 254) (See display ad page129)*
This school in the Hotel Ritz offers 1- to 6-week Cesar Ritz Diploma and Pastry Diploma Courses (year-round), an advanced level 12-week Ritz-Escoffier Diploma Course (January, April, September), and short courses for professionals and enthusiasts. Founded in 1988 and named for the hotel's first chef, Auguste Escoffier. Courses begin each week and are limited to 8-10 students. The 2,000-square-foot custom-designed facility includes a main kitchen, pastry kitchen, conference room/library, and changing rooms.

COURSES: Each week of the Cesar Ritz and Pastry Diploma Courses consists of 25 to 28 hours of demonstrations, hands-on practice, and theory. Students who complete 1 to 5 weeks receive the Cesar Ritz or Pastry Certificate; those who complete the 6-week course and pass a practical exam are awarded the Cesar Ritz or Pastry Diploma. Candidates for the advanced course must have the Cesar Ritz Diploma or equivalent experience and enroll for twelve 32-hour weeks. Pastry Diploma recipients may apply for an internship in the Hotel Ritz's main pastry kitchen; Ritz-Escoffier Diploma recipients are invited to apply for internships in the kitchens of the Espadon, the Michelin two-star Hotel Ritz restaurant.

FACULTY: School director Marie-Anne Dufeu has been in the cooking school field for 10 years. The 3 full-time instructors are Chefs de Cuisine Jean-Louis Taillebaud and Aimé Barroyer and Chef Patissier Bruno Neveu. Ritz Executive Chef Guy Legay and Master Baker Bernard Burban were each elected Meilleur Ouvrier de France; Chief Sommelier Jean-Michel Deluc teaches the wine courses.

COSTS: In 1995, Cesar Ritz Diploma Course 5,750 FF per week, Pastry Diploma Course 5,350 FF per week, Ritz-Escoffier Diploma Course 69,600 FF. A 25% deposit must accompany enrollment with balance due 4 weeks before course. Written cancellations 4 weeks prior forfeit 500 FF; no refunds thereafter. A list of nearby lodging is provided; special rates at the Hotel Ritz are available.

LOCATION: Central Paris, near 3 main subway entrances and most major department stores.

CONTACT: Susan Sturman, Assistant Manager, Ritz-Escoffier Ecole de Gastronomie Francaise, 15, Place Vendome, 75041 Paris Cedex 01, France; (33) 1-43-16-30-50, Fax (33) 1-43-16-31-50; (800) 966-5758 (in U.S.).

HONG KONG

CHOPSTICKS COOKING CENTRE
Kowloon/September-November, March-April *(See also page256)*
This private trade school offers 4- to 17-week certificates in Chinese cuisine. Founded 1971. Calendar: quarter. Curriculum: culinary. Admission dates February, March, August, September,

RITZ-ESCOFFIER
ECOLE DE GASTRONOMIE FRANÇAISE

The ultimate gourmet French cooking school is located in the legendary Ritz Hotel where renowned Chef Auguste Escoffier reigned in the kitchens a century ago. Food lovers and professionals discover the art of fine cuisine in a most exceptional environment.

- *Diploma Courses for Professionals*
- *Week-long Courses for Passionate Amateurs*
- *Daily Demonstration Classes for Paris Visitors*

All courses taught in French with English translation.

Information:

HÔTEL RITZ
15 place Vendome
75041 Paris cedex 01
Tel.: 33 (1) 43 16 30 50
Fax: 33 (1) 43 16 31 50
USA (800) 966 5758

October. Total enrollment 20; 90% of applicants accepted; 10% under age 25; 70% age 25 to 44; 20% age 45 or over; 95% part-time students; 12 students per instructor; 90% of students obtain employment. Classes are held in a professional restaurant kitchen.

COURSES: Include chinese regional dishes, dim sums, chinese roasts, cakes and pastries, and breads. Schedule: 8 to 12 hours per week. Part-time and evening options available.

FACULTY: School principal Cecilia J. Au-Yang, a domestic science graduate and author of a series of 20 cookbooks; professional chefs from various hotels and restaurants.

COSTS: Range from $2,200-$6,000. Nonrefundable application deposit is $300; registration fee is $40. All fees are nonrefundable. Application deadline 3-6 months in advance. Part-time employment is available. Local lodging averages $1,000 per month.

CONTACT: Cecilia Au-Yang, Principal, Chopsticks Cooking Centre, 108 Boundary St., G/Fl., Kowloon, Hong Kong; (852) 2336-8433 or 2336-8037, Fax (852) 2338-1462.

IRELAND

ALIX GARDNER'S COOKERY SCHOOL
Dublin/Year-round

This school offers a three-month certificate course and a variety of classes and courses for cooking enthusiasts (page 130). Founded 1978. Admission dates September, January, April. Facilities: two demonstration rooms and a practical room with 16 workspaces.

COURSES: Modern and traditional cookery, with emphasis on the principles of Escoffier. Vegetarians, coeliacs, diabetics, and other special dietary needs are accommodated. Schedule: 9:30 am to 4 pm Monday-Friday.

FACULTY: Proprietor Alix Gardner is a graduate of the London Cordon Bleu and the Prue Leith School of Food & Wine.

COSTS: IR £2,900. A 1-year scholarship is open to anyone under the age of 24.

CONTACT: Alix Gardner's Cookery School, Kensington Hall, Grove Park, Dublin 6, Ireland; (353) 1-4960045, Fax (353) 1-6686578.

BALLYMALOE COOKERY SCHOOL
Midleton/April-September, December-January *(See also page 257)*

This proprietary school offers a 12-week Certificate Course in Food & Wine and a variety of short courses. Program started in 1983. Calendar: quarter. Curriculum: culinary. Admission dates September, January. Total enrollment 44; 90% of applicants accepted; 50% under age 25; 40% age 25 to 44; 10% age 45 or over; 6 students per instructor; 100% of graduates obtain employment. Facilities include a specially-designed kitchen with gas and electric cookers, a mirrored demonstration area, and vegetable, fruit and herb gardens that supply fresh produce.

COURSES: Most courses are hands-on and emphasize traditional Irish and French classic cookery, international cuisine, vegetarian, and seafood cooking. Schedule: 40 hours per week.

FACULTY: The 4 full- and 4 part-time faculty include school Principal Darina Allen, a Certified Teacher and Food Professional by the IACP and her brother, Rory O'Connell, both trained in the Ballymaloe House restaurant kitchen, and her husband Tim Allen. Guest chefs include Marcella Hazan, Madhur Jaffrey, and Anne Willan.

COSTS: The 12-week course is IR £3,575. The school can arrange for airport and train station pick-up. Students live in cottages adjoining the school and may assist in the Ballymaloe House restaurant kitchen. Self-catering cottage lodging is provided for 44 students at IR £35 per week (double occupancy), IR £48 (single).

LOCATION: A mile from the sea, outside the village of Shanagarry in southern Ireland, a 4-hour drive from Dublin Airport and 1 hour from Cork Airport.

CONTACT: Tim Allen, The Ballymaloe Cookery School, Kinoith, Shanagarry, County Cork, Midleton, Ireland; (353) 21-646785, Fax (353) 21-646909.

THE COOKERY CENTRE OF IRELAND
(See also page 257) **Dublin/Year-round**

This school offers a full-time 12-week Certificate Course and a variety of nonvocational courses. Admission dates September and January. Essentially 100% of applicants are admitted and 100% of graduates obtain employment.

COURSES: Emphasis is on basic and advanced cordon bleu cookery along with food preservation, menu planning, wine appreciation, and flower arranging. Visits to meat manufacturers, a fish smoking house, bakeries, and hotel kitchens are also scheduled. After 6 weeks, students spend 1 day a week for 4 weeks working in a Dublin-area restaurant or hotel kitchen. A certificate is awarded those who pass theoretical and practical exams.

FACULTY: Mrs. Bee Mannix-Walsh, D.Sc.I., Cordon Bleu (London) is an experienced home economics teacher and City & Guilds (London) chef. She has prepared food for magazines and television commercials.

COSTS: IR £2,400 for the 12-week Certificate Course A nonrefundable deposit of 10% of course fee is required with balance due at class.

LOCATION: In central Dalkey, close to the DART and No. 8 bus terminal.

CONTACT: The Cookery Centre of Ireland, 2A St. Patrick's Ave., Dalkey, Co. Dublin, Ireland; (353) 1 2858728, Fax (353) 1 2853805.

ITALY

MASTER CLASSES IN VENICE WITH MARCELLA & VICTOR HAZAN
March-October except July and August

This 5-day participation Master Class, offered once a month and limited to 6 students, follows a loosely structured format, focusing on the techniques and improvisation of classic Italian cuisine. Classes are scheduled from 10 am to 3 pm for 5 consecutive days. Other activities include a visit to the Rialto market and dinner at a fine local restaurant.

FACULTY: Italian cook Marcella Hazan, author of *Marcella's Italian Kitchen* and other books. Her husband, Victor, discusses wines from their cellar.

COSTS: Master Class is $2,500. A $200 deposit is required, which becomes nonrefundable when class date is confirmed and accepted. Balance due 120 days prior. Cancellations 45 days prior receive a 60% refund unless space is filled. A list of recommended hotels is provided.

LOCATION: The Hazan home atop a 16th century palazzo in Venice.

CONTACT: Susan Cox, Hazan Classics, P.O. Box 285, Circleville, NY 10919; (914) 692-7104, Fax (914) 692-2659.

SCUOLA DI ARTE CULINARIA "CORDON BLEU"
(See also page 269) **Florence/October-May**

This school offers professional programs from October–December and January–May, as well as nonvocational and vacation programs (page 269). The fall (spring) curriculum consists of 10 (17) one- to ten-session hands-on courses, a total of 260 (360) hours of instruction. Morning, afternoon, evening, and customized schedules are available. Facilities: the school's 40-square-meter teaching kitchen.

COURSES: Include basic to advanced cooking, pastry, breads, holiday menus, regional specialties, specific subjects.

FACULTY: Cristina Blasi and Gabriella Mari, professional teachers for 10 years, are sommeliers and olive oil experts who authored a book on ancient Roman cooking and are members of the Commanderie des Cordons Bleus de France, Italian Association of Professional Chefs, and the IACP; part-time instructors include Fabio Onasti, Aldo Biondi, and other professional chefs.

COSTS: Tuition: 5,000,000 Lira (6,700,000 Lira) for the fall (spring) program, 7,500,000 Lira for both.

LOCATION: Central Florence.

CONTACT: Gabriella Mari, Cristina Blasi, Co-Directors, Scuola di Arte Culinaria Cordon Bleu, Via di Mezzo, 55/R, 50121 Firenze - Florence, Italy; (39) 55-2345468 (phone/fax).

MEXICO

SEASONS OF MY HEART COOKING SCHOOL
Oaxaca/January-April, September-December *(See also page 273)*
This school offers a 1-week course for culinary professionals. Cost is $1,295, including meals, lodging, and planned activities. A $200 deposit is required; $100 is nonrefundable. Cancellations 2 weeks prior forfeit $200, no refund thereafter unless space is sold.

NEW ZEALAND

CENTRAL INSTITUTE OF TECHNOLOGY
New Zealand/Year-round
This trade school offers a 3-year diploma and a 1-year certificate in Hospitality Operations-Management. Program started 1978. Accredited by State. Calendar: semester. Curriculum: core. Admission dates: August. Total enrollment 300; 90 enrollees each admission period; 50% of applicants accepted; 40% financial aid recipients; 65% under age 25; 14 students per instructor; 50% of graduates obtain employment. Facilities: 3 kitchens, 20 classrooms, 2 restaurants.

COURSES: 1480 hours (diploma), 500 hours (certificate) of culinary courses required for graduation. Schedule: 20 hours per week, 30 weeks.

FACULTY: 24 full-time.

COSTS: Tuition: in-country NZ$1,600, out-of-country NZ$10,500. Application deadlines: August 15. Admission requirements: high school diploma or equivalent and admission test. On-campus housing cost: NZ$130 per week.

CONTACT: Tim Locker, Head of Department, Faculty of Business & Tourism Management, Central Institute of Technology, P.O. Box 40-740, Upper Hutt, New Zealand; (64) 4-5276398, Fax (64) 4-5276364.

THE NEW ZEALAND SCHOOL OF FOOD AND WINE
Christchurch/Year-round
This proprietary institution offers a 15-week full-time Certificate in Foundation Cookery Skills and a 20-week full-time course, Food and the Family, in conjunction with the New Zealand College of Early Childhood Education. Established 1994. Registered with the New Zealand Qualifications Authority (NZQA); students eligible for student visas. Admission dates for Foundation Skills: January 20, May 6, August 26, 1996; Food and the Family: July 15. Facilities: demonstration kitchen with overhead mirrors, practical kitchen with commercial equipment.

COURSES: Foundation Skills instruction is structured around the textbook *Leith's Bible* and covers

CAREER/PROFESSIONAL SCOTLAND

the basic concepts of French cuisine, food presentation, menu planning, costing, catering, and the developing cuisines of Australasia, and includes wine and vineyard tours. Food and the Family integrates the skills of early childhood education with cookery, and includes basics of classical French cuisine, menu planning, costing, and catering.

FACULTY: Ten full- and part-time tutors.

COSTS: Tuition for Foundation Skills is NZ$3,750 (plus tax); Food and the Family, NZ$4,400 (plus tax). A NZ$250 deposit is required; balance due 20 days prior. Full refund until day 7 of the course.

LOCATION: Christchurch, a city of 300,000 in South Island.

CONTACT: Celia Hay, New Zealand School of Food and Wine, 63 Victoria St., Box 25217, Christchurch, South Island, New Zealand; (61) 3-3797-501 (phone/fax).

SCOTLAND

EDINBURGH COOKERY SCHOOL
September-July

This school offers full-time 10-week Foundation, Intermediate, and Advanced Certificate courses, a 22-week Intensive Certificate course, and a 1-year Combined Cookery, Secretarial and French Certificate course in conjunction with Basil Paterson College. Established in 1988 by Jill Davidson. Admission dates: September, October, January, April. Hands-on classes are limited to 12. Facilities include domestic and commercial gas cookers, electric ovens, and Aga cookers.

COSTS: Tuition, exclusive of VAT, is £3,500 for the Intensive Certificate course, £1,650 for the other certificate courses, £700 for the 4-week summer courses.

CONTACT: Edinburgh Cookery School, The Coach House, Newliston, Kirkliston, Edinburgh, EH29 9EB, Scotland; (44) 31-333-1501.

TOP TIER SUGARCRAFT
Inverness/Year-round

Established in 1984, this school and mail order business offers 1-, 2-, and 3- week demonstration and participation courses (limit 8 students) for beginners and experts. Facilities: 600-square-foot classroom with specialized equipment. Other activities include sightseeing in the Highlands. Also available: day and weekend courses.

COURSES: Sugarpaste, royal, floral, chocolate, marzipan, pastillage, and personalized wedding cake instruction. Schedule: 10 am to 3 pm daily.

FACULTY: Principal teacher Diana Turner, British Sugarcraft Guild member and judge, has more than 10 years of experience in sugarcraft work.

COSTS: Day classes begin at £25 ; weekend courses begin at £36; week-long programs cost £750 per week, including meals and accommodations with a Scottish family. A £100 deposit is required; full refund with 1 month notice.

LOCATION: A mile from Culloden Battlefield, 5 miles from Inverness.

CONTACT: Top Tier Sugarcraft, 10 Meadow Rd., Balloch, Inverness, IV1 2JR, Scotland; (44) 1463-790456 (phone/fax).

SOUTH AFRICA

SILWOOD KITCHEN CORDONS BLEUS COOKERY SCHOOL
Rondebosch Cape/Year-round

This school offers three 1-year culinary career courses that begin each January: the Certificate course, the Diploma course, and the Grande Diploma. Founded in 1964 by Leslie Faull. Enrollment is limited to 40 students, divided into groups of 10. The school facility is a 200-year-old coach-house converted into a demonstration and experimental kitchen, 3 additional kitchens, demonstration hall, and a library.

FACULTY: The 11-member faculty includes school principal Alicia Wilkinson, Jeanette Rietmann, Steven van der Merwe, Alisa Smith, Louise Faull, Peggy Loebenberg, and Nikki Black.

COSTS: Tuition is R14,706 for the Certificate course, R6,110.40 for the Diploma course, and R638.40 for the Grande Diploma. A R800 deposit must accompany application.

CONTACT: Mrs. Alicia Wilkinson, Silwood Kitchen, Silwood Rd., Rondebosch Cape, South Africa; (27) 21-686-4894.

National Apprenticeship Training Program for Cooks

American Culinary Federation Educational Institute (ACFEI)

Culinary Apprenticeship is a three-year on-the-job training program complemented by related instruction from an educational institution. The program began under the Carter Administration in 1976 with a grant from the U.S. government and is now the 7th largest apprenticeship program in the United States, with over 17,000 cooks being trained since its inception.

The apprenticeship program offers career-oriented cooks an alternative to private culinary institutions and vocational-technical schools. Apprentices, who generally range in age from 18 to 40 (average age 24), receive three years (6,000 hours) of on-the-job training while earning an income. The first 500 hours are a probationary period, after which the apprentice is eligible to join the ACFEI and become registered with the Department of Labor. In addition to a 40-hour work week, the apprentice attends school part-time (a minimum of 192 hours per year) and may also have the opportunity to earn an associate degree. The average hourly wage for an apprentice starts at $5 with a recommended increase of $.25 every six months. The average cost for school is between $500 and $3,000 during a three-year period.

To qualify for the program, applicant must be at least 17 years of age, have a high school diploma or equivalent, and have passed all entry-level academic and aptitude examinations as prescribed by the Apprenticeship Committee of the ACFEI. Consideration is given to those who have had high school foodservice training or on-the-job experience. A five-step screening process includes an orientation seminar, documentation of prior experience, and personal interviews.

The program is planned in six semi-annual stages, which can be shortened or lengthened according to the individual's ability. The apprentice keeps a weekly Log Book in which recipes and food preparation techniques are recorded. Those who complete the apprenticeship can: prepare, season, and cook soups, sauces, salads, meats, fish, poultry, game, vegetables, and desserts; produce baked goods and pastries; fabricate meat portions from primal cuts; prepare a buffet dinner; select and develop recipes; plan, write, and design complete menus; plan food consumption, purchasing, and requisitioning; operate a working budget in food and labor costing; recognize quality standards in fresh vegetables, meats, fish, and poultry; demonstrate supervisory abilities and inter-relate with other departments in a food operation; and demonstrate basic artistic culinary skills, including ice carving, tallow sculpturing, cake decorating, and garniture display work.

In addition to work skills, the apprentice completes 30 hours minimum class time at an accredited post-secondary institution in each of 12 areas of related instruction: 1) Introduction to Food Service (Industry Survey); 2) Sanitation and Safety; 3) Basic Food Preparation (Introduction to Cooking); 4) Business Math (Food Cost Accounting); 5) Food and Beverage Service; 6) Nutrition; 7) Garde Manger; 8) Menu Planning and Design; 9) Baking; 10) Purchasing; 11) Supervisory Management; 12) Advanced Food preparation.

On completion of the program, the apprentice is identified as a Certified Cook and may be offered employment at the training establishment or recommended for job placement. Upon graduation, an apprentice can earn an annual income of between $18,000 and $25,000.

For more information, contact: ACFEI Programs Coordinator, American Culinary Federation, P.O. Box 3466, 10 San Bartola Rd., St. Augustine, FL 32085; (800) 624-9458 or (904) 824-4468, Fax (904) 825-4758.

The following list of the 97 ACFEI apprenticeship programs in effect on May 19, 1995 was provided by the American Culinary Federation. Many of the program coordinators provided additional information about their programs.

ALABAMA

ACF BIRMINGHAM CHAPTER

This chapter has 25 apprentices, 15 under age 25, 10 age 25 or over. Costs are $3,500 in-state and $5,000 out-of-state; beginning salary is $5 per hour, with 40 cent increases every 6 months. The 15 locations are country club, restaurant, hotel, corporate dining room and private club. Most desirable settings are local fine-dining restaurants and country clubs. Housing cost is $350-$500 per month. Degree program available through Jefferson State Community College.

CONTACT: Ana Gray, MS, CSC, Apprenticeship Chairperson, Hospitality Management, Jefferson State Community College, 2601 Carson Rd., Birmingham, AL 35215; (205) 856-7898 (work), Fax (205) 853-0701.

ACF GREATER MONTGOMERY CHAPTER

CONTACT: Mary Ann Ward, CEC, CCE, Trenhom State Technical College, 1225 Air Base Blvd., Montgomery, AL 36108; (205) 262-4728 (work), (205) 272-7245 (home).

ARKANSAS

ACF LITTLE ROCK, ARKANSAS CHAPTER

This chapter has 11 apprentices, 4 under age 25, 7 age 25 or over. Costs are $650 per year; beginning salary is $4.75 per hour, with 5% increases every 6 months. There are 8 locations. Most desirable settings are hotel, restaurant, country club.

CONTACT: Chris Ames, Director, 8309 Patricia Lynn Ln., Sherwood, AR 72120; (501) 565-8465 (work), (501) 834-0666 (home), Fax (501) 834-9406.

ARIZONA

RESORT & COUNTRY CLUB CHEFS — NEW SOUTHWEST ACF

CONTACT: Robert Chantos,CEC, 8787 East Mt. View Rd., #1130, Scottsdale, AZ 85258; (602) 890-4816(work).

CHEFS ASSOCIATION OF GREATER PHOENIX

This chapter has 8 apprentices, 50 under age 25. The 9 locations are resort. Degree program available through Scottsdale Community College and Phoenix Community College. Baking apprenticeship available.

CONTACT: Camron Clarkson, CWC, 2210 E. Sunnyside Dr., Phoenix, AZ 85028; (602) 404-9566.

CHEFS ASSOCIATION OF SOUTHERN ARIZONA, TUCSON

CONTACT: Bob Shell, CWC, CCE, P.O. Box 13895, Tucson, AZ 85732; (602) 791-9106 (work).

CALIFORNIA

ACF CHEFS ASSOCIATION SAN JOAQUIN VALLEY
Contact: Bill McComas, 810 Bliss, Clovis, CA 93612; (209) 298-4900, Fax (209) 298-8837.

ACF SAN FRANCISCO CHAPTER
Contact: Kay Stickney, 1650 S. Amphlett Blvd., Suite 312, San Mateo, CA 94402; (415) 574-6700.

CALIFORNIA CAPITOL CHEFS ASSOCIATION
This chapter has 43 apprentices, 33 under age 25, 10 age 25 or over. Waiting list is about about 1 year. Costs are $150 for books and materials; beginning salary is $5.40, with increases every 6 months. The 26 locations are restaurant and convalescent home. Most desirable settings are Red Lion Hotel and El Paso Country Club. Housing cost is $425 per month. Degree program available through Sierra College. Baking apprenticeship available.
Contact: Jon Greenwalt CEC, 5475 Asby Ln., Granite Bay, CA 95746; (916) 791-2554 (work).

CHEFS DE CUISINE ASSOCIATION OF CALIFORNIA
This chapter has 15 apprentices, 14 under age 25, 1 age 25 or over. Costs are approximately $150; beginning salary is variable, with increases every 6 months. Most desirable settings are hotel, private club, restaurant. Housing cost is variable. Degree program available through California Polytechnic is completed by 100 of apprentices. Baking apprenticeship available.
Contact: LeRoy Blanchard, CEC, c/o Westin Bonaventure Hotel, 400 N. Washington Blvd., Los Angeles, CA 90015; (213) 744-9480 (work), (310) 514-0427 (home), Fax (213) 748-7334.

CHEFS DE CUISINE OF BAKERSFIELD
This chapter has 3 apprentices, age 25 or over. Waiting list is about about 1 year. Costs are approximately $500; beginning salary is $5 per hour, with increases every 6 months. The 2 locations are county club and hotel. Most desirable setting is Red Lion Corporation. Housing cost is from $1,000 per month. Degree program available through Bakersfield Community College.
Contact: William P. Coyle, CCE, Bakersfield College-Food Service, 1801 Panorama Drive, Bakersfield, CA 93305; (805) 395-4345 (work), (805) 397-7271 (home), Fax (805) 395-4241.

NORTHERN CALIFORNIA CHEFS ASSOCIATION
Contact: Michael Piccinino, CEC, CCE, 6945 Pine Dr., Anderson, CA 96007; (916) 225-4829, Fax (916) 225-4881.

ORANGE EMPIRE CHEFS ASSOCIATION
This chapter has 15 apprentices, Costs are $100 one-time ACF fee, $55 annually and $13 per unit; beginning salary and increases negotiable. The 30 locations are hotel, country club and restaurant. Most desirable: Ritz Carlton, Laguna Niguel, Meridien, and Westin. Housing cost: $400-$4,600 per month. Degree program available through Orange Coast College. Baking apprenticeship available.
Contact: Bill Barber, CWC, c/o Orange Coast Community College, 2701 Fairview Rd., P.O. Box 5005, Costa Mesa, CA 92628-5005; (714) 432-5835 (work), (714) 831-3065 (home).

SAN FRANCISCO CULINARY/PASTRY PROGRAM
This chapter has 15 apprentices, 15 under age 25. Waiting list is about 12 to 18 months. beginning salary is 55% of journeyman wage, with 5% increases every 5 months. The 5 to 7 locations are

full-service hotels and restaurants. Baking apprenticeship available.

CONTACT: Joan Ortega, 760 Market St., Ste. 1066, San Francisco, CA 94102; (415) 989-8726 (work), Fax (415) 989-2920.

SANTA BARBARA CHEFS ASSOCIATION

CONTACT: Tim Fox, 208 Natoma, #2, Santa Barbara, CA 93101; (805) 564-4333 (work).

SOUTHERN CALIFORNIA INLAND EMPIRE CHEFS ASSOCIATION

CONTACT: John Webster, CC, 27677 Rainbow Ct., Highland, CA 92346; (909) 381-8811, ext. 4166 (work), Fax (909) 862-6462.

COLORADO

ACF CULINARIANS OF COLORADO

This chapter has 33 apprentices, 3 under age 25, 30 age 25 or over. Costs are approximately $1,000; beginning salary is 70% of journeyman's wages, with 5% increases every 6 months. The 30 locations are restaurant, hotel, club, hospital, and caterer. Most desirable settings are located in Denver. Housing cost is $300 per month and up. Degree program available through Community College of Denver is completed by less than 5% of apprentices.

CONTACT: Hans K. Amstein, CEC, Chairman Apprentice Committee, 820-16th St., Ste. 421, Denver, CO 80202; (303) 571-5653 (work), (303) 985-7996 (home), Fax (303) 571-4050.

ACF TOP OF THE ROCKIES CHEFS ASSOCIATION

This chapter has 25 apprentices, 12 under age 25, 12 age 25 or over. Costs are approximately $3,900 for 3 years with AAS degree; beginning salary is $6.50 per hour, with 50 cent-$1 increases based on merit. The 9 locations are resort and restaurant. Most desirable settings are Keystone Ranch, Ski Tip Lodge/Pastry Shop. On-site housing cost is from $260 per month. Degree program available through Colorado Mountain College.

CONTACT: Doug Schwartz, Director Culin. Educ., P.O. Box 38, Dillon, CO 80435; (303) 468-4153.

DISTRICT OF COLUMBIA

ACF NATION'S CAPITAL CHEFS

This chapter has 12 apprentices, 7 under age 25, 5 age 25 or over. Waiting list is about about 1 year. Costs are approximately $2,500 per year; beginning salary is $6.75 per hour, with increases every 6 months. The 12 locations are restaurant, hotel and country club. Most desirable settings are ANA Hotel, Congressional Country Club, Vista International Hotel. Degree program available through North Virginia Community College.

CONTACT: Forest Bell, 6289 Dunaway Ct., McLean, VA 22101; (301) 469-2018 (work), (703) 893-3823 (home), Fax (301) 469-2035.

FLORIDA

ACF CENTRAL FLORIDA CHAPTER

This chapter has 300 apprentices, 80 under age 25, 20 age 25 or over. Costs are approximately $615; beginning salary is $6.50 per hour, with 25 cent increases yearly. The 50 locations are restaurant, corporate and resorts. Most desirable settings are Swan (Westin) Hotel, Hyatt Grand Cypress, Alagua Country Club. Baking apprenticeship available.

CONTACT: Valerie Shelton, Mid Florida Tech, 2900 W. Oakridge Rd., Orlando, FL 32809; (407) 855-5880, ext.286 (work), Fax (407) 855-5880, ext. 700.

ACF FIRST COAST CHAPTER

This chapter has 25 apprentices, 15 under age 25, 10 age 25 or over. Waiting list is about 3 months. Costs are $300 per year; beginning salary is $5.50 per hour, with 25 cent increases semi-annually. The 20 locations are restaurant, hotel, resort, private club, country club. Most desirable settings are River Club (private), Ritz Carlton Amelia Island (resort), Omni Hotel (hotel). Housing cost is approximately $400 per month. Degree program available through Florida Community College at Jacksonville is completed by 70% of apprentices. Baking apprenticeship available.

CONTACT: Don Pleau, CWC, Executive Chef, American Culinary Federation, 200 Ponte Vedra Blvd., Ponte Vedra Beach, FL 32082; (904) 285-1111 (work), Fax (904) 285-2111.

ACF GREATER FORT LAUDERDALE CHAPTER

This chapter has 22 apprentices, 6 under age 25, 16 age 25 or over. Costs are approximately $200; beginning salary is $6-$8, with 25-50 cent increases every 3 to 6 months. The 12 locations are restaurant, resort and hospital. Most desirable settings are Marriot Harbor Beach Resort, Bonaventure Hotel Resort, Lauderdale Yacht Club. Degree program available through Atlantic Vocational Technical Center and ACF. Baking apprenticeship available.

CONTACT: Kenneth P. Carver, CEC, AAC, Apprenticeship Coordinator, 8200 S.W. 3rd St., North Lauderdale, FL 33068; (305) 360-8638 (work), Fax (305) 977-2019.

ACF GULF TO LAKES CHAPTER

This chapter has 16 apprentices, 5 under age 25, 11 age 25 or over. Costs paid by school; beginning salary subject to local wage scales; 25 cent increases every 6 months. The 12 locations are restaurant, corporate, resort, hotel, inn and nursing care home. Most desirable settings are full service resorts, hotels and restaurants. Degree program through Lake County Vocational Tech. Center.

CONTACT: James Aro, CEC, 2001 Kurt St., Eustis, FL 32726; (904) 742-6486 ext.152 (work), (904) 483-2546 (home).

ACF PALM BEACH COUNTY CHEFS

This chapter has 28 apprentices, Costs are $300 per year; beginning salary is $6 per hour, with 50 cent increases every 6 months. The 10 locations are restaurant, hotel, resort, private club, country club, corporate dining room. Housing cost is $400 per month. Degree program available through Palm Beach Community College is completed by 80% of apprentices.

CONTACT: Ken Wade, CEC, AAC, Apprenticeship Chairman, 3926 Bluebell St., Palm Beach Gardens, FL 33410; (407) 744-1300 (work), (407) 694-2444 (home), Fax (407) 744-9948.

ACF TREASURE COAST CHAPTER

This chapter has 30 apprentices, 10 under age 25, 20 age 25 or over. Costs are about $160 plus texts and materials; beginning salary is $5-$6 per hour; increases quarterly upon evaluation. The 15 locations are country club, resort, corporate, institutional and restaurant. Most desirable are Indian River Plantation, Harbor Ridge CC, Indian River Estates. Degree program through ACF.

CONTACT: George Vecchio, Martin County High School, 2801 S. Kanner Hwy., Stuart, FL 34994; (407) 287-0710 ext. 478 (work), (407) 467-0600 (home), Fax (407) 223-1648.

DISNEY CULINARY APPRENTICESHIP

This chapter has 137 apprentices. Costs are $2,175 for 3 years; beginning salary is $6.20 per hour. Certificate program available through WDW is completed by 70% of apprentices.

CONTACT: Alex Edgemon, General Employement, Disney Culinary Apprenticeship, Walt Disney World Co., P.O. Box 10,000, Lake Buena Vista, FL 32830-1000; (407) 934-7595 (work).

GULF COAST CULINARY ASSOCIATION
CONTACT: Jim O'Brien, CWC, P.O. Box 208, Pensacola, FL 32597; (904) 432-3707 (work).

SARASOTA BAY CHEFS ASSOCIATION
CONTACT: Heinz Schellenberger, CCE, 4748 Beneva Rd., Sarasota, FL 34232; (813) 924-1365, ext. 255 (work).

SOUTHWEST FLORIDA CHEFS ASSOCIATION
This chapter has 20 apprentices, 80 under age 25, 20 age 25 or over. Costs are approximately $150; beginning salary is $6, with 50 cent increases every 6 months. Locations: country clubs, fine restaurants. Most desirable settings: Wildcat Run and Forrest Country Clubs, Peters La Cuisine. Housing cost is from $300-$400. Degree program through ACF and Edison Community College.
CONTACT: Jack Lowy, CEC, CCE, 3800 Michigan Ave., Ft. Myers, FL 33916; (813) 549-0055 (work), Fax (813) 332-4839.

TAMPA BAY CHEFS ASSOCIATION
This chapter has variable number of apprentices. Costs are $34 per credit, a total of approximately $1,200; beginning salary is open. Apartment housing near college. Degree program available through Hillsborough Community College is completed by 70% of apprentices. Baking apprenticeship available.
CONTACT: Deborah Ferris, 2086 San Marino Way, N., Clearwater, FL 34623; (813) 221-5300 (work), (813) 222-0263 (home).

VOLUSIA COUNTY CHEFS AND COOKS
This chapter has 138 apprentices, 25 under age 25, 113 age 25 or over. Waiting list is about about 1 year. Costs are free (state funded); beginning salary is $5 per hour to $32,000 per year, with increases depend on employer. The 90 locations are restaurant and hotel. Most desirable settings are country clubs, hotels and gourmet restaurants. Housing cost is $400-$500 per month. Degree program available through Daytona Beach Community College. Baking apprenticeship available.
CONTACT: Brian Clarke, CEC, Daytona Beach Community College, 1200 International Dr., Daytona Beach, FL 32120-2881; (904) 255-8131 ext. 3735 (work), Fax (904) 254-4492.

GEORGIA

ACF INC., GREATER ATLANTA CHAPTER
CONTACT: John Brantley, CEC, 3571 Forrest Glen Tr., Lawrenceville, GA 30244; (404) 806-0336.

HAWAII

CHEFS DE CUISINE ASSOCIATION OF HAWAII
CONTACT: William Trask, Ilikai Hotel, 1777 Ala Moana Blvd., Honolulu, HI 96816; (808) 949-3811 (work), (808) 735-5641 (home).

H.A.R.I.E.T.T.
This chapter has 22 apprentices, 6 under age 25, 16 age 25 or over. Waiting list is about about 1

APPRENTICESHIPS · IOWA

year. Costs are approximately $40 annual junior membership in ACF; beginning salary is 70% of dinner cook rate, with 5% increases every 1,000 hours. The 15 locations are hotel. Most desirable settings are any one; all are well-rounded placements. Housing cost from $800 per month. Degree program available through ACF. Baking apprenticeship available.

CONTACT: Cheryl E. Kincaid, Training Coordinator, Hawaii Hotel and Restaurant Industry Employment and Training Trust, 1400 Kapiolani Blvd., B-347, Honolulu, HI 96814; (808) 949-8812 (work), Fax (808) 941-4777.

MAUI CHEFS & COOKS ASSOCIATION

This chapter has 6 apprentices, 4 under age 25, 2 age 25 or over. Costs are in-state $261 per semester, out-of-state $1,557 per semester; beginning salary is $10.50-$11 per hour (no less than 50% of Cook I rate), with increases from 50%-100% of Cook I rate every 6 months. The 3 locations are resort and restaurant. Most desirable settings are Westin Maui and Kea Lani Resort. Limited on-campus dormitory housing; nearby apartments available. Housing cost is $600-$800 per month. Mandatory degree program available through Maui Community College is completed by 50% of apprentices.

CONTACT: Chris Speere, Culinary Educator, c/o Maui Community College, 310 Kaahumanu Ave., Kahului, HI 96732; (808) 242-1210/1225 (work), (808) 575-2353 (home), Fax (808) 242-1251.

ILLINOIS

ACF CHICAGO CHEFS OF CUISINE

CONTACT: Jeff M. Lemke, CWC, 40 Shoreline Rd., Barrington, IL 60016; (708) 382-4240 (work).

INDIANA

ACF GREATER INDIANAPOLIS CHAPTER

CONTACT: Frank Lee, CWC, Hillview CC, 180 East King St., Franklin, IN 46131; (317) 736-5555.

ACF SOUTH BEND CHAPTER

This chapter has 16 apprentices, 5 under age 25, 11 age 25 or over. Costs are $3,825 for 3 years (6,000 hours); beginning salary is $7.50 per hour (average), with approximately 8% increases every 1,000 hours. The 14 locations are restaurant, hotel, private club, country club, college, hospital. Most desirable settings are restaurant, hotel, country club. Certificate program available through Lake Michigan College is completed by 65% of apprentices.

CONTACT: Denis F. Ellis, CEC, AAC, Chairman Apprenticeship Committee, University of Notre Dame, Box 1043, Notre Dame, IN 46556; (219) 631-5416 (work), (219) 271-9171 (home), Fax (219) 631-7994., E-Mail denis.f.ellis.1@nd.edu

IOWA

ACF CHEF DE CUISINE/QUAD CITIES

This chapter has 25 apprentices, 13 under age 25, 12 age 25 or over. Waiting list is at most 1 year. Costs are approximately $4,500 for 3 years; beginning salary is $5 per hour, with 25 cent increases every 6 months. The 22 locations are country club, hotel and restaurant. Most desirable settings are based on apprentice's location. Housing cost is from $300-$350 per month. Degree program available through Scott Community College.

CONTACT: Jennifer Cook-DeRosa, ACF Culinary Arts Apprenticeship Facilitator, 500 Belmont Rd., Bettendorf, IA 52722; (319) 359-7531 ext. 278 (work), (319) 764-1700 (home).

ACF GREATER DES MOINES CULINARY ASSOCIATION

CONTACT: Robert Anderson, Des Moines Area CC, 2006 S. Ankeny Blvd., Ankeny, IA 50021; (515) 964-6200 (work).

LOUISIANA

ACF NEW ORLEANS CHAPTER

This chapter has 190 apprentices, 65% under age 25, 35% age 25 or over. Applications accepted fall semesters only. Costs are approximately $3,600; 25 cent salary increases every 6 months. The 75 locations are restaurant, hotel, country club, private club. Housing in nearby apartment complexes; housing cost is $350-$550 and up. Degree program available through Delgado Community College is completed by 90% of apprentices.

CONTACT: Iva Bergeron, CCE, Director, Delgado Community College, 615 City Park Ave., New Orleans, LA 70119; (504) 483-4208 (work), Fax (504) 483-4893.

MARYLAND

CENTRAL MARYLAND CHEFS ASSOCIATION

This chapter has 26 apprentices, 24 under age 25, 1 age 25 or over. Beginning salary is $5 minimum, with increases twice a year. Most desirable settings are hotel, country club, restaurant. Degree program available through Anne Arundel Community College. Baking apprenticeship available.

CONTACT: Terry Green, CCE, Apprenticeship Chairman, Western School, 100 Kenwood, Baltimore, MD 21228; (410) 887-0852 (work), (301) 855-4018 (home), Fax (410) 887-1024.

MASSACHUSETTS

EPICUREAN CLUB OF BOSTON

CONTACT: Christoph Leu, The Westin Hotel, 10 Huntington Ave., Boston, MA 02116-5798; (617) 424-7524 (work).

MICHIGAN

ACF MICHIGAN CHEFS DE CUISINE

This chapter has 65 apprentices. Costs are approximately $1,500; beginning salary is $6, with increases every 6 months. The 60 locations are hotel, restaurant, country and city club, and hospital. Most desirable settings are in Oakland County. Degree program available through Oakland Community College.

CONTACT: Kevin Enright, CEC, Chef-Coordinator, Oakland Community College, 27055 Orchard Lake Rd., Farmington Hills, MI 48334; (810) 471-7500 (work).

ACF OF NORTHWESTERN MICHIGAN

This chapter has 36 apprentices. Costs are approximately $2,880 for 3 years, $18 per week; beginning salary is $6 per hour, with increases every 6 months. The 22 to 25 locations are institutional, hotel, country club and restaurant. Housing cost is from $280 per month. Degree program available through Lake Michigan College.

CONTACT: Suzanne Beckley, Hospitality Management Coordinator, Lake Michigan College, 27555 East Napier Ave., Benton Harbor, MI 49022; (616) 927-8100 ext. 5004 (work).

MISSOURI

ACF CHEFS AND COOKS OF SPRINGFIELD/OZARK

This chapter has 19 apprentices, 19 under age 25. Beginning salary is minimum wage, with increases every 6 months. The 6 to 8 locations are hotel, country club, and restaurant. .

CONTACT: Gunter Rinderspacher, Lake of Ozarks CC, 1417 N. Jefferson, Springfield, MO 65802, (417) 895-7282 (work), (417) 532-8801 (home).

ACF GREATER KANSAS CITY CHEFS ASSOCIATION

CONTACT: Patrick Sweeney, CEC, Johnson County CC, 12345 College at Quivira, Overland Park, KS 66210; (913) 469-8500, ext. 3611.

CHEFS DE CUISINE OF ST. LOUIS

CONTACT: Ralph Wehner, CWC, 362 Novara, Ballwin, MO 63021; (314) 362-1406 (work).

MONTANA

CHEFS AND COOKS OF MONTANA

This chapter has 3 apprentices, all over age 25. Costs are free; beginning salary is $5.25 to $6 per hour, with 25 to 50 cent increases every 6 months. The 1 location is a private club. Housing cost is from $250 per month. Degree program available through Montana Vocational-Technical Center.

CONTACT: Jack Hemsing, CEC, Billings Petroleum Club, Box 1957, Billings, MT 59103; (406) 252-6702 (work), (406) 652-1149 (home).

NEBRASKA

ACF PROFESSIONAL CHEFS OF OMAHA

CONTACT: Jim Trebbien, CCE, Metropolitan CC, Bldg. 10, P.O. Box 3777, 30th & Fort Sts., Omaha, NE 68103-0777; (402) 449-8394 (work), (402) 238-2199 (home), Fax (402) 449-8333.

NEVADA

ACF COLORADO RIVER CHEFS ASSOCIATION

CONTACT: Tracey Yamamoto, Harrahs Casino, Harrahs Casino, 2900 S. Casino Dr., Laughlin, NV 89029; (702) 298-6814 (work).

THE FRATERNITY OF EXECUTIVE CHEFS OF LAS VEGAS

This chapter has 11 apprentices, 11 under age 25. Waiting list is flexible. Costs are approximately $165; beginning salary is 80% of cook's helper's wages, with increases yearly. The 4 locations are resort. Most desirable settings are Mirage, Caesar's, Hilton. Housing cost is $350-$500. Degree program available through University of Las Vegas. Baking apprenticeship available.

CONTACT: Joe DelRosario, CWC, CCE, Community College of Southern Nevada, 3200 E. Cheyenne, North Las Vegas, NV 89030; (702) 651-4192 (work), (702) 438-1330.

HIGH SIERRA CHEFS ASSOCIATION

This chapter has 12 apprentices, 2 under age 25, 10 age 25 or over. Costs are approximately $185 dues, required college courses $500 to $1,000 over 3 years; beginning salary is $6.87 per hour, with increases yearly. The 6 locations are hotel and casino. Most desirable settings are Harrah's, Horizon, Harvey's. Housing cost is $300-$500 per month. Degree program available through Lake Tahoe Community College. Baking apprenticeship available.

CONTACT: Paul Lee, CWC, Harrah's Lake Tahoe, P.O. Box 8, Lake Tahoe, NV 89449; (702) 588-6611 ext. 2202 (work), Fax (702) 586-6609.

NEW HAMPSHIRE

GREATER NORTH NEW HAMPSHIRE CHAPTER

This chapter has 20 apprentices, 19 under age 25, 1 age 25 or over. Beginning salary is $4.50, with increases every 1,000 hours. The 12 locations include Balsams Resort Hotel, Waldorf-Astoria (NY), The Greenbrier (WV), The Cloister (GA), Hyatt Regency (Orlando). Free dormitory lodging is provided at The Balsams.

CONTACT: Phil Learned, CEC, The Balsams Resort Hotel, Box 112, Dixville Notch, NH 03576; (603) 255-3861 (work), Fax (603) 255-4670.

NEW JERSEY

ACF NORTHERN NEW JERSEY CHAPTER

CONTACT: George D. Theos, CCE, CEC, W. 207 Midland Ave., Paramus, NJ 07652; (201) 986-0008, ext. 413 (work), (201) 445-5913 (home).

PROFESSIONAL CHEFS OF SOUTH JERSEY

CONTACT: John Carbone, CCE, CEC, AAC, P.O. Box 157, Port Republic, NJ 08241; (609) 646-4950 (work), (609) 652-1726 (home).

NEW MEXICO

ACF CHEFS OF SANTA FE

CONTACT: Maurice Zeck, 100 E. San Francisco St., Santa Fe, NM 87501; (505) 982-5511 (work).

ACF "PASO DEL NORTE" CHAPTER

CONTACT: Richard Cannarsa, P.O. Box 371, Santa Teresa, NM 88008-5858; (915) 594-2056.

ACF RIO GRANDE VALLEY CHAPTER

This chapter has 15 apprentices. AA degree available. Baking apprenticeship available.

CONTACT: Kayleigh Carabajal, CCE, CEPC, Academic Advisor, Albuquerque Tech-Voc Institute, 525 Buena Vista S.E., Albuquerque, NM 87106; (505) 224-3765 (work), Fax (505) 224-3720.

ACF SOUTHWEST NEW MEXICO & TEXAS

CONTACT: Paul R. Bellegarde, CWC, 1922B Amysue Rd., El Paso, TX 79936; (915) 577-6059.

NEW YORK

ACF CAPITOL DISTRICT CENTRAL NY

CONTACT: Michael Loporto, CEC, 85 Fourth Street, Troy, NY 12180; (518) 273-8546 (work).

ACF OF GREATER BUFFALO

This chapter has 3 apprentices, 3 under age 25, Costs are fees and college tuition; beginning salary is negotiable. Locations are private clubs. Most desirable settings are full service with extensive catering. Degree program available through Niagara County Community College or Erie Community College is completed by 100% of apprentices. Baking apprenticeship available.

CONTACT: Samuel J. Sheusi, CEC, CCE, AAC, 5084 Dana Dr., Lewiston, NY 14092; (716) 731-4101 (work), (716) 297-4551 (home), Fax (716) 297-4551.

ACF PROFESSIONAL CHEFS/COOKS ASSN. OF ROCHESTER

This chapter has 4 apprentices, 3 under age 25, 1 age 25 or over. Costs are approximately $150 plus $3,000 per year; beginning salary is $4.25-$5 per hour, with increases every 6 months. The 10 locations are country club and hotel. Most desirable settings are Locust Hill Country Club, Lodge of Woodcliffe Hotel and Country Club, Mario's Restaurant. Degree program available through Monroe Community College.

CONTACT: Jeffrey S. Clark, CEC, Apprenticeship Chairman, Professional Chefs/Cooks Association of Rochester, 3 Broezel St., Rochester, NY 14613; (800) 851-3951 (work), (716) 458-7277 (home).

CHEFS OF WESTCHESTER AND LOWER CONNECTICUT

CONTACT: Brian Martin, Black Goose Grille, 927 Post Rd., Darien, CT 06820; (203) 655-7107, (work), (914) 667-0984 (home).

NORTH CAROLINA

ACF CHARLOTTE CHAPTER

CONTACT: John McAllister, 5709 Cornflower Circle, Charlotte, NC 28212; (704) 786-3104.

ACF SANDHILLS/CROSS CREEK CHEFS ASSOCIATION

CONTACT: Joe Greene, CWC, P.O. Box 4000, Carolina Vista, Pinehurst, NC 28374; (919) 295-6565 (work), (919) 692-5872 (home).

ACF TRIANGLE CHEFS

This chapter has 3 apprentices, all under age 25. Costs are approximately $13.25 per credit hour; beginning salary is variable, with increases every 6 months. The numerous locations are restaurant, hotel and country club. Degree program available through Wake Technical Community College. Baking apprenticeship available.

CONTACT: Fredi Morf, Culinary Instructor, 1316 Hickory Hollow Ln., Raleigh, NC 27610; (919) 839-0691 (work), (919) 231-7769 (home).

TRIAD PROFESSIONAL CHEFS ASSOCIATION

CONTACT: S. Mitchell Mack, c/o HIFS, 3121 High Point Rd., Greensboro, NC 27407; (919) 242-9161, ext. 4112 (work).

OHIO

ACF CLEVELAND CHAPTER

CONTACT: Richard Fulchiron, CEC, Cuyahoga Community College, 2900 Community College Ave., Cleveland, OH 44115; (216) 987-4087 (work), (216) 243-0714 (home), Fax (216) 987-4096.

ACF COLUMBUS CHEFS CHAPTER

This chapter has 70 apprentices, 50 under age 25, 20 age 25 or over. Program begins once a year in September (application deadline May 15). Costs are $6,000 for 3 year program; beginning salary is $5 per hour, with increases usually every 6 months. The 40 locations are hotel, country club, private club, restaurant. Most desirable settings are restaurant, hotel, club. AAS degree program available through Columbus State Community College must be earned to complete program.

CONTACT: Carol Kizer, CCE, Chairperson Hospitality Mgt. Dept., Columbus State Community College, 550 E. Spring St., Columbus, OH 43215; (614) 227-2579 (work), Fax (614) 227-5146.

OKLAHOMA

ACF CULINARY ARTS OF OKLAHOMA

This chapter has 12 apprentices. Beginning salary is minimum wage. The 6 locations are restaurant, hotel, resort, country club. Most desirable settings are country clubs. Associate degree program available through OSU-Oklahoma City. Baking apprenticeship available.

CONTACT: Geni Thomas, CEPC, CEC, CCE, AAC, 4337 Dahoon Dr., Oklahoma City, OK 73120; (405) 749-3155 (work), (405) 752-1279 (home), Fax (405) 749-3214.

ACF TULSA CHAPTER

CONTACT: Robert M. Boyce, CWC, 5531 S. Toledo Pl., Tulsa, OK 74135-4325; (918) 486-6575 (work), (918) 496-3221 (home), Fax (918) 486-6576.

PENNSYLVANIA

ACF BERKS LEHIGH CHEFS

CONTACT: James Lesniak, 1244 Chestnut St., Reading, PA 19602; (215) 374-7115 (work).

ACF LAUREL HIGHLANDS CHAPTER

This chapter has 61 apprentices, 64% under age 25, 36% age 25 or over. Costs are $3,120 for 3 years (1995 semester); beginning salary is minimum wage, with increases every 1,000 hours. The 35 locations are restaurant, hotel, club, resort and institution. Most desirable settings are club, hotel, restaurant. Degree program available through Westmoreland County Community College.

CONTACT: Mary Zappone, CCE, Professor, Westmoreland County Community College, Culinary Arts, Westmoreland Community College, Armbrust Rd., Youngwood, PA 15697-1895; (412) 925-4015 (work), Fax (412) 925-4293.

ACF PITTSBURGH CHAPTER

This chapter has 60 apprentices, 40 under age 25, 20 age 25 or over. Costs are $4,000 including books and fees; beginning salary is negotiable, with 25 cent increases every 6 months. Most desirable settings are hotels, clubs, restaurants. Degree program available through Community College of Allegheny County is completed by 80% of apprentices. Baking apprenticeship available.

CONTACT: Willie Stinson, CEC, AAC, Coordinator, Culinary Arts, Community College of Allegheny City, 808 Ridge Ave., Jones Hall, Rm. 012, Pittsburgh, PA 15212; (412) 237-2698 (work), E-Mail w.stinson culinary

DELAWARE VALLEY CHEFS ASSOCIATION

CONTACT: William Tillinghast, 3602 Belgrade, Philadelphia, PA 19135; (215) 895-1146 (work), (215) 533-0325 (home), Fax (215) 895-1143.

SOUTH CAROLINA

SOUTH CAROLINA UPSTATE PROFESSIONAL CHEFS

This chapter has 7 apprentices. Costs are approximately $500 per semester; beginning salary is $5.50 per hour, with increases every 6 months. The 5 locations are hotel, city club, corporate, hospital and college. Most desirable settings are Hyatt Regency, Milliken Corporation, Pointsett Club. Housing cost ranges from $250 per month. Degree program available through Greenville Technical College.

CONTACT: Ben Black, CSC, Greenville Technical College, P.O. Box 5616, Greenville, SC 29606-5616; (803) 250-8030 (work).

TENNESSEE

ACF MIDDLE TENNESSEE CHAPTER

This chapter has 45 apprentices, Waiting list is about about 1 year. Costs are free; beginning salary is minimum wage, with increases yearly. The 1 location is hotel. Degree program available through Volunteer State Community College.

CONTACT: Stanley B. Jensen, CEC, AAC, 116 Connie Dr., Hendersonville, TN 37075; (615) 264-1436 (work)

OPRYLAND HOTEL CULINARY INSTITUTE

This chapter has 50 apprentices, 50% under age 25, Waiting list is up to 1 year. Beginning salary is $5.25 per hour, with 25 cent increases every 6 months. All rotations are within the restaurant, hotel, club kitchens, in-house butcher shop, bakery, and pastry shops of the Opryland complex. Housing in nearby apartments. Mandatory AAS degree program through Volunteer State Community College is completed by all apprentices.

CONTACT: Dina Starks, RD, Apprenticeship Coordinator, 2800 Opryland Dr., Nashville, TN 37214; (615) 871-7765 (work), Fax (615) 871-6942.

TEXAS

ACF CAPITOL OF TEXAS CHEFS

This chapter has 8 apprentices, all under age 25. Costs are about $500 per year; beginning salary is $6-$7 per hour, with 25 cent-40 cent increases twice a year. The 12 Austin locations are hotel, resort, country club, conference centers. Most desirable settings are Hill country, downtown, university area. Diploma available through Austin Community College is completed by 50%-60% of apprentices.

CONTACT: Thomas G. Ciapi, CEC, CCE, CWC, Executive Sous Chef/Apprentice Culinary Educator-Lakeway Inn, 101 Lakeway Dr., Austin, TX 78734; (512) 261-7339 (work), (512) 836-6534 (home), Fax (512) 261-7322.

ACF PROFESSIONAL CHEFS ASSOCIATION OF HOUSTON

CONTACT: Fritz Gitschner, CMC, Houston Country Club, 1 Potomac Dr., Houston, TX 77057; (713) 465-8381 (work).

TCA-BRAZOS VALLEY CHAPTER

This chapter has 13 apprentices. Waiting list is about about 30 applicants long. Costs are free;

beginning salary is $6 per hour, with state mandated percentage increases granted yearly. The 5 locations are educational and institutional. Most desirable settings are at Texas A&M University. Housing cost ranges from $450 per month. Baking apprenticeship available.

CONTACT: Victoria Beck, Administrative Dietician, Food Service Department, Texas A&M University, College Station, TX 77843-1374; (409) 845-3005 (work), (409) 696-8721 (home).

TCA-DALLAS

CONTACT: James Goering, CCE, CEC, El Centro College, Main @ Lamar, Dallas, TX 75202-3604; (214) 746-2217 (work), (214) 241-4487 (home).

TCA-HEART OF TEXAS CHAPTER

This chapter has 4 apprentices. Costs are approximately $1,500 over 3 years plus fees; beginning salary is minimum wage, with increases every 6 months. The 1 location is university. Most desirable setting is Baylor University. Housing cost is from $250 per month.

CONTACT: Allen Meyers, CEC, P.O. Box 1401, Mexia, TX 76667; (817) 755-3432 (work).

TCA-HOUSTON

CONTACT: Francois Lefebvre, CWC, 8618 Crystal Cove Ct., Houston, TX 77044; (713) 623-2500 , ext. 4578 (work), (713) 458-6282 (home).

TCA-SAN ANTONIO

CONTACT: Dan Block, La Mangion Del Rio Hotel, 112 College St., San Antonio, TX 78205; (210) 225-2581(work).

TEXAS CHEFS ASSOCIATION

CONTACT: Robert Sutten, CEC, TCA Apprenticeship Chairman, 3215 Modella, Dallas, TX 75229; (210) 377-1092 (work).

UTAH

ACF BEEHIVE STATE CHEFS CHAPTER

This chapter has 80-100 apprentices, average age 27. Costs are $1,550; beginning salary is $6.50 per hour, with increases based on merit. The Utah locations are restaurant, hotel, retirement home, club. Housing cost is approximately $650 per month. Degree program available through Salt Lake Community College is completed by more than 34% of apprentices. Baking apprenticeship available.

CONTACT: Joe Mulvey, Director of Apprenticeship, Apprenticeship Office, Salt Lake Community College, 4600 S. Redwood Rd., Salt Lake City, UT 84119; (801) 957-4066 (work), Fax (801) 957-4612., E-Mail mulveyjo@slcc.edu

VERMONT

NORTH VERMONT CHEFS & COOKS ASSOCIATION

This chapter has a varied number of apprentices. Costs are $835 per year. There are 15 locations. Most desirable settings are Marriott, Perry Restaurant Group, restaurants in Stowe locations. Baking apprenticeship available.

CONTACT: Krista Willett, Apprenticeship Chair, RD1, Box 282, Richmond, VT 05477; (802) 434-3148 (work), (802) 434-4297 (home).

VIRGINIA

ACF TIDEWATER CHAPTER
CONTACT: Art Elvins, CEC, Chapter President, 2428 Alameda Ave., #170, Norfolk, VA 23513; (804) 855-1835 (work), (804) 482-6464 (home), Fax (804) 857-4869.

BLUE RIDGE CHEFS ASSOCIATION
CONTACT: Bill King, CEC, 3425 Pippin Ln., Charlottesville, VA 22903; (703) 894-5436 (work), (804) 295-0614 (home), Fax (703) 894-0534.

NATIONAL GUILD OF PASTRY & BAKING PROFESSIONALS
CONTACT: Marcel Walter, CEPC, P.O. Box 125, Williamsburg VA 23187; (804) 220-7673 (work), (804) 566-4124 (home).

VIRGINIA CHEFS ASSOCIATION
This chapter has 25 apprentices, 22 under age 25, 3 age 25 or over. Costs are approximately $3,000 in-state plus $1,250 for books and materials; beginning salary is $6.50 per hour, with 25 cent increases yearly. The 20 locations are restaurant, country club, hotel, grocery store, central commissary and hospital. Most desirable settings are Colonial Williamsburg, Tobacco Company Restaurant. Housing cost ranges from $300-$500 per month. Degree program available through J. Sargeant Reynolds Community College is completed by 100% of apprentices. Baking apprenticeship available.

CONTACT: David J. Barrish, CHA, Program Head, Hospitality Management, J. Sargeant Reynolds Community College, P.O. Box 85622, Richmond, VA 23285-5622; (804) 367-8880 (work), Fax (804) 367-2703.

WASHINGTON

WASHINGTON STATE CHEFS ASSOCIATION
CONTACT: John V. Melchior, 1325 Sixth Ave., P.O. Box 1709, Seattle, WA 98111; (206) 464-3084 (work), (206) 464-3058 (home).

WEST VIRGINIA

ACF WEST VIRGINIA CHAPTER
CONTACT: Dan Ferguson, CWC, Edgewood CC, 216 Rockledge Dr., Nitro, WV 25143; (304) 343-5557 (work), (304) 776-3559 (home) Fax (206) 464-3958.

WISCONSIN

ACF CHEFS OF MILWAUKEE, INC.
This chapter has 24 apprentices, 13 under age 25, 11 age 25 or over. Costs are $2,200; beginning salary is $5-$6 per hour, with 25 cent increases every 6 months. The 48 locations are restaurant, hotel, private club, country club, catering. Most desirable settings are restaurant, hotel, country club. Degree program available through Milwaukee Area Technical College is completed by 60% of apprentices.

CONTACT: Knut Apitz, 747 N. Broadway @ Mason, Milwaukee, WI 53202; (414) 276-0747 (work), (414) 276-1424 (home).

ACF FOX VALLEY CHAPTER

This chapter has 27 apprentices. Costs are approximately $1,400 for 3 years; beginning salary is $5 per hour, with increases each semester. The 19 locations are restaurant, hotel, resort, convention center, country club. Most desirable settings are American Club Resort, Paper Valley Hotel, Oneida Golf and Riding Club. Housing cost is from $300 per month. Degree program available through Fox Valley Technical College.

CONTACT: Albert Exenberger, ACF Fox Valley Chapter, Fox Valley Technical College, 1825 N. Bluemound Dr., Appleton, WI 54913; (414) 735-5600 (work), (414) 722-7960 (home).

ACF MIDDLE WISCONSIN CHEFS

CONTACT: Gregory Krzyminski, Mid-State Technical College, 500 32nd St. North, Wisconsin Rapids, WI 54494; (715) 423-5650 (work), (715) 422-5345 (home) Fax (715) 422-5345.

BAHAMAS

BAHAMAS CULINARY ASSOCIATION

This chapter has 53 apprentices. Costs are $150; beginning salary is $120 per week, with increases annually. The 208 locations include Princess Towers Hotel, Sun International, and Carnival's Crystal Palace Hotel. Degree program available through Bahamas Hotel Training College.

CONTACT: Christopher Smith, CCE, P.O. Box N4896, Nassau, Bahamas; (809) 326-5860 (work), Fax (809) 325-2459.

BAHAMAS HOTEL TRAINING COLLEGE

This chapter has 25 apprentices. Waiting list is about about 1 year. Costs are about $1,000 per year; beginning salary is $120 per week, with increases yearly. The 8 locations are resort, hotel and restaurant. Most desirable settings are Bahamas Princess Country CC, Lucaya Beach Hotel, Princess Casino. Degree program through ACF and SACS. Baking apprenticeship available.

CONTACT: Bernard Dawkins, Box F-41679, Freeport, Grand Bahamas; (809) 352-2896 (work), (809) 352-9002 (fax).

2

Non-Vocational and Vacation Programs

ALABAMA

SOUTHERN LIVING COOKING SCHOOL
Birmingham/Spring and Fall

Since 1975, *Southern Living* magazine has presented cooking shows that are co-sponsored by nationally-recognized food brands and local newspapers and feature the demonstration of more than a dozen recipes containing sponsors' products.

EMPHASIS: Southern dishes.

FACULTY: Professional home economists from *Southern Living*.

COSTS, ACCOMMODATIONS: Range from $1-$10, depending on location.

LOCATION: Auditoriums and community centers in Birmingham and other southern cities

CONTACT: *Southern Living* Cooking School, P.O. Box 2581, Birmingham, AL 35202; (205) 877-6000.

ARIZONA

CUISINES OF THE WORLD — HACKETT HOUSE
Tempe/September-April

Since 1986, the nonprofit Tempe Sister City Corporation has conducted demonstration (limit 12 students) and participation (limit 12 to 100) classes as part of its program to support Tempe's cultural ties with sister cities in Europe and Asia. The Reader's Digest Foundation Award-winning Cuisines of the World program features 30 to 50 sessions per year. Facilities: commercial kitchen and patio area of Hackett House, a restored 19th-century bakery. Also available: family and private classes and a children's program that combines instruction in international cuisine, music, literature, dance, and art.

FACULTY: Local and well-known food professionals have included Madeleine Kamman, Martin Yan, Diana Kennedy, Merle Ellis. Barbara Colleary chairs the cuisine programs.

COSTS: Adult classes are $25-$50; children's classes are $8-$10; $5 is tax deductible. Refund granted 4 days prior. Credit cards accepted.

LOCATION: Old Town Tempe.

CONTACT: Barbara Colleary, Cuisine Coordinator, Cuisines of the World, Hackett House, 95 W. 4th St., Tempe, AZ 85281; (602) 350-8181.

CULINARY CONCEPTS
Tucson/Year-round

Founded in 1994, this retail kitchenware store and school offers 40 mostly participation classes (limit 28 students) per month that include single sessions, 9-session certificate courses, series for children and teens, and dinner workshops. Facilities: 700-sq.-ft. teaching kitchen with 7 workspaces. Also available: wine appreciation, beer-making instruction, private classes, party planning.

EMPHASIS: A variety of topics, guest chef specialties.

FACULTY: Includes proprietor Judith Berger, cookbook author Rita Rosenberg, and chefs Sandra Joy Paul, CEPC, and Sarah Kevorkian.

COSTS: Range from $35-$45 per session. Refund with 72 hours notice.

LOCATION: A Southwestern shopping plaza in north-central Tucson.

CONTACT: Judith B. Berger, Culinary Concepts, Plaza Palomino, 2930 N. Swan, #126, Tucson, AZ 85712; (520) 321-0968, Fax (520) 321-0375.

THE HOUSE OF RICE STORE
Scottsdale/Year-round

Founded in 1977, this retail store/school offers 1-session participation courses (limit 12 students). Also available: private group classes.

EMPHASIS: Chinese, Japanese, Vietnamese, and Thai cuisines.

FACULTY: School owner Kiyoko Goldhardt, Chau Liaw, Lan Nguyen, and Mark Gerding.

COSTS: $16 to $25 per class. Pre-payment is required; refunds granted cancellations a week prior.

LOCATION: One mile east of downtown Scottsdale

CONTACT: Kiyoko Goldhardt, The House of Rice Store, 3221 N. Hayden Rd., Scottsdale, AZ 85251; (602) 947-6698 or (602) 949-9681, Fax (602) 947-0889.

LES GOURMETTES ON THE CAMEL'S BACK
Scottsdale/January-May, October-November

Started in 1994 by Barbara Pool Fenzl, this *destination* resort offers one or two 1-, 2- and 5-day cooking vacations per month. Instructional format: demonstration. Class size: 22 maximum. Three hours of instruction daily. Other activities: visits to markets and specialty shops. Also available: private lessons.

EMPHASIS: Southwestern cuisine, guest chef specialties.

FACULTY: Barbara Fenzl, owner of Les Gourmettes Cooking School, and the Food and Beverage staff of John Gardiner's. Guest chefs: Clark Knutson, Vincent Guerithault, and Christopher Gross.

COSTS, ACCOMMODATIONS: Ranges from approximately $700 (2 days) to $2,200 (5 days), which includes double occupancy standard lodging at John Gardiner's Tennis Ranch on Camelback, all meals, and use of tennis courts and fitness corral. Commuter, single occupancy, and casita lodging rates are available.

LOCATION: 15 miles from the Phoenix/Sky Harbor airport.

CONTACT: Bob Marshall, Director of Sales & Marketing, John Gardiner's Tennis Ranch on Camelback, 5700 E. McDonald Dr., Scottsdale, AZ 85253; (800) 245-2051 or (602) 948-2100, Fax (602) 483-3386.

LES GOURMETTES COOKING SCHOOL
Phoenix/September-May

Founded in 1982, this school offers 10 to 15 demonstration classes and series (limit 15 students) quarterly. Also available: summer classes for children, culinary trips in the U.S. and abroad, 3-day sessions at John Gardiner's Tennis Ranch in Scottsdale.

EMPHASIS: French and Southwest and a variety of other cuisines.

FACULTY: School proprietor Barbara Fenzl, CCP studied at the Cordon Bleu, Ecole Lenotre, and with James Beard and Julia Child. Guest instructors have included Giuliano Bugialli, Hugh Carpenter, Lydie Marshall, and Jacques Pepin.

COSTS: Guest chef classes from $40-$85; 3-session courses are $105. Advance payment required.

LOCATION: Central Phoenix.

CONTACT: Barbara Fenzl, Les Gourmettes Cooking School, 6610 N. Central Ave., Phoenix, AZ 85012; (602) 240-6767, Fax (602) 266-2706

SCOTTSDALE CULINARY INSTITUTE *(See page 2)*
Scottsdale/Year-round

This career school also offers classes for nonprofessionals.

SWEET BASIL GOURMETWARE & COOKING SCHOOL
Scottsdale/Year-round

Established in 1993, this cookware store offers occasional demonstrations (limit 25 students) and

NONVOCATIONAL/VACATION   **CALIFORNIA**   **155**

15-20 one- to three-session participation courses (limit 12) per month. Facilities: 400-square-foot kitchen with six workspaces and gas and electric appliances.

EMPHASIS: Various topics, including low fat cooking, ethnic and regional cuisines, specific subjects.

FACULTY: The eight instructors include school director Stacey Schulz, IACP award winner Barbara Colleary, and nutritionist TJ Majeras.

COSTS: $25-$75 per course.

LOCATION: 12 miles from Phoenix and Sky Harbor Airport.

CONTACT: Martha Sullivan, Owner, Sweet Basil Gourmetware & Cooking School, 10701 N. Scottsdale Rd., #101, Scottsdale, AZ 85260; (602) 596-5628.

THE TASTING SPOON
Tucson/September-May

Founded in 1978, this school in a private residence offers 3 to 4 weekly classes and 2 to 3 Lunch and Learn sessions per month, 12-session diploma courses in spring and fall, and a 10-session International Series. Also available: wine tastings, demonstrations by local chefs.

EMPHASIS: Techniques, beginning to advanced recipes, international cuisines.

FACULTY: Chefs Jeff Azersky, Doug Levy, James Murphy, Donna Nordin, Todd Seligman.

COSTS: Classes range from $30-$40, Lunch and Learn sessions are $12, and series are $375. Full payment or deposit required with registration; refund for cancellations 72 hours prior. Credit cards accepted.

LOCATION: Northwest Tucson.

CONTACT: Virginia Selby, Director, The Tasting Spoon, P.O. Box 44013, Tucson, AZ 85733-4013; (602) 327-8174.

ARKANSAS

HARRIET NEIMAN
Fayetteville

Established in 1992, this catering facility offers 3 to 4 morning demonstration and participation (limit 8 to 13 students) classes per month. Facilities: 36-square-foot demonstration station. Also available: children's classes, private instruction.

EMPHASIS: Ethnic, especially Mediterranean, easy cooking techniques.

FACULTY: Harriet Neiman studied at La Varenne, Linda Gaddy studied at Le Cordon Bleu.

LOCATION: 2 hours from Tulsa, 4 hours from Little Rock.

CONTACT: Harriet Neiman, 40 N. Crossover Rd., Fayetteville, AR 72701; (501) 521-3739.

CALIFORNIA

ACADEMY OF COOKING — BEVERLY HILLS
Beverly Hills/Year-round except January and August

Established in 1990, caterer Meredith Jo Mischen offers 12 participation classes (limit 10 students) per month. Facilities: restaurant kitchen with 10 work stations. Also available: children's and private classes, culinary tours in Southern California.

EMPHASIS: Afternoon tea, buffet, brunch menus; California, international,, vegetarian cuisines.

FACULTY: Meredith Jo Mischen studied with chefs at New York's Plaza and Waldorf Astoria Hotels and operates Meredith's Marvelous Morsels.

COSTS: Classes are $50. Credit for cancellations 72 hours prior

CONTACT: Meredith Jo Mischen, Director, Academy of Cooking-Beverly Hills, 400 S. Beverly Dr., #214, Beverly Hills, CA 90212; (310) 284-4940.

AMY MALONE SCHOOL OF CAKE DECORATING
La Mesa/Year-round

Founded in Virginia in 1977, this school offers approximately 40 morning and evening participation (limit 14 students) and demonstration (limit 30) classes each quarter.

EMPHASIS: Cake decorating, special occasion creations, confectionery calligraphy, candymaking, creative garnishes.

FACULTY: Amy Malone is a graduate of the Wilton, Betty Newman May, John McNamara, Mary Howard, Josepha Baroloco and Frances Kuyper schools of cake decorating and was guest instructor at L'Academie de Cuisine.

COSTS: Range from $15-$75 per class. $10 deposit is refundable for cancellations 5 days prior.

LOCATION: East of San Diego

CONTACT: Amy Malone, Amy Malone School of Cake Decorating, 4212 Camino Alegre, La Mesa, CA 91941; (619) 660-1900.

BORDER GRILL
Los Angeles/Year-round

Since 1992, this restaurant has offered monthly demonstrations (limit 65 students) of its specialties.

EMPHASIS: French, Latin, and city cuisines.

FACULTY: Susan Feniger and Mary Sue Milliken, chef-owners of the Border Grill and City Restaurant and authors of *City Cuisine*.

COSTS: Range from $30-$40 per session. Credit cards accepted

CONTACT: Susan Feniger/Mary Sue Milliken, Border Grill, 1445-4th St., Los Angeles, CA 90401; (310) 451-1655.

BRISTOL FARMS COOK 'N' THINGS
Pasadena & Anaheim/Year-round

Established in 1985, this cookware store offers approximately 20 one- to six-session demonstration (limit 40 students) and participation (limit 20) courses per month. Facilities: kitchen with 6-burner stove, grill, 3 convection ovens, and video system. Also available: children's and private classes, field trips, and tours.

EMPHASIS: International and regional cuisine, baking, low-fat cooking, techniques.

FACULTY: Director Claudia McQuillan, CCP, and Theresa Parra; guest s have included Stephen Pyles, Patricia Wells, Jacques Pepin, and Julia Child.

COSTS: Range from $25-$75 per session, payable at least 4 days prior. Cancellations 24 hours prior receive class credit.

LOCATION: Next door to the South Pasadena Market, 15 minutes from Los Angeles; Anaheim Hills in Orange County.

CONTACT: Theresa Parra, Cooking School Manager, Bristol Farms Cook 'N' Things, 606 Fair Oaks Ave., S. Pasadena, CA 91030; (818) 441-5588, Fax (818) 441-8994. 5580 E. Santa Ana Canyon Rd., Anaheim Hills, CA 92807, (714) 974-5588, Fax (714) 924-1175.

CAKEBREAD CELLARS
Napa Valley/January, April, July, November *(See also page 4)*

This winery offers four demonstration classes a year that focus on seasonal events.

FACULTY: Resident chef Brian Streeter, a New England Culinary Institute graduate, and guest chefs.

COSTS: $75 per class.

CONTACT: Cakebread Cellars, 8300 St. Helena Hwy., Box 216, Rutherford, CA 94573-0216; (707) 963-5221, Fax (707) 963-1067.

CALIFORNIA CULINARY ACADEMY
San Francisco/Year-round

(See ad page 5)

This career institution's Consumer Education Department offers hands-on and demonstration classes for food and wine enthusiasts of all levels. Topics include such basics as knife skills, sauce workshops, and baking fundamentals; more specialized courses on ice carving, food styling, and winepairing; classes on international cuisines; and Saturday sessions for teens.

CAROLE BLOOM, PATISSIERE
Carlsbad/Year-round

Established in 1978, Carole Bloom teaches demonstration (limit 12 students) and participation (limit 8) classes 2 or 3 times a week.in pastry and desserts. Facilities: a specially-equipped professional kitchen. Also available: private instruction.

EMPHASIS: Swiss, French, Italian, and Austrian pastries and desserts, chocolate, pralines, special occasion cakes, ice creams.

FACULTY: Carole Bloom contributes to *Fine Cooking* and *Bon Appétit*, produces a cooking show, and is author of *Truffles, Candies, & Confections* and *The International Dictionary of Desserts, Pastries, and Confections*, and *The Candy Cookbook*.

COSTS: $85 per class must accompany reservation. Refunds granted 48 hours prior.

LOCATION: 15 miles north of San Diego

CONTACT: Carole Bloom, 7067 Rockrose Terr., Carlsbad, CA 92009; (619) 931-5920, Fax (619) 931-0423; E-Mail: golivas@cyber.net.

CASTROVILLE ARTICHOKE FESTIVAL
Castroville/September

First held in 1959, this annual 2-day festival in the artichoke capitol features specialty dishes and activities.

EMPHASIS: Artichoke preparations.

COSTS: General admission is $3. A list of nearby lodging is available.

LOCATION: The Monterey peninsula, 50 miles south of San Jose

CONTACT: Carmen Kloncz, Chairperson, Castroville Festivals, Inc., P.O. Box 1041, Castroville, CA 95102; (408) 633-2465; Fax (408) 633-0485.

CHEZ LINDA COOKING
Los Gatos/Year-round

Established in 1995 by Linda Vandermarliere, this school offers ten 4-session demonstration and participation courses (limit 12-15 students) and children's classes per month and two 1-week vacations (limit 10) to Burgundy, France, per year.Facilities: 500-square-foot home kitchen. Also available: children's classes, wine instruction. The trips feature 8 hours of cooking demonstrations; visits to wineries, food producers, and markets; dining at fine restaurants; sightseeing.

EMPHASIS: California and Southwestern cuisine, low-fat cooking, French and Italian menus.

FACULTY: The three instructors include Linda Vandermarliere, who graduated from La Varenne and studied with Madeleine Kamman, Gordon Heyder, David Lawrence, guest chefs.

COSTS, ACCOMMODATIONS: Classes are $39 each. The trip to France is $3,000, which includes meals, lodging, and planned activities. A 50% deposit is required; balance due 60 days prior.

LOCATION: Five miles from the airport in San Jose.

CONTACT: Linda Vandermarliere, Chez Linda Cooking, 469 N. Santa Cruz Ave., Los Gatos, CA 95030; (408) 395-5979.

CONKLIN-CHASE, THE FINE ART OF COOKING
Fresno/Year-round

Established in 1993, this kitchenware store offers approximately a hundred 4- to 8-session demonstration courses (limit 30 to 50 students) annually. Facilities: 2,100-square-foot modern teaching kitchen with 4 work stations, Wolf range, and video monitors. Also available: children's classes, hands-on and master classes, guest chef sessions, annual culinary tours to France and Italy, international cruises.

EMPHASIS: International cuisines, including French, Italian, Mediterranean, Thai, American Southwest, Caribbean.

FACULTY: Charles Hiigel is an IACP member and studied with Anne Willan, La Varenne and at the Paris Cordon Bleu. He is resident chef at the Culinary Shoppe in Danville, teaches at Draeger's in Menlo Park, and.lectures for Royal Cruiuse Lines. Guest chefs include Giuliano Bugialli, Giuliano Hazan, Hugh Carpenter, Perla Meyers.

COSTS: $35 per session, $75 for hands-on. No refunds.

LOCATION: Central San Joaquin Valley

CONTACT: Charles Hiigel, Owner, Conklin-Chase, The Fine Art of Cooking, 1752 W. Bullard, Fresno, CA 93711; (209) 439-5000.

THE COOKING SCHOOL AT JORDANO'S MARKETPLACE
Santa Barbara/Year-round

Established in 1990, this cookware store and school offers 16 to 20 one- to four-session demonstration (limit 30 students) and participation (limit 18) courses per month. Facilities: the 14,000-sq.-ft. space has a large counter, overhead mirror, and professional appliances. Also available: farms and winery tours, wine tastings, private group and children's classes, culinary tours of Europe.

EMPHASIS: Basic techniques, ethnic and regional cuisines, holiday and entertaining menus, breads and pastries, guest chef specialties.

FACULTY: Director Pamela Sheldon, CCP, author of *The Healthy Gourmet Cookbook*, and more than 30 instructors, cookbook authors, and guest chefs, including Giuliano Bugialli, Hugh Carpenter, Ken Hom, Deborah Madison, and Nick Malgieri.

COSTS: Range from $25-$95. Advance paymentrequired; cancellations 1 week prior receive class credit. Positions available for volunteer kitchen assistants.

LOCATION: 90 minutes north of Los Angeles. There is an airport in Santa Barbara.

CONTACT: Pamela Sheldon Johns, Director, The Cooking School at Jordano's Marketplace, 614 Chapala St., Santa Barbara, CA 93101; (805) 564-7773, Fax (805) 564-4939.

COOKS AND BOOKS COOKING SCHOOL
Danville/Year-round

Established in 1991, this cookbook store and school offers more than 100 demonstration and participation courses per year. Facilities: 1,600-square-foot teaching area. Also available: local shopping excursions, culinary tours.

EMPHASIS: International cuisines, seasonal and holiday menus, nutritious foods, wine and food pairing, guest chef specialties.

FACULTY: In-house instructor D.J. Rae is a CCA graduate. Other instructors are San Francisco-area chefs, teachers, and cookbook authors.

COSTS: $35-$50 per session. Cancellations 7 days prior receive a refund; store credit 72 hours to 7 days prior.

LOCATION: 30 miles east of San Francisco.

CONTACT: D.J. Rae, Cooks and Books, 472 Hartz Ave., Danville, CA 94526; (510) 831-0708.

CUISINE SUR LA MER
Manhattan Beach/Spring and fall

Established in 1980, this gourmet shop and school offers evening demonstrations.

FACULTY: Includes caterer Hollie Evans and Disneyland pastry chef George Geary.

COSTS: $35.per class.

LOCATION: The Los Angeles area, on the Pacific Coast.

CONTACT: Cuisine Sur La Mer, 919 Manhattan Ave., Manhattan Beach, CA; 90266; (310) 374-3103.

CULINARY ADVENTURES, INC.
Malibu/Year-round

Cooking instructor Doris Felts conducts day-long tours (limit 25 participants), that include lectures, demonstrations, and visits to specialty markets, growers, and manufacturers. Also available: consultations, private tours, trips to Napa/Sonoma, New Orleans, and Santa Fe.

EMPHASIS: Food product information for serious cooks.

FACULTY: Doris Felts has taught cooking since 1976, conducts tours for organizations, and consults on southern California food products and sources.

COSTS: Day tours range from $65-$95, including lunch and transportation.

LOCATION: Los Angeles area.

CONTACT: Doris Felts, Culinary Adventures, Inc., 23908 DeVille Way, Malibu, CA 90265; (310) 456-2484, Fax (310) 456-3429.

DEPOT
Torrance/Year-round

Since 1992, this restaurant has offered 1 or 2 Saturday afternoon demonstrations (limit 60 students) a month. Facilities: a private dining room of the restaurant.

EMPHASIS: Italian, grilling, holiday meals, soups, chef specialties, wine pairing.

FACULTY: Michael S. Shafer, CEC, chef and general manager of Depot, an Urban Grill Room and Bar, also oversees operations in Fino, Misto, and Chez Melange. He received the Gold Medal in the 1988 Culinary Olympics. California winemakers also teach.

COSTS: $35 per session, booked in advance, paid at session.

LOCATION: A Los Angeles suburb.

CONTACT: Michael S. Shafer, Depot, 1250 Cabrillo, Torrance, CA 90501; (310) 787-7501.

DRAEGER'S CULINARY CENTER
Menlo Park/Year-round

Established in 1991 in Draeger's Supermarket, this school offers 350 demonstrations (limit 35 students) per year. Facilities: 36-seat classroom with kitchen and overhead mirror. Also available: wine classes and dinners, market tours, private classes.

EMPHASIS: Ethnic and regional cuisines, fundamentals, baking, vegetarian and healthful foods, entertaining menus, food history.

FACULTY: Guest instructors include well-known chefs, cookbook authors, culinary professionals.

COSTS: Range from $20-$65 per session. Credit cards accepted. Full payment with reservation. Refund up to two weeks prior to class.

LOCATION: Menlo Park, about 35 miles south of San Francisco.

CONTACT: William K. Wallace, Culinary Director, Draeger's Culinary Center, Draeger's Supermarket, 1010 University Dr., Menlo Park, CA 94025; (415) 688-0688, Fax (415) 326-3718.

ELDERBERRY HOUSE COOKING SCHOOL
Oakhurst\March and November

Founded in 1985, the Chateau du Sureau (Estate by the Elderberries) offers two 3-day participation programs (limit 12 students) per year. Eight hours of daily cooking instruction are devoted to preparing a 6-course menu. Facilities: Erna's Elderberry Restaurant's full commercial kitchen, herb garden, local organic vegetable farm. Other activities: bass fishing, golf, hiking, tennis, and visits to Yosemite National Park.

EMPHASIS: Sauces, soups, seafood and meat cookery, desserts.

FACULTY: Chef-Proprietor Erna Kubin-Clanin has 30 years of culinary and restaurant experience.

COSTS, ACCOMMODATIONS: Meals and class only $450 ($175 per day). Nine 2-person guest rooms range from $260-$360 including breakfast. 10% student discount. 50% deposit required; refund granted 7 days prior minus 10% cancellation fee.

LOCATION: The chateau, a member of Relais & Chateaux, is in a mountain village near Yosemite, 45 minutes from Fresno, 4 hours north of Los Angeles, and less than 4 hours from San Francisco.

CONTACT: Erna Kubin-Clanin, Proprietor, Elderberry House Cooking School, 48688 Victoria Ln., Box 577, Oakhurst, CA 93644; (209) 683-6800; Fax (209) 683-0800.

THE ELIZABETH THOMAS COOKING SCHOOL
Berkeley/Year-round

Established in 1977, this school in a private residence offers 6 four-session demonstration courses (limit 8 students) per year. Facilities: a remodeled teaching kitchen. Also available: classes for youngsters, theme classes, private lessons, 1-week intensives, and culinary tours of Berkeley and Napa Valley

EMPHASIS: French, Italian, American, California, British, and other ethnic cuisines; techniques.

FACULTY: Elizabeth Thomas, a graduate of the London Cordon Bleu, studied with Jacques Pepin and Lorenza de Medici and taught in San Francisco, Washington, China, Crete, and the West Indies.

COSTS: $40 per session, $150 per 4-session course. Payment with reservation.

LOCATION: Overlooking the Golden Gate Bridge, 35 minutes from San Francisco

CONTACT: The Elizabeth Thomas Cooking School, 1372 Summit Rd., Berkeley, CA 94708; (510) 843-3422.

EPICUREAN SCHOOL OF CULINARY ARTS
Los Angeles/Year-round *(See page 8)*

Founded in 1985, this school offers a variety of demonstration (limit 30 students) and participation courses (limit 15). Facilities: kitchen with 5 participation areas.

EMPHASIS: Theme-baking and vegetarian cooking.

COSTS: Approximately $60 per class. Cancellations with 48 hours notice receive credit.

GARLIC & SAPPHIRES
Del Mar/Year-round

Founded in 1988, this school offers 2 demonstrations per week, 3 weeks per month. Theme changes 3 times per year. Also available: limited hands-on classes.

EMPHASIS: Natural gourmet.

FACULTY: Lesa Heebner, author of *Cooking with the Seasons* and TV chef on a San Diego CBS-affiliate.

COSTS: $55 per class. Full refund 10 days prior.

LOCATION: 25 minutes from San Diego airport.

CONTACT: Lesa Heebner, Garlic & Sapphires, P.O. Box 2974, Del Mar, CA 92014; (619) 755-7773; Fax (619) 755-7909.

THE GREAT CHEFS AT THE ROBERT MONDAVI WINERY
Oakville/Spring and Fall

Since 1976, the Robert Mondavi Winery has hosted two to four 1- to 3-day weekend programs per season that feature cooking demonstrations and seminars by noted chefs, private winery tours, and theme lunches and dinners.

EMPHASIS: International cuisines, table setting, flower arranging, food and wine pairing.

FACULTY: Has included Barbara Tropp, Stephan Pyles, Lydia Shire, and Michel and Claude Troisgros.

COSTS, ACCOMMODATIONS: One-day sessions range from $120-$150; two-day program is $650; three-day program is $1,550, including transportation and lodging. Payment must accompany application and credit cards accepted. Cancellations 6 weeks prior forfeit 10%, 50% within 6 weeks.

LOCATION: Napa Valley.

CONTACT: Valerie Varachi, The Great Chefs at the Robert Mondavi Winery, P.O. Box 106, Oakville, CA 94562; (707) 944-2866, Fax (707) 944-8517.

HOMECHEF COOKING SCHOOL
San Francisco/Year-round

Founded in 1972, this cookware store offers 30 demonstration (limit 60 students) and participation (limit 20) courses per month and a 14-week Certificate in Basic Cooking course adapted from a professional curriculum. Facilities: 1,000-square-foot classroom, kitchen, and dining area. Also available: children's classes, private classes, and San Francisco walking tours.

FACULTY: Founder Judith Ets-Hokin, CCP, author of the *The Dinner Party Cookbook* and *The Homechef, Fine Cooking Made Simple*, holds certificates from cooking schools in England, France, and Italy. Other faculty includes head instructor Rebecca Ets-Hokin, Nicole Monier, Julie Khademi, Barbara Shenson, Gail Seche, Lynne Devereux, and Lisa Futterman.

COSTS: The Basic Cooking course is $392 (assistants $185); single classes are $39 per demonstration, $45 per participation.

CONTACT: Rebecca Ets-Hokin, Director, Homechef Cooking School, 3525 California St., San Francisco, CA 94118; (415) 668-3191, Fax (415) 668-0902.

HUGH CARPENTER'S NAPA VALLEY FOOD & WINE ADVENTURE
Napa Valley/May-October

Conducted since 1992 by chef and cookbook author Hugh Carpenter, these 6-day food and wine tours (limit 15 participants) feature participation classes, dining in fine restaurants, private winery tours, seminars on food and wine pairing, and a croquet tournament. Facilities: Cakebread Cellars Winery kitchen. Also available: hot-air ballooning, Calistoga spa, golf, and tennis.

EMPHASIS: California-Asian and cross-cultural cuisine; winery chef specialties.

FACULTY: Hugh Carpenter, founding chef of six Chopstix restaurants in Los Angeles and a Napa Valley resident, is author of the IACP-award-winning *Pacific Flavors*, *Chopstix*, and *Fusion Food Cookbook*. Cakebreads Cellars Executive Chef Brian Streeter also instructs.

COSTS, ACCOMMODATIONS: Cost is $860, which includes some meals and planned itinerary. A $100 deposit is required; balance due/refund granted 30 days prior. A list of recommended lodging is available.

LOCATION: Napa Valley, 50 miles northeast of San Francisco

CONTACT: Hugh Carpenter, Creative Food Concepts, P.O. Box 114, Oakville, CA 94562; (707) 944-9112, Fax (707) 944-2221.

JC'S KITCHEN COMPANY
San Diego/Year-round

Established in 1991, this cookware store and school offers 16 demonstration (limit 30 students)

and participation (limit 12) courses per month. Facilities: a specially-designed teaching kitchen. Also available: children's classes, wine instruction, private classes, market visits.

EMPHASIS: International and regional cuisines, guest chef specialties, cooking for health.

FACULTY: Local and celebrity guest chefs, including Giuliano Bugialli, Hugh Carpenter, Perla Meyers, and Jacques Pepin.

Costs: Range from $25-$85 per class.

Location: San Diego.

CONTACT: Jana Cason, JC's Kitchen Co., 4223 Genesee Ave., #110, San Diego, CA 92117; (619) 541-1990, Fax (619) 541-2237.

THE JEAN BRADY COOKING SCHOOL
Santa Monica/September-July

Established in 1973, this school in a private residence offers 8 to 12 seven-session demonstration (limit 15 students) and participation (limit 6 to 8) classes per month. Facilities: a commercially-equipped home kitchen featured in *Bon Appétit*; Campanile restaurant kitchen. Also available: childrens' classes, market visits, 1-week seminars for private groups, culinary tours to Europe.

EMPHASIS: A variety of topics; low-fat savories; menus for easy entertaining; guest chef specialties.

FACULTY: Proprietor Jean Brady studied with Lydie Marshall, Jacques Pepin, and Paula Wolfert and attended the Cordon Bleu and La Varenne. Guest chefs include Lydie Marshall, Jacques Pepin, Paula Wolfert, and top local chefs in their restaurant kitchens.

Costs: Guest chef classes range from $60-$90; 7-session classes are $250.

LOCATION: 20 minutes from Beverly Hills.

CONTACT: The Jean Brady Cooking School, 680 Brooktree Rd., Santa Monica, CA 90402; (310) 454-4220 (phone/fax).

KITCHEN WITCH GOURMET SHOP
Encinitas/September-July

Founded in 1981, this gourmet shop and school offers 45 demonstrations (limit 14 students) monthly. Also available: after-school classes for children, private group lessons.

EMPHASIS: Ethnic and regional cuisines, nutrition, vegetarian, macrobiotic, breads, holiday menus, pastries, chocolate, microwave and food processor techniques.

FACULTY: Includes Carole Bloom, Phillis Carey, Suzy Eisenman, Kay Pastorius, Dee Biller, Nadia Frigeri, and Nancy Brown.

Costs: Range from $16-$27. Credit cards accepted. Deposit 30 days in advance. Refunds granted 3 days prior.

LOCATION: North of San Diego, on the Pacific Coast

CONTACT: Marie Santucci, Kitchen Witch Gourmet Shop, 127 N. El Camino Real, Suite D; Encinitas, CA 92024; (619) 942-3228.

LE TROU RESTAURANT AND COOKING SCHOOL
Deux Sevres/Year-round *(See pages 9, 126, 252)*

Individuals and small groups desiring a cooking vacation can enroll for 1- or 2-week classes and tours to France and Italy.

LET'S GET COOKIN'
Westlake Village/Year-round

In addition to professional courses, this school offers more than 50 morning and evening demonstration and participation classes each quarter, classes for children, 5 to 12-session demonstration courses in basic to advanced creative cooking techniques, culinary day trips, and tours abroad.

Costs: Range from $40-$75 per session, children's classes are $25.

NONVOCATIONAL/VACATION **CALIFORNIA** **163**

LILY LOH'S CHINESE COOKING CLASSES
Solana Beach/Fall, Winter, Spring

Founded 1976, this school in a private home offers five 4- to 5-session demonstration and participation courses (limit 9 students) each season. Facilities: professionally-designed home kitchen. Also available: summer 4-session Teenager's Course, culinary tours in southern California.

FACULTY: Shanghai-born Lily Loh has a home ec. degree from Purdue University and a masters degree from Cornell, is author of *Lily Loh's Chinese Seafood and Vegetables* and host of two videos.

COST: Each course is $190, teen course is $150. A $50 nonrefundable deposit is required.

LOCATION: Solana Beach, 20 minutes from San Diego airport.

CONTACT: Lily Loh, P.O. Box 1232, Solana Beach, CA 92075; (619) 755-5345, Fax (619) 755-3028.

MANDOLINE COOKING SCHOOL
Sunnyvale/Year-round

Established in 1992, this school in a private residence offers 50 afternoon and evening participation classes (limit 6 students) per year. Facilities: a large kitchen with 5 work stations. Also available: private classes for groups.

EMPHASIS: Regional Italian, Mediterranean, regional American, vegetarian, and French bistro cuisine, pastry, desserts, bread making, wine pairing, techniques, seasonal ingredients, equipment selection.

FACULTY: Paula Barbarito-Levitt, an IACP-member, studied at Le Cordon Bleu, the New York Restaurant School, the California Culinary Academy and with Giuliano Bugialli and Lydie Marshall.

COSTS: Range from $35-$150; 50% deposit required; 2-week cancellation policy.

LOCATION: A 50-minute drive south of San Francisco and 10 minutes north of San Jose.

CONTACT: Paula Barbarito-Levitt, Mandoline Cooking School, 1083 Robbia Dr., Sunnyvale, CA 94087; (408) 733-4224, Fax (408) 773-1863.

MON CHERI COOKING SCHOOL/UC EXTENSION
Santa Cruz/Year-round

Founded in 1983, this university extension-private school cooperative program offers a half dozen 1- to 4-session participation workshops and courses per month. Class size: 18-20. Facilities: historic house with modern commercial kitchen. Also available: culinary vacations in U.S. and abroad (New Orleans, Seattle, Australia/New Zealand in 1996), classes for youngsters.

EMPHASIS: Stress relief cooking and a variety of other topics.

FACULTY: Director Sharon Shipley, an IACP member who received certificates from La Varenne and Le Cordon Bleu; noted guest chefs.

COSTS: Range from $85 for a single session to $155 for four. Credit cards accepted.

LOCATION: Silicon Valley, 40 miles south of San Francisco.

CONTACT: Culinary Arts, UC Extension, Humanities Dept., 740 Front St., #155, Santa Cruz, CA 95060; (408) 427-6695, Fax (408) 427-6608. Sharon Shipley (408) 736-0892, Fax (408) 736-0932.

MONTANA MERCANTILE
Los Angeles/Year-round

Founded in 1976, this school offers private instruction, informal demonstrations, participation classes for beginners, in-house instruction in English and Spanish for employed household cooks, and a wine tasting series.

CONTACT: Rachel Dourec, Box 17178, Beverly Hills, CA 90209; (310) 472-3220; Fax (310) 472-8846.

NAPA VALLEY COLLEGE — CENTER FOR CULINARY ARTS
(See page 11) **St. Helena/Year-round**

Established in 1990, this school offers 65 one- to six-session demonstration (limit 35 students) and participation (limit 14) courses per year. Facilities: new kitchen with 18 burners, 4 ovens, large demonstration counter, and outdoor dining area. Also available: wine and food classes, farmers market visits, catering seminars, and culinary tours abroad.

EMPHASIS: Various topics, including basic cake decorating, Indian cuisine, gumbo, root vegetables.

FACULTY: Includes Bruce Aidells, Jan Birnbaum, Catherine Brandel, Mark Dierkhising, and Laxmi Hiremath.

COSTS: Demonstration classes range from $55-$65, participation classes are $65. Cancellations 5 days prior receive refund less a $5 processing fee.

LOCATION: The Upper Valley campus, 75 minutes from San Francisco; St. Supery Winery in Rutherford.

CONTACT: Sue Farley: (707) 967-2930.

NATURAL FOODS COOKING SCHOOL
Woodland Hills/Year-round

This school offers a 12-month basic natural foods curriculum that includes two group classes per month and weekend retreats year-round.

EMPHASIS: Grains, pasta, vegetables, breads, fermented foods, catering, food and healing.

FACULTY: Donna Wilson, who also owns the Ginkgo Leaf Bookstore, has operated natural foods stores and restaurants in southern California since 1978.

COSTS: Individual evaluation is $25, nonrefundable; group classes are $25 each, $75 for a series of 5; private classes are $50 per hour.

LOCATION: Woodland Hills.

CONTACT: Donna Wilson, The Ginkgo Leaf, (818) 716-6332; E-Mail: donnaw7359@aol.com

NORTHERN CALIFORNIA CENTER FOR THE CULINARY ARTS
San Francisco/January-December

Established in 1992 to promote chefs conducting classes in their own establishments, the NCCCA offers more than 20 hands-on classes (8 to 16 students) each season. Also available: tours of bakeries, sausage makers, and wineries;weekend stays at fine resorts.

FACULTY: Includes Julian Serrano, Hubert Keller, Gary Danko, George Morrone, and David Hale.

COSTS: Chefs' classes range from $75-$140. Full payment is required with registration.

LOCATION: San Francisco and Northern California, including Napa, Marin, and Sonoma Counties, the East Bay, San Mateo, and Santa Clara County to Monterey

CONTACT: Northern California Center for the Culinary Arts, Box 181, 2570 Ocean Ave, San Francisco, CA 94132; (800) 773-7979 (CA only) or (415) 397-7345, Fax (415) 397-6309.

NUTRITIOUSLY GOURMET
Orinda/Year-round

Established in 1991, this private facility offers 6 morning and evening classes (limit 12 students) per season.

EMPHASIS: Creative low-fat cuisine using seasonal ingredients; plant foods, maximizing fibers, new equipment that minimizes fats.

FACULTY: Jane A. Rubey, M.P.H., R.D. has taught nutrition courses at the California Culinary Academy and is a regular on KGO radio. She is the author of *Lowfat International Cuisine* and *Fabulous Fiber Cookery*.

COSTS: $30 per class. Class credit for cancellations.

LOCATION: Across the bay from San Francisco, 40 minutes from the airport

CONTACT: Jane A. Rubey, Nutritiously Gourmet, P.O. Box 1356, Orinda, California 94563; (510) 254-7582.

PATINA RESTAURANT AND PINOT BISTRO
Los Angeles/March-May

These restaurants offer Saturday morning demonstration and participation classes (limit 12 students) and A Day in Patina's Kitchen, a full-day class that includes an early morning shopping expedition, preparation of a 5-course menu of the student's choice, and dinner for eight.

EMPHASIS: Restaurant specialties, pastries, chocolate truffles, bistro cooking, children's favorites.

FACULTY: Joachim Splichal, chef-owner of Pinot Bistro and Patina Restaurant, which was ranked first in Southern California in 1992 and 1993 by the Zagat Restaurant Survey; Bruno Feldeisen, pastry chef of Patina and Pinot Bistro; and Octavio Becerra, executive chef of Pinot Bistro.

COSTS: Saturday classes from $55-$75. Full-day class $1,250, including dinner and wines for eight.

CONTACT: Shannon Baer, Patina Restaurant, 5955 Melrose Ave., Los Angeles, CA 90038; (213) 960-1762, Fax (213) 467-1924.

PEGGY RAHN COOKS
Pasadena/Year-round

Founded in 1974, this school in a 1918-vintage home offers 50 one- to two-session demonstration (limit 20 students) and participation (limit 10) workshops per year. Facilities: well-equipped, home kitchen with overhead mirror. Also available: private classes, small group excursions to markets, party classes, and culinary trips.

EMPHASIS: Ethnic cuisines, technique classes, healthful eating.

FACULTY: Peggy Rahn, CCP, is a food and travel columnist, cookbook and restaurant reviewer, and co-host of CBS's "Meet the Cook". She teaches at UCLA and has studied at La Varenne, Le Cordon Bleu, and the Ritz Escoffier. Guest faculty has included Giuliano Bugialli, Madeleine Kamman, and Paula Wolfert.

COSTS: Range from $50-$75 per course, pre-paid to reserve space. Refund with 24 hour notice.

LOCATION: Ten minutes from downtown Los Angeles, 20 minutes from Burbank

CONTACT: Peggy Rahn Cooks, 484 Bellefontaine St., Pasadena, CA 91105; (818) 441-2075, Fax (818) 441-5286.

THE RITZ-CARLTON
San Francisco

Established in 1993 at The Ritz-Carlton on Nob Hill, The Gastronomic School offers weekend and half-day participation classes.

EMPHASIS: A variety of topics.

FACULTY: Master Sommelier Emmanuel Kemiji and Chef Gary Danko.

CONTACT: The Gastronomic School, The Ritz-Carlton, 600 Stockton St., San Francisco, CA 94115; (415) 296-7465.

SEASONAL TABLE COOKING SCHOOL
Santa Monica/Year-round

Established in 1994, this school offers two-three 1- to 4-session demonstration courses (limit 25 students) per week. Facilities: commercially-equipped restaurant kitchen. Also available: wine instruction, market visits, private classes for individuals, companies, and special events.

EMPHASIS: A variety of topics, including techniques, seasonal and entertaining menus, wine, breads, restaurant specialties, ethnic cuisines.

FACULTY: Co-owners Karen Berk, founder of Incredible Edibles Cooking School and co-editor of the Southern California Zagat restaurant and marketplace surveys, and Jean Brady of the Jean Brady Cooking School; guest chefs, cookbook authors, and culinary professionals.

COSTS, ACCOMMODATIONS: Average $50 per session. Full payment in advance; credit with 72 hours notice.

LOCATION: 20 minutes from Beverly Hills, 15 minutes from Los Angeles International Airport, 1 block from the beach.

CONTACT: Karen Berk, The Seasonal Table Cooking School, 12618 Homewood Way, Los Angeles, CA 90049; (310)472-4475, Fax (310) 471-3904.

SIAMESE PRINCESS RESTAURANT
Los Angeles/June -March

Since 1987, this restaurant has offered Sunday classes. Facilities: the dining room and kitchen.

EMPHASIS: Royal Thai cuisine.

FACULTY: Executive Chef Victor Sodsook, author of *I Love Thai Food* and *True Thai*.

COSTS: Classes are $35. Credit cards accepted.

CONTACT: The Siamese Princess, 8048 W. Third St., Los Angeles, CA 90048; (213) 653-2643, Fax (213) 653-1291.

SOUTHERN CALIFORNIA SCHOOL OF CULINARY ARTS
South Pasadena/Year-round   *(See page 14)*

This non-profit vocational school (page 14) offers about 12 participation classes (limit 12 students) per month for cooking enthusiasts. Also available: workshops for children ages 8-14.

EMPHASIS: A variety of topics, including international cuisines, entertaining menus, low-fat cooking, food and wine pairing.

FACULTY: The school's professional faculty.

COSTS: $45-$55 per class.

A STORE FOR COOKS
Laguna Niguel/Year-round

Founded 1981, this cookware store and school offers 12 to 14 morning and evening demonstration classes (limit 25 students) per month and Lunch and Learn classes once a week. Also available: classes for private groups.

EMPHASIS: Ethnic and regional cuisines, holiday and seasonal foods, guest chef specialties.

FACULTY: Proprietor and cookbook author Susan Vollmer, Hugh Carpenter, Phillis Carey, Tarla Fallgatter, cookbook authors, and local chefs.

COSTS: Lunch and Learn classes are $12; demonstrations range from $30-$75. Credit cards accepted. Refunds are granted 72 hours prior.

LOCATION: On the Pacific coast, 55 miles south of Los Angeles.

CONTACT: Susan Vollmer, A Store for Cooks, 30100 Town Center Dr., Suite R, Laguna Niguel, CA 92677; (714) 495-0445, Fax (714) 495-2139.

SUGAR 'N SPICE CAKE DECORATING SCHOOL
San Francisco/Year-round

Established in 1973, this baking supply store and school offers more than 50 one- to six-session participation courses (limit 14 students) a year.

EMPHASIS: Cake decorating and candy making.

FACULTY: Jeanne Lutz is a graduate of Edith Gate's Cake Decorating School and studied with several professionals. Guest instructors are also featured.

COSTS: Range from $20 for one session to $75 for a 6-session course.

CONTACT: Sugar 'n Spice Cake Decorating School, 3200 Balboa St., San Francisco, CA 94121; (415) 387-1722.

NONVOCATIONAL/VACATION   **CALIFORNIA**   **167**

SUNNYSIDE SCHOOL
Sonoma/Year-round

Established in 1993, this school offers 8 demonstration (limit 16 students) and participation classes (limit 12) per month.

EMPHASIS: Guest chef selections, wine themes, local specialties.

FACULTY: Prominent restaurant and hotel chefs and caterers from the Bay area.

COSTS: Range from $35-$50 per class. Refund is 50% with 36-hour notice.

LOCATION: A 45-minute drive from the Golden Gate Bridge.

CONTACT: Charles Saunders, Chef/Owner, Sunnyside School, 140 E. Napa St., Sonoma, CA 95476; (707) 935-0366, Fax (707) 939-9845.

TANTE MARIE'S COOKING SCHOOL
(See page 15)   **San Francisco/Year-round**

In addition to its career courses, this school offers demonstration (limit 38 students) and participation (limit 16) courses and culinary travel programs. Students who enroll for a week attend class with the certificate students; 6-session participation courses meet one evening a week, and and weekend classes focus on a single topic. Also available: single sessions on a space available basis.

EMPHASIS: General and specific topics, including pastries and regional cuisines.

COSTS: One-week courses are $500; 6-session evening courses are $420; afternoon demonstrations are $40 (5 for $150); and participation classes are $70. Weekend 1-day classes range from $35 to $100. The $100 deposit for 1-week and evening courses is refundable 4 weeks prior.

UCLA EXTENSION, HOSPITALITY/FOODSERVICE MANAGEMENT
(See page 16)   **Los Angeles/Year-round**

In addition to certificate courses, this school offers a variety of 1- to 10-session demonstration and participation courses, 1-day seminars, and culinary tours.

EMPHASIS: Ethnic and regional cuisines, guest chef specialties, wine and beer appreciation.

COSTS: From $45-$60 per session. Full payment is required and is refundable, less $25, 5 days prior.

LOCATION: Private homes and local facilities.

VALLEY OAKS COOKING SCHOOL
Hopland/Year-round

Established in 1991 by Fetzer Vineyards, this school offers Saturday classes (limit 36 students) once or twice per month, demonstration and participation sessions, wine and food pairing seminars, a tour of Fetzer's bio-dynamic organic garden, and a tasting of seasonal produce.

FACULTY: Culinary Director John Ash. Guest chefs include Susanna Foo, Gerald Boyd, Rosina Wilson, Chris Yeo, and Danny Mellman.

LOCATION: In Mendocino County, 2 hours north of San Francisco.

CONTACT: Fetzer Food & Wine Center at Valley Oaks, P.O. Box 611, Hopland, CA 95449; (707) 744-1250.

WEIR COOKING
San Francisco/Year-round

Established in 1989, this school in a private home offers weekend and 5-day participation courses (limit 8 students) that include Napa and Sonoma Valley tours and dining at fine restaurants. Facilities: a newly-designed professional commercial kitchen with wood-fired Tuscan oven and 4 work stations. Also available: private classes and visits to restaurants, wineries, and markets.

EMPHASIS: French, Italian, Mediterranean, and American regional cuisines.

FACULTY: Joanne Weir was a cook at Berkeley's Chez Panisse restaurant, studied for a year with

Madeleine Kamman, teaches in Canada, New Zealand, and Australia, and is author of *From Tapas to Meze* and several books in the Williams Sonoma Kitchen Library series.

COSTS: Tuition ranges from $80-$100 per class. A 50% deposit, half of which is refundable for cancellations 2 weeks prior, must accompany registration.

LOCATION: Pacific Heights, San Francisco.

CONTACT: Joanne Weir, Weir Cooking, 2107 Pine St., San Francisco, CA 94115; (415) 776-4200, Fax (415) 776-0318.

YAN CAN INTERNATIONAL COOKING SCHOOL
Foster City/Year-round

Founded in 1985 by Martin Yan, host of the "Yan Can Cook" television show, this school offers classes. Facilities: two full kitchens and an overhead mirror.

EMPHASIS: Chinese cuisines and other topics.

FACULTY: The more than 15-member faculty includes Martin Yan, Bruce Aidells, Peggy Fallon, Flo Braker, and Joyce Jue.

COSTS: Range from $35-$75.

LOCATION: In Foster City, 10 minutes from the San Francisco airport

CONTACT: Susan Yan, School Director, Yan Can International Cooking School, Charter Square, 1064 G Shell Blvd., Foster City, CA 94404; (415) 574-7788.

YANKEE HILL WINERY-WHAT'S COOKING AT THE WINERY
Columbia/Year-round

This winery, established in 1970, started offering weekly cooking and wine classes in 1995. Demonstrations limited to 30 students, participation classes 12. Facilities: 2,500-sq.-ft. area with 12 workspaces, Swiss baking ovens, pizza oven, candy stove, sausage and salami-making equipment, smoker, wine-making equipment. Also: classes for youngsters, private classes, facility rental.

EMPHASIS: Baking, international cuisines taught by native instructors, in a relaxed environment.

FACULTY: The 10 instructors include Yankee Hill Winery owner Ron Erickson, Denise Ganino, Jerry Phillips, Gretchen Erickson, and Ken Churches; guest chefs.

COSTS: $25-$100 per class.

LOCATION: Two hours south of Sacramento, in the grape-growing regions of Tuolumne and Calaveras Counties.

CONTACT: Ron Erickson, Owner, Yankee Hill Winery, P.O. Box 330, Columbia, CA 95310; 209-533-2417 or 800-497-WINE, Fax 209-533-2417.

YOSEMITE CHEFS' & VINTNERS' HOLIDAYS
Yosemite National Park/November-February

Since 1982, Yosemite Concession Services Corporation has offered a series of eight 2-day/3-night Chefs' Holidays and Vintners' Holidays (limit 250 attendees) that feature four cooking demonstrations or wine seminars and a concluding banquet. Facilities: Great Lounge of The Ahwahnee hotel.

EMPHASIS: Cuisines of Western chefs, California wines.

FACULTY: Each program features four noted cooking instructors or four wineries. Executive Chef Robert Anderson and his staff prepare the banquet.

COSTS, ACCOMMODATIONS: Chefs' and Vintners' Holiday Packages are $695 each, which includes lodging and banquet for two at the Ahwahnee hotel. Reservations more than 21 days prior require a deposit. Credit cards accepted.

LOCATION: Yosemite National Park, 90 miles from Fresno and 175 miles from San Francisco.

CONTACT: Yosemite Chefs' Holidays & Vintners' Holidays, Yosemite Concession Services Corp., Box 578, Yosemite, CA 95389; (209) 252-4848, Fax (209) 372-1362.

COLORADO

ASIAN COOKERY
Colorado Springs/Year-round

Founded in 1989, this school in a private residence offers 36 demonstration (limit 10 to 12) and participation (limit 8) classes per year. Facilities: specially-designed teaching kitchen. Also available: private classes, specialty classes, dinner parties.

EMPHASIS: Chinese, Malaysian, Thai, Vietnamese, Indian, low-fat, and vegetarian cuisines.

FACULTY: Peng Jones, CCP, studied at the International School of Home Cookery in Malaysia and trained in Oriental food and vegetable carving.

COSTS: Range from $25-$35 per session, payable with registration. Full refund 1 week prior.

LOCATION: A 20-minute drive from the Colorado Springs airport; about 60 miles south of Denver.

CONTACT: Peng Jones, Owner, Asian Cookery, P.O. Box 62674, Colorado Springs, CO 80962; (719) 590-7768.

AUTHENTIC VEGETARIAN CUISINE FROM INDIA
Boulder/Year-round

Founded in 1993, this school and catering service in a private residence offers six 1- to 3-session demonstration (limit 20 students) and participation (limit 6 to 16) courses per quarter. Also available: a newsletter, private classes.

EMPHASIS: Western Indian cuisine (without curry powder), techniques, spices, flat breads, chutneys, appetizers, fast foods.

FACULTY: Jessica Shah, a native of Bombay, has 14 years cooking experience, owns a catering service, and writes for local and national publications.

COSTS: Range from $25 to $75. Advance payment required.

LOCATION: Boulder, 45 minutes from Denver.

CONTACT: Jessica Shah, 971 Clover Circle, Lafayette, CO 80026; (303) 665-2000 (phone/fax).

COOKING SCHOOL OF THE ROCKIES
(See page 17) **Boulder/Year-round**

Founded in 1991. This school and cookware store offers a diploma program, demonstration (limit 40 students) and participation (limit 10 to 20) classes, short courses, and 5-day summer basic techniques intensives that emphasize creativity, organization, and presentation. Facilities: a specially-designed new 2,000-square-foot facility.

EMPHASIS: Basic French techniques, pastry, baking, nutrition, ethnic cuisines, wine appreciation.

FACULTY: Director Joan Brett apprenticed with Chef Boris Bless and studied with Julia Child, Jacques Pepin, and Peter Kump's New York Cooking School; Mary Copeland, Michael Comstedt.

COSTS: Classes range from $35-$75; intensives are $365; $100 nonrefundable deposit required.

EXPLORE
Vail Valley/September

The White River Institute, which is dedicated to education, global awareness, and healthy living, sponsors a yearly 1-week educational retreat for physically-active over-50 adults. The program consists of symposia that focus on a specific theme, hands-on workshops (cooking, photography, painting), outdoor recreational clinics (fly fishing, golf), keynote dinner speaker, and tour of the Betty Ford Alpine Gardens.

FACULTY: Program organizers are Vonnie Wheeler and John Horan-Kates. The faculty includes academicians, authors, artists, and other professionals. Joan Brett of the Cooking School of the

Rockies conducts the cooking workshop.

COSTS, ACCOMMODATIONS: Cost is $1,775, including double occupancy lodging (single supplement $375) at the Hyatt Regency Beaver Creek resort, most meals, and resort amenities. Cost without lodging is $1,350. A $750 deposit is required; $100 is charged cancellations 45 days prior.

LOCATION: The Hyatt Regency and locations in the Vail Valley area

CONTACT: Explore, White River Institute, 100 E. Thomas Pl., Drawer 2770, Avon, CO 81620; Travel Desk (800) 323-4386, Fax (303) 9494699.

FOOD & WINE MAGAZINE CLASSIC
Aspen/June 14-16, 1996

Established in 1983 and sponsored by *Food & Wine Magazine*, this annual 3-day weekend festival features a variety of events for food and wine enthusiasts and professionals. The 20-hour program offers over 80 lectures, demonstrations, panels, and tastings; a benefit auction; and fine dining.

EMPHASIS: Trade seminars for chefs and restaurateurs cover employee relations, marketing, direct mail, customer relations, insurance; consumer events include chef demonstrations and tastings from over 250 vintners and more than 50 food and specialty exhibitors.

FACULTY: Has included Michael Broadbent, Julia Child, Marcella Hazan, Jacques Pepin, Frank Prial.

COSTS: Three-day tickets are about $475. Reserve tastings are $75 to $200 extra. A list of accommodations is provided.

CONTACT: *Food & Wine Magazine* Classic, 425 Rio Grande Plaza, Aspen, CO 81611-9938; (800) 4-WINE-95 or (303) 494-6396.

NATURALLY GRAND JUNCTION COOKING SCHOOL
Grand Junction/Year-round

A cooking instructor since 1971, Rebecca Wood offers a 15-hour demonstration course (limit 15 students) and weekend and one-week programs for out-of-towners. Facilities: private home. Also available: advanced courses.

EMPHASIS: Health-building grain-based diet, low-fat vegetarian dishes.

FACULTY: Rebecca Wood authored five books on food and health and taught cooking in London, Rome, and Dublin. Anpetu Ohenikshi studied ethnic cuisine and agriculture in native cultures.

COSTS: Tuition is $225 for the 15-hour course. A $100 deposit is required 2 weeks prior; 10% senior discount.

LOCATION: Western Colorado, midway between Salt Lake City and Denver.

CONTACT: Rebecca Wood, NATURALLY GRAND Junction Cooking School, 2837 Elm Ave., Grand Junction, CO 81501; (970) 256-9697 or (800) 833-1336, Fax (970) 242-7796.

SCHOOL OF NATURAL COOKERY
Boulder, Denver, Minneapolis, Seattle/Year-round *(See page 18)*

Founded in 1985, this vegetarian cooking school offers a 3-part, 15-session, flexible schedule series (limit 12 students) 4 times a year.

EMPHASIS: Theory and techniques for preparing whole grains, beans, vegetables; innovative dishes.

COSTS: Tuition is $250 for Parts I and II, $125 for Part III; materials fee $50-$55. A 50% tuition deposit plus fee is due 3 prior. Refund granted 3 weeks prior to class.

THE SEASONED CHEF
Denver/Year-round

Established in 1993, this school offers 12 demonstration (limit 35 students) and participation (limit 12-15) classes per month. Facilities: Well-equipped home kitchen. Also available: classes for youngsters, wine appreciation, market visits, private instruction.

EMPHASIS: Topics include basic techniques, healthful cooking, ethnic cuisines, menu planning.

FACULTY: Area cooking school instructors, restaurant chefs, guest chefs and cookbook authors.

COSTS: $35-$45 per class. Payment with registration, refund for cancellation one week prior.

CONTACT: Sarah Leffen, The Seasoned Chef, 999 Jasmine St., #100, Denver, CO 80220; (303) 377-3222.

TELLURIDE WINE FESTIVAL
Telluride/Last weekend in June

Established in 1981, this annual weekend festival features luncheon programs with guest chefs, seminars, tastings of over 200 wines, and a cooking class.

EMPHASIS: Wine and food pairing.

CONTACT: Keith Hampton, Program Director, Telluride Wine Festival, Box 1677, Telluride, CO 81435; (303) 728-3178, Fax (303) 728-4865.

CONNECTICUT

BOBBI COOKS COOKING SCHOOL
North Canton/Year-round

Established in 1977, this school in a private residence offers more than 100 demonstration (limit 25 students) and participation (limit 18) classes a year. Facilities: 800-square-foot kitchen with professional range/oven. Also available: kids in the kitchen, wine and food pairing, couples' classes, private instruction.

EMPHASIS: Include entertaining, grilling, heart healthy, herbs, techniques.

FACULTY: Bobbi Leavitt studied at Johnson & Wales and Michael James French Chef School and is an IACP member. Occasional guest instructors.

COSTS: $25-$38 per class. Deposit required.

Location: Farmington Valley, 30 minutes from Hartford and Bradley International Airport.

CONTACT: Bobbi Leavitt, Bobbi Cooks Cooking School and Catering Service, 516 Cherrybrook Rd., North Canton, CT 06059; (203) 693-4931 (phone/fax).

THE COMPLETE KITCHEN COOKING SCHOOL
Darien/Spring and Fall

Established in 1980, this school in a kitchenware store offers more than 30 morning and evening demonstrations (limit 20 students) per term.

FACULTY: School Director Sigrid Laughlin and guest instructors, including Julia della Croce, Nicole Routhier, Stephen Schmidt, Patricia Wells.

COSTS: $45-$75 per session. Refunds are granted 48 hours prior.

LOCATION: 40 miles from New York City and New Haven.

CONTACT: Sigrid Laughlin, Director, The Complete Kitchen Cooking School, 863 Post Rd., Darien, CT 06820; (203) 655-4055, Fax (203) 655-0121.

CONNECTICUT CULINARY INSTITUTE
Farmington/Year-round

In addition to its career program, this school offers about 15 to 20 one- to ten-session demonstration (limit 40 students) and participation (limit 12) courses per month for nonprofessional cooks. Also available: Children's classes.

COSTS: $25-$55 per session.

THE COOK STORE
Storrs/Year-round

Established in Willimantic in 1991, this cookware and specialty food shop offers 6 to 8 demonstration classes (limit 14 students) per month. Facilities: fully-equipped teaching kitchen. Also available: children's after-school and summer classes (physically challenged are encouraged to attend).

EMPHASIS: Ethnic cuisines, breads, topics per request. For children: knife skills, kitchen safety, cooking for the family.

FACULTY: Proprietor Charles R. Caro, is a former caterer and restaurateur. Other faculty includes Robert Tavarnesi, Barbara Tashman, children's instructor Phyllis J. Caron-Taylor, and sign interpreter Suzanne Silva.

COSTS: Usually $10-$15 for adult classes, $5 for children's classes. Food cost is additional. Registration is nonrefundable and payable in advance.

LOCATION: Mansfield, a half-mile from the University of Connecticut's main campus and 45 minutes from Hartford.

CONTACT: The Cook Store, 1132 Storrs Rd., Storrs, CT 06268-2304.

CUCINA CASALINGA
Wilton and Italy/Spring and Fall

Established in 1981, this Wilton cooking school offers demonstration (limit 20 students) and participation (limit 12) classes and culinary tours (limit 20) to Italy. Facilities: an open-plan home kitchen. Also available: private group classes, couples' classes, children's summer camp, wine tastings, excursions in the Northeast, tours of Italian neighborhoods in the Bronx.

EMPHASIS: Italian regional cuisine.

FACULTY: Owner/instructor Sally Ann Maraventano graduated from Georgetown University, studied at the University of Florence, and learned to cook from her mother and Sicilian grandfather who owned an Italian bakery. Guest instructors include European chefs and American culinarians.

COSTS, ACCOMMODATIONS: Adult (children's) classes are $65 ($35) per session, $185 ($100) for a series of 3. Reservations required and payment must be received 7 days before class. Tour land costs range from $2,500-$3,500, including double occupancy lodging, meals, and planned itinerary.

LOCATION: Lower Fairfield County, 1 hour north of Manhattan by car or train. Tours for 1996 include schools in Umbria, Publia, Amalfi, and Venice.

CONTACT: Sally Ann Maraventano, Owner, Cucina Casalinga, 171 Drum Hill Rd., Wilton, CT 06897; (203) 762-0767, Fax (203) 762-0768.

FOODSEARCH PLUS
Ridgefield/Year-round

Established in 1991, this cooking school and food consulting business offers 1- to 4-session participation courses (limit 8 students) and 2-day workshops that feature 3-4 hours of hands-on instruction. Facilities: A converted barn in a country setting with full service test kitchen. Also available: professional instruction and childrens' classes.

EMPHASIS: Basic culinary techniques, entertaining menus and presentation, home cooking, reduced fat menus.

FACULTY: Karen Hanson and Barbara Somers, whose experience encompasses food writing, menu and recipe development, and teaching at New School Culinary Arts and New York University.

COSTS: $35-$55 per session, $100 to $250 for multiple sessions. Discounts on two or more classes.

CONTACT: Karen Hanson and Barbara Somers, Foodsearch+, 258 Florida Rd, Ridgefield, CT 06877; (203) 438-0422.

HAY DAY COOKING SCHOOL
Westport, Ridgefield, Greenwich, Scarsdale/Year-round

Founded in 1982, this school offers approximately fifteen 3-hour demonstration classes per year at each of its 4 locations. Facilities: professional demonstration kitchen-classroom with seating for 40 students, overhead mirror, stovetop, and P.A. system.

NONVOCATIONAL/VACATION **CONNECTICUT** **173**

EMPHASIS: Ethnic and regional cuisines, classic techniques and methods, food history and folklore.

FACULTY: Guest chefs have included Bradley Ogden, Jacques Pepin, Marcella Hazan, Michael Romano, and Martha Stewart.

COSTS: $60-$75 per class.

LOCATION: The Riverside section of Greenwich, a 45-minute drive from New York City; Governor St. in Ridgefield, a 70-minute drive; Post Rd. East in Westport, a 1-hour drive; and a location in Scarsdale, NY, a 30-minute drive

CONTACT: Nicole Courtemanche, Reservations, Hay Day, Inc., 1071 Post Rd. East, Westport, CT; 06880 (203) 221-0100; Fax (203) 454-4923.

PRUDENCE SLOANE'S COOKING SCHOOL
Hampton/September-July

Established in 1993, this school in a private residence offers 6 to 10 participation workshops (limit 8 students), demonstrations (limit 20), and dinner demonstrations (limit 16) per month. Facilities: well-equipped teaching kitchen. Also available: private classes, culinary weekends, wine tasting, food styling, kitchen design.

EMPHASIS: Ethnic and regional cuisines, techniques, theory, food history and flavoring principles, seasonal and holiday menus.

FACULTY: Prudence Sloane, an IACP member, was awarded the Blue Ribbon Professional diploma from Peter Kump's New York Cooking School, is a food stylist and has studied kitchen design; guest chefs and instructors.

COSTS: $20-$60 per session. Full paymentto reserve space.

LOCATION: Northeastern Connecticut, 90 minutes from Boston and 3 hours from New York City.

CONTACT: Prudence Sloane, Owner, Prudence Sloane's Cooking School, 245 Main St., Hampton, CT 06247; (203) 455-0596.

RONNIE FEIN SCHOOL OF CREATIVE COOKING
Stamford/Spring and Fall

Since 1971, Ronnie Fein has taught demonstration (limit 16 students) and participation (limit 10) classes that emphasize ingredients and techniques. Facilities: fully-equipped home teaching kitchen. Also available: children's classes, private instruction year-round.

EMPHASIS: Regional cuisines, seasonal and holiday menus, food gifts, low-fat cuisine.

FACULTY: Ronnie Fein writes for food publications and attended the China Institute and Four Seasons Cooking School. She is author of *The Complete Idiot's Guide to Cooking Basics*.

COSTS: $45-$55. Refund for cancellations 24 hours prior.

LOCATION: North Stamford, 45 minutes from New York City.

CONTACT: Ronnie Fein School of Creative Cooking, 438 Hunting Ridge Rd., Stamford, CT 06903; (203) 322-7114, Fax (203) 329-3366.

THE SILO COOKING SCHOOL
New Milford/March-December

Founded in 1972 by former restauranteur Ruth Henderson and her husband, New York Pops founder and music director Skitch, this gourmet foods store and art gallery housed in a fomer cattle barn offers more than 70 demonstration (limit 30 to 35 students) and participation (limit 14) courses per year. Facilities: well-equipped teaching kitchen. Also available: custom group and children's classes.

EMPHASIS: Ethnic and regional cuisines, holiday menus, baking, guest chef specialties, wine selection.

FACULTY: Has included Giuliano Bugialli, Skitch Henderson, Michael Romano, Daniel Leader, Jacques Pepin, Madeleine Kamman, and Sheila Lukins.

COSTS: About $75-$85 for master chef classes, $45-$75 for others. Payment with application.

LOCATION: About 80 miles from New York City on the Henderson's 200-acre Hunt Hill Farm in the Litchfield Hills

CONTACT: Sandra Daniels, Director, Silo Cooking School, Upland Rd., New Milford, CT 06776; (203) 355-0300, Fax (203) 350-5495.

DELAWARE

WHAT'S COOKING AT THE KITCHEN SINK
Hockessin/September-June

Established in 1991, this school in a kitchenware store offers 12 to 16 demonstration classes (limit 16 students) per month. Facilities: 300-square-foot, 16-seat teaching area with overhead mirror. Also available: children's workshops, private and party classes.

EMPHASIS: Special occasion menus, guest chef specialties, specific subjects.

FACULTY: Director Lee Wooding, an IACP member, and CIA graduate Scott Daniels, executive chef of The Back Burner Restaurant.

COSTS: $22-$45 per class. Refund for cancellation 1 week prior.

LOCATION: A Wilmington suburb 40 miles from Philadelphia and 75 miles from Baltimore

CONTACT: Lee Wooding, Director, What's Cooking at the Kitchen Sink, P.O. Box 1300, Hockessin Corner, Hockessin, DE 19707; (302) 239-7066, Fax (302) 239-7665.

DISTRICT OF COLUMBIA

PETER KUMP'S SCHOOL OF CULINARY ARTS *(see page 202)*

PARIS COOKS
District of Columbia/October-April

A cooking instructor since 1977, Elizabeth Esterling teaches 5-session demonstration and participation courses (limit 5 students) that stress easy, elegant, do-ahead menus. Facilities: home kitchen.

EMPHASIS: Intermediate and advanced low fat French cuisine.

FACULTY: Elizabeth Esterling has a degree from La Varenne and is Chevalier du Tastevin, Clos Vougeot. She has written the *Le Cookbook* and contributed to *Small Feasts* and *Simple Feasts*.

COSTS: Five sessions are $200.

CONTACT: Elizabeth Esterling, Paris Cooks, 1619 34th St., N.W., Washington, DC 20007; (202) 333-4451 (phone/fax).

THE PASTRY INSTITUTE OF WASHINGTON DC
Washington, D.C./Year-round *(See page 21)*

This professional school offers 3 or 4 demonstrations (limit 30 students) and hands-on workshops (limit 15) per month.

EMPHASIS: French pastry, cakes, chocolates, decoration, holiday desserts.

FACULTY: School instructors and local restaurant chefs.

COSTS: $40-$60 per session. Full payment with registration.

SMITHSONIAN INSTITUTION
District of Columbia/Year-round

The Smithsonian Associates Program, which provides educational opportunities for Associates and the general public, offers 2 or 3 programs per year that include cooking demonstrations, lectures, and visits to cultural attractions.

NONVOCATIONAL/VACATION / **FLORIDA** 175

Costs, Accommodations: Include double occupancy lodging, some meals, all planned activities.
Location: Includes Seattle, New Orleans, Paris.
Contact: Mary Beth Mullen, Smithsonian Associates, Study Tours and Seminars, 1100 Jefferson Dr., S.W., Room 3045, Washington, DC 20008; (202) 357-4700, Fax (202) 633-9250.

FLORIDA

ARIANA'S COOKING SCHOOL
Miami/Year-round

Founded in 1976, this cookware store and school offers more than 50 demonstration and participation (limit 28 students) classes per quarter. Facilities: a 400-sq.-ft. kitchen with overhead mirror.

Faculty: The more than 15-member faculty includes Wendy Kallergis, Carole Kotkin, Ariana Kumpis, Bobbi Garber, Mario Martinez.

Costs: $25-$100 per session.

Contact: Ariana M. Kumpis, Ariana's Cooking School, 7251 S.W. 57th Ct., Miami, FL 33143; (305) 667-5957.

ART INSTITUTE OF FORT LAUDERDALE
(See page 21) **Ft. Lauderdale/Year-round**

This career school (page 21) offers a continuing education program that is open to nonprofessional cooks.

CHEF ALLEN'S
Miami/Spring, Summer, Fall

Since 1986, Chef Allen Susser has offered instruction that includes demonstration and hands-on classes (limit 10 students) and one-on-one sessions in which the student works along with the restaurant staff. Facilities: Chef Allen's restaurant in North Miami Beach.

Emphasis: New World cuisine, local fish, tropical fruits, Latin root vegetables.

Faculty: Chef Susser is a graduate and on the faculty of Florida International University School of Hospitality & Restaurant Management. Author of *Allen Susser's New World Cuisine and Cookery*, he studied at Le Cordon Bleu and was chef at Paris' Bristol Hotel.

Costs: Group classes range from $35-$50. Individual session is $195. Reserve 3 weeks prior.

Contact: Chef Allen Susser, Chef Allen's, 19088 Northeast 29th Ave., N. Miami Beach, FL 33180; (305) 935-2900, Fax (305) 935-9062.

CREATIVE CUISINE COOKING SCHOOL *(See page 221)*

DAMIANO'S AT THE TARRIMORE HOUSE
Delray Beach/June-October

This restaurant offers Wednesday evening theme classes that feature low-fat .or fat-free cooking. Facilities: a demonstration kitchen in the restaurant dining room.

Emphasis: Italian, Southwest, and Asian cuisines.

Faculty: Chef Anthony Basil Damiano.

Costs: $100 for three classes.

Contact: Lisa Damiano, Damiano's at the Tarrimore House, 52 N. Swinton Ave., Delray Beach, FL 33444; (407) 272-4706.

GOING SOLO IN THE KITCHEN
(See display ad page 176) **Apalachicola/Year-round**

Jane Doerfer conducts bimonthly 5-day participation courses (limit 12 students) that are geared to the needs of the solo cook. Instruction is scheduled mornings and evenings; afternoons are free. Facilities: the instructor's 19th-century Key West-style home, overlooking the Apalachicola River.

FACULTY: *Going Solo* newsletter publisher Jane Doerfer's cookbook credits include *The Victory Garden Cookbook* (collaborator), *The Legal Sea Foods Cookbook*, and *Going Solo in the Kitchen*.

COSTS: Tuition is $975, which includes lodging and meals.

LOCATION: Apalachicola, a Natural Estuarine Sanctuary in the Florida Panhandle, is 75 miles from Tallahassee

CONTACT: Jane Doerfer, Going Solo in the Kitchen, P.O. Box 123, Apalachicola, FL 32329; (904) 653-8848 or Regatta Travel (800) 445-7685.

GOING SOLO IN THE KITCHEN

Combine beachcombing and cooking at Going Solo in the Kitchen, a 4½ day learning vacation in the unspoiled Florida panhandle. Participatory classes, which are taught by cookbook author Jane Doerfer, are held in a teaching kitchen designed by the noted architect Hugh Newell Jacobsen. Beginners are welcome. For reservations call (800) 445-7685.

HARRIET'S KITCHEN WHOLE FOODS COOKING SCHOOL
Winter Park/September-June

Founded in 1987, this school offers 12 to 15 demonstration (limit 35 students) and participation (limit 16) classes per month. Facilities: a 500-square-foot teaching kitchen. Also available: classes for youngsters, a 9-session Healing Macrobiotic series, sourdough whole grain bread classes, and a 5-day macrobiotic weekend intensive at St. George Island every fall.

EMPHASIS: Macrobiotic and gourmet vegetarian cuisines.

FACULTY: Director Harriet McNear, a Kushi certified teacher and licensed nutrition counselor, studied at the Kushi Institute and the Natural Gourmet Cookery School. Local chefs include Tim Rosendahl, Clair Epting, Richard Blanke, Marc van Couwenberghe, M.D.

COSTS: Classes range from $20-$40, 5-day intensive $500-$800, the 9-session course $180. A 50% deposit is required and refund is granted cancellations 5 days prior. Spouses receive a 30% discount. Work-study and assistantship positions are available.

Location: Near Walt Disney World, 15 miles from Orlando International Airport.

CONTACT: Harriet McNear, Director, Harriet's Kitchen, 1136 Oaks Blvd., Winter Park, FL 32789; (407) 644-2167 (phone/fax).

KEY WEST COOKING SCHOOL
Key West/Year-round

Founded in 1994, this school offers group demonstration classes (minimum 10 students). Facilities: an outdoor garden adjacent to a restaurant. Also available: bed & breakfast culinary packages during midweek.

EMPHASIS: Island cuisine, Key West specialties, Cuban and Caribbean cuisines.

FACULTY: Owner Donna Shields, IACP member and former instructor at the CIA; Key West restaurant chefs.

COSTS: $35 per class.

LOCATION: In old town Key West, 10 minutes from Key West airport, a 3-hour drive from Miami.

NONVOCATIONAL/VACATION   **FLORIDA**

CONTACT: Donna Shields, Owner, Key West Cooking School, P.O. Box 1636, Key West, FL 33041; 1-800-32-FOODS; Fax (305) 295-9305.

KITCHEN HEARTH
Miami Beach/January-July, September-November

Established in 1994, this cookware store offers four demonstration (limit 18 students) and participation classes (limit 10) per month. Facilities: kitchen with 10 workspaces. Also available: classes for youngsters, market visits.

EMPHASIS: A variety of topics, including Italian, Thai, Chinese, and Indian cuisines; baking and cake decorating; low-fat cooking.

FACULTY: Guest chefs from noted local restaurants.

COSTS, ACCOMMODATIONS: $30 for adult classes, $15 for children's classes. Payment with registration; refund with 3 days notice.

LOCATION: Two miles from the historic South Beach district and 15 minutes from Miami International Airport.

CONTACT: Gail Fix, The Kitchen Hearth, 456 Arthur Godfrey Rd., Miami Beach, FL 33140; (305) 538-3358, Fax (305) 538-3431.

THE RITZ-CARLTON COOKING SCHOOL
Amelia Island/Year-round

This hotel offers monthly two-day participation courses that focus on a theme. Facilities: The Grill kitchen. Other activities: a tour of the food preparation facilities.

EMPHASIS: Seasonal and entertaining menus, regional and ethnic cuisines, macrobiotic recipes.

FACULTY: Matthew Medure, AAA 5-diamond chef of The Grill; the hotel's food and beverage staff.

COSTS, ACCOMMODATIONS: Cost is $650 per person, $964 per couple, which includes lodging, most meals, and resort amenities.

LOCATION: On the Atlantic Ocean, 25 minutes north of Jacksonville.

CONTACT: The Ritz-Carlton, 4750 Amelia Island Pkwy., Amelia Island, FL 32034; (800) 241-3333 or (904) 277-1100, Fax (904) 277-1145.

SARASOTA FOOD AND WINE ACADEMY
Sarasota/Year-round

Established in 1995, this wine and gourmet food store offers 20 demonstration (limit 40 students) and participation (limit 15) courses per year. Facilities: a 350-square-foot central teaching station and kitchen. Also available: wine courses.

FACULTY: Special events coordinator Anthony Blue; guest chefs.

COSTS: Range from $25-$100.

LOCATION: Adjacent to Michael's On East restaurant, 60 miles south of Tampa

CONTACT: Michael Klauber, Director, Sarasota Food and Wine Academy, 1212 East Ave. S., Sarasota, FL 34239; (813) 362-9463.

GEORGIA

THE COOKING SCENE
Alpharetta/Year-round

Founded in 1993, the Georgia Lifestyles Learning Center offers approximately 25 different demonstration (limit 25 to 50 students) and participation (limit 15) 1- to 4-session courses per month. Facilities: the new 32,000-square-foot, 60-seat teaching kitchen with 10 work areas has an audio system, overhead mirror, full prep kitchen, cookware and book store, private dining area, and banquet room. Also available: cooking camps for youngsters, couples and singles classes, private classes, lectures, and culinary trips abroad.

EMPHASIS: Ethnic and regional cuisines, special occasion dishes, baking and pastry, decorating and candy making, healthy and vegetarian menus, wine tasting, specific subjects.

FACULTY: Ray Overton, culinary director, apprenticed with Nathalie Dupree and is a member of the IACP and AIWF. Guest instructors have included Lydie Marshall, Shirley Fong-Torres, Fabrizio Bottero, and Virginia Willis.

COSTS: Demonstrations are $20-$25 per class; hands-on sessions begin at $100. Tuition is required with registration. Credit cards accepted.

LOCATION: One mile from Harry's Farmers Market and 16 miles north of midtown Atlanta.

CONTACT: Ray L. Overton, III, Culinary Director, The Cooking Scene/Georgia Lifestyles Learning Center, 1790 Hembree Rd., Alpharetta, GA 30201; (404) 442-8053, Fax (404) 667-1310.

DIANE WILKINSON'S COOKING SCHOOL
Atlanta

Founded 1974, Diane Wilkinson offers 5 five-day intensive techniques courses and several short courses per year. Facilities: remodeled Mediterranean-style kitchen with 2 fireplaces, one built for open-hearth cooking. Also available: private classes for individuals and groups.

EMPHASIS: French and Italian techniques, seasonal foods, reduced fat recipes.

FACULTY: Diane Wilkinson, certified by the IACP as a CCP, studied at Le Cordon Bleu, La Varenne, with Marcella Hazan, and has worked in kitchens in France and Italy, including those of Michael Guerard, Claude Deligne, Guenther Seeger, and L'Oustan de Beaumanière.

COSTS: Classes are $50, five sessions are $225, the intensive is $650. A $200 deposit is required for the intensive, refundable 3 weeks prior

CONTACT: Diane Wilkinson, 4365 Harris Trail, Atlanta, GA 30327; (404) 233-0366, Fax (404) 233-0051; E-Mail: 71177, 1411 compuserve.com.

ESCAPADES, INC.
Roswell/Year-round

Founded in 1994, this gourmet carry-out/bakery offers three 1-session demonstration (limit 30) and participation (limit 12) classes per month. Facilities: restaurant kitchen with home-style appliances and 12 work stations.

EMPHASIS: Breads, holiday foods, gourmet meals, French technique, cake decorating.

FACULTY: Owner and bread expert Betsy Oppenneer, CCP, authored two books and a newsletter, produced two videos, and started a baking catalog. She has judged cooking contests, taught at more than 70 schools, appeared on radio and television, and consulted with food companies. Executive Chef Nancy Eichler, CCP, owned two catering companies, taughtin Chicago and Atlanta, and consulted with cookware companies and community cookbooks. Both studied under Julia Child and Madeleine Kamman.

COSTS: Demonstrations are $25-$30, participation classes are $30-$40 per session. Payment in advance. No refunds 48 hours before class.

LOCATION: A 15-minute drive north of Atlanta.

CONTACT: Nancy Eichler, Escapades, 1570 Holcomb Bridge Rd., Suite 210, Roswell, GA 30076; (404) 518-2800; Fax (404) 518-2888.

KITCHEN FARE COOKING SCHOOL
Atlanta/Year-round

Founded in 1983, this school in a cookware store offers over 125 evening demonstrations (limit 25 students) per year. Facilities: a large, home-style kitchen.

EMPHASIS: Ethnic and regional cuisines, healthy cooking, fish, poultry, holiday menus.

FACULTY: A revolving staff of local chefs and professionals.

COSTS: $20 per class. Class credit for cancellations more than 24 hours prior. Credit cards accepted.

CONTACT: Laura Shapiro, Kitchen Fare Cooking School, 2385 Peachtree Rd., NE, Atlanta, GA 30305; (404) 233-8849.

MR. C'S COOKING CASTLE
Chamblee/March-July, September-November

Established in 1975, this school offers up to four 1- to 4-session participation courses (limit 15 students) per month. Facilities: 1,200-square-foot kitchen with 4 workspaces. Also: private classes.

EMPHASIS: Cooking techniques, cake decorating.

FACULTY: Caterers and party planners Cass Chapman, CEC, and Pauline Chapman, Sous Chef.

COSTS, ACCOMMODATIONS: $25 per class, 10% deposit.

LOCATION: 10 miles from Atlanta.

CONTACT: Cassius L. Chapman, Mr. C's Cooking Castle, P.O. Box 81261, Chamblee, GA 30366; (404) 493-9068.

URSULA'S COOKING SCHOOL, INC.
Atlanta/September-May

Founded in 1966 by Ursula Knaeusel, this school offers three 4-session demonstration courses (limit 40 students) per year. Facilities: 3-level classroom with 18-foot mirror over a 22-foot granite counter. Also available: Gingerbread house, cutting and decorating classes, bridal shower classes, couples classes.

EMPHASIS: Nouvelle cuisine, time-saving methods and advance preparation,.

FACULTY: Ursula Knaeusel's over 40 years of experience include supervising kitchens, managing guest houses, operating restaurants in Europe and the U.S., and teaching in Central America, the Caribbean, and the U.S.

COSTS: Tuition is $85 for the 4-session course. Payment with registration. Refunds granted cancellations prior to course.

LOCATION: One mile from Interstate 75 and 85 and 4 miles from downtown Atlanta.

CONTACT: Ursula Knaeusel, President, Ursula's Cooking School, Inc., 1764 Cheshire Bridge Rd., N.E., Atlanta, GA 30324; (404) 876-7463.

HAWAII

BIG ISLAND BOUNTY
Hawaii/May

First held in 1992, this annual 4-day festival showcases Hawaii's regional cuisine and features gastronomic field trips, seminars on traditional Hawaiian foods, roundtable discussions, and receptions and dinners. Also available: farmers market, golf, tennis, scuba, fishing, bicycling.

EMPHASIS: Foods of Hawaii.

FACULTY: Noted chefs and culinarians; has included Amy Ferguson-Ota, Peter Merriman, and Alan Wong.

COSTS, ACCOMMODATIONS: A variety of package plans, which include lodging at The Ritz-Carlton-Mauna Lani, are available. Meals and events can also be purchased separately.

LOCATION: The Ritz-Carlton on the Kohala Coast of the Big Island of Hawaii, 20 miles north of the Keahole-Kona airport.

CONTACT: Elizabeth DeMotte, Director of Public Relations, The RitzCarlton, Mauna Lani, One North Kaniku Dr., Kohala Coast, HI 96743; (808) 885-2000, (800) 845-9905; Fax (808) 885-1064.

A CELEBRATION OF HAWAII REGIONAL CUISINE
Maui/Year-round

Begun in 1994 by Interactive Events, these culinary vacation programs incorporate half-day hands-on classes and evening dining events. Other activities: spa treatments, golf, tennis, cultural and art tours, and enrichment seminars that include floral design, herb gardening, decorative table displays, cooking with condiments, and wine tasting.

EMPHASIS: Hawaiian regional cuisine, Pacific Rim, vegetarian, using local ingredients.

FACULTY: The founding chefs of Hawaii Regional Cuisine: Peter Merriman (Hula Grill), Roger Dikon (Makena Resort), Mark Ellman (Avalon), Jean-Marie Josselin (A Pacific Cafe), Roy Yamaguchi (Roy's Kahana Bar & Grill), Beverly Gannon (Haliimaile General Store).

COSTS, ACCOMMODATIONS: Land package cost is approximately $2,000, which includes most meals, ground transport, and first class lodging. A $500 deposit is required; balance due 60 days prior; cancellations over 60 days prior forfeit $250.

CONTACT: Noelle Edwards, Interactive Events, 2810 Puuhoolai St., Wailea, HI 96753; (800) 961-9196 or (808) 875-8808, Fax (808) 875-1565, E-mail events@maui.net.

COOKING WITH THE MASTER CHEFS ON MAUI
Wailea, Maui/Year-round

Starting in early 1996 at the Kea Lani Hotel, these week-long food and wine education programs are offered every five or six weeks. Activities: cooking classes, wine seminars, and field trips to wineries, specialty markets, and produce farms. Facilities: Kea Lani Hotel kitchens and classrooms.

EMPHASIS: Cuisines of the Pacific Rim and international guest chefs; wine and food pairing.

FACULTY: Each program features a Pacific Rim chef, a noted guest chef, and a wine expert.

COSTS, ACCOMMODATIONS: A variety of packages, including all-suite and villa lodging, available.

CONTACT: The Kea Lani Hotel, Wailea, Maui, HI 96753; (808) 875-4100, Fax (808) 875-1200.

CUISINES OF THE SUN
Kohala Coast/July

Since 1990 the Mauna Lani Bay Hotel has offered an annual 5-day culinary vacation (limit 200 participants) that features daily demonstrations of tropical recipes, nightly receptions, and other attractions. Facilities: on-stage demonstration kitchen. Also available: resort amenities, including golf, tennis, spa.

EMPHASIS: Tropical cuisines. Theme and region changes each year.

Faculty: Noted chefs and beverage makers from the regions featured.

COSTS, ACCOMMODATIONS: Approximately $1,500 single, $2,200 double occupancy, which includes some meals, planned activities, and lodging. Daily and individual event options available. Prepayment required for events only; full refund 4 days prior.

LOCATION: The AAA 5-Diamond Mauna Lani Bay Hotel and Bungalows is on the Kohala Coast of Hawaii's Big Island, 20 miles from the airport

CONTACT: Sharon Bianco, Director of Catering, The Mauna Lani Bay Hotel and Bungalows, One Mauna Lani Drive, Kohala Coast, Hawaii, 96743; (800) 367-2323, Fax (808) 885-4556.

JMD EDUCATIONAL CENTER FOR WINE AND FOOD
Aiea/Year-round

Established in 1990 and acquired by the University of Hawaii College of Continuing Education in 1992, the Center offers 15 culinary classes per semester and a fine wine series. Facilities: professional kitchen, exhibition hall, banquet room, wine cellar, garden lanai. Also available: California wine tours, cultural programs, catering and event planning and facilities.

EMPHASIS: A variety of topics; wine appreciation.

NONVOCATIONAL/VACATION   ILLINOIS

FACULTY: Director David J. Hill managed a restaurant for more than 25 years. The 11-member faculty includes chefs, cookbook authors, and Richard Dean, Master Sommelier, who coordinates the wine series.

COSTS: $35 per class. Payment with registration, refund with one working day notice.

LOCATION: The Halawa Valley, near Honolulu.

CONTACT: David J. Hill, JMD Educational Center for Wine and Food, 99-1269 Iwaena St., Aiea, HI 96701; (808) 486-5638, Fax (808) 487-2043.

ILLINOIS

ARG COOKING SCHOOL AND SUPPLY CO.
LaGrange/Fall, Winter, Spring

Founded in 1993, this gourmet equipment catalog supply company and cooking school offers demonstration and participation classes (limit 4-12 students). Facilities: a well-equipped private home kitchen and professional restaurant-style kitchen. Also available: guided tours of specialty markets and kitchen equipment emporiums.

EMPHASIS: Basic and intermediate Mexican, Caribbean, Latin, and Mediterranean cuisines.

FACULTY: Owner Anthony Garcia has taught Latin and Mediterranean cooking in the Chicago area for 10 years. He trained in Italian restaurants and is primarily self-taught.

COSTS: $40-$60 per class, payable 10 days in advance.

LOCATION: Two locations in the near western suburbs of Chicago

CONTACT: Anthony Garcia, ARG Cooking School and Supply Co., 106 W. Calendar Court, Ste. 223, LaGrange, IL 60625; (708) 485-4876; Fax (708) 354-8773.

BEAUTIFUL FOOD
Glenview/Spring and Fall

A cooking instructor since 1973, Charie MacDonald teaches approximately 20 participation classes (limit 20 students) a year. Facilities: the 2,800-square-foot commercial kitchen of Beautiful Food, her catering and wholesale specialty food business. Also available: Culinary tours.

EMPHASIS: Fresh foods, techniques, breads, pastas, pastries, soups, low-cholesterol foods.

FACULTY: Charie MacDonald studied at Le Cordon Bleu, the Ecole des Trois Gourmands (Provence), and with Simone Beck. An IACP charter member, she founded Beautiful Food in 1982.

COSTS: Class fee is $45, payable in advance. The trip cost of $5,000 includes airfare to/from Nice, meals, lodging, and ground transport. A deposit of $2,000 is required by December 1.

LOCATION: Glenview, northwest of Chicago near O'Hare International Airport

CONTACT: Beautiful Food, 1872 John's Dr., Glenview, IL 60025; (708) 657-8403, Fax (708) 657-8685.

CARLOS' RESTAURANT
Highland Park/Year-round

Since 1993, Carlos' Restaurant has offered luncheon demonstrations (limit 25 students) and A Day in the Kitchen individual participation classes.

EMPHASIS: Contemporary French cooking.

FACULTY: Executive Chef Jacky Pluton.

COSTS: Luncheon classes are $40; the full-day class is $140 per person, which includes the class for one and dinner for two.

Location: Highland Park, 25 miles north of Chicago.

CONTACT: Carlos' & Debbie Nieto, Owners, Carlos' Restaurant, 429 Temple Ave., Highland Park, IL 60035; (708) 432-0770, Fax (708) 432-2047.

CHEZ MADELAINE
Hinsdale/Fall, Winter, Spring

Founded in 1977, this school in a private home offers 35 to 40 one- to three-session demonstration and participation classes (limit 6 students) per year. Also available: evening menu classes.

EMPHASIS: Basics, techniques, ethnic cuisines, seasonal and holiday menus, preserving, soups, stocks, baking.

FACULTY: Madelaine Bullwinkel received the Diplome from L'Academie de Cuisine, is author of *Gourmet Preserves, Chez Madelaine*, and is a member of Les Dames d'Escoffier. Occasional guest instructors and cookbook authors.

COSTS: From $60-$75. Payment must accompany application.

LOCATION: Hinsdale, 20 miles west of Chicago, 20 minutes from O'Hare airport

CONTACT: Madelaine Bullwinkel, Owner, Chez Madelaine Cooking School, 211 N. Washington St., Hinsdale, IL 60521; (708) 325-4177, Fax (708) 655-0355.

COOKING CRAFT, INC.
St. Charles/September-May

Founded in 1982, this gourmet shop and deli offers 2 to 3 evening demonstrations (limit 24 students) per week and some participation courses. Also available: classes for children, private sessions.

EMPHASIS: Basics.

FACULTY: The main instructor has over 10 years of teaching experience. Other instructors specialize in ethnic topics.

COSTS: $18-$22 per class. Payment upon registration; full refund with 72 hours notice.

LOCATION: Mid-size commuter town on the Fox River, 40 miles west of Chicago

CONTACT: Anne Lorenz, Owner/Director, Cooking Craft, Inc., 1415 W. Main Street, St. Charles, IL 60174; (708) 377-1730; Fax (708) 377-3665.

THE COOKING AND HOSPITALITY INSTITUTE OF CHICAGO
Chicago/Year-round *(See page 32)*

In addition to career programs, this school offers more than a dozen classes and series for nonprofessionals.

EMPHASIS: Topics include seafood, herbs, pasta; charcuterie, catering, techniques.

COSTS: $40-$50 per session, $125-$150 for full-day programs.

CUISINE COOKING SCHOOL
Moline/September-June

Established in 1979, this school in a private residence offers approximately 50 participation classes (limit 10 students) a year. Facilities: remodeled large kitchen with 5 work stations and AGA range. Also available: food and wine pairing, classes for youngsters, private instruction, culinary tours.

EMPHASIS: French and Italian cuisines.

FACULTY: Owner/teacher Marysue Salmon studied at La Varenne and with Simone Beck and earned a BS degree in Food Science from Iowa State University.

COSTS: $37.50 per class. A 50% deposit is required; refund 1 week prior.

LOCATION: 3 hours west of Chicago, 3 hours east of Des Moines

CONTACT: Marysue Salmon, Cuisine Cooking School, 1100 - 23rd Ave., Moline, IL 61265; (309) 797-8613, Fax (309) 797-8641.

FOOD FESTS
Five U.S. locations

Established by publicist Gail Guggenheim in 1984, these cooking school weekends feature cooking classes, seminars, and tastings. Facilities: a complete kitchen with overhead mirrors set up on a stage; closed-circuit monitors. Also available: hotel amenities.

EMPHASIS: Entertaining menus, new food trends, ethnic specialties, techniques, gourmet products.

Faculty: Area chefs and cooking teachers, usually Certified Members of the IACP.

COSTS, ACCOMMODATIONS: Range from $189-$229 per couple for two nights, including continental breakfasts. Refund policy varies with location.

LOCATION: The Kahler Hotel in Rochester, Minn.; Sheraton San Marcos Resort in Chandler/Phoenix; Lakeview Resort in Morgantown, W.Va.; Olympia Park Hotel in Park City, Ut.; Plaza One Hotel in Rock Island, Ill.

CONTACT: Food Fests, 125 Country Lane, Highland Park, IL 60035; (708) 831-4265, Fax (708) 831-4266.

FRONTERA GRILL
Chicago, Oaxaca/October

Since 1992, Rick Bayless has conducted demonstrations (limit 25 students) and an annual 1 one-week culinary tour of Oaxaca, Mexico. Facilities: Frontera Grill restaurant kitchen

EMPHASIS: Mexican cuisine.

FACULTY: Rick Bayless graduated from the University of Oklahoma, hosted a PBS television Mexican cooking series, and, with his wife Deann, authored *Authentic Mexican*, and established Chicago's Frontera Grill and Topolobampo restaurants, both 3-star rated by the Chicago Tribune. In 1991, Rick received the James Beard Award as the Best America Chef, Midwest.

COSTS: Demonstrations are $45; the 1-week tour is $2,000.

LOCATION: River North section of Chicago; Oaxaca, Mexico

CONTACT: Pat Schloeman, Frontera Grill, 445 N. Clark, Chicago, IL 60610; (312) 661-1434, Fax (312) 661-1830; E-Mail: rickbayl10475@aol.com.

LA VENTURÉ
Skokie/November-May

Founded in 1980, this school in a private residence offers 30 six-session participation courses (limit 12 students) per month. Facilities: a 600-square-foot professional-style kitchen. Also available: private classes, classes for children.

EMPHASIS: French, Italian, and Chinese cuisines; candy making and cake decorating; baking.

FACULTY: Director-owner Sandra Bisceglie attended the French School Dumas Pere and Harrington Institute of Interior Design and has a certificate of completion from the National Institute for the Foodservice Industry.

COSTS: Range from $289-$359. Refund for cancellations with 10 days notice.

LOCATION: Skokie is adjacent to Chicago, 3 miles from O'Hare airport

CONTACT: Sandra Bisceglie, La Venturé, 5100 West Jarlath, Skokie, IL 60077; (708) 679-8845.

ORIENTAL FOOD MARKET & COOKING SCHOOL, INC.
Chicago/Year-round

Established in 1971, this market and catering service offers 1- and 6-session demonstration classes (limit 50 students) each month, and a 19-day culinary and cultural tour to China (limit 15 participants) in July.

EMPHASIS: Thai, Indonesian, Japanese, Korean, Vietnamese, Chinese, and Philippine cuisines.

FACULTY: Pansy and Chu-Yen Luke have operated the market and school since its inception.

COSTS: From $15-$25 per session; the tour is $3,500, including ground transport and airfare

CONTACT: Oriental Food Market and Cooking School, 2801 West Howard St., Chicago, IL 60645; (312) 274-2826.

TRUFFLES, INC.
O'Fallon/September-June

Founded in 1980, this school in a private home offers 2-session demonstration and participation courses (limit 8 to 15 students). Facilities: professional home kitchen with grill and double ovens.

EMPHASIS: Regional and international food, bread and pastry, party themes.

FACULTY: Caterer and food consultant Kathy Kneedler, CCP, has taught cooking for 15 years and is a past newsletter editor for the St. Louis Culinary Society.

COSTS: $20-$25. Deposit required; refunds granted 3 days before class.

LOCATION: About 45 minutes from a major airport and 20 minutes from St. Louis.

CONTACT: Kathy A. Kneedler, President and Director, Truffles Inc., 910 Indian Springs Rd., O'Fallon, IL, 62269; (618) 632-9461, Fax (618) 624-2267.

WHAT'S COOKING
Hinsdale and locations in Asia

Established in 1980, this school offers demonstration and participation courses (limit 15 students) in light, healthy Pacific Rim cooking and conducts Far East culinary tours that feature classes with professional chefs, gourmet dining, sightseeing, and visits to food markets.

EMPHASIS: The cuisines of China, Thailand, Singapore, Malaysia, Indonesia, India, Korea, the Philippines, Japan, and Hawaii.

FACULTY: Ruth Law, a graduate of Domas Pere French Cooking School and a Certified Member of the IACP, is author of *Indian Light Cooking,* a 1994 nominee for *The Julia Child Cookbook* and *Dim Sum-Fast and Festive Chinese Cooking.*

Location: Hinsdale, a Chicago suburb. Tours visit China, Hong Kong, Thailand, Singapore, Malaysia, Indonesia, India

CONTACT: Ruth Law, What's Cooking, P.O. Box 323, Hinsdale, IL 60522; (708) 986-1595, Fax (708) 655-0912.

INDIANA

COUNTRY KITCHEN
Fort Wayne/Year-round

Founded in 1964, this school offers basic to advanced cake decorating courses 3 times a year and more than 35 demonstration (limit 60 students) and participation (limit 35) classes on candies, desserts, and other topics. Facilities: classroom with tiered work and observation seating. Also available: classes for groups, children's parties.

FACULTY: More than 10 instructors.

COSTS: Cake decorating courses range from $65-$70 each. Demonstrations range from $10-$30. Full payment in advance; refunds granted a week prior

CONTACT: Vi Whittington, Country Kitchen, 3225 Wells St., Ft. Wayne, IN 46808; (219) 482-4835.

KITCHEN AFFAIRS
Evansville/January-November

Established in 1987, this cookware store and school offers 15 demonstration (limit 20 students) and participation (limit 12) classes per month. Facilities: a 350-square-foot kitchen with 4 work stations. Also available: children's classes, private classes.

EMPHASIS: Basic techniques, ethnic cuisines, menu planning.

FACULTY: Restaurant chefs, professional instructors, cookbook authors, and school owners Shelly and Mike Sackett. Many instructors are IACP members.

COSTS: From $15-$60. Credit cards accepted. Full payment in advance; refund 10 days prior.

Location: Across from Evansville's largest shopping mall.

CONTACT: Shelly Sackett, Director, Kitchen Affairs, Woodland Center, 4610 Vogel Rd., Evansville, IN 47715; (800) 782-6762 or (812) 474-1131.

IOWA

COOKING WITH LIZ CLARK
Keokuk/Year-round

Opened in 1977, this school offers about 10 demonstration (limit 16 students) and participation (limit 12) classes each quarter. Facilities: Elizabeth Clark's renovated antebellum home, which also houses her restaurant. Also available: weekend intensives that offer continuing education units, culinary tours in the U.S. and abroad.

EMPHASIS: Seasonal and holiday menus and guest chef specialties.

Faculty: Liz Clark has studied in Italy and France, received her diploma in the Cours Intensifs from La Varenne, and studied at the Moulin de Mougins with Roger Verge and at The Oriental in Bangkok. Other instructors have included Barbara Kafka, Janeen Sarlin, Peter Kump, Betsy Oppenneer, Shirley Corriher, and Nick Malgieri.

COSTS, ACCOMMODATIONS: Classes are $36-$60 each, pre-paid 1 week before. Housing is $30 per night. Credit or refund is granted cancellations 3 days prior to class.

LOCATION: 50 miles south of Burlington airport

CONTACT: Southeastern Community College, Box 6007, Keokuk, IA 52632; (319) 752-2731, Fax (319) 524-3221, ext 409.

KANSAS

COOKING AT BONNIE'S PLACE
Wichita/September-May

Established in 1990 by Bonnie Aeschliman, this school offers 4-6 demonstrations (limit 25 students) per month. Facilities: demonstration kitchen.

EMPHASIS: A variety of topics.

FACULTY: Bonnie Aeschliman, CCP, has a master's degreee in food and nutrition; Dr. Phil Aeschliman is a member of the IACP.

COSTS, ACCOMMODATIONS: $20-$30 per class.

LOCATION: One mile from Wichita.

CONTACT: Bonnie Aeschliman, Cooking at Bonnie's Place, 5900 E. 47th St., North, Wichita, KS 67220; (316) 744-1981.

KENTUCKY

THE COOKBOOK COTTAGE
Louisville/Year-round

Established in 1986, this cookbook store and school offers more than 150 demonstration (limit 20 students) and participation (limit 10) classes per year. Facilities: 1,200-square-foot classroom, which seats 30 and has overhead mirrors.

EMPHASIS: Herb and spice cookery, breads, international and regional cuisines, holiday and seasonal menus, guest chef specialties.

FACULTY: Proprietor/instructor Stephen J. Lee earned a degree in Culinary Arts from the University of Kentucky, is food columnist for the *Louisville Entertainer* and a member of the IACP. Other faculty includes local cooking teachers and guest chefs.

COSTS: Range from $15-$30 for most classes, $48 for guest chefs. Advance registration and payment is required. Credit cards accepted.

LOCATION: Louisville.

CONTACT: Stephen J. Lee, Proprietor, The Cookbook Cottage, 1279 Bardstown Rd., Louisville, KY 40204; (502) 458-5227.

RANDALL'S SCHOOL OF COOKING
Lexington/Year-round

Established in 1991, this school offers 140 one- to four-session demonstration (limit 16 students) and participation (limit 12) courses per year. Facilities: a 180-square-foot self-contained kitchen with overhead mirror in Randall Foods Market. Also available: private group classes, children's classes, birthday parties.

EMPHASIS: Ethnic and regional cuisines, techniques, pastry, cake decorating, guest chef specialties.

FACULTY: Instructors include IACP and ACF members, registered dieticians, and guest chefs Beatrice Ojakangas, Nathalie Dupree, Joanne Weir, and Jude Theriot.

COSTS: Range from $10 to $34. Payment within 3 days of enrollment. Cancellations 2 days prior receive refund.

Location: Three miles from downtown Lexington.

CONTACT: Dianne Holleran, Consumer Affairs Director, Randall's School of Cooking, 344 Romany Rd., Lexington, KY 40502; (606) 269-1034, Fax (606) 269-5380.

LOUISIANA

CAJUN COOKING CONVERSATIONS COOKING SCHOOL
Breaux Bridge/Year-round

Founded in 1993, this school offers one or two demonstrations (limit 60 students) per day and 10-15 local one-day tours per year. Facilities: 4,800-square-foot demonstration kitchen, restaurant kitchens. Also available: private classes, manufacturing/processing plant tours, visits to markets, restaurants, and food manufacturers, sightseeing.

EMPHASIS: Cajun cooking of Southwest Louisiana (Acadiana).

FACULTY: Stan Gauthier, a self-taught cook who developed a line of Cajun spices and seasonings; ACF-accredited chefs and cooks of the region.

COSTS, ACCOMMODATIONS: Class prices range from $15-$75. For large groups, a 50% deposit is required 30 days prior. Credit cards accepted.

LOCATION: Southwest Louisiana, bordered by the Atchafalaya Swamp & Basin, an hour from Baton Rouge, and 2 hours from New Orleans.

CONTACT: Carole Purcell, Cajun Cooking Conversations Cooking School, All Cajun Food Co., 1019 Delcambre Rd., Breaux Bridge, LA 70517; (800) 467-3613 or (318) 332-3613, Fax 318-332-1467.

COOKIN' CAJUN COOKING SCHOOL
New Orleans/Year-round

Established in 1988 by Creole Delicacies, a firm specializing in Cajun and Creole gourmet items, this school offers demonstration classes (limit 50 to 80 students) Monday through Saturday mornings. Facilities: theatre-style mirrored kitchen overlooking the Mississippi River. Also available: private classes, parties, fish classes for anglers.

EMPHASIS: Cajun and Creole cuisine.

FACULTY: Susan Murphy and several other instructors.

COSTS: $15 per class. Advance reservations are required. Mention ShawGuides for a 10% discount.

NONVOCATIONAL/VACATION **LOUISIANA** **187**

LOCATION: Riverwalk Marketplace near the New Orleans Convention Center

CONTACT: Cookin' Cajun Cooking School, #1 Poydras, Store #116, New Orleans, LA 70130; (504) 523-6425, Fax (504) 523-4787.

CREOLE COOK SYMPOSIUM
New Orleans/March

Since 1992, the Hermann-Grima Historic House has sponsored an annual 3-day symposium that features lectures, seminars, a hands-on cooking workshop in a mid-19th-century open-hearth kitchen, a French Quarter walking tour, and dinner in a private home.

EMPHASIS: New Orleans food, wine, culture, and history.

COSTS, ACCOMMODATIONS: Fee is $225, which includes lectures, seminars, and one lunch and dinner. Cooking class is $50 extra. Payment required with registration; refunds 8 weeks prior. Hotel information is provided.

LOCATION: The French Quarter.

CONTACT: Creole Cook Symposium, Hermann-Grima Historic House, 820 St. Louis St., New Orleans, LA 70112; (504) 525-5661, Fax (504) 525-5663.

KAY EWING'S EVERYDAY GOURMET
Baton Rouge/Year-round

Since 1985, Kay Ewing has taught 10 to 12 participation classes per year (limit 6 students). Facilities: The Panhandler, a gourmet kitchen store. Also available: classes for youngsters held in the summer and during holidays.

EMPHASIS: International and cajun cuisines, full participation, menu classes.

FACULTY: Kay Ewing is a member of the IACP and author of *Kay Ewing's Cooking School Cookbook.*

COSTS: Tuition is $30 for adults, $15 for children. Payment 1 week after class is booked; refund 48 hours prior

CONTACT: Kay Ewing, c/o The Panhandler, 9259 Florida Blvd., Monterrey Plaza, Baton Rouge, LA 70815; (504) 927-4371.

THE NEW ORLEANS SCHOOL OF COOKING
Year-round

Founded in 1980 by Joe Cahn, this school offers morning demonstrations Monday through Saturday. Facilities: a large mirrored kitchen. Also available: classes for private groups.

EMPHASIS: Cajun and Creole cuisine.

FACULTY: Kevin Belton is a self-taught cook and television personality.

COSTS: $20 per class. Credit cards accepted.

LOCATION: The Jax Brewery adjacent to the Louisiana General Store, overlooking the Mississippi River and the French Quarter.

CONTACT: The New Orleans School of Cooking, 620 Decatur St., New Orleans, LA 70130; (504) 525-2665, Fax (504) 731-6108. Group reservations: Laura Schneider, (504) 731-6100.

MAINE

THE WHIP AND SPOON
Portland/Spring and Fall

Established in 1980, this gourmet foods and cookware store offers approximately 25 to 30 demonstration classes (limit 25 students) each quarter. Facilities: a well-equipped teaching kitchen.

EMPHASIS: Ethnic and regional cuisines, healthful foods, guest chef specialties.

FACULTY: Local cooks, chefs, and caterers, including Rosemarie DeAngelis, Barbara Gulino, Cheryl Lewis, Rick Perry, and Avis Layman.

COSTS: $15 per class. Refund with 48 hours notice. Credit cards accepted.

LOCATION: The Old Port Exchange on Portland's waterfront.

CONTACT: The Whip and Spoon, 161 Commercial St., Portland, ME 04112; (800) 937-9447, (207) 774-4020.

MARYLAND

CAKE COTTAGE, INC.
Baltimore/Year-round

Founded in 1977, this candy shop and school offers participation courses (limit 30 students) in basic and advanced cake decorating and demonstration (limit 50) and participation classes in candies, cake writing, puff pastry, petit fours, butter cream flowers, air brush decorating, and party foods. Also available: children's courses.

FACULTY: Carole studied at the Wilton School and has taught for over 20 years; Donna studied candymaking with chocolatiers in the U.S. and abroad for over 19 years.

COSTS: The basic decorating course is $35, advanced course is $40, the children's course is $25. Single sessions range from $8-$40. Full nonrefundable payment must accompany registration.

LOCATION: Baltimore's northeast section, 20 minutes from BWI airport.

CONTACT: The Cake Cottage, Inc., 8716 Belair Rd., Baltimore, MD 21236; (410) 529-0200, Fax (410) 529-6867.

THE CHINESE COOKERY, INC.
Silver Spring/Year-round

Founded by cooking educator and biochemist Joan Shih in 1975, this school offers 8 levels of participation and demonstration (limit 5 students) courses in Chinese cuisine. Facilities: classroom/lab equipped for Chinese cooking, outdoor Chinese brick oven. Also available: Japanese sushi class, classes for teenagers, private lessons for cooking professionals, market visits, restaurant kitchen tours, and culinary tours to the Far East.

EMPHASIS: Eight levels of instruction in Chinese cuisine, including Szechuan, Hunan, vegetarian.

FACULTY: Joan Shih, a chemist at the National Institute of Health, received a certificate in Chinese cuisine in Taiwan and has taught Chinese and Japanese cooking on television and in schools.

COSTS: Five-session courses are $135 and the sushi class is $35. A nonrefundable deposit of $30 is required. Classes are arranged by appointment

CONTACT: Joan Shih, The Chinese Cookery, Inc., 14209 Sturtevant Rd., Silver Spring, MD 20905; (301) 236-5311.

L'ACADEMIE DE CUISINE
Bethesda/Year-round *(See page 49)*

In addition to its career programs, this school offers 35 to 40 one- to four-session demonstration (limit 25 students) and participation (limit 21) courses per month and one-week French culinary vacations that include trips to an Armagnac distillery, Bordeaux wineries, and a duck farm, and dining at Michelin-star restaurants. Also available: children's classes and parties, private dinners, guest chef demonstrations.

EMPHASIS: Techniques, international and regional cuisines, nutritional and low-fat foods, pastry, wine and food pairing, breads, entertaining menus.

FACULTY: Francois Dionot, Director. More than 20 teachers with varied backgrounds.

COSTS: From $27-$55 per session. Full payment required; refund with 3 business days notice.

NONVOCATIONAL/VACATION   **MASSACHUSETTS**

LOCATION: For classes, the school's Bethesda campus; for trips, Domaine de Bassibe in Gascony.

CONTACT: Susan Watterson, L'Academie de Cuisine, 5021 Wilson Ln., Bethesda, MD 20814; (301) 986-9490, Fax (301) 652-7970.

MASSACHUSETTS

BOSTON UNIVERSITY SEMINARS IN THE CULINARY ARTS

The Seminars in the Culinary Arts program, started in 1984, features 1- to 3-session demonstration (limit 130) and participation (limit 24) courses (See also page 50). Facilities: large demonstration room with overhead mirror and kitchen with 8 work stations. Also available: children's classes, market visits, food and wine pairing, domestic and foreign tours hosted by a well-known culinary historian familiar with the regions' food and wine.

EMPHASIS: Guest chef specialties.

FACULTY: Has included Julia Child, Jacques Pepin, Nancy Harmon Jenkins, Jasper White, Jody Adams.

COSTS: Seminars range from $10-$125; full-day classes and 3-session courses range from $150-$300. Payment must accompany registration; refund with 24 hours notice.

THE CAMBRIDGE SCHOOL OF CULINARY ARTS
(See page 51)   **Cambridge/July-August**

This career school's Continuing Education Program offers 1- to 4-session courses and culinary tours.

EMPHASIS: Ethnic and regional cuisines, vegetarian meals, breads, pastries, event planning, appetizers, desserts.

COSTS: Range from $45-$55 per session; payment with registration; refunds 10 days prior.

KUSHI INSTITUTE COOKING SEMINARS
Becket/Year-round

This nonprofit educational facility, founded in 1978 by Michio and Aveline Kushi, offers 3 different one-week programs (limit 16 students) that each feature 10 cooking classes, morning exercise sessions, and informal evening lectures. Other activities: shiatsu massage, personal consultation.

EMPHASIS: International cuisine, home style cooking, healing foods using macrobiotic menus and cooking techniques.

Faculty: Wendy Esko, Diane Avoli, Carry Wolf, Michelle Nemer, Mayumi Nishimura, Warren Kramer, Palma O'Sullivan.

COSTS, ACCOMMODATIONS: The $985 cost includes meals and double occupancy country manor lodging with shared bath; $75 discount with 30-day pre-registration and payment. Private bath and single lodging are additional. A $100 deposit is required with balance due on arrival. Airport pick-up is $75 one-way. Credit cards accepted.

LOCATION: The Berkshire mountains, a 3-hour drive from Boston and New York City, near Lenox, Mass.

CONTACT: Mercedes Gallagher, The Kushi Institute, P.O. Box 7, Becket, MA 01223; (413) 623-5741, Fax (413) 623-8827.

LE PETIT GOURMET COOKING SCHOOL
Wayland/Year-round

In operation from 1979-1984 and re-opened in 1993, this school offers eight 1- to 4-session demonstration/participation courses (limit 8 students) per month. Facilities: 330-square-foot kitchen with two workspaces. Also available: private classes.

EMPHASIS: Beginning to advanced French cuisine, low fat cooking, specific subjects.

FACULTY: Fran Rosenheim studied with local chefs and at Le Cordon Bleu and La Varenne in Paris.

COSTS, ACCOMMODATIONS: $50 per session.

LOCATION: 30 minutes from Boston.

CONTACT: Fran Rosenheim, Le Petit Gourmet Cooking School, 19 Charena Rd., Wayland, MA 01778; (508) 358-4219, Fax (508) 358-4291.

MARGE COHEN
Needham Heights/September-June

Since 1980, Marge Cohen has taught 5-session demonstration and participation courses. Facilities: her home kitchen. Also available: Private classes, men-only courses, local culinary tours.

EMPHASIS: Basic to advanced Chinese and other ethnic cuisines.

FACULTY: Marge Cohen has certificates from the Le Cordon Bleu and Weichuan Cooking School in Taiwan and has hosted a cable TV program.

COSTS: Each 5-session course is $100; culinary tours are $25.

Location: Twenty minutes west of Boston.

CONTACT: Marge Cohen, P.O. Box 53, Needham Heights, MA 02194; (617) 449-2688, Fax (617) 449-7878.

TERENCE JANERICCO COOKING CLASSES
Boston/September-June

Founded in 1966, this school in a private residence offers 17 one- and six-session demonstration (limit 14 students) and participation (limit 6) courses per month. Also available: private classes.

EMPHASIS: Gourmet cooking, baking, ethnic and regional cuisines, specific subjects.

FACULTY: Terence Janericco has operated a catering firm for more than 25 years and teaches at adult education centers in Boston and at schools in New England and Michigan. He is author of 12 books, including *The Book of Great Soups*, *The Gourmet Galley*, *Vegetable Cookery*, and *The Book of Great Desserts*.

COSTS: Six-session courses are $360, single-sessions are $60. A $60 deposit is required with balance due at first class; refund 1 week prior

CONTACT: Terence Janericco Cooking Classes, 42 Fayette St., Boston, MA 02116; (617) 426-7458.

MICHIGAN

KITCHEN GLAMOR
Grand River/Year-round

Founded in 1949, this gourmet cookware store and cooking school offers 3 to 5 demonstration (limit 125 students) and participation (limit 25) courses per month and 15 to 20 pre-registration classes (limit 12 to 16) and guest chef classes each season. Facilities: the kitchen auditorium has a 12-foot counter, 2 four-range burners, and overhead mirror.

FACULTY: Includes award-winning cake decorator Mary Ann Hollen, food authority Jeanne Sarna, and local chefs. Guest chefs have included Joanne Weir, Madeleine Kamman, and Alice Medrich.

COSTS: Demonstrations are $3 each, $30 for 12; pre-registration classes are $40 for local chefs, $25-$35 for others; guest chef demonstrations range up to $80 per session. Credit cards accepted. No refunds.

Location: The West Bloomfield School is in the Orchard Mall; the Rochester school is in the Great Oaks Mall, Walton at Livernols; the Novi location is at the Novi Town Center. The closest major city is Detroit.

CONTACT: Kitchen Glamor, 26770 Grand River, Redford Township, MI 48240; (313) 537-1300.

LUCY'S KITCHEN
Ann Arbor/Year-round

Lucy Seligman offers private monthly cooking classes (limit 6 students) that are either demonstrations or hands-on. Facilities: Lucy's kitchen or students' home kitchens. Also available: children's classes, event planning, kitchen organization, private meal preparation.

EMPHASIS: Various topics, including Japanese, Russian, Turkish, and American regional cuisines.

FACULTY: Lucy Seligman graduated from Boston University's Culinary Arts program, owned a cooking school in Japan, and studied cooking in Paris, Bangkok, Tokyo, Florence, and Los Angeles. She publishes a newsletter on Japanese cuisine and is fluent in Japanese and French.

COSTS: Range from $32-$36 per class.

LOCATION: Near North Campus in Ann Arbor.

CONTACT: Lucy Seligman, Lucy's Kitchen, 631 Watersedge Dr., Ann Arbor, MI 48105; (313) 662-5572, Fax (313) 662-4212.

NELL BENEDICT COOKING CLASSES
Birmingham/September-May

Since 1970, Nell Benedict has taught evening demonstration classes (limit 45 students). Facilities: the teaching kitchen at The Community House.

EMPHASIS: Ethnic cuisines, breads, restaurant specialties.

FACULTY: Nell Benedict studied at Le Cordon Bleu, La Varenne, and L'Arts Culinara and with James Beard, Jacques Pepin, and Roger Verge. She has taught on television and is a Charter Member of the IACP.

COSTS: Each session is $16. Refund for cancellations 48 hours prior.

Location: Approximately 8 miles north of Detroit.

CONTACT: Nell Benedict, The Community House, 380 S. Bates St., Birmingham, MI 48009; (313) 644-5832 or write: International Cuisine, 18769 Alhambra, Lathrup Village, MI 48076.

MINNESOTA

BYERLY'S SCHOOL OF CULINARY ARTS
St. Louis Park/Year-round

Founded in 1980, this school in an upscale supermarket offers an average of 20 one-session demonstration (limit 25 students) and participation (limit 14) classes each month. Facilities: a large teaching kitchen with overhead mirror. Also available: private and couple's classes, children's birthday classes.

EMPHASIS: Chinese, Indian, Italian, and Thai cuisine; baking, entertaining, healthy cooking.

FACULTY: Manager Mary Evans studied at La Varenne and Lenotre. Other instructors: cookbook author Antonio Cecconi, registered dietitian Nancy Cooper, CIA graduate John Schumacher, syndicated columnist Mary Carroll, and L'Academie de Cuisine graduate Deidre Schipani.

COSTS: Average $20 per class. Full refund with 3 days notice.

Location: St. Louis Park, a suburb of Minneapolis, 15 minutes from downtown Minneapolis.

CONTACT: Mary Evans, Manager, Byerly's School of Culinary Arts, 3777 Park Center Blvd., St. Louis Park, MN 55416; (612) 929-2492, Fax (612) 929-7756.

COOKS OF CROCUS HILL
St. Paul/Year-round

Founded in 1976, this school in a cookware store offers 20 to 25 one-, three-, and five-session demonstration (limit 25 students) and participation (limit 12) courses per month. Also available: private group classes.

EMPHASIS: Basics, ethnic cuisines, holiday and seasonal menus, specific subjects, guest chef specialties, wine and beer tastings.

FACULTY: The 21-member faculty includes owner Martha Kaemmer, BJ Carpenter, Jennifer Holloway, and Yvonne Moody. Guest chefs include Hugh Carpenter, Jim Dodge, and Joanne Weir.

COSTS: The 3-session course is $120, the 5-session is $185. Classes range from $40-$65. Payment required within 5 working days of registration; refund with 48 hours notice. Credit cards accepted

CONTACT: Jennifer Holloway, Director, Cook's of Crocus Hill, 877 Grand Ave., St. Paul, MN 55105; (612) 228-1333.

MISSISSIPPI

THE EVERYDAY GOURMET
Jackson/January-November

Founded in 1982, this school in a cookware store offers approximately 12 demonstration (limit 24) and participation (limit 12 to 15) classes each month. Also available: guest chefs, lunch sessions, and classes for children.

FACULTY: Includes Martha McIntosh, Gayle Stone, Butchie Nations, Cheryl Welch, and school director Chan Patterson.

COSTS: Range from $20-$40; children's classes are $15. Advance payment is requested; refund with 48 hours notice. Credit cards accepted

CONTACT: The Everyday Gourmet, Inc., 2905 Old Canton Rd., Jackson, MS 39216; (601) 362-0723 or (800) 898-0122.

OFFSHORE COOKING SCHOOL
Ocean Springs/Year-round *(See page 59)*

This vocational school also offers courses in cajun and southern cooking for nonprofessionals.

MISSOURI

CULINARY INSTITUTE OF SMOKE-COOKING (CISC)
Cape Girardeau/Year-round

Founded in 1992, CISC's Master BBQ-Cook's School offers 8 train-at-home master lessons in the student's backyard using own equipment of BBQ pit/smoker/grill, meat, and thermometers. Also available: private lessons, BBQ restaurant consulting, and on-site classroom demonstrations.

EMPHASIS: Southern-style barbecuing and grilling.

FACULTY: Owners Charles and Ruth Knote, authors of *Barbecuing and Sausage Making Secrets* (CISC textbook), are graduates of Memphis-in-May BBQ Judging School and have 42 years of barbecuing experience.

COSTS: Master BBQ Cook's School is $100 cash or $30 plus four $20 payments.

Location: Train-at-home (correspondence school) format.

CONTACT: Charles Knote, President, CISC's Master BBQ Cook's School, 2323 A Brookwood Drive, Cape Girardeau, MO 63701; (314) 334-4621 (phone/fax).

DIERBERGS SCHOOL OF COOKING
St. Louis/Year-round

Founded in 1978, these 4 schools offer 80 one-session demonstration and participation courses (limit 18 students) per month. Facilities: sound-proof enclosures in Dierbergs Supermarkets. Also available: classes for couples, children's classes, parent-child sessions.

FACULTY: In addition to the more than 30-member faculty of home economists and cooking

NONVOCATIONAL/VACATION **MISSOURI** **193**

instructors, guest teachers include Gerard Germain, executive chef, Tony's Restaurant; industry spokespersons, traveling chefs, and cookbook authors.

Costs: Adult classes range from $16-$20, guest classes are $20-$40. Payment within 3 days of enrollment; refund with 4 days notice.

Contact: Dierbergs, 11481 Olive St. Rd., Creve Coeur, MO 63141; (314) 432-6561/6505; 1322 Clarkson/Clayton Center, Ellisville, MO 63011; (314) 394-9543; 12420 Tesson Ferry Rd., St. Louis, MO 63128; (314) 849-3698; 290 Mid Rivers Dr., St. Peters, MO 63376; (314) 928-1117.

JASPER'S
Kansas City/August-June

Established in 1954, this restaurant offers 2 demonstration classes (limit 45 students) per month and holiday luncheon classes. Also available: private classes for groups of 20 or more, children's and couples' classes, wine classes.

Emphasis: Northern Italian cuisine.

Faculty: Executive Chef Jasper J. Mirabile, Jr., son of Jasper's founder, studied at La Varenne, the Gritti Palace, and the University of Nevada. Jasper's has received the Travel/Holiday Award, the Mobil 4-Star award, and the AAA 4-Diamond award.

Costs: Each class is $35; refund with 48 hours notice. Credit cards accepted.

Location: South Kansas City.

Contact: Jasper J. Mirabile, Jr., Jasper's, 405 W. 75th St., Kansas City, MO 64114; (816) 363-3003, Fax (816) 361-2284.

KEMPER CENTER COOKING SCHOOL
St. Louis/Year-round

The Kemper Center of the Missouri Botanical Garden offers more than 20 one- to three-session demonstration and participation courses each season. Also available: gardening, arts & crafts.

Emphasis: A variety of topics.

Faculty: Includes caterers, nutritionists, cookbook authors, and cooking teachers.

Costs, Accommodations: $30-$35 per session. Members receive a discount. Refund with 4 days notice.

Contact: Glenn E. Kopp, Coordinator, Kemper Center Cooking School, Missouri Botanical Garden, P.O. Box 299, St. Louis, MO 63166-0299; (314) 577-5100.

KITCHEN CONSERVATORY
St. Louis/Year-round

Established in 1984, this school in a gourmet shop offers 25 to 30 demonstration and participation classes (limit 18 students) quarterly at each of its two locations. Also available: day trips to restaurants and shops, classes for children and teens.

Emphasis: Ethnic and regional cuisines, seasonal and entertaining menus, guest chef specialties.

Faculty: Local chefs, restaurateurs, caterers, dietitians, home economists, and IACP members. Guests have included Hugh Carpenter, Merle Ellis, Martin Yan, Paula Wolfert, and Perla Meyers.

Costs: Range from $28-$75. Credit cards accepted. Refund with 2 weeks notice.

Location: The Belleville, Illinois store is 15 minutes from downtown St. Louis; the St. Louis store, in Clayton, is minutes from downtown.

Contact: Kitchen Conservatory, 8021 Clayton Rd., St Louis, MO 63117; (314) 862-COOK (2665); 6948 West Main Street, Belleville, IL 62223; (618) 398-COOK (2665).

SUZANNE CORBETT — CULINARY RESOURCES
St. Louis/Year-round

Started in 1976, Suzanne Corbett teaches 10 participation (limit 16 students) courses per year.

Facilities: her home kitchen, vocational schools, historic sites. Also available: wine instruction.

EMPHASIS: Historic American foods, hearth-style baking, regional dishes, international cuisines, wok cookery.

FACULTY: Suzanne Corbett, who specializes in foods from the past, is the food editor of the *St. Louis Bugle*, has been a home economics instructor and a contributing editor to Rodale Press and *Victoria Magazine*, and is a certified instructor for vocational foodservice and Certified Culinary Professional by the IACP. She also offers video/film workshops featuring food subjects

COSTS: $25 to $50 per class. Refund with 48 hours notice

CONTACT: Suzanne Corbett — Culinary Resources, St. Louis Community College, 5850 Pebble Oak, St. Louis, MO 63128-1412; (314) 487-5205, Fax (314) 487-5335.

TAKE PLEASURE IN COOKING!
Kansas City/Year-round

Founded 1988, this school in a private residence offers 4 demonstration (limit 20 students) and 3 to 4 participation (limit 6) classes per month. Facilities: a 280-square-foot home kitchen with overhead mirror. Also available: private classes and workshops.

EMPHASIS: Culinary arts for the home, herbs, yeast doughs, regional cuisines, creative techniques, ease of preparation. .

FACULTY: Gloria Martin, owner, is an IACP member and has taught cooking for 17 years.

COSTS: Range from $30-$40. Refund with 24 hours notice.

LOCATION: The Kansas City suburb of Raytown, 15 miles from downtown

CONTACT: Gloria Martin, Take Pleasure in Cooking!, 8612 E. 84th St., Kansas City, MO 64138; (816) 353-6022.

NEBRASKA

WILLOW HOLLOW GOURMET
Lincoln

Established in 1974, this school in a private residence offers personalized demonstration (limit 20 students) and participation (limit 15) sessions. Also available: private classes at student's home for groups of 8 or more.

Faculty: Jackie Swanson, IACP member since 1973.

CONTACT: Jackie Swanson, President, Willow Hollow Gourmet, 1265 So. Cotner Blvd., Lincoln, NE 68502; (402) 483-2665, (800) 397-0230.

NEW HAMPSHIRE

A TASTE OF THE MOUNTAINS COOKING SCHOOL
Glen and Ossipee/Year-round except foliage

Founded in 1980 at the Bernerhof Inn (Glen), this school offers weekend courses in May, June and November and day courses every Wednesday and Thursday during the summer and winter. The hands-on classes are limited to ten students and custom seminars for groups of seven or more are available. Classes are also held at the Whittier House restaurant (Ossipee).

EMPHASIS: Basic techniques including knife handling, sauces, sauteeing, breads.

Faculty: Chefs Scott Willard and Richard Spencer, CWC, both culinary school graduates and ACF Chef of the Year recipients; Northern New England area guest chefs.

COSTS, ACCOMMODATIONS: Per person rates for weekend courses, which include double occupancy lodging and meals, range from $399 (standard room) to $499 (suite); day rate is $205 for the weekend; class rate is $45-$55. A 50% deposit is required; balance due on arrival. Refunds for weekend courses granted 30 days prior. Credit cards accepted.

LOCATION: Bernerhof Inn and Whittier House, in the White Mountains, are near Conway, 3 hours north of Boston and 90 minutes west of Portland, Me

CONTACT: A Taste of the Mountains Cooking School, Box 240, Glen, NH 03838; (603) 383-9132 or (800) 548-8007; Fax (603) 383-0809.

NEW JERSEY

COOKINGSTUDIO
West Caldwell/Year-round

This school offers 30 to 35 one- to eight-session demonstration and participation courses (limit 15 students) per month. Also available: Sunday With a Chef classes, celebrity chef demonstrations, classes for couples and singles, classes for children.

EMPHASIS: Basic and advanced Principles of Cooking, Mastery of Baking and other topics.

FACULTY: The more than 15-member resident and guest faculty includes Rick Rodgers, Carole Walter, and Jean Yueh. Guest chefs have included Giuliano Bugialli and Jacques Pepin. The school is a member of the IACP.

COSTS: Principles courses range from $55-$60 per session. Individual sessions range from $15-$45. Children's classes are $25-$35. Payment must accompany registration. Credit cards accepted. Full refund with 3 days notice.

LOCATION: Short Hills, Bedminster and Verona locations

CONTACT: Susan Loden, Cookingstudios, 2 Dedrick Pl., West Caldwell, NJ 07006; (201) 808-4277.

COOKTIQUE
Tenafly/Spring and Fall

Founded in 1976, this school offers approximately 150 evening demonstration (limit 25 students) and participation (limit 14) sessions a year. Facilities: a 400-square-foot demonstration kitchen with overhead mirror. Also available: children's classes, and birthday parties.

EMPHASIS: Techniques, sauces, fish, guest chef specialties.

FACULTY: Culinary professionals and master chefs. Guest chefs have included Giuliano Bugialli, Marcella Hazan, Nicholas Malgieri, Giuliano Hazan, Lorenza de' Medici, and Jacques Pepin.

COSTS: Begin at $25; guest chef classes $50-$100. Refund with 10 days notice. Credit cards accepted.

Location: 16 miles from New York City.

CONTACT: Cathy McCauley, Director, Cooktique, 9 W. Railroad Ave., Tenafly, NJ 07670; (201) 568-7990.

EDIBLES...NATURALLY! COOKING SCHOOL
Princeton Junction/Year-round

Established in 1994, this cafe and cooking school offers 8-10 evening demonstration (limit 24 students) and participation (limit 12) classes per month. Also available: children's, senior citizen's, and private singles' classes, market visits, field trips.

EMPHASIS: American regional, fusion, herbs, spices, vegetarian, low fat, macrobiotic, baking, basics.

FACULTY: Guest chefs and cookbook authors, including Giuliano Hazan, Craig Shelton, Olivier de St.Martin, Anne Casale; owner.

COSTS: Range from $35-$60 per class. Payment required with registration; full refund with 7 days notice. Credit cards accepted.

Location: Central New Jersey, an hour from Philadelphia and New York City.

CONTACT: Alice Miller, Director, Edibles...Naturally! Cooking School, 14 Washington Rd., Princeton Junction, NJ 08550; (609) 936-8200, Fax (609) 936-8855.

GOURMET LONG LIFE COOKING SCHOOLS
Springfield/Year-round

Established in 1984, this school offers 3-session demonstration courses (limit 9 students) for individuals concerned with weight control, sound nutrition, and/or medical conditions requiring a modified diet. Facilities: a 300-square-foot teaching kitchen.

EMPHASIS: Nutritional counseling; gourmet cooking without added salt, sugar, fats, or oils; vegetarian diets, cultural and ethnic foods; analysis of product labels.

FACULTY: Gloria Rose is author of *Cooking for Good Health*, included in the program materials. Instructors are gourmet cooks, registered dietitians or nurses affiliated with New Jersey hospitals.

COSTS: The $285 cost per course includes textbook and private nutritional counseling. A $150 nonrefundable deposit is required. Classes are booked 3 months in advance.

LOCATION: The central New Jersey school is 8 miles from Newark; the north Jersey school is 30 minutes from Manhattan.

CONTACT: Gloria Rose Gourmet Long Life Cooking School, 48 Norwood Rd., Springfield, NJ 07081; (201) 376-0942.

HOPEWELL-PENNINGTON COOKING CENTER
Hopewell/Year-round

Founded in 1994, this kitchen design showroom offers more than 80 demonstration (limit 25 students) and participation (limit 10) classes per year. Facilities: a 600-square-foot kitchen equipped with 3 work stations, overhead mirror, and the newest home kitchen appliances. Also: classes for children, teens, singles, and couples; wine appreciation seminars; private corporate classes.

EMPHASIS: Guest chef specialties, ethnic, regional, spa cuisine, special occasion, basic skills, etiquette.

FACULTY: Cooking teachers, guest chefs, and cookbook authors, including Carole Walter, Anne Casale, and Norman Weinstein.

COSTS: Range from $40-$85. Full payment with registration. Credit cards accepted.

LOCATION: Hopewell, a small town known for its antique dealers, is midway between New York City (55 miles) and Philadelphia (45 miles).

CONTACT: Ellen Schostak, Director, Hopewell-Pennington Cooking Center, 31 W. Broad St., Hopewell, NJ 08525; (609) 466-2066, Fax (609) 466-8491.

PETER KUMP'S SCHOOL OF CULINARY ARTS *(see page 202)*

PRINCETON COOKING SCHOOL
Year-round

Established in 1982, this school offers 1 five-session demonstration (limit 20 students) or participation (limit 8) course per season in Mexican and international cuisines. Facilities: a professional restaurant kitchen. Also available: private classes by appointment, tours of New York markets.

EMPHASIS: Mexican and international cuisines.

FACULTY: IACP-member Ruth Alegria is chef-owner of The Mexican Village restaurant.

COSTS: The 5-session course is $250, individual demonstrations range from $45-$60. Refund granted cancellations prior to course.

CONTACT: Ruth Alegria, Princeton Cooking School at Mexican Village Restaurant, 42 Leigh Ave., Princeton, NJ 08540; (609) 683-5818 (phone/fax).

NEW MEXICO

JANE BUTEL'S COOKING SCHOOL
Albuquerque/Year-round

Founded in 1983, Southwest regional cooking authority Jane Butel teaches 10 five-day and weekend participation courses (limit 15 students) per year as well as demonstration sessions that are scheduled on an on-going basis. Facilities: new 2,000-square-foot tiled kitchen with 5 work stations, demonstration area, and overhead mirror. Also available: advanced and private group lessons, sightseeing, ballooning, visits to markets and wineries.

EMPHASIS: Traditional, innovative, and low-fat New Mexican and Southwestern cuisine.

FACULTY: Jane Butel, author of 13 cookbooks, including *Jane Butel's Southwestern Kitchen and Fiesta*, and founder of the Pecos Valley Spice Co.; selected guest chefs and speakers.

COSTS, ACCOMMODATIONS: The $1,495 ($495) five-day (weekend) course fee includes some meals and double occupancy lodging at the Old Town Sheraton Inn; single supplement is $210 ($84); non-participant rate is $150 ($75), which includes meals. Deposit of $350 ($200) is nonrefundable but can be credited to another course. Demonstrations average $40 each.

LOCATION: Old Town Albuquerque.

CONTACT: Jane Butel's Cooking School, 800 Rio Grande NW #14, Albuquerque, NM 87104; (800) 473-TACO or (505) 243-2622, Fax (505) 243-8297; E-Mail: Compuserve 74547,1727.

SANTA FE SCHOOL OF COOKING
Year-round

Founded in 1989, this school and food market offers demonstration (limit 44 students) and participation (limit 15) classes several times weekly and smaller hands-on classes that include shopping at the Farmer's Market. Facilities: a Santa Fe-style kitchen with overhead mirrors. Also available: private classes, shopping trips to the Farmer's Market in August and September, culinary tours of northern New Mexico.

EMPHASIS: New Mexican and contemporary Southwestern cuisines, vegetarian, Mexican light cooking, and Native American.

FACULTY: Includes owner/director Susan Curtis, author of *Santa Fe School of Cooking Cookbook*; cookbook authors Cheryl Alters Jamison and Kathi Long; and guest chefs Mark Miller and Deborah Madison.

COSTS: Classes range from $25-$60; tours are approximately $800, which includes several meals and field trips.

LOCATION: The historic downtown district, 50 miles from Albuquerque International Airport

CONTACT: Susan Curtis, Owner/Director, Santa Fe School of Cooking, 116 W. San Francisco St., Santa Fe, NM 87501; (505) 983-4511, Fax (505) 983-7540.

NEW YORK

A LA BONNE COCOTTE
New York and Provence/Year-round

Founded in 1971, this school offers beginner, intermediate, and advanced four-session participation courses (limit 10 students). Facilities: a large country kitchen. Also available: Cooking and Living with Lydie in Provence, a five-day summer program (limit 6), that features cooking classes and sightseeing.

EMPHASIS: French cuisine, from simple regional recipes to haute cuisine.

Faculty: Mme. Lydie Pinoy Marshall, author of *Cooking with Lydie Marshall*, *A Passion for Potatoes*, and *Chez Nous*.

COSTS, ACCOMMODATIONS: Fee for a series of five classes is $400 and a $100 deposit must accompany application. Money-back refund policy for cancellations. Fee for the summer residential program is $1,100 and $350 deposit is refundable only if space can be filled. Participants are lodged at Lydie Marshall's small chateau.

LOCATION: New York City and Nyon, France, about 45 miles northeast of Avignon

Contact: Mme. Lydie P. Marshall, A La Bonne Cocotte, 23 Eighth Ave., New York, NY 10014; (212) 675-7736 or Le Chateau Feodal, 26110 Nyons, France; (33) 75 26 45 31.

ANNA TERESA CALLEN ITALIAN COOKING SCHOOL
New York/Year-round

Established in 1978, this school in a private residence offers 8 five-session participation courses (limit 6 students) per year. Facilities: an efficient home kitchen. Also: culinary tours to Italy.

Faculty: Anna Teresa Callen, a member of the IACP and the New York Association of Cooking Teachers, is author of *The Wonderful World of Pizzas, Quiches and Savory Pies*, and *Anna Teresa Callen's Menus for Pasta*. She teaches at Peter Kump's New York Cooking School and New York University, where she also lectures on history of gastronomy.

Costs: $620 for course, $120 advance for registration. Refund with 2 weeks notice.

Location: Downtown Manhattan.

Contact: Anna Teresa Callen, Anna Teresa Callen Italian Cooking School, 59 West 12th St., New York, NY 10011; (212) 929-5640.

CAROL'S CUISINE, INC.
Staten Island/Year-round

Founded in 1972, this school in a restaurant offers more than 130 one- to six-session demonstration (limit 25 students) and participation courses (limit 17) per year. Facilities: fully-equipped professional teaching kitchen with overhead mirror. Also available: private lessons, wine classes.

Emphasis: Techniques, baking, cake decorating, international and Italian cuisine.

Faculty: Owner-director Carol Frazzetta, a charter member of the New York Association of Cooking Teachers, was accredited by the IACP and holds an advanced certificate from Le Cordon Bleu. She studied at the CIA, the Wilton School of Cake Decorating, Marcella Hazan's School in Bologna, and the L'Academie de Cuisine. Leonard Pickell is a wine consultant and Wine Master at the James Beard House.

Costs: Range from $37-$45 per session. Deposit required. Partial refund for cancellations with 10 days notice.

Location: Central Staten Island, 1 hour from Manhattan by ferry or bus.

Contact: Carol Frazzetta, Carol's Cuisine, Inc., 1571 Richmond Rd., Staten Island, New York, NY 10304; (718) 979-5600.

CLUB CUISINE
New York/Year-round

Founded in 1985, this club rents its model recipe-testing kitchen for television and photo sessions, guest chef demonstrations and food promotion events. Also: culinary trips to southern France, breakfast at Fulton Fish Market, visits to a food photographer's studio, yacht excursions. wine tastings, French conversation courses, fund raising events, media training, and book signing parties.

Emphasis: French and Italian cuisine, etiquette, food and wine pairing, food-related events.

Faculty: Founder-president Michele Lyster trained at La Varenne and in her family's restaurant. A food stylist and consultant to the food industry, she is also on the program committee of the James Beard Foundation. Guest chefs have included Martin Yan, Anna Teresa Callen, Steven Schmidt, and Jack Ubaldi.

Costs: Trips to France range from $2,000 to $2,500, which includes meals and lodging.

Location: Various sites in New York City; trips to France

Contact: Nancy Hoffman, Club Cuisine, Inc., 244 Madison Ave., New York, NY 10016; (212) 557-5702, Fax (212) 286-0214; E-Mail: rqys90a@prodigy.com.

COOKHAMPTON — SILVIA LEHRER
Water Mill/Summer and Fall

Founded in 1988, this school offers 1- to 4-session demonstration (limit 20 students) and participation (limit 8) courses under the auspices of the Southampton Cultural Center. Facilities: a 400-square-foot teaching kitchen. Also available: culinary tours.

FACULTY: IACP-Certified instructor Silvia Lehrer, former owner of Cooktique in Tenafly, New Jersey, is author of *Cooking at Cooktique* and studied with James Beard, Simca Beck, and Giuliano Bugialli. Guest chefs of the Hamptons.

EMPHASIS: a variety of topics, including seasonal and entertaining menus, Italian cuisine, and chef specialties.

COSTS: Range from $75-$85 per session, $100 to $125 for guest chefs.

LOCATION: The summer resort area of Southampton township.

CONTACT: Silvia Lehrer, Cookhampton, P.O. Box 765, Water Mill, NY 11976; (516) 537-7831.

COOKING BY THE BOOK, INC.
New York/September-July

Founded in 1989, this school in a Tribeca loft offers 4 evening participation classes (limit 20 students) each month that focus on a selected cookbook or chef menu. Facilities: a fully-equipped 500-square-foot kitchen with 7 work stations. Also available: private parties and cooking instruction, corporate events, children's programs, wine instruction, customized classes.

EMPHASIS: Menus selected from a variety of cookbooks, such as Jacques Pépin's *Cuisine Economique*, Steven Raichlen's *Miami Spice*, and Julia Child's *Cooking with Master Chefs*.

FACULTY: Suzen and Brian O'Rourke; authors occasionally present.

COSTS: $55 per class, payable in advance. Refund with 48 hours notice.

Location: Downtown Manhattan, 25 minutes from Newark and La Guardia airports.

CONTACT: Suzen O'Rourke, President, Cooking by the Book, Inc., 13 Worth St., New York, NY 10013; (212) 966-9799; Fax (212) 925-1074.

CORNELL'S ADULT UNIVERSITY
Ithaca/July and August

Established in 1968, Cornell's Adult University offers an annual on-campus 4-week summer program consisting of 1-week workshops and courses (limit 12 to 20 participants) in subjects that include cooking, history, current events, ecology, music, literature, architecture, and art. Also available: a supervised youth program offers activities geared to 5 age groups.

EMPHASIS: The yearly culinary workshop focuses on menu planning and techniques for creating appetizing and nutritionally sound meals.

Faculty: Cornell University faculty and staff.

COSTS, ACCOMMODATIONS: Approximately $700 per week for adults and $250-$385 for children, which includes tuition, double occupancy dormitory lodging (single supplement available), meals, and planned activities. A $30 materials fee is extra. A $25 nonrefundable deposit is required; balance is due 30 days prior.

LOCATION: The 13,000-acre campus is in New York's Finger Lakes region

CONTACT: Cornell's Adult University, 626 Thurston Ave., Ithaca, NY 14850-2490; (607) 255-6260.

THE CULINARY INSTITUTE OF AMERICA
Hyde Park/Spring and Fall

(See page 68)

This school's Continuing Education Department offers a variety of Adult Education courses for cooking enthusiasts and home gourmets. All courses are taught on campus by the Institute's chefs and instructors. Continuing education brochure: (800) 888-7850.

DE GUSTIBUS AT MACY'S
New York/Fall and Spring

Established in 1980, this school in Macy's department store conducts about a half dozen 1- to 5-session demonstration (limit 65 students) and participation (limit 20) classes each season. Facilities: a professionally-equipped teaching kitchen. Also available: wine seminars, a recipe-writing course, and a media skills class.

EMPHASIS: Regional American cuisine, French and Italian cuisines; wine selection; menus for entertaining; guest chef specialties.

FACULTY: Guest chefs and cookbook authors include David Bouley, Daniel Boulud, Bobby Flay, Anne Rosenzweig, and Alain Sailhac.

COSTS: Range from $70 for 1 session to $260 for a series of 4. Credit cards accepted. Cancellations receive class credit.

LOCATION: Macy's Herald Square store at 34th Street and 7th Avenue.

CONTACT: Arlene Feltman Sailhac, De Gustibus at Macy's, 343 E. 74 St., Apt. 9G, New York, NY 10021; (212) 439-1714.

THE EPICUREAN GALLERY
New York/Year-round

Founded in 1977, this school and catering service in a private residence offers 26 six-session participation courses (limit 5 students) per year. Also available: seasonal and private classes.

EMPHASIS: Italian, French, American cuisine; baking; recipe modification and menu planning.

FACULTY: Gilda Latzky has taught French and Italian cooking and baking for more than 27 years in New York City, and also teaches in New Mexico, Colorado, Dallas, and Scottsdale. She studied in France and Italy and at the CIA.

COSTS: Each 6-session course is $375. A $75 deposit is required; refunds only if space is filled.

LOCATION: Greenwich Village. Classes also in Colorado, New Mexico, Texas, and Arizona.

CONTACT: Gilda Latzky, The Epicurean Gallery, 808 Broadway, New York, NY 10003; (212) 460-8243.

KAREN LEE IMAGINATIVE COOKING CLASSES & CATERING
New York/Year-round

Established in 1972, Karen Lee conducts participation classes (limit 9 students) that include two 5-day courses for out-of-towners, three 4-session courses that meet once weekly, and weekend seminars.

EMPHASIS: Nouvelle and traditional Chinese cuisine, Italian cuisine, basic technique, vegetarian, entertaining menus.

FACULTY: Owner and caterer Karen Lee apprenticed with Madame Grace Zia Chu and is author of *Nouvelle Chinese Cuisine*, *Soup*, *Chinese Cooking Secrets*, and *The Occasional Vegetarian*.

COSTS: Tuition, which includes a copy of Ms. Lee's latest book, is $630 for the 5-day course, $440 for the 4-session course ($125/single class), and $280 for the weekend course. A $150 nonrefundable deposit is required; cancellations receive credit

CONTACT: Karen Lee Imaginative Cooking Classes & Catering, 142 West End Ave., New York, NY 10023; (212) 787-2222.

LA CUISINE SANS PEUR
New York/Year-round

Founded in 1978, this school in a private residence offers more than twenty 5- and 6-session demonstration courses (limit 4 students) per year. Also available: 1-week cooking vacations in Provence. The more than 20 courses taught during the year include the 6-session basic course and the 5-session intermediate, advanced, and baking courses. Specialty classes include desserts, fish and game, and the cooking of Alsace and Provence.

EMPHASIS: The regional cooking of France with emphasis on Alsace and Provence, cooking without recipes, basic to advanced baking, fish, game, vegetable, and dessert courses.

FACULTY: Chef and proprietor Henri-Etienne Lévy trained and worked in restaurant kitchens in France and Germany for 15 years.

COSTS: Tuition is $450 per course. Payment is due 4 weeks prior. No cash refunds.

LOCATION: On Manhattan's Upper West Side, 10 minutes from Lincoln Center

CONTACT: Henri-Etienne Lévy, chef/proprietor, La Cuisine Sans Peur, 216 W. 89th St., New York, NY 10024; (212) 362-0638, Fax (212) 873-2029.

LAUREN GROVEMAN'S KITCHEN
Larchmont/Year-round

Established in 1990, Lauren Groveman conducts 5-session participation courses (limit 6 students) and individual classes on specific subjects.

EMPHASIS: Techniques and preparation of comfort foods, breads, appetizers, edible gifts.

FACULTY: Cookbook author and columnist Lauren Groveman.

COSTS: Tuition (deposit) is $375 ($100) for the 5-session course, $100 ($30) for a specialty class.

Location: About 30 minutes from New York City.

CONTACT: Lauren Groveman, President, Lauren Groveman's Kitchen, Inc., 55 Prospect Ave., Larchmont, NY 10538; (914) 834-1372, Fax (914) 834-3802.

LOOK WHO'S COOKING, INC.
Oyster Bay/Year-round

Established in 1994, this school offers 20 one- to four-session demonstration (limit 20 students) and participation courses (limit 10) per month. Facilities: 800-square-foot well-equipped kitchen with 10 workspaces.

EMPHASIS: Gourmet cooking for the everyday cook; low fat cooking; baking; fundamentals and techniques; entertaining menus.

FACULTY: Barbara Sheridan, graduate of N.Y. Institute of Technology Culinary Arts Program; Wayne Warner; visiting chefs.

COSTS, ACCOMMODATIONS: $50 per session. A 50% deposit is required; refund with 24 hours notice.

LOCATION: Long Island, 20 miles from New York City.

CONTACT: Barbara M. Sheridan, Look Who's Cooking, Inc., 7 West Main St., Oyster Bay, NY 11771; (516) 922-2400.

MARY BETH CLARK
New York/Year-round

(See page 263)

In addition to The International Cooking School of Italian Food and Wine, Ms. Clark offers private instruction in Italian cuisine in Manhattan. Tuition for a 3-hour session is $275 plus ingredients; $100 deposit is refundable a week prior.

MIETTE
New York/September-June

Since 1995, Tartine restaurant has offered an 8-session hands-on course (limit 12 youngsters, ages 8-16) that meets Monday afternoons in the restaurant kitchen and concludes with a student-prepared dinner for parents.

EMPHASIS: French and other cuisines, etiquette, table setting, French language, healthful recipes.

FACULTY: Chef Paul Vandewoude and his assistant, Mariette Bermowitz.

COSTS: $25 per class.

CONTACT: Mariette Bermowitz, Miette, 253 W. 11th St., New York, NY 10014; (212) 229-2611 or (718) 336-4009.

THE NATURAL GOURMET COOKERY SCHOOL
New York/Year-round *(See page 72)*

In addition to career programs, this school offers 2-week (45-hour) basic intensives each summer, a 1-week advanced intensive, approximately 40 partial participation evening and Saturday classes and series each quarter, and lectures on health-related topics.

EMPHASIS: Vegetarian cooking, low/no fat, recipe adaptation, medicinal cooking, tofu, tempeh, and seitan, food and healing, international cuisines.

COSTS: Tuition is $595 per week for the summer intensives; classes and series are $30-$60 per session. A $50 or 50% deposit is required. Persons over 65 receive a 10% discount.

NEW SCHOOL CULINARY ARTS
New York/Year-round *(See page 72)*

In addition to career programs, this school offers more than 100 one- to eight-session participation courses (limit 14 students) each trimester as well as on-site restaurant chef demonstrations (limit 10 to 20), weekend workshops (limit 12), lectures on culture and cuisine, demonstration classes (limit 12), classes for youngsters, and wine courses.

EMPHASIS: Culinary techniques, ethnic and regional cuisines, holiday menus, home entertaining, baking, and light-style cooking.

COSTS: Range from $65-$80 per session, children's classes are $40, lectures are $10, weekend workshops are $325, wine courses average $45-$65 per session. Full refund, less $15, for written cancellations prior to class.

NEW YORK UNIVERSITY CENTER FOR FOODS & FOOD MGT.
New York/Year-round *(See page 75)*

In addition to its food business courses, NYU offers classes on ethnic and regional cuisines, special occasion menus, chocolates, local restaurant specialties and wine, beer, cheese, and coffee tastings.

Costs: Range from $50-$60 per class.

NORMAN WEINSTEIN'S BROOKLYN COOKING SCHOOL
September-June

Since 1974, caterer Norman Weinstein has taught Oriental cooking. Facilities: Hot Wok Catering's 150-square-foot kitchen. Also available: private classes.

EMPHASIS: Asian cuisines, authentic Western barbecue, knife skills workshops, Asian tasting dinners, Chinatown walking tours.

FACULTY: Norman Weinstein is author of two cookbooks and has operated Hot Wok Catering for more than 15 years.

COSTS: Range from $40-$50 per session.

LOCATION: Brooklyn's Kensington area, accessible via subway from Manhattan

CONTACT: Norman Weinstein's Brooklyn Cooking School, 412 E. 2nd St., Brooklyn, NY 11218; (718) 438-0177.

PETER KUMP'S SCHOOL OF CULINARY ARTS
New York/Year-round *(See page 76) (See display ad page 203)*

In addition to career programs (page 76), this school offers more than 500 avocational hands-on courses or workshops a year. These include the 5-session, 25-hour Techniques of Fine Cooking series, offered at least monthly as a 5-day intensive, and other Techniques series covering spa cuisine, Italian cooking, pastry and baking, and cake decorating. Other courses include ethnic and regional cuisines, business topics, wine tasting, holiday menus, and specific subjects. A demonstration series at the 23rd Street facility features noted chefs.

COSTS: Hands-on classes range from $18-$25 per hour. Credit cards accepted; deposits required. Housing and restaurant suggestions are provided to out-of-towners.

LOCATIONS: In addition to the 23rd and 92nd St. New York City locations, classes are offered at satellite schools in Merrick and Larchmont, NY, Hohokus, NJ, Pittsburgh, PA, and Washington, DC.

CONTACT: Peter Kump's School of Culinary Arts (800) 522-4610.

PETER KUMP'S SCHOOL OF CULINARY ARTS

One-Week Intensives 23rd Our Year

Our one-week intensive programs are the ideal way to expand your cooking knowledge. Programs include Techniques of Fine Cooking, Italian and spa cuisine, cake decorating and Pastry & Baking. Other day, evening and weekend classes cover a full range of culinary topics. Most are taught at our brand-new **23rd** Street location.

(800) 522-4610   307 West 92nd Street, NYC 10128

SAPORE DI MARE
Wainscott/June-September

Since 1990, this regional Italian restaurant has offered participation classes (limit 15 students) up to three times weeklyFacilities: the restaurant kitchen.

EMPHASIS: Appetizers, pasta, main courses, pizza, breads, grilling, desserts.

FACULTY: Restaurateur Pino Luongo, author of *A Tuscan in the Kitchen,* owner of Sapore di Mare in the Hamptons and Le Madri and Coco Pazzo in New York. Instructors include the chefs from the restaurants.

COSTS: Nonrefundable tuition is $150 per class.

Location: Long Island, 90 miles from New York City.

CONTACT: Kristen Dell'Aguzzo, Director, Sapore di mare Summer Cooking Classes, P.O. Box 1357 (Wainscott Stone Rd. & Montauk Hwy.), Wainscott, NY 11975; (516) 324-5045, Fax (516) 537-1828.

THE SEASONAL KITCHEN
Pittsford/Year-round

Since 1980, Ginger and Dick Howell have offered approximately 26 weeks of morning and evening demonstrations annually. Facilities: a well-equipped country kitchen. Also available: classes for men, couples, and groups

EMPHASIS: Easy-to-prepare and seasonal recipes. .

FACULTY: Ginger and Dick Howell are members of the IACP.

COSTS: Range from $30-$35. Cancellations receive a 50% refund.

LOCATION: A suburb of Rochester.

CONTACT: The Seasonal Kitchen, 610 W. Bloomfield Rd., Pittsford, NY 14534; (716) 624-3242.

SEMINARS AT MAD. 61
New York/Year-round

Established in 1994, this cooking school at a restaurant and retail market offers approximately 30 demonstration (limit 15-25 students) classes per year.

EMPHASIS: Seasonal recipes.

FACULTY: Marta Pulini, exec. chef, mad. 61; Cesare Casella, ex-chef, Coco Pazzo, Il Toscanaccio.

COSTS: $50 per seminar, advance payment in full. Refund with 24- hour notice.
LOCATION: Barneys New York store on Madison Avenue.
CONTACT: Jennifer Duffy, mad. 61 restaurant, 10 E. 61st St., New York, NY 10021; (212) 833-2218.

TOPS INTERNATIONAL SUPER CENTER COOKING SCHOOL
Amherst and Greece/Year-round
Established in 1991, this school in a supermarket offers 20 to 25 one- to eight-session demonstration (limit 30 students) and participation courses (limit 15 students) per month. Facilities: modern kitchens with overhead mirrors and seminar seating. Also available: children's classes, private classes for groups.

FACULTY: Includes CIA-educated restaurant chefs, caterers, home economists, and registered dietitians. Guest chefs have included Paul Prudhomme, Tommy Tang, CIA Culinary Dean Fritz Sonnenschmid, and Ron Pickarski.

COSTS: Range from free to $20. Pre-registration and pre-payment required.

LOCATION: Amherst and Greece are 15 minutes from the Buffalo and Rochester airports.

CONTACT: Patricia Pollock, Manager, The Cooking School, Tops International Super Center, 3980 Maple Rd., Amherst, NY 14226; (716) 834-5177, Fax (716) 834-9679.

NORTH CAROLINA

COOK'S CORNER, LTD.
Greensboro/January-November
Founded in 1983, this cookware store offers 15-18 demonstration (limit 24 students) classes per month. Facilities: fully-equipped teaching kitchen with overhead mirror. Also available: wine tastings, classes for private groups.

FACULTY: Mary James Lawrence, CCP, and Lucy Hamilton, who holds a Cordon Bleu certificate; guest chefs.

COSTS: Range from $9-$50, payable by credit card; refund with 48 hours notice.

LOCATION: A restored area of Greensboro.

CONTACT: Cook's Corner, Ltd., 401 State St., Greensboro, NC 27405; (910) 272-2665, Fax (910) 379-9022.

COOKS & CONNOISSEURS COOKING SCHOOL
New Bern/February-October
Established in 1983, this cookware store and school offers demonstration and participation classes. Facilities: a 200-square-foot teaching kitchen.

EMPHASIS: Chinese, Italian, French, and regional American cuisines, seasonal and local chef specialties, cookbook recipes, wine selection.

FACULTY: Proprietor Candace H. Lynn and staff, including Laurie Hayes, Willard Doxey, and Karen Askew.

COSTS: One-day classes range from $15-$20; 4-week series, $60-$80.

LOCATION: Near Tryon Palace Restoration and 30 miles from beaches

CONTACT: Cooks & Connoisseurs Cooking School, 2500 Trent Rd., #24, New Bern, NC 28562; (919) 633-2665.

THE GRANDE GOURMET COOKING SCHOOL
Wilmington/Year-round
Founded in 1989, this school in a private residence offers a half dozen demonstration (limit 25 students) and participation (limit 10) classes per month. Also: children's and private classes.

NONVOCATIONAL/VACATION **NORTH CAROLINA 205**

EMPHASIS: Italian, Chinese, and French cuisines, techniques, low-fat cookery, cake decorating, entertaining menus, wine tastings.

FACULTY: Owner Robin Hackney studied with Nick Malgieri, Karen Lee, and others; Occasional guest instructors.

COSTS: Range from $30-$45 per session. A deposit is required; refund with 10 days notice.

LOCATION: The southeastern beach resort of Wilmington, 2 hours from Raleigh.

CONTACT: Robin Hackney, Owner, The Grande Gourmet Cooking School, 1108 Princeton Dr., Wilmington, NC, 28403; (910) 763-1764; Fax (910) 763-0658.

THE JANE THOMPSON COOKING SCHOOL
Raleigh/Year-round

Founded in 1988 in New York and relocated to Raleigh, this school offers participation and demonstration classes (limit 16 students).

EMPHASIS: French and Italian cuisine, including fish, poultry, stocks, and sauces.

FACULTY: Jane Thompson, former managing editor of *Master Chef* magazine, has studied in Europe and the U.S. with Simone Beck, Jacques Pepin, Madeleine Kamman, and Giuliano Bugialli.

COSTS: Each class is $45. Reservations are required; full refund with 14 days notice.

LOCATION: Throughout the Triangle

CONTACT: The Jane Thompson Cooking School, 3725 Graham Sherron Rd., Wake Forest, NC 27587; (919) 554-2699.

THE STOCKED POT & CO.
Winston-Salem/Year-round

Founded in 1980, this school and catering firm offers 30 classes (limit 34 students) per quarter. Facilities: well-equipped teaching kitchen with overhead mirror. Also available: bridal shower cooking classes. Also available: Lunch and Learn sessions, children's and family classes.

EMPHASIS: Ethnic and regional cuisines, seasonal dishes, nutritional foods, wine seminars.

FACULTY: Owner/chef Donald C. McMillan, CEC, who also owns and operates Gisele's Fine Foods Restaurant and Simple Elegance Catering, Lucy Herrman, Tom Peters, Tim Booras, and Bob Werth, CEC. Guest teachers include Hugh Carpenter and Giuliano Hazan.

COSTS: Range from $18-$30 per class; Lunch and Learn classes are $10-$12; children's classes are $15; celebrity chef classes are $45. Advance payment required; refund with 72 hours notice, 2 weeks notice for guest chefs.

LOCATION: Winston-Salem's Reynolda Village, the former Richard Joshua Reynolds estate, about 20 miles from the Piedmont airport.

CONTACT: Nancy Barnes, The Stocked Pot & Co., 111-B Reynolda Village, Winston-Salem, NC 27106; (910) 722-3663.

OHIO

BUEHLER'S FOOD MARKETS
Year-round

Since 1983, this food market has offered demonstration (limit 30 students) and participation (limit 12) classes at its 5 locations. Facilities: teaching areas with theater-type seating and overhead mirrors. Also available: child, teen, and parent-child classes.

EMPHASIS: Seasonal menus, nutrition, pasta, desserts.

FACULTY: Staff home economists and guest instructors.

COSTS: Range from $5-$20 per session.

LOCATION: Delaware, Dover, Medina, Wadsworth, and Wooster, Ohio

CONTACT: Mary McMillen, Director of Consumer Affairs, Buehler's Food Markets, Box 196, 1401 Old Mansfield Rd., Wooster, OH 44691; (216) 264-4355, Ext. 256.

THE CLEVELAND RESTAURANT COOKING SCHOOL *(See page 81)*
This career school also offers hands-on basic, pastry, and specialty classes, a series of demonstrations, and wine dinners.

COOKS'WARES CULINARY CLASSES
Cincinnati/Spring and Fall
Since 1992, this kitchenware store has offered more than 70 demonstration (limit 24 students) and participation (limit 10) classes per year. Facilities: a 300-square-foot teaching kitchen with overhead mirror. Also available: wine tasting, private instruction, children's classes.

EMPHASIS: Basics, ethnic and regional cuisines, aspecific subjects.

FACULTY: Includes Trina Liss, Kathleen Baker, Jude Theriot, Marilyn Harris, and Kathleen Sweeney.

COSTS: Range from $20-$40, $15 for youngsters, payable in advance; refund with .5 days notice. Credit cards accepted.

LOCATION: Approximately 20 miles from central Cincinnati.

CONTACT: Trina Liss, Director, Cooks'Wares Culinary Classes, 11344 Montgomery Rd., Cincinnati, OH 45249; (513) 489-6400, Fax (513) 489-1211.

DOROTHY LANE MARKET SCHOOL OF COOKING
Dayton/September-May
Established in 1984, this supermarket offers 60-80 demonstrations (limit 20 students) and a few participation classes (limit 10) per year. Facilities: 400-square-foot teaching kitchen with overhead mirror and new appliances. Also: children's classes, wine instruction, market visits, private lessons.

EMPHASIS: A variety of topics, including basic techniques, ethnic and regional cuisines, entertaining menus, guest chef specialties, specific subjects.

FACULTY: Includes professional chefs, caterers, cookbook authors, home economists, and dietitians. Guest chefs have included Giuliano Bugialli, Hugh Carpenter, Sara Leah Chase, Giuliano Hazan, and Perla Meyers.

COSTS: Range from $20 for children's classes to $65 for guest chefs. Most classes are $35. Prepayment is required. Refund with 7 days notice. Credit cards accepted.

CONTACT: Deb Lackey, Dorothy Lane Market School of Cooking, 2710 Far Hills Ave., Dayton, OH 45419; (513) 299-5132 or (513) 299-3561, Fax (513) 299-3568.

GOURMET CURIOSITIES, ETC.
Sylvania/Spring, Fall, Summer
Established in 1978, this cookware store's Creative Cooking School offers approximately 75 demonstration (limit 34 students) and participation (limit 16) courses per year. Facilities: a 1,000-square-foot kitchen with overhead mirror. Also available: children's classes, wine tastings, private classes, market visits, demonstrations at off-site functions.

FACULTY: Owners Geneva and Bruce Williams attended La Varenne, are members of the ACF, have served on consumer panels, and had recipes accepted for publication. Other instructors include area chefs.

COSTS: Range from $20-$30 per session. Payment with registration; refund with 3 days notice.

LOCATION: 11 miles from Toledo and 60 miles from Detroit.

CONTACT: Bruce C. Williams, Gourmet Curiosities, Etc., Starlite Plaza, 5700 Monroe St., Sylvania, OH 43560; (419) 882-2323.

HANDKE'S CUISINE COOKING CLASS
Columbus/September-June

Since 1991, Chef Hartmut Handke has conducted demonstrations (limit 32 students).

EMPHASIS: American and European cuisine.

FACULTY: Hartmut Handke, CMC

COSTS: $39 plus tax and gratuity. Credit cards accepted. Refund with 48 hours notice

CONTACT: Katie Dougherty, Catering Director, Handke's Cuisine Cooking Class, 520 S. Front St., Columbus, OH 43215; (614) 621-2500, Fax (614) 621-2626.

LA BELLE POMME
Columbus,/Year-round

Established in 1976, this school in a department store offers more than 40 demonstrations (average 30 students) each quarter. Facilities: large overhead mirror, 8 burners, 3 ovens.

EMPHASIS: Techniques, entertaining menus, ethnic cuisines, guest chef specialities, wine.

FACULTY: School director Betty Rosbottom attended La Varenne and the Greenbrier Cooking School and is author of *Betty Rosbottom's Cooking School Cookbook*. Other instructors include Carolyn Claycomb and Marsha and Harry Allen. Guest chefs have included Giuliano Bugialli and Sheila Lukins.

COSTS: Range from $24-$45. Refund, less $5, with 10 days notice.

LOCATION: Lazarus Department Store in downtown Columbus.

CONTACT: La Belle Pomme at Lazarus, 141 S. High St., Columbus, OH 43215; (614) 463-2665.

THE LORETTA PAGANINI SCHOOL OF COOKING
Chesterland/Year-round

This gourmet shop and school offers more than 300 one- to four-session demonstration (limit 28 students) and participation (limit 15) courses per year. Facilities: fully-equipped 600-square-foot professional kitchen and overhead mirror. Also available: couples classes. a young gourmet series, gastronomic tours to Italy, New York City and the Finger lakes, local trips to food-related sites.

EMPHASIS: Professional techniques.

FACULTY: School owner/director Loretta Paganini, born and schooled in Italy, serves as a culinary consultant to area restaurants , and is a food writer for the local newspaper and guest chef on local TV. Guest faculty includes local chefs and teachers and visiting professionals.

COSTS: Range from $15-$35 per session. One week advance registration is required; refund with 5 days notice.

LOCATION: 25 miles east of Cleveland

CONTACT: Loretta Paganini, The Loretta Paganini School of Cooking, Gingerbread House, 8613 Mayfield Rd., Chesterland, OH 44026; (216) 729-1110 or (216) 729-COOK, Fax (216) 729-6459.

WHAT'S COOKING?, INC.
Akron/Year-round

Founded in 1984, this cookware store offers 14 one-to-six session demonstration (limit 21 students) and participation (limit 14) courses per month. Facilities: teaching kitchen with overhead mirror. Also available: classes for couples and groups, market visits.

EMPHASIS: Fundamentals, regional American and international cuisine, health-conscious and quick cooking.

FACULTY: John and Bev Shaffer studied with James Beard and Julie Dannenbaum. They are winners of over 120 cooking prizes and producers of a cable TV show. Occasional guest instructors.

COSTS: Start at $24. Full payment to register.

LOCATION: Suburban area, 30 miles southeast of Cleveland Airport.

CONTACT: Bev & John Shaffer, What's Cooking?, Inc., 843 N. Cleveland Massillon Rd., Akron, OH 44333-2174; (216) 666-3663.

ZONA SPRAY COOKING SCHOOL
Hudson/Year-round

Founded in 1972, this cookware store offers 26 five- to six-session demonstration (limit 38 students) and participation courses (limit 10) per month and 8 to 10 professional technique participation courses (limit 10) per year. Facilities: a 500-square-foot kitchen with 3 ovens and 3 work stations. Also available: private and children's classes, market visits, sessions on catering and food writing, gastronomic bicycle tours.

EMPHASIS: Techniques, basics, pastry, low-fat cuisine, Japanese cuisine, herbs and spices, cake decorating, breads.

FACULTY: Proprietor Zona Spray and 15-20 professional chefs, caterers, and cookbook authors. Guest chefs have included Rick Bayless, Shirley Corriher, Joe Ortiz, Barbara Tropp, Alice Medrich, and Joanne Weir.

COSTS: Demonstrations are $25, $40 with visiting chef or author; professional programs are $495; gastronomic tours are $850 to $3,000. Advance registration is required; refund with 48 hours notice (3 weeks for professional program). Credit cards accepted.

LOCATION: Western Reserve in Ohio, 20 miles south of Cleveland, 15 miles east of Akron.

CONTACT: Zona Spray, Zona Spray Cooking School, 140 N. Main, Hudson, OH 44236; (216) 650-1665, Fax (216) 656-2665.

OKLAHOMA

COOKING SCHOOL OF TULSA
Tulsa/Year-round

Founded in 1991, this cookware shop offers more than 130 demonstration (limit 20 students) and participation (limit 8) classes per year. Facilities: fully-equipped teaching kitchen with overhead mirror. Also available: wine tastings.

EMPHASIS: Simple techniques, menus for entertaining, ethnic cuisines, guest chef specialties.

FACULTY: Proprietor Keith Lindenberg, local chefs, visiting guest chefs, nutritionists.

COST: Classes range from $25-$45. Advance registration and payment required. No refunds within 7 days of class. Credit cards accepted.

CONTACT: Cooking School of Tulsa, 8264 S. Lewis, Tulsa, OK 74137; (918) 298-7110.

GOURMET GADGETRE, LTD.
Lawton/October-June

Established in 1980, this cookware store offers demonstrations (limit 20 students).

EMPHASIS: Breads, candies, ethnic cuisines.

FACULTY: Restaurateurs Hazel Wong and Patty Quarles; June Harris.

COSTS: $15 per class. Refund with 48 hours notice.

CONTACT: Gourmet Gadgetre, Ltd., 1105 Ferris, Lawton, OK 73507; (405) 248-1837.

OREGON

CARL'S CUISINE
Salem/Year-round

Since 1978, this specialty kitchen store and has offered demonstration classes (limit 12 students).

NONVOCATIONAL/VACATION **PENNSYLVANIA** **209**

EMPHASIS: Ethnic and regional cuisines, seasonal menus, specific subjects.

FACULTY: Proprietor Carl Meisel has travelled and studied in Europe, Thailand, and regions of the U.S. He is a consultant on menu planning, travel, and kitchen design.

COSTS: $20 per class. Advance rservations required.

LOCATION: Downtown Salem.

CONTACT: Carl's Cuisine, 333 Chemeketa St. NE, Salem, OR 97301; (503) 363-1612, Fax (503) 363-5014.

PENNSYLVANIA

CHARLOTTE-ANN ALBERTSON'S COOKING SCHOOL
Philadelphia (Florida)/Year-round (Winter)

Founded in 1973, this school offers more than 75 one- to four-session demonstration (limit 25 students) and some participation (limit 15) courses per year. Facilities: Madsen Design Center and commercial kitchens. Also: market tours, children's classes, wine seminars and dinners; European culinary vacations (limit 20), offered in conjunction with the CIA and granting continuing education credit, feature cooking demonstrations, market and city tours, winery visits, and fine dining.

EMPHASIS: Ethnic cuisines, holiday menus, grilling, wine, kitchen design, food science, food marketing.

FACULTY: Charlotte-Ann Albertson, a charter member and Certified Teacher of the IACP, studied at La Varenne and Le Cordon Bleu. Other faculty include CIA-trained Philadelphia chefs and caterers and guest experts such as Shirley Corriher and Barbara Tropp. The CIA-sponsored trips are accompanied by a CIA master chef/instructor.

COSTS, ACCOMMODATIONS: Classes range from $25-$45 per session. Advance payment required. No cash refunds. Trip costs approximately $3,000, which includes airfare from New York, hotel lodging, most meals, and planned excursions.

LOCATION: Madsen Design Center, 8 miles from downtown Philadelphia and suburban commercial kitchens; in private homes in Florida.

CONTACT: Charlotte-Ann Albertson, P.O. Box 27, Wynnewood, PA 19096-0027; (610) 649-9290 (phone/fax). Marco Island, FL (813) 642-6550.

COOKING WITH CLASS
Shohola/Spring-Summer

Established in 1993, this school offers more than 40 hands-on classes and series each season. Facilities: commercial kitchen studio and cookbook library. Private instruction available.

EMPHASIS: Basics, ethnic and regional cuisines, special occasion dishes, cake decorating, sugar artistry and design, guest chef specialties, specific subjects.

FACULTY: Founder Sheila Kaye-Stepkin. guest chefs from New York City and surrounding area.

COSTS: Range from $50-$150 per session.

LOCATION: On Twin Lakes, 90 minutes from Manhattan and 5 minutes from Milford.

CONTACT: Sheila Kaye-Stepkin, Cooking with Class, 2221 Twin Lakes Rd., Shohola, PA 18458; (800) 226-6540, Fax (717) 296-2627; E-Mail: jgek68a@prodigy.com.

THE COOKING COTTAGE AT CEDAR SPRING FARM
Sellersville/Year-round

Founded in 1992, this cooking school offers 65 demonstration classes and specialized series (limit 12 students) per year. Facilities: demonstration kitchen with overhead mirror. Also available: private group classes and market trips, trips to France.

FACULTY: Winnie McClennen and her daughter, Peggi Clauhs.

COSTS: Range from $35-$45; payment with reservation.

LOCATION: Rural Upper Bucks County, between Allentown and Philadelphia

CONTACT: Peggi Clauhs, The Cooking Cottage at Cedar Spring Farm, 1731 B Old Beth. Pike, Sellersville, PA 18960; (215) 453-1828; Fax (215) 257-6177.

THE COOK'S CORNER, INC.
Yardley/Year-round

Founded in 1987, this school in a cookware store offers 1 demonstration class (limit 35 students) per week. Facilities: full demonstration kitchen with overhead mirror.

EMPHASIS: Ethnic and regional cuisines, desserts, pastas, breads, salads, guest chef specialties, wine appreciation.

FACULTY: Owner Catherine Rowan and guest cookbook authors, professional instructors, and restaurant chefs.

COSTS: Range from $40-$45. Nonrefundable payment must accompany registration.

LOCATION: Yardley is 30 miles north of Philadelphia and 1 mile from Trenton, N.J.

CONTACT: The Cook's Corner, 90 W. Afton Ave., Yardley, PA 19067; (215) 493-9093.

CRATE
Pittsburgh/Fall and Spring

Established in 1978, this retail kitchenware store offers 80 to 90 day and evening demonstration (limit 40 students) and participation (limit 12) courses per year. Facilities: new demonstration kitchen with 8 burners, regular, convection, and microwave ovens, overhead mirror.

EMPHASIS: Italian, Chinese, Mediterranean, and French cuisines; vegetarian, bread, herbs, biscotti, filo, cookies and cake; guest specialties.

FACULTY: Includes chefs and owners of top local restaurants, owners of culinary businesses, and professional caterers. Guests have included Mary Beth Clark, Joanne Weir, Alice Medrich, Perla Meyers, and Marlene Sorosky.

COSTS: Average class cost is $25-$30; guests are higher. Payment required with registration.

LOCATION: In Pittsburgh's South Hills-Scott Township.

CONTACT: Linda Wernikoff, Owner, Crate, Greentree Road Shopping Ctr., Pittsburgh, PA 15220; (412) 341-5700.

JACQUALIN ET CIE CUISINIERE
Lahaska/Year-round

Fou nded in 1978, this cooking school and catering firm offers 25 to 30 mostly demonstration classes (limit 10 students) and full-day bread workshops (limit 6) each quarter. Facilities: French country kitchen. Also available: day trips to Philadelphia and New York markets, gastronomic tours of France.

EMPHASIS: French and Italian cuisines.

FACULTY: Proprietor Jacqualin Giles, who studied in France and Italy, and her daughter and partner Christine Hutkin.

COSTS: Range from $35-$45, bread making workshop is $65. Tuition must accompany reservation. No refunds.

LOCATION: Lahaska, an hour from Philadelphia.

CONTACT: Jacqualin Giles or Christine G. Hutkin, Jacqualin et Cie Cuisiniere, P.O. Box 303, Route 202, Lahaska, PA 18931; (215) 794-7316, Fax (215) 794-7693.

JANE CITRON COOKING CLASSES
Pittsburgh/Year-round except summer

Established in 1978, this school in a private home offers 20 demonstration (limit 12 students) classes per year. Facilities: well-equipped home kitchen. Also available: private classes, market vis-

NONVOCATIONAL/VACATION **PENNSYLVANIA** **211**

its, culinary tours of Napa Valley and Europe.

FACULTY: Jane Citron studied with Marcella Hazan, Madeleine Kamman, Jacques Pepin, and Roger Verge. She is Food Editor and writes a food column for *Pittsburgh Magazine*.

COSTS: $55 per class. Advance payment required. Refund if replacement found.

LOCATION: The Murdoch Farms section of Pittsburgh

CONTACT: Jane Citron, 1314 Squirrel Hill Ave., Pittsburgh, PA 15217; (412) 621-0311, Fax (412) 765-2511.

KATHY D'ADDARIO'S COOKING TECHNIQUES
Ambler/Year-round

Established in 1994, this school offers 70 ten-session participation courses (limit 6-8 students) per year. Facilities: Large home kitchen. Also available: wine instruction, market visits, private classes.

EMPHASIS: Traditional techniques.

FACULTY: Kathy D'Addario is a graduate of the Restaurant School and studied at Le Cordon Bleu, Giuliano Bugialli's in Florence, and Peter Kump's New York Cooking School.

COSTS: Range from $30 to $48 per session. Payment in advance; refund with 1 week notice.

LOCATION: a 30-minute drive from Philadelphia.

CONTACT: Kathy D'Addario's Cooking Techniques, 858 Tennis Ave., Ambler, PA 19002; (215) 643-5883, Fax (215) 257-6681.

THE KITCHEN SHOPPE OF CARLISLE
Carlisle/September-May

Founded in 1975, this cookware store offers a dozen 1-session demonstration (limit 40 students) and participation (limit 12) courses each month. Facilities: demonstration kitchen with 6 work stations. Also available: Classes for youngsters and private groups.

EMPHASIS: Entertaining menus, ethnic cuisines, guest specialties.

FACULTY: Proprietor Suzanne Hoffman, a Certified Member of the IACP, and instructors Sherry Ball and Diana Povis. Guest chefs have included Giuliano Bugialli, Hugh Carpenter, Marlene Sorosky, and Martin Yan.

COSTS: From $25-$45 per session; children's classes $15. Full payment required with registration.

LOCATION: 20 minutes from Harrisburg and 2 hours from Philadelphia.

CONTACT: Suzanne Hoffman, The Kitchen Shoppe of Carlisle, 101 Shady Lane, Carlisle, PA 17013; (800) 391-COOK or (717) 243-0906, Fax (717) 245-0606.

LE BEC-FIN
Philadelphia/Spring and Fall

Since 1992, Georges Perrier has conducted about 8 morning demonstration classes (limit 60 students) per year. Facilities: demonstration kitchen at Assouline & Ting gourmet food distributor.

EMPHASIS: Classic French cuisine with a nouvelle influence.

FACULTY: Georges Perrier, chef-owner of Le Bec-Fin.

COSTS: Tuition is $75, payable in advance by check or credit card.

CONTACT: Wendy Handler, Le Bec-Fin, 1523 Walnut St., Philadelphia, PA 19102; (215) 567-1000, Fax (215) 568-1151.

PETER KUMP'S SCHOOL OF CULINARY ARTS *(see page 202)*

RANIA'S COOKING SCHOOL
Pittsburgh/Spring and Fall

Opened in 1984, this restaurant offers over 20 demonstrations (limit 24 students) each season. Also available: children's classes, wine instruction, private classes.

EMPHASIS: Ethnic and regional cuisines, holiday foods, appetizers to desserts.

FACULTY: Proprietor Rania Harris and chefs Michael Barbato (Westin Wm. Penn), Joe Nolan (Cafe Allegro), Mike Bennetti (Bankovitz Seafood), and David Indorato (Hyatt); and Sharryn Campbell, wine tasting.

COSTS: Tuititon is $30 per class; children's class is $18. No refunds

CONTACT: Rania's Cooking School, 100 Central Sq., Pittsburgh, PA 15228; (412) 531-2222.

RHODE ISLAND

SAKONNET MASTER CHEFS SERIES
Little Compton/September-June

Started in 1980, Sakonnet Vineyards offers 10 full-day demonstration and participation classes (limit 12 students) per year. Facilities: a large main work table and counter, which serves as individual work areas.

EMPHASIS: Guest chef specialties; wine selection and food pairing.

FACULTY: Has included Johanne Killeen and George Germon of Al Forno Restaurant in Providence; Maureen Pothier of the Bluepoint Oyster Bar and Restaurant; Jasper White of Jasper's in Boston; Nancy Verde Barr, backstage chef to Julia Child; and Todd English of Olives in Boston.

COSTS: Range from $80-$100. Advance reservation required. Accommodations can be arranged.

LOCATION: 30 minutes from the New Bedford and Fall River, Mass., 40 minutes from Providence, and 75 minutes from Boston.

CONTACT: Sakonnet Vineyards, P.O. Box 197, Little Compton, RI 02837; (401) 635-8486.

SWINBURNE SCHOOL
Newport/Year-round

Founded in 1924 by the Civic League of Newport, Inc., this adult education center offers 300 classes annually on a variety of topics, including cooking.

EMPHASIS: Ethnic cuisines, vegetarian foods, seasonal and special occasion menus, breads, sauces, cake decorating, wine appreciation.

FACULTY: Local cooks, chefs, and cookbook authors.

COSTS: Ranges from $30-$75 per session. No refunds within 1 week of class unless space can be filled. Credit cards accepted.

CONTACT: Lee Rush, Program Coordinator, Swinburne School, 115 Pelham St., Newport, RI 02840; (401) 846-1496.

SOUTH CAROLINA

IN GOOD TASTE
Charleston/Year-round

Founded in 1983, this gourmet shop offers demonstration and participation classes. Facilities: a well-equipped teaching kitchen. Also available: bed and breakfast tours, classes for youngsters.

EMPHASIS: Ethnic and regional cuisines, techniques, breads, wine appreciation.

FACULTY: School owner Jacki Boyd, Roland Gilg, Mary Wichmann, Donna Florio, Celia Strong.

COSTS: Range from $12-$25 per session.

CONTACT: Jacki Boyd, In Good Taste, 1901 Ashley River Rd., Charleston, SC 29407; (803) 763-5597.

TENNESSEE

CHEF DOUGH DOUGH & CO.
Memphis/Year-round

Since 1989, Dolores Katsotis (Chef Dough Dough) has conducted demonstration (limit 20 students) and participation classes (limit 12) for adults and youngsters.

EMPHASIS: A variety of topics.

FACULTY: Dolores Katsotis, a CIA graduate and author of *Cooking Adventures with Chef Dough Dough*, is the daughter of the late John Grisanti, a Memphis restaurateur and wine connoisseur.

LOCATION: Community centers and museums.

CONTACT: Dolores Katsotis, Chef Dough Dough & Co., 8370 Stavenger Cove, Cordova, TN 38018; (901) 754-0698 (phone/fax).

CLASSIC GOURMET COOKING SCHOOL
Nashville/Year-round except August and December

Established in 1991, this cookware store offers more than 125 demonstration (limit 30 students) and participation classes per year. Facilities: teaching kitchen with overhead mirror. Also available: wine and food classes, private classes.

EMPHASIS: French techniques, Oriental, Italian, dinner parties.

FACULTY: Owner/Chef Hilda Pope, Mary Clarke, Susan Hudgens, and Rachel Blair. Guest chefs include area chefs and cookbook authors.

COSTS: Range from $32-$50. Full payment with reservation. Refund with 48 hours notice.

LOCATION: Near Opryland, The Hermitage, and Belle Meade Mansion.

CONTACT: Hilda Pope, Classic Gourmet Cooking School, Hillsboro Plaza, 3900 Hillsboro Rd., Nashville, TN 37215; (615) 383-8700, Fax (615) 383-8788.

CULINARY CLASSICS COOKING SCHOOL
Nashville/Year-round

Founded in 1963, this school in a private home offers 3-session lecture-demonstrations (limit 12 students). Also available: culinary tours.

EMPHASIS: Ethnic cuisines, techniques, presentation, economy, creative substitution, purchasing, historical information, relationship of different cuisines.

FACULTY: Gloria Olson, a chef rotisseur member of Chaine des Rotisseurs and author of *Culinary Classics*, is a consultant on menu planning, travel, and kitchen design.

COSTS: $30 per class, $70 per 3-session course, $25 per 1-hour consultation.

LOCATION: Belle Meade and Forrest Hills area

CONTACT: Gloria Olson, Culinary Classics Cooking School, 1145 Balbade Dr., Nashville, TN 37215; (615) 665-0893.

RAJI RESTAURANT
Memphis/February and November

This restaurant offers full-day workshops (limit 15 students). Facilities: Raji Restaurant kitchen.

EMPHASIS: Fusion (French Indian) cooking.

FACULTY: Chef Raji Jallepalli.

COSTS: Workshop tuition is $250. Credit cards accepted.

CONTACT: Raji Jallepalli, Raji Restaurant, 712 W. Brookhaven Circle, Memphis, TN 38117; (901) 685-8723.

BLANCO RIVER COOKING SCHOOL
Wimberley/Spring and Fall
Founded in 1989 by Leslie McGrath, this school offers more than 50 demonstration (limit 20 students) and participation (limit 15) classes a year. Facilities: the 575-square-foot kitchen of Ms. McGrath's 450-acre ranch.

EMPHASIS: International and regional cuisines.

FACULTY: Guest chefs have included Bruce Auden, Rick Bayless, John Ash, Debra Madison and Guiliano Bugialli.

COSTS: $85, payable within 5 days of registration.

LOCATION: 35 miles from Austin and 40 miles from San Antonio

CONTACT: Blanco River Cooking School, 3701 River Rd., Wimberley, TX 78676; (512) 847-2583.

CREATING CULINARY OPPORTUNITIES
Houston/February and October
Since 1993, Ann Iverson has offered 1- and 2-day participation courses (limit 12 students) that meet 4 hours daily. Facilities: a 340-square-foot private kitchen with 12 work areas.

EMPHASIS: Northern Italian cuisine

FACULTY: Ann Iverson, who studied with Giuliano Bugialli, Mary Beth Clark, Marcella and Victor Hazan, and Lorenza di Medici.

COSTS: $160 per day. Full payment with registration; refund with 3 weeks notice.

CONTACT: Ann Iverson, Owner, Creating Culinary Opportunities, 2902 West Lane Dr., Unit E, Houston, TX 77027; (713) 622-6936, Fax (713) 622-2924.

CUISINE CONCEPTS
Ft. Worth/September-April
Founded in 1979, this school in a private residence offers personalized classes and wine education (limit one to two students). Group instruction is also available (limit 26 students).

EMPHASIS: Designed to the student's needs and requests.

FACULTY: Author, food stylist, and food and wine writer Renie Steves, CCP, is owner of The French Apron and Cuisine Concepts cooking schools and has studied with Madeleine Kamman, James Beard, Julia Child, Nick Malgieri, and Marcella and Victor Hazan. She was elected to *Who's Who in Food and Wine in Texas, 1994.*

COSTS: $75 per hour for one student, $100 for two, plus a $6 per hour assistant fee and minimal marketing expense. A 50% deposit is required 7 days in advance. Lessons can be rescheduled.

LOCATION: Ft. Worth's west side, near the Kimbell Museum; 35 minutes west of DFW Airport.

CONTACT: Renie Steves, Cuisine Concepts, 1406 Thomas Pl., Ft. Worth, TX 76107-2432; (817) 732-4758, Fax (817) 732-3247.

CUISINE INTERNATIONAL
Dallas and Europe/Year-round
Cuisine International represents cooking schools and culinary tours in Italy (Badia Coltibuono in Tuscany, the Luna Convento Hotel in Amalfi, Hotel Le Sirenuse in Positano, Venetian Cooking in a Venetian Palace, The World of Regaleali in Sicily, Italian Cookery Weeks in Umbria, Il Melograno in Puglia), France (Mas de Cornud), England (Raymond Blanc's Le Petit Blanc Ecole de Cuisine).

EMPHASIS: Culinary tours to Europe.

FACULTY: Owner Judy Ebrey, CCP.

CONTACT: Judy Ebrey, P.O. Box 25228, Dallas, TX 75225; (214) 373-1161, Fax (214) 373-1162; E-Mail: CuisineInt@aol.com

DESIGNER EVENTS COOKING SCHOOL
Bryan/Year-round

Established in 1992 by Merrill Bonarrigo, this school offers one participation class per month, limited to 15 students. Food and wine pairing seminars are provided by Messina Hof Wine Cellars.

EMPHASIS: Menus prepared by Texas chefs.

COSTS: $65-$75 per session.

LOCATION: The Messina Hof Winery estate in the Brazos Valley, 100 miles from Houston.

CONTACT: Merrill Bonarrigo, Designer Events Cooking School, 4545 Old Reliance Rd., Bryan, TX 77808; (409) 778-9463, Fax (409) 778-1729.

DOLORES SNYDER HAUTE CUISINE
Irving/Spring and Fall

Founded in 1976, this school in a private residence offers 30 three-session demonstration (limit 16 students) and participation (limit 10) courses per year. Facilities: a 320-square-foot teaching kitchen with 8 work areas. Also available: private classes.

EMPHASIS: International cuisines, theory and techniques, seafood, guest specialties, entertaining with English tea.

FACULTY: Dolores Snyder, CCP, received a BS in Home Economics from the University of Texas and attended La Varenne, the Cordon Bleu, the Ritz-Escoffier Ecole de Cuisine, and The Oriental Thai Cooking School.

COSTS: $35 for demonstrations, $135 for a 3-session series. Full payment reserves a space. Refund with 1 week notice.

LOCATION: Six miles from Dallas, 5 miles from DFW Airport

CONTACT: Dolores Snyder, Director, Gourmet Cookery School, Box 140071, Irving, TX 75014-0071; (214) 717-4189.

HEART OF TEXAS COOKING SCHOOL
September-May

Established in 1980, this traveling cooking school presents 30 to 35 demonstration classes (limit 50 to 500 students) per year through county agents, home economics teachers, churches, clubs, and organizations in Texas.

EMPHASIS: Heart healthy, down home, Southwest regional cuisines.

FACULTY: Lenore Angel has written 9 cookbooks, is a former food editor and stylist, and had a cable TV series. Joan Lyons has a degree in food research, was a food and drug agent, and co-authored 2 cookbooks.

COSTS: Sponsors Pioneer Flour Mills, Fiesta Seasonings, and Chantal Cookware pay for the classes.

LOCATION: Throughout Texas.

CONTACT: Lenore Angel, Heart of Texas, 4080 Menger, San Antonio, TX 78259; (210) 497-3151.

THE KITCHEN SHOP AT THE GREEN BEANERY
Beaumont/Year-round

Established in 1992, this cafe and cookware store offers about 75 demonstration (limit 30 students) and limited participation (limit 15) classes a year. Facilities: a 20-seat demonstration kitchen area. Also available: culinary tours.

EMPHASIS: Basics, ethnic and regional cuisines, pastries, specific subjects.

FACULTY: Glenn Watz, chef/owner of the Green Beanery Cafe for 19 years; local and visiting instructors.

COSTS: Range from $20-$35 per class. Credit cards accepted.

LOCATION: Beaumont is 90 miles east of Houston.

CONTACT: Glenn Watz, Owner, or Carolyn Wood, Manager, The Kitchen Shop at the Green Beanery, 2121 McFaddin Ave., Beaumont, TX 77701; (409) 832-9738, Fax (409) 832-9738.

LE PANIER
Houston/Year-round

Established in 1980, this cooking school offers approximately 200 demonstration (limit 45 students) and participation (limit 15) classes a year. Facilities: a well-equipped teaching area that offers theater seating, a large overhead mirror, and several cooking and work spaces. Also available: classes for youngsters, basic techniques series, catering courses.

EMPHASIS: Ethnic cuisines, breads, entertaining menus, cooking for health, main course dishes, pastries and desserts.

FACULTY: Owner/Director LaVerl Daily teaches Basic Techniques. Most other classes are taught by guest chefs, teachers, and cookbook authors, including Giuliano Bugialli, Giuliano Hazan, Nicholas Malgieri, Hugh Carpenter, and Shirley Corrihe.

COSTS: Range from $35-$60 per session, children's classes are $20. Phone reservations are required; payment is due 3 days prior.

LOCATION: Between Kirby and Holcombe Streets

CONTACT: LaVerl Daily, Director, Le Panier, 7275 Brompton Rd., Houston, TX 77025; (713) 664-9848 or (713) 666-2038, Fax (713) 666-2037.

LOEWS ANATOLE HOTEL'S YOUNG CULINARIANS
Dallas/July-August

Since 1987, this resort hotel has conducted a 5-day summer cooking school (limit 20 students) for youngsters, ages 8 to 15. Facilities: the hotel's L'Entrecote Restaurant kitchen. Also available: advanced camp for prior attendees.

FACULTY: L'Entrecote Chef Lindell Mendoza.

CONTACT: Jay Allison, The Young Culinarians-Loews Anatole Hotel, 2201 Stemmons Fwy., Dallas, TX 75207; (214) 761-7230.

THE MANSION ON TURTLE CREEK
Dallas/Year-round

Each month this hotel and restaurant hosts a demonstration class, special dinner, or both. Facilities: usually the Pavilion Ballroom.

EMPHASIS: Specific cuisines.

FACULTY: Chef Dean Fearing co-hosts the classes. Guest chefs have included Wolfgang Puck, Julia Child, Robert Del Grande, and Charlie Palmer.

COSTS, ACCOMMODATIONS: Classes range from $145-$185, including tax. Special room rates begin at $195 per night.

CONTACT: Tamara Deel, The Mansion on Turtle Creek, 2821 Turtle Creek Blvd., Dallas, TX 75219; (214) 559-2100, Fax (214) 520-5896.

NATURAL FOODS COOKING SCHOOL
Houston/September-July

Established in 1989, this school offers 8 demonstrations (limit 30 students) per month. Facilities: Houston locations. Also available: classes for youngsters, market tours, private classes.

EMPHASIS: Macrobiotic cuisine.

FACULTY: Nutritional counselor Marian Bell has taught for more than 15 years. Guest instructors include Chef Carl of Moveable Feast.

COSTS: Range from $10-$15 per class; cancellations receive a full refund

CONTACT: Natural Foods Cooking School, 4418 Woodvalley, Houston, TX 77096; (713) 523-0171.

RICE EPICUREAN MARKETS COOKING SCHOOL
Houston/Year-round

Established in 1990, this school offers 30 three-session demonstration (limit 45 students) and participation (limit 16) courses per month. Facilities: a 1,100-square-foot classroom with overhead mirror. Also available: private classes, children's classes and cooking camp, market tours.

FACULTY: Local and out-of-town chefs, including Mark Miller, Emeril Lagasse, Stephen Pyles, Martin Yan, and Tommy Tang.

COSTS: Range from $20-$60 per session, $100 for a 3-session course. Payment is required with registration; refund with 72 hours notice. Credit cards accepted.

LOCATION: On a major road in a fine residential area.

CONTACT: Peg Lee, Director, The Cooking School, Rice Epicurean Markets, 6425 San Felipe, Houston, TX 77057; (713) 789-6233/5426, Fax (713) 789-9853.

STAR CANYON COOKING SCHOOL
Dallas/Year-round

Established in 1994, this school in a restaurant offers 4 demonstration courses (limit 50 students) per month. Facilities: demonstration kitchen, classroom, and closed-circuit TV monitors.

EMPHASIS: New Texas cuisine.

FACULTY: Chef Stephan Pyles, a founder of Southwestern cuisine.

COSTS: Demonstration and tasting is $50, demonstration and lunch is $75.

LOCATION: Minutes from Love Field, 5 minutes from downtown.

CONTACT: Kellye, Star Canyon, 3102 Oak Lawn Ave., No. 144, Dallas, TX 75219; (214) 520-7827 (STAR), Fax (214) 520-2667.

VERMONT

CULINARY MAGIC COOKING SEMINARS
Ludlow/June-August, October

Started in 1992, the Mobil 4-Star Governor's Inn sponsors four 3-day weekend hands-on cooking vacations (limit 16 participants) per year. Other activities: winery tour and visit to an antique cooperative.

EMPHASIS: The Inn's healthy gourmet specialties, presentation.

FACULTY: Deedy Marble, innkeeper and chef since 1982, studied with Madeleine Kamman, Lorenza de Medici, and Roger Vergé. She and her husband, Charlie, have received 14 national culinary awards and placed fifth in the World Chef Competition.

COSTS: Cost is $370-$390 double, $531 single occupancy,, including Inn lodging, all tax and gratuity, most meals, planned activities. Full payment with registration; refund with 20 days notice.

LOCATION: The Okemo Valley, 132 miles from Hartford Airport, 135 miles from Boston, and 230 miles from New York

CONTACT: Chef Deedy Marble, Culinary Magic Cooking Seminars, The Governor's Inn, Ludlow, VT 05149; (800) 468-3766 or (802) 228-8830.

NEW ENGLAND CULINARY INSTITUTE
Essex

(See page 101)

This degree-granting institution offers 4 culinary vacation weekends (limit 112 students) a year. Other activities: sightseeing.

EMPHASIS: Each vacation focuses on a different theme.

COSTS, ACCOMMODATIONS: Cost is $400, which includes double occupancy lodging at The Inn at Essex. Single supplement $75.

VERMONT OFF BEAT
East Burke/June-October

This special interest vacation provider offers weekend workshops on a variety of topics, including healthful cooking. Other programs: writing, photography, quilting, antiquing, flyfishing, gardening.

EMPHASIS: Low fat, high carbohydrate cooking.

FACULTY: Terry Blonder, who taught at the Pritikin Center and is author of *Wholehearted Cooking* and *For Goodness' Sake*.

COSTS, ACCOMMODATIONS: Cost of $370 includes lodging at the 440-acre Mountain View Creamery and meals. Payment with registration. Refund less $35 with 21 days notice.

LOCATION: Northeastern Vermont, near Route 91.

CONTACT: Carol Maurer, Vermont Off Beat, P.O. Box 4366, S. Burlington, VT 05406-4366; (802) 863-2535, Fax (802) 863-2535.

VIRGINIA

CHANNEL BASS INN COOKING VACATIONS
Chincoteague Island/Year-round

Established in 1972, this Inn offers 2-day participation programs (limit 3 participants or 2 couples) that are tailored to the interests of the group. Facilities: the Inn's restaurant kitchen. Also available: fishing, bird watching, boating, swimming.

EMPHASIS: Sauces, soups, desserts, and seafoods prepared in the French and Spanish style.

FACULTY: Innkeeper and chef James S. Hanretta, a master chef for more than 20 years.

COSTS, ACCOMMODATIONS: The $750 fee ($1,250 per couple) covers 3 continental breakfasts, 2 brunches, 2 dinners, and Inn lodging. A 50% deposit is required with balance due on arrival. Refund with 2 weeks notice.

LOCATION: The Fodor 4-Star rated Channel Bass Inn, a 100-year-old frame house with 10 guest rooms, is on the Delmarva Peninsula near Chincoteague Wildlife Refuge and Assateague Seashore

CONTACT: Inn Reservations, The Channel Bass Inn Cooking Vacations, 6228 Church St., Chincoteague Island, VA 23336; (800) 249-0818 or (804) 336-6148.

HELEN WORTH'S CULINARY INSTRUCTION
Charlottesville (Ivy)/Year-round

Helen Worth offers private one-on-one lessons in her fully-equipped kitchen.

EMPHASIS: Essential skills, cooking equipment, kitchen efficiency, food purchasing, aesthetics, table refinements, wine appreciation.

FACULTY: Helen Worth, author of *Cooking Without Recipes*, *Hostess Without Help* and others. The Helen Worth Cooking School founded in Cleveland, 1940; established Manhattan, 1947; Ivy, Virginia, 1980. She initiated a food and wine appreciation course at Columbia University and subsequently at Charlottesville's University of Virginia.

COSTS: $75 per hour. A $25 nonrefundable deposit is required.

LOCATION: 68 miles west of Richmond, 118 miles from Washington, D.C

CONTACT: Helen Worth, 1701 Owensville Rd., Charlottesville (Ivy), VA 22901-8825; (804) 296-4380.

JUDY HARRIS' COOKING SCHOOL
Alexandria/September-June

Founded in 1978, this school offers more than 60 participation (limit 12 students) and demonstration (limit 20) classes per year. Facilities: a large, well-equipped kitchen, culinary herb and vegetable garden.

EMPHASIS: Ethnic cuisines, food processor, herbs, baking, techniques, dinner parties, cooking for health. Also available: private and restaurant classes, culinary tours.

FACULTY: Judy Harris, who studied French cuisine in Paris and cooked in Washington, D.C., restaurants; well-known chefs and cookbook authors.

COSTS: Range from $32-$60. Refund with 5 days notice.

LOCATION: Ten miles from Washington, D.C., five miles from Old Town Alexandria.

CONTACT: Judy Harris, 2402 Nordok Place, Alexandria, Virginia 22306; (703) 768-3767.

WASHINGTON

BON VIVANT SCHOOL OF COOKING
Seattle/Year-round

Founded in 1977 by Louise Hasson, this school offers two 9-session certificate courses, two 4-session certificate courses, and over 150 demonstration classes (limit 20 students) per year. Facilities: Students' home kitchens. Also available: assistant program for graduates of certificate courses.

EMPHASIS: Basic techniques, breads, pastry, seasonal specialties, regional, international cuisines.

FACULTY: Louise Hasson has a BA in education, 20 years of teaching and catering experience, and is a certified member of the IACP. She studied at the Cordon Bleu. Badia a Coltibuono and Regalaeli. Other instructors include Northwest chefs and teachers.

COSTS: Tuition is $295 for 12 classes, $275 for an additional 12 classes. Credit cards and installment payments are accepted. No refunds.

LOCATION: Seattle and suburban areas

CONTACT: Louise Hasson, Bon Vivant School of Cooking, 4925 N.E. 86th, Seattle, WA 98115; (206) 525-7537.

COOK'S WORLD COOKING SCHOOL
Seattle/Year-round

Founded in 1990, this cookware store offers 20 demonstration (limit 20 students) and participation (limit 12) courses per month. Facilities: a 400-square-foot professionally-designed instruction kitchen with overhead mirrors. Also available: wine instruction, private classes.

EMPHASIS: Basics, French, Italian, Indian, Pacific Northwest, gourmet vegetarian.

FACULTY: Nancie Brecher, IACP member, who studied at the CIA, Peter Kump's, and La Varenne; local chefs.

COSTS: Range from $20-$32 per class. Deposit required; refund with 1 week notice.

CONTACT: Nancie Brechner, Cook's World, 2900 NE Blakeley St. Seattle, WA 98105; (206) 528-8192.

EVERYDAY GOURMET SCHOOL OF COOKING
Seattle/Year-round

Founded in 1988 by Beverly Gruber, this school offers 10- and 18-session hands-on certificate courses (limit 12 students) and 1- to 6-session participation and demonstration (limit 36) courses. Facilities: large, multi-station work island in Larry's Markets,. Also available: apprentice/assistant program, custom classes.

EMPHASIS: Basic techniques, pastry, kitchen survival skills, ethnic foods.

FACULTY: Beverly Gruber is a cum laude graduate of Madeleine Kamman's 2-year professional cooking school, an IACP-Certified Teacher, and has taught professionally for more than 10 years.

COSTS: Range from $30-$35 per session. A $35-$50 nonrefundable deposit is required with balance due 15 days prior to class. No refunds thereafter.

LOCATION: Larry's Market in Bellevue.

CONTACT: Beverly Gruber, Director, Everyday Gourmet School of Cooking, Larry's Market, 677 120th Ave. NE, #155, Bellevue, WA 98006; (206) 363-1602 (office phone/fax), (206) 451-2080 (school phone/fax).

THE GOURMET'S GALLEY/IN SEASON
Friday Harbor/Year-round

First offered in 1991, this school in a private residence conducts 2 to 4 demonstration (limit 12 students) and participation (limit 8) classes per month. Facilities: large commercial kitchen with professional range and refrigerator.

EMPHASIS: Northwest cuisine, seafood, island-grown vegetables, bistro food.

FACULTY: Greg Atkinson, CCP, is executive chef at Friday Harbor House, writes weekly newspaper columns and authored a cookbook.

COSTS: $35-$65 per class, payable with registration. Accommodation list on request.

LOCATION: San Juan Island, northwest of Seattle, 30 minutes by air from Seatac.

CONTACT: Patricia DeStaffany, The Gourmet's Galley, P.O. Box 578/9 Spring St. W, Friday Harbor, WA 98250; (206) 378-2251.

THE HERBFARM
Fall City/Year-round

Established in 1974, this restaurant and herb nursery offers more than 300 demonstration classes (limit 28 students) and events each year. Facilities: the open kitchen of The Herbfarm Restaurant, top-rated in the Northwest by the Zagat Guide. Also available: classes in horticulture, basketry, herbal crafts, herbal medicine, wines of the Pacific Northwest, a Father's Day weekend microbrewery festival, and the Northwest Wine Festival in August.

EMPHASIS: Pacific Northwest cuisines, herbs.

FACULTY: Jerry Traunfeld, The Herbfarm Restaurant chef and co-author of *Seasonal Favorites from The Herbfarm*, and local guest chefs.

COSTS: Range from $27-$45 per class. Refund with 48 hours notice. Credit cards accepted.

LOCATION: Situated on 13 rural acres 30 minutes east of Seattle, The Herbfarm has 17 public gardens, an organic garden, and a gift shop

CONTACT: Ellen Pardee, Cooking School Director, The Herbfarm, 32804 Issaquah-Fall City Rd., Fall City, WA 98024; (206) 784-2222, Fax (206) 789-2279.

KITCHEN/KITCHEN COOKING SCHOOL
Bellevue/Year-round

Founded in 1983, this cookware store offers approximately 100 evening demonstrations (limit 22 students) and occasional specialized participation classes (limit 8) each year.

EMPHASIS: Ethnic and regional cuisines, entertaining menus, baking, herb cooking, seafood.

FACULTY: Includes Bonita Atkins, Susan Fowler, Carol Foster, Mary Jane Landau, Northwest cookbook authors, and guest chefs.

COSTS: Range from $25-$35.

LOCATION: Bellevue, east of Lake Washington, is 10 miles from Seattle

CONTACT: Donna Lundquist, Kitchen/Kitchen Cooking School, 242 Bellevue Sq., Bellevue, WA 98004; (206) 451-9507.

LE GOURMAND RESTAURANT
Seattle/Year-round

Established in 1986, this restaurant offers a demonstration class (limit 20 students) the last Sunday and Monday of each month.

EMPHASIS: French and Northwest regional cuisine.

NONVOCATIONAL/VACATION   **WEST VIRGINIA**

FACULTY: Le Gourmand Chef Bruce Naftaly, a founder of the Northwest cuisine movement.
COSTS: The $30 fee must accompany reservation. Refund with 1 week notice.
LOCATION: Near Seattle's Ballard District, 25 minutes from SEATAC airport
CONTACT: Le Gourmand Restaurant, 425 N.W. Market St., Seattle, WA 98107; (206) 784-3463.

RECIPE CLUB, KASPAR'S RESTAURANT
Seattle/September-June

Since 1989, this restaurant has offered monthly demonstrations.
EMPHASIS: Creative contemporary and Pacific Northwest cuisines.
FACULTY: Kaspar Donier, Swiss-trained chef of Kaspar's Restaurant.
COSTS: $30 per session.
CONTACT: Nancy Donier, Owner, Recipe Club, Kaspar's Restaurant, 2701 First Ave., Seattle, WA 98121; (206) 441-4805, Fax (206) 441-1659.

WEST VIRGINIA

LA VARENNE AT THE GREENBRIER
White Sulphur Springs/February-May

Each spring, this luxury resort offers eight 5-day cooking vacations (limit 60 students each) that feature daily demonstration classes and optional hands-on instruction. Facilities: large demonstration kitchen with overhead mirror. Other activities: receptions, dinners, resort amenities.
EMPHASIS: Contemporary American cuisine, French technique, wine pairing.
FACULTY: Anne Willan, founder and director of Ecole de Cuisine La Varenne, food columnist, TV show food host, and author of more than a dozen cookbooks; Greenbrier chefs; guest food personalities.
COSTS, ACCOMMODATIONS: Tuition of $1,850 includes lodging and meals. Hands-on class is $100 extra. Deposit required. Resort amenities include golf, tennis, horseback riding, skeet and trap, hiking, spa, swimming, concerts, live music, dancing.
LOCATION: The Mobil 5-Star, AAA 5-Diamond resort is in the Allegheny mountains, 15 minutes from the Greenbrier Valley Airport in Lewisburg. Amtrak service is available.
CONTACT: Riki Senn, Cooking School Coordinator, La Varenne at The Greenbrier, Box 1075-Station A, White Sulphur Springs, WV 24986; (800) 624-6070 or (304)

WISCONSIN

CREATIVE CUISINE COOKING SCHOOL
Milwaukee; Naples/April-December; December-April

Founded in 1977, this school offers 2 or 3 demonstrations (limit 20 students) per week. Also available: private demonstrations, programs for groups.
EMPHASIS: Ethnic cuisines, food processor, pasta, vegetarian, heart-healthy, entertaining menus.
FACULTY: Food consultant and IACP-Certified Member Karen Maihofer studied with Julia Child, James Beard, and Guiliano Bugialli. She is author of 5 cookbooks, including *Foods For Entertaining, Holiday Cuisine,* and *Salads & Muffins.*
COSTS: Range from $25-$30 per class. No refunds.
LOCATION: Twenty minutes from downtown Milwaukee; Naples, on Florida's Gulf Coast.
CONTACT: Karen Maihofer, Creative Cuisine Cooking School, P.O. Box 17664, Milwaukee, Wisconsin 53217; (414) 352-0975 and 20962 Blacksmith Forge, Estero, FL 33928; (813) 947-9879

ECOLE DE CUISINE
Kohler/Year-round

Established in 1987, this school in a resort offers more than 30 five-day participation (limit 10 students) and demonstration (limit 60) courses, 50 to 75 demonstration classes, several weekend getaways, and 2 culinary tours each year. Facilities: the new 1,300-square-foot school is equipped with 5 Viking ovens and specialized appliances; cookware shop next door. Also available: visits to cheese producers, a tour of The American Club kitchens, classes for children.

EMPHASIS: Basic, intermediate, and advanced French classic cuisine, French pastry, wine and food pairing, cheese, table service, ice carving, sugarwork.

FACULTY: Jill Prescott, who completed certified courses at Ecole Lenotre, Ecole de Cuisine Gastronomie Ritz-Escoffier, and Ecole de Cuisine La Varenne; American Club executive chefs Rhys Lewis and Jack Kaestner and executive pastry chef Richard Palm; guest chefs.

COSTS, ACCOMMODATIONS: Five-day (weekend) courses are $1,425 ($580), which includes double occupancy lodging and meals; non-cook rate is $825 ($330); private room is $70 per night extra; rates without meals and lodging are available. Demonstrations are $30. Full payment is required with registration. Cancellations within 30 days forfeit $300. The American Club, a AAA 3-Diamond resort, offers health and racquet facilities, 7 restaurants, and golf.

LOCATION: The Woodlake Mall shopping village, 55 miles from Mitchell International Airport in Milwaukee. Nearby attractions include the Kohler Design Center and a 600-acre wilderness preserve.

CONTACT: Jill Prescott, Ecole de Cuisine, 765 N. Woodlake Dr., Kohler, WI 53044; (800) 344-2838 (for brochure) or (414) 451-9151 (for school), Fax (414) 457-0299.

WISCONSIN SCHOOL OF COOKERY
Cascade/Year-round

Founded in 1991, this school offers 2 demonstrations (limit 35 students) per month. Facilities vary.

FACULTY: Richard Baumann, member of ICP and FWA, writes for *Lake Home* and *Home Gallery* magazines and is the author of *Wisecrackers*.

COSTS: $20 per session.

CONTACT: Wisconsin School of Cookery, W6248 Lake Ellen Dr., Cascade, WI 53011-1322; (414) 528-8015.

ASIA

EXPLORING THE KITCHENS OF ASIA WITH JOYCE JUE
September-October or April-May

Established in 1981, InnerAsia Expeditions travel company offers an annual 15-day tour (limit 20 participants) that features cooking demonstrations at Hong Kong's Mandarin Oriental Hotel and Bangkok's Oriental Hotel. Other activities: private lesson in Singapore, visits to country markets and the Kodari experimental farm in Hong Kong, dining at noted restaurants, shopping, sightseeing, 3-day optional Bali extension with kitchen tour and lecture on Indonesian cooking.

EMPHASIS: Asian cuisine.

FACULTY: Joyce Jue, Asian food editor for the *San Francisco Chronicle* and author of *Wok and Stir Fry Cooking* and *Asian Appetizers*; Singaporean food writer Violet Oon; Chef Genn of Amandari's restaurant in Bali.

LOCATION: Hong Kong, Macau, Bangkok, Singapore, and Bali.

CONTACT: InnerAsia Expeditions, 2627 Lombard St., San Francisco, CA 94123; (800) 777-8183 or (415) 922-0448, Fax (415) 346-5535.

ACCOUTREMENT COOKING SCHOOL
Sydney/April-October

Established in 1976, this school offers culinary tours and approximately 100 sessions a year.

EMPHASIS: Thai, Japanese, Italian, French, Middle Eastern, and Indian cuisines, seafood, salads, desserts, guest chef specialties.

FACULTY: Proprietor Susan Jenkins, who trained at Ecole Lenotre and worked with many chefs; Australian guest chefs; chefs from abroad.

CONTACT: Accoutrement, 611 Military Rd., Mosman, Sydney, NSW, Australia; (61) 2-969-1031.

ARTE AL DENTE
Sydney/February-April, July-October

Established in 1991, this school in a private home offers approximately 10 three-session demonstration courses (limit 8 students) in per year. Also: culinary courses near Rome in spring and fall.

EMPHASIS: Italian home cooking, specializing in Roman cuisine.

FACULTY: Libby Mangosi, a resident of Italy for 26 years.

COSTS: A$170 per course. Culinary tours are approximately A$2,195, which includes lodging.

LOCATION: Five minutes from city center.

CONTACT: Libby Mangosi, Arte al Dente, P.O. Box 277, Double Bay, 2028, Australia; Phone/Fax (61) 2-3654684.

AUSTRALIAN GAS COOKING SCHOOL
North Sydney/February-November

This school offers evening courses and all-day Saturday workshops. Facilities: well-equipped gas kitchen. Also available: gourmet tours hosted by food personalities.

EMPHASIS: Basic techniques, guest chef specialties, specific topics.

FACULTY: Head of School Lyn Sykes, author of magazine and newspaper columns with 25 years of food experience; qualified cooking instructors; guest chefs from Australia and abroad.

COSTS: Range from A$35-A$150. Nonrefundable tuition must accompany application. Credit cards accepted. No refunds

CONTACT: The Australian Gas Cooking School, AGL Centre, 111 Pacific Highway, North Sydney, NSW, 2060, Australia; (61) 2-922-8400/8608.

BEVERLEY SUTHERLAND SMITH COOKING SCHOOL
Mt. Waverly/Year-round

Established in 1967, this school offers 2 to 3 one- to three-session demonstration courses (limit 25 students) per month. Facilities: mirrored teaching kitchen that overlooks an herb garden.

EMPHASIS: Instructor and guest chef specialties, ethnic and regional dishes.

FACULTY: Beverley Sutherland Smith, a Grand Dame Chaine des Rotisseurs, has contributed to *Epicurean* and *Gourmet*, is author of 15 books and winner of the Australian Gold Book award, food writer for *The Age* and *The Weekly Times* newspapers and *New Idea* magazine.

COSTS: Start at A$43.

LOCATION: Mt. Waverley, a Melbourne suburb, is about 12 miles from city center.

CONTACT: Beverley Sutherland Smith, 29 Regent St., Mt. Waverley, Victoria 3149, Australia; (61) 3 9802 5544, Fax (61) 3 9802 7683.

BORAL GAS COOKERY SERVICE
Queensland/Year-round except January

Established by the Gas Corporation of Queensland in 1950 and upgraded in 1982 and 1989, this school offers 1- to 2-session demonstration (limit 60 students) and 3- to 4-session participation (limit 16) courses that utilize gas cookery. Facilities: auditorium with overhead mirror and individual work areas with 2-person bays.

EMPHASIS: Australian and Asian cuisines, vegetarian recipes, regional foods.

FACULTY: Cookery School Head Barbara Harman, trained home economists Joanne Capper and Carol Weeks, guest chefs.

COSTS: Range from A$20-A$60 per session, A$30-A$60 for visiting chef classes. Payment is due 1 week prior to course.

LOCATION: Five minutes from Brisbane in the John Oxley Centre

CONTACT: Boral Gas Cookery Service, Gas Corp. of Queensland, John Oxley Centre, 339 Coronation Dr., Milton, QLD, 4064, Australia; (61) 7-858-0444, Fax (61) 7-368-1513.

CARRINGTON HOUSE RESTAURANT AND COOKING SCHOOL
Newcastle/March-October

Founded in 1985, this school offers demonstration (limit 50 students) and participation (limit 10) classes approximately 8 to 10 times per year. Also: shopping excursions in Newcastle and Sydney.

EMPHASIS: Australian and guest chef specialties, holiday menus, low fat cookery.

FACULTY: Chef-proprietor and radio food commentator Barry Meiklejohn has more than 15 years international culinary experience.

COSTS: A$45-A$70 per class, payable by cash or credit card

CONTACT: Barry Meiklejohn, Proprietor, Carrington House Restaurant and Cooking School, 130 Young St., Carrington, Newcastle, NSW, 2294, Australia; (61) 4-961-3564.

CLARE GOURMET WEEKEND
Adelaide/May

This 2-day food and wine festival, sponsored by the Clare Valley Winemakers, features a structured vintage tasting, anniversary dinner, and gourmet food day.

COSTS: A$7 admission. Events are priced individually.

CONTACT: Sarah Harris, National Media Coordinator, SATC, GPO Box 1205, Sydney, NSW, 2001, Australia; (61) 02-261-5098, Fax (61) 02-264-3941.

THE COOK, THE ARTIST COOKERY SCHOOL
Brisbane/Year-round except January

Founded in 1992, this school in a private residence offers 3-session demonstration (limit 12 to 40 students) and participation (limit 12) courses. Facilities: domestic and tertiary college kitchen. Also available: escorted overseas cooking tours.

EMPHASIS: Italian, Thai and other Asian cuisines.

FACULTY: Director Roz MacAllan and home economist Leisel Rogers. The school publishes *Food Art*, a quarterly newsletter.

COSTS: A$50 per session, A$150 per course, payable in advance.

LOCATION: About 3 miles from city center.

CONTACT: Ms. Roz MacAllan, Director, The Cook, The Artist Cookery School, P.O. Box 152, Brisbane Market, Brisbane, QLD, 4106, Australia; (61) 7-846-3725; Fax (61) 7-846-2032.

COUNCIL OF ADULT EDUCATION
Melbourne/Year-round

This educational organization offers more than 70 two to six-session cooking and catering courses and full-day classes.per year. Also available: on-going classes, short courses, workshops, and travel programs on a wide range of topics, including art, crafts, photography, performing arts, recreation, personal development, history, writing, languages, literature, and nature.

EMPHASIS: International cuisines, microwave, breads, vegetarian cookery, catering, wine.

FACULTY: Cooking instructors and guest chefs.

COSTS: Nonrefundable tuition ranges from A$20-A$40 per session for multi-session courses and from A$60-A$75 for a full-day class. Discounts for seniors and pensioners. Credit cards accepted

CONTACT: Council of Adult Education, 256 Flinders, St., Melbourne, VIC, 3000, Australia; (61) 3-652-0611, Fax (61) 3-654-6759.

DAVID EGAN COOKING SCHOOL
Applecross/Year-round

Established in 1991, this school offers 7-session demonstration courses (limit 8 students). Facilities: a 750-square-foot room with overhead mirror and individual work spaces.

EMPHASIS: Vegetarian Chinese, Indian, Italian, French, Mexican, and Australian cuisines; eggless cakes and desserts.

FACULTY: A cook and chef since 1968, David Egan has worked in London, France, Switzerland, and as a chef at the Southern Cross Intercontinental Hotel in Melbourne and the Sheraton Perth Hotel. He is an associate member of the Catering Institute of Australia.

COSTS: A$140 per course. A videotape of the 7 lessons is A$45, payable by bank draft.

CONTACT: David Egan, P.O. Box 435, Applecross, 6153, Western Australia; (61) 9-337-9514, Fax (61) 9-330-6808.

DIANA MARSLAND COOKING
Armadale/Year-round except January

Founded in 1981, this school offers 1- to 5-session demonstration and participation courses and culinary tours. Facilities: a large kitchen with overhead mirror.

FACULTY: Diana Marsland studied at Le Cordon Bleu and Leith's School in London.

COSTS: Range from A$40-A$50 per session.

LOCATION: A residential suburb of Melbourne.

CONTACT: Diana Marsland, 24 Barkly Ave., Armadale, VIC, 3143, Australia; (61) 3-509-3971 (phone/fax).

ELISE PASCOE COOKING SCHOOL
Darling Point/Fall, Summer, Spring

Established in 1975, this school in a private residence offers 50 one- to three-session demonstration (limit 30 students) and participation (limit 6) courses and weekend workshops per year. Facilities: home kitchen with 3 work stations and overhead mirror. Also available: private and men only classes, culinary tours of Australia.

EMPHASIS: Technique, and theory, Mediterranean, Italian and Thai cuisines, pastry, yeast doughs.

FACULTY: Elise Pascoe is a free-lance food writer, television presenter, and author of 5 cook books. She trained at Le Cordon Bleu and La Varenne in Paris, with Roger Verge in France and Angelo Paracucchi in Italy, and has been a guest instructor at schools in Europe and the U.S.

COSTS: A$170 per 3-session course, single session A$60, workshop A$100. Full payment required with booking. Credit cards accepted.

LOCATION: Sydney's Eastern suburbs, 10 minutes from central Sydney and 30 minutes from airport

CONTACT: Elise Pascoe, Principal, Elise Pascoe Cooking School, 1/44 Darling Point Rd., Darling Point, NSW, 2027, Australia; (61) 2-363-0406, Fax (61) 2-363-3122.

ELIZABETH CHONG COOKING SCHOOL AND GOURMET TOURS
Melbourne/Year-round

Founded in 1961, this school offers participation courses (limit 30 students). Facilities: kitchen with overhead mirror and individual work areas. Also available: an annual culinary tour to China, Hong Kong, Taiwan.

EMPHASIS: Chinese cuisine.

FACULTY: School founder Elizabeth Chong, author of 5 books, including *The Heritage of Chinese Cooking*, a food writer for periodicals, and recipient of the Prix La Mazille, 1994.

COSTS: Range from A$120-A$195 (single lesson, A$50). A A$30 nonrefundable deposit is required with balance due 2 weeks prior.

LOCATION: Near public transportation.

CONTACT: Elizabeth Chong Cooking School, 68 Hawthorn Grove, Hawthorn, Melbourne, VIC, 3122, Australia; (61) 3-9819-3666, Fax (61) 3-9818-1870.

THE FRENCH KITCHEN
Armadale/Year-round

Established in 1969, this school offers 1- to 5-session demonstration courses (limit 25 students), two levels of 5-day hands-on intensives (limit 15), and local and international guest chefs. Facilities: French country-style kitchen, which has an overhead mirror.

EMPHASIS: Classic French cuisine and its modern derivatives.

FACULTY: School director Diane Holuigue studied at Le Cordon Bleu, Ecole Lenotre, and with Paul Bocuse, Julia Child, and Roger Verge. She is former food editor of *Home Beautiful* and *Epicurean* magazines and currently food editor of *The Australian Newspaper*.

COSTS: Range from A$40-A$75 per session; A$640 for the 5-day intensive.

LOCATION: A residential suburb of Melbourne.

CONTACT: The French Kitchen, 3 Avondale Rd., Armadale, VIC, 3143, Australia; (61) 3-509-3638, Fax (61) 3-500-9650.

GRETTA ANNA SCHOOL OF COOKING
Sydney/Year-round

Established in 1958, this school offers 3-session demonstrations (limit 32 students) and 4-day live-in courses. Facilities: lecture room, commercial kitchen, shop, herb garden.

EMPHASIS: French, Continental, and Italian cuisines.

FACULTY: Gretta Anna Teplitzky studied at Le Cordon Bleu, has worked in Michelin 3-star restaurants in France, writes cookbooks and articles for food magazines, and has appeared regularly on TV and radio.

COSTS: Each 3-hour lesson is A$41.

LOCATION: Demonstrations are held at the school, in a Sydney suburb; live-in courses are held in the country, where meals and lodging are provided at a nominal extra cost

CONTACT: Gretta Anna School of Cooking, 67 Clissold Rd., Wahroonga, Sydney, NSW, 2076, Australia; (61) 2-487-2425.

HARRY'S CHINESE COOKING CLASSES
Sydney/February-December

Established in 1977, this school offers three 7-session demonstration courses (limit 25 students) on a rotating basis. Facilities: rented halls and schools with kitchen facilities. Also available: children's classes, private classes, 4-week courses.

EMPHASIS: Basic Chinese, advanced Chinese, and Thai cuisines.

FACULTY: A third generation chef, Harry Quay has more than 30 years experience.

COSTS: A$18 per session, payable at class.

CONTACT: Harry Quay, Proprietor, Harry's Chinese Cooking Classes, 47 Bruce St., Brighton-le-Sands, Sydney, NSW, 2216, Australia; (61) 2-567-6353.

NONVOCATIONAL/VACATION **AUSTRALIA**

HOWQUA-DALE GOURMET RETREAT
Mansfield/March-November

Established as a small country house-hotel in 1977 with a cooking school added in 1984, this resort offers a dozen 4-day and weekend participation courses (limit 12 students) and 3-4 six-day gourmet cycling tours of Australia's wine regions per year. Facilities: a horse-shoe shaped pavilion with specialized equipment. Also: fishing, skiing, swimming, horseback riding, bird-watching.

EMPHASIS: Fresh local foods and modern Australian cuisine; wine appreciation.

FACULTY: Co-owner Marieke Brugman, a noted food writer and cooking demonstrator, conducts the classes. Her partner, Sarah Stegley, acts as hostess and instructs in wine selection.

COSTS, ACCOMMODATIONS: All-inclusive fee is approximately A$600 for the weekend course, A$1,100 for the 4-day course, and A$2,200 for the tour, excluding transport. Deposit is A$200, nonrefundable unless space is filled.

LOCATION: A 40-acre estate on the Howqua River 18 miles from Mansfield, a country town 128 miles northeast of Melbourne

CONTACT: Marieke Brugman or Sarah Stegley, Howqua Dale Gourmet Retreat, Howqua River Rd., P.O. Box 379, Mansfield, VIC, 3722, Australia; (61) 5-7773503, Fax (61) 5-777-3896.

MA CUISINE COOKING SCHOOL
Perth/Year-round

Established in 1982, this cookware store offers 80 to 90 two- to three-session demonstration (limit 35 students) and participation (limit 16) courses per year. Facilities: teaching kitchen with overhead mirror and individual work areas. Also available: Culinary tours to France.

FACULTY: School director is IACP-member Beverly Sprague. Instruction is given by prominent Australian and international culinary professionals.

COSTS: Range from A$30-A$70 per session; series range from A$70-A$160. Full payment required; no refunds.

LOCATION: The beach-side suburb of Perth, Western Australia's capitol

CONTACT: Beverley Sprague, Ma Cuisine Cooking School, AMANO, 12 Station St., Cottesloe, Perth, 6011, Australia; (61) 9-384-0378, Fax (61) 9-384-5790.

MARGARET RIVER WINE & FOOD FESTIVAL
Margaret River/February

This annual event features a 3-day master class sponsored by Ma Cuisine Cooking School at a wine estate.

CONTACT: The Margaret River Wine & Food Festival, Augusta Margaret River Tourist Bureau, Bussell Hwy., Margaret River, 6285, Australia; (61) 97-572911, Fax (61) 97-573287.

MELBOURNE FOOD AND WINE FESTIVAL
Belgrave/February-March

Established in 1993, this annual 3-week festival features more than 18 events, including tours of markets and vineyards, dinners with chefs and vintners, and a 2-day cooking master class conducted by an international faculty.

COSTS: Events range from A$20-A$185 each.

CONTACT: Sylvia Johnson, Manager, P.O. Box 128, Belgrave, VIC, 3160, Australia; (61) 3-754-2722 (phone/fax).

NATURAL FOODS VEGETARIAN COOKING SCHOOL
Sydney/May and November

Founded in 1987, this school in a private residence offers 2 five-session demonstration (limit 36 students) and participation (limit 4-12) courses per year. Facilities: private kitchen with 4 work stations.

EMPHASIS: Nutrition, fruits, legumes, wholegrains.

FACULTY: Certified cooking demonstrator Myrna Fenn.

COSTS: A$100.

CONTACT: Myrna Fenn, Cooking School Coordinator, Natural Foods Vegetarian Cooking School, 20/21 Rangers Rd., Cremorne, Sydney, NSW, 2090, Australia; (61) 2-953-7175.

ROSA MATTO COOKING SCHOOL
Adelaide

Chef Rosa Matto conducts cooking classes that emphasize European and Italian cuisines.

CONTACT: Rosa Matto Cooking School, 1a Union St., Goodwood, SA 5034, Australia; (61) 8 344 7419 or (61) 8 373 6106.

SYDNEY SEAFOOD SCHOOL
Pyrmont/Year-round

Established by the Fish Marketing Authority in 1989, this school offers a half dozen 1- to 4-session demonstration (limit 60 students) and participation (limit 40) courses per month. Facilities: a practical kitchen and 66-seat demonstration auditorium with tiered seating and overhead mirror. Also available: children's classes, trade program for commercial cooks, gourmet tours in Sydney.

EMPHASIS: Seafood cookery, guest chef specialties, advanced techniques, seafood buying and handling, sushi and sashimi.

FACULTY: Qualified home economists who are seafood specialists; guest chefs.

COSTS: Nonrefundable tuition, payable in advance, ranges from A$30-A$110 per course; credit cards accepted.

LOCATION: The Sydney Fish Market, a complex that incorporates the Fish Marketing Authority, fish auction hall, fish retail outlets, and a sushi bar

CONTACT: Annie Foord, Manager, Sydney Seafood School, Fish Marketing Authority, Blackwattle Bay, Pyrmont, NSW, 2009, Australia; (61) 2-660-1611, Fax (61) 2-552-3632.

TAMARA'S KITCHEN
Melbourne/Year-round

Established in 1989, this cookware store and school offers forty 3- to 5-session demonstration and participation courses (limit 12 students) per year. Facilities: Large shopfront with 12 workspaces. Also available: market visits, private classes.

EMPHASIS: Breadmaking, pasta, risotto, Italian and Jewish menus, desserts, specific subjects.

FACULTY: The instructors include Tamara Milstein, who trained in Europe and the U.S.

COSTS, ACCOMMODATIONS: A$90-A$190 per course. A A$50 deposit is required.

CONTACT: Tamara Milstein, Tamara's Kitchen, 490 Tooronga Rd., Hawthorn East, VIC 3123, Australia; (61) 3-9882-1450, Fax (61) 3-9882-3436.

THORN PARK COOKING SCHOOL
Clare Valley

Chef David Hay and Michael Speers conduct weekend classes in their historic home.

EMPHASIS: Various topics, including seasonal and entertaining menus, wines, specific subjects.

CONTACT: Thorn Park Country House, College Rd., Sevenhill, SA 5453, Australia; (61) 88 843 4304, Fax (61) 88 843 4296.

VICTORIA'S KITCHEN OF CREATIVE COOKING
Mt. Hawthorn/February-September

Established in 1981, this school offers 12 to 15 one and two-session demonstration courses a year.

EMPHASIS: International cuisines, entertaining menus, vegetarian cookery, microwave, beef, poultry and seafood preparation, purchasing, storage, economy.

FACULTY: Food consultant.Victoria Blackadder was named *Australian Women's Weekly* Best Cook in Australia in 1981 and established a catering business in 1986. She is author of *Victoria's Kitchen*.

COSTS: Range from A$14-A$20 per session, payable in advance.

LOCATION: Home Base Exhibition Centre Auditorium, 10 minutes from Perth city center.

CONTACT: Victoria Blackadder, Victoria's Kitchen, P.O. Box 278, Mt. Hawthorn 6016, Western Australia; (61) 9-443-2266.

(See page 112) **WILLIAM ANGLISS COLLEGE**

This career institution also offers 2- to 8-session courses in ethnic cuisines, cake decorating, breads, nutrition, sausages, chocolates, cakes and pastries, and beginning to advanced wine study.

COSTS: Range from A$110-A$320. Credit cards accepted.

YALUMBA WINERY COOKING SCHOOL
Barossa Valley

This winery offers classes and one-day and weekend workshops.

CONTACT: Jane Ferrari, Yalumba Winery Cooking School, P.O. Box 10, Angaston SA 5353, Australia; (61) 85 613200, Fax (61) 85 613393.

CANADA

ACADEMIE DE CUISINE ENR.
Dollard des Ormeaux/May, June, September-January

Established in 1974, this school offers 12 seven-session demonstration (limit 12 students) and participation (limit 8) courses per year. Facilities: a 500-square-foot kitchen with overhead mirror. Also available: children's classes, wine tasting, private classes, culinary tours in Canada, the U.S., and Italy.

EMPHASIS: Regional Italian and international cuisines; cake decorating.

FACULTY: Mario Novati received his training in Venice and at the Lewis Hotel Training School in Washington, D.C. He has published 3 cookbooks and hosted a weekly television cooking series in Ottawa and Montreal.

COSTS: Range from C$38-C$50 per session, payable in advance. A nonrefundable 50% deposit is required.

CONTACT: Chef Mario Novati, Academie de Cuisine Enr., 60 Paddington Pl., Dollard des Ormeaux, QB, H9G 2S4, Canada; (514) 696-6110, Fax (514) 685-7055.

ART OF FOOD COOKING SCHOOL
Toronto/Year-round

Established in 1991, this school in a private residence offers 3 weekly demonstration classes (limit 10 students). Also available: fall culinary tours to Provence, private instruction.

EMPHASIS: International cuisines and special occasion menus.

FACULTY: Merla McMenomy, IACP member, who studied at Peter Kump's New York Cooking School and La Varenne; local guest chefs.

COSTS: $65, payable with registration.

LOCATION: Mid-town Toronto, 15 miles from Toronto International Airport

CONTACT: Merla McMenomy, Art of Food Cooking School, 98 Walker Ave., Toronto, ON, M4V 1G2, Canada; (416) 975-5088; (416) 960-9337.

BENKRIS COOKING SCHOOL
Calgary/September-June

Founded in 1979, this cookware store offers 20 one- to six-session demonstration (limit 40 students) and participation (limit 24) courses per month. Facilities: well-equipped, mirrored kitchen. Also available: kids' camp, wine seminars, private classes, tourist programs, Italian market tours.

EMPHASIS: Ethnic and regional cuisines, breads, wine and food harmonies.

FACULTY: Owner Richard Durvin, senior assistant Becky Monroe, J. Webb Wine Merchants, and more than 20 local chefs and caterers. Guest instructors include Hugh Carpenter, Deborah Madison, Caren McSherry-Valagao, Perla Meyers, Giuliano Hazan, and Bonnie Stern.

COSTS: Range from C$45-C$85 per class, full payment upon registration. Credit cards accepted. Cancellations 48 hours prior to class receive credit.

LOCATION: Calgary, in the downtown Eau Claire Market

CONTACT: Richard Durvin, Co-owner, Benkris Cooking School, Box 102, 200 Barclay Parade SW, Calgary, AB, T2P 4R5, Canada; (403) 290-1952, Fax (403) 290-0430.

BIRTHE MARIE'S COOKING SCHOOL
Brampton/September-June

Since 1977, Birthe MacDonald has offered 1-2 demonstrations per week. Facilities: a home kitchen.

FACULTY: Toronto Culinary Guild and IACP-member Birthe MacDonald learned to cook in Denmark.

COSTS: Approximately C$50 per session.

CONTACT: Birthe MacDonald, 88 Hillside Dr., Brampton, ON, L6S 1A6, Canada; (416) 453-6647.

THE BONNIE STERN SCHOOL OF COOKING
Toronto/Year-round

Founded in 1973, this school offers 12 to 15 demonstration (limit 30 students) and participation (limit 15) classes and series per month. Facilities: interchangeable demonstration/participation area with overhead mirror. Also available: wine instruction, private group classes.

EMPHASIS: Basic techniques, ethnic and regional cuisines, low fat cookery, holiday menus.

FACULTY: School proprietor Bonnie Stern, a George Brown College graduate who has studied with Simone Beck and Marcella Hazan and is author of 6 cookbooks, including *Simply Heartsmart Cooking* and *Bonnie Stern's Appetizers*; Linda Stephens, a George Brown College graduate; and guest instructors, including Biba Caggiano, Giuliano Bugialli, and Madeleine Kamman.

COSTS: C$70 per session, C$260 per 6-week course. A C$45 deposit is required. Cancellations with 1 week notice forfeit C$20

CONTACT: Maureen Lollar, The Bonnie Stern School of Cooking, 6 Erskine Ave., Toronto, ON, M4P 1Y2, Canada; (416) 484-4810, Fax (416) 484-4820.

CAREN'S COOKING SCHOOL
Vancouver/September-May

Founded in 1978, this school offers 60 three- to four-session evening demonstration courses (limit 32 students) per year. Facilities: an overhead mirror, butcher block demonstration table, 8 gas burners. Also available: wine classes, classes for children, culinary tours to Europe.

EMPHASIS: Italian, French, and Continental Asian cuisine.

FACULTY: Owner Caren McSherry-Valagao, CCP, trained at the Cordon Bleu, the CIA, and The Oriental in Bangkok. She studied with Julia Child, Jacques Pepin, and Paul Prudhomme. Guest chefs have included John Ash, Giuliano Bugialli, Jane Butel, Hugh Carpenter, and Jacques Pepin.

COSTS: Range from C$40-C$50 per class. Cancellations with 1 week notice receive credit.

LOCATION: Ten minutes from downtown, near Victoria and Hastings St

NONVOCATIONAL/VACATION **CANADA**

CONTACT: Cindy Burridge, Administrator, Caren's Cooking School, 1856 Pandora St., Vancouver, BC, V5L 1M5, Canada; (604) 255-5119, Fax (604) 253-1331.

COOKING LITE
Montreal/September-May

Since 1989, Marilyn Calder Flaherty has offered demonstration and participation classes. Facilities: a suburban home kitchen.

EMPHASIS: Healthful foods.

FACULTY: Marilyn Flaherty earned a bachelor's degree in Home Economics.

COSTS: A 3-class series is C$75.

LOCATION: Pointe Claire, a Montreal suburb.

CONTACT: M. Calder Flaherty, 29 Cedar Ave., Pointe Claire, QB, H9S 4X9, Canada; (514) 695-4117.

THE COOKING STUDIO
Winnipeg/Year-round except Summer

Established in September, this school offers 4- and 6-session demonstration (limit 25 students) and participation courses (limit 12). Facilities: 1,000-foot commercial kitchen. Also available: children's birthday parties, private dinners, Saturday workshops, excursions to France.

EMPHASIS: Ethnic and regional cuisines, nutrition, guest chef specialties.

FACULTY: Owner Marisa Curatolo earned a degree in Foods and Nutrition from the University of Manitoba, completed Chef Training at the Dubrulle French Culinary School, and studied at Peter Kump's New York School, Ecole LeNotre and Le Cordon Bleu.

COSTS: The 6-session course is $220, 4-session course is $150; Saturday workshops range from $40-$45 each. Full payment prior to class.

CONTACT: The Cooking Studio, 3200 Roblin Blvd., Winnipeg, Manitoba, Canada R3R 2Z9; (204) 896-5174, Fax (204) 888-0628.

COOKING WITH SUSAN LEE
London/Year-round except April, August, December

Established in 1988, this school in a private residence offers 3-hour participation classes (limit 12 students). Facilities: large family kitchen. Also available: Private lessons.

EMPHASIS: Seasonal foods, ethnic and regional cuisines, entertaining menus.

FACULTY: Home economist and food writer Susan Lee and local chefs.

COSTS: Classes are C$40 each. Refund with 2 days notice.

CONTACT: Cooking with Susan Lee, 1011, Wellington St., London, ON, N6A 3T5, Canada; (519) 439-1423.

THE COOKING WORKSHOP
Toronto/Fall, Winter, Spring

Established in 1985, this school offers 15 participation weekend workshops (limit 12 students) per year. Facilities: the industrial kitchen of Dufflet Pastries, a bakery equipped with skylights and double ovens; a private home kitchen. Also available: winemaking at home, private classes, culinary tours to Italy.

EMPHASIS: Italian cuisine, breads, pastry, foundations (soups, stocks, sauces, dressings).

FACULTY: Maria Pace, owner, studied at La Varenne and with Marcella Hazan and has taught cooking since 1981 in Toronto and on CTV's "What's Cooking". Professional baker Paula Bambrick trained at George Brown College and worked at Dufflet Pastries for 6 years. Doris Eisen develops bread and pastry recipes for home cooks.

COSTS: Range from C$65-C$90. Advance nonrefundable payment is required.

LOCATION: Three blocks west of Bathurst Street in Toronto's "Little Italy"; Dufflet Pastries (787 Queen St. West)

CONTACT: Maria Pace, The Cooking Workshop, M. Pace & Associates, 33 Clinton St., Toronto, ON, M6J 3H9, Canada; (416) 588-1954.

THE COOKSCHOOL AT THE COOKSHOP
Vancouver/Year-round

Established in 1992, this cookware store offers 26 evening demonstration (limit 20 students) and participation (limit 8) courses per month. Facilities: a 1,000-square-foot area with overhead mirror. Also available: classes for youngsters, wine instruction, private lessons.

EMPHASIS: Include Thai cuisine, salmon cooking, northern Italian food and wines, pastries, Caribbean food, sushi.

FACULTY: School director, restaurateur, and teacher Nathan Hyam; 40 guest chefs from area hotels and restaurants.

COSTS: Range from C$26-C$99 per class. Payment in advance.

LOCATION: Downtown Vancouver.

CONTACT: Peter Haseltine, Owner, 3-555 W. 12th Ave., Vancouver, BC, V5Z 3X7, Canada; (604) 873-5683; Fax (604) 876-4391.

DUBRULLE FRENCH CULINARY SCHOOL
Vancouver/Year-round *(See page 113)*

This career school also offers hands-on classes for the serious amateur.

EMPIRE COOKING SCHOOL
Woodstock

Since 1983, home economist and cookbook author Charlotte Empringham has taught microwave cookery. Demonstration classes are given in participants' homes.

COSTS: C$25 per hour for private classes, C$185 for a group, plus food and mileage.

CONTACT: Charlotte Empringham, Empire Cooking School, 124 John Davies Dr., Woodstock, ON, N4T 1N2, Canada; (519) 421-2837.

ENTREE NOUS COOKING SCHOOL
Toronto/Year-round

Established in 1994 by Pam Gilbert, this school offers 12-16 one- to four-session participation courses (limit 6-10 students) per month. Facilities: a student's home kitchen (student usually organizes the group).

EMPHASIS: Regional French, classic French patisserie, northern Italian, Thai.

FACULTY: Pam Gilbert is a graduate of Le Cordon Bleu and studied with Giuliano Bugialli and Vatcharin Bhumichitr.

COSTS, ACCOMMODATIONS: C$65 per class.

CONTACT: Pam Gilbert, Entree Nous Cooking School, 330 Spadina Rd., #602, Toronto, ON, M5R 2V9, Canada; (416) 921-8033, Fax (416) 921-0864.

GEORGE BROWN COLLEGE
Toronto/Year-round *(See page 113)*

In addition to career programs, this college offers more than a dozen part-time nonvocational cooking courses each semester. Topics include vegetarian cookery, Chinese cuisine, baking, cake decorating, sausage making, wine appreciation, and junior gourmet.

NONVOCATIONAL/VACATION   **CANADA**   **233**

GREAT COOKS
Toronto/September-May

Established in 1989, this cooking school located in a pastry shop offers more than 60 afternoon and evening demonstration classes (limit 21 students) annually. Facilities: a 600-square-foot teaching kitchen with overhead mirrors. Also available: wine tastings, group classes, cooking trips.

EMPHASIS: International and regional cuisines, menus for entertaining, vegetarian meals, local and out of town guest chef specialties, wine appreciation.

FACULTY: More than 30 Toronto chefs, including Mark McEwan, Arpi Magyar, Jean Pierre Challet, Martin Kouprie and Dufflet Rosenberg, owner of Dufflet Pastries.

COSTS: Range from C$70-C$100 per class. A 5% discount is granted those who register for 3 classes or more. Credit with 48 hours notice. Credit cards accepted.

LOCATION: Downtown Toronto.

CONTACT: Esther Rosenberg, Great Cooks, 787 Queen St. W., Toronto, ON, M6J 1G1, Canada; (416) 594-0388, Fax (416) 594-9832.

HOLLYHOCK FARM
Cortes Island/May-November

Established in 1983, Hollyhock offers more than 70 workshops annually in the practical, creative, spiritual, and healing arts, including cooking. Also available: yoga, meditation, birdwalks, body work, star talks,
drawing, painting, dancing, drum-making, ceramics, photography, writing, kayaking.

EMPHASIS: Open-pit style cooking of seafood and fresh produce.

FACULTY: Includes cook, teacher, and author James Barber.

COSTS, ACCOMMODATIONS: Workshop cost, which includes dormitory or semi-private lodging and meals, is C$800. A C$250 deposit is required with balance due on arrival. Cancellations 3 weeks prior receive a C$200 refund or credit.

LOCATION: About 100 miles north of Vancouver, Canada.

CONTACT: Hollyhock, Box 127, Manson's Landing, Cortes Island, BC, V0P 1K0, Canada; (800) 933-6339, Fax (604) 935-6424.

THE INN AT BAY FORTUNE
Souris/May-October

Since 1992, this country inn, rated three stars by *Where to Eat in Canada*, has offered 2-day participation sessions (limit 4 students) that feature enhancing tasting ability and understanding of ingredients through recipe development and service participation. Facilities: large fully-equipped professional kitchen, library, herb gardens. Other activities: wild mushroom picking, herb and vegetable gardening, field trips.

EMPHASIS: Contemporary creative cuisine.

FACULTY: New York chef Michael Smith, a CIA graduate.

COSTS, ACCOMMODATIONS: Tuition is C$225 per person. Double occupancy country inn rooms are C$115 to C$165 with full breakfast. C$100 deposit required.

LOCATION: 45 minutes from the nearest airport in Charlottetown.

CONTACT: Michael Smith, The Inn at Bay Fortune, Bay Fortune, Souris RR4, PEI, C0A 2B0, Canada; (902) 687-3745 or (860) 296-1348 (winter); Fax (902) 687-3540.

JAPANESE CANADIAN CULTURAL CENTRE OF MONTREAL
Montreal/Year-round

First offered in 1989, this cultural center conducts three 4-session demonstrations (limit 18 students) per year.

EMPHASIS: Japanese cuisine.

FACULTY: Japanese chefs from Montreal restaurants.

COSTS: C$60 per course.

CONTACT: Susan Levesque, Program Director, Japanese Canadian Cultural Centre of Montreal, 8155 Rousselot St., Montreal, QB, H2E 1Z7, Canada; (514) 728-5580 (phone/fax).

LANGDON HALL COUNTRY HOUSE HOTEL
Cambridge/January-March

Since 1991, this country house hotel has offered 3- and 4-day demonstration (limit 12 students) and participation (limit 6) courses.

EMPHASIS: International and regional Canadian cuisine.

FACULTY: Ms. Louise Duhamel and guest chefs.

COSTS, ACCOMMODATIONS: Costs vary. Lodging is provided in the 38-room Langdon Hall, situated on 200 acres of gardens and woodlands. Amenities include a tennis court, croquet, heated pool, and exercise facilities.

LOCATION: An hour from Toronto, 45 minutes from Pearson International Airport.

CONTACT: Langdon Hall Country House Hotel, R.R. #33, Cambridge, ON, N3H 4R8, Canada; (800) 268-1898 or (519) 740-2100, Fax (519) 740-8161.

LE CORDON BLEU PARIS COOKING SCHOOL
Ottawa/Year-round *(See page 115)*

This school's Cuisine and Pastry certificate courses are also taken by nonprofessional cooks. Single subject short courses and evening classes are scheduled each session and demonstrations are open to the public.

MAISON SANGUINET COOKING SCHOOL
Montreal/September-July

Established in 1990, this school offers 40 to 80 demonstration (limit 15 students) and participation (limit 9) courses per year. Facilities: 500-square-foot commercially-equipped home kitchen with overhead mirror and 3 work-stations. Also available: Chinatown walking tours and an Asian Dinner Club.

EMPHASIS: Southeast Asian and Italian cuisines.

FACULTY: Thomas Robson, owner/director, trained at Montreal's l'Institut de Tourisme et d'Hotellerie du Quebec and worked in restaurants, catering firms, and private settings.

COSTS: C$60; discounts for groups of 6 or more. Reservations are required.

LOCATION: A 19th-century greystone on the edge of Old Montreal, 30 minutes from airport.

CONTACT: Thomas Robson, Owner/Director, Maison Sanguinet Cooking School, 1711 rue Sanguinet, Montreal, QB, H2X 3G5, Canada; (514) 287-7529 (phone/fax).

MANOR CUISINE'S CREATIVE COOKING
Pointe Claire/September-June

Established in 1984, this school offers about ten 6- to 8-session beginner to advanced courses (7 levels) per year.

EMPHASIS: Techniques, creative presentation, boning and butterflying, garnishing, napkin folding, cake decorating, contemporary low fat and low cholesterol cuisine, and fruit, vegetable, and ice sculpture.

FACULTY: Ausma Groskaufmanis, B.Sc.

COSTS: C$23 to C$25 per session. No refunds.

NONVOCATIONAL/VACATION ENGLAND 235

LOCATION: Montreal.

CONTACT: Ausma Groskaufmanis, Creative Cooking, 6 Manor Crescent, Pointe Claire, QB, H9R 4S9 Canada; (514) 697-7015.

MC CALL'S SCHOOL OF CAKE DECORATION, INC.
(See page 115) **Etobicoke/September-May**

In addition to professional courses, this school offers all-day workshops and 1- to 4-session cake decorating, baking, chocolate and specialty participation courses for nonprofessionals.

COSTS: Range from C$40 to C$90 per session.

THE NATURAL FOODS COOKING SCHOOL
Montreal/Year-round

Founded in 1988, The Basics of Healthy and Inter-natural Cooking program consists of 6-session participation classes (limit 8 students) and Saturday workshops. Facilities: private kitchen with large gas stove and oven, a convenient working island. Also available: individual instruction and group classes on specific themes.

EMPHASIS: Healthy and low-fat foods, food history, ethnic cuisine, cutting techniques.

FACULTY: Founder Bonnie Tees has 10 years' experience in natural cooking. She was head cook at the Macrobiotic Institute of Switzerland and studied at The Natural Gourmet Cooking School in New York.

COSTS: C$175 for 6 sessions. C$150 is refundable after first class, C$100 after second, no refunds thereafter.

CONTACT: Bonnie Tees, The Natural Foods Cooking School, 4865 Harvard, #6, Montreal, QB, H3X 3P1, Canada; (514) 482-1508.

NEELAM KUMAR'S NORTH INDIAN CUISINE
Kirkland/January, April, September

Established in 1984, this school in a private home offers 4 six-session participation courses per year. Facilities: a 140-square-foot kitchen.

EMPHASIS: Vegetarian and non-vegetarian Indian cuisine.

FACULTY: Neelam Kumar has a university degree in Home Science.

COSTS: C$100.

LOCATION: Western Montreal.

CONTACT: Neelam Kumar, 6 Daudelin, Kirkland, QB, H9J 1L8, Canada; (514) 6974029.

SHERWOOD INN COUNTRY COOKING WEEKENDS
Port Carling/November-January, March, May

Since 1992, this country inn has offered hands-on theme weekends. Other activities: wine discussion and restaurant kitchen tour.

EMPHASIS: Italian, French, and Oriental cuisines; chocolate and sugar work, healthy eating options, Christmas menus.

FACULTY: The chefs of Sherwood Inn.

COSTS, ACCOMMODATIONS: Cost ranges from C$338 to C$427, depending on accommodation, and includes lodging, most meals, health club, mountain biking, and cross country skiing equipment in the winter.

LOCATION: The CAA/AAA 4-Diamond Sherwood Inn, a member of Romantik Hotels and Restaurants International group, is 2 hours north of Toronto.

CONTACT: Philip Meyer, General Manager, Sherwood Inn, P.O. Box 400, Port Carling, ON, P0B 1J0, Canada; (705) 765-3131; Fax (705) 765-6668.

CHAA CREEK SCHOOL OF CARIBBEAN COOKERY
Belize/May-August, October-November
Established in 1993, this jungle lodge offers 1-week hands-on cooking vacations (limit 10 participants). Facilities: the Chaa Creek hotel kitchen, which has 8 work stations. Other activities: market visits, a canoe trip, a class in a native kitchen, visits to the Mayan sites of Cahal Pech and Xunantunich, shopping in Guatemala.

EMPHASIS: Belizean, Mexican, and Caribbean cuisines.

FACULTY: Bill Altman, a chef and restaurant owner since 1972, has taught cooking in Washington and Arizona and has more than 20 years of experience with tropical cuisines.

COSTS, ACCOMMODATIONS: Cost is $1,065, which includes meals, ground transport, planned activities, and double occupancy lodging at Chaa Creek Cottages. Single supplement is $205. A $350 deposit is required with balance due 90 days prior to arrival. Full refund less $50 for cancellations 90 days prior.

LOCATION: On the Macal River, 8 miles from San Ignacio, in western Belize

CONTACT: Chef Bill Altman, Food & Beverage Dept., Chaa Creek School of Caribbean Cookery, P.O. Box 53, San Ignacio, Belize, Central America; (501) 92-2037, Fax (501) 92-2501.

ENGLAND

ACORN ACTIVITIES
Herefordshire/April, June, September, November
Established in 1989, this activity holiday provider offers a 2-day gourmet cooking course (limit 12 students). Facilities: a well-equipped kitchen with individual work areas and cookers. Also available: study tours, courses, and programs relating to air sports, water sports, ball sports, horseback riding, hunting, shooting, falconry, fishing, motor sports, arts & crafts, music, and languages.

EMPHASIS: Low-fat gourmet cooking.

FACULTY: A professional chef who has appeared on the BBC2 Food and Drink program.

COSTS, ACCOMMODATIONS: Tuition is £100. Accommodations, including breakfast, range from farmhouses and cottages at £20 per night to luxury hotels at £95 per night. A £20 deposit is required with balance due/refund granted 60 days prior.

LOCATION: Herefordshire, near the Welsh border, 120 miles (3 hours by train) west of London.

CONTACT: Acorn Activities, P.O. Box 120, Hereford, HR4 8YB, England; (44) 1432-830083, Fax (44) 1432-830110.

AGA WORKSHOP
Buckinghamshire/Year-round except August and December
This school in a private residence offers about 50 one and two-day Aga demonstration workshops (limit 20 students) per year. Facilities: the kitchen of Watercroft, Mary Berry's home.

EMPHASIS: Using the Aga cooker for grilling and frying, saving fuel, fresh herbs and vegetables, entertaining and holiday cookery, specialized equipment.

FACULTY: Mary Berry studied at the Paris Cordon Bleu and the Bath College of Home Economics and has a City and Guilds teaching qualification. Author of 20 cookery books, she was cookery editor of *Ideal Home Magazine*, is a contributor to *Family Circle*, and has had television programs.

COSTS, ACCOMMODATIONS: One-day (two-day) workshop is £76 (£146), which includes lunch and VAT. Group bookings of 4 or more for 1 day are £71 per person. Payment with booking is required; refund with 4 weeks notice. A list of nearby bed and breakfasts is provided.

LOCATION: Watercroft, situated on 3 acres of informal garden, is 30 miles from London and Heathrow airport, accessible by railway from London Marylebone.

CONTACT: Mary Berry, Aga Workshop, Watercroft, Church Rd., Penn, Buckinghamshire, HP10 8NX, England; (44) 49481-6535 (phone/fax).

THE BATH SCHOOL OF COOKERY
Bath, Avon/Year-round

Established in 1988 in Bassett House, an 18th-century country house, this private school offers over thirty 1-day, weekend, 4-day, and 4-week demonstration and participation courses (limit 10 students) per year. Facilities: a large kitchen equipped with Aga cookers, microwaves, and modern appliances and a smaller kitchen for vegetable/salad preparation, pastry, and chocolate work.

EMPHASIS: Everyday French, basic to advanced food preparation and technique, creative cuisine, seasonal, holiday, and special occasion dishes, ethnic menus.

FACULTY: Sallie Caldwell studied in France and the Far East, operated a catering firm and restaurant in Bath, and was principal teacher of a cookery school.

COSTS, ACCOMMODATIONS: Resident (non-resident) tuition, which includes meals, is £420 (£360) for the 4-day courses, £1,490 (£1,290) for the 4-week Master Course; day demonstrations are £55 each. Deposit (£150 for 4-week course, £50 for others) is required with balance due/refund granted 6 weeks prior. Bassett House is situated on 6 acres in a woodland setting with a 2-acre herb, fruit, and vegetable garden.

LOCATION: A 70-minute train ride from London.

CONTACT: D.K.S. Caldwell, Director, The Bath School of Cookery, Bassett House, Claverton, Bath, Avon, BA2 7BL, England; (44) 225-722498.

BONNE BOUCHE/GLOBAL GOURMET
West Country/Year-round

Established in 1987, Bonne Bouche offers week-long hands-on cooking courses and gourmet tours (limit 6 students) that include dining at private manors and Michelin-starred restaurants as well as other related food activity. Also available: customized programs for one day or more. The Global Gourmet offers 2- to 10-day food, wine, and cooking courses in Europe, Asia and elsewhere.

EMPHASIS: Classical, regional, and modern cuisines of European and Asian countries.

FACULTY: Anne Nicholls, of Flemish heritage, worked with Michelin-star chef Michel Brunneau at La Bourride in Caen; Sonia Stevenson and cookery writer Sri-Owen.

COSTS, ACCOMMODATIONS: Range from £95 to £1,200 and include single or double lodging at Bonne Bouche's 16th-century Devon longhouse and meals. Overseas tours range from £200 to £2,000, including lodging, meals, and some transportation.

CONTACT: Anne or Gerald Nicholls, Lower Beers House, Brithem Bottom, Cullompton, Devon, EX15 1NB, England; (44) 1884-32257 (phone/fax).

CAROLINE HOLMES — HERBS
Suffolk/Year-round

Established in 1983, Caroline Holmes offers 1-day demonstration (limit 16 students) courses and 1-week tours that visit local food producers and herb gardens in Northern France and the Loire Valley.

EMPHASIS: Growing, maintaining, and using herbs.

FACULTY: Caroline Holmes holds a Certificate in Gourmet Cookery and City and Guilds Horticulture. She works with the Museum of Garden History, Hintlesham Hall, *Historic Garden* magazine, and organizes seminars for the Council of the Herb Society.

COSTS, ACCOMMODATIONS: One-day courses begin at £35; 1-week courses, U.K.-based, from £100 and accommodation costs begin at £20 per night; French-based from £330 including accommodations.

LOCATION: London, Ipswich, Scotland, and France

CONTACT: Caroline Holmes, Denham End Farm, Bury St. Edmonds, Suffolk, IP29 5EE, England; (44) 284-810653, Fax (44) 284-850228.

CLOS DU ROY AT BOX HOUSE
Wiltshire/Spring and Fall

Since 1989, the Box House country house hotel has offered 3-day demonstration (limit 10 students) and participation (limit 6) courses. Facilities: the kitchen of the hotel's Clos du Roy restaurant.

EMPHASIS: French regional, traditional, classic, and modern cuisines.

FACULTY: Philippe Roy, chef patron of the Clos du Roy.

COSTS, ACCOMMODATIONS: Cost is £390, including double occupancy room and private bath, meals, and VAT. Full payment required and refund granted cancellations one month prior. Box House, a Georgian mansion, has a heated swimming pool and 7 acres of pastures and gardens.

LOCATION: West Country, 15 minutes from Bath and less than 2 hours from London

CONTACT: Philippe Roy, Clos du Roy, Box House, Box, Wiltshire, SN14 9NR, England; (44) 22574447, Fax (44) 225-743971.

COOKERY AT THE GRANGE
Frome, Somerset/March-April, June, September, December *(See page 118)*

In addition to its certificate program, this school offers 4 four-day and 4 to 5 weekend participation (limit 14 participants) courses per year. Facilities: main kitchen, preparation area, and walled herb garden.

EMPHASIS: European cuisine, herbs, wine appreciation.

FACULTY: Robin Witt and teaching staff.

COSTS, ACCOMMODATIONS: All-inclusive rates are £390 for the 4-day program and £235-£245 for weekend. A nonrefundable deposit of £75 (4-day) and £60 (weekend) is required.

COOKERY HOLIDAYS FOR CHILDREN
Chichester, West Sussex/August

Established in 1983 to encourage young people to learn more about food, the Young Cooks Club offers 2 five-day summer cooking and activity vacations (limit 20 students ages 11 to 16). Other activities: restaurant tour, competitions, swimming, tennis, riding, organized sports.

EMPHASIS: Breads, casseroles, roasts, stir-fry, fish, sauces, meringue, pastries.

FACULTY: Food writers Sophie Grigson, Janet Laurence, and Rosemary Moon.

COSTS, ACCOMMODATIONS: Cost of £280 includes meals, lodging in a 16th century farmhouse, planned activities, and lunch for a guest the last day of class. A £80 deposit is required, refundable only if space can be filled.

CONTACT: Anna Best, Young Cooks of Britain, Bridge Courtyard, Chichester, W. Sussex, P020 7PP, England; (44) 243-779239, Fax (44) 243784241.

THE CORDON VERT COOKERY SCHOOL
Altrincham, Cheshire/Year-round *(See also page 119)*

The Vegetarian Society UK, a registered charity and membership organization, offers demonstration (limit 14) and participation (limit 12) courses that include four 1-week Foundation Courses leading to the Cordon Vert Diploma; weekend courses on specific topics; 1-day demonstrations, and one 4-day professional course leading to the Professional Cordon Vert Diploma.

EMPHASIS: Basic and advanced techniques of vegetarian cookery; international cuisines; puff pastries, garnishes, and breads; exotic ingredients.

FACULTY: Sarah Brown began the courses in 1982, based on her BBC-TV series, *Vegetarian Kitchen*. Tutors include Ursula Ferrigno, Rachel Tyldsley, Lyn Weller, Deborah Clarke, Jane Coleman, and Jane Billinge.

COSTS: Range from £255 nonresident (£315 resident)-£260 (£320) for Foundation Courses, from £150 (£180)-£160 (£190) for weekend courses; professional courses are £420; 1-day classes are £45. Resident tuition includes full board and lodging in twin-bedded rooms in the school's Lodge. A nonrefundable deposit is required; balance due 5 weeks prior. Credit cards accepted.

LOCATION: Ten miles south of Manchester

CONTACT: Heather Mairs, The Cordon Vert Cookery School, The Vegetarian Society, Parkdale, Dunham Rd., Altrincham, Cheshire, WA14 4QG, England; (44) 161-928-0793; Fax (44) 161-926-9182.

THE CREATIVE COOKERY SCHOOL AT OLD HALL LEISURE
Chester/Year-round except January

Established in 1990, this school in a renovated turn-of-the-century farmhouse offers 1-day and once monthly 3-day weekend mainly demonstration courses (limit 10 students). Facilities: the well-equipped teaching kitchen of Old Hall Leisure. Also available: clay pigeon shooting, swimming, tennis, golf, classes for youngsters, wine instruction, private classes, market visits.

EMPHASIS: Mediterranean, Thai, and Indian cuisines.

FACULTY: Su Bloomberg graduated from the California Culinary Academy and worked in several restaurants, including her own in St. Annes on Sea. Guest chefs include Italian vegetarian food writer Ursula Ferrigano.

COSTS, ACCOMMODATIONS: Tuition, which includes VAT, is £43 for the 1-day class, £115 for the weekend course, which includes meals, exercise classes, and use of facilities. Nightly lodging at Old Hall Leisure ranges from £25-£50, including VAT. All rooms have en-suite shower or bath. Amenities include indoor and outdoor pools, tennis courts, gymnasium, therapy center, beauty spa, and Cafe-Bar. Full payment required with booking.

LOCATION: The Cheshire countryside, less than 5 minutes from Chester and 30 minutes from Manchester airport.

CONTACT: Su Bloomberg, The Creative Cookery School at Old Hall Leisure, Aldford Rd., Huntington, Chester, CH3 6EA, England; (44) 1244-350873, Fax (44) 1244-313785.

THE EARNLEY CONCOURSE
Chichester, Sussex/Year-round

Established in 1975 by the Earnley Trust, Ltd., an educational charity founded in 1951, this residential center for courses and conferences offers about 15 weekend demonstration and participation courses (limit 12 students) annually. Facilities: the center's fully-equipped kitchen workshop, which has demonstration and dining areas.

EMPHASIS: Indian and Chinese cookery, cooking for health, vegetarian dishes, advanced techniques, special occasion dishes.

FACULTY: Includes Savita Burke, Deh-Ta Hsiung, Steven Page, and Mary Whiting.

COSTS, ACCOMMODATIONS: Each course is priced from £135, which includes lodging, meals, and VAT. Nonresident tuition is £94, which includes lunch and VAT. The cost of ingredients is additional. Amenities include arts and crafts studios, computer room, heated pool, squash court, and gardens. A deposit is required with balance due 28 days prior; cancellations 28 days prior receive 50% deposit refund.

LOCATION: A rural setting in West Sussex, 6 miles south of Chichester.

CONTACT: The Earnley Concourse, Earnley, Chichester, Sussex, PO20 7JL, England; (44) 1243 670392, Fax (44) 1243 670831.

FRANCES KITCHIN COOKERY SCHOOL
Somerset/January -December

Founded in 1987, this school in a private home offers demonstration (limit 10 students) courses each month and a 3-day Cooking and Candlelit Dinners course. Facilities: large kitchen in a country house. Also available: flower arranging courses, color and style, summer tours to France.

EMPHASIS: English, French, Italian, and Indian cuisine.

FACULTY: Frances Kitchin, a qualified home economist and chef who has lectured at Strode College for 21 years, is a freelance writer and author of 2 cookbooks, and has a weekly cookery spot on radio.

COSTS, ACCOMMODATIONS: Cooking and Candlelit Dinners are £210, including breakfasts, dinners and lodging. A nonrefundable £50 deposit is required. Day courses are £20, including lunch.

LOCATION: Stoney Mead, a country house, is 12 miles from Taunton, on the railway line from Paddington (London).

CONTACT: Frances Kitchin, Stoney Mead, Curry Rivel, Langport, Somerset, TA10 0HW, England; (44) 1458-251203 (phone/fax).

HINTLESHAM HALL
Suffolk/Year-round

This luxury country hotel offers approximately 20 demonstration classes (limit 12 students) a year.

EMPHASIS: Vegetarian and fish dishes, seasonal menus, herb cookery, sugarcraft, specific topics.

FACULTY: Hintlesham's Chef Alan Ford and guest instructors.

COSTS, ACCOMMODATIONS: Each class is £48. Nightly lodging, which includes continental breakfast and VAT, begins at £85 single, £110 double occupancy. Credit cards accepted. Hintlesham Hall, built in the 16th century and situated on 175 acres, was refurbished in the 1990's to create 33 bedrooms and suites. Amenities include an 18-hole golf course, tennis, snooker, trout fishing, clay pigeon shooting, horseback riding, pool, and spa.

LOCATION: About five miles west of Ipswich, Suffolk, an hour drive from Stansted Airport, and an hour train ride from London.

CONTACT: Claire Hills, Hintlesham Hall Ltd., Hintlesham, Ipswich, Suffolk, IP8 3NS, England; (44) 473-652334 or (44) 473-652268, Fax (44) 473-652463.

JILL PROBERT'S COOKERY DEMONSTRATION COURSES
Cheshire/Spring and Fall

Since 1983, this school in a private residence has offered 6-session intermediate and advanced courses (limit 14). Facilities: a 17th century farmhouse kitchen.

EMPHASIS: Dinner party/freezer cookery and food processor techniques.

FACULTY: Jill Probert, a magazine and newspaper food editor, is a member of the Guild of Food Writers and the Institute of Home Economics.

COSTS: Each course is £38.

LOCATION: On the Welsh border, 2 miles from Chester.

CONTACT: Jill Probert, Bretton Hall, Chester, Cheshire, CH4 ODF, England; (44) 244-660209.

KEN LO'S MEMORIES OF CHINA CHINESE COOKERY SCHOOL
London/Year-round

This school, an extension of the Memories of China restaurant, offers several 4- to 10-session demonstration courses (limit 18 students).

EMPHASIS: Chinese cuisine, including ingredients, timing and heat control, cutting techniques, blending of textures, colors, and shapes, and menu creation.

FACULTY: Kenneth Lo was author of 36 books on Chinese cooking;. Instructors include Chef Kam-Po But of the Memories of China restaurant; cookbook author Terry Tan; and Mr. Deh-Ta Hsiung.

COSTS: Range from £15-£23 per session. A £15 deposit is required; refund with 2 days notice.

NONVOCATIONAL/VACATION **ENGLAND** **241**

Location: The basement beneath the reataurant's Chinese grocery shop,

Contact: Memories of China Cookery School, Ken Lo's Kitchen, 14 Eccleston St., London, SW1, England; (44) 71-730-4276/7734.

LA CUISINE IMAGINAIRE VEGETARIAN COOKERY SCHOOL
Hertfordshire/Year-round

Founded in 1989, this school offers one- and half-day demonstration courses (limit 12 students) and a four-day practical certificate course (limit 6). Facilities: a well-equipped kitchen and lounge in St. Albans. Also available: private instruction.

Emphasis: Vegetarian cuisine, including quick meals, dinner parties, international dishes.

Faculty: Director and instructor Roselyne Masselin is a food writer, cookbook author, qualified home economist, and runs Catering Imaginaire.

Costs: One-day London course is £50, half-day St. Albans course is £30, four-day course is £330; all include lunch and notes. Full payment is required for short courses, deposit for four-day courses; cancellations receive course credit where possible.

Location: Shepherds Bush in London; St. Albans, Hertfordshire, 30 minutes from Heathrow airport and central London

Contact: Roselyne Masselin, La Cuisine Imaginaire Cookery School, 18 Belmont Ct., Belmont Hill, St. Albans, Hertfordshire, AL1 1RB, England; (44) 727 837643, Fax (44) 727-847646.

LA PETITE CUISINE
London/Year-round

Founded in 1977, this school offers twice-monthly demonstrations. Facilities: a small theatre in Divertimenti cookware store. Also available: private hands-on 5-lesson sessions in Lyn Hall's home teaching kitchen.

Emphasis: Modern gourmet cuisine, French, Italian, Chinese, Thai, guest chef specialties.

Faculty: Owner Lyn Hall, BA, MFCA holds certificates in wine, bread, cake decorating, and butchery, and is an Olympic Culinary Gold Medalist. Guest chefs include British cookbook writers and TV chefs.

Costs: Private classes are £80 per lesson for five sessions, or £40 per hour. Demonstrations are £24.

Location: South Kensington in French London; Divertimenti, 139 Fulham Road, Chelsea, London SW3 6SD; (44) 71-581-8065, Fax (44) 71-823-9429

Contact: Mrs. Lyn Hall, 21 Queen's Gate Terrace, London SW7 5PR; (44) 71-5846841, Fax (44) 71-225-0169.

LE CORDON BLEU
London/Year-round
(See page 120)

In addition to the certificate and diploma courses, courses for all levels include A Taste of Le Cordon Bleu and Patisserie a la Carte (each 5 days), Cuisine Legere and Boulangerie (each 4 days), and A Taste of France (3 days). Also available: Saturday workshop series for children, evening entertaining and bachelor's courses, guest chef demonstrations.

Costs: Tuition ranges from £180 to £385 for short courses, payable in full with registration and refundable (less 10%) 4 weeks prior.

LEITH'S SCHOOL OF FOOD AND WINE, LTD.
London/Year-round

This career school offers nonprofessionals the Basic Certificate in Food and Wine participation course, 10-session beginner and advanced participation evening courses, Saturday demonstrations, a 10-session Advanced Certificate in Wine course, and specialty wine classes.

Costs: Basic Certificate course is £1,270, 10-session courses are £310-£320, demonstrations are £40, Advanced Certificate in Wine course is £400.

THE MANOR SCHOOL OF FINE CUISINE
Widmerpool, Nottinghamshire/Year-round

In addition to its certificate course, this school offers a 5-day Foundation course, a 4-day Entertaining course, theme weekends, and day and evening courses. Also available: water sports, clay pigeon, shooting, horseback riding, golf.

EMPHASIS: Healthy eating, holiday cookery, seasonal menus, Aga cookery, specific topics.

COSTS, ACCOMMODATIONS: The Foundation course (nonresident) is £340.75 (£293.75), Entertaining course £329 (£282), weekends are £130. All prices are inclusive of VAT. Lodging is at the manor. A nonrefundable deposit of £50 is required with balance due/refund granted 6 weeks prior.

MILLER HOWE COOKERY COURSES
Cumbria/Spring and Fall

Founded in 1971, this country house and school offers residential 5-day courses (limit 15 students). Facilities: the main restaurant kitchen.

EMPHASIS: Fresh ingredients, starters, main courses, sweets, tea accompaniments, sauces, garnishes.

FACULTY: Miller Howe chef-proprietor John Tovey, a graduate of Le Cordon Bleu, cookbook author, and TV chef.

COSTS, ACCOMMODATIONS: All-inclusive cost is £400 (includes VAT). Refund for cancellation only if space is filled. Miller Howe, an Edwardian country house, has three lounges, a conservatory overlooking the lake, and 13 centrally-heated private bedrooms. Credit cards accepted.

LOCATION: In The Lakes district above Lake Windermere near the Langdale Pikes and accessible to London by train

CONTACT: John J. Tovey, Chef Patron, Miller Howe, Windermere, The English Lakes, Cumbria, LA23 1EY, England; (44) 5394-42536.

RAYMOND BLANC'S LE PETIT BLANC ECOLE DE CUISINE
Oxford/October-April

Established in 1991 in a 15th century Cotswold manor house, this 5-day cooking vacation school (limit 8 participants) is offered as a beginner course 12 times yearly and as an intermediate course 8-10 times a year. Facilities: individual work areas in the restaurant kitchen.

EMPHASIS: Contemporary French cuisine, including appetizers, fish and vegetables, meat and vegetables, pastries.

FACULTY: Chef Raymond Blanc owns and operates Le Manoir. Sessions are taught by head chef Clive Fretwell.

COSTS: Course cost of £1,150 includes all meals, service, VAT, and lodging at Le Manoir aux Quat' Saisons, which has the highest classification of Relais & Chateaux. Lodging is free for non-cooking guests. A £150 deposit is required with balance due four weeks priorNo refunds unless space can be filled.

LOCATION: Seven miles from Oxford and 40 miles from London.

CONTACT: Le Petit Blanc, Ecole de Cuisine, Blanc Restaurants Ltd., Church Rd., Great Milton, Oxford, OX44 7PD, England; (44) 844 278881, Fax (44) 844 278847. In U.S., **CONTACT:** Judy Ebrey, P.O. Box 25228, Dallas, TX 75225; (214) 373-1161, Fax (214) 373-1162. E-Mail: CuisineInt@aol.com

SQUIRES KITCHEN SUGARCRAFT SCHOOL OF CAKE DECORATING
Surrey/Year-round

This school offers 1-hour to 3-day demonstration (limit 35 students) and participation (limit 12 students) courses. Facilities: teaching kitchen with specialized equipment. Also available: children's courses, private classes, customized courses for groups.

COSTS: Range from £20-£40 per session. A 25% deposit is required.

TANTE MARIE SCHOOL OF COOKERY
(See page 122) — **Surrey/Year-round**

In addition to its diploma courses, this school offers a 12-week certificate course thrice yearly that includes demonstration (limit 36 students) and participation (limit 12) classes. Facilities: 10,000 sq. ft. cookery school with 5 kitchens, each accommodating 12 students. Also available: 3- to 5-day participation courses, 1-day theme demonstrations, private group demonstrations.

EMPHASIS: Basic and advanced skills, wine appreciation, specific subjects.

COSTS: Certificate program is £2,600. A £250 transferable but nonrefundable booking fee is required.

EUROPE

THE ANNEMARIE VICTORY ORGANIZATION, INC.
(See page 253) — **Europe/Year-round**

Since 1978, this travel company has conducted and represented deluxe culinary tours and cooking school programs to France and Italy (Provence Cooking School at Chateau de la Messardiere in St. Tropez, A Gourmet Experience at the Hotel Ritz in Paris, The Italian Art of Eating with Faith Willinger at La Posta Vecchia, Ruffino's Tuscan Experience).

EMPHASIS: Deluxe culinary travel programs.

FACULTY: Austrian-born Annemarie Victory studied at the Sorbonne, attended the hotel and interpreter school in Switzerland, and currently hosts the Discovery Channel's TV series, *World Class Cuisine*.

LOCATION: Europe, including France, Italy, Belgium, Austria, Switzerland, Ireland.

CONTACT: The Annemarie Victory Organization, Inc., 136 E. 64th St., New York, NY 10021; (212) 486-0353, Fax (212) 751-3149.

CAPITAL TOURS LTD.
Italy and France/Spring and Fall

This tour operator offers monthly 5-day cooking vacations (limit 15 participants) that feature market visits and daily hands-on classes in restaurant kitchens.

EMPHASIS: Regional cooking of Tuscany, Umbria, and the Cote d'Azur.

FACULTY: Restaurant chefs.

COSTS, ACCOMMODATIONS: The cost of $3,000 includes airfare from Toronto, Montreal, or Ottawa.

LOCATION: In Italy: Florence and Rome. In France: Nice.

CONTACT: Carlo Bertasi, Capital Tours Ltd., 427 Preston St., #204, Ottawa, ON, K1S 4N3, Canada; (613) 230-1955, Fax (613) 230-8811.

EUROPEAN CULINARY ADVENTURES
Gascony and Tuscany/Spring, Summer, Fall

Since 1987, Kate Ratliffe has conducted culinary travel programs to Europe and now offers week-long cooks tours to the Southwest of France and Tuscany and Umbria. Facilities: farmhouse kitchens. Other activities: visits to markets, villas, foie gras farms, Armagnac and wine cellars, and fine restaurants.

EMPHASIS: Regional country cooking of Gascony and Tuscany.

FACULTY: Kate Ratliffe, owner/chef of the luxury canal barge, the *Julia Hoyt*, has lived and worked in Europe since 1987 and is author of *A Culinary Journey in Gascony*; local chefs, restaurateurs, and food producers.

COSTS: Land cost is $2,250 per person for Gascony, which includes double occupancy lodging in a 3-star hotel, meals, and planned activities.

LOCATION: The Duchy of Gascony, an area of southwestern France between Bordeaux and Toulouse. Participants are met in Agen, a 4-hour train ride from Paris. Italian tours are based near Cortona and explore the hill towns of southern Tuscany and Umbria. Participants arrive by train from Florence or Rome.

CONTACT: Kate Ratliffe, European Culinary Adventures, 5 Ledgewood Way, #6, Peabody, MA 01960; (800) 852-2625 or (508) 535-5738.

SARA MONICK CULINARY TOURS
France, Italy, Spain/Spring, Fall

Since 1986, Sara Monick has conducted 5- to 11-day hands-on culinary tours (limit 8-14 participants) in France (Hostellerie de Crillon le Brave in Provence), Spain (Madrid and the South of Spain), and Italy (Hotel Le Sirenuse). Other activities: visits to markets, food producers, wineries, and private homes and gardens; dining at fine restaurants; sightseeing; language classes.

EMPHASIS: French, Italian, and Spanish cuisines.

FACULTY: Sara Monick, a cooking instructor since 1977 and Certified Member of the IACP, owns The Cookery in Minneapolis. She studied with Madeleine Kamman, Jacques Pepin, Nicholas Malgieri, and Giuliano Bugialli. Tour classes are taught by local and guest chefs and teachers.

COSTS, ACCOMMODATIONS: Cost, which includes double occupancy lodging, most meals, and planned excursions, ranges from $2,300-$4,000. A $500 deposit is required; cancellation penalty ranges from $50 (60 days prior) to $500 (less than 45 days prior). No refunds within 7 days

CONTACT: Sara Monick or Diane Hilliard, Hilliard & Olander, Ltd., 608 Second Avenue South, Minneapolis, MN 55402; (612) 374-2444 or 333-1440 or (800) 2298407, Fax (612) 333-3554.

TRAVEL CONCEPTS
Europe/Year-round

Founded in 1982, this travel company specializes in customized European culinary and wine tours for groups, including Champagne and Cuisine With Mrs. Charles Heidsieck, An Irish Gourmet Experience, and The Swiss Gourmet Experience.

EMPHASIS: Culinary and wine travel programs.

COSTS: Group rates vary. Some programs can accommodate individuals who are not members of the group.

LOCATION: The Loire Valley, northern France, northern Burgundy, northern Italy, England, Ireland, and Switzerland.

CONTACT: Dr. Patricia A. McNally, Director, Travel Concepts, 62 Commonwealth Ave., #3, Boston, MA 02116; (617) 266-8450, Fax (617) 267-2477.

THE WANDERING SPOON
Greece and Portugal/Spring and Fall

Since 1983, Lucille Haley Schechter has conducted 1-week hands-on culinary programs (limit 10 participants) for private groups. Other activities: dining in fine restaurants, visits to markets, vineyards, and cultural centers.

EMPHASIS: Mediterranean and international cooking techniques

FACULTY: Former *Harper's Bazaar* magazine editor Lucille Haley Schechter is co-author of *The International Menu Diabetic Cookbook* and is a Professional Member of the James Beard Foundation.

COSTS, ACCOMMODATIONS: One-week session, excluding airfare, is $1,990, double occupancy. Students often are housed in deluxe Mediterranean hotels.

LOCATION: Greece and Portugal, including Crete, Corfu, Santorini, and the Algarve.

CONTACT: Lucille Haley Schechter, The Wandering Spoon, 340 E. 57th St., New York, NY 10022; (212) 751-4532, Fax (212) 753-1714.

FRANCE

ANDRE DAGUIN HOTEL DE FRANCE
Gascogne/October-April

Established in 1985, this hotel offers 3-day to 2-week courses (limit 6 students). Facilities: the hotel's restaurant kitchen. Other activities: a tour of the Armagnac region with visits to wine cellars, a foie gras duck farm, and a farmer's market.

EMPHASIS: The cuisine of Gascony; foie gras, confit de canard, and other duck preparations.

FACULTY: Includes J. Francois Leclerc, under supervision of Chef Andre Daguin, proprietor.

COSTS, ACCOMMODATIONS: Fee, which includes meals and hotel lodging, is approximately 2,850 FF for 3 days. A 25% deposit is required with balance due 3 weeks prior. Credit cards accepted.

LOCATION: Auch en Gascogne.

CONTACT: Andre Daguin, Hotel de France, Place de la Liberation, 32000 Auch en Gascogne, France; (33) 62-05-00-44, Fax (33) 62-05-88-44.

AT HOME WITH PATRICIA WELLS: COOKING IN PROVENCE
Provence/May, June, September

Established in 1995 by American journalist and author Patricia Wells, these five-day cooking vacations (limit 6 participants) feature four hours of daily hands-on instruction in her 18th-century farmhouse kitchen, which has a wood-fired bread oven. Other activities: visits to local markets, wine tastings, dinner at a fine restaurant.

EMPHASIS: Provencal cuisine.

FACULTY: Patricia Wells has lived in France since 1980, is restaurant critic of *The International Herald Tribune*, and authored five books, including *Bistro Cooking* and *Simply French*.

COSTS, ACCOMMODATIONS: Fee is $2,500 ($2,000 for non-cooks), which includes most meals and planned activities. A $400 deposit is required; balance is due 90 days prior. A list of recommended lodging is supplied.

LOCATION: Ms. Wells' hilltop home is just outside Vaison-la-Romaine, about 30 miles northeast of Avignon.

CONTACT: Patricia Wells, Cooking in Provence, 18, Rue Daru, Paris,75008, France; (33) 1-42-27-43-40, Fax (33) 1-42-67-53-52.

THE CHATEAU COUNTRY COOKING SCHOOL
Montbazon-en-Touraine/Spring and Fall

Since 1986, Denise Olivereau-Capron and her son, Xavier, have hosted 6-day participation courses (limit 15 participants). Facilities: the chateau's renovated L'Orangerie restaurant. Other activities: dining at fine restaurants and visits to the Tours flower market, the chateaux of the region, a goat cheese farm, the Chinon markets, and the caves of Vouvray.

EMPHASIS: French regional cuisine.

FACULTY: Chef Edouard Wehrlin.

COSTS, ACCOMMODATIONS: Course fee of 14,000 FF single, 13,500 FF double, includes chateau lodging, meals, wine tastings, and planned excursions.

LOCATION: Le Domaine de la Tortiniere, a 19th century manor-house chateau, is in the Loire Valley.

CONTACT: Mme. Denise Olivereau-Capron, Le Domaine de le Tortiniere, 37250 Montbazon-en-Touraine, France; (33) 47-26-00-19, Fax (33) 47-65-95-70 or Sara Monick, The Cookery, 4215 Poplar Dr., Minneapolis, MN 55422; (612) 374-2444, Fax (612) 333-3554.

COOKERY LESSONS AND TOURAINE VISIT
Brehemont/Spring and Fall

Established in 1983 by Maxime and Eliane Rochereau and scheduled six times a year, these one-week hands-on vacation programs (limit 15 participants) in the 18th-century Le Castel de Bray et Monts feature three hours of instruction daily. Facilities: the manor's restaurant kitchen. Other activities: visits to chateaux, wineries, pastry shops, sightseeing, shopping.

EMPHASIS: French cuisine.

FACULTY: Chef Maxime Rochereau, who was chef at the Ritz Hotel in Paris.

COSTS, ACCOMMODATIONS: Cost is 5,800 FF (10% discount for a couple), including lodging at the manor, meals, and planned activities. A $150 deposit is required; refund with 30 days notice.

LOCATION: A vineyard village on the Loire River in the chateau region, 16 miles from Tours and a one-hour train ride from Paris.

CONTACT: Maxime Rochereau, Cookery Lessons and Touraine Visit, Le Castel de Bray et Monts, Brehemont, Langeais, 37130 France; (33) 47-96-70-47 or (33) 47-96-63-98, Fax (33) 47-96-57-36.

COOKING AT THE ABBEY
Salon-de-Provence/March-April, November-December

Started in 1987, the Hostellerie Abbaye de Sainte Croix resort offers 3-, 4-, and 7-day vacation participation courses (limit 12 students). Facilities: the restaurant kitchen, which has 4 ovens and 12 work stations. Other activities: local sightseeing and vineyard visits.

EMPHASIS: Provencal cuisine.

FACULTY: Chef P. Morel of the Abbaye's Michelin 1-star restaurant.

COSTS, ACCOMMODATIONS: Cost (single supplement) ranges from 3,495 FF (365 FF) for 3 days to 9,700 FF (1,500 FF) for 7 days, which includes most meals, lodging, and planned activities.

LOCATION: The Abbaye, a member of Relais & Chateaux, is 2 miles from Salon, 20 miles northeast of the nearest airport, and 20 miles west of Aix-en-Provence

CONTACT: Cooking at the Abbey, Host. Abbaye de Ste. Croix, Rte. du Val de Cuech, 13300 Salon-de-Provence, France; (33) 90-56-24-55, Fax (33) 90-56-3112.

COOKING WITH FRIENDS IN FRANCE
Chateauneuf de Grasse/Year-round *(See display ad page 247)*

Established in 1993 on the property once shared by Julia Child and Simone Beck, this vacation school offers 28-30 six-day participation courses (limit 8 students) per year. Other activities: visits to the Forville Market, a butcher shop, cheese ripener, cutlery shop, and Michelin 2-star restaurant kitchens; demonstration by a French chef.

EMPHASIS: French cuisine, including techniques, tricks, menu-planning, lighter dishes.

FACULTY: Proprietor/instructor Kathie Alex apprenticed at Roger Verge's Le Moulin de Mougins, assisted well-known chefs at the Robert Mondavi Winery, studied catering at Ecole Lenotre, and studied with and assisted Simone Beck at her school.

COSTS, ACCOMMODATIONS: Cost is $1,850, which includes double occupancy lodging (some private baths), breakfasts and lunches, wine tastings, and planned excursions (car required). A $450 deposit is required and $375 is refunded for cancellations 90 days prior. Students stay in either La Pitchoune or La Campanette, private homes originally owned by Julia Child and Simone Beck. Golf and horseback riding are nearby.

LOCATION: On the Cote d'Azur, about 9 miles from Cannes, 4 miles from Grasse, and 20 miles from Nice International Airport.

NONVOCATIONAL/VACATION — FRANCE

CONTACT: Kathie Alex, Cooking with Friends in France, La Pitchoune, Domaine de Bramafam, Chateauneuf de Grasse, 06740, France; (33) 93-60-10-56 (phone/fax). For brochure: Jackson & Co., 29 Commonwealth Ave., Boston, MA 02116; (617) 350-3837, Fax (617) 247-6149.

cooking with friends in F R A N C E

Come cook with us in Julia Child's Provence kitchen! This weeklong cultural immersion includes classes in English given by French chefs, most meals, market/village tours, restaurant visits, and accommodations. Afternoons free to explore the French Riviera.

United States: (617) 350.3837   **France:** (33) 93.60.10.56

COOKING WITH THE MASTERS
Bouilland and Tecomah/Fall, Winter, Spring

Established in 1990, Michel Bouit organizes six 1- to 4-week participation programs (limit 15 students) per session. Facilities: full service restaurant/hotel kitchens. Other activities: excursions to local artisans, markets, and vineyards; sightseeing and shopping in Paris.

EMPHASIS: Classical and regional French cuisine, culinary terms and service, industry-related visits, customized tours.

FACULTY: Jean-Pierre Silva, chef-proprietor of Le Vieux Moulin; Alain LeCourtois, director of Tecomah; 1989 ACF National Chef of the Year Michel Bouit, CEC, AAC, president of MBI Inc., specializing in culinary tours, competitions, consulting, and public relations.

COSTS, ACCOMMODATIONS: Course fee of $2,550 includes airfare, lodging, ground transport, most meals, and excursions; single supplement is $200. Deposit is 50%, balance is due 60 days prior to departure, $100 penalty for cancellation 30 days prior. Credit cards accepted.

LOCATION: Le Vieux Moulin, Bouilland, 9 miles from the 15th century city of Beaune, wine capitol of Burgundy. Tecomah, Jouy-en-Josas, a suburb of Paris

CONTACT: Michel Bouit, President, MBI, Inc., P.O. Box 1801, Chicago, IL 60690; (312) 663-5701, Fax (312) 663-5702.

COOKING IN PROVENCE
Crillon le Brave/March, April, November

Since 1992, Hostellerie de Crillon le Brave has sponsored five 6-day cooking vacations (limit 8 participants) a year. Classes are hands-on with preparation of a complete menu. Facilities: the hotel's restaurant kitchen. Other activities: market visits, winery tour, visits to Avignon and other Provence sites, dining at the hotel and fine restaurants, golf, tennis, cycling, hiking.

EMPHASIS: Provencal and Mediterranean cuisine.

FACULTY: Chef de Cuisine Philippe Monti, a native of Provence, trained at Pic, l'Esperance, Auberge de l'Ill, and Taillevent.

COSTS, ACCOMMODATIONS: Cost is $2,500 ($2,800), which includes meals, double (single) occupancy lodging at Hostellerie de Crillon le Brave, and planned excursions; supplement for noncooking partners is $850. An $800 deposit is required, refundable 60 days in advance.

LOCATION: Hostellerie de Crillon le Brave, a member of Relais & Chateaux and named "Country House Hotel of the Year" in 1992 by Andrew Harper's Hideaway Report, is at the foot of Mont Ventoux, about 25 miles from Avignon and 30 minutes from the antique center of Provence.

CONTACT: Craig Miller, Hostellerie de Crillon le Brave, Place de l'Eglise, 84410 Crillon le Brave, France; (33) 9065-61-61, Fax (33) 90-65-62-86.

COOKING IN PROVENCE
Provence/Spring and Fall

Travel agent Cathy Kinloch offers 12 one-week cooking vacations (limit 8 participants) per year. In addition to 4 hours of daily hands-on instruction, activities include visits to markets and wineries.

EMPHASIS: Provencal cuisine.

FACULTY: Chef Sylvie L'Allemande.

COSTS, ACCOMMODATIONS: Cost: 2,400 FF, including meals and lodging. A 25% deposit is required.

LOCATION: One hour from Avignon.

CONTACT: Cathy Kinloch, Cooking in Provence, Teachers' Travel Service, Ltd., 21 St. Clair Ave. E., #1003, Toronto, ON, M4T 1L9, Canada; (800) 268-7229 or (416) 922-2232, Fax (416) 922-8410.

CUISINIERES DU MONDE
Chavagnac/Year-round

Daniele Delpeuch conducts 1 and 2-week participation courses (limit 7 students) year-round and Foie Gras and Truffles Weekends during the winter. Facilities: Ms. Delpeuch's 16th-century stone farmhouse. Other activities: visits to the market, neighboring farms, a well-known baker, a foie gras farm, the region's prehistoric caves, and a 17th century walnut oil mill.

EMPHASIS: Traditional French cooking; duck and goose preparations.

FACULTY: Daniele Delpeuch contributed to the Time-Life *Great Meals in Minutes* series, served as guest lecturer at La Varenne, conducted workshops in the U.S., and was private chef to French president M. Francois Mitterrand. She tours as a cooking teacher and is a restaurant consultant.

COSTS, ACCOMMODATIONS: Cost, which includes meals, farmhouse lodging, and all planned activities, is approximately $2,000 per week.

LOCATION: The Perigord region, near the town of Sarlat.

CONTACT: Daniele Mazet-Delpeuch, Cuisinieres du Monde, la Borderie, 24120 Chavagnac, France; (33) 53-51-00-24, Fax (33) 53-50-53-71.

ECOLE DES ARTS CULINAIRES ET DE L'HOTELLERIE
Ecully/June, July, September
(See page 123)

In addition to career courses, this school offers four 1-week participation courses (limit 20 students) during the summer.

EMPHASIS: French cuisine and pastry, menu composition, restaurant-quality desserts and decorative accompaniments, wines.

COSTS: The 5,200 FF fee includes 3 meals daily. Residence hall lodging is 1,000 FF per week.

ECOLE DES TROIS PONTS
Roanne/June, August-October

This language school in a chateau offers three 1-week Cooking and French Courses (limit 20 guests per week, 6 students per instructor) that feature morning language classes, afternoon hands-on cooking classes, and an optional wine course. Also available: a cooking-only option (instruction in English), courses in general and intensive French, a stress management course, courses for professional florists, and a Fine Food Lover's Tour.

EMPHASIS: Provincial French cuisine and sauces; French language instruction.

COSTS, ACCOMMODATIONS: Cost ranges from 5,900 FF to 6,600 FF for Cooking and French and from 4,700 FF to 6,100 FF for the cooking only option, which includes lodging, most meals and planned excursions.

LOCATION: The 17th-century Chateau de Matel is set in 32 acres of park and woodland, 5

NONVOCATIONAL/VACATION **FRANCE**

minutes from the center of Roanne in the Burgundy/Beaujolais region, near Lyons and Vichy.

CONTACT: Mrs. O'Loan, Director, Ecole des Trois Ponts, Chateau de Matel, 42300 Roanne, France; (33) 77-71-53-00, Fax (33) 77-70-80-01. U.S. Contact; Michael Giammarella, EMI International, P.O. Box 640713, Oakland Gardens, New York 11364-0713; (718) 631-0096; Fax (718) 631-0316.

ECOLE LENOTRE
(See page 124)
This school for culinary professionals also offers 2- to 4-day gastronomy courses for amateur cooks.

EMPHASIS: Basics, regional specialties, pastries, wine and food pairing, theme menus.

COSTS: Range from 2,400 FF (1,500 FF) for French residents (non-residents) to 4,800 FF (4,000 FF).

ETOILE BLEU MARINE
La Rochelle/Spring and Fall

Established in 1991 by Maybelle Iribe, these one-week vacations (limit 8 participants) featuring 9 hours of hands-on cooking instruction are offered six times per year. Facilities: A 200-square-foot kitchen with garden. Other activities: visits to wineries, food producers, and markets, sightseeing.

EMPHASIS: Regional French cooking and seafood.

FACULTY: Emi Taya, a graduate of the University of Tokyo; restaurateurs Fred Nillson and Mirko Bettini, oenologist George Caviste.

COSTS, ACCOMMODATIONS: Cost is $2,000, which includes meals, lodging, and planned activities.

LOCATION: La Rochelle is three hours from Paris and 2 hours from the airport in Bordeaux.

CONTACT: Maybelle Iribe, Etoile Bleu Marine, 33, rue Thiers, La Rochelle, 17000, France; (33) 46-41-62-63, Fax (33) 46-41-10-76. In the U.S.: Ms. M.J. Drinkwater, Town & Country Travel, Sacramento, CA; (916) 483-4621.

FOOD IN FRANCE
Gourge/May-July, August-October

Founded in 1990, this village house offers eleven 6-day participation courses (limit 7 participants) per year. Facilities: 2 well-equipped domestic kitchens with 7 work stations. Other activities: market visits, wineries, cheese producers, and restaurants, cycling. Also available: water-color sketching.

EMPHASIS: French regional cuisine, wine appreciation.

FACULTY: Pat Cove has taught cookery courses in Adult and Further Education colleges for the Inner London Education Authority and specialized in French regional cuisines at Morley College in London; David Normand-Harris holds the advanced diploma of the Wine and Spirit Education Trust.

COSTS, ACCOMMODATIONS: £395 per person (20% less for non-participating partners) includes lodging and full board. Lodging is at Les Belles Etoiles, 2 adjoining houses in the center of the village. A 10% nonrefundable deposit is required with balance due 6 weeks prior.

LOCATION: Gourge, a rural village in the Deux Sevres, is 25 miles west of Poitiers and 185 miles southwest of Paris.

CONTACT: Pat Cove, Food in France, 14 Thorpewood Ave., London, SE26 4BX, England; (44) 181-699-3437 (phone/fax).

FRANCE AUTHENTIQUE
Domfront, Normandy/Year-round

Established in 1994, France on Your Plate is a 1-week customized vacation program (limit 8 to 10 participants) that features cooking classes in restaurant kitchens. Other activities: visits to local food producers, the copper-making center of Villedieu-les-Poeles, and the World War II landing beaches. Also available: cycling, fishing, horseback riding, swimming, tennis, and golf.

EMPHASIS: Cuisine of Normandy.

FACULTY: Prominent local chefs.

COSTS, ACCOMMODATIONS: $1,200-$2,000 per week, which includes most meals, planned activities, and lodging at La Maison de la Resistance.

LOCATION: The Normandy region, 3 hours from Paris.

CONTACT: William T. Fleming, Jr., President, France Authentique, 1413 Sandhurst Pl., W. Vancouver, BC, V7S 2P4, Canada; (604) 925-3095, Fax (604) 9261084.

FRENCH LANGUAGE AND COOKING PROGRAM
St. Malo/July

This two-week program (limit 12 participants) features 20 hours of hands-on cooking and 5 hours of French language instruction per week.

EMPHASIS: Sauces, pastries, seasonings, and wine. Language classes focus on conversation.

FACULTY: Local chefs and French language instructors.

COSTS, ACCOMMODATIONS: Cost is $2,030, which includes half-board lodging in a private home. Nonrefundable $100 registration fee is required.

LOCATION: About three hours from Paris by train.

CONTACT: Maria McDonald, Director, Lingua Service Worldwide, 216 E. 45th St., 17th Flr., New York, NY 10017; (800) 394-LEARN or (212) 867-1225, Fax (212) 867-7666.

HOLIDAYS IN THE SUN IN THE SOUTH OF FRANCE
Gordes/Spring, Fall, December

Since 1980, this school in a private country home, Les Megalithes, has offered 1-week participation courses (limit 6 participants) with instruction in English, French, and German. Facilities: indoor and outdoor home kitchen. Other activities: market visits, horseback and bicycle riding, handicraft shopping, visits to museums and historic sites

EMPHASIS: Cuisine of Provence, including appetizers, main courses, breads, jellies, holiday dishes.

FACULTY: Sylvie Lallemand, president/founder of the Association des amis de la cuisine et des traditions provencales, learned to cook from her mother and grandmother and studied with Roger Vergé.

COSTS, ACCOMMODATIONS: Tuition is 3,000 FF, which includes private room and bath at Les Megalithes, pool, and meals. A nonrefundable 200 FF deposit is required.

LOCATION: Gordes, near Avignon, a 3 -hour drive from Nice

CONTACT: Sylvie Lallemand, Les Megalithes, 84220 Gordes, France; (33) 90-72-23-41.

LA CUISINE DE MARIE BLANCHE
Paris/Year-round except August

Founded in 1976, this school (formerly Princess Ere 2001) in a private apartment offers 1- to 4-week participation courses (limit 6 to 8 participants) with instruction in French, English, or Spanish. Facilities: 300-square-foot kitchen with 6 work stations. Also available: food-related visits to museums and champagne caves in Reims.

EMPHASIS: French cuisine for at-home entertaining.

FACULTY: Marie-Blanche de Broglie, founder-director, holds the Cordon Bleu Grand Diplome and is author of *The Cuisine of Normandy*; Gerard Salle is head chef of the Michelin 1-star Plaza Athenee.

COSTS: One class is 600 FF (670 FF with Chef Salle) 10 classes are 5,000 FF and 20 classes are 9,000 FF. A 10% nonrefundable deposit is required.

LOCATION: Near the Eiffel Tower

CONTACT: Marie-Blanche de Broglie, Director, La Cuisine de Marie Blanche, 18, Av. de la Motte-Picquet, 75007 Paris, France; (33) 1-45-51-36-34, Fax (33) 145-51-90-19.

LA MIRANDE — COOKING IN PROVENCE
Avignon/Spring and Fall

Since 1994, this hotel-restaurant has offered 1- or 4-day participation courses (limit 10 participants). Facilities: restored 19th century kitchen with its original wood-fired cast-iron stove and restored counters. Other activities: daily trips to the Avignon market.

EMPHASIS: Provencal cuisine.

FACULTY: Olga Manguin, a specialist in Provencal cuisine, and Christian Etienne, Robert Brunel, Eric Coisel.

COSTS, ACCOMMODATIONS: 1,700 FF daily (6,450 FF 4 days) in double room, 2,345 FF (9,000 FF) in single room, 1,145 FF (4,100 FF) for non-cooking partner, includes breakfast and lunch. A 25% deposit is required. Cancellations 3 weeks prior forfeit 350 FF.

LOCATION: La Mirande, a period town house, is about 65 miles from Marseille international airport and 6 miles from Avignon's domestic airport.

CONTACT: Martin Stein, Creative Director, La Mirande, 4, Place de La Mirande, 84000 Avignon, France; (33) 90-85-93-93, Fax (33) 90-86-26-85.

THE ULTIMATE FOOD & WINE VACATION

Come to Burgundy, France to the Château du Feÿ, as featured on PBS. La Varenne's Visitor Programs, directed by Anne Willan include one-week summer series courses, the *French Cooking Today* series and the fall Gastronomic courses.

La Varenne

US (800) 537-6486
(202) 337-0073
France 86 63 18 34

LA VARENNE
(See page 125) (See display above) — **Burgundy/May-November**

In addition to its residential courses, La Varenne offers several 1-week programs (limit 15 participants) for cooking and wine enthusiasts. The Summer Series, held weekly June and July, features different specialties and chef-instructors each week, 5 half-day participation classes and 3 demonstrations, a wine tasting, visits to Joigny and Chablis, and dinner at a fine country restaurant. The Grand Luxe Gastronomic Course, scheduled in the fall and hosted by Anne and her husband Mark Cherniavsky, includes 4 practical classes, a master chef demonstration, 3 wine tastings, visits to a cheese producer, baker, and Chablis vineyard, and dining at two noted restaurants.

EMPHASIS: Classic, contemporary, and regional French cuisine, bistro cooking, pastry, wine appreciation, guest chef specialties.

COSTS: Fee, which includes transportation from Paris, full board, shared twin lodging at Château du Feÿ, and planned activities, is $2,795 Summer Series, $3,495 Grand Luxe. Single supplement is $400. Full payment is required; cancellations more than 90 days prior forfeit $100.

(See page 49) — **L'ACADEMIE DE CUISINE**

LE CORDON BLEU
(See page 126) — **Paris/Year-round**

In addition to the Cuisine and Pastry certificate courses, which are also taken by nonprofessional cooks, this culinary school offers 1-day, 1-week, and 1-month demonstration and hands-on (limit 8 to 12 students) sessions and Thursday afternoon guest chef demonstrations. Also available: French floral art, children's classes, guided tours of Paris markets, Saturday classes, special courses for individuals or groups.

EMPHASIS: French cuisine and pastry and specific subjects, including special occasion menus, souffles, oenology.

COSTS: Range from 9,950 FF-13,150 FF for 1-month courses, 3,200 FF-4,590 FF for 1-week courses, 950 FF-1,375 FF for 1-day courses, and 200 FF for demonstrations. Full payment is required and refundable (less 500 FF) for cancellations 6 weeks prior (no refund for 1-day courses).

LE TROU RESTAURANT AND COOKING SCHOOL
Deux Sevres/Year-round *(See pages 9, 126, 162)*
Individuals and small groups desiring a cooking vacation can enroll for 1- or 2-week classes and tours to France and Italy.

L'ECOLE DE CUISINE DU DOMAINE D'ESPERANCE
Gascony/September, November-January, May-June
Established in 1993, this 18th-century country house hosts six 1-week participation vacations (limit 9 students) a year. Facilities: large country kitchen with 8 work areas. Other activities: market trip and visits to nearby wine cellars. Also available: weekend courses for groups of 6 or more.

EMPHASIS: Seasonal French cuisine.

FACULTY: Natalia Arizmendi, recipient of the Cordon Bleu Grand Diplome, has taught cooking and pastry for over 10 years. She is tri-lingual in French, English, and Spanish.

COSTS, ACCOMMODATIONS: Cost is 8,500 FF, including double occupancy lodging (private bath) and meals at the domaine. A nonrefundable 10% deposit is required, balance due 10 days prior.

LOCATION: Gascony, in southwest France, 90 minutes from Bordeaux.

CONTACT: Claire de Montesquiou, Domaine d'Esperance Cooking Course, Mauvezin d'Armagnac, 40240 La Bastide d'Armagnac, France; (33) 58-44-68-33, Fax (33) 58-44-85-93.

LES CASSEROLES DU MIDI
Avignon/August-June
Established in 1992, this school in an 18th-century country home offers weekly 1-week participation courses (limit 4 students). Other activities: shopping for ingredients, visits to farms, wineries, and food producers, sightseeing in Provence, swimming and tennis.

EMPHASIS: Provencal cuisine.

FACULTY: Italian-born Olga Manguin was owner/chef of Le Cafe des Nattes in Avignon for 15 years.

COSTS: The daily rate of 1,000 FF includes meals, double occupancy lodging, ground transport, and excursions; a deposit of 1,000 FF is required with booking. The Manguin home has 4 bedrooms, 2 with ensuite bath.

CONTACT: Mme. Olga Manguin, Les Casseroles du Midi, L'Anastasy, Ile de la Barthelasse, Avignon, 84000, France; (33) 90-85-55-94, Fax (33) 90-82-59-40.

LES LIAISONS DELICIEUSES
France/Fall, Winter, Spring
Established in 1994, this culinary tour company offers three one-week vacations (limit 10 participants) per year that feature 15 hours of hands-on cooking instruction. Facilities: hotel and restaurant kitchens with individual workspaces. Other activities: visits to wineries, food producers, markets, and restaurants, sightseeing, hiking and biking.

EMPHASIS: French regional cuisine.

FACULTY: Founder Patti Ravenscroft is tour director and translator. Classes are taught by Michelin-star restaurant chefs and proprietors.

COSTS, ACCOMMODATIONS: Cost ranges from $1,950-$2,490, which includes lodging, meals, and

NONVOCATIONAL/VACATION FRANCE

planned activities. A $600-$800 deposit is required. Refund less $100 for cancellations more than 45 days prior.

LOCATION: Includes Hotel Les Pyrenees in the Basque region, Hostellerie du Vieux Moulin in Burgundy, and L'Auberge de la Truffe in the Dordogne.

CONTACT: Patty R. Ravenscroft, Les Liaisons Delicieuses, 4710 - 30th St. N.W., Washington, DC 20008; (202) 966-4091, Fax (202) 966-4091.

MAS DE CORNUD
St. Remy-de-Provence/Year-round

Since 1993, David and Nitockrees Carpita have operated a cooking school in their 18th-century Provencal country inn. The one-week Home Cooking in Provence course (limit 6 participants) features daily participation classes. Facilities: the inn's well-equipped kitchen. Other activities: visits to artisan bakers, markets and cheese and olive oil producers, wine tastings, sightseeing. Also available: customized culinary programs.

EMPHASIS: Provencal and Mediterranean cuisine.

FACULTY: Nitockrees Carpita is a member of the IACP and trained in France. Guest chefs include Jean-Andre Charial of l'Oustau Baumanière, Philippe Theme and Jean-Pierre Novi of La Riboto de Taven, and Alain Assaud of Le Marceau .

COSTS, ACCOMMODATIONS: Cost of $1,950 ($2,450) includes double (single) occupancy lodging ($1,750 for non-participant guest) at Mas de Cornud, most meals, ground transport, and planned activities. The inn has a swimming pool and boules court.

LOCATION: Two miles from Saint-Remy, accessible by TGV from Paris to Avignon or by air to Avignon or Marseille.

CONTACT: David and Nitockrees Carpita, Mas de Cornud, Rte. de Mas-Blanc, 13210, St. Remy-de-Provence, France; (33) 90-92-39-32, Fax (33) 90-92-55-99, E-Mail 74333,237@compuserve.com

PROVENÇAL GETAWAY VACATIONS
Currier/May-July, September-October

First offered in 1994, cooking instructor Eileen Dwillies conducts seven 6-day vacations (limit 4 participants) per year in her restored 16th century house. Facilities: participation cooking in home-style kitchen. Other activities: daily tours of outdoor markets, vintners caves, artists' workshops, and olive mills.

EMPHASIS: Provençal cuisine.

FACULTY: Eileen Dwillies, author of 9 cookbooks, has taught cooking for 20 years and is a former food editor and TV show host.

COSTS, ACCOMMODATIONS: C$950 includes meals, tours, and twin lodging with shared bath. C$350 deposit is nonrefundable unless replacement is found

CONTACT: Eileen Dwillies, Provençal Getaway Vacations, 525 Wheelhouse Sq., Ste. 222, Vancouver, BC, V5Z 4L8, Canada; (604) 876-8722, Fax (604) 876-1497.

PROVENCE COOKING SCHOOL
St. Tropez/May-October

(See display ad page 254)

The Chateau de la Messardiere offers four to six week-long cooking vacations per year. In addition to daily participation classes, activities include sightseeing in Provence, visits to food markets, wineries, and museums, dining at fine restaurants.

EMPHASIS: Provence cuisine.

COSTS, ACCOMMODATIONS: All-inclusive land cost is $2,800, single supplement $750.

LOCATION: Overlooking St. Tropez and the Mediterranean.

CONTACT: Annemarie Victory Organization, Inc., 136 E. 64th St., New York, NY 10021; (212) 486-0353, Fax (212) 751-3149.

Provence

COOKING SCHOOL AT CHATEAU DE LA MESSARDIERE IN ST. TROPEZ
Experience the light and healthy cuisine of Provence.
Learn about its wines, olive oils, cheeses and herbs. Explore its beauty
Seven-day programs from May to October.
Write or call for a detailed brochure.
THE ANNEMARIE VICTORY ORGANIZATION, INC. • 136 EAST 64TH ST., NEW YORK, NY 10021
212-486-0353 • FAX: 212-751-3149

RITZ-ESCOFFIER ECOLE DE GASTRONOMIE FRANCAISE
Paris/Year-round *(See page 128) (See display ad page 129)*
In addition to its professional and diploma courses, this school in the Hotel Ritz offers 1-week theme courses in June, July. and September, and a holiday celebration course and wine course in December. Demonstration classes are held Monday through Thursday afternoons, alternate Tuesday evenings, and the last Saturday morning of each month. Also available: Custom-designed programs for groups.

EMPHASIS: Themes include holiday menus, brasserie & bistro cooking, fish, Provencal specialties, sauces, and wildgame.

COSTS: Demonstrations are 230 FF each (6 for the price of 5), holiday and summer courses range from 5,650 FF to 10,000 FF per week. Demonstration reservations must be made by noon the day of class. Lodging packages are available on a limited basis.

ROGER VERGÉ COOKING SCHOOL
Mougins/September-July
Established in 1984, this school in Restaurant l'Amandier offers 2-hour demonstrations (limit 20) from Tuesday through Saturday. Facilities: the restaurant kitchen.

EMPHASIS: Seasonal menus, Provencal cuisine.

FACULTY: Michel Duhamel and other chefs from the Moulin de Mougins restaurant.

COSTS: 300 FF per class, 1,350 FF for 5 classes. Booking is desired 48 hours in advance.

LOCATION: Near Cannes

CONTACT: Ecole du Moulin, Restaurant l'Amandier, 06250 Mougins Village, France; (33) 93-75-35-70, Fax (33) 93-90-18-55.

TRADITIONAL FAMILY COOKING IN THE QUERCY
Brassac/May-February
Established in 1978, the Midi-Pyrenees travel agency offers a 5-day hands-on family cooking course (limit 6 students) from May to November and a 2-day goose foie gras and confit course (limit 8) from November to February.

EMPHASIS: French country cooking; goose recipes.

FACULTY: Accomplished French farm cooks.

COSTS, ACCOMMODATIONS: The 5-day course, which includes lodging, breakfasts, and lunches, ranges from 2,230 FF double (700 FF single supplement)-3,980 FF (1,200 FF), depending on accommodations. The 2-day session, which includes hotel lodging and meals, is 725 FF (70 FF) plus the cost of goose and foie gras. A 25% deposit is required; balance due 45 days prior.

LOCATION: Southwest France near Montauban, a 5-hour train ride from Paris or a 2-hour plane ride from Orly Airport.

NONVOCATIONAL/VACATION **FRANCE** **255**

Contact: Andre Pochat, Agence de Voyages Midi-Pyrenees, Vignes, Brassac, 82190 Bourg-de-Visa, France; (33) 63-94-24-30.

VACANCES CUISINE EN PROVENCE
Provence/April-October

Established in 1990 by Anthony and Sarah Beerbohm, these 8-day cooking and cultural vacations (limit 16-20 participants) focus on the gastronomy, culture, and lifestyle of Provence and feature 3 cooking demonstrations. Other activities: market visits; wine, olive oil, and honey tastings; guided excursions to museums, wine estates, pottery workshops, and Cezanne's studio; golf, tennis, cycling, and horseback riding for non-cooking guests. Also: special programs during black truffle season (Nov.-Feb.), historic garden programs.
Emphasis: Provencal, Mediterranean, and French country cooking using fresh, local ingredients; truffles in winter.
Faculty: Designer and experienced cook Sarah Beerbohm, who studied with noted Provencal chefs, directs and translates the sessions given by local home cooks and guest restaurant chefs. Anthony Beerbohm conducts wine tastings.
Costs, Accommodations: Cost of $2,456 ($2,946) includes double (single) occupancy 3-star hotel lodging, 2 meals daily, scheduled excursions, and ground transport.
Location: Five days are spent in Cotignac, a rural village in the Cote de Provence wine-producing region of the Centre-Var; three days are in Aix-en-Provence, which is 90 minutes from the Nice and Marseille airports and 30 minutes from the Paris train connection.
Contact: Sarah Beerbohm, Vacances Cuisine en Provence, Mas de Robernier, 83570 Montfort-sur-Argens, Provence, France; (33) 94-04-78-96, Fax (33) 94-04-78-97. U.S. Contact: Churchill & Turen, Ltd., Tower Crossing, 1504 N. Napier Blvd., Ste. 152, Naperville, IL 60563; (800) 445-7979 or (708) 717-7777, Fax (708) 505-9521.

A WEEK IN BORDEAUX
Bordeaux/June-September

First held in 1988, Jean-Pierre and Denise Moulle offer four 6-day culinary participation vacations (limit 8 participants) each summer. Facilities: the professional kitchen of Chateau La Louviere and a small farmhouse kitchen with a grilling fireplace. Other activities: visits to chateaux, wine estates, markets, cheese shops, medieval villages, oyster beds, regional inns, and Michelin-starred restaurants. Also available: sight-seeing and shopping.
Emphasis: French classic cuisine, regional cuisine of Gascony, wine appreciation.
Faculty: Jean-Pierre Moulle graduated from Ecole Hoteliere in Toulouse, served as chef at Chez Panisse, and now consults for restaurants and cooks part-time at Chez Panisse. Bordeaux native Denise Moulle opened 2 wine shops in California's Bay Area and markets her family's French chateau wines in the U.S.
Costs, Accommodations: Cost of $2,800 (single supplement $200) includes lodging, meals, planned excursions, and ground transport. Lodging is at the private Chateau Mouchac. Deposit of $500 required with balance due 45 days prior; cancellations more than 45 days prior forfeit $150.
Location: France's Bordeaux region.
Contact: Jean-Pierre Moulle, A Week in Bordeaux, P.O. Box 8191, Berkeley, CA 94707; (510) 845-8741, Fax (510) 845-3100.

A WEEK IN PROVENCE
Gordes/February-June, September-December

Established in 1995 by Sarah and Michael Brown, these week-long vacation programs, scheduled every other week and limited to 6 participants, feature daily cooking demonstrations. Other activities: visits to food markets and wineries, sightseeing. Also: library, hiking, riding, biking, golfing.

EMPHASIS: Provence cuisine.

FACULTY: Sarah Brown spent her childhood in France, has a Ph.D. in Art History, and studied cooking since she was 7; gallery owner Michael Brown represented agricultural and food interests as a lobbyist in Washington, DC, and exports wines to the U.S.

COSTS, ACCOMMODATIONS: Cost of $1,500 includes lodging in the Brown's converted village farmhouse, two meals daily, and morning tours. A $500 deposit is required; balance is due 30 days prior. Cancellations more than 45 days prior forfeit $150.

LOCATION: Near the Marseilles-Provence airport and Avignon.

CONTACT: Sarah & Michael Brown, A Week in Provence, Les Martins, 84220 Gordes, France; (33) 90-72-26-56, Fax (33) 90-72-23-83 or Sheppard Ferguson, c/o Schoenhof's Foreign Books, 486 Green St., Cambridge, MA 02139; (617) 547-8534, Fax (617) 547-8565.

THE WINE ENTHUSIAST ULTIMATE WINE COURSES
France and Italy/Spring, Summer, Fall

The Wine Enthusiast offers 1-week wine course vacations (limit 14 participants) that feature daily wine instruction, a cooking demonstration by a noted restaurateur, and tours of wineries and chateaux.

FACULTY: Masters of Wine and noted restaurateurs.

COSTS: About $4,000, which includes double occupancy lodging, meals, and planned activities.

LOCATION: Bordeaux, Champagne and Burgundy.

CONTACT: Mark Golodetz, Director Travel Services, Wine Enthusiast Cos., 8 Saw Mill River Rd., Hawthorne, NY 10532; (800) 356-8466, ext. 7724, Fax (800) 8338466.

HONG KONG

CHOPSTICKS COOKING CENTRE
Kowloon/Year-round

Founded in 1971, this school in a private residence offers 1-week demonstration courses for groups (limit 30 students) and participation courses for professionals (limit 8). Facilities: a large restaurant kitchen. Other activities: market and restaurant kitchen visits. Also available: private classes, non-residential classes.

EMPHASIS: Chinese cuisine.

COSTS: Range from $40 per session to $900 for a 1-week course, excluding meals, lodging, and airfare. Nonrefundable fees include a $40 registration fee and a 50% deposit.

HONG KONG FOOD FESTIVAL
Hong Kong/March

This annual two-week event features approximately 20 *Cooking with Great Chefs* demonstration classes (limit 12 students) that are held in the kitchens of participating hotels and restaurants. Other activities: Culinary Awards Photo Exhibition, t'ai chi lessons, theme parties and banquets, and tours of tea companies, wedding cake bakeries, and Sai Kung villages.

EMPHASIS: Thai, Cantonese, Chinese, Japanese, and European specialties.

COSTS: Cooking classes are HK$350 each. Costs of other events vary.

CONTACT: Hong Kong Tourist Assn., 11th Flr, Citicorp Centre, 18 Whitfield Rd., North Point, Hong Kong; (852) 801 7177. Food Festival Hotline (852) 187 8887. Offices in the U.S. (212) 869-5008 and other countries.

NONVOCATIONAL/VACATION   **IRELAND**   **257**

BALLYMALOE COOKERY SCHOOL
(See page 130)   **Midleton/April-September, December-January**

This school offers 1- to 5-day vacation programs that include a 1-day Christmas Cooking demonstration and a week-end Entertaining Course. Also available: fishing and golf.

FACULTY: A well-known international chef is guest instructor.

COSTS: One-day courses are IR £85, weekend courses are IR £225, 5-day courses are IR £355. Local lodging is approximately IR £48, single occupancy and IR£35, sharing.

BALTIMORE INTERNATIONAL CULINARY COLLEGE
(See page 48)   **Lough Ramor/March-October**

The Centre's programs are also open to cooking enthusiasts. Also available: golf, tennis, fishing, boating.

THE COOKERY CENTRE OF IRELAND
(See page 131)   **Dublin/Year-round**

This school offers 6-session participation (limit 18 students) and demonstration (limit 40) courses and a 2-week hands-on summer program for 11 to 16-year-olds.

COSTS: IR £140 (IR £85) for the 6-week participation (demonstration) course, IR £100 for the children's course; no refund unless management cancels.

COUNTRY HOUSE COOKERY — BERRY LODGE
Miltown Malbay, County Clare/Year-round

Established in 1994, this school in a country house offers day, weekend, and week-long participation courses (limit 10 students). Facilities: a modern traditional farmhouse kitchen. Other activities: two mornings of cookery in summer with lunch and wine, day tour of local cultural and historical sites, dinners at local restaurants. Also available: golf, fishing, swimming, sightseeing.

EMPHASIS: Traditional and modern Irish country cuisine, French and international cuisine.

FACULTY: Rita Meade learned to cook from her mother and qualified as a Home Economist. She studied in England, France and Italy and has taught cooking for nearly 30 years.

COSTS, ACCOMMODATIONS: One-week tuition is IR£250. Dinner is IR£20. Lodging at Berry Lodge, a 19th-century country house, is IR£20 per night. A IR£150 deposit is required; balance is due 4 weeks prior. Two morning summer program is IR£70.

LOCATION: Rural western Ireland, 200 yards from the sea in West Clare, 160 miles from Dublin, and 38 miles from Shannon International Airport

CONTACT: Rita Meade, Berry Lodge-Country House Cookery, Annagh, Miltown Malbay, Co. Clare, Ireland; (353) 65-87022 (phone/fax).

ISRAEL

TNUVA, TRAINING CENTER FOR FOOD CULTURE
Tel Aviv/Year-round except August

Tnuva, the largest food distributing company in Israel, established its training center for food culture in 1973 and offers classes that teach adults and children how to prepare food inexpensively and efficiently. Sessions taught in English can be arranged for groups of 25 or more.

EMPHASIS: Russian, Middle Eastern, Moroccan, Italian, and Chinese cuisines; microwave, vegetarian, and nutritional cookery.

FACULTY: School director Tova Aran and a teaching staff of food writers, home economics instructors, restaurant chefs, pastry chefs, and caterers.

COSTS: 40 Shekels per class.

LOCATION: Central Tel-Aviv.

CONTACT: Tova Aran, Tnuva, Training Center for Food Culture, 47 Ben-Gurion Blvd., Tel-Aviv, Israel; (972) 3-5243-157/8, Fax (972)3-5230-055.

ITALY

ADA PARASILITI COOKING SCHOOL
Milan/September-June

Established in 1969, this school offers demonstration (limit 15) and participation (limit 8) courses. Facilities: apartment used exclusively for the school has a kitchen with overhead mirror and ample work space.

EMPHASIS: Italian and international cuisines.

FACULTY: Ada Parasiliti is an Accredited Teacher with the IACP.

COSTS: Range from $60-$100 per session.

LOCATION: The historical center of Milan.

CONTACT: Ada Parasiliti, L'Angolo-Scuola di Cucina, Via Ponte Vetero 13, 20121 Milan, Italy; (39) 2-876398.

ALASTAIR LITTLE COOKERY WEEKS - LA CACCIATA
Orvieto/May-July, September, early October

Established 1994 on the Belcapo estate, La Cacciata offers four 7-day mostly demonstration courses (limit 20 students) a month (17 per year). Facilities: a 12-square-meter kitchen area with inglenook fireplace, wood-fired oven outside. Other activities: visits to such local towns as Perugia, Assissi or Siena, Orvieto market, dinner with estate owners.

EMPHASIS: Simple, fresh Italian food preparation, including risottos, pastas, truffles, focaccia, breads, pizza, and gelati.

FACULTY: Alastair Little, British chef and owner of a restaurant in London's Soho district, rated first in Britain by *The Times*. He is co-author of *Keep It Simple* and a weekly food column. Local Italian chefs.

COSTS, ACCOMMODATIONS: Cost of £800 includes lodging, meals, and planned excursions. A £200 deposit is required, balance due 8 weeks prior. Lodging in bedrooms (with bathrooms) in converted farmhouses. The estate, a working farm noted for its extra virgin olive oil, has a swimming pool and riding school.

LOCATION: Overlooking the medieval city of Orvieto in Umbria, 90 miles north of Rome

CONTACT: Sarah Robson, Manager, La Cacciata, Alastair Little Cookery, 15 Dawson Place, London W2 4TH, England; (44) 71-243-8042 (phone/fax).

BADIA A COLTIBUONO
Siena/May-July, September-October

Founded in 1985 by Lorenza de' Medici, this 5-day vacation course (limit 14 students) is scheduled about a dozen weeks a year at her 11th century estate. Facilities: a large teaching kitchen. Other activities: visits to food producers and wineries, tours of Tuscany, dining at private villas and chateaux, a trip to the Palio races (July), and dinner at one of the contradas in Siena.

EMPHASIS: Regional Italian cooking and wines.

FACULTY: Lorenza de' Medici, author of several cookbooks and a series of cooking manuals; master of wine Nicolas Belfrage.

COSTS, ACCOMMODATIONS: The all-inclusive (except airfare) fee is $4,500 single occupancy, $3,900 double. Lodging is at Badia a Coltibuono, which produces wines, extra virgin olive oil, and other products. Amenities include a cookbook library, swimming pool, and sauna.

LOCATION: About 20 miles north of Siena and 40 miles south of Florence.

NONVOCATIONAL/VACATION **ITALY** 259

CONTACT: Lorenza de' Medici, Badia a Coltibuono, 53013 Gaiole in Chianti (Siena) Italy; Fax (39) 577-749235. In the U.S.: Judy Ebrey, P.O. Box 25228, Dallas, TX 75225; 373-1162, E-Mail: VillaTable@aol.com

BED AND BREAKFAST IN TUSCANY
May, October, November

Established in 1985, restaurateur and caterer Lucia Ana Luhan offers 3 or 4 one-week and mini-courses (limit 10 students) per year at her family farm/bed and breakfast. Facilities: the farm's kitchen, which has individual work areas. Other activities: shopping and sightseeing.

EMPHASIS: Tuscan cuisine, including pastas and pizza.

FACULTY: Lucia Luhan completed her master's degree studies in public relations from Boston University and studied in Europe and South America. She is proprietor of What's Cooking? in Newport Beach and Luciana's Ristorante in Dana Point.

COSTS, ACCOMMODATIONS: The $1,540 1-week fee includes lodging and most meals. Regular bed and breakfast daily rate is $100 single, $130 double occupancy.

LOCATION: The wine country of central Italy, a 5-minute drive from Montecatini Terme, less than 30 minutes from Florence, 90 minutes from Siena.

CONTACT: Food and Wine Appreciation Program, B & B in Tuscany, 24312 Del Prado, Dana Point, CA 92629; (714) 661-6500. In Italy (39) 572-628-817.

BETWEEN PAST & PRESENT — CHIANTI COOKING
Siena/Spring and Fall

Established in 1995 by Diana Place, these one-week cooking vacations (limit 10 participants) featuring 3 hours of daily hands-on instruction are offered 20 times per year. Facilities: modern kitchen with 10 workspaces and brick oven. Other activities: sightseeing, visits to wineries, food producers, markets, fine restaurants.

EMPHASIS: Tuscan cooking and ingredients.

FACULTY: Chef Helene Stoquelet, owner Franco Camella, translator/guide Diana Place.

COSTS, ACCOMMODATIONS: Cost of $1,800 includes double occupancy lodging in a private villa at the Villa a Sesta, meals, and planned excursions. A $600 deposit is required; refund less $50 for cancellations 30 days prior.

LOCATION: A small village in Chianti, 90 minutes from Florence and 2 hours from Pisa.

CONTACT: Diana Place, Essence of Italy, P.O. Box 956, Boca Raton, FL 33429; (407) 361-0301, Fax (407) 361-0301.

CHIANTI IN TUSCANY — ITALIAN COOKERY AND WINE
Gaiole/March-October

Established in 1986, Countesses Paola and Simonetta Bevilacqua de'Mari conduct continuous 1-week hands-on cooking courses (limit 10 participants) and Italian language lessons in their home, Podere Le Rose. Facilities: a well-equipped typical country kitchen. Other activities: a wine lesson, market visit, winery tour.

EMPHASIS: Northern and southern Italian cookery, fresh ingredients, easy-to-make recipes; Italian language.

FACULTY: Simonetta and Paola Bevilacqua de'Mari di Altamura, who learned from their mother, Contessa Maria Giulia di Bevilacqua, and worked with Italian restaurant chefs; Alvaro Luddi, formerly chef in a well-known Tuscan restaurant; guest chefs; wine lessons by Luigi de'Mari. The school is accredited by the Italian Ministry of Foreign Affairs.

COSTS, ACCOMMODATIONS: Cost of 5 days of classes is 900,000 Lira. Lodging for one (two), including breakfast, ranges from 350,000 Lira-500,000 Lira (280,000 Lira-600,000 Lira). Complete package cost of 1,600,000 Lira includes lodging, most meals, ground transport, and planned excursions. A 30% deposit is required and full refund, less expenses, is granted with 30 days notice.

LOCATION: The 13th century Podere Le Rose, a restored Italian farmhouse, is a half hour drive from Siena, an hour from Florence

CONTACT: Simonetta de'Mari di Altamura, Chianti in Tuscany, Centro Pontevecchio, Podere Le Rose, Poggio S. Polo 2, 53010, Lecchi - Gaiole, Italy; (39) 55-294511, Fax (39) 55-2396887.

CUCINA TOSCANA
Florence/Year-round

Established in 1983, this travel service tailors 1-day to 1-month gastronomic excursions in Italy for groups of 2 to 25. Facilities: restaurant kitchens. Other activities: antique hunting, garden visits. Also available: Walking tours of Florence, insider shopping, excursions to the Tuscan countryside.

EMPHASIS: Regional Italian cuisine.

FACULTY: Proprietor Faith Heller Willinger has studied Italian cooking for 20 years, is author of *Eating in Italy: A Traveler's Guide to the Gastronomic Pleasures of Northern Italy*, and directs the Cipriani Culinary program in Venice. Laura Kramer, tour guide/research assistant, has a degree in Medieval and Renaissance studies and is an experienced leader of art/history/shopping tours of Tuscany.

COSTS: Rates begin at $275 per day plus expenses for up to 3 people. Group day rates, which include meals and transport, start at $150 per person. Rates for longer trips are lower.

CONTACT: Faith Heller Willinger, Cucina Toscana, Via della Chiesa, 7, 50125 Florence, Italy; (39) 55-2337014 (phone/fax). In the U.S. **CONTACT:** Vivian, (708) 432-1889 (phone/fax).

CUCINARE AT CASTELLO DI SPALTENNA
Gaiole/March, November-December

First held in 1994, The Castello di Spaltenna hotel offers 4 or 5 one-week and three-day participation courses each year. Other activities: excursions in the Chianti region, tours of private castles, visits to wineries and food producers, dinners at fine restaurants. Also available: short classes for a minimum of 6 participants.

EMPHASIS: Tuscan specialties.

FACULTY: Hotel co-owners Chef Seamus de Pentheny O'Kelly, a student of Paul Bocuse who received his degree in Hotel and Catering from Middlesex Polytechnic of London and had his own restaurant in England, and Tuscan native Julia Scartozzoni, an interior designer specializing in hand-painted furnishings.

COSTS, ACCOMMODATIONS: Cost is $2,500 ($2,900), which includes meals, double (single) occupancy lodging at the 21-room luxury hotel, and planned activities. Non-cook rate is $1,900. A $400 deposit is required with balance due 30 days prior; refund with 3 months notice.

LOCATION: The Chianti region, about 15 miles north of Siena and 30 miles south of Florence

CONTACT: Julia Scartozzoni, Castello di Spaltenna, 53013, Gaiole in Chianti (Siena); (39) 577-749843; Fax (39) 577-742969.

CULINARY STUDIOS IN TUSCANY
Florence, Chianti/March, April, September, October

Established in 1992, the Florentine Culinary Studio offers a 10-day Italy's Culinary Secrets vacation (limit 18 participants) that includes 50 hours of cooking instruction and a 7-day tour of Chianti (limit 18 participants). Facilities: the professional kitchen of the Grand Hotel, rustic trattorias. Other activities: Italian language classes, trips to the Florentine Central Food Market, an olive oil demonstration, winery visits, dining at fine restaurants.

EMPHASIS: Italian regional specialties, desserts, wines.

FACULTY: Professional chefs and cookbook authors, including Executive Chef Monti of the

Excelsior, Giovanna Folonari-Ruffino, sommelier Enrico Bolognini, the head chef of Sabatini's and Arnolfo's restaurants, and a representative from La Molisana pasta company.

Costs, Accommodations: The 10-day program: $3,995, including single occupancy lodging at The Excelsior, most meals, tours, language classes, and ground transport. The 7-day Chianti program: $2,300, including single occupancy lodging, all meals, wine tours, and ground transport. A 25% nonrefundable deposit is required 6 weeks prior.

Location: The Hotel Excelsior is a 5-star Ciga Hotel and former palace situated on the banks of Arno in Florence's historic center.

Contact: TravelAdvisors, Mrs. Becky Steere, 619 East Blithdale Ave., Mill Valley, CA 94941-1468; (415) 383-2323, Fax (415) 383-8929; Marco Berarducci, Il Rinascimento, Borgo dei Greci, 16, Florence, Italy; (39) 55-247-9621 (phone/fax).

CULINARY TOUR OF FLORENCE
Florence/September-November

First offered in 1994. Becky Steere of the Travel Advisors travel agency conducts a 14-day tour that features daily classes at the Florentine Culinary Studio. Other activities: Italian language instruction, winery tour, visits to restaurants and Parma proscuitto and cheese producers.

Emphasis: Tuscan cuisine.

Faculty: Tour host Becky Steere is a culinary graduate of Le Cordon Rouge. Instructors are noted chefs, cookbook authors, and winemakers.

Costs, Accommodations: Cost is $3,995, including meals, double occupancy lodging at the Mobil 5-Star Excelsior Hotel and planned excursions. Single supplement available.

Contact: Becky Steere, Travel Advisors, 619 E. Blithedale Ave., Mill Valley, CA 94941; (415) 383-2323, Fax (415) 383-8929.

DIANE SEED'S IL MELEGRANO CULINARY EXPERIENCE
Puglia/May, September, October

Since 1994, this chateau hotel has offered six 6-day hands-on cooking vacations (limit 20 participants) per year. Other activities: visits to a cheese maker, olive grove, and oil production plant.

Emphasis: Regional Italian cuisine.

Faculty: Diane Seed, prominent British cooking teacher and author, who has lived in Rome for 28 years.

Costs, Accommodations: Cost of $2,500 includes meals and lodging in a luxury 5-star 16th century relais and chateau massaria, with a swimming pool and health center. Deposit of $300 is required with balance due 30 days prior; refundable if space can be filled.

Location: The Truilly region on the Adriatic, south of Bari.

Contact: Judy Ebrey, P.O. Box 25228, Dallas, TX 75225; (214) 373-1161, Fax (214) 373-1162, E-Mail: CuisineInt@aol.com

ENRICO FRANZESE'S COOKING CLASSES
Amalfi/March, April, September, October

Established in 1991, this 1-week culinary vacation features 4 morning demonstration and participation classes. Facilities: Luna Convento Hotel's Saracen Tower. Other activities: guided excursions to Sorrento, Ravello, Pompeii, and Amalfi.

Faculty: Enrico Franzese, trained at the Cipriani in Venice and the Hassler in Rome, won the 1990 Parma Ham Chef's Competition in Bologna, and appears on Italian television.

Costs, Accommodations: Cost is $2,000, which includes meals, planned excursions, transportation from Naples, and first class double occupancy lodging and private bath at the Luna Convento Hotel, a restored 13th century convent.

Location: Amalfi, a resort area on Italy's west coast, is about 150 miles south of Rome and 40

miles south of Naples

CONTACT: Judy Ebrey, P.O. Box 25228, Dallas, TX 75225; (214) 373-1161, Fax (214) 373-1162, E-Mail: CuisineInt@aol.com

ETRUSCA SCHOOL OF COOKING
Tuscany/Spring-Fall

First offered in 1995, Susan Westbrook's Sojourns in Tuscany tour company conducts 1-week hands-on vacation programs (limit 10 participants) at the Torre di Cala Piccola Hotel and in Siena and Montepulciano. Facilities: a classroom in the hotel's former conference area. Other activities: tours of wine and cheese producers, dining at local restaurants, sightseeing in Etruscan towns, a visit to the baths at Saturnia, shopping excursions to Siena and Florence.

EMPHASIS: Specialties of the Maremma region of southern Tuscany.

FACULTY: Siena native Laura Ciatti worked at the Enoteca (wine library) in the Medici Fortress in Siena and is writing a cookbook on Tuscan cuisine. Susan Westbrook has a Cornell degree in art history and has traveled extensively in Tuscany.

COSTS, ACCOMMODATIONS: Lodging is at the Torre di Cala Piccola Hotel, a complex of 1-bedroom villas. The hotel has a pool and is a half mile from the sea.

LOCATION: The Argentario peninsula in southern Tuscany, 90 minutes north of Rome.

CONTACT: Susan Westbrook, Sojourns in Tuscany, Inc., 133 Caroline Depot Rd., Brooktondale, NY 14817; (607) 539-6023 (evenings).

GIULIANO BUGIALLI'S COOKING IN FLORENCE

On sabbatical in 1996.

CONTACT: Giuliano Bugialli's Cooking in Florence, P.O. Box 1650, Canal St. Station, New York, NY 10013; (212) 966-5325, Fax (212) 226-0601.

GRITTI PALACE SCHOOL OF FINE COOKING
Venice/January, March, July, October-November

Started in 1974, this luxury hotel offers 5-day vacation demonstration (limit 22 to 25 participants) courses. All courses are held in Italian with simultaneous English translation. Facilities: specially-equipped mirrored room fitted with a stove.

EMPHASIS: Regional Italian cuisine, seasonal ingredients, wine selection, setting of a table, flower arrangements.

FACULTY: Gritti's chef Celestino Giacomello.

COSTS, ACCOMMODATIONS: Tax-inclusive course fee is 600,000 Lira. Room rates for 5 nights with breakfasts are 3,550,000 Lira double occupancy (cooking course for two), 2,950,000 Lira double occupancy (cooking course for one); 2,250,000 Lira single occupancy.

LOCATION: The hotel Gritti Palace, palace of Doge Andrea Gritti in the 15th century, is 30 minutes by boat from Venice.

CONTACT: Ms. Laura Fanecco, Gritti Palace School of Fine Cooking, Campo Santa Maria del Giglio, 2467 Venice, Italy 30124; (800) 221-2340, Canada (800) 9552442; Fax (212) 421-5929.

HOTEL CIPRIANI COOKING SCHOOL
Venice/April, September-November

Founded in 1978, this resort offers seven 5-day demonstration programs (limit 24 students) per year. Facilities: demonstration kitchen in a large meeting room overlooking the Venetian lagoon, video, 3 gas burners and oven. Other activities: a visit to the Rialto market, a lagoon or mainland excursion, wine presentations, restaurant visits, concluding banquet.

EMPHASIS: Italian and international cuisines utilizing the foods and wines of Venice.

FACULTY: Well-known instructors, including Julia Child, Giuliano Hazan, Darina Allen, and Carol Field. Program coordinator is Faith Willinger.

COSTS, ACCOMMODATIONS: Cost is $2,750, which includes 5 nights double occupancy deluxe lodging at the Hotel Cipriani, meals, and planned activities. Non-participant guest fee $2,250; single supplement $250. Full payment with booking; full refund 15 days prior to arrival. Hotel amenities include a heated pool, tennis, and sauna.

LOCATION: Approximately 30 minutes by water-taxi from the airport.

CONTACT: Mr. Sandro Fabris, Director, or Fabienne Chapuis, P.R., Hotel Cipriani Cooking School, Giudecca, 10, Venice, 30133, Italy; (39) 41-5207744, Fax (39) 41-5203930; In the U.S., Orient Express Hotels: (800) 237-1236 or (212) 838-7874.

IL BORGHETTO COOKING SCHOOL
Florence/April, May, September, October

Since 1995, this country villa has offered 6-day vacation programs (limit 8 participants). Facilities: a newly constructed restaurant kitchen with 4 work areas. Other activities: visits to local markets and castles, guided tours, shopping in Florence and Siena.

EMPHASIS: The theoretical and practical aspects of Tuscan cuisine, including ingredient selection and techniques.

FACULTY: Francesca Cianchi, former chef at Mezzaluna in New York City.

COSTS, ACCOMMODATIONS: The $3,000 fee includes lodging and meals; $1,000 additional for nonparticipant in double room. 35% deposit to reserve, balance 3 weeks prior; 25% cancellation penalty a month prior. The 15th-century Il Borghetto is on a 30-hectare estate with olive groves, medieval grain silos, swimming pool, and cookbook library. All rooms have en-suite bathrooms.

LOCATION: The central Chianti region, 10 miles south of Florence

CONTACT: Francesca Cianchi and Roberto Cavallini, Il Borghetto Cooking School, 50020 San Casciano Val di Pesa, Florence, Italy; (39) 55-8244442/8244352, Fax (39) 55-8244247. Elaine Muoio, Italian Rentals, 3801 Ingomar Street, N.W., Washington, DC 20015; (202) 244-5345, Fax (202) 362-0520.

THE INTERNATIONAL COOKING SCHOOL OF ITALIAN FOOD & WINE
(See display ad page 264) **Bologna/Year-round**

Established 1987 by Mary Beth Clark, this school offers 5 participation courses (limit 14 students) per year that include the 6-day Basic certificate course and the 7-day Piedmont Truffle Festival. Facilities: modern, professional kitchen. Other activities: visits to food producers and markets, olive oil tastings, private winery tours, a truffle hunt, dining in Michelin-star restaurants with private demonstrations.

EMPHASIS: Traditional and new light Italian cuisines with fresh ingredients and ease of prepara tion, traditional and new techniques, antipasti, pasta, risotto, truffle dishes, seasonal, desserts.

FACULTY: Mary Beth Clark, owner of International Food And Wine Consultants, Inc., is chef trained, has taught since 1977, is author of *Trattoria* and contributor to *Italy: A Culinary Journey*, is a feature writer for magazines, and has a cooking video. Other instructors: noted Italian chefs.

COSTS, ACCOMMODATIONS: Cost ranges from $3,000-$3,450 ($2,400-$3,100 for non-cooking guest, $275 single supplement), including most meals, first class lodging, ground transport, and planned activities. A $300 deposit ($150 nonrefundable) is required; balance due 60 days prior.

LOCATION: Central Bologna

CONTACT: Mary Beth Clark, The International Cooking School Of Italian Food And Wine, 201 E. 28th St., Suite 15B, New York, NY 10016; (212) 779-1921, Fax (212) 779-3248.

ITALIAN COOKERY WEEKS
Orvieto and Ostuni/May-September

Established in 1990, this school offers weekly 6-day hands-on courses (limit 20 participants) in

The International Cooking School of Italian Food and Wine
in Bologna, Italy

Join Mary Beth Clark, award-winning cooking teacher and author, for hands-on cooking in the "Gastronomic Capital of Italy". Learn delectable meals from *l'antipasto* through *il dolce*. Special techniques of traditional and new light cooking. Conducted in English in a modern professional kitchen.

Dine in Michelin-starred restaurants. Exclusive estate visits. Truffle hunt!

Recommended as the <u>only</u> school in Italy for "The Best Cooking Class Vacations." Exceptional week-long courses in May, July, September, October. Video available.

BROCHURE: THE INTERNATIONAL COOKING SCHOOL OF ITALIAN FOOD AND WINE
201 East 28 Street, Suite 15B, New York, NY 10016-8538
Telephone (212) 779-1921 Fax (212) 779-3248

Orvieto and Ostuni. Other activities: shopping at the local market, sightseeing in Assisi and Perugia (Orvieto) and Lecce and Alberobello (Ostuni), truffle hunt. Also available: tailor-made group classes, swimming, golf, horseback riding.
EMPHASIS: Italian regional cuisine.
FACULTY: Susanna Gelmetti, who was chef at London's Accademia Italiana delle Arti; well-known Italian chefs and guest English chefs.
COSTS: Cost of £800 includes meals, lodging at 15th and 16th century farm estates with en-suite baths, and planned excursions.
LOCATION: Montebello, a farm estate in Orvieto, and Lo Spagnulo, a converted 15th century castle near Ostuni.
CONTACT: Susanna Gelmetti, Italian Cookery Weeks, P.O. Box 2482, London, NW10 1HW, England; (44) 181-208-0112, Fax (44) 171-401-8763. In the U.S.: Judy Ebrey, P.O. Box 25828, Dallas, TX 75225; (214) 373 1161, Fax (214) 373-1162, E-Mail: CuisineInt@aol.com

---

ITALIAN COUNTRY COOKING CLASSES WITH DIANA FOLONARI
Positano/May-June, September-October
Since 1980, Diana Folonari has taught 1-week participation courses (limit 12 students). Facilities: Ms. Folonari's home.
EMPHASIS: Italian cuisine.
FACULTY: Diana and Vic Folonari.
COSTS, ACCOMMODATIONS: Fee for classes is $1,500; cost of 8 nights at the Villa Franca Hotel (other hotels available) is $690-$840 per person; one-way transfer from Naples is $115 A $300 deposit is required. balance due 60 days prior; $100 penalty for cancellation at least 60 days prior.

NONVOCATIONAL/VACATION   **ITALY**   **265**

Location: Via del Canovaccio 10 in Positano, which is accessible by train and limousine from airports in Rome and Naples

Contact: E & M Associates, 211 E. 43rd St., New York, NY 10017; (800) 223-9832 or (212) 599-8280.

ITALIAN CUISINE IN FLORENCE
Year-round

Founded in 1983, this school in a private apartment offers a dozen 3- to 5-day demonstration (limit 18 students) and participation (limit 8) courses per year. Facilities: a 300-sq.-ft. kitchen with modern equipment. Also: demonstrations for groups, private instruction. Courses: Classical, regional, and new Italian cuisine; desserts.

Faculty: Masha Innocenti, CCP, has a diploma from Scuola di Arte Culinaria Cordon Bleu and is a member of the Associazione Italiana Sommeliers and Commanderie des Cordons Bleus de France.

Costs: 1,300,000 Lira for the gourmet cuisine courses, 850,000 Lira for the desserts course. Rates include meals. Private classes are 300,000 Lira per day. A nonrefundable 30% deposit is required; balance is due 6 weeks prior. Payment by bank check in Italian currency.

Location: Near the center of Florence.

Contact: Mrs. Masha Innocenti, Director, Italian Cuisine in Florence, Via Trieste 1, Florence, 50139, Italy; (39) 55-480041 (phone/fax) or (39) 55499503. For information write to: Wm. Grossi, RDI, 82 Four Clover Rd., Ancramdale, NY 12503; (518) 329-1141.

ITALIAN LANGUAGE AND CUISINE
Siena/Year-round

Since 1990, this sponsor of language learning vacations has offered 4-week participation courses (limit 12 students) that feature daily cooking and language instruction. Other activities: cocktail parties, movies, guided museum visits, excursions, conferences.

Emphasis: Tuscan cuisine, pasta; Italian language.

Faculty: Local chefs and native Italian language instructors.

Costs, Accommodations: Cost is $1,545, which includes half-board lodging in a private home. Nonrefundable deposit of $100 is required.

Location: Siena, 90 minutes by train from Florence.

Contact: Maria McDonald, Director, Lingua Service Worldwide, 216 E. 45th St., 17th Fl., New York, NY 10017; (800) 394-LEARN or (212) 867-1225, Fax (212) 867-7666.

L'AMORE DI CUCINA ITALIANA
Pomino/April-May, September-October

Since 1992, this travel company has offered 1-week hands-on culinary vacations. Facilities: the kitchen of the Locanda di Praticino. Other activities: shopping expeditions; visits to an outdoor market, a winery, cheese and olive oil producers, and the museum of a noted porcelain manufacturer; a cultural evening in Florence; dining at fine restaurants.

Emphasis: Tuscan and regional Italian cuisines.

Faculty: Cristina Blasi and Gabriella Mari, owners of a cooking school in Florence and authors of a book about the cooking of ancient Rome; wine and olive oil experts.

Costs: Land cost $1,975 ($1,775 for non-cook guest), including meals, double occupancy lodging ($300 single supplement) at Locanda di Praticino, and planned activities. A $400 deposit is required; balance due 30 days prior. Cancellations 60 days prior forfeit $100; no refund thereafter.

Location: Pomino, about a half-hour drive from Florence.

Contact: Ralph P. Slone, l'Amore di Cucina Italiana, Inland Services, Inc., 360 Lexington Ave., New York, NY 10017; (212) 687-9898.

LA CUCINA AL FOCOLARE
Valdarno Valley/March-May, October-November *(See display ad below)*

Founded in 1992, the Fattoria Degli Usignoli, a converted 15th-century friary, conducts ten 1-week hands-on culinary vacations (limit 25 participants) a year. Facilities: the converted wine cellar has a demonstration kitchen with wood-burning oven, rotisserie, and individual work stations. Other: tours of outdoor markets, museum visits, sightseeing in Florence, Siena, and San Gimignano.

EMPHASIS: Tuscan specialties, pizza, breads, grill and rotisserie dishes, table setting, napkin folding, culinary history, wine appreciation.

FACULTY: Owner Sylvia Pincitori, Chef Fortunato Domenici, and the staff of Ristorante Fattoria Degli Usignoli.

COSTS, ACCOMMODATIONS: Cost is $2,500 ($2,250, $1,950, $1,800), which includes single (double, triple, quadruple) occupancy apartment with private kitchen, meals, planned activities, and transport from Florence. The Fattoria, situated on 55 acres, produces its own Chianti and extra virgin olive oil. Amenities include tennis, horseback riding, and swimming. A $400 deposit is required; balance due 45 days prior. Cancellations 45 days prior forfeit $100.

LOCATION: Overlooking the Valdarno Valley, 18 miles southeast of Florence

CONTACT: Peggy Markel, Director, La Cucina al Focolare, Box 646, Boulder, CO 80306-0646; (800) 988-2851, Fax (303) 440-8598.

LA CUCINA AL FOCOLARE
Florence, Italy
Immerse yourself into the breadth of Tuscan cuisine.
Hands-on cooking, Wine Courses
1-800-988-2851 • Free brochure

LA CUCINA KASHER IN TOSCANA
Pomino/April-October

Since 1995, this travel company has offered 1-week hands-on kocher culinary vacations. Facilities: the kitchen of Locanda di Praticino, with a full-time mashgiach. Other activities: visits to markets, olive oil producers, and a porcelain museum, shopping, a cultural evening in Florence, an Italian language lesson, synagogue visits.

EMPHASIS: Cuisines of the Jews of Rome, Tuscany, Venice, and other regions.

FACULTY: Edda Servi Machlin, a teacher of Italian-Jewish cuisine and historian of Italian-Jewish life.

COSTS, ACCOMMODATIONS: Land cost is $2,400 ($2,200 for non-cook guest), which includes meals, double occupancy lodging at the Locanda di Praticino, and planned activities. A $400 deposit is required; balance is due 30 days prior. Cancellations 60 days prior forfeit $150.

LOCATION: A 30-minute drive from Florence.

CONTACT: Ralph Slone, La Cucina Kasher in Toscana, Inland Services, Inc., 360 Lexington Ave., New York, NY 10017; (212) 687-9898.

LAURA NICCOLAI COOKING SCHOOL
S.Agata sui Due Golfi/Summer

Founded in 1987 by Laura Niccolai, this school features ten 1-week participation courses (limit 10 students) each summer. Facilities: a well equipped, professional kitchen in the historic Niccolai Villa. In addition to daily classes, activities include dinners in selected restaurants, visits to

NONVOCATIONAL/VACATION **ITALY**

Limoncello liqueur and mozzarella factories, and guided tours to Capri and Positano. Also available: day classes, private lessons.

EMPHASIS: Traditional and modern Italian and Neapolitan cuisine, emphasis on healthful recipes.

FACULTY: IACP member Laura Niccolai studied with Michelin three-star chef Gualtiero Marchesi and French pastry chef Jain Bellouet.

COSTS, ACCOMMODATIONS: Fee is $3,000 ($2,200 for non-cook guest), which includes double occupancy lodging in a Sorrento hotel, meals, planned activities, and transport from/to the Naples airport. A $250 deposit is required, balance is due 60 days prior. Refund less $50 for cancellation 30 days prior.

LOCATION: Between Sorrento and Positano, 30 miles south of Naples.

CONTACT: Laura Niccolai, Laura Niccolai Cooking School, 730 Columbus Ave., #9H, New York, NY 10025; (212) 666-1436, Fax (212)_666-1436, E-mail LNCooking@aol.com. In Italy: Laura Niccolai Cooking School, Via Termine 9, S. Agata sui Due Golfi, 80064 (NA), Italy; (39) 81-878-0152.

A LESSON IN FLAVORS — DONNA FRANCA TOURS
Tuscany, Lombardy, Venetia, Umbria/May-October

Established in 1967, this tour operator offers 8-10 eleven-day hands-on culinary tours (limit 20 participants) per year. Facilities: kitchens of private villas. Other activities: winery visits, private viewings of Venice gardens, visits to a prosciutto factory and balsamic vinegar gourmet shops, a medieval banquet, and excursions to Lake Como, Ferrara, Modena, Siena, San Gimignano, Florence, Perugia, and Spoleto.

FACULTY: Donna Franca studied with Marcella Hazan and has operated culinary tours since 1972. A member of Les Dames d'Escoffier, she conducts lessons in her private villa in Cetona, Siena.

COSTS, ACCOMMODATIONS: Land cost is approximately $3,000, which includes double occupancy lodging in castles and villas, most meals, land transport, and planned excursions. Single supplement is $550. A $250 deposit is required, balance due 45 days prior.

CONTACT: Donna Franca Tours, 470 Commonwealth Ave., Boston, MA 02215; (800) 225-6290 or (617) 227-3111, Fax (617) 266-1062.

LIGURIAN SCHOOL OF POETIC COOKING
Tellaro/Spring and Fall

Established by Peggy Markel of La Cucina al Focolare (page 266) in 1996, this 5-day vacation program includes daily participation classes, market visits, sightseeing, and a boat excursion to Cinque Terre.

EMPHASIS: Fish, sauces, Ligurian cuisine.

FACULTY: Self-taught chef Angelo Cabani, owner of the Michelin 1-star Locanda Miranda Inn.

COSTS, ACCOMMODATIONS: $2,500 includes meals, lodging at the Inn, and planned excursions.

LOCATION: Overlooking the Gulf of La Spezia.

CONTACT: Peggy Markel, P.O. Box 646, Boulder, CO 80306-0646; (800) 988-2851, Fax (303) 440-8598.

MANGIA: A TASTE OF FLORENCE
Florence/September-July

Since 1988, Judy Witts has conducted 1- and 3-day demonstration (limit 10 students) and participation (limit 6) classes in her Florence apartment and twice yearly 5-day culinary vacations (limit 6) at a country villa in Chianti. Facilities: apartment kitchen with traditional Tuscan kitchen utensils. Other activities: dinners at local restaurants, visits to markets, kitchen shops, wineries and cheese makers.

EMPHASIS: Italian-Tuscan regional cuisine, including pastas, breads, desserts, antipasti.

FACULTY: IACP member Judy Witts, CCP, received pastry training at San Francisco's Stanford Court Hotel and studied at Tante Marie's Cooking School, Florence Cordon Bleu, and Roger Vergé Cooking School.

COSTS: $100 per class. The 5-day Chianti vacation is $1,500, including meals and lodging. Villa amenities include private baths and a pool. Deposit required.

LOCATION: Florence, overlooking the central market; Chianti vacation is 10 minutes from Florence, 2 hours from Rome airport.

CONTACT: Judy Witts, Mangia, Via Taddea, 31, 50123 Florence, Italy; (39) 55-29-25-78 (phone/fax).

MARGHERITA AND VALERIA SIMILI'S COOKING COURSES
Bologna/Fall, Winter Spring

This school offers more than 100 hands-on classes a year. Also available: one-week intensives for groups of no more than 10.

EMPHASIS: Most classes focus on breads. Other topics include pasta, sausage, and holiday desserts.

FACULTY: Margherita and Valeria Simili.

COSTS: $80-$100 per class.

Contact: Margherita and Valeria Simili, 116 Via San Felice, Bologna, 40122, Italy; (39) 51-52-37-71 or (39) 51-55-44-94, Fax (39) 51-52-37-71.

MARIA BATTAGLIA — LA CUCINA ITALIANA, INC.
Verona/October-May

Established in 1981, this school offers week-long cooking programs each season at La Foresteria Serego Alighieri, a 14th century villa in Valpolicella. Other activities: a trip to the Verona market, a demonstration at the Ferron Rice Mill, and tours of the Masi winery and Serego Alighieri Estate.

EMPHASIS: Northern, central, and southern Italian cuisine.

FACULTY: Maria Battaglia studied Italian cooking in Bologna, Florence, Messina, Sardinia, and Milan. She was a recipe consultant and spokesperson for Contadina Foods and was awarded the Diploma di Merito by the Federazione Italiana Cuochi in Milan and Verona.

COSTS, ACCOMMODATIONS: $3,200 per person, including breakfast, double occupancy lodging at the La Foresteria villa apartments, which have private kitchens, and all cooking classes and excursions. A $300 deposit is required with balance due 6 weeks prior.

LOCATION: A 25-minute drive north of Verona, 10 minutes from Catullo airport in Villafranca.

CONTACT: Maria Battaglia, La Cucina Italiana, P.O. Box 6528, Evanston, IL 60204; (708) 328-1144, Fax (708) 328-1787.

MARINER TOURS
Florence/Spring and Fall

Established in 1991, this special interest tour operator offers six weekend to week-long hands-on cooking vacations (limit 12 participants) per year. Facilities: kitchens of country inns, the Cordon Bleu school in Florence. In addition to daily instruction, activities include visits to wineries and balsamic vigear and olive oil producers, truffle hunting, shopping in local markets, restaurant dining, and sightseeing.

EMPHASIS: Regional Italian cuisine; wine appreciation.

FACULTY: Include Rosi Cavollini of Il Borghetto, Mary Ann Esposito of PBS' Ciao Halio, Cristina Blasi and Gabriella Mari of the Scuola di Arte Culinaria Cordon Bleu, and a Master of Wine.

COSTS, ACCOMMODATIONS: Cost, whichy ranges from $750 for weekend trips in the U.S. to $3,200 for a week in Italy, includes lodging, meals, and planned activities. A $200-$1,000 deposit is required, refundable with 45 days notice.

Location: U.S. and Florence, Italy.

Contact: Gail Hohweiler, Mariner Tours, 405 North Hill Rd., Stowe, VT 05672; (802) 253-7514, Fax (802) 253-6869.

PHEASANT HILL
Tuscany/Spring and Fall

Established by Peggy Markel of La Cucina al Focolare (page 266) in 1996, this week-long vacation program includes daily participation classes, mushroom picking, olive oil tastings, winery visits, and dining in local restaurants.

Emphasis: Tuscan and medieval cuisine.

Faculty: Janet Hansen, a founding member of the Arcigola SlowFood Movement in Italy and author of a book on medieval recipes.

Costs, Accommodations: $1,800, including meals and farmhouse lodging with shared baths.

Location: Collefagiano, an organic farm that produces olive oil and artichokes, is near Grosetto, in southern Tuscany.

Contact: Peggy Markel, Box 646, Boulder, CO 80306-0646; (800) 988-2851, Fax (303) 440-8598.

THE SCHOOL OF TRADITIONAL NEAPOLITAN CUISINE
Positano/March-April, October-November

Since 1993, Hotel Le Sirenuse has offered 5-day demonstration culinary vacations (limit 20 students). Facilities: Include an original wood-burning pizza oven. Other activities: visits to mozzarella, pasta, and limoncino factories, a fish monger, and Oplontis, Amalfi, and Ravello.

Emphasis: Regional Neapolitan cuisine; wines.

Faculty: Hotel Le Sirenuse Chef Alfonso Mazzacano and Alfonso Iaccarino, chef-owner of the Michelin 2-star Don Alfonso restaurant. Hotel manager Antonio Sersale translates.

Costs, Accommodations: The $2,300 to $2,800 cost includes lodging, all meals, and planned excursions. The 60-room Hotel Le Sireneuse, an 18th century palazzo and member of the Leading Hotels of the World, was built as a summer home for the Marchese Sersale, whose family continues to run it today.

Location: Positano, a fishing village in southern Italy, is 40 miles from Naples

Contact: Antonio Sersale, Manager, The School of Traditional Neapolitan Cuisine, Hotel Le Sirenuse, Via C. Colombo 30, 84017, Positano, Salerno, Italy; (39) 89-875066, Fax (39) 89-811798. In the U.S.: Judy Ebrey, P.O. Box 25228, Dallas, TX 75225; (214) 373-1161, Fax (214) 373-1162, E-Mail: CuisineInt@aol.com

SCUOLA DI ARTE CULINARIA "CORDON BLEU"
(See page 131) **Florence, Siena, Pomino/Year-round**

Established in 1985 as a branch of the Italian Cordon Bleu School, this private school offers 1-, 3-, and 7-day cooking vacations (limit 12 students) at a medieval hamlet near Siena, 7-day cooking and art vacations at a farmhouse in Tuscany, and 1- to 8-session courses at the school in central Florence. Facilities: 30-square-meter professional kitchen in Siena, 50-square-meter Tuscan country-style kitchen with fireplace and brick oven, the school's 40-square-meter teaching kitchen. Other activities: professional programs during winter, visits to markets, food producers, wineries and artisans' workshops, dining in trattorias and fine restaurants, cultural programs, sightseeing.

Emphasis: Basic, advanced, Tuscan, new Italian cuisine; bread; ice cream; history, nutrition; wines.

Faculty: Cristina Blasi and Gabriella Mari are sommeliers and olive oil experts who authored a book on ancient Roman cooking and are members of the Commanderie des Cordons Bleus de France, Italian Association of Professional Chefs, and the IACP; part-time instructors include Fabio Onesti.

COSTS, ACCOMMODATIONS: Costs range from $300 for 1 day to $3,000 for the 7-day program at the Hotel Relais Borgo San Felice near Siena, which includes meals and lodging. Amenities include tennis, swimming, and billiards. A 30% deposit is required; balance due 2 weeks prior. The 7-day Tuscany program is $2,500 all-inclusive. Lodging is at a farmhouse with swimming pool and winery. A $300 nonrefundable deposit is required. Classes and series in Florence begin at 120,000 Lira per session. Local lodging starts at $30 per day.

LOCATION: A rural hamlet 10 miles from Siena; Pomino, a rural community 45 minutes northeast of Florence; central Florence, an hour drive from the Pisa airport

CONTACT: Gabriella Mari, Director, Scuola di Arte Culinaria Cordon Bleu, Via di Mezzo, 55/R, 50121 Firenze - Florence, Italy; (39) 55-2345468 (phone/fax).

SICILIAN COOKING ADVENTURE
Catania/April and May

Marina Tudisco offers a 9-day hands-on culinary travel program (limit 12 students). Other activities: a trip to the active volcano, Mt. Etna; a visit to Caltagirone, the ceramics center of Sicily; an afternoon in Taormina; an archeological tour of Syracuse; sightseeing in Catania; dinners at specialty restaurants. Also available: Mediterranean Cooking, an abbreviated course for English-speaking foreigners living in Italy.

FACULTY: Marina Tudisco, director of the Cordon Bleu Culinary Arts School in Catania since 1978, studied with Enrica Jarratt at the Cordon Bleu in Rome, is Accademico della Cucina Italiana e Commandeur des Cordons Bleus de France, and teaches Mediterranean cooking in North America.

COSTS, ACCOMMODATIONS: Land price is approximately $2,100 ($1,800 for nonparticipant) double, single supplement $350. A $300 deposit is required, $50 of which is nonrefundable; balance is due 90 days prior. Lodging is at the Grand Hotel Excelsior.

CONTACT: Mr. Davide Ciancio, c/o Nicober Viaggi, Via Androne 43, 95100 Catania, Italy; (39) 95-312164, Fax (39) 95-327936.

TASTING ITALY
March-June, September-November

Founded in 1992, Tasting Italy sponsors more than 20 one-week hands-on cookery courses (limit 12-16 students) a year to different regions of Italy. Facilities: well-equipped kitchens with pizza ovens, grills, and open fire cooking. Other activities: visits to markets, vineyards, restaurants, and wine tastings.

EMPHASIS: Italian regional cooking; wine tasting.

FACULTY: Valentina Harris, author and presenter of BBC's *Regional Italian Cookery;* Carla Tomasi, author and proprietor of Turnaround Cooks; Alvaro Maccioni, owner of London's La Famiglia; journalist and food stylist Maxine Clark.

COSTS, ACCOMMODATIONS: Cost from £850, which includes full accommodation (based on sharing), food and wine.

LOCATION: Sicily: the Ravida family's 18th century palazzo on the southern coast. Tuscany: the hotel Fattoria Montelluci near Arezzo. Piedmont: La Camilla near Gavi, the country home of the Scavia family. Veneto: the hunting lodge, La Foresteria, near Verona.

CONTACT: Sara Schwartz, Tasting Italy, 97 Bravington Rd., London, W9 3AA, England; (44) 181-964-5839, Fax (44) 181-960-3919.

TENUTA DI CAPEZZANA CULINARY PROGRAM IN TUSCANY
Florence/Spring & Fall

Established in 1993, this school in a 15th century Medici villa offers 12 week-long sessions per year. Instructional format: participation. Class size: 12 maximum. Facilities: Capezzana's family kitchen. Other activities: visits to markets, specialty shops, sausage and cheese makers, bakeries;

wine instruction; comparative tastings, demonstrations and dining at fine restaurants.

EMPHASIS: Italian wines, basics, ingredients, wine and food pairing, antipasti, home-style cooking of Tuscany.

FACULTY: Culinary director is Rolando Beramendi, owner of Italian import company Manicaretti and general manager of Capezzana. Instructors include Contessa Lisa Bonacossi, Fabbio Picchi of Cibr??o, Chef Carlo of Da Delfina, and Master of Wine Nicholas Belfrage.

COSTS, ACCOMMODATIONS: Cost is $2,300, which includes double occupancy lodging in the villa, all meals, ground transportation, and planned activities. A $500 deposit is required, balance due 30 days prior. Full refund with 60 days notice. Food and wine professionals receive a discount.

LOCATION: A 20-minute drive from Florence. The villa is a working olive oil and wine-producing estate.

CONTACT: Pamela Sheldon Johns, U.S. Representative, 1324-G State St., Santa Barbara, CA 93101; (805) 963-0230 (phone/fax).

VENETIAN COOKING IN A VENETIAN PALACE
Venice/January-March, June, September-October

Since 1984, Fulvia Sesani has conducted cooking classes (limit 10 students) at her home in a 13th century Venetian palace. Facilities: the palace's modern, fully-equipped kitchen. Other activities: shopping in the Rialto market, visits to the Ducal palace, museums, and private homes, dinner at Harry's Bar, and the Palazzo Morosini. Also available: day classes and private lessons.

EMPHASIS: Traditional Venetian cooking, edible works of art.

FACULTY: Fulvia Sesani.

COSTS: All-inclusive land costs range from $2,950 to $3,250.

LOCATION: The Palazzo Morosini is in the Santa Maria Formosa area of Venice

CONTACT: Fulvia Sesani, Palazzo Morosini, Castello 6140, Venice, 30122, Italy; (39) 41-5228923. U.S. **CONTACT:** Judy Ebrey, P.O. Box 25228, Dallas, TX 75225; (214) 373-1161, Fax (214) 373-1162, E-Mail: CuisineInt@aol.com

VILLA CENNINA/THE ART OF ITALIAN CUISINE
Siena/Year-round

Established in 1983, this organization offers 15 one- to two-week hands-on cooking vacations (limit 15 participants) per year at the 16th century Villa Cennina under the sponsorship of the nonprofit Cultural Society of Siena. Instruction: 4 to 8 hours daily.Other activities: visits to wineries, food producers, markets, restaurants, tours to culinary and cultural arts centers. Facilities: restaurant kitchen.

EMPHASIS: Tuscan cuisine.

FACULTY: Gian Luca Pardini, owner/chef of Ristorante Mecenate in Lucca and consultant to a chain of Italian restaurants in Japan.

COSTS, ACCOMMODATIONS: Ranges from $1,800-$2,800, which includes lodging, meals, ground transport, and planned activities. Villa amenities include swimming pool, tennis courts, horseback riding, hiking trails, private baths.

LOCATION: 30 miles from Florence.

CONTACT: Pat Kuh, Villa Cennina/The Art of Italian Cuisine, Transitions Abroad, Inc., 197 W. 16th St., Chicago Heights, IL 60411; (708) 756-3655, Fax (708) 756-3420.

THE WORLD OF REGALEALI
Sicily/April-May, October-November

Founded 1989, Marchesa Anna Tasca Lanza offers weekly 2- and 5-day demonstration courses (limit 12 students) in Regaleali, her ancestral family home. Facilities: large professional kitchen with wood-burning oven in an 18th century farm house; adjoining estate and winery. Other activities: visits to archeological sites, markets, and programs on the estate's agricultural enterprises, which include wines, ricotta, and breads. Also available: classes for private groups.

EMPHASIS: Sicilian cooking utilizing meats, cheeses, vegetables, and wines from the estate.

FACULTY: Anna Tasca Lanza, author of *The Heart of Italy*; Mario Lo Menzo, the family chef; other local and guest chefs.

COSTS, ACCOMMODATIONS: The $1,200 ($2,200) cost includes all meals and 2 (5) days lodging at Regaleali. $500 deposit required, remainder due upon arrival.

LOCATION: 2 hours by train from Palermo, in central Sicily.

CONTACT: Judy Ebrey, P.O. Box 25228, Dallas, TX 75225; (214) 373-1161. Fax: (214) 373-1162, E-Mail: CuisineInt@aol.com

JAPAN

KONISHI JAPANESE COOKING CLASS
Tokyo/Year-round

Established in 1969, this school offers 40 participation classes (limit 10 students) per year. Facilities: 300-square-foot kitchen with Japanese utensils. Also available: classes for youngsters, market visits, private classes.

EMPHASIS: Healthy Japanese cooking with artistic presentation, including sushi, tempura, sukiyaki, soba, and nabemono (one-pot table cooking).

FACULTY: Mrs. Kiyoko Konishi has taught in English-speaking foreigners for 26 years and is author of *Japanese Cooking for Health and Fitness*, *Entertaining with a Japanese Flavor*, and three bilingual cooking videos. Her assistant is Naoko Morioka.

COSTS: 3,700 yen per session, payable in advance. Refund with 48 hours notice.

LOCATION: Central Tokyo.

CONTACT: Kiyoko Konishi, Konishi Japanese Cooking Class, 3-1-7-1405, Meguro, Meguro-ku, Tokyo, 153, Japan; (81) 3-3714-0085, Fax (81) 3-3714-0085.

TASTE OF CULTURE
Tokyo/Year-round

Established in 1970 by Elizabeth Andoh, this school offers four to six 1- to 4-session slide-illustrated lecture-demonstration (limit 25 students) and participation (limit 4) courses per year. Facilities: small home-style kitchen, fully equipped for Japanese cooking. Other activities: market field trips, private classes.

EMPHASIS: Japanese cooking: basics, vegetarian temple food, seasonal and ceremonial menus

FACULTY: Elizabeth Andoh is an IACP member and graduate of the Yanagihara School of Classical Cuisine.

COSTS, ACCOMMODATIONS: From 5,000 yen for demonstration class to 22,000 yen for 4-session participation course. Deposit is 5,000 yen for local residents (no refunds) and full fee for overseas students (refund minus 20% for cancellation 3 weeks prior). A list of nearby hotels is available.

CONTACT: Elizabeth Andoh, A Taste of Culture, 3-8-16 Yoga (Hilltop 109 #202), Setagaya-ku, Tokyo, 158, Japan; (813) 3-5716-5751, Fax (813) 3-5716-5751.

MEXICO

THE FLAVORS OF MEXICO—CULINARY ADVENTURES, INC.
Veracruz, Puebla, Oaxaca, Michoacan

Established in 1988, Marilyn Tausend's Culinary Adventures conducts 7- to 10-day hands-on cooking vacations to different regions of Mexico. Facilities: typically indoor and outdoor home and restaurant kitchens. Other activities: visits to food markets and cottage industries where food and food-related products are prepared, tours of historical and archaeological sites, and artisans' workshop.

EMPHASIS: Regional Mexican cuisine.

FACULTY: Marilyn Tausend, co-author of *Mexico the Beautiful Cookbook*; Mexican cooking authority Diana Kennedy, author of *The Art of Mexican Cooking* and *Mexican Regional Cooking*; Maria Dolores Torres Yzabal of the Instituto de Cultura Gastronomica, an organization dedicated to preserving traditional Mexican cookery; Shelley Wiseman, director of La Place, Ecole de Cuisine in Mexico City; Carmen Barnard, coordinator.

COSTS, ACCOMMODATIONS: Costs range from $2,000-$2,550, which includes meals, double occupancy lodging in small hotels, planned excursions, and local transport. A $300 deposit (50% nonrefundable) is required with balance due a month prior.

LOCATION: Oaxaca, Veracruz, and Michoacan are less than an hour's flight from Mexico City; Puebla is a 2-hour drive.

CONTACT: Marilyn Tausend, Culinary Adventures, Inc., 6023 Reid Dr. N.W., Gig Harbor, WA 98335; (206) 851-7676, Fax (206) 851-9532.

MEXICAN CUISINE SEMINARS WITH LULA BERTRAN
San Miguel de Allende/Early March, June, September

Since 1980, Lula Bertran has conducted hands-on seminars (limit 10 students) and personalized programs for individuals and groups. Facilities: conference room, fully-equipped kitchen. Other activities: guided market visits, dining at traditional restaurants, and short trips to nearby towns.

EMPHASIS: Mexican cuisine, food history, and eating customs; pre-Hispanic Indian cooking.

FACULTY: Food writer and author Lula Bertran is founding member of "The Mexican Culinary Circle" and academic investigator and board member of the Mexican Society of Gastronomy and Oenology.

COSTS, ACCOMMODATIONS: Single class (up to 4 people) is approximately $500; lodging ranges from $80 to $300, which usually includes breakfasts. A 50% deposit is required 60 days prior; balance is due 45 days prior. Cancellations more than 45 days prior forfeit 30% of deposit.

LOCATION: Mexico City, colonial cities, and beach resorts.

CONTACT: Lula Bertran, 9297 Siempre Viva Rd., Ste. MX-60-158, San Diego, CA 92173-3628; (525) 202-7251, Fax (525) 540-3633.

SEASONS OF MY HEART COOKING SCHOOL
(See also page 132) **Oaxaca/January-April, September-December**

Founded in 1993, this vacation school in a country farm setting offers hands-on cooking programs that include 1-week tours (limit 12 students), a 1-week professionals' course, 4-day weekend bed & breakfast courses (limit 2), and day class/market tours (limit 12). Facilities: Rancho Aurora, a working farm, has a large, handmade kitchen with 5 stations and an outdoor kitchen with parilla, wood-fire, and pre-Hispanic cooking utensils. Other activities: visits to corn and chocolate mills, mezcal factory, markets, archaeological sites, cheese and bread makers, farms, weavers, pottery makers and Spanish classes. Also available: private group tours and lectures.

EMPHASIS: Native and pre-Hispanic foods, wild plants and herbs, contemporary dishes.

FACULTY: Susana Trilling, IACP-member, chef, caterer, teacher and writer. Local chefs, cooks, farmers, and cheese and chocolate makers.

COSTS, ACCOMMODATIONS: Daily classes begin at $65; 4-day B&B $600; 1-week courses $1,295, including meals, lodging, and planned activities. Lodging in Oaxaca hotel (Casa Colonial) and private casita for B&B. Deposit ranges from A$150-A$200, of which A$100-A$200 is non-refundable.

LOCATION: A ranch surrounded by archaeological sites in the mountains outside Oaxaca.

CONTACT: Susana Trilling, Director, Seasons of My Heart Cooking School, Rancho Aurora Apto. 42, Admon 3, Oaxaca 68101, Mexico; (951) 6-52-80 (phone/fax). In U.S., Lee Lehto, booking agent, (800) 758-1697.

MOROCCO

LA CARAVANE ADVENTURES IN FOOD AND TRAVEL
Morocco/February or November
Since 1983, Kitty Morse has conducted an annual 2-week Morocco tour (limit 22 participants) that includes cooking demonstrations. by local experts. Other activities: travel to the seashore and the Sahara dunes, excursions to historic locales, shopping in souks and bazaars, dinner in a Marrakesh palm grove, visit with personal friends.

EMPHASIS: Moroccan cuisine and culture.

FACULTY: Kitty Morse was born in Casablanca and is author of *The Vegetarian Table: North Africa* and *The California Farm Cookbook*. She is a member of the Southern California Culinary Guild and the IACP. She also leads farm tours in Southern California.

COSTS, ACCOMMODATIONS: About $3,500, which includes airfare from New York, land transportation, double occupancy deluxe or first class lodging, two meals daily, and planned activities. A $500 deposit is usually required.

LOCATION: The coastal cities of Casablanca and Essaouira, historic cities of Fez, Marrakesh, Meknes, and Rabat, and desert kasbahs of Erfoud, Rissani, Ouarzazate, Taliouine, and Taroudant

CONTACT: Kitty Morse, La Caravane Adventures, P.O. Box 433, Vista, CA 92085; (619) 758-8631 (phone/fax).

NETHERLANDS

LA CUISINE FRANCAISE
Amsterdam/September-June
Established in 1980. This school offers 60 one- or four-session demonstration (limit 25 students) and participation (limit 16) courses per year. Facilities: a 90-square-meter kitchen rebuilt in 1994. Also available: sessions in English for groups, private classes, and market visits.

EMPHASIS: French, Italian, and English/Dutch cuisines

FACULTY: School owner and instructor Patricia I. van den Wall Bake-Thompson was born in Great Britain and studied home economics at Harrow Technical College. She serves as a consultant to food companies.

COSTS: Each session is $45 (75-105 Dutch guilder), payable in advance. A 10% deposit is required. Credit cards accepted.

LOCATION: In an 18th century canal house, which also houses a private restaurant, close to central Amsterdam and 10 minutes from the airport

CONTACT: La Cuisine Francaise, Herengracht 314, 1016 CD Amsterdam, Netherlands; (31) 20-6278725, Fax (31) 20-6203491.

NEW ZEALAND

THE EPICUREAN WORKSHOP
Auckland/Year-round
Established in 1989, this cookware store and school offers 80 demonstration (limit 35-40 students) and participation (limit 8) classes per year, and 1-hour Gourmet on the Run classes twice weekly. Facilities: teaching kitchen with overhead mirrors. Also available: children's and young adult's classes, Taste of New Zealand classes for visitors, private classes, and 5-day vacation programs.

EMPHASIS: Seasonal themes, classics, technique and method, ethnic cuisines, local and overseas guest chef specialties.

FACULTY: Director Catherine Bell is a graduate of Leith's School in London and an IACP member. Local chefs include Ray McVinnie, Greg Heffernan, and Peter Chichester

COSTS: Demonstrations range from NZ$6-NZ$57; weekend intensive basics is NZ$325; hands-on classes from NZ$100, young chef classes from NZ$43. Full payment required with booking; refund with 14 days notice, credit with 7 days notice.

LOCATION: Newmarket, a major shopping center in Auckland

CONTACT: The Epicurean Workshop, 27 Morrow St., P.O. Box 9255, Newmarket, Auckland, New Zealand; (64) 9-5240-906, Fax (64) 9-5242-017.

THE NEW ZEALAND SCHOOL OF FOOD AND WINE
(See page 132) — Christchurch/Year-round

This career school offers a foundation skills course three times a year, demonstration and practical classes, children's classes, and wine seminars. Students can sit in on full-time courses.

EMPHASIS: Classical French cuisine, developing cuisine of Australasia, understanding food and wine.

FACULTY: School founder Celia Hay, Graham Brown, Deborah Crosby, Catherine Bell, Jo Seagar.

COSTS: Range from NZ$30-NZ$250.

SCOTLAND

EDINBURGH COOKERY SCHOOL
(See page 133) — September-July

In addition to career courses, this school offers demonstration classes and 1- to 4-week beginner to advanced summer courses for all levels.

EMPHASIS: Various topics include Aga cookery, sugarcraft, vegetarian recipes, entertaining menus.

COSTS: Tuition, exclusive of VAT, is £700 for 4-week summer courses.

SPAIN

ALAMBIQUE SCHOOL
Madrid/October-June

Established in 1973 by Clara Maria Amezua, this school in a cookware store offers 2- to 4-session demonstration (limit 35-40 students) and participation (limit 10-12) courses for beginners and professionals. Facilities: 2 teaching kitchens equipped with microwave, gas, and electric ovens and overhead mirrors. Also available: classes for children, tailor-made courses, tours.

EMPHASIS: Classic and regional Spanish cuisines, international cuisines.

FACULTY: Victoria Llamas, Gloria Zunzunegui, Georgette Sournac, Marga Velasco, Isabel Maestre.

COSTS: Single sessions range from $22-$37, courses from $100-$700.

LOCATION: Alambique has outlets in Vigo.

CONTACT: Clara Maria Amezua de Llamas, Owner, Alambique, S.A., c/o Encarnacion, 2, Madrid 28013, Spain; (34) 547 8827 or 547 4220, Fax (34) 559 7802.

TAIWAN

TAIPEI CHINESE FOOD FESTIVAL
Taipei/August

This annual 3-day event features lectures on culinary culture, demonstrations by noted chefs, and professional cooking competitions. Taipei travel agencies organize gourmet tours that include visits to the National Palace Museum, the Fu Hsing Dramatic Arts Academy, the Tsushih Temple at Sanhsia, and the pottery kilns at Yingko.

LOCATION: Sungshan Domestic Airport Exhibition Hall.

CONTACT: Alex Hsiao, Taiwan Visitors Assn., One World Trade Ctr., Ste. 7953, New York, NY 10048; (212) 466-0691, Fax (212) 432-6436.

THAILAND

SALA SIAM — BOLDER ADVENTURES
Bangkok/Year-round
Since 1991, this tour company has offered weekly programs that include daily participation classes (limit 5 students). Facilities: a 1,000-square-foot kitchen with 3 work areas.

EMPHASIS: Thai cuisine.

FACULTY: Thai cook Peep Chinsanaboom.

COSTS, ACCOMMODATIONS: Approximately $125 per day. Standard stay is 4 days. Lodging is in a private teak villa.

LOCATION: Bangkok.

CONTACT: Rusty Staff, President, Bolder Adventures, P.O. Box 1279, Boulder, CO 80306; (800) 642-2742, Fax (303) 443-7078.

THE THAI COOKING SCHOOL AT THE ORIENTAL
Bangkok/Year-round
Since 1986, the Oriental Hotel has offered weekly 5-day demonstration courses (limit 25 students). Facilities: classroom, participation/demonstration room, kitchen, eating area.

EMPHASIS: Authentic Thai cuisine, including fruit and vegetable carving, flower arrangement, curries and condiments, stir-fried, steamed, and fried dishes, desserts, menu selection, substitute ingredients.

COSTS, ACCOMMODATIONS: Cost, which includes 5 nights lodging at The Oriental Hotel, most meals, and all planned activities, is $1,452 double occupancy ($1,965 single), $948 for non-cooking guest. $250 deposit is refundable a month prior, balance due a month prior. Hotel amenities include swimming pools, sports center, tennis and squash, oriental spa and health center.

LOCATION: Overlooking the Chao Phraya River, 15 minutes from main business district.

CONTACT: Ms. Mayuree Laolugsanalerd, Administrative Manager, The Thai Cooking School at The Oriental, 48 Oriental Ave., Bangkok 10500, Thailand; (662) 2360400/20, Fax (662) 236-1937-9. In the U.S., Mandarin Oriental Hotel Group; (800) 526-6566.

TURKEY

TOHUM CENTER FOR NATURAL LIVING AND HEALING ARTS
Çukurbag Village/May-June
Established in 1993, Tohum offers a 9-day trip that includes a 5-day, 15-hour, mostly demonstration course (limit 15 participants) that features a grain-based diet designed to individual health needs, utilizing organic produce from the Center's gardens. Facilities: outdoor clay pot cooking over a wood fire; indoor brick oven baking. Other activities: a 3-day Mediterranean yacht trip.

EMPHASIS: Traditional, healthful Anatolian cuisine, including bulghur, whole wheat, flatbreads, grupe molasses, and tahini.

FACULTY: Rebecca Wood, a natural foods industry consultant and author of *Whole Foods Encyclopedia* and *Quinoa: the Supergrain*; Aysogul Yuçesan of Çukurbag; Atilla Sevilmis, co-founder of Tohum, who teaches herbal medicine; folk dancer Okan Nalçaci; and village cooks.

NONVOCATIONAL/VACATION   **WEST INDIES**   **277**

COSTS, ACCOMMODATIONS: Cost is $1,950, which includes yacht trip, lodging, meals, ground transport, and all planned activities. A $500 deposit is required; balance due 45 days prior.

LOCATION: Southwestern Turkey, 8 miles from the Mediterranean.

CONTACT: Rebecca Wood, NATURALLY GRAND Junction Cooking School, 2837 Elm Ave., Grand Junction, CO 81501; (800) 838-1336, Fax (970) 242-7796.

WEST INDIES

COOKING IN PARADISE
St. Barthelemy/April

Since 1979, Steven Raichlen has conducted programs that include Cooking in Paradise, a 1-week hands-on culinary vacation (limit 10 participants) in the Caribbean. Facilities: open-air kitchen. Other activities: visits to top island restaurants, gourmet picnic, and sailing cruise. Also available: swimming, fishing, scuba diving, shopping in the capital of Gustavia.

EMPHASIS: Healthy Caribbean cuisine.

FACULTY: Cooking teacher, food writer, and syndicated columnist Steven Raichlen contributes to *Eating Well* and *Prevention* magazines, and the Los Angeles Times Syndicate. He is author of several cookbooks, including IACP Julia Child award-winner *Miami Spice* and *The New Caribbean Pantry*.

COSTS, ACCOMMODATIONS: Cost of $2,995 ($2,495 for non-cooking companion) includes meals, activities, and lodging at the Seahorse Hotel, which overlooks the ocean. Deposit of $500 is required with balance due February 1; no refunds after March 1.

LOCATION: St. Barthelemy's 8 square miles of beaches and hills are 8 miles from the island of St. Maarten.

CONTACT: Steven Raichlen, Director, Cooking in Paradise, P.O. Box 1597, Coconut Grove, FL 33233; (305) 854-9550, Fax (305) 854-2232.

LA SAMANNA
St. Martin/April

This island resort offers special interest weeks, one of which is a 1-week culinary vacation featuring signature dishes of Rosewood Hotels executive chefs. Other activities: swimming, sailing, wind-surfing, snorkeling, water-skiing, tennis. Also available: chartered sightseeing and deep-sea fishing cruises, shopping in Marigot and Philipsburg.

EMPHASIS: Southwestern and other regional cuisines, traditional British cooking, French provincial cooking.

FACULTY: Includes Dean Fearing, CIA's 1991 Chef of the Year; Paul Gayler, Marc Ehrler.

COSTS, ACCOMMODATIONS: Start at $590 per couple per day and include breakfast and dinner, hotel amenities, gratuities, and lodging in the 80-room residential-style La Samanna hotel. Full payment due within 10 days of reservation; refund with 21 days notice.

LOCATION: On 55 acres of beachfront property 10 minutes from Juliana International Airport and 5 minutes from Marigot, the capitol of French St. Martin.

CONTACT: La Samanna, P.O. Box 4077, 97064 St. Martin CEDEX, French West Indies, France; (590) 875122; Fax (590) 876400; Reservations in New York, MaryAnne DeMatteo, 509 Madison Avenue, Suite 1800, New York, NY 10022; 1-800-8542252; (212) 319-5191; Fax (212) 832-5390.

WORLDWIDE

THE ADVENTUROUS APPETITE
Turkey, India, Caribbean, Brazil/Spring, Summer, Fall

Established in 1994 by Bonnie Kassel, these 2-week culinary vacations are scheduled six times yearly and limited to 10 participants. The programs feature daily instruction, visits to wineries and food producers, dining at fine restaurants, cruises, shopping, and sightseeing.

EMPHASIS: Traditional regional cuisines.

FACULTY: Restaurant chefs, village women.

COSTS, ACCOMMODATIONS: Costs range from $3,000-$3,500, which includes airfare, lodging, meals, and all planned activities. A $500 deposit is required, refundable 60 days prior.

LOCATION: Destinations include the state of Goa in India, the colonial Caribbean, Bahia in northeastern Brazil, and cruising along the coast of Turkey.

CONTACT: Bonnie Kassel, The Adventurous Appetite, 56 W. 70th St., New York, NY 10023; (212) 873-9067, Fax (212) 496-1846.

CUISINE ECLAIREE
England, Sweden, U.S./February-July, September-November

Established in 1994, this company offers six hands-on 5-day vacation courses (limit 10-15 participants) per month. Facilities: 10 workspaces. Other activities: market and restaurant visits, wine tastings, sightseeing.

COSTS, ACCOMMODATIONS: Vary. A 10% nonrefundable deposit is required.

LOCATION: Stockholm, New Orleans, locations in the United Kingdom.

CONTACT: Elaine M. Lemm, Cuisine Eclairee, 5, the Poplars, Newton-on-Ouse, York, Y06 2BL, England; (44) 1347-848557.

CULINARY TRAVEL COMPANY
Worldwide/Year-round

Established in 1995, this tour operator offers 8-10 cooking vacations (limit 6-18 participants) per year that feature hands-on instruction as well as winery tours, visits to markets and food producers, dining at fine restaurants, and sightseeing.

EMPHASIS: Food, history, and culture.

FACULTY: Dan Strebel, proprietor, and experienced teachers in the countries visited.

COSTS, ACCOMMODATIONS: Costs vary.

LOCATION: The 1996 destinations include Mexico, Italy, France, Belize, Spain, and Asia.

CONTACT: Dan Strebel, The Culinary Travel Company, 210 W. Pickwick Rd., Arlington Heights, IL 60005; 708-640-6569 or 800-266-5319.

SPA & CULINARY ADVENTURES
Worldwide/Year-round

Established in 1994, this tour operator offers more than ten 5-day to 2-week cooking vacations per year. Instructional format: demonstration and participation. Class size: 20 students maximum. Two to six hours of instruction daily. Other activities: visits to wineries, food producers, markets; dining in private homes and fine restaurants; sightseeing.

EMPHASIS: Culture, history, and cuisines of the countries visited.

FACULTY: Resident culinary experts.

COSTS, ACCOMMODATIONS: Cost ranges from $650 to $3,000. A $150 deposit is required, balance is due 45 days prior.

CONTACT: Lynn Nicholson, President, Spa & Culinary Adventures, 13106 NW Germantown Rd., Portland, OR 97231; (800) 300-1565 or (503) 286-0333, Fax (503) 286-0733.

3

Wine Courses

Taught by Members of the American Wine Society (AWS) and the Society of Wine Educators (SWE)

The Guide to Cooking Schools 1996

CALIFORNIA

MICHAEL A. AMOROSE
San Francisco/Year-round

First offered 1974. 25 1-session courses per year. Enrollment 20 to 35 per class. Specialties: California and Pacific Northwest wines; 9 wines sampled per session; current vintages; price range $15 to $40 per bottle. Source of wines: instructor's cellar and current purchases. Instructor is author of seven books on wine. Tuition: $25 per session. Class location: meetings and conventions.

CONTACT: Michael A. Amorose, 555 California St., #1700, San Francisco, CA 94104; (415) 951-3377, Fax (415) 951-3296.

MARIAN W. BALDY
Chico/Spring

First offered 1972. One 15-week, 45-session course per year. Enrollment 180 students per class. Specialties: sensory evaluation, label reading, wine & food combining, table & sparkling wine production, viticulture; 4 wines sampled per session; 1994 to 1982 vintages; price range $5 to $85 per bottle. Source of wines: California. Instructor has AB degree in Microbiology and PhD in Genetics, experience as wine maker in commercial cellar, and wrote The University Wine Course and teacher's manual. Tuition: $295. Class location: California State University, Chico.

CONTACT: Marian W. Baldy, PhD, School of Agriculture, California State University, First & Normal Sts., Chico, CA 95929-0310; (916) 898-6250, Fax (916) 898-4675, E-Mail mbaldy@davax.csuchico.edu

ROBERT BECK
Rocklin/Fall, Spring

First offered 1987. 4 4-session courses per year. Enrollment 20 students per class. Specialties: worldwide, some California emphasis, wine & food; 7 to 8 wines sampled per session; various vintages; price range $4 to $60 per bottle. Instructor is member of SWE, grape grower, and wine maker. Tuition: $40 to $50 plus $15 to $20 lab fee.

CONTACT: Robert Beck, Sierra College, Rocklin, CA 96788; (916) 781-0590, Fax (916) 878-7878.

MICHAEL R. BOTWIN
San Luis Obispo/Fall, Winter, Spring

First offered 1983. 3 5-session courses per year. Enrollment approximately 15 students per class. Specialties: California wines with emphasis on central coast; 8 wines sampled per session; current vintages; price range $6 to $20 per bottle. Source of wines: local wine shops. Instructor is member of SWE with 20 years teaching experience. Tuition: $105. Class location: California Polytechnic State University (San Luis Obispo).

CONTACT: Michael R. Botwin, California Polytechnic State University, San Luis Obispo, CA 93407; (805) 543-1200 (home).

JOHN BUECHSENSTEIN
Northern California sites/Year-round

First offered 1978. Year-rond 1- or 2-day workshops and multiple session seminars. Enrollment 25-50 students per class. Specialties: sensory evaluation and winemaking; 12-24 wines sampled per session; current vintages to early 1980's; price range $5 to $60 per bottle. Instructor is wine maker with BS from U.C. Davis, and member of AWS, IFT, SWE, and ASEV. Tuition: $150 to $300 per course. Class location: University of California-Davis and other sites.

CONTACT: John Buechsenstein, Wine Education & Consultation, 309 Hillview Ave., Ukiah, CA 95482; (707) 468-8245, Fax (707)468-8245.

JAMES D. CRUM, PH.D.
San Bernardino/Fall, Winter, Spring
First offered 1980. 3 4-session courses per year. Enrollment 15 students per class. Specialties: getting to know wine, sensory evaluation, visits to local wineries; 10 to 12 wines sampled per session; 1994 to 1980 vintages; price range $5 to $20. Source of wines: purchased by instructor. Instructor is professor and Dean Emeritus, CSU-San Bernardino, International Wine Master, consultant, and lecturer. Tuition: $50 per session plus $25 wine fee. Class location: California State University Extension, San Bernardino.

CONTACT: James D. Crum, Ph.D, 5132 Sepulveda, San Bernardino, CA 92404-1134; (909) 886-3186, Fax (909) 886-3186.

ROBERT VERNON HOULEHAN
Berkeley/Year-round
First offered 1973. 3 6-session courses per year. Enrollment 12 students per class. Specialties: European and California wines; 5 wines sampled per session; current vintages to 20 years old; price range $7.50 to $20 per bottle. Instructor is member of SWE; travels to Europe twice a year. Tuition: $120 per course. Class location: private homes of students.

CONTACT: Robert V. Houlehan, 1320 Addison St., #C327, Berkeley, CA 94702; (510) 841-2829.

DENIS KELLY
Oakland/Year-round
First offered 1975. 3 to 5 10-session courses per year. Enrollment 14 to 30 students per class. Specialties: wines of Europe and America; 5 wines sampled per session; price range $7 to $75 per bottle. Instructor writes for *Wines & Spirits, Gourmet,* and other publications; author or co-author of 4 wine books, member of SWE. Tuition: $190 to $215 per course. Class location: University of California Extension-Berkeley, Diablo Valley College, private classes in Oakland and Berkeley.

CONTACT: Denis Kelly, 4482 Montgomery St., Oakland, CA 94611; (510) 658-8615, Fax (510) 428-1456.

FRED McMILLIN
San Francisco/Spring, Summer, Fall
First offered 1965. 5 to 6 3-session courses per year. Enrollment 15 students per class. Specialties: wine history, California wine history, ranking the great varietals; 20-30 wines sampled per session; current vintages to 1987; price range $8 to $30 per bottle. Source of wines: worldwide. Instructor has 2 degrees in chemical engineering, was offered teaching position in philosophy. Tuition: $60 to $90 plus $20 wine fee. Class location: San Francisco State University-Extended Education, San Francisco City College-Ft. Mason Campus.

CONTACT: Fred McMillin, 2121 Broadway, #6, San Francisco, CA 94115; (415) 563-5712.

G. M. "POOCH" PUCILOWSKI
Sacramento/Year-round
First offered 1973. 10 to 12 1- to 6-session courses per year. Enrollment 15 to 40 students per class. Specialties: California wines; 6 to 9 wines sampled per session; current vintages; price range $5 to $40 per bottle. Instructor and past-president of SWE; offers commercial courses to restaurants, wineries, and wholesalers. Tuition: $50 to $100 per course. Class location: local restaurants.

CONTACT: G.M. "Pooch" Pucilowski, 2701 E St., Sacramento, CA 95815; (916) 448-3664, Fax (916) 448-9115.

MARILYNN VILAS
Davis/October-June
First offered 1940. 10 2- to 3-hour classes per quarter. Enrollment 20 to 30 students per class. Specialties: enology & viticulture; Instructors all have Ph.D's. Tuition: in-state $4,500, out-of-state

WINE COURSES — FLORIDA

$14,000 per year. Class location: University of California-Davis.

CONTACT: Marilynn Vilas, University of California, Department of Viticulture & Enology, Davis, CA 95615; (916) 752-2260, Fax (916) 752-0382.

ALAN YOUNG
San Francisco/Year-round

First offered 1974. 20 6-session courses per year. Enrollment 10 students per class. Specialties: Winelovers' Bootcamp 3-day courses and home study programs; 8 wines sampled per session; 1994 to 1980 vintages; price range $3 to $150 per bottle. Source of wines: international. Instructor is Australian wine consultant and author of 12 books. Other faculty members are internationally known winemakers and writers. Tuition: $247 to $347 per course. Class location: Napa and Sonoma Valleys, Long Island, Australia, New Zealand, Europe.

CONTACT: Dr. Alan Young, President, International Wine Academy, 38 Portola Drive, San Francisco, CA 94131-1518; (415) 641-4767, Fax (415) 641-7348.

CONNECTICUT

ROMOLO D. TEDESCHI
Bethany/Fall, Spring

First offered 1981. 2 6-session courses per year. Enrollment 15 to 20 students per class. Specialties: California, European, and Australian wines; 4 wines sampled per session; current vintages; price range under $10 per bottle. Instructor was awarded Order of Merit and 2 Scholar of Wine awards from Les Amis du Vin and is a member of SWE. Tuition: $125 per 6-week course. Class location: Sacred Heart University, Fairfield.

CONTACT: Romolo D. Tedeschi, 4 Glenwood Ct., Bethany, CT 06524; (203) 393-3796.

FLORIDA

CHARLES FAIRES
Ft. Lauderdale/Fall, Spring

First offered 1980. 2 6 to 8-session courses per year. Enrollment 18. 8 to 12 wines sampled per session; price range $6 to $20 per bottle. Instructor is member of AWS. Tuition: $90 per course. Class location: University of Tennessee/Non-credit Program, Knoxville, TN.

CONTACT: Charles Faires, P.O. Box 290367, Ft. Lauderdale, FL 33329; (305) 563-7738.

JOSEPH J. SCHAGRIN
Ft. Lauderdale/Year-round

First offered 1961. 10 2-session courses per year. Enrollment 12 students per class. Specialties: worldwide varieties; 8 wines sampled per session; 2 to 20 year old vintages; price range $5 to $50 per bottle. Instructor is President and National Director of Tasters Guild with 30 years teaching experience. Tuition: $150 per course. Class location: home and office.

CONTACT: Joseph J. Schagrin, 1451 W. Cypress Creek Rd., #300, Ft. Lauderdale, FL 33309; (305) 928-2823, Fax (305) 928-2624.

GEORGIA

ANITA LOUISE LARAIA
Atlanta/January, March, May, October

First offered 1978. 4 6-session courses per year. Enrollment 60 students per class. Specialties: worldwide varieties, home study course book & audio cassettes; 6 wines sampled per session; current vintages to 1970; price range $6 to $80 per bottle. Instructor has Certificate from the Wine &

Spirits Guild of Great Britain, wine writer for *Atlanta Homes* magazine, and is member of SWE. Tuition: $200 per 6-session course. Class location: Wyndham Garden Hotel, Buckhead; private restaurant and corporate classes.

CONTACT: Anita Louise LaRaia, Director, The Wine School, P.O. Box 52723, Atlanta, GA 30355; (404) 901-9433.

ILLINOIS

PAUL ERNST
Darien/Year-round

First offered 1977. Enrollment 40 to 50 students per class. 6 to 30 wines sampled per session; current vintages to 1960's; price range $5 to $100 per bottle. Instructor is past president of Midwest SWE, Director of Chicago Les Amis du Vin and Wine Lovers Intl. Tuition: $120 per 6-session course, $10 to $95 per single session. Class location: hotels and restaurants.

CONTACT: Paul Ernst, 8321-B Portsmouth Dr., Darien, IL 60561; (708) 654-WINE, Fax 708-789-8186.

PATRICK W. FEGAN
Chicago/Year-round

First offered 1984. 6 semesters of four 5-week levels and five 1-night seminars 5-session courses per year. Enrollment 100 to 150 students per semester. 5 to 10 wines sampled per session; current to older vintages; price range price range $1.99 to $50 per bottle. Source of wines: retail shops. Instructor is wine columnist and writer, wine judge with 20 years teaching experience. Tuition: $140 to $225 per 5-week course, $35-$50 per 1-night seminar.

CONTACT: Patrick W. Fegan, Director, Chicago Wine School, 1633 N. Halsted St., Chicago, IL 60614; (312) 266-9463, Fax (312) 266-9769, E-Mail pwfegan@aol.com

IRENE HUFFMAN
Milan/Spring, Fall

First offered 1985. 2 to 6 4-session courses per year. Enrollment 10 to 15 students per class. 8 to 10 wines sampled per session; price range $6 to $60 per bottle. Source of wines: purchased. Instructor board member SWE, wine columnist, wine judge. Tuition: $95/4-sessions, $25 to $40 for classes. Class location: Plaza One Hotel (Black Hawk College Outreach Program).

CONTACT: Irene Huffman, Saelens Beverages, Inc., 1225 W. 5th St., Milan, IL 61264; (309) 787-6941, Fax (309) 787-0863.

KANSAS

LLOYD DAVENPORT
Manhattan/Fall, Spring

First offered 1968. 2 5-session courses per year. Enrollment 20 students per class. Specialties: worldwide varieties, viticulture; 6 to 8 wines sampled per session; price range $5 to $30 per bottle. Instructor is member of SWE. Tuition: $50 per course.

CONTACT: Lloyd Davenport, 2909 Sunnyside Dr., Manhattan, KS 66502.

LOUISIANA

FORREST K. DOWTY
Lafayette/Fall, Spring

First offered 1978. Enrollment 50 students per class. Specialties: worldwide varieties, occasional wine trips; 8 wines sampled per session; price range $2 to $100 per bottle. Instructor owns

Magnolia & Reliable Marketing of Lafayette (wine wholesaler), has SWE Certificate of Proficiency, and 50 year wine experience. Tuition: $100 beginners, $150 advanced.

CONTACT: Forrest K. Dowty, Box 3587, Lafayette, LA 70502; (318) 233-9244, Fax (318) 261-3570.

MASSACHUSETTS

MICHAEL APSTEIN, MD
Boston/Year-round

First offered 1980. 6 6-session courses per year. Enrollment 30 students per class. Specialties: worldwide varieties; 5 wines sampled per session; current vintages to 1983; price range $5 to $35 per bottle. Instructor is wine writer and educator for 15 years, wine editor of Grand Diplome Cooking Course, judge in national and international competition, and gastroenterologist specializing in liver disease. Tuition: $129 per course. Class location: Boston Center for Adult Education.

CONTACT: Michael Apstein, MD, Boston Center for Adult Education, 5 Commonwealth Ave., Boston, MA 02116; (617) 267-4430.

JERRY GOLDMAN
N. Andover/Fall, Winter, Spring

First offered 1972. 4 6 to 8-session courses per year. Enrollment 20 students per class. Specialties: wine appreciation, specific regions; 6 wines sampled per session; current vintages to late 1970's; price range $10 to $50 per bottle. Instructor is SWE and AWS member, appears on TV and radio talk shows, and taught at Northern Essex Community College and Merrimac College. Tuition: $65 to $85 per course. Class location: Messina's Liquor Store, N. Andover.

CONTACT: Jerry Goldman, Messina's Liquor Store, 117 Main St., N. Andover, MA 01845; (508) 686-9649, Fax (508) 681-8498.

DIANE L. HENAULT
Scituate/Year-round

First offered 1976. 5 1 to 6-session courses per year. Enrollment 9 to 16 students per class. Specialties: Italian, German, and Spanish wines; 6 to 8 wines sampled per session. Instructor is author of *Wines of New England, 1981,* and member of SWE. Tuition: $40 to $85 per single session. Class location: Cambridge Center for Adult Education, Cambridge.

CONTACT: Diane L. Henault, Cambridge Center for Adult Education, 39 Ladds Way, Scituate, MA 02066; (617) 545-7309, Fax (617) 545-0344.

MARYLAND

LISA AIREY
Baltimore/Year-round

First offered 1992. 8 3-session courses per year. Enrollment 25 to 35 students per class. 6 wines sampled per session; current vintages to 1985; price range $4 to $20 per bottle. Instructor is wine consultant for Kronheim Co. (wine wholesaler) and member of AWS. Tuition: $65 per course. Class location: Notre Dame Prep School, Towson.

CONTACT: Lisa Airey, 99 Ray Rd., Baltimore, MD 21227; (410) 242-8000, Fax (410) 242-3493.

MINNESOTA

GEORGE RENIER
Duluth/Fall, Spring

First offered 1979. 2 8-10-session courses per year. Enrollment 18-35 students per class. Specialties: wine & beer making at home; 3 wines sampled per session. Instructor is AWS judge and winemaker since 1950. Tuition: $15 to $20 per course plus fee. Class location: Duluth Jr. High Schools.

CONTACT: George Renier, 2418 E. 4th St., Duluth, MN 55812; (218) 724-2558.

MONTANA

GREGORY B. CARTER
Missoula/Year-round
First offered 1982. 6 6-session courses per year. Enrollment 25 to 30 students per class. Specialties: California, French, and German wines, local wine education & restaurant tours; 4 to 5 wines sampled per session; current vintages to 15 years old. Instructor is member of SWE. Tuition: $50 per course. Class location: local restaurants.

CONTACT: Gregory B. Carter, P.O. Box 5596, Missoula, MT 59806; (406) 543-6634, Fax (406) 728-4405.

NEW JERSEY

JOSEPH FIOLA
Cream Ridge/Fall, Spring, Summer
First offered 1989. 2 to 3 single-session-session courses per year. Enrollment 50 to 100 students per class. Specialties: Northeastern U.S. wines; 3 to 8 wines sampled per session. Instructor has Ph.D in Horticulture; won the AWS gold and bronze awards for wines produced. Tuition: $50 per course. Class location: Rutgers University-Cooper Extension, New Brunswick.

CONTACT: Joseph Fiola, 283 Rte. 539, Cream Ridge, NJ 08514; (609) 758-7311, Fax (609) 758-7085.

ROBERT LEVINE
Princeton/Fall, Spring
First offered 1970. 2 5-session courses per year. Enrollment 32 students per class. Specialties: classical varietals, label reading, component identification, recognizing spoiled wines; 5 to 8 wines sampled per session; current vintages to 1965; price range $5 to $100 per bottle. Instructor Founder & President Emeritus of SWE, member AWS, conducts many seminars in NY, Paris and elsewhere. Tuition: $110 per course. Class location: Princeton Adult School.

CONTACT: Robert Levine, 29 Linwood Circle, Princeton, NJ 08540; (609) 924-6328.

GARY C. PAVLIS, PH.D.
Mays Landing/Fall, Spring
First offered 1992. 2 14-session courses per year. Enrollment 25 students per class. Specialties: worldwide; 6 wines sampled per session; 1974 to 1994 vintages; price range $3 to $30 per bottle. Source of wines: various. Instructor is member of SWE and AWS Certified Judge. Tuition: $125. Class location: Rutgers University.

CONTACT: Gary C. Pavlis, PhD., 6260 Old Harding Hwy., Mays Landing, NJ 08330; (609) 625-0056, Fax (609) 625-3646.

NEW YORK

GREG GIORGIO
Altamonte/Year-round
First offered 1987. 1 to 2 single-session-session courses per year. Enrollment 20 students per class. Specialties: current vintages; 3 to 4 wines sampled per session; price range $7 to $15 per bottle. Instructor is SWE member. Tuition: $10 to $20 per session. Class location: local restaurants.

CONTACT: Greg Giorgio, P.O. Box 74, Altamonte, NY 12009.

WINE COURSES   NEW YORK

INTERNATIONAL WINE CENTER
New York/Year-round

First offered 1981. 25 to 30 1 to 14-session courses per year. Enrollment 12 to 35 students per class. Specialties: worldwide; 7 to 10 wines sampled per session; various vintages; price range $3 to $40 per bottle. Source of wines: purchased. Instructors with various backgrounds and director Mary Ewing Mulligan. a Master of Wine. Tuition: $40 to $950. Class location: International Wine Center.

CONTACT: Steven Miller, Manager, International Wine Center, 231 W. 29th St., New York, NY 10001; (212) 268-7517, Fax (212) 239-4497.

RONALD A. KAPON
New York/Fall, Spring

First offered 1969. 2 6-session courses per year. Enrollment 20 to 100 students per class. Specialties: worldwide; 6 to 12 wines sampled per session; price range $6 to $80 per bottle. Instructor is graduate of German Wine Academy and a Ph.D. in Economics. Tuition: $100. Class location: Queens College, Gramercy Park Hotel, Wine Workshop.

CONTACT: Ronald Kapon, 230 W. 79th St., #42, New York, NY 10024; (212) 799-6311.

HARRIET LEMBECK
New York City/Fall, Spring, Summer

First offered 1975. Enrollment 60 students (N.Y. Helmsley), 30 students (New School). Specialties: worldwide wines and spirits; 6-10 wines sampled per session; all current, some old vintages; price range $5 to $125 per bottle. Source of wines: retail stores, private cellar, industry samples. Instructor is author of *Grossman's Guide to Wines, Beers, & Spirits, 7th ed.* and Director of New School wine and wine & spirits program. Tuition: $525/10-session course, $700 with spirits ($200 spirits alone), $60 to $225/course at New School. Class location: N.Y. Helmsley Hotel, Pen & Pencil Restaurant (New School).

CONTACT: Harriet Lembeck, Director, Wine & Spirits Program, 54 Continental Ave., Forest Hills, NY 11375; (718) 263-3134, Fax (718) 263-3750.

HARVARD LYMAN
Stony Brook/Fall

First offered 1974. 1 15-session courses per year. Enrollment 25 to 40 students per course. Specialties: all major regions, wine making styles, grapes, wine and health, wine economics; 6 wines sampled per session; 3 to 5 year-old vintages; price range $5 to $30 per bottle. Source of wines: local. Instructor is member of AWS and Charter Member SWE. Tuition: $90 per credit (1 or 3 credits). Class location: SUNY-Stony Brook.

CONTACT: Harvard Lyman, Dept. Biochemistry/Cell Biology, SUNY-Stony Brook, Stony Brook, NY 11794-5215; (516) 632-8534, Fax (516) 632-8575, E-Mail hlyman@cc.allin1.sunysb.edu

DAVID G MALE
Williamsville/Fall, Spring

First offered 1986. 2 10-session courses per year. Enrollment 30 students per class. Specialties: all wines, wines and foods of the world; 6-8 wines sampled per session; 1975 to 1994 vintages; price range $7-$50 per bottle. Instructor: vice-president of Intervin (intl. wine competition) with 30 years teaching experience. Tuition: $235. Class location: Eagle House Restaurant, Williamsville.

CONTACT: David G. Male, President, Vintage House, 441 Sprucewood Terr., Williamsville, NY 14221-3910; (716) 634-2456, Fax (716) 634-7061.

PAUL S. MANDALA, M.D.
West Islip/Fall, Winter, Spring

First offered 1980. 5 to 6 5-session courses per year. Enrollment 12 students per class. Specialties: worldwide; 8 wines sampled per session; Instructor is member SWE. Tuition: $200 to $250. Class location: office.

CONTACT: Paul S. Mandala M.D., 1111 Montauk Hwy, W. Islip, NY 11795; (516) 665-8098, Fax (516) 665-8098.

TAO PORCHON-LYNCH
White Plains/Fall, Winter, Spring

First offered 1985. 3 6- to 8-session courses per year. Enrollment 12 to 20 students. Specialties: France, Spain, Australia, and regional U.S.; 8 wines sampled per session; price range $10 to $75 per bottle. Instructor is a member of AWS (Life), SWE, a wine judge, and wine writer/publisher. Tuition: $100. Class location: Harvest Moon in Nyack, J.C.C. in Ardsley, La Reserve.

CONTACT: Tao Porchon-Lynch, Les Amoreux Du Vin, 5 Barker Ave., #501, White Plains, NY 10601; (914) 761-7700 ext.2501, Fax (914) 997-2617.

DR. HERBERT F. SPASSER
New York/Fall

First offered 1976. 2 5-session courses per year. Enrollment 20 students. Specialties: Italy, France, Germany, U.S.; 5 to 6 wines sampled per session; 1978 to 1992 vintages; price range $7 to $40 per bottle. Source of wines: purchased and donated. Instructor is Certificate Member of SWE, Chevalier/Commandeur Chaine de Rotisseurs, and wine advisor to the Restaurant Society of N.Y. Tuition: $225. Class location: Midtown Manhattan.

CONTACT: Dr. Herbert F. Spasser, 116 Central Park So., New York, NY 10019; (212)765-1877.

THE WINE SCHOOL AT WINDOWS ON THE WORLD
New York/Spring, Summer, Fall

First offered 1976. 5 8-session courses per year. Enrollment 125 students per class. Specialties: major wine regions of the world; 10 wines sampled per session; 1970's to present vintages; price range $10 to $150 per bottle. Source of wines: purchased. Instructor is Wine Director of Windows on the World, author of *Windows on the World Complete Wine Course,* Board member SWE, 1993 James Beard Wine & Spirits Professional of the Year. Tuition: $425. Class location: World Trade Center.

CONTACT: Rebecca Chapa, Coordinator, The Wine School at Windows on the World, 106th floor, World Trade Center, New York, NY 10048-0605; (212) 912-0344, Fax (212) 775-0847.

OHIO

MATTHEW CITRIGLIA
Cleveland/Year-round

First offered 1988. 2 1-session courses per year. Enrollment 8 to 25 students per class. 5 to 6 wines sampled per session; price range $8 to $25 per bottle. Instructor is AWS certified judge. Tuition: $20 to $25.

CONTACT: Matthew Citriglia, 2967 W. 14th St., Cleveland, OH 44113; (216) 574-4360, Fax (216) 248-9242.

JAMES HEMESATH
Middletown/Fall, Winter

First offered 1983. 2 6-session courses per year. Enrollment 20 students per class. Specialties: worldwide; 6-9 wines sampled per session; current to early 1970's vintages; price range up to $100 per bottle. Instructor is SWE member and wine judge. Tuition: $150. Class location: Arts in Middletown Building.

CONTACT: James Hemesath, 639 DaVinci Dr,, Middletown, OH 45042; (513) 425-0788.

ROBERT LINER/MATTHEW ELSEN — WINE MERCHANTS
Portland/Winter, Summer, Fall

First offered 1990. 3 3-session courses per year. Enrollment 20 students per class. Specialties: France and West Coast U.S.; 8 wines sampled per session; 1985 to current vintages; price range $10 to $80 per bottle. Instructors have 17 to 20 years experience. Tuition: $85. Class location: in store.

CONTACT: , Liner & Elsen Wine Merchants, 202 N.W. 21st Ave., Portland, OR 97209; (503) 241-9463, Fax (503) 243-6706.

PENNSYLVANIA

WILLIAM H. CLARK
Longhorne/Fall, Spring

First offered 1976. 2 10-session courses per year. Enrollment 30 students per class. Specialties: U.S. and European; 5 wines sampled per session; price range $10 to $30 per bottle. Instructor is member SWE. Tuition: $100. Class location: Neshaminy Adult School.

CONTACT: William H. Clark, 74 Hollybrooke Dr., Longhorne, PA 19047.

LOUIS J. DIGIACOMO
Paoli/Spring, Fall

First offered 1979. 4 8-session courses per year. Enrollment 42 students. Specialties: all regions; 6 wines sampled per session; current vintages; price range $7 to $25 per bottle. Source of wines: local. Instructor is a wine writer/lecturer. Tuition: $60. Class location: Main Line School Night, Radnor.

CONTACT: Louis J. DiGiacomo, 204 Country Rd., Berwyn, PA 19312; (215) 563-7700, Fax (215) 563-3337.

JOHN ELD
Pittsburgh/Spring, Summer, Fall

First offered 1988. 6 4-session courses per year. Enrollment 16 students per class. Specialties: California; 5 to 6 wines sampled per session. Instructor is wine wholesaler and AWS member. Tuition: $42.

CONTACT: John Eld, Community College of Allegheny County, 8701 Perry Hwy., Pittsburgh, PA 15237-9987; (412) 369-3736.

ALTON LONG
Bryn Mawr/Year-round

Instructor is member of AIWF. Tuition: $25 per seminar, $48 per dinner. Class location: Yangming restaurant.

CONTACT: Charlotte Ann Albertson, P.O. Box 27, Wynnewood, PA 19096-0027; (610) 649-9290.

SHIRLEY MARTIN COUNTRY WINES
Pittsburgh/September-October

First offered 1975. 2 3-session courses per year. Enrollment 5 to 20 students per class. Specialties: wine making. Instructor is a member of AWS and a graduate of Penn. State University with a major in home economics. Tuition: $18. Class location: Country Wines, Pittsburgh.

CONTACT: Shirley Martin, 3333 Babcock Blvd., Pittsburgh, PA 15237; (412) 366-0151, Fax (412) 366-9809.

PAUL G. MOFFITI
Drexel Hill/Fall, Spring

First offered 1989. 2 8-session courses per year. Enrollment 20 students per class. Specialties: wine evaluation-judging; 6 wines sampled per session; varied vintages; price range $5 to $15 per bottle. Source of wines: local. Instructor is AWS certified judge and teaches AWS certification classes. Tuition: $60. Class location: Main Line school night adult education.

CONTACT: Paul G. Moffiti, 834 Alexander Ave., Drexel Hill, PA 19026; (215) 789-0198.

DICK NAYLOR
Stewartstown/Year-round

First offered 1980. 2 6-session courses per year. Enrollment 20 to 30 students per class. Specialties: dry red wine; 4 to 6 wines sampled per session; current to late 1980's vintages; price range $5 to $15 per bottle. Instructor is AWS and SWE member and lecturer. Tuition: $55. Class location: Naylor Wine Cellars.

CONTACT: Dick Naylor, Naylor Wine Cellars, RFD #3, Box 424, Stewartstown, PA 17363; (717) 993-2431, Fax (717) 993-9460.

RICHARD SAUL
Slatington

First offered 1986. Specialties: all regions and subjects; price range varies. Instructor is AWS member and wine judge examiner. Tuition: varies.

CONTACT: Richard Saul, 2391 Rockdale Rd., Slatington, PA 18080; (610) 767-0282.

SYLVIA H. SCHRAFF
Altoona/Spring, Fall

First offered 1987. 2 2-session courses per year. Enrollment 25 students. Specialties: basic wine appreciation; 5-6 wines sampled per session; 1989 to 1994 vintages; price range $6 to $12 per bottle. Instructor is owner/wine maker of Oak Spring Winery and has M.S. degree in Nursing Science. Tuition: $25. Class location: Oak Spring Winery.

CONTACT: Sylvia Schraff, President, Oak Spring Winery, R.D.1, Box 612, Altoona, PA 16601; (814) 946-3799.

EDWARD TURBA
Pittsburgh/Winter, Summer

First offered 1988. Specialties: worldwide; 5 wines sampled per session; Instructor is SWE member, taught at Intl. Culinary Academy, Le Mont restaurant sommelier for 8 years. Tuition: $200/3-hour session excl. wine. Class location: privately arranged.

CONTACT: Edward Turba, Sommelier, 3 Soffel St., Pittsburgh, PA 15211; (412) 431-2467.

PUERTO RICO

PEDRO J. BORRAS
Guaynabo/Year-round except June-July

First offered 1978. 4 5 to 8-session courses and one-day seminars per year. Enrollment 25 to 30 students per class. 5 to 8 wines sampled per session; current to late 1970's vintages; price range $8 to $60 per bottle. Instructor is SWE member. Tuition: $185 to $225. Class location: local cooking school.

CONTACT: Pedro J. Barras, Green Hill, G-2, Garden Hill, Guaynabo, PR 00966; (809) 759-6105.

TENNESSEE

SHIELDS T. HOOD
Memphis/Fall, Spring

First offered 1978. 5 3-session courses per year. Enrollment 18 to 30 students per class. Specialties:

WINE COURSES TENNESSEE 291

California and worldwide; 10 wines sampled per session; current vintages; price range $5 to $50 per bottle. Instructor is SWE certified with 23 years wine experience. Tuition: $20 per session. Class location: local restaurants.

CONTACT: Shields T. Hood, 905 James St., Memphis, TN 38106; (901) 774-8888, Fax (901) 946-4751.

JOHN IACOVINO
Oak Ridge/Fall, Spring, Summer

First offered 1989. 3 4- to 6-session courses per year. Enrollment 25 to 30 students per class. 6 to 9 wines sampled per session; current to early 1980's vintages; price range $8 to $80 per bottle. Source of wines: local stores, winery direct, personal cellar. Instructor is member AWS, Senechal of Ducal Order of Croix du Burgogne, and judge for Tennessee Intl. Wine Festival. Tuition: $100 to $125. Class location: local restaurants and homes.

CONTACT: John Iacovino, 120 Westlook Circle, Oak Ridge, TN 37830; (615) 483-8330, Fax (615) 482-2495.

RAYMOND SKINNER, JR.
Memphis/Fall, Winter

First offered 1983. 1 6-session course per year. Enrollment 20 students per class. Specialties: southern U.S.; 4 to 5 wines sampled per session; current vintages; price range $5 to $20 per bottle. Instructor is member SWE. Tuition: $40 to $60. Class location: includes local wineries.

CONTACT: Raymond Skinner, Jr., 1370 Madison, Memphis, TN 38104; (901) 725-9128.

JAMES D. STOUT
Knoxville/

First offered 1978. 3 7-session courses per year. Enrollment 18 students per class. Specialties: French, Italian, Australian, Chilean, California and eastern U.S.; 7 to 8 wines sampled per session; 1970 to 1990 vintages; price range $6 to $35 per bottle. Source of wines: retail outlets. Instructor is member AWS and Cross of Burgundy Wine Society with 20 years teaching experience. Tuition: $110. Class location: University of Tennessee.

CONTACT: Jack Stiles, Program Coordinator, University of Tennessee, 600 Henley St., Ste. 105, Knoxville, TN 37902; (615) 574-0150.

VIRGINIA

DR. JOSEPH FORMICA
Richmond/Fall

First offered 1992. 1 15-session courses per year. Enrollment 20 students. Specialties: sensory evaluation, physical and chemical compatibilities with food; 6 wines sampled per session; late 1980's to current vintages; price range $7 to $50 per bottle. Source of wines: local. Instructor is SWE member, certified by Wine & Spirit Education Trust of England, and a Ph.D. in microbiology. Tuition: $135 plus $75 lab fee. Class location: J. Sargent Reynolds Community College.

CONTACT: Dr. Joseph Formica, Director, The Wine School, 8402 Gaylord Rd., Richmond, VA 23229-4126; (804) 747-8163.

STEFAN GRABINSKI
Richmond/Spring, Fall, Winter

First offered 1970. 3 to 6 8-session courses per year. Enrollment 16 students per class. Specialties: wine countries and regions, wine making and evaluations; 6 wines sampled per session; 1970 to current vintages; price range $7 to $20 per bottle. Source of wines: local. Instructor is SWE and AWS member, founding member of Richmond Wine Society, and former vineyard owner. Tuition:

$100 plus wine fee. Class location: local college and restaurants.

CONTACT: Stefan Grabinski, 4944 Farrell Ct., Richmond, VA 23228; (804) 270-6255.

JOHN KEATING
Poquoson/Fall, Spring

First offered 1977. 2 8-session courses per year. Enrollment 20 students per class. Specialties: worldwide; 6 wines sampled per session; price range $10 per bottle. Instructor teaches at Johnson & Wales. Tuition: $150. Class location: College of William & Mary.

CONTACT: John E. Keating, 7 Roberts Landing, Poquoson, VA 23662; (804) 868-7543.

SHARON LIVINGSTON
Fredericksburg/Fall and Spring

First offered 1985. 2 10-session courses per year. Enrollment 20 students per class. Specialties: overview; 4 wines sampled per session; price range $5 to $20 per bottle. Source of wines: wine shops and Virginia wineries. Instructor is past president of Virginia Vineyards Assn, publisher of Virginia Wine Line and author *Virginia Wine of the Month Club Journal*. Tuition: $100. Class location: local restaurant.

CONTACT: Sharon Livingston, Sharline, 586 Truslow Rd., Fredericksburg, VA 22406-5500; (703) 373-1371.

CANADA

MICHAEL BOTNER, C.A. — ACCOUNTING FOR TASTE
Ottawa/Fall, Winter, Spring

First offered 1992. 2 15-session courses per year. Enrollment 24 students per class. Specialties: sommelier certificate program, advanced theory and practicum; 7 to 8 wines sampled per session; 1970 and later vintages; price range averages $15 to $20 per bottle. Instructor is a wine judge and consultant and a wine writer/columnist since 1979. Tuition: $250. Class location: Algonquin College.

CONTACT: Michael Botner, Accounting for Taste, 929 Fairlawn Ave., Ottawa, ON K2A 3S6 ; (613) 728-5480, Fax (613) 728-5480.

JIM CRAWFORD —MANITOBA LIQUOR CONTROL COMMISSION
Winnipeg/Year-round

First offered 1992. 5 to 10 5-session courses per year. Enrollment 20 students per class. Specialties: all major wine regions; 12 wines sampled per session; last 10 years vintages; price range $5 to $100 per bottle. Instructors are graduates of British Wine & Spirit Education Certificate course. Tuition: $50. Class location: in-house.

CONTACT: Jim Crawford, Coordinator Product Education, Manitoba Liquor Control Commission, P.O. Box 1023, Winnipeg, MB R3T 1L9; (204) 474-5553, Fax (474) 475-7686.

HANS W. TEUNISSEN
Willowdale/Irregularly year-round

First offered 1983. 2 to 3 10-session courses per year. Enrollment 15 students per class. Specialties: worldwide; 8 wines sampled per session; varied vintages; price range $5 to $50 per bottle. Instructor is SWE member. Tuition: C$120. Class location: community college.

CONTACT: Hans Teunissen, 31 Wedgewood Dr., Willowdale, ON M2M 2H2; (416) 733-9441.

4

Food & Wine Organizations

ORGANIZATIONS 295

AMERICAN CULINARY FEDERATION (ACF)
St. Augustine, Florida

Founded in 1929. Membership 25,000. Oldest nationwide professional cooks' association recognized by other leading food service organizations. Objectives: to further the advancement of the profession and offer training, education, and fellowship. More than 280 local chapters in the U.S. and Caribbean. Membership benefits include: educational seminars at national and regional meetings; monthly magazine, *The National Culinary Review*, competitions for medals in culinary arts shows sponsored by local chapters. The ACF and the NRA jointly sponsor the United States Culinary "Olympic" Team, which competes in the Culinary "Olympics" every 4 years in Germany.

The American Culinary Federation Educational Institute (ACFEI), an ACF subsidiary, accredits culinary schools through its Accrediting Commission (page XX), certifies chefs on the basis of knowledge and experience, awards loans and scholarships to students, and provides a U.S. Department of Labor recognized 3-year National Apprenticeship Training Program for Cooks. Certification categories include Certified Cook/Pastry Cook (CC, CPC), Certified Sous Chef/Certified Chef de Cuisine and/or Pastry Chef (CSC, CCC, CPC), Certified Culinary Educator (CCE), Certified Executive Chef and/or Executive Pastry Chef (CEC, CEPC), and the highest level, Certified Master Chef/Pastry Chef (CMC, CMPC). Another ACF subsidiary, The American Academy of Chefs, is the honor society of American chefs.

CONTACT: ACF, P.O. Box 3466, St. Augustine, FL 32085; (800) 624-9458 or (904) 824-4468, Fax (904) 825-4758.

AMERICAN DIETETIC ASSOCIATION (ADA)
Chicago, Illinois

Founded in 1917. Membership 66,000, 75% registered dietitians. Mission is to promote sound nutrition information for the public via publications, national events, and media and marketing programs. Establishes and enforces quality standards for training and practice in clinical nutrition, foodservice systems management, community dietetics; lobbies for federal legislation. Total scholarships awarded last year $165,000 (approximately 165 awarded at $1,000 each). Includes 50 state and 220 district affiliates. Established nonprofit ADA Foundation.

CONTACT: American Dietetic Association, 216 W. Jackson Blvd., Ste. 800, Chicago, IL 60606-6995; (312) 899-4802, Fax (312) 899-4845.

AMERICAN INSTITUTE OF BAKING (AIB)
Manhattan, Kansas

Founded in 1919. This non-profit educational organization's objective is to promote the cause of education in nutrition, baking, and bakery management. Employs 135 full-time personnel; is supported by contributions of over 600 member companies. Programs include the 16-week Baking Science and Technology course for those desiring supervisory positions in the industry, the 10-week Bakery Maintenance Engineering program, and short courses and seminars (page XX). Correspondence courses include Science of Baking, Bakery Maintenance Engineering, and Warehouse Sanitation. Scholarships (40 awarded last year, averaging $1,750 each) and financial aid are available. The AIB's Certified Baker Program provides companies with on-the-job training; the research department develops new techniques; the Technical Assistance group provides information on technical, and regulatory subjects; the Department of Food Product Safety offers training and in-plant inspection for food sanitation; the Department of Safety Education offers training and in-plant audits; and the Library responds to information requests.

CONTACT: AIB, 1213 Bakers Way, Manhattan, KS 66502; (800) 633-5137 or (913) 537-4750.

AMERICAN INSTITUTE OF WINE & FOOD (AIWF)
San Francisco, California

Founded in 1981 by Julia Child, Robert Mondavi, and Richard Graff. Membership nearly 10,000. This non-profit educational organization's objectives are to advance the appreciation of wine and food and stimulate greater scholarly education in gastronomy. Membership is open to all and benefits include a discounted invitation to the annual Conference on Gastronomy, invitations to national and chapter programs, special prices on national educational conferences and seminars, and savings on wine and food publications. Publications include the annual *Journal of Gastronomy* and *American Wine & Food* newsletter. There are more than 30 AIWF chapters in the U.S. and abroad. Annual membership contributions range from $35 for students to $500 for corporations.

CONTACT: AIWF, 1550 Bryant St., Ste. 700, San Francisco, CA 94103; (415) 255-3000, (800) 274-AIWF.

AMERICAN WINE SOCIETY (AWS)
Rochester, New York
Founded in 1967. 5,000 members. Non-profit consumer organization dedicated to bringing together wine lovers and educating people about wine production and use. The national conference, held in November, features tastings, contests, tours of wineries and vineyards, and well-known speakers. Publications include a quarterly journal, specialized technical manuals, and lists of related books and publications. The organization assists in publicizing regional events and helps organize local chapters (currently 90), which sponsor tastings, tours, wine making and other social and educational events. Members with at least 2 years of chapter comparative tastings or equivalent are eligible for the AWS Wine Judge Certification Program. Membership is open to all and annual dues are $36 per individual or couple. Professional Memberships are $58 per year and Lifetime Memberships, for ages 60 and over, are $280.

CONTACT: AWS, 3006 Latta Rd., Rochester, NY 14612; (716) 225-7613.

BREAD BAKERS GUILD OF AMERICA
Pittsburgh, Pennsylvania
Nonprofit educational organization founded in 1993 by bakery owner Tom McMahon. Objectives are to bring together individuals involved in the production of high quality bread products, to raise professional standards, and to encourage the education and training of people interested in careers as bread baking professionals. It also seeks to promote the exchange of information between artisan bakers, their suppliers, and specialists in the science of baking and baking ingredients. The Guild publishes a newsletter and sponsors seminars and workshops in the U.S. and abroad, as well as regional and national baking competitions. Membership is open to anyone but the focus of the Guild is professional bread bakers; annual dues are $45.

CONTACT: Tom McMahon, Bread Bakers Guild of America, P.O. Box 22254, Pittsburgh, PA 15222; (412) 322-8275.

CONFRERIE DE LA CHAINE DES ROTISSEURS
International gastronomic organization, originally founded in Paris in 1248 as a guild of masters in the art of roasting geese for the royal table, disbanded in 1791, reincorporated in 1950. In the U.S. the Chaine has approximately 140 local chapters with about 7,000 members. Its purpose is to encourage educational functions and promote fellowship among individuals with a serious interest in wine and cuisine. The nonprofit, tax-exempt Chaine Education Fund supports educational and charitable programs. Membership benefits at the local level include gastronomic functions, usually 4-6 formal dinners per year supplemented by 2-4 smaller events. On a regional and national level, members can join in Chaine-sponsored excursions, attend the national convention, and share, by invitation, activities of other chapters. Professionals make up approximately 30% of the membership and include authors, critics, and food service professionals. Membership is normally by invitation only. Interested individuals who do not know a member should contact the National Office for information.

CONTACT: Confrerie de la Chaine des Rotisseurs, National Administrative Office: 980 Madison Ave., New York, NY 10021; (212) 570-1302, Fax (212) 517-7195 or National Executive Office: P.O. Box 6648, Malibu, CA 90264-6648.

ORGANIZATIONS 297

COOKING TOGETHER FOUNDATION (CTF)
Williamsburg, Virginia

Founded in 1995. This nonprofit educational organization is dedicated to teaching children to cook and bake. Activities include workshops conducted by culinary professionals for children and their parents or caregivers. Annual dues range from $5 for youths/$25 for individuals to $500 for corporations.

CONTACT: Allison Brody, Executive Director, Cooking Together Foundation, P.O. Box 149, Williamsburg, VA 23187; (804) 253-7543 (phone/fax).

COUNCIL ON HOTEL, REST. AND INSTIT. EDUCATION (CHRIE)
Washington, D.C.

Founded in 1946. 2,400 members from 50 countries. This trade and professional organization's mission is to foster the international advancement of teaching and training in the field of hospitality and tourism management and facilitate the professional development of its members, who include administrators, educators, industry professionals, and government executives. Membership benefits include an annual conference and several publications: The *CHRIE Communique* semi-monthly newsletter, the *Hospitality & Tourism Educator* interdisciplinary quarterly, the 3 times yearly *Hospitality Research Journal*, *HOSTEUR* magazine for students at member schools, and the *Annual Directory of CHRIE Members*. CHRIE also publishes *A Guide to College Programs in Hospitality & Tourism*, which describes curricula, admission requirements, scholarships, and internships.

CONTACT: CHRIE, 1200 17th St., N.W., Washington, DC 20036-3097; (202) 331-5990, Fax (202) 785-2511.

EDUCATIONAL FOUNDATION OF THE NRA
Chicago, Illinois

Established in 1987. Nonprofit organization created to advance the professional standards of foodservice management through education. The Foundation develops courses, video training, seminars, and other programs that help managers gain proficiency. The Professional Management Program (ProMgmt.), for undergraduate hospitality students, covers five foodservice areas: unit revenue/cost management, risk management, human resources/diversity management, operations, and marketing. Students receive a certificate upon completion of the course and program. The organization also offers ProMgmt. scholarships (75 awarded last year, avg. $850 ea). More than 150 schoools are partners in the program.

CONTACT: Educational Foundation of the National Restaurant Assn., 250 S. Wacker Dr., Ste. 1400, Chicago, IL 60606; (312) 715-1010.

INTERNATIONAL ASSN. OF CULINARY PROFESSIONALS (IACP)
(See display ad page 298) **Louisville, Kentucky**

Founded in 1978. More than 2,500 members representing over 32 countries. This not-for-profit professional association's objectives include: providing continuing education and professional development, sponsoring of the annual IACP Julia Child Cookbook Awards, promoting the exchange of culinary information among members of the professional food community, establishing professional and ethical standards, and funding scholarships (80 awarded last year, avg. $2,300 ea). Membership benefits include the annual spring and regional conferences, newsletters and research reports, the annual IACP Membership Directory, the Certified Culinary Professional (CCP) certification program.

Annual dues are $150 (plus $50 one-time fee) for Professional Members, $250 (plus $50) for Cooking School Members, $300 (plus $50) for Business Members; $750 (plus $100) for Corporate Members, and $50 for Student/Apprentice Members.

CONTACT: IACP, 304 W. Liberty St., Suite 201, Louisville, KY 40202; (502) 581-9786, Fax (502) 589-3602.

Tuition-Credit Scholarships
Cash-Award Scholarships Sojourns

Approximately 75 awards for partial or full tuition credit in a wide range of schools and culinary programs and for sojourns (unpaid apprenticeships). Respected food professionals review all complete applications and make awards. For more information, contact the IACP Foundation at 304 West Liberty Street, Suite 201, Louisville, Kentucky 40202; Telephone 502-587-7953, Fax 502-589-3602.

INTL. ASSN. OF WOMEN CHEFS AND RESTAURATEURS (IAWCR)
San Francisco, California

Established in 1993 by eight noted women chefs and restaurateurs. Mission: to promote the education and advancement of women in the restaurant industry. The IAWCR publishes the quarterly newsletter *Entrez!*, and conducts an annual convention and regional events to promote such issues as flexible working arrangements, job sharing, and child care. Future activities include job bank, membership and service directories, an apprentice and mentor program, and awarding grants and scholarships. Membership categories/annual dues include Executive (restaurant chef/owners)/$175, Professional (employed in the restaurant industry)/$75, Student/$35, Affiliate (supporting the association's mission)/$125, Small Business/$250, and Corporate/$1,500.

CONTACT: IAWCR, 110 Sutter St., Ste. 305, San Francisco, CA 94104; (415) 362-7336, Fax (415) 362-7335.

INTERNATIONAL FOOD SERVICE EXECUTIVES ASSOCIATION
Margate, Florida

Founded 1901. Membership 4,000. Nonprofit educational and community service organization. Services include student scholarships (20 awarded last year averaging $500 each), monthly gatherings, savings on travel, and *Hotline Magazine*. Also has certification program for executives, chefs, managers and others. Memberships are Active (management, ownership, purchasing), Associate (supplier/vendor), Member-at-Large (reside more than 50 miles from an IFSEA branch) and Corporate. Annual dues: $130 for certification only, $150 for certification and IFSEA membership.

CONTACT: IFSEA, 1100 S. State Road 7, Suite 103, Margate, Florida 33068; (305) 977-0767, Fax (305) 977-0874.

INTERNATIONAL FOODSERVICE EDITORIAL COUNCIL (IFEC)
Hyde Park, New York

Founded in 1956 by a group of foodservice magazine editors and public relations executives. Membership 200. This nonprofit association is dedicated to improving the quality of media communications in the foodservice industry. Membership benefits include an annual directory and conference, newsletter, and networking. Four scholarships ranging from $1,000-$2,500 were awarded last year to students whose career aspirations combine foodservice and communications. Membership is open to individuals employed in editorial functions within the industry.

CONTACT: Carol Metz, Executive Director, IFEC, P.O. Box 491, Hyde Park, NY 12538; (914) 452-4345, Fax (914) 452-0532.

JAMES BEARD FOUNDATION, INC.
New York, New York

Established in 1986. Nonprofit organization whose mission is to keep alive the ideals and activities that made James Beard the "Father of American Cooking" and to maintain his home as the first historical culinary center in North America. Membership benefits include discounts on the more

ORGANIZATIONS 299

than 200 events (workshops and dinners featuring well-known American chefs) each year; a subscription to *Beard House* magazine; the Foundation directory, which lists professional members; and the annual James Beard Awards (first weekend in May), which includes cookbook, journalism, chef, and restaurant categories. A scholarship and apprenticeship program and library have been developed. Last year $200,000 in scholarships were awarded (35 for up to $20,000 each). Applications are available each fall and are awarded for one year only. Annual dues begin at $60 for nonprofessionals and $125 ($250 for members within 75 miles of Manhattan) for professionals.

CONTACT: James Beard Foundation, Inc., 167 W. 12th St., New York, NY 10011; (212) 675-4984, (800)-36-BEARD, Fax (212) 645-1438.

NAPA VALLEY WINE LIBRARY ASSOCIATION (NVWLA)
St. Helena, California

Established in 1963. Dedicated to preserving and sharing information regarding viticulture, enology, and wine lore, particularly as it pertains to the Napa Valley. Acquires books and other publications for the Napa Valley Wine Library, a more than 4,000-title collection including oral history transcripts and historic photographs, which is housed at the St. Helena Public Library. Membership benefits include the seasonal *Wine Library Report*, first notice of wine appreciation weekends and one-day seminars, and admission to the annual winetasting, an August event that presents the wines of more than 100 Napa Valley wineries. Membership is open to anyone and dues are $20 per year.

CONTACT: Napa Valley Wine Library Association, P.O. Box 328, St. Helena, CA 94574; (707) 963-5145.

NATIONAL RESTAURANT ASSOCIATION (NRA)
Washington, D.C.

Established in 1919. Membership 25,000. This national trade association for the foodservice industry provides educational, research, communications, convention, and government services; interacts with legislators and political leaders; offers a media relations program and speech bank; has a toll-free information hotline. The nonprofit Educational Foundation subsidiary advances industry professional standards. Publications: the monthly *Restaurants USA* magazine, *Washington Weekly* political report, operations manuals. Sponsors Restaurant, Hotel-Motel Show in Chicago each May. Membership is open to any entity that operates facilities and/or supplies meal service to others on a regular basis. Dues are revenue-based and begin at $140 for annual sales under $250,000.

CONTACT: National Restaurant Association, 1200-17th St., NW, Washington, DC 20036-3097; (202) 331-5900, Fax (202) 331-2429.

NATIONAL ASSN. FOR THE SPECIALTY FOOD TRADE, INC.
New York, New York

Established in 1952. Membership 1,750 companies in the U.S. and overseas. Nonprofit business trade association that fosters trade, commerce, and interest in the specialty food industry. Sponsors the semi-annual International Fancy Food and Confection Show every winter (West Coast) and summer (East Coast), attracting 15,000-30,000 attendees. Other services include the Annual Product Awards held every summer, the Scholarship and Research Fund, and the bimonthly *Showcase Magazine*. Membership requires that a company be in business for a minimum of one year. The Admissions Committee reviews applications and makes recommendations to the Board of Directors for a final decision. Annual dues are $200 (for annual sales under $1 million), $400 ($1-$5 million), and $600 (over $5 million).

CONTACT: Josephine McCarthy, NASFT, 8 West 40th Street, New York, NY 10018; (212) 921-1690, Fax (212) 921-1898.

OLDWAYS PRESERVATION AND EXCHANGE TRUST
Boston, Massachusetts
Established 1990. This nonprofit educational institution is dedicated to preserving healthy food traditions and fostering cultural exchange in the fields of food, cooking, and agriculture. The Chefs Collaborative: 2000, an educational initiative launched in 1993, works to expand links between chefs and growers who are committed to farming in an ecologically responsible way. It jointly founded and is a cosponsor of Chefs Helping to Enhance Food Safety (C.H.E.F.S). Conferences, retreats, workshops, and a fund-raising campaign are planned. Membership is open to all; benefits include the Chef Collaborative and Oldways newsletters. Annual dues are $50.

CONTACT: Oldways Preservation and Exchange Trust, 25 First St., Cambridge, MA 02141; (617) 621-3000, Fax (617) 621-1230.

SOCIETY OF WINE EDUCATORS (SWE)
East Longmeadow, Massachusetts
Formed in 1977. Membership 1,500. Nonprofit organization dedicated to improving information about the various aspects of wine making, including wine service, wine and food pairing, wine and health. Membership services include the annual conference (held near a different wine-producing area each summer), educational programs, and trips to wine regions worldwide. The Society provides an annual test of proficiency and awards a Certificate of Proficiency. Publications include the quarterly *SWE Chronicle*, the yearly *Wine Educator*, and the *SWE Resource Manual* of teaching materials. Annual dues are $55 (single), $82.50 (couple), plus a $15 application fee the first year. Industry membership is $200 annually in addition to a $15 application fee.

CONTACT: SWE, 132 Shaker Rd., Ste. 14, East Longmeadow, MA 01028; (413) 567-8272, Fax (413) 567-2051.

TASTERS GUILD
Ft. Lauderdale, Florida
Established in 1985 by wine consultant Joseph J. Schagrin. Objective: promote the appreciation and moderate use of wine and food through education, tastings, consumer benefits, and travel opportunities. Conducts Annual International Wine Judging each spring, publishes *Tasters Guild Journal*, and sponsors an annual Food and Wine Cruise and other excursions. Local Guilds sponsor wine and food events and discounts are offered to members by affiliated wine and gourmet establishments. Annual membership dues: $35 per family, $18 for hospitality education students.

CONTACT: Joseph J. Schagrin, President, Tasters Guild, International, 1451 W. Cypress Creek Rd., Ste. 300-26, Ft. Lauderdale, FL 33309; (305) 928-2823, Fax (305) 928-2624.

WINE INSTITUTE
San Francisco, California
Formed in 1934. Membership 400 California winemakers. Trade association dedicated to initiating and advocating public policy to enhance the environment for the responsible consumption and enjoyment of wine. Individuals and companies providing goods and services to the industry can become associate members. Based in San Francisco, with offices in Sacramento, Washington, DC, 6 regions of the United States, and 8 foreign countries.

CONTACT: Wine Institute, 425 Market St., Ste. 1000, San Francisco, CA 94105; (415) 512-0151, Fax (415) 442-0742.

5

Appendix

AMERICAN CULINARY FEDERATION EDUCATIONAL INSTITUTE (ACFEI) ACCREDITING COMMISSION

Annapolis, Maryland

Accreditation by the American Culinary Federation Educational Institute Accrediting Commission, the educational arm of the American Culinary Federation and a U. S. Department of Education-recognized accrediting agency, is a review process that evaluates the quality of an educationally-accredited post-secondary institution's program in culinary arts and foodservice management. The program's objectives, staff, facilities, policies, curriculum, instructional methods, and procedures are examined to determine if they meet ACFEI standards, which were developed to meet the requirements for entry-level culinarians. To be eligible, a program must contain a majority of required competencies; must be offered by a school that is accredited by an agency recognized by the U.S. Dept. of Education; must be full-time, include at least 1,000 contact hours, and result in a certificate, diploma, or degree; must have a full-time coordinator who has qualifications equivalent to a Certified Culinary Educator, Executive Chef, or Executive Pastry Chef, or has earned a master's degree in an appropriate discipline; and must have been in continuous existence for at least two years and have graduated a sufficient number of students in order to be evaluated. Application for accreditation must be authorized by the department Dean and 50% of the full-time faculty in the technical phase of the program must have credentials equivalent to an ACFEI Certified Culinary Educator, Sous Chef, or Pastry Chef.

CONTACT: For a current list of accredited programs: The Educational Institute, American Culinary Federation, P.O. Box 3466, St. Augustine, FL 32085; (904) 824-4468. For accreditation application: The American Culinary Federation Educational Institute Accrediting Commission, 959 Melvin Rd., Annapolis, MD 21403; (410) 268-5659, Fax (410) 263-3110.

ACFEI-Accredited schools as of July, 1995:

ALABAMA

JEFFERSON STATE COMMUNITY COLLEGE
Pinson Valley Pkwy. at 2601 Carson Rd., Birmingham, AL 35215 **CONTACT:** (205) 853-1200

ARIZONA

SCOTTSDALE CULINARY INSTITUTE
8100 Camelback Road, Scottsdale, AZ 85251 **CONTACT:** Elizabeth Leite (602) 990-3773

CALIFORNIA

CALIFORNIA CULINARY ACADEMY
625 Polk Street, San Francisco, CA 94102 **CONTACT:** Admissions office (800) 229-2433

CITY COLLEGE OF SAN FRANCISCO
50 Phelan Ave., San Francisco, CA 94112 **CONTACT:** Frank Ambrozic (415) 239-3154

DIABLO VALLEY COLLEGE
321 Golf Club Road, Pleasant Hill, CA 94523 **CONTACT:** Jack Hendrickson (510) 685-1230, ext. 556

LOS ANGELES TRADE-TECH. COLLEGE
400 W. Washington Blvd., Los Angeles, CA 90015 **CONTACT:** Ernest W. Green (213) 744-9480

ORANGE COAST COLLEGE
2710 Fairview Blvd., Costa Mesa, CA 92635 **CONTACT:** Daniel Beard (714) 432-5835

SANTA BARBARA CITY COLLEGE
721 Cliff Drive, Santa Barbara, CA 93100 CONTACT: John Dunn (805) 965-0581

CONNECTICUT

MANCHESTER COMMUNITY COLLEGE
P.O. Box 1046, 60 Bidwell St., Manchester, CT 06040 CONTACT: Sandra Jenkins (203) 647-6121

FLORIDA

ART INSTITUTE OF FT. LAUDERDALE
1799 S.E. 17th St., Ft. Lauderdale, FL 33316 CONTACT: Klaus Friedenreich (305) 463-3000, ext. 208

ATLANTIC VOCATIONAL TECHNICAL CENTER
4700 Coconut Creek Parkway, Coconut Creek, FL 33066 CONTACT: Moses Ball (305) 977-2066

FLORIDA COMMUNITY COLLEGE AT JAX
4501 Capper Road, Jacksonville, FL 32218 CONTACT: Al Fricke (904) 766-6652

THE FLORIDA CULINARY INSTITUTE
a Division of New England Tech. 1126 53rd Court, West Palm Beach, FL 33407
CONTACT: David Pantone (407) 842-8324

GULF COAST COMMUNITY COLLEGE
5230 W. U.S. Highway 98, Panama City, FL 32401 CONTACT: Travis Herr (904) 769-1551, ext. 3850

PINELLAS TECHNICAL EDUCATION CENTER CLEARWATER CAMPUS
6100 154th Avenue, North Clearwater, FL 33516 CONTACT: Vincent Calandra (813) 531-3531

PINELLAS TECHNICAL EDUCATION CENTER
St. Petersburg Campus, 901 34th St. South, St. Petersburg, FL 33711
CONTACT: Alvin Miller (813) 327-3671, ext. 284

SOUTHEAST INST. OF CULINARY ARTS
Collins at Del Monte Ave., St. Augustine, FL 32084 CONTACT: Hal Holanchock (904) 824-4401

GEORGIA

ART INSTITUTE OF ATLANTA/SCHOOL OF CULINARY ARTS
3391 Peachtree Rd., NE, Atlanta, GA 30326 CONTACT: Jim Morris (404) 266-1341, ext. 227

SAVANNAH TECHNICAL INSTITUTE
5717 White Bluff Rd., Savannah, GA 31499 CONTACT: Marvis Hinson (912) 351-6362, ext. 360

HAWAII

KAPIOLANI COMMUNITY COLLEGE
University of Hawaii, 4303 Diamond Head Rd., Honolulu, HI 96816 CONTACT: Frank Leake (808) 734-9483

LEEWARD COMMUNITY COLLEGE
96-045 Ala Ike, Pearl City, HI 96782 CONTACT: Fern Tomisato (808) 455-0375

MAUI COMMUNITY COLLEGE
Food Service Department, 310 Kaahumanu Ave., Kahului, HI 96732
CONTACT: Karen Tanaka (808) 242-1225

APPENDIX

IDAHO

BOISE STATE UNIVERSITY
1910 University Drive, Boise, ID 83725 **CONTACT:** Manly Ed Slough (208) 385-1532

ILLINOIS

COLLEGE OF DUPAGE
22nd St. and Lambert Rd., Glen Ellyn, IL 60137 **CONTACT:** George Macht (708) 858-2800, ext. 2315

ELGIN COMMUNITY COLLEGE
1700 Spartan Dr., Elgin, IL 60120 **CONTACT:** Mike Zema (708) 697-1000, ext. 7461

JOLIET JUNIOR COLLEGE
1216 Houbolt Ave., Joliet, IL 60436 **CONTACT:** Patrick Hagerty (815) 729-9020, ext. 2448

KENDALL COLLEGE
2408 Orrington Ave., Evanston, IL 60201 **CONTACT:** Michael Carmel (708) 866-1300

INDIANA

IVY TECH STATE COLLEGE
3800 N. Anthony Blvd., Ft. Wayne, IN 46805 **CONTACT:** Bob Moghaddam (219) 480-4240

IVY TECH STATE COLLEGE
One West 26th St., Indianapolis, IN 46208 **CONTACT:** Vincent Kinkade (317) 921-4619

IOWA

DES MOINES AREA COMMUNITY COLLEGE
2006 South Ankeny Blvd., Ankeny, IA 50021 **CONTACT:** Robert Anderson (515) 964-6532

KIRKWOOD COMMUNITY COLLEGE
6301 Kirkwood Blvd., P.O. Box 2068 Cedar Rapids, IA 52406 **CONTACT:** Carol Wohlleben (319) 398-5468

KANSAS

JOHNSON COUNTY COMMUNITY COLLEGE
12345 College at Quivira, Overland Park, KS 66210 **CONTACT:** Jerry Vincent (913) 469-8500

KENTUCKY

JEFFERSON COMMUNITY COLLEGE
109 East Broadway, Louisville, KY 40202 **CONTACT:** Patricia Heyman (502) 584-0181, ext. 317

NATIONAL CENTER FOR HOSPITALITY STUDIES AT SULLIVAN COLLEGE
3101 Bardstown Rd., Louisville, KY 40232 **CONTACT:** Thomas Hickey (502) 456-6504, ext. 329

LOUISIANA

BOSSIER PARISH COMMUNITY COLLEGE
2719 Airline Dr., N., Bossier City, LA 71111 **CONTACT:** Nancy Underwood (318) 746-6120

DELGADO COMMUNITY COLLEGE
615 City Park Ave., New Orleans, LA 70119 **CONTACT:** Iva Bergeron (504) 483-4208

GRAND RAPIDS COMMUNITY COLLEGE
151 Fountain, N.E., Grand Rapids, MI 49503 **CONTACT:** Robert Garlough (616) 771-3690

HENRY FORD COMMUNITY COLLEGE
5101 Evergreen Road, Dearborn, MI 48128 **CONTACT:** Dennis Konarski (313) 845-6360

MICHIGAN

MONROE COUNTY COMMUNITY COLLEGE
1555 S. Raisinville Rd., Monroe, MI 48161 **CONTACT:** Kevin Thomas (313) 242-7300

NORTHWESTERN MICHIGAN COLLEGE
1701 East Front St., Traverse City, MI 49684 **CONTACT:** Fred Laughlin (616) 922-1197

OAKLAND COMMUNITY COLLEGE
27055 Orchard Lake Rd., Farmington Hills, MI 48018 **CONTACT:** Susan Baier (313) 471-7779

MINNESOTA

HENNEPIN TECHNICAL COLLEGE
Brooklyn Park Campus, 9000 Brooklyn Blvd., Brooklyn Park, MN 55445
Eden Prairie Campus, 9200 Flying Cloud Dr., Eden Prairie, MN 55445
CONTACT: Mike Jung (612) 425-3800, ext. 2553

ST. PAUL TECHNICAL COLLEGE
235 Marshall Ave., St. Paul, MN 55102 **CONTACT:** Eberhard Werthmann (612) 221-1300

MONTANA

COLLEGE OF TECHNOLOGY UNIVERSITY OF MONTANA — MISSOULA
909 S. Avenue West, Missoula, MT 59801 **CONTACT:** Dennis Lerum (406) 542-6811

NEBRASKA

METROPOLITAN COMMUNITY COLLEGE
P.O. Box 3777, Omaha, NE 68103 **CONTACT:** Mr. Dana Goodrich (402) 449-8309

NEW HAMPSHIRE

NEW HAMPSHIRE COLLEGE – THE CULINARY INSTITUTE
2500 North River Rd., Manchester, NH 03104 **CONTACT:** Paul Dittmer (603) 644-3128

NEW YORK

PAUL SMITH'S COLLEGE
Paul Smiths, New York 12970 **CONTACT:** Paul Sorgule (518) 327-6218

SCHENECTADY COUNTY COMMUNITY COLLEGE
78 Washington Ave., Schenectady, NY 12035 **CONTACT:** Anthony Strianese (518) 346-6211

SULLIVAN COUNTY COMMUNITY COLLEGE — HOSPITALITY DEPT.
Box 4002, Le Roy Rd. Loch Sheldrake, NY 12759 **CONTACT:** Ed Nadeau (914) 434-5750

SUNY/COBLESKILL AG. & TECH. COLLEGE
P.O. Box 4002, Cobleskill, NY 12043 **CONTACT:** Alan Roer (518) 234-5425

APPENDIX

OHIO

CINCINNATI TECHNICAL COLLEGE
3520 Central Parkway, Cincinnati, OH 45223 **CONTACT:** Richard Hendrix (513) 569-1662

COLUMBUS STATE COMMUNITY COLLEGE
550 East Spring St., Columbus, OH 43215 **CONTACT:** Carol Kizer (614) 227-2579

HOCKING TECHNICAL COLLEGE
3301 Hocking Parkway, Nelsonville, OH 45764 **CONTACT:** Doug Weber (614) 753-3591

OREGON

WESTERN CULINARY INSTITUTE
316 SW 13th Ave., Portland, OR 97201 **CONTACT:** Mary Harris, Dir. of Admissions (503) 223-2245

PENNSYLVANIA

INDIANA UNIVERSITY OF PA (IUP) CULINARY SCHOOL
125 S. Gilpin St., Punxsutawney, PA 15767 **CONTACT:** Al Wutsch (800) 438-6424

INTERNATIONAL CULINARY ACADEMY
107 Sixth St., Fulton Bldg., Pittsburgh, PA 15222 **CONTACT:** Larry Brudy (412) 471-9330

PENNSYLVANIA INSTITUTE OF CULINARY ARTS
700 Clark Bldg., 717 Liberty Ave. Pittsburgh, PA 15222 **CONTACT:** Dieter Kiessling (412) 566-2444

PENNSYLVANIA COLLEGE OF TECHNOLOGY
One College Ave., Williamsport, PA 17701 **CONTACT:** Deborah Wilson (713) 326-3761

WESTMORELAND COUNTY COMMUNITY COLLEGE
Armbrust Rd., College Station Youngwood, PA 15697 **CONTACT:** Mary Zappone (412) 925-4016

SOUTH CAROLINA

GREENVILLE TECHNICAL COLLEGE
P.O. Box 5616, Station B, Greenville, SC 19606 **CONTACT:** Dr. Margaret Condrasky (803) 250-8000, ext. 8404

HORRY-GEORGETOWN TECHNICAL COLLEGE
P.O. Box 1966, Hwy. 501 East, Conway, SC 29526 **CONTACT:** Mr. Carmen Catino (803) 347-3186

TRIDENT TECHNICAL COLLEGE
P.O. Box 118067, Charleston, SC 29423-8067 **CONTACT:** Ward Morgan (803) 722-5571

TENNESSEE

OPRYLAND HOTEL INSTITUTE
2800 Opreyland Drive, Nashville, TN 37214 **CONTACT:** Dina Starks (615) 871-7765

TEXAS

ST. PHILIP'S COLLEGE
2111 Nevada St., San Antonio, TX 78203 **CONTACT:** Mary Kunz (512) 531-3315

UTAH

SALT LAKE COMMUNITY COLLEGE
4600 S. Redwood Rd., Salt Lake City UT 84130 **CONTACT:** LeslieSeiferle/Ricco Renzetti (801) 957-4066

WASHINGTON

BELLINGHAM TECHNICAL COLLEGE
3028 Lindbergh Ave., Bellingham, WA 98225 **CONTACT:** Patricia McKeown (206) 676-7761

RENTON TECHNICAL COLLEGE
3000 Northeast Fourth St., Renton, WA 98056 **CONTACT:** Kristi Frambach (206) 235-2372

SEATTLE CENTRAL COMMUNITY COLLEGE
1701 Broadway, Seattle, WA 98122 **CONTACT:** Linda Hierholzer (206) 344-4331

SOUTH SEATTLE COMMUNITY COLLEGE
6000 16th Avenue, SW, Seattle, WA 98106 **CONTACT:** Dan Cassidy (206) 764-5344

SPOKANE COMMUNITY COLLEGE
North 1810 Greene St., Spokane, WA 99207 **CONTACT:** Doug Fisher (509) 533-7284

WISCONSIN

BLACKHAWK TECHNICAL COLLEGE
6004 Prairie Rd., P.O. Box 5009, Janesville, WI 53547 **CONTACT:** Joe Wollinger (608) 757-7690

MADISON AREA TECHNICAL COLLEGE
3550 Anderson St., Madison, WI 53704 **CONTACT:** Mary Hill (608) 246-6368

MILWAUKEE AREA TECHNICAL COLLEGE
1015 N. Sixth St., Milwaukee, WI 53203 **CONTACT:** Gus Kelly (414) 278-6507

WAUKESHA COUNTY TECHNICAL COLLEGE
800 Main Street, Pewaukee, WI 53072 **CONTACT:** William Griesemer (414) 691-5254

APPENDIX

RECOMMENDED READING

In addition to the following newsletters, magazines, and books, many culinary food and wine organizations (pages 295-300) offer publications as a membership benefit.

THE ART OF EATING
Quarterly newsletter. Established 1986. Address: Box 242, Peacham, VT 05862; Fax (802) 592-3400. Writer: Edward Behr. Annual subscription: $30 worldwide.

Monographs about food, and occasionally wine, emphasizing tradition and the relationship of food to place.

ART CULINAIRE
Quarterly magazine. Established 1986. Publisher: Culinaire, Inc., 40 Mills St., Morristown, NJ 07960; (201) 993-5500, Fax (201) 993-8779. Editor: Jennifer N. Lindner. Per issue (annual subscription) price: $18 ($59) U.S., $22 ($75) other countries. Subscriptions: P.O. Box 9268, Morristown, NJ 07963. Online 102475.3651 @ Compuserve.com.

Hardcover magazine with 80 pages of color photographs, industry-related articles, recipes.

BBC GOOD FOOD
Monthly magazine. Established 1989. Publisher: BBC Worldwide Publishing, Woodlands, 80 Wood Lane, London W12 OTT, England; (44)81-576-2000. Editor: Mitzie Wilson. Annual subscription £49.35. Subscriptions: P.O. Box 425, Woking GU21 1GP; (44) 483-733724 (order line), (44) 483-733754 (inquiry line).

BBC VEGETARIAN GOOD FOOD
Monthly magazine. Established 1992. Publisher: BBC Worldwide Publishing, Woodlands, 80 Wood Lane, London W12 OTT, England; (44)81-576-2000. Editor: Mary Gwynn. Annual subscription £45.60. Subscriptions: P.O. Box 425, Woking GU21 1GP; (44) 483-733712 (order line), (44) 483-733742 (inquiry line).

BECOMING A CHEF
320-page paperback. Published in 1995 by Van Nostrand Reinhold, 115 Fifth Ave., New York, NY 10003; (212) 254-3232. Authors: Andrew Dornenburg and Karen Page. ISBN 0-442-01513-5. Price $29.95. Orders: International Thomson Publishing, Inc. (800) 842-3636 or (606) 525-6600, Fax (606) 525-7778.

Interviews with over 60 noted U.S. chefs about their early influences, training, personal and career experiences, restaurants; includes recipes.

BON APPÉTIT
Monthly magazine. Established 1955. Publisher: Conde Nast Publications, 6300 Wilshire Blvd., Los Angeles, CA 90048; (213) 965-3600, Fax (213) 937-1206. Editor: William J. Garry. Per issue (annual subscription) price: $2.95 ($18) in U.S.; ($30) in Canada & abroad. Subscriptions: P.O. Box 59191, Boulder, CO 80322; (800) 765-9419.

Features kitchen & tableware design, chefs, travel & restaurants, recipes for home cooks, wine & spirits tasting panel, wine reviews, articles about vineyards.

CAREER OPPORTUNITIES IN THE FOOD & BEVERAGE INDUSTRY
240-page paperback. Published in 1994 by Facts on File, Inc., 460 Park Ave. South, New York, NY 10016; (212) 683-2244. Author: Barbara Sims-Bell. ISBN 0-8160-2913-X. Price $14.95. Orders: (800) 322-8755 or (212) 683-2244, Fax (212) 213-4578.

Provides career profiles of 70 jobs, including duties, salary range, employment and advancement prospects, prerequisites, best locations.

CHEF
Monthly magazine. Established 1952. Publisher: Talcott Communications Corp., 20 North Wacker Dr., Ste. 3230, Chicago, IL 60606; (312) 849-2220, Fax (312) 849-2174. Editor: Paul Clarke. Per issue (annual subscription) price: $2.95 ($24) U.S., ($35) Canada, ($60) other.

Information on current news and trends, interviews with chefs, columns on marketing, management, career mobility, menu and restaurant design.

CHILE PEPPER
Bimonthly magazine. Established 1987. Address: P.O. Box 80780, Albuquerque, NM 87198; (505) 266-8322, Fax (505) 266-2127, E-mail Chile@USA.net. Editor: Dave DeWitt. Per issue (annual subscription) price: $3.95 ($18.95); sample issue free. Subscriptions: P.O. Box 769, Mt. Morris, IL 61054-8234; (800) 959-5468.

Cooking and travel magazine devoted to spicy foods from around the world.

CHOCOLATIER
Bimonthly magazine. Established 1984. Publisher: Haymarket, 45 W. 34th St., Room 600, New York, NY 10001; (212) 239-0855, Fax (212) 967-4184. Editor: Mike Schneider. Per issue (annual subscription) price: $4.95 ($23.95).

Focuses on chocolate and elegant desserts, their preparation and presentation, with photographs and recipes.

COFFEE JOURNAL
Quarterly magazine. Established 1995. Publisher: Tiger Oak Publications, 119 N. 4th St. Ste. 211, Minneapolis, MN 55401; (612) 338-4125, Fax (612) 338-0532, E-mail coffeejrnl@aol.com. Editor: Susan Bonne. Per issue (annual subscription) price: $3.95 ($12.97)U.S., $4.95 Canada. Subscriptions: P.O. Box 3000, Denville, NJ 07834-9479; (800) 783-4903. Online through the electric newstand at http://www.enews.com.

Lifestyle magazine featuring gourmet coffees and teas, new blends, brewing techniques, exotic travel, recipes, fiction, recommendations.

COOK'S ILLUSTRATED
Bimonthly magazine. Established 1992. Publisher: Boston Common Press, 17 Station St., Box 569, Brookline, MA 02147-0569; (617) 232-1000, Fax (617) 232-1572, E-mail cooksill@aol.com. Publisher & Editor: Christopher Kimball. Per issue (annual subscription) price: $4 ($19.95) U.S., $4.95 Canada. Subscriptions: Box 7444, Red Oak, IA 51591-0444; (800) 526-8442.

Magazine for home cooks emphasizing cooking technique; narrowly focused articles cover topics in depth and include comparisons of kitchen-tested methods and products.

COOKING LIGHT
Ten issues per year. Established 1987. Publisher: Southern Progress Corp., 2100 Lakeshore Drive, Birmingham, AL 35209; (205) 877-6000, Fax (205) 877-6469, E-mail cooklight@aol.com or cookinglight@msn.com. Editor: Doug Crichton. Per issue (annual subscription) price: $2.95 ($18) U.S.,

$3.50 ($24) Canada, ($24) other countries. Subscriptions: Box 830656, Birmingham, AL 35282-9086; (800) 999-1750, Fax (205) 877-6504. Online Microsoft Network and Pathfinder; digital cookbook on CD-ROM.

Healthy lifestyle magazine; 65% devoted to food & preparation, 35% to personal care and fitness.

CULINARY TRENDS

Quarterly magazine. Established 1990. Address: 6285 East Spring St., Ste 107, Long Beach, CA 90808-9927; (310) 989-5444, Fax (310) 989-5447. Editor: Tim Linden. Subscription price: $21.60/yr U.S., $40/yr foreign.

Features stories and recipes of interest to the career culinarian, as well as home chefs.

EATING WELL

Bimonthly magazine. Established 1990. Publisher: EW Communications, LP, Ferry Road, Charlotte, VT 05445; (802) 425-3961, Fax (802) 425-3675, E-mail EwellEdit@aol.com. Editor: Marcelle Langan Di Falco. Per issue (annual subscription) price: $2.95 ($18) U.S., $3.95 ($24) Canada, Subscriptions: P.O. Box 52919, Boulder, CO 80322; (800) 678-0541. Online EWellEdit@aol.com.

Healthy eating magazine; reports and comments on the dietary movement in America; nutrition reports, food and cooking articles and recipes.

FINE COOKING

Bimonthly magazine. Established 1994. Publisher: The Taunton Press, 63 South Main St., Newtown, CT 06470; (203) 426-8171, Fax (203) 426-3434. Editor: Martha Holmberg. Per issue (annual subscription) price: $4.95 ($26) U.S., $5.95 ($32) other. Subscriptions: P.O. Box 5507, Newtown, CT 06470-9879; (800) 888-8286. For editorial only: America Online: FINECOOKNG; Compuserve: 74602,2651.

Features cooking techniques, food & preparation, recipes relating to cooking methods.

FOOD & WINE

Monthly magazine. Established 1978. Publisher: American Express Co., 1120 6th Ave., New York, NY 10036; (212) 382-5618, Fax (212) 764-2177. Editor: Dana Cowin. Per issue (annual subscription) price: $2.95 ($28). Subscriptions: P.O. Box 3003, Harlan, IA, 51593-0022. Web address available early 1996.

Lifestyle magazine that focuses on food stories, recipes, tabletop design stories, travel.

FOOD ARTS

Ten issues per year. Established 1988. Publisher: M. Shanken Communications, 387 Park Ave. South, New York, NY 10016; (212) 684-4224, Fax (212) 481-1540. Editor: Michael & Ariane Batterberry. Per issue (annual subscription) price: $4 ($30) U.S., $5 Canada, $7 other. Subscriptions: P.O. Box 10681, Riverton, NJ 08076; Fax (212) 481-0722.

Magazine designed for chefs, restaurateurs, food & beverage directors, caterers; provides editorial on various aspects of the food business.

GOURMET

Monthly magazine. Established 1941. Publisher: Conde Nast Publications, 560 Lexington Ave., New York, NY 10022; (212) 880-8800, Fax (212) 751-4139. Editor: Gail Zweigenthal. Per issue (annual subscription) price: $2.95 ($20) U.S., $3.50 ($34) Canada. Subscriptions: P.O. Box 51422, Boulder, CO 80321-1422. Internet: "Epicurious" http://www.epicurious.com.

Lifestyle magazine; balanced coverage of travel, food, culture, and entertainment.

THE JOURNAL OF ITALIAN FOOD & WINE
Bimonthly magazine. Established 1991. Address: 609 W. 114th St., #77, New York, NY 10025; (212) 316-3026, Fax (212) 316-3476. Editor: Robert Dilallo. Per issue (annual subscription) price: $5 ($17), newstand price $2.95 U.S., $4.25 Canads. Subscriptions: (800)-438-2385.

Covers food & wine in Italy, North America, and other countries; recipes, book reviews, restaurant and chef profiles, regional Italian articles, wine reviews, commentary.

NATION'S RESTAURANT NEWS
Weekly. Established 1956. Publisher: Lebhar-Friedman, Inc., 425 Park Ave., New York, NY 10022; (212) 756-5000, Fax (212) 756-5215. Editor: Rick Van Warner. Per issue (annual subscription) price: $5 ($34.50) U.S., $44.50 Canada, $295 other. Subscriptions: P.O. Box 31182, Tampa, Fl 33631; (813) 664-6700; Fax (813) 664-6884. CD-ROM: Buyer's Advantage; an electronic database of non-food products, services, and vendors.

News publication covering the foodservice industry; editorially directed to foodservice decision-makers.

NORTH CAROLINA'S TASTE FULL
Bimonthly magazine. Established 1990. Publisher: Taste Full Magazine, 202 N. Third St., P.O. Box 1712, Wilmington, NC 28402; (910) 763-1601, Fax (910) 763-0321. Editor: Elizabeth K. Norfleet. Annual subscription: $19.95 U.S., $27.50 Canada, $32 other.

Focuses on food, travel, and entertaining in N.C. with emphasis on the state's current culture and talent; explores national food trends from a Tarheel perspective.

NW PALATE
Bimonthly magazine. Established 1987. Publisher: NW Palate Magazine, P.O. Box 10860, Portland, OR 97210; (503) 224-6039, Fax (503) 222-5312. Editor: Cameron Nagel. Per issue (annual subscription) price: $3.95 ($21) U.S., $5.95 ($33) Canada.

Features food, wine, and lifestyles of the Pacific Northwest; includes recipes, wine & food personalities, getaways, wine reviews, news and events.

PASTRY ART & DESIGN
Quarterly magazine. Established 1995. Publisher: Hay Market, 45 W. 34th St., Room 600, New York, NY 10001; (212) 239-0855, Fax (212) 967-4184. Editor: Mike Schneider. Per issue (annual subscription) price: $5.95 ($30).

Features articles on pastry kitchen/bakery profitability, kitchen equipment, dessert beverages, tabletop presentations, pastry school curricula; includes interviews, techniques, trends, competition updates, an employment hotline.

SAVEUR
Bimonthly magazine. Established 1994. Publisher: Meigher Communications, 100 Ave. of the Americas, New York, NY 10013; (212) 334-1212. Editor: Dorothy Kalins. Per issue (annual subscription) price: $5 ($24) U.S. ($38) other. Subscriptions: (800) 462-0209.

Details the people, places, and cultures where traditional and well-known foods come from; includes recipes and other cooking lifestyle information.

SIMPLE COOKING
Bimonthly newsletter. Established 1980. Address: P.O. Box 8, Steuben, ME 04680; Fax (207) 546-2115, E-mail OUTLAWCOOK@AOL.COM. Editors: John & Matt Lewis Thorne. Per issue (annual subscription) price: $4 ($24) U.S., $4.25 Canada, $5 other.

APPENDIX 313

Features essays on food, cooking and the culinary life; includes recipes, food book reviews, product notes for the home cook.

SIMPLY SEAFOOD
Quarterly magazine. Established 1991. Publisher: Waterfront Press, 5305 Shilshole Ave., Ste. 200, Seattle, WA 98107; (206) 789-6506, Fax (206) 789-9193. Editor: Peter Redmayne. Per issue (annual subscription) price: $2.35 ($8.95) U.S., $2.95 ($11) Canada.

Informational writing, practical instruction, recipes related to handling and preparation of seafood.

VEGETARIAN GOURMET
Five issues per year. Established 1992. Publisher: Chariot Publishing, Inc., 2 Public Ave., Montrose, PA 18801; (717) 278-1984, Fax (717) 278-2223. Editor: Jessica Dubey. Per issue (annual subscription) price: $3.95 ($15.95) U.S., $4.95 ($21.95) Canada; Subscriptions: (800) 628-8244.

Magazine focusing on healthy cooking; features recipes, articles, and a low-fat special issue each year.

VEGETARIAN JOURNAL
Bimonthly magazine. Established 1990. Publisher: The Vegetarian Resource Group, P.O. Box 1463, Baltimore, MD 21203; (410) 366-8343, E-mail TheVRG@aol.com. Editor: Debra Wasserman. Per issue (annual subscription) price: $3 ($20) U.S., ($30) Canada. Internet: www:http://envirolink.org/arrs/VRG/home.html.

Covers vegetarian meal planning, nutrition, recipes, and natural food product reviews. Nutrition articles reviewed by registered dietician or medical doctor. Advertising not accepted.

VEGETARIAN JOURNAL'S FOODSERVICE UPDATE
Quarterly magazine. Established 1993. Publisher: The Vegetarian Resource Group, P.O. Box 1463, Baltimore, MD 21203; (410) 366-8343, E-mail TheVRG@aol.com. Editor: Charles Stahler & Debra Wasserman. Annual subscription: $20 U.S., $30 Canada. For free sample issue send SASE. Internet: www:http://envirolink.org/arrs/VRG/home.html.

For foodservice personnel in schools, restaurants, hospitals, and other institutions; offers advice and recipes, spotlights industry leaders.

VEGETARIAN TIMES
Monthly magazine. Established 1974. Address: 1140 Lake St., Ste. 500, Oak Park, IL 60301; (708) 848-8100, Fax (708) 848-8175, E-mail 74651.21500compuserve.com. Editor: Toni Apgar. Per issue (annual subscription) price: $3.50 ($29.95) U.S., ($41.95) Canada, ($54.91) other. Subscriptions: P.O. Box 446, Mt. Morris, IL 61054-9894; (800) 435-9610 or (815) 734-5824.

Features vegetarian recipes, nutritional breakdowns, photography; articles on health, nutrition, fitness; profiles, product news and reviews.

VEGGIE LIFE
Bimonthly magazine. Established 1993. Publisher: EGW Publishing Co., 1041 Shary Circle, Concord, CA 94518; (800) 777-1164. Editor: Margo M. Lemas. Per issue (annual subscription) price: $2.95 ($17.70) U.S., $3.50 ($23.70) Canada, ($23.70) other. Subscriptions: Box 412, Mt. Morris, IL 61054-8163.

Focuses on vegetarian cooking, gardening, nutrition.

AUSTRALIAN GOURMET TRAVELLER
Monthly magazine. Established 1969. Publisher: Australian Consolidated Press, 54 Park St., Sydney NSW, 2000, Australia; (61) 2-282-8000. Editor Carolyn Lockhart. Per issue (annual subscription)

APPENDIX

price A$5.95 (A$59 in Australia, A$118.80 overseas air). Subscriptions: ACP Subscriptions Services, GPO Box 5252, Sydney, NSW 2001, Australia.

Features food and travel.

VOGUE AUSTRALIA ENTERTAINING GUIDE
Bimonthly magazine. Publisher: Conde Nast Publications Pty Ltd, Locked Bag 2550, Crows Nest, NSW 2065, Australia; (61) 2-964-3888, Fax (61) 2-964-3882. Editor: Sharyn Storrier Lyneham. Annual subscription: A$33 in Australia.

Lifestyle magazine featuring food, entertaining, travel.

WEIGHT WATCHERS MAGAZINE
Monthly magazine. Established 1968. Publisher: Weight Watchers Publishing Group, 360 Lexington Ave., New York, NY 10017; (212) 370-0644, Fax (212) 687-4398. Editor: Nancy Gagliardi. Per issue price: $1.95 U.S., $2.50 Canada. Subscriptions: (800) 876-8441.

Information and news on women's health, wellness, nutrition, and fitness; low-fat cooking techniques and recipes.

THE WINE ADVOCATE
Bimonthly newsletter. Established 1978. Address: P.O. Box 311, Monkton, MD 21111; (410) 329-6477, Fax (410) 357-4504. Editor: Robert M. Parker, Jr. Annual subscription: $40 U.S., $50 Canada, $70 other. On-line Prodigy.

Consumer guide to fine wine; accepts no advertising.

THE WINE ENTHUSIAST
Monthly magazine. Established 1988. Address: 8 Saw Mill River Rd., Hawthorne, NY 10532; (800) 356-8466, Fax (914) 345-3028, E-mail wineenth@aol.com. Editor: W.R. Tish. Annual subscription: $11.99 U.S., $23.98 other. Subscriptions: (800) 356-8466 ext. 8915. All tasting notes can be found on America Online at the Food & Drink Network.

Focuses on wine for both new and experienced wine drinkers.

THE WINE SPECTATOR
Twenty issues per year. Established 1976. Publisher: M. Shanken Communications Inc., 387 Park Ave. South, New York, NY 10016; (212) 684-4224, Fax (212) 684-5424. Editor: Jim Gordon. Per issue price: $2.95 ($40) U.S., $3.95 ($53.50) Canada, 39FF, L2.50 ($110) other countries. Subscriptions: P.O. Box 50463, Boulder, CO 80323-0463, (800) 395-3364.

Magazine featuring fine dining and wine, cooking and entertaining, world travel and the arts, unusual shopping and collectibles.

APPENDIX

CAREER SCHOOL TUITION RANKINGS

Use this index for guidance only. Programs are indexed by total tuition for those that are less than nine months and by annual tuition for those that are nine months or more. Additional costs, such as housing, meals, fees, books, and supplies are not included. Schools whose in-state (in-county, in-district) and out-of-state (out-of-country) tuition costs fall in different categories are indicated by IS (IC, ID) or OS (OC) following the state or country. Consult individual listings and schools for more specific information.

TOTAL TUITION FOR PROGRAMS OF LESS THAN NINE MONTHS

LESS THAN $2,500

Epicurean Ckg. School (CA)
Le Trou (CA)
Let's Get Cookin' (CA)
New School Culinary Arts (NY)
Northampton Comm. College (PA) IS
San Juaquin Delta (CA)
School of Natural Cookery (CO)
Sclafani's Cooking School

$2,500 TO $4,999

Cleveland Restaurant School (OH)
Cookery Centre of Ireland (Ireland)
Ecole Superieure de Cuisine (France)
Le Chef College (TX)
Missouri Culinary Inst. (MO)
New Zealand School of Food & Wine (NZ)
Orleans Technical Institute (PA)
Pastry Institute of Washington DC (DC)

$5,000 TO $9,999

Ballymaloe Cookery School (Ireland)
Boston University (MA)
CBI Culinary Academy (CT)
Ckg. & Hosp. Inst. of Chicago (IL)
Connecticut Culinary Institute (CT)
Dubrulle French Cul. Schl. (Canada)
Lederwolff (CA)
Natural Gourmet Cookery School (NY)
New York Restaurant School (NY)
Northampton Comm. College (PA) OS
Southeastern Academy (FL)

$10,000 OR OVER

California Cul. Academy (CA)

Cooking School of the Rockies (CO)
Ecole des Arts Culinaires (France)
French Culinary Institute (NY)
Le Cordon Bleu-London (England)
New York Restaurant School (NY)
Ritz-Escoffier (France)
Southern California School Culinary Arts (CA)
Tante Marie's (CA)

ANNUAL TUITION FOR PROGRAMS OF NINE MONTHS OR LONGER

LESS THAN $1,000

Asheville Buncombe (NC) IS
Atlanta Area Tech. School (GA)
Atlantic Voc-Tech Ctr. (FL)
Augusta Technical Institute (GA)
Baton Rouge Reg. Tech. (LA)
Burlington County College (NJ) IS
Central Community College (NE) IS
Central Piedmont Comm. College (NC) IS
City College of SF (CA) IS
Clark County Comm. College (NV) IS
College of DuPage (IL)
Colorado Mntn. Cul. Inst. (CO)
Columbia College (CA) IS
Contra Costa College (CA)
Crows Nest College of TAFE (Australia)
Cuyahoga Community College (OH)
Cypress College (CA) IS
Daytona Beach Comm. College (FL)
Diablo Valley College (CA)
El Centro College (TX) IS
Elizabethtn. State Voc-Tech (KY) IS
Galveston College (TX)
Glendale Comm. College (CA) IS
Great Plains Voc-Tech (OK)

Grossmont College (CA) IS
Guilford Tech (NC) IS
Gulf Coast Comm. College (FL) IS
Humber College (Canada) IS
Inst. of So. for Hosp. (FL) IS
Jefferson Community College (KY) IS
Joliet Junior College (IL) IS
Kansas City Ks. Voc-Tech (KS)
Kapiolani Community College (HI) IS
Kentucky Tech-Daviess (KY)
Lawson State (AL)
Los Angeles Trade-Tech (CA)
Manchester Community College (CT) IS
Massasoit Community College (MA) IS
Maui Community College (HI) IS
Metropolitan Comm. College (NE) IS
Monroe Cty. Comm. College (MI)
Moorhead Technical College (MN) IS
NE Ks Area Voc-Tech (KS) IS
No. Tech. Education Ctr. (FL)
Odessa College (TX)
Okaloosa-Walton (FL) IS
Oklahoma State University (OK)
Olympic College (WA)
Orange Coast College (CA) IS
Oxnard College (CA) IS
Pima Comm. College (AZ) IS
Pinellas Tech-Clearwater (FL)
Pinellas Tech-St. Pete (FL)
Pioneer Area Voc-Tech (OK)
San Joaquin Delta (CA) IS
Santa Barbara City College (CA) IS
Santa Fe Community College (NM) IS
Santa Rosa Jr. College (CA) IS
Savannah Technical Institute (GA)
SE Inst. of Culinary Art (FL) IS
Shasta College (CA) IS
Sheridan Voc Tech (FL)
Sinclair Comm. College (OH) IS
So. Oklahoma Area Voc-Tech (OK)
So. Puget Sound Comm. College (WA) IS
Southeast Community College (NE)
Spokane Community College (WA) IS
St. Philip's College (TX)

Truckee Meadows (NV) IS
Utah Valley Comm. College (UT) IS
West Ky State Voc-Tech (KY)

$1,000 TO $1,999

Adirondack Community College (NY)
Algonquin College (Canada) IS
Black Hawk College (IL) IS
Boise State University (ID)
Bucks County Community College (PA)
Bunker Hill Community College (MA) IS
Burlington County College (NJ) OS
Canadore College (Canada) IS
Central Community College (NE) OS
Chippewa Valley Tech (WI) IS
Clark College (WA)
College of Lake County (IL)
Columbus State Community College (OH) IS
Comm. College-Allegheny Cty. (PA) IS
Del Mar College (TX)
Des Moines Comm. College (IA) IS
Edmonds Community College (WA) IS
Elgin Community College (IL)
Elizabethtn. State Voc-Tech (KY) OS
Erie Community College (NY) IS
Essex Ag-Tech Inst. (MA) IS
Food Arts Studio (IL)
Fox Valley Tech. Institute (WI) IS
Gateway Comm-Tech College (CT) IS
George Brown College (Canada) IS
Georgian College (Canada) IS
Greenville Tech. College (SC)
Hocking Technical College (OH) IS
Horry-Georgetown (SC) IS
Hudson County Comm. College (NJ) IS
Indian Meridian Voc-Tech (OK)
Iowa Western Comm. College (IA) IS
Ivy Tech-Ft. Wayne (IN) IS
Ivy Tech-Gary (IN) IS
Ivy Tech-Indianapolis (IN)
Jefferson Community College (NY) IS
Johnson Cty. Comm. College (KS) IS
Kirkwood Community College (IA) IS
Lane Community College (OR) IS
Linn-Benton Community College (OR) IS

APPENDIX

Macomb Community College (MI) IS
Madison Area Tech. College (WI)
Massasoit Community College (MA) OS
Metropolitan Comm. College (NE) OS
Missoula Voc-Tech Center (MT) IS
Mitchell Technical Institute (SD)
Mohawk Valley Comm. College (NY) IS
Moorhead Technical College (MN) OS
Moraine Park Technical College (WI)
Niagara College (Canada) IS
Niagara County Comm. College (NY)
North Dakota State College (ND) IS
North Seattle Comm. College (WA) IS
Northwest Technical College (MN) IS
Northwestern Mich. College (MI)
Oakland Community College (MI)
Onondaga Community College (NY) IS
Renton Technical College (WA)
Richardson Researches (CA)
St. Clair College (Canada) IS
St. Louis Comm. College (MO)
St. Paul Technical College (MN) IS
Salt Lake Comm. College (UT) IS
Santa Fe Community College (NM) OS
Schenectady Cty. Comm. College (NY) IS
Schoolcraft College (MI)
Scott Community College (IA)
Scottsdale Comm. College (AZ) IS
SE Inst. of Culinary Art (FL) OS
Seattle Central Comm. College (WA) IS
Sinclair Comm. College (OH) OS
Skagit Valley College (WA) IS
So. Alberta Inst. (Canada) IS
So. Seattle Comm. College (WA) IS
South Central Tech. College (MN) IS
Stratford Chefs School (Canada) IS
Trident Technical College (SC) IS
Triton College (IL)
Univ. College of Cariboo (Canada)
University of Alaska (AK) IS
Vincennes University (IN) IS
W, Va. Northern Comm. College (WV) IS
Wallace State (AL)
Warren Occup-Tech Ctr. (CO) IS

Washtenaw Community College (MI) IS
Waukesha County Tech. College (WI) IS
Westchester Community College (NY)
Westmoreland Cty. Comm. College (PA)
Wichita Area Voc-Tech (KS)
William Rainey Harper (IL) IS

$2,000 TO $2,999

Berkshire Community College (MA) IS
Bristol Community College (MA) IS
Clark County Comm. College (NV) OS
Columbia College (CA) OS
Comm. College-Allegheny Cty. (PA) OS
Cypress College (CA) OS
El Centro College (TX) OS
Glendale Comm. College (CA) OS
Grossmont College (CA) OS
Hennepin Tech (MN) IS
Holyoke Community College (MA) IS
Horry-Georgetown (SC) OS
Hudson County Comm. College (NJ) OS
Instituto del Arte Moderno (PR)
Iowa Lakes Comm. College (IA) IS
Iowa Western Comm. College (IA) OS
Jefferson Community College (KY) OS
Jefferson Community College (NY) OS
Kapiolani Community College (HI) OS
Kirkwood Community College (IA) OS
Laney College (CA)
Manchester Community College (CT) OS
Maui Community College (HI) OS
Middlesex County College (NJ) IS
Milwaukee Area Tech. College (WI) IS
Missoula Voc-Tech Center (MT) OS
Monroe Community College (NY)
New Hampshire Tech (NH) IS
New York City Technical College (NY) IS
North Dakota State College (ND) OS
Northern Mich. University (MI) IS
Northwest Technical College (MN) OS
Okaloosa-Walton (FL) OS
Onondaga Community College (NY) OS
Orange Coast College (CA) OS
Oxnard College (CA) OS
Penn Valley Comm. College (MO) OS

Salem County Voc-Tech (NJ)
San Joaquin Delta (CA) OS
Santa Rosa Jr. College (CA) OS
Shasta College (CA) OS
South Central Tech. College (CA) OS
Southern Maine Tech (ME) IS
St. Paul Technical College (MN) OS
Sullivan County Comm. College (NY) IS
SUNY-Cobleskill (NY) IS
Trident Technical College (SC) OS
Truckee Meadows (NV) OS
University of Akron (OH) IS
University of Toledo (OH) IS
Utah Valley Comm. College (UT) OS
Wake Tech. Comm. College (NC)
Washtenaw Community College (MI) OS
Waukesha County Tech. College (WI) OS

$3,000 TO $4,999

American Institute of Baking (KS)
Bossier Parish Comm. College (LA)
Bunker Hill Community College (MA) OS
Central Piedmont Comm. College (NC) OS
Cincinnati Technical College (OH) IS
City College of SF (CA) OS
Columbus State Community College (OH) OS
Cooking Academy of Chicago (IL)
Cul. Inst. of Col. Sprgs. (CO)
Des Moines Comm. College (IA) OS
Dunwoody Institute (MN)
Ecole Superieure de Cuisine ()
Edmonds Community College (WA) OS
Erie Community College (NY) OS
Essex Ag-Tech Inst. (MA) OS
Gateway Comm-Tech College () OS
Grand Rapids Comm. College (MI) IS
Guilford Tech (NC) OS
Gulf Coast Comm. College (FL) OS
Harrisburg Area Comm. College (PA)
Hennepin Tech-Brooklyn Pk. () OS
Hennepin Tech-Eden Prairie (MN) OS
Hocking Technical College (OH) OS
Indian Hills Comm. College (IA)
Inst. of So. for Hosp. (FL) OS
Iowa Lakes Comm. College (IA) OS

Ivy Tech-Ft. Wayne (IN) OS
Ivy Tech-Gary (IN) OS
Johnson Cty. Comm. College (KS) OS
Joliet Junior College (IL) OS
Lane Community College (OR) OS
Le Cordon Bleu Paris (Canada)
Macomb Community College (MI) OS
Memphis Culinary Academy (TN)
Middlesex County College (NJ) OS
Mohawk Valley Comm. College (NY) OS
Northern Mich. University (MI) OS
Pastry Institute of DC (DC)
Pima Comm. Colege (AZ) OS
Salt Lake Comm. College (UT) OS
Santa Barbara City College (CA) OS
Schenectady Cty. Comm. College (NY) OS
Seattle Central Comm. College (WA) OS
Silwood Kitchen (South Africa)
So. Alberta Inst. (Canada) OS
So. Puget Sound Comm. College (WA) OS
Southern Maine Tech (ME) OS
Spokane Community College (WA) OS
Sullivan County Comm. College (NY) OS
SUNY-Cobleskill (NY) OS
Univ. of New Hampshire (NH) IS
University of Toledo (OH) OS
Vincennes University (IN) OS
W, Va. Northern Comm. College (WV) OS
Warren Occup-Tech Ctr. (CO) OS
Washburne Trade School (IL)

$5,000 TO $7,499

Academy of Culinary Arts (NJ)
Algonquin College (Canada) OS
Asheville Buncombe (NC) OS
Berkshire Community College (MA) OS
Black Hawk College (IL) OS
Bristol Community College (MA) OS
Century Business College (CA)
Cincinnati Technical College (OH) OS
Ckg. & Hosp. Inst. of Chicago (IL) IS
Dandenong College (Australia)
Grand Rapids Comm. College (MI) OS
Holyoke Community College (MA) OS
Humber College (Canada) OS

APPENDIX 319

Indiana University of Pa. (PA)
Int. Culinary Academy (PA)
Lexington Institute (IL)
Linn-Benton Community College (OR) OS
Minuteman Tech (MA)
NE KS Area Voc-Tech (KS) OS
New Hampshire Tech (NH) OS
New York City Technical College (NY) OS
New York Food & Hotel Mgmt. Schl. (NY)
North Seattle Comm. College (WA) OS
Pa. College of Technology (PA)
Scottsdale Comm. College (AZ) OS
Skagit Valley College (WA) OS
So. Seattle Comm. College (WA) OS
St. Clair College (Canada) OS
Thames Valley University (England)
UCLA Extension (CA)
University of Akron (OH) OS
University of Alaska (AK) OS
William Rainey Harper (IL) OS

$7,500 TO $9,999

Art Inst. of Ft. Lauderdale (FL) ATI
ATI Career Institute (VA)
Baltimore Int. Cul. College (MD)
Cambridge School (MA)
Canadore College (Canada) OS
Chippewa Valley Tech (WI) OS
Colorado Inst. of Art (CO)
Fla. Culinary Institute (FL)
George Brown College (Canada) OS
Georgian College (Canada) OS
Lederwolff Culinary Academy (CA) IS
Milwaukee Area Tech. College (WI) OS
New Hamp. College Cul. Inst. (NH)
Newbury College (MA)
Niagara College (Canada) OS
Pa. Institute of Cul. Arts (PA)
Paul Smith's College (NY)
Peter Kump's NY Cooking Schl. (NY)
Sullivan College (KY)

$10,000 OR OVER

Art Institute of Atlanta (GA)
Art Institute of Houston (TX)

Cul. Arts Inst. of La. (LA)
Cul. Schl. of Kendall College (IL)
Culinary Institute of America (NY)
Fox Valley Tech. Institute (WI) OS
Johnson & Wales Univ. (RI)
L'Academie de Cuisine (MD)
Le Chef Culinary Arts (TX) OS
Lederwolff Culinary Academy (CA) OS
Los Angeles Culinary Inst. (CA)
New England Cul. Institute (VT)
New York Institute Restaurant School (NY)
Restaurant School (PA)
Scottsdale Culinary Inst. (AZ)
Stratford Chefs School (Canada) OS
Tante Marie School of Cookery (England)
Univ. of New Hampshire (NH) OS
Western Culinary Institute (OR)

SCHOOLS & ORGANIZATIONS THAT OFFER SCHOLARSHIPS

See individual listings for specific information about number and dollar amount awarded last year.

Adirondack Community College, 66
American Culinary Federation, 295
American Dietetic Assn., 295
American Institute of Baking, 295
Art Institute of Ft. Lauderdale, 21
Art Institute of Houston, 97
Asheville Buncombe Tech Comm. College, 79
ATI Career Institute, 103
Baltimore International Culinary College, 48
Black Hawk College, 30
Boston University Metro College, 50
Bucks County Community College, 86
Burlington County College, 65
California Culinary Academy, 4
Cambridge School of Culinary Arts, 51
Central Community College, 61

APPENDIX

Central Piedmont Community College, 79
Cincinnati State Tech. & Comm. College, 81
City College of San Francisco, 6
Clark College, 104
College of Dupage, 31*31*
College of Lake County, 31
College of Technology-U of MT, 60
Colorado Mountain Culinary Inst., 16
Columbus State Community College, 81
Cooking Academy of Chicago, 32
Culinary Arts Institute of Louisiana, 45
Culinary Institute of America, 68
Culinary Institute of Col. Springs, 18
Culinary School of Kendall College, 32
Cuyahoga Community College, 82
Cypress College, 7
Del Mar College, 98
Des Moines Area Community College, 38
Diablo Valley College, 7
Dunwoody Institute, 57
Edmonds Community College, 104
Educational Foundation of the NRA, 297
Elgin Community College, 33
Erie Community College, 68
Florida Culinary Institute, 22
Fox Valley Technical Institute, 109
Glendale Community College, 8
Grand Rapids Community College, 54
Greenville Technical College, 95
Guilford Technical Community College, 80
Gulf Coast Community College, 23
Indian Hills Community College, 39
Indiana University of Pa., 89
Instituto de Educacion Univ., 94
Intl. Assn. of Culinary Professionals, 297
Intl. Assn. Women Chefs & Restaurateurs, 298
Intl. Food Service Executives Assn., 298
Intl. Foodservice Editorial Council, 298

Ivy Tech-E. Chicago, 37
Ivy Tech-Ft. Wayne, 36
James Beard Foundation, 298
Johnson & Wales University, 103
Kapiolani Community College, 29
Kentucky Tech Elizabethtown, 43
Kentucky Tech-Daviess County, 43
Kirkwood Community College, 40
Lane Community College, 85
Laney College, 9
Linn-Benton Community College, 85
Los Angeles Culinary Institute, 10
Los Angeles Trade-Technical College, 10
Madison Area Technical College, 109
Maui Community College, 29
Metropolitan Community College, 61
Minuteman Tech, 53
Mitchell Technical Institute, 97
Mohawk Valley Community College, 71
Monroe County Community College, 54
Moraine Park Technical College, 110
Natl. Assn. for the Specialty Food Trade, 299
New England Culinary Institute, 101
New Hampshire Technical College, 63
New York City Technical College, 73
New York Food & Hotel Mgmt. School, 73
New York Restaurant School, 74
Newbury College, 53
North Dakota State College of Science, 80
Northampton Community College, 89
Northwestern Michigan College, 55
Oakland Community College, 56
Okaloosa-Walton Community College, 25
Olympic College, 105
Orange Coast College, 11
Oxnard College, 12
Paul Smith's College, 76
Pennsylvania College of Technology, 90

APPENDIX

Pennsylvania Inst. of Culinary Arts, *92*
Peter Kump's NY Cooking School, *76*
Pima Community College, *1*
Pinellas Tech-N. Clearwater, *25*
Pinellas Tech-St. Pete, *25*
Restaurant School, *92*
Saint Louis Community College, *60*
Salt Lake Community College, *100*
San Joaquin Delta College, *12*
Santa Barbara City College, *13*
Santa Fe Community College, *66*
Savannah Technical Institute, *28*
School for American Chefs, *14*
Schoolcraft College, *56*
Scott Community College, *40*
Scottsdale Community College, *2*
Scottsdale Culinary Institute, *2*
South Seattle Community College, *107*
Southeast Inst. of Culinary Arts, *26*
Southern Cal. School of Culinary Arts, *14*
Sullivan County Community College, *78*
Trident Technical College, *96*
Triton College, *35*
Truckee Meadows Community College, *62*
Utah Valley Community College, *101*
Vincennes University, *38*
Warren Occupational Technical Ctr., *19*
Washtenaw Community College, *56*
Waukesha County Technical College, *110*
Westchester Community College, *78*
Westmoreland County Comm. College, *93*
William Rainey Harper College, *36*

SCHOOLS THAT OFFER CLASSES FOR CHILDREN AND TEENS

Academie de Cuisine, *229*
Academy of Cooking, *155*
Alambique School, S.A., *275*

Albertson, Charlotte-Ann, *209*
Benkris Cooking School, *230*
Bobbi Cooks Cooking School, *171*
Boston University Metro College, *189*
Bristol Farms Cook'N'Things, *156*
Buehler's Food Markets, *205*
Byerly's School of Culinary Arts, *191*
Cake Cottage, Inc., *188*
California Culinary Academy, *157*
Caren's Cooking School, *230*
Chef Dough Dough & Co., *213*
Chez Linda Cooking, *157*
Conklin-Chase, *158*
Connecticut Culinary Institute, *171*
Cook Store, *171*
Cookery Centre of Ireland, *257*
Cookery Holidays for Children, *238*
Cooking by the Book, Inc., *199*
Cooking Craft, Inc., *182*
Cooking Scene, *177*
Cooking School at Jordano's, *158*
Cooking Studio, *231*
Cookingstudio, *195*
Cooks' Wares Culinary Classes, *206*
CookSchool at the CookShop, *232*
Cooktique, *195*
Cornell's Adult University, *199*
Country Kitchen, *184*
Creative Cookery School, *239*
Cucina Casalinga, *172*
Cuisine Cooking School, *182*
Culinary Institute of America, *199*
Dierbergs School of Cooking, *192*
Dorothy Lane Market, *206*
Ecole de Cuisine, *222*
Edibles...Naturally!, *195*
Elizabeth Thomas Cooking School, *160*
Epicurean Workshop, *274*

Everyday Gourmet, *192*
Foodsearch Plus, *172*
George Brown College, *232*
Gourmet Curiosities, Etc., *206*
Grande Gourmet Cooking School, *204*
Hackett House, *153*
Harriet Neiman, *155*
Harriet's Kitchen, *176*
Harry's Chinese Cooking Classes, *226*
HomeChef Cooking School, *161*
Hopewell-Pennington Cooking Ctr., *196*
In Good Taste, *212*
Jasper's Cooking Classes, *193* JC's Kitchen Company, *161*
Kay Ewing's Everyday Gourmet, *187*
Kitchen Affairs, *184*
Kitchen Conservatory, *193*
Kitchen Hearth, *177*
Kitchen Shoppe of Carlisle, *211*
Kitchen Witch Gourmet Shop, *162*
Konishi Japanese Cooking Class, *272*
L'Academie de Cuisine, *188*
La Venture, *183*
Le Cordon Bleu-London, *241*
Le Cordon Bleu-Paris, *251*

Le Panier, *216*
Les Gourmettes Cooking School, *154*
Let's Get Cookin', *162*
Loews Anatole Hotel's Young Culinarians, *216*
Loretta Paganini School, *207*
Lucy's Kitchen, *191*
Miette, *201*
Mon Cheri Cooking School, *163*
Natural Foods Cooking School, *216*
New School Culinary Arts, *202*
Peter Kump's School, *202*
Randall's School of Cooking, *186*
Rania's Cooking School, *211*
Rice Epicurean Markets, *217*
Ronnie Fein School, *173*
Seasoned Chef, *170*
Silo Cooking School, *173*
Southern Cal. School of Culinary Arts, *166*
Stocked Pot & Co., *205*
Sydney Seafood School, *228*
Tops Int. Super Ctr. Cooking Schl., *204*
What's Cooking @ Kitchen Sink, *174*
Yankee Hill Winery, *168*
Zona Spray Cooking School, *208*

APPENDIX 323

ABBREVIATIONS

ACCREDITING AGENCIES
ACCSCT Accrediting Commission of Career Schools/Colleges of Technology
ACFEI American Culinary Federation Educational Institute
MSA Middle States Association of Colleges and Schools
NASC Northwest Association of Schools and Colleges
NCA North Central Association of Colleges and Schools
NEASC New England Association of Schools and Colleges
SACS Southern Association of Colleges and Schools
State State Department of Education
WASC Western Association of Schools and Colleges

ASSOCIATE DEGREES
AA Associate in Arts
AAS Associate in Applied Science
AOS Associate in Occupational Studies
AS Associate in Science

CURRENCY CONVERSION TABLE   *(as of September 7, 1995)*

Country	Currency per U.S. $1	Country	Currency per U.S. $1
Australia (A$)	1.33	Israel (Shekel)	3.05
Canada (C$)	1.34	Italy (Lira)	1621.00
France (FF)	5.09	New Zealand (NZ$)	1.53
Great Britain (£)	.64	South Africa (R)	3.66
Ireland (IR£)	.63	Spain (Pts)	128.85

APPENDIX

INDEX OF ADVERTISERS

Name of School	Page
California Culinary Academy	5
Clark College Culinary Arts Program	104
Cooking Hospitality Institute of Chicago	33
Cooking School of the Rockies	17
Cooking with Friends in France	247
Culinary Arts Institute of Louisiana	45
The Culinary Institute of America	67
Ecole des Arts Culinaires et de l'Hotellerie	124
French Culinary Institute	69
Going Solo in the Kitchen	176
IACP Foundation	298
International Cooking School of Italian Food and Wine	264
International School of Confectionery Arts, Inc.	49
L'Academie de Cuisine	50
L'Ecole de Patisserie Francaise	128
La Cucina al Focolare	266
La Varenne	125, 251
Le Cordon Bleu	127
Mohawk Valley Community College	71
Napa Valley Cooking School	11
New England Culinary Institute	102
New York Restaurant School	75
Pastry Institute of Washington DC	21
Pennsylvania Institute of Culinary Arts	91
Peter Kump's New York Cooking School	77
Peter Kump's School of Culinary Arts	203
Provence Cooking School	254
Restaurant School	93
Richardson Researches, Inc.	13
Ritz-Escoffier Ecole de Gastronomie Francaise	129
Sclafani Cooking School, Inc.	47
Scottsdale Culinary Institute	3
Tante Marie's Cooking School	15
Western Culinary Institute	87

6

Index

INDEX

A

A La Bonne Cocotte, *197*
Academie de Cuisine, *49, 229*
Academy of Cooking, *155*
Academy of Culinary Arts, *64*
Accoutrement Cooking School, *223*
Acorn Activities, *236*
Ada Parasiliti Cooking School, *258*
Adirondack Community College, *66*
Adventurous Appetite, *278*
Aeschliman, Bonnie, *185*
Aga Workshop, *236*
Alambique School, S.A., *275*
Alastair Little Cookery Weeks, *258*
Albertson, Charlotte-Ann, *209*
Albuquerque Tech-Voc, *66*
Alex, Kathie, *246*
Algonquin College, *112*
Alix Gardner's Cookery School, *130*
American Culinary Federation, *295*
American Dietetic Assn., *295*
American Harvest Workshop, *4*
American Institute of Baking, *41, 295*
American Institute of Wine & Food, *295*
American Wine Society, *296*
Amy Malone School, *156*
Andoh, Elizabeth, *272*
Andre Daguin Hotel de France, *245*
Anna Teresa Callen, *198*
Annemarie Victory Organization, *243, 253*
Area Technical Trade Center, *62*
ARG Cooking School, *181*
Ariana's Cooking School, *175*
Art Institute of Atlanta, *27*
Art Institute of Ft. Lauderdale, *21, 175*
Art Institute of Houston, *97*
Art of Food Cooking School, *229*
Art of Italian Cuisine, *271*
Arte al Dente, *223*
Asheville Buncombe Tech Comm. College, *79*
Asian Cookery, *169*
At Home With Patricia Wells, *245*
ATI Career Institute, *103*
Atkinson, Greg, *220*
Atlanta Area Technical School, *27*
Atlantic Community College, *64*
Atlantic Vocational Technical Center, *22*
Augusta Technical Institute, *28*
Australian Gas Cooking School, *223*
Authentic Vegetarian Cuisine, *169*

B

Badia a Coltibuono, *258*
Bake-Thompson, Patricia, *274*
Ballymaloe Cookery School, *130, 257*
Baltimore Intl. Culinary College, *48, 257*
Bath School of Cookery, *237*
Baton Rouge Regional Tech, *44*
Battaglia, Maria, *268*
Beautiful Food, Inc., *181*
Bed and Breakfast in Tuscany, *259*
Bell, Catherine, *274*
Bellouet-Conseil, *124*
Benedict, Nell, *191*
Benkris Cooking School, *230*
Beringer Vineyards, *14*
Berkshire Community College, *50*
Berry Lodge, *257*
Bertran, Lula, *273*
Between Past & Present, *259*
Beverley Sutherland Smith, *223*
Big Island Bounty, *179*
Birthe Marie's Cooking School, *230*
Bisceglie, Sandra, *183*
Black Hawk College, *30*

INDEX

Blackadder, Victoria, *228*
Blanc, Raymond, *242*
Blanco River Cooking School, *214*
Bloom, Carole, *157*
Bobbi Cooks Cooking School, *171*
Boise State University, *30*
Bolder Adventures, *276*
Bon Vivant School of Cooking, *219*
Bonne Bouche, *118, 237*
Bonnie Stern School of Cooking, *230*
Boral Gas Cookery Service, *223*
Border Grill, *156*
Bossier Parish Community College, *44*
Boston University Metro College, *50, 189*
Bouit, Michael, *247*
Brady, Jean, *162*
Bread Bakers Guild of America, *296*
Bristol Community College, *51*
Bristol Farms Cook'N'Things, *156*
Broglie, Marie-Blanche de, *250*
Brown, Sarah, *255*
Bucks County Community College, *86*
Buehler's Food Markets, *205*
Bugialli, Giuliano, *262*
Bullwinkel, Madelaine, *182*
Bunker Hill Community College, *51*
Burlington County College, *65*
Butel, Jane, *196*
Byerly's School of Culinary Arts, *191*

C

Cajun Cooking Conversations, *186*
Cake Cottage, Inc., *188*
Cake Icing Course, *118*
Cakebread Cellars, *4, 156*
California Culinary Academy, *4, 157*
Callen, Anna, *198*
Cambridge School of Culinary Arts, *51, 189*

Camelot Career College, *45*
Canadore College, *113*
Canberra Institute of Technology, *111*
Capital Tours Ltd., *243*
Career Development Center, *53*
Caren's Cooking School, *230*
Carl's Cuisine, *208*
Carlos' Restaurant, *181*
Carol's Cuisine, Inc., *198*
Carole Bloom, Patissiere, *157*
Caroline Holmes-Herbs, *237*
Carpenter, Hugh, *161*
Carpita, David & Nitockrees, *253*
Carrington House Restaurant, *224*
Castello di Spaltenna, *260*
Castroville Artichoke Festival, *157*
CBI Culinary Academy, *19*
Cedar Spring Farm, *209*
Celebration of Hawaii, *180*
Central Community College, *61*
Central Institute of Technology, *132*
Central Piedmont Community College, *79*
Century Business College, *6*
Chaa Creek School, *236*
Channel Bass Inn Cooking Vacations, *218*
Charlotte-Ann Albertson, *209*
Chateau Country Cooking School, *245*
Chef Allen's, *175*
Chef Dough Dough & Co., *213*
Chez Linda Cooking, *157*
Chez Madelaine, *182*
Chianti in Tuscany, *259*
Chinese Cookery, Inc., *188*
Chippewa Valley Technical College, *108*
Chocolate Gallery, *67*
Chong, Elizabeth, *225*
Chopsticks Cooking Centre, *128, 256*
Cincinnati State Tech. & Comm. College, *81*

INDEX

Cipriani Hotel, *262*
Citron, Jane, *210*
City College of San Francisco, *6*
Clare Gourmet Weekend, *224*
Clark College Culinary Arts, *104*
Clark County Community College, *62*
Clark, Liz, *185*
Clark, Mary Beth, *201, 263*
Classic Gourmet Cooking School, *213*
Clea's Castle Cooking School, *30*
Cleveland Restaurant Cooking School, *81, 206*
Clos du Roy at Box House, *238*
Club Cuisine, *198*
Cohen, Marge, *190*
College of DuPage, *31*
College of Lake County, *31*
College of Southern Idaho, *30*
College of Technology-U of MT, *60*
College of Tourism and Hospitality, *111*
Colorado Institute of Art, *16*
Colorado Mountain Culinary Inst., *16*
Columbia College, *6*
Columbus State Community College, *81*
Comm. College of Allegheny County, *86, 88*
Comm. College of Southern Nevada, *62*
Complete Kitchen, *171*
Confrerie de la Chaine des Rotisseurs, *296*
Conklin-Chase, *158*
Connecticut Culinary Institute, *19, 171*
Contra Costa College, *7*
Cook Store, *171*
Cook's Corner, Inc., *210*
Cook's Corner, Ltd., *204*
Cook's of Crocus Hill, *191*
Cook's World, *219*
Cook, The Artist Cookery School, *224*
Cookbook Cottage, *185*
Cookery at the Grange, *118, 238*

Cookery Centre of Ireland, *131, 257*
Cookery Holidays for Children, *238*
Cookery Lessons & Touraine Visit, *246*
Cookhampton, *199*
Cookin' Cajun Cooking School, *186*
Cooking at the Abbey, *246*
Cooking Academy of Chicago, *32*
Cooking at Bonnie's Place, *185*
Cooking by the Book, Inc., *199*
Cooking with Class, *209*
Cooking Cottage, *209*
Cooking Craft, Inc., *182*
Cooking with Friends in France, *246*
Cooking & Hosp. Inst. of Chicago, *32, 182*
Cooking Lite, *231*
Cooking With Liz Clark, *185*
Cooking with Master Chefs on Maui, *180*
Cooking with the Masters, *247*
Cooking in Paradise, *277*
Cooking in Provence, *247*
Cooking in Provence, *248*
Cooking Scene, *177*
Cooking School at Jordano's, *158*
Cooking School of the Rockies, *17, 169*
Cooking School of Tulsa, *208*
Cooking Studio, *231*
Cooking with Susan Lee, *231*
Cooking Together Foundation, *297*
Cooking Workshop, *231*
Cookingstudio, *195*
Cooks and Books Cooking School, *158*
Cooks & Connoisseurs Ckg. School, *204*
CookSchool at the CookShop, *232*
Cooks'Wares Culinary Classes, *206*
Cooktique, *195*
Corbett, Suzanne, *193*
Cordon Bleu-London, *241*
Cordon Bleu Scuola, *131, 269*

Cordon Bleu-Paris, *251*
Cordon Vert Cookery School, *119, 238*
Cornell's Adult University, *199*
Council of Adult Education, *224*
Council on Hotel, Rest. & Inst. Ed., *297*
Country House Cookery-Berry Lodge, *257*
Country Kitchen, *184*
Crate, *210*
Creating Culinary Opportunities, *214*
Creative Cookery School, *239*
Creative Cuisine Cooking School, *221*
Creole Cook Symposium, *187*
Crow's Nest College of Tafe, *111*
Cucina Casalinga, *172*
Cucina Toscana, *260*
Cucinare at Castello di Spaltenna, *260*
Cuisine Concepts, *214*
Cuisine Cooking School, *182*
Cuisine Eclairee, *278*
Cuisine International, *214*
Cuisine Sur La Mer, *159*
Cuisines of the Sun, *180*
Cuisinieres du Monde, *248*
Culinary Adventures, Inc., *159*
Culinary Arts Institute of Louisiana, *45*
Culinary Classics Cooking School, *213*
Culinary Concepts, *153*
Culinary Institute of America, *68, 199*
Culinary Institute of Col. Springs, *18*
Culinary Institute of Smoke Cooking, *192*
Culinary Magic Cooking Seminars, *217*
Culinary School of Kendall College, *32*
Culinary Studios in Tuscany, *260*
Culinary Tour of Florence, *261*
Culinary Travel Company, *278*
Cuyahoga Community College, *82*
Cypress College, *7*

D

D'Addario, Kathy, *211*
Daguin, Andre, *245*
Damiano's at the Tarrimore House, *175*
Dandenong College, *112*
David Egan Cooking School, *225*
Daytona Beach Community College, *22*
De Gustibus at Macy's, *200*
Del Mar College, *98*
Depot, *159*
Des Moines Area Community College, *38*
Designer Events Cooking School, *215*
Diablo Valley College, *7*
Diana Marsland Cooking, *225*
Diane Seed's Il Melegrano, *261*
Diane Wilkinson's Cooking School, *178*
Dierbergs School of Cooking, *192*
Doerfer, Jane, *175*
Dolores Snyder Haute Cuisine, *215*
Donna Franca Tours, *267*
Dorothy Lane Market, *206*
Draeger's Culinary Center, *159*
Dubrulle French Culinary School, *113, 232*
Dunwoody Institute, *57*
Dwillies, Eileen, *253*

E

Earnley Concourse, *239*
Eastbourne College, *119*
Ebrey, Judy, *214*
Ecole des Arts Culinaires, *123, 248*
Ecole de Cuisine, *222*
Ecole Gast. Bellouet-Conseil, *124*
Ecole Lenotre, *124, 249*
Ecole Superieure-Ferrandi, *125*
Ecole des Trois Ponts, *248*

INDEX

Edibles...Naturally!, *195*
Edinburgh Cookery School, *133, 275*
Edmonds Community College, *104*
Educational Foundation of the NRA, *297*
Egan, David, *225*
El Centro College, *98*
Elderberry House Cooking School, *160*
Elgin Community College, *33*
Elisabeth Russell, *120*
Elise Pascoe Cooking School, *225*
Elizabeth Chong Cooking School, *225*
Elizabeth Thomas Cooking School, *160*
Empire Cooking School, *232*
Empringham, Charlotte, *232*
Enrico Franzese's Cooking Classes, *261*
Entree Nous Cooking School, *232*
Epicurean Gallery, Ltd., *200*
Epicurean School of Culinary Arts, *8, 160*
Epicurean Workshop, *274*
Erie Community College, *68*
Escapades, *178*
Essence of Italy, *259*
Essex Agricultural & Technical Inst., *52*
Esterling, Elizabeth, *174*
Etoile Bleu Marine, *249*
Etrusca School of Cooking, *262*
European Culinary Adventures, *243*
Everyday Gourmet (MS), *192*
Everyday Gourmet (WA), *219*
Ewing, Kay, *187*
Explore, *169*
Exploring the Kitchens of Asia, *222*

F

Fein, Ronnie, *173*
Felts, Doris, *159*
Ferrandi, *125*
Flaherty, Marilyn, *231*

Flavors of Mexico, *272*
Florentine Culinary Studio, *260*
Florida Culinary Institute, *22*
Folonari, Diana, *264*
Food Arts Studio, *34*
Food Fests, *182*
Food in France, *249*
Food & Wine Magazine Classic, *170*
Foodsearch Plus, *172*
Fox Valley Technical Institute, *109*
France Authentique, *249*
Frances Kitchin Cooking Courses, *239*
Franzese, Enrico, *261*
Frazetta, Carol, *198*
French Culinary Institute, *70*
French Kitchen, *226*
French Language and Cooking, *250*
Frontera Grill, *183*

G

Galveston College, *98*
Gardner, Alix, *130*
Garlic & Sapphires, *160*
Garnet Career Center, *108*
Gateway Community-Technical College, *20*
George Brown College, *113, 232*
Georgia Lifestyles Center, *177*
Georgian College, *114*
Gilbert, Pam, *232*
Giuliano Bugialli Cooking Programs, *262*
Glendale Community College, *8*
Going Solo in the Kitchen, *175*
Gourmet Curiosities, Etc., *206*
Gourmet Gadgetre, Ltd., *208*
Gourmet Long Life Cooking Schools, *196*
Gourmet's Galley/In Season, *220*
Grand Rapids Community College, *54*
Grande Gourmet Cooking School, *204*

INDEX

Great Chefs @ Robert Mondavi Winery, *161*
Great Cooks, *233*
Great Plains Area Voc-Tech, *83*
Greenbrier, *108*
Greenville Technical College, *95*
Gretta Anna School of Cooking, *226*
Gritti Palace School of Fine Cooking, *262*
Groskaufmanis, Ausma, *234*
Grossmont College, *8*
Groveman, Lauren, *201*
Gruber, Beverly, *219*
Guilford Technical Community College, *80*
Gulf Coast Community College, *23*

H

Hackett House, *153*
Hall, Lyn, *241*
Handke's Cuisine Cooking Class, *207*
Harriet Neiman, *155*
Harriet's Kitchen, *176*
Harris, Judy, *218*
Harrisburg Area Community College, *88*
Harry's Chinese Cooking Classes, *226*
Hasson, Louise, *219*
Hay Day Cooking School, *172*
Hazan Classics, *131*
Heart of Texas Cooking School, *215*
Heebner, Lesa, *160*
Helen Worth's Culinary Inst., *218*
Hennepin Tech, *57*
Henry Ford Community College, *54*
Herbfarm, *220*
Hintlesham Hall, *240*
Hiram G. Andrews Center, *88*
Hocking Technical College, *82*
Holidays in the sun, *250*
Hollyhock Farm, *233*
Holmes, Caroline, *237*

Holuigue, Diane, *226*
Holyoke Community College, *52*
HomeChef Cooking School, *161*
Hong Kong Food Festival, *256*
Honolulu Community College, *29*
Hopewell-Pennington Cooking Ctr., *196*
Horry-Georgetown Technical College, *95*
Hostellerie de Crillon le Brave, *248*
Hotel Cipriani Cooking School, *262*
Hotel Le Sireneuse, *269*
House of Rice Store, *154*
Howell, Ginger & Dick, *203*
Howqua-Dale Gourmet Retreat, *227*
Hudson County Community College, *65*
Hugh Carpenter, *161*
Humber College, *114*

I

Il Borghetto Cooking School, *263*
In Good Taste, *212*
Indian Hills Community College, *39*
Indiana University of Pa., *89*
Inn at Bay Fortune, *233*
Innocenti, Masha, *265*
Institute of the South for Hospitality, *23*
Instituto de Educacion Univ., *94*
Instituto del Arte Moderno, Inc., *94*
Int. Cooking School Italian Food & Wine, *263*
Interactive Events, *180*
Int. Assn. of Culinary Professionals, *297*
Int. Assn. Women Chefs & Restaurateurs, *298*
Int. Culinary Academy, *89*
Int. Food Service Executives Assn., *298*
Int. Foodservice Editorial Council, *298*
Int. School of Baking, *84*
Int. School of Confectionery Arts, *48*
Iowa Lakes Community College, *39*
Iowa Western Community College, *39*

INDEX

Italian Cookery Weeks, *263*
Italian Country Cooking Classes, *264*
Italian Cuisine in Florence, *265*
Italian Language and Cuisine, *265*
Iverson, Ann, *214*
Ivy Tech-E. Chicago, *37*
Ivy Tech-Ft. Wayne, *36*
Ivy Tech-Indianapolis, *37*
Jacqualin Et Cie Cuisiniere, *210*
James Beard Foundation, *298*
Jane Butel's SW Cookery School, *196*
Jane Citron Cooking Classes, *210*
Jane Thompson Cooking School, *205*
Janericco, Terence, *190*
Japanese Canadian Cultural Centre, *233*
Jasper's Cooking Classes, *193*
JC's Kitchen Company, *161*
Jean Brady Cooking School, *162*
Jefferson Community College, *42*
Jefferson Community College, *70*
Jill Probert's Cookery Courses, *240*
JMD Educational Center, *180*
John Gardiner's Tennis Ranch, *154*
Johnson County Community College, *41*
Johnson & Wales University, *18, 24, 94, 96, 103*
Joliet Junior College, *34*
Jones, Peng, *169*
Jordano's Marketplace, *158*
Judy Harris' Cooking School, *218*
Julie Sahni's School, *70*

K

Kansas City Ks. Area Voc-Tech, *41*
Kapiolani Community College, *29*
Karen Lee, *200*
Kaspar's Restaurant, *221*
Kathy D'Addario's Techniques, *211*
Katsotis, Dolores, *213*
Kay Ewing's Everyday Gourmet, *187*
Kea Lani Hotel, *180*
Kemper Center Cooking School, *193*
Ken Lo's Memories of China, *240*
Kendall College, *32*
Kentucky Tech Elizabethtown, *43*
Kentucky Tech-Daviess County, *43*
Key West Cooking School, *176*
King's Chocolate House, *71*
Kirkwood Community College, *40*
Kitchen Affairs, *184*
Kitchen Conservatory, *193*
Kitchen Fare Cooking School, *178*
Kitchen Glamor, *190*
Kitchen Hearth, *177*
Kitchen/Kitchen Cooking School, *220*
Kitchen Shop @ Green Beanery, *215*
Kitchen Shoppe of Carlisle, *211*
Kitchen Witch Gourmet Shop, *162*
Kitchin, Frances, *239*
Konishi Japanese Cooking Class, *272*
Kumar, Neelam, *235*
Kump, Peter, *76, 202*
Kuony, Liane, *110*
Kushi Institute, *189*

L

La Belle Pomme, *207*
La Cacciata, *258*
La Caravane Adventures, *274*
La Cucina al Focolare, *266*
La Cucina Italiana, *268*
La Cucina Kasher in Toscana, *266*
La Cuisine Francaise, *274*
La Cuisine Imaginaire, *241*
La Cuisine de Marie Blanche, *250*
La Cuisine Sans Peur, *200*
La Mirande-Cooking in Provence, *251*

INDEX

La Petite Cuisine, *241*
La Samanna, *277*
La Varenne, *125, 251*
La Varenne at the Greenbrier, *221*
La Venture, *183*
L'Academie de Cuisine, *49, 188*
Lafayette Regional Technical Inst., *45*
Lafferty, Donna, *34*
Lallemand, Sylvie, *250*
L'Amore di Cucina Italiana, *265*
Lane Community College, *85*
Laney College, *9*
Langdon Hall Country House Hotel, *234*
Lanza, Anna Tasca, *271*
Latzky, Gilda, *200*
Laura Niccolai Cooking School, *266*
Lauren Groveman's Kitchen, *201*
Law, Ruth, *184*
Lawson State Community College, *1*
Le Bec-Fin, *211*
Le Chef College of Hosp. Careers, *99*
Le Cordon Bleu-London, *120, 241*
Le Cordon Bleu-Paris, *126, 251*
Le Cordon Bleu Paris, *115, 234*
Le Gourmand Restaurant, *220*
Le Panier, *216*
Le Petit Gourmet Cooking School, *189*
Le Trou, *9, 126, 162, 252*
Leavitt, Bobbi, *171*
L'Ecole de Cuisine, *252*
L'Ecole de Patisserie Francaise, *127*
Lederwolff Culinary Academy, *9*
Lee, Karen, *200*
Lee, Susan, *231*
Lehrer, Silvia, *199*
Leith's School of Food & Wine, *121, 241*
Lenotre, *249*
Les Casseroles du Midi, *252*
Les Gourmettes Cooking School, *154*
Les Liaisons Delicieuses, *252*
Lesson in Flavors, *267*
Let's Get Cookin', *10, 162*
Levy, Henri, *200*
Lexington College, *34*
Ligurian School of Poetic Cooking, *267*
Lily Loh's Chinese Cooking Classes, *163*
Linn-Benton Community College, *85*
Lo, Ken, *240*
Loews Anatole Hotel's Young Culinarians, *216*
Loh, Lily, *163*
Look Who's Cooking, Inc., *201*
Loretta Paganini School, *207*
Los Angeles Culinary Institute, *10*
Los Angeles Trade-Technical College, *10*
Lucy's Kitchen, *191*
Luhan, Lucia, *259*

M

Ma Cuisine Cooking School, *227*
MacDonald, Birthe, *230*
Macomb Community College, *54*
Mad.61, *203*
Madison Area Technical College, *109*
Maison Sanguinet, *234*
Malone, Amy, *156*
Manchester Community College, *20*
Mandoline Cooking School, *163*
Mangia: A Taste of Florence, *267*
Manguin, Olga, *252*
Manor Cuisine's Creative Cooking, *234*
Manor School of Fine Cuisine, *121, 242*
Mansion on Turtle Creek, *216*
Maraventano, Sally Ann, *172*
Margaret River Wine & Food Festival, *227*
Marge Cohen, *190*
Margherita and Valeria Simili, *268*

INDEX

Mari, Paola & Simonetta, *259*
Maria Battaglia, *268*
Mariner Tours, *268*
Markel, Peggy, *266, 267, 269*
Marshall, Lydie, *197*
Marsland, Diana, *225*
Martin, Gloria, *194*
Mary Beth Clark, *201, 263*
Mas de Cornud, *253*
Massasoit Community College, *52*
Masselin, Roslyne, *241*
Master Classes w Marcella Hazan, *131*
Matto, Rosa, *228*
Maui Community College, *29*
McCall's School, *115, 235*
McMenomy, Merla, *229*
McSherry-Valagao, Caren, *230*
Medici, Lorenza de, *258*
Melbourne Food & Wine Festival, *227*
Memphis Culinary Academy, *97*
Meridian Technology Center, *83*
Metropolitan Community College, *61*
Mexican Cuisine Seminars, *273*
Mid-Florida Technical Institute, *24*
Middlesex County College, *65*
Miette, *201*
Miller Howe Cookery Courses, *242*
Milstein, Tamara, *228*
Milwaukee Area Technical College, *109*
Minuteman Tech, *53*
Mischen, Meredith, *155*
Missouri Culinary Institute, *59*
Mister C's Cooking Castle, *179*
Mitchell Technical Institute, *97*
Mohawk Valley Community College, *71*
Mon Cheri Cooking School, *163*
Monick, Sara, *244*
Monroe Community College, *72*

Monroe County Community College, *54*
Montana Mercantile, *163*
Moorhead Technical College, *58*
Moraine Park Technical College, *110*
Morse, Kitty, *274*
Moulle, Jean-Pierre, *255*

N

Napa Valley College, *11, 163*
Napa Valley Wine Library Association, *299*
Natl. Assn. for the Specialty Food Trade, *299*
Natl. Restaurant Association, *299*
Natural Foods Cooking School (CA), *164*
Natural Foods Cooking School (TX), *216*
Natural Foods Cooking School (Can), *235*
Natural Foods Vegetarian Ckg. Schl., *227*
Natural Gourmet Cookery School, *72, 202*
Naturally Grand Junction, *170*
Neelam Kumar's North Indian Cuisine, *235*
Neiman, Harriet, *155*
Nell Benedict Cooking Classes, *191*
New England Culinary Institute, *101, 217*
New England Tech, *22*
New Hampshire College Culinary Inst., *63*
New Hampshire Technical College, *63*
New Orleans Regional Vo-Tech, *45*
New Orleans School of Cooking, *187*
New School Culinary Arts, *72, 202*
New York City Technical College, *73*
New York Food & Hotel Mgmt. School, *73*
New York Institute of Technology, *74*
New York Restaurant School, *74*
New York University Center, *75, 202*
New Zealand School of Food & Wine, *132, 275*
Newbury College, *53*
Niagara College, *115*
Niagara County Community College, *76*
Niccolai, Laura, *266*

INDEX

Nicolet Area Technical College, 110
Norman Weinstein, 202
North Dakota State College of Science, 80
North Seattle Community College, 105
North Technical Education Center, 24
Northampton Community College, 89
Northeast Kansas Area Voc-Tech, 42
Northern California Center, 164
Northern Michigan University, 55
Northwest Technical College, 58
Northwestern Michigan College, 55
Nutritiously Gourmet, 164

O

Oakland Community College, 56
Odessa College, 99
Offshore Cooking School, 59, 192
Okaloosa-Walton Community College, 25
Oklahoma State University, 84
Old Hall Leisure, 239
Oldways Preservation, 300
Olsen, Gloria, 213
Olympic College, 105
Onondaga Community College, 76
Oppenneer, Betsy, 178
Orange Coast College, 11
Oriental Food Market/Cooking School, 183
Oriental Hotel, 276
Orleans Technical Institute, 90
Oxford Symposium on Food & Cookery, 121
Oxnard College, 12

P

Pace, Maria, 231
Paganini, Loretta, 207
Parasiliti, Ada, 258
Paris Cooks, 174
Pascoe, Elise, 225

Pastry Institute of Washington DC, 21, 174
Patina Restaurant, 165
Paul Smith's College, 76
Peggy Rahn Cooks, 165
Pennsylvania College of Technology, 90
Pennsylvania Inst. of Culinary Arts, 92
Peter Kump's NY Cooking School, 76
Peter Kump's School of Cul. Arts, 202
Pheasant Hill, 269
Pima Community College, 1
Pinellas Tech-N. Clearwater, 25
Pinellas Tech-St. Pete, 25
Pioneer Area Voc-Tech School, 84
Postilion School of Culinary Art, 110
Princeton Cooking School, 196
Probert, Jill, 240
Provencal Getaway Vacations, 253
Provence Cooking School, 253
Prudence Sloane's Cooking School, 173

Q

Quay, Harry, 226

R

Rahn, Peggy, 165
Raichlen, Steven, 277
Raji Restaurant, 213
Randall's School of Cooking, 186
Rania's Cooking School, 211
Ratliffe, Kate, 243
Raymond Blanc, 242
Recipe Club, Kaspar's Restaurant, 221
Renton Technical College, 105
Restaurant School, 92
Rice Epicurean Markets, 217
Richardson Researches, Inc., 12
Ritz-Carlton, Amelia Island, 177
Ritz-Carlton, Mauna Lani, 179

INDEX

Ritz-Carlton, San Francisco, *165*
Ritz-Escoffier, *128, 254*
Robert Mondavi Winery, *161*
Rochereau, Maxime, *246*
Roger Verge Cooking School, *254*
Ronnie Fein School, *173*
Rosa Matto Cooking School, *228*
Rose, Gloria, *196*
Rubey, Jane, *164*

S

Sahni, Julie, *70*
Saint Clair College, *116*
Saint Louis Community College, *60*
Saint Paul Technical College, *58*
Saint Philip's College, *100*
Sakonnet Master Chefs Series, *212*
Sala Siam-Bolder Adventures, *276*
Salem County Voc-Tech, *66*
Salmon, Marysue, *182*
Salt Lake Community College, *100*
Saltzman, Joanne, *18*
San Jacinto College North, *100*
San Joaquin Delta College, *12*
Santa Barbara City College, *13*
Santa Fe Community College, *66*
Santa Fe School of Cooking, *197*
Santa Rosa Junior College, *13*
Sapore di Mare, *203*
Sara Monick Culinary Tours, *244*
Sarasota County Technical Inst., *26*
Sarasota Food & Wine Academy, *177*
Savannah Technical Institute, *28*
Schechter, Lucille, *244*
Schenectady County Comm. College, *77*
School for American Chefs, *14*
School of Natural Cookery, *18, 170*
School of Traditional Neapolitan Cuisine, *269*

Schoolcraft College, *56*
Sclafani's Cooking School, Inc., *46*
Scott Community College, *40*
Scottsdale Community College, *2*
Scottsdale Culinary Institute, *2, 154*
Scuola di Arte Culinaria, *131, 269*
Seasonal Kitchen, *203*
Seasonal Table Cooking School, *165*
Seasoned Chef, *170*
Seasons of My Heart, *132, 273*
Seattle Central Community College, *106*
Seed, Diane, *261*
Seligman, Lucy, *191*
Sesani, Fulvia, *271*
Shah, Jessica, *169*
Shasta College, *14*
Sheridan Vo. Tech Center, *26*
Sherwood Inn, *235*
Siamese Princess Restaurant, *166*
Sicilian Cooking Adventure, *270*
Sidney N. Collier Voc-Tech, *46*
Silo Cooking School, *173*
Silwood Kitchen Cordons Bleus, *134*
Simili, Margherita & Valeria, *268*
Sinclair Community College, *82*
Skagit Valley College, *106*
Sloane, Prudence, *173*
Smith, Beverley, *223*
Smithsonian Institution, *174*
Snyder, Dolores, *215*
Society of Wine Educators, *300*
Sonia Stevenson, *122*
Soujourns in Tuscany, *262*
South Central Technical College, *59*
South Puget Sound Community College, *107*
South Seattle Community College, *107*
Southeast Community College, *61*
Southeast Inst. of Culinary Arts, *26*

Southeastern Academy, 27
Southern Alberta Inst., 116
Southern Cal. School of Culinary Arts, 14, 166
Southern Living Cooking School, 153
Southern Maine Technical College, 46
Southern Oklahoma Area Voc-Tech, 84
Spa & Culinary Adventures, 278
Spokane Community College, 107
Spray, Zona, 208
Squires Kitchen School, 122, 242
Star Canyon Cooking School, 217
Steere, Becky, 261
Stern, Bonnie, 230
Steves, Renie, 214
Stocked Pot & Co., 205
Store for Cooks, 166
Stratford Chefs School, 117
Sugar 'n Spice Cake Decorating School, 166
Sullivan College, 43
Sullivan County Community College, 78
Sunnyside School, 167
SUNY College of Agriculture & Tech, 78
Susser, Allen, 175
Suzanne Corbett, 193
Swanson, Jackie, 194
Sweet Basil Cooking School, 154
Swinburne School, 212
Sydney Seafood School, 228
Symposium for Prof. Food Writers, 108

T

Taipei Chinese Food Festival, 275
Take Pleasure in Cooking!, 194
Tamara's Kitchen, 228
Tante Marie School of Cookery, 122, 243
Tante Marie's Cooking School, 15, 167
Taste of Culture, 272
Taste of the Mountains, 194

Tasters Guild, 300
Tasting Italy, 270
Tasting Spoon, 155
Tausend, Marilyn, 272
Tees, Bonnie, 235
Telluride Wine Festival, 171
Tenuta di Capezzana, 270
Teplitzky, Gretta Anna, 226
Terence Janericco Cooking Classes, 190
Thai Cooking School at the Oriental, 276
Thames Valley University, 123
Thomas, Elizabeth, 160
Thompson, Jane, 205
Thorn Park Cooking School, 228
Tnuva, 257
Tohum Center, 276
Top Tier Sugarcraft, 133
Tops Int. Super Center Cooking Schl., 204
Traditional Family Cooking, 254
Travel Concepts, 244
Trident Technical College, 96
Trilling, Susana, 273
Triton College, 35
Truckee Meadows Community College, 62
Truffles, Inc., 184
Tudisco, Marina, 270

U

UC Extension-Santa Cruz, 163
UCLA Extension, 16, 167
University of Akron, 83
University of Alaska-Fairbanks, 1
University College of the Cariboo, 117
University of Montana, 60
University of New Hampshire, 64
University of Toledo, 83
Ursula's Cooking School, 179
Utah Valley Community College, 101

INDEX

V

Vacances Cuisine, *255*
Valley Oaks Cooking School, *167*
Vandermarliere, Linda, *157*
Venetian Cooking in a Venetian Palace, *271*
Verge, Roger, *254*
Vermont Off Beat, *218*
Victoria's Kitchen, *228*
Victory, Annemarie, *243, 253*
Villa Cennina, *271*
Vincennes University, *38*

W

Wake Technical Community College, *80*
Wallace State Community College, *1*
Wandering Spoon, *244*
Warren Occupational Technical Ctr., *19*
Washburne Trade School, *35*
Washtenaw Community College, *56*
Waukesha County Technical College, *110*
Week in Bordeaux, *255*
Week in Provence, *255*
Weinstein, Norman, *202*
Weir Cooking, *167*
Wells, Patricia, *245*
West Kentucky State Voc-Tech, *44*
West Virginia Northern Comm. College, *108*
Westchester Community College, *78*
Western Culinary Institute, *86*
Westmoreland County Comm. College, *93*
What's Cooking (IL), *184*
What's Cooking @ Kitchen Sink, *174*
What's Cooking? Inc. (OH), *207*
Whip and Spoon, *187*
White River Institute, *169*
Wichita Area Voc-Tech, *42*
Wilkinson, Diane, *178*
William Angliss College, *112, 229*
William Rainey Harper College, *36*
Willinger, Faith, *260*
Willow Hollow Gourmet, *194*
Wilton School of Cake Decorating, *36*
Wine Enthusiast, *256*
Wine Institute, *300*
Wisconsin School of Cookery, *222*
Witts, Judy, *267*
Wood, Rebecca, *170, 277*
World of Regaleali, *271*
Worth, Helen, *218*

Y

Yalumba Winery Cooking School, *229*
Yan Can Cooking School, *168*
Yankee Hill Winery, *168*
Yosemite Chefs' Holidays, *168*

Z

Zona Spray Cooking School, *208*

*Shaw*Guides

THE LEARNING VACATION AND CREATIVE CAREER SPECIALISTS

ShawGuides contain descriptions of more than 2,000 programs throughout the world. Detailed listings include program description, daily schedule, faculty credentials, costs and refund policies, and contact information.

☐ *The Guide to Cooking Schools*, 8th (1996) Edition. Contains 322 career programs, 448 nonvocational and vacation programs, 100 earn-as-you-learn apprenticeships, 65 wine courses, and 21 food and wine organizations. Encompasses 48 states and 19 countries. ISBN 0-945834-21-7. PRICE: **$19.95**.

☐ *The Guide to Art & Craft Workshops*, 2nd Edition. Over 400 learning vacations in 45 states and 23 countries. Includes drawing, painting, sculpture, fibers, metals, wood, pottery, decorative art, and boat and house building. Also contains more than 50 artist colonies. ISBN 0-945834-11-X. PRICE: **$16.95**.

☐ *The Guide to Photography Workshops & Schools*, 4th Edition. More than 300 workshops and tours, over 200 career and college programs, nearly 40 artist colonies with photographic facilities, and 22 photography organizations. Worldwide. ISBN 0-945834-19-5. PRICE: **$19.95**.

☐ *The Guide to Golf Schools & Camps*, 2nd Edition. Nearly 200 programs, including 109 schools for adults, 87 camps for youngsters, and 9 career programs in golf facility management. Encompasses 44 states and 13 countries. Also contains information about 11 national, 92 international, and 104 state and local organizations. ISBN 0-945834-17-9. PRICE: **$16.95**.

☐ *The Guide to Academic Travel*, 2nd Edition. Hundreds of mind-expanding vacations sponsored by colleges, universities, museums, and educational organizations. Includes more than 300 sponsors, whose offerings range from archaeology to zoology. Also contains information about 145 total immersion language schools in 26 countries. ISBN 0-945834-12-8. PRICE: **$16.95**.

☐ *The Guide to Writers Conferences*, 4th Edition. Over 370 workshops, conferences, residencies, and retreats in 45 states and 10 countries. Most offer manuscript critique and opportunities to meet editors and agents. Also includes 114 writer organizations. ISBN 0-945834-15-2. PRICE: **$16.95**.

If not available at your local bookstore, use this convenient coupon.

*Shaw*Guides
P.O. 1295, New York, NY 10023

Please send me the books I have checked above.

☐ I am enclosing a check or money order for $ ____
(add $3 postage for 1 book, $1 for each additional).

☐ Please charge to MasterCard, VISA, or American Express.

Card # _____ Exp. Date _____

Signature _____

Name _____

Address _____

City _____ State _____ Zip _____

For faster service on credit card orders, call (800) 247-6553.